Trusting Ourselves

Trusting Ourselves

Ourselves

The Sourcebook on Psychology for Women

KAREN JOHNSON, M.D.,

AND *TOM FERGUSON, M.D.*

THE ATLANTIC MONTHLY PRESS
NEW YORK

Published simultaneously in Canada
Printed in the United States of America

Library of Congress Cataloging-in-Publication Data

Johnson, Karen.
    Trusting ourselves: the sourcebook on psychology for women/
Karen Johnson and Tom Ferguson.
    ISBN 0-87113-346-6
    1. Women—Psychology. 2. Women and psychoanalysis. I. Ferguson,
Tom, 1943– . II. Title.
HQ1206.J59   1990   155.6′33—dc20   89-38637

Design by Melinda Grosser for *silk*

The Atlantic Monthly Press
19 Union Square West
New York, NY 10003

First printing

With love and appreciation to my grandmother, Opal June Hyde Johnson, who encouraged me to acquire an education, and my father, Dean R. Johnson, who made its acquisition possible.

Acknowledgments

This book is like a child, the product of two parents, a woman and a man.

The idea for the book arose out of a lecture series I began giving in 1982 on the psychology of women. The lectures were intended for the lay public, and my co-author, Tom Ferguson, had been transforming some of them into small pieces for a magazine he edits, *Medical Self-Care.* He knew that I had always wanted to write, but I was anxious and uncertain about pursuing a dream that I did not know if I had the talent or skill to achieve.

Tom nagged, prodded, and encouraged—finally volunteering to be my partner and doing almost all the early work to move this project along. He contacted his agent, Charlotte Sheedy, who agreed to represent me—for which I remain enormously thankful. He wrote the book proposal, which he and Charlotte shepherded through various publishers while I stayed in the background, intimidated by the process. When I was called to New York to meet potential publishers, only one, Ann Godoff, seemed excited by the concept of making reliable psychological information easily accessible to women. Her interest should have come as no surprise, since she had earlier supported the groundbreaking women's health book *The New Our Bodies, Ourselves.* I consider myself blessed to have her as my editor and cannot express enough my gratitude for who she is as a person and a professional.

During the actual writing Tom and Ann provided valuable editorial assistance for most of the chapters, but a few received special attention from other associates. Diane Goldstein and Nanette Gartrell provided critical advice for the chapter on primary relationships with women, and Peter O. Ways did the same for the chapter on alcohol. Backing Ann at Atlantic Monthly Press were Nancy Lewin,

Bonnie Levy, and Amy Ryan, all of whom provided superior editorial support and without whom this book would have been even more stilted than it is. After all, its "mother" was trained as a doctor, not a writer, and I needed a lot of help learning new skills.

As a professional, I have many people to thank for helping me gain the qualifications to do my work. Among them is Andrew Hunt, first Dean of the College of Human Medicine at Michigan State University, who envisioned and nurtured an unconventional medical school that emphasized a humanistic approach to health care long before it became popular. Within the same university I found a creative and flexible psychiatry department chaired by Norbert Enzer, which permitted me to design and implement a unique training program in the psychiatric care of women. During those years I received training and supervision from many dedicated clinicians and educators. I am especially glad to have been under the tutelage of Terry Stein, John Schneider, Marcia and Cyril Worby, and Lucy Ferguson. My deepest appreciation, however, is reserved for Teresa Bernardez, who took me under her wing and made herself available to me during the entire four years of my psychiatric residency. Without her generous support, encouragement, and training I would not be able to do the work I do today. Finally, as role models and senior colleagues, Lillian B. Rubin and Jean Baker Miller deserve special thanks. Both women have given of themselves personally and professionally in spite of many demands on their time. As a fledgling author I found their encouragement and support invaluable.

Over the years I have been fortunate to work as a psychiatrist and educator at several sites that have challenged and nurtured my development. At Women's Health Resources at Illinois Masonic Hospital and Medical Center in Chicago and at Health Works for Women at Mount Zion Hospital and Medical Center and BaySpring Women's Medical Group in San Francisco, I was able to care for women patients as well as participate in educational programs. At Women's Health Resources Alice Cottingham was my "right-hand woman." My growth was exponential during the time we worked together. I am happy this relationship has survived a geographical separation and can now be proclaimed a solid friendship of peers. Gloria Weiss, a private practitioner in Evanston, Illinois, expressed faith in my work by honoring me with the role of supervisor for three years. We used the phone and the mail to bridge the two thousand miles between us.

The "gestation" of this book was almost five years, although the last eighteen months were especially demanding. My most important relationships were stretched to their limits in accommodating this endeavor, and I want to express sincere appreciation to my friends and family who hung in there even when I had little to offer in return. Particular debt is owed to my life partner and fellow feminist, Michael Martin. Michael proved to be a fair and loving companion who kept our relationship and household alive while I devoted almost all of my waking hours to work. I feel very fortunate to have him in my life.

Those to whom I owe an even greater debt are my patients. Protecting their confidentiality means being unable to acknowledge directly their contributions. Yet without the privilege of being allowed into the most private areas of their lives, I could not have written a single chapter of this book. Additionally, I am thankful for the many women who attended my presentations over the years and offered challenges to my ideas as well as nourishment to my efforts.

Finally, were it not for the many courageous women and men who have struggled for—and continue to work toward—a world where room is made for women's voices and women's experiences as equal to those of men . . . none of us would be reading these words.

Thanks to you all.

KAREN JOHNSON
San Francisco, California
November 1989

Contents

PART 1 | A Summary of the Psychology of Women

Psychological theories are people's ideas about what make human beings tick. The psychology of women represents our ideas about why women are the way they are.

No psychology is independent of the time in which it is developed or the personal and professional bias of its creator. Psychology is both art and science. Psychological theory, while often eloquent and persuasive, lacks the precision of the more traditional physical sciences like chemistry and physics. As a result, it is more vulnerable to the subjectivity of its inventors.

Human beings are not raised in a social vacuum, and we are not able to study them independent of the families and societies in which they develop. When we ask whether certain traits or behaviors are uniquely female or male, we cannot answer the question without considering the historical and cultural pressures that inevitably color individual psychology even as they influence the inventors of psychological theory.

The roots of all psychological theory go back to the beginning of recorded history.[1] Aristotle (384–322 B.C.) is considered to have created the intellectual climate that eventually led to the development of psychology. By blending philosophy and science, he planted the seeds for the emergence of an entirely new field of study.

Psychology did not actually appear as a distinct academic field until the mid–nineteenth century. By using considerable political savvy combined with extensive education, training, and clinical experience, two professional groups, psychologists and psychiatrists, acquired the ability to define psychological health and illness. They were thus able to greatly influence the care given to emotionally distressed people.

Academic psychologists, who often work within universities, conduct scientific animal and human experiments. Their controlled, laboratory-like studies allow them to look at very specific variables while keeping other factors to a minimum, permitting observations that are less contaminated by the ordinary and complex events of life. However, their studies are often conducted under artificial and contrived conditions.

On the other hand, psychiatrists, like most physicians, tend to draw their conclusions about human behavior from the people they see in their clinical practices. These patients discuss all of the messy realities of everyday life, making it almost impossible to isolate one variable for intense scrutiny.

Together, these two disciplines can provide a broader understanding of human psychology than either alone. Unfortunately, the competition between these professionals can be fierce, and collaboration is rare. Although psychologists develop many different and often conflicting beliefs about what motivates human behavior, they view the conclusions drawn from their studies as having more validity than hypotheses based on clinical experience. Yet within the medical hierarchy where many psychologists work, the physician enjoys much greater status, prestige, and power than the psychologist.

For example, it was the clinically based theories of a physician, Sigmund Freud, that gained early prominence within both of these professional communities, rather than the theories of one of the many psychologists who were his contemporaries. While women, people of color, and members of the labor movement were instrumental in putting psychological theory into everyday practice, particularly on behalf of the poor and disadvantaged, few were physicians. Their contributions have received little acknowledgment.[2] Even today, psychologists are battling with psychiatrists over the right to be admitted to certain training centers and to admit their own patients to the hospital without having to transfer their care to a psychiatrist.

In spite of the rivalry among these mental-health professionals, each has made substantial contributions to our understanding of human beings. They have also perpetuated a number of shared biases, one of which is of particular interest to us: the overrepresentation of the male perspective in psychological theory.

As we review the history of psychological theory and the contributions from psychologists (people with Ph.D.s specializing in psychology), psychiatrists (people with M.D.s specializing in psychology), and other mental-health providers,[3] we will see a tapestry that reflects a predominantly male bias. As we move closer to examine the individual threads more clearly, we begin to see even in the early stages themes that contrast with this dominant bias. Initially, these themes were either broken or overwhelmed by the broader strokes of the male-influenced weavers of psychological theory. Eventually, however, the challengers began to take hold; as their numbers increase, their contributions take on more prominence. We see theories that revise the earlier male-biased psychological models and attempt to incorporate women's perspectives. In addition, we see new threads develop as theorists struggle with the completely original models that arise from an exclusively woman-oriented psychological theory. The patterns created by these weavers are as varied and complex as those of their predecessors.

In the past, challenges to a male-dominated theory were either ignored, minimized, or drowned out by the male perspective that reinforced society's values. It would be a tragedy if this were to happen again. The purpose of this book is to share clinical and experimental material on the psychology of women in a readily digestible format. Professionals alone do not assure the survival of any psychological theory. New theories can only thrive in the context of a receptive and knowledgeable lay community. It was just this combination of professional invention and community readiness that allowed Freud's new ideas to flourish in Victorian Vienna.

Challenges to Freud's misconceptions about women were raised immediately, but they could not break through the resistance of the more powerful male-dominated society of the day. I hope that this kind of suppression will not occur again. To that end, an informed community of women is essential to assure the survival of the fledgling psychological theories being developed by contemporary theorists. These theories aim to reflect a woman's perspective as accurately and comprehensively as previous models have reflected a man's. An informed public will tip the balance in the power struggle about who decides which theories will set the tone for the psychological services our society provides.

All clinicians are exposed to a male-influenced perspective of psychological theory. Upon reading this book, you will be knowledgeable about the basic aspects of a female-influenced perspective. As you are exposed to psychology in any of the forms in which it appears in our culture—popular books, educational programs, religious services, or medical care—you will do so with a more balanced perspective. If you actually seek the services of a mental-health professional, you will be able to assess their clinical bias. An informed public will assure that a female-influenced perspective cannot be ignored by any theorist or clinician who wishes to offer quality care.

So let's move on to examine the development of psychological theory from a historical perspective. The larger tapestry will serve as the context in which we follow the threads of the development of the psychology of women.

NOTES

1. George Mora, "History of Psychiatry," in *Comprehensive Textbook of Psychiatry*, 4th ed., ed. Harold I. Kaplan and Benjamin Sadock (Baltimore: Williams and Wilkins, 1985), pp. 2034–54.

2. Dorothea Dix, Julia Lanthrop, and Jane Addams were leaders in initiating reforms in the treatment of people with emotional problems. Along with others, especially the National Child Labor Committee, the National Women's Trade Union League, and the National Association for the Advancement of Colored People, they were instrumental in adding a social perspective to our understanding of psychological distress.

3. Mental-health services are provided by professionals in nursing, social work, education, and religion. No one practitioner, theorist, or professional orientation is necessarily superior to any other. Each has something to offer.

1 | Historical Perspective

The most famous physician-theorist was Sigmund Freud (1856–1939) who popularized psychological theory and invented psychoanalysis. At the age of thirty, Freud opened his practice in Vienna; nine years later, in 1895, he published his first book, *Studies in Hysteria: General Theory of Sexual Development*. At the center of Freudian theory was the premise that people were motivated by a self-centered desire for pleasure[1] and that this desire needed to be carefully controlled lest it cause serious trouble. We now know that the avant-garde theories proposed by Freud were fraught with distortions as well as intriguing concepts. Few of his ideas have stood the test of time intact, and modern clinicians and researchers have altered and refined classic Freudian psychoanalytic theory. But at the turn of the century, Freud's dramatic and heady proposals seemed to explain the emotional distress reported by many of the affluent clientele who sought his ministrations.

Freudian Theory: The Roots of Psychoanalysis

Freud argued that rather than exercising conscious control of free will, people were motivated by unconscious forces. While a woman might have a rational explanation for why she did what she did, she often did not know the "real" reason for her actions. Her genuine motivation was presumed to be outside her conscious awareness. The discipline of psychoanalysis attempted to understand these unconscious forces.

In Freudian psychoanalysis, patients experiencing distress were encouraged to talk freely about themselves. The psychoanalyst instructed the patient to say anything that came into her mind, no matter how strange or seemingly inconsequential. The therapist then listened carefully while the patient described her thoughts and expressed her feelings. These "free associations," as Freud called them, were presumed to offer clues to underlying unconscious motivations. Dreams were believed to be "the royal road to the knowledge of the unconscious,"[2] and patients were encouraged to report these as well. This material, when listened to attentively by a trained clinician, was believed to reveal unconscious patterns of thought and emotional reactions that the astute clinician could identify and help the patient to understand. By becoming aware of her unconscious patterns, it was assumed that the patient understood herself better and could then use rational free choice to direct her life rather than being driven to act by unconscious factors.

The interpretations of these dreams and free associations were, however, more in the hands of the psychoanalyst than the patient; contrary to the common assumptions among the analytic and lay community, these interpretations were not value free. They very much depended upon the beliefs and attitudes of the individual clinician.

Freud's View of Women

Freud's beliefs about women and their proper role revealed itself early in his career when he strongly criticized John Stuart Mill's *On the Subjection of Women*. Mill felt that women deserved the opportunity to become economically independent and to participate fully in public life. Freud rejected these arguments. He insisted that a woman could not earn as much as a man because her domestic responsibilities demanded her full attention. Employment, Freud wrote, "would require the suppression of her tender attribute, the ideal of womanhood, determined by law through her beauty, charm, and sweetness . . . Law and custom have much to give women that has been withheld from them, but the position of women will surely be what it is: in youth an adored darling and in mature years a loved wife."

Freud believed that for both females and males, there was only one basic pattern of human personality development. His psychosexual stages were based on the premise that each child was born with an undifferentiated sexual energy. This energy was organized around specific body areas, and each child moved through successive stages until she reached the final stage, mature genital heterosexuality. Anything other than this "normal" course of development was considered a sign of psychological illness.

Freud believed that at each stage, certain areas of the body were responsive to pleasurable stimulation. He called these areas erotogenic zones. The first erotogenic zone was the mouth. Infants in the first year of life, the period designated the *oral stage* by Freud, derive gratification and pleasure from feeding. Freud thought that any sucking activities not strictly necessary for nutrition were motivated by a rudimentary sexual drive.

During the second and third year of life, children develop more self-control. Freud saw this as especially evident in a child's growing ability to control her bowel movements. He designated this the *anal stage*. He suggested that children obtain pleasure from holding on to and releasing their bowel movements. He speculated that this phase was particularly important to children because proper performance would result in parental approval.

Strangely enough, Freud labeled years three through five the *phallic stage* (not clitoral stage) of development.[3] By this age, a child is usually quite well coordinated and can manipulate almost any part of her body. Freud believed that during these years, the focus of sexual pleasure shifts to the genitals.

Together, these three stages were called infantile sexuality (or, more recently, the pre-Oedipal period) and were believed to be repressed as part of the unconscious. But even though these experiences, thoughts, and feelings were no longer a part of an adult's conscious awareness, Freud believed that they had great influence on personality and behavior.

The next stage of development, which Freud called *latency*, began around age six and lasted until puberty. It was believed that during this period, there was little outward sign of sexually motivated behavior. With the surge of sexual impulses that accompanied puberty, the young person entered the *genital stage*. When these sexual feelings were directed toward someone of the opposite sex, it was assumed that the person had achieved maturity.

Girls versus Boys

Freud believed that female and male development were similar until the phallic stage. At that point, certain critical events were believed to occur that led to the development of "normal" feminine or masculine behavior. Freud called these events the Oedipus complex because it reminded him of Sophocles' fifth-century B.C. play, *Oedipus Rex*.

At the beginning of the play, a soothsayer tells the king that the child his wife is carrying will grow up to kill his father (the king) and marry his mother (the queen). To prevent his own death, the king orders a slave to abandon the newborn baby, Oedipus, in a remote mountain wilderness. But the child is rescued. He grows to adulthood, and unknowingly kills his own father in battle. He marries his mother, unaware of their relationship, and they have four children. Later, when he learns the truth of his past, he is horrified by what he has done and puts out his own eyes.

Freud thought that this story represented a universal theme for all small boys.[4] He believed that every young boy was in love with his mother and viewed his father as a rival for her affections. These feelings were unacceptable and caused the little boy considerable anxiety. When he discovered that boys and men have penises while girls and women do not, he imagined that females have lost their penises as punishment for such unacceptable feelings. He feared that he may lose his as well. This fear of castration was so intense that he was forced to abandon his mother as a sexual love object. He did this by relegating his forbidden Oedipal wish to his unconscious. At this point, he enters the latency stage and moves into an identification with his father and other men.

It is not too difficult to understand how the Oedipus story might have seemed to represent the experience of some boys. But it is almost inconceivable that Freud was able to convince himself that this same line of thinking also applied to girls. It was this assumption that led him into the dangerous quagmire of penis envy.

Penis Envy

Freud hypothesized that as a girl enters the phallic stage, she notices that the male's penis was larger than her clitoris. This discrepancy would appear quite unfair, and she would feel jealous and resentful. Freud speculated that these feelings resulted in a permanent sense of inferiority.

Freud further reasoned that as she came to realize that all females lacked penises, the little girl would grow up seeing women as inferior to men. He believed that this penis envy was pushed out of consciousness, but a woman's lingering unconscious resentment would give rise to a profound jealousy. Freud believed that this explained why women seemed far more prone to jealousy than men.[5]

Freud believed that healthy development required a girl to go through a period in which she rejected her mother as a love object, blaming her mother for the fact that neither mother nor daughter possessed a penis. The focus of the girl's interest and pleasure then became her father, who replaced her mother as her love object. Thereafter, Mother was presumably viewed as a rival.

Once the girl accepts the fact that she will never have a penis, Freud believed, she wishes for a child as a substitute. Thus, she makes her father, not her mother, her love object by substituting a desire to have a baby for the missing penis. In this way, the little girl is assumed to adopt a feminine attitude toward her father and imagines one day taking her mother's place.

Freud believed that a young girl's normal development could be diverted in two principal ways, either of which resulted in a psychological disturbance:

- If her penis envy left her dissatisfied with her inadequate clitoris and overshadowed any enjoyment she had previously found in clitoral stimulation, she would repress her sexual impulses. She would then become frigid—sexually disinterested or inhibited—and labeled neurotic.[6]
- If she refused to see herself as castrated and continued genital masturbation, she might develop what Freud called the masculinity complex. By this he meant that she was reluctant to accept her appropriate feminine role, that she harbored fantasies of being like a man, and that she was vulnerable to homosexuality.

Female Characteristics

According to Freud, the pathway to maturity was more difficult for heterosexual women than for heterosexual men. After all, boys learned to treat women—their mothers—as their original love objects. Shifting their affection and sexual attraction from mother to other women was not difficult. But girls' development seemed to take a much more circuitous route. Freud believed that girls had to switch from their original love objects, their mothers, to their fathers and from there to male lovers.

In addition, Freud believed that girls had to switch their erotogenic zone from their clitoris to their vagina. He believed that any woman who required clitoral stimulation to achieve orgasm was psychosexually immature. A normal adult woman, according to Freud, would be able to have an orgasm by vaginal stimulation alone.

Freud thought that women had several other psychological vulnerabilities that were uncommon in men, particularly narcissism, vanity, and shame. He observed that many girls and young women enjoyed dressing themselves up in pretty clothes and jewelry. He viewed this presumed preoccupation with themselves as a strong need to be loved and admired. He called this characteristic narcissism.[7] He believed that women were vain and placed special value on their physical attractiveness to compensate for their sense of inferiority. The source of their shame and sense of deficiency was the awareness that women's genitals were inferior to men's.

To his credit, Freud acknowledged his ignorance about the psychology of women, even as late as 1926. Unfortunately, this did not prevent his theories from gaining wide acceptance.

Freud's Model of the Psyche

In Freud's model, the mind was composed of three parts:

- the id, which represented unconscious instinctual desires and impulses,
- the superego, or conscience, which was formed through the child's identification with her parents, and
- the ego, the mediator between the instinctual demands of the id and the rules of the superego, which allowed the individual to adapt and mature according to society's wishes and restrictions.

Freud believed that a young man would reach mature adulthood through enduring the psychological pain of resolving the Oedipus complex under the threat of castration. By going through this process, Freud believed that a particularly strong superego or moral conscience was formed in men, which permitted them to function as autonomous, impersonal people, independent of emotion. Since a little girl was, in Freud's view, already castrated, she lacked the castration anxiety necessary to form a mature superego. Consequently, Freud believed that women had a weaker moral conscience than men. He believed that this was reflected in an inferior sense of justice, a weaker social interest, and a tendency to be ruled by their emotions to such an extent that they were incapable of objective judgment.

There are several other prominent ideas of Freudian psychology well-known even to those who have never read his original work:

- Unconscious drives and feelings threatening to the ego or superego are repressed by defense mechanisms, which preserve an internal conflict between the id and ego or superego in an attempt to stave off feelings of anxiety.
- There is considerable conscious and unconscious resistance to allowing this repressed material to emerge into an individual's awareness.
- People demonstrate a tendency to transfer to others feelings and attitudes that were originally associated with important figures in early childhood, particularly parents. Freud called this phenomenon transference.

Freud's Critics

In spite of the ingenuity of his theories, Freud seemed relatively blind to the restrictions on personality development caused by the reality of life in the Victorian era. This led to several psychological myths, many of which have been perpetuated by the psychologists and psychiatrists who have succeeded Freud.[8]

Myth 1: "It's all in your head"—Traditional theory assumes that individual psychology can be understood in the abstract, that is apart from the specific society in which a woman lives. This belief does not recognize the complex interrelationship between an individual's psychological development and the family and social structure within which she evolves and lives.

Debunking Myth 1: "Trusting your thoughts and feelings"—Every society contributes to the creation of people with specific personality types. There are different expectations of the roles to be played by women and men, therefore different psychological developments will be encouraged. People who adapt to these differing psychologies will be viewed as "normal."

Emotional distress often signals a reluctance to adapt to these roles or norms. This conflict is not confined to the internal struggle between personal desires and moral conscience, although this may certainly occur. A substantial amount of conflict arises from the struggle between the individual's longing to be authentic and the limitations to that authenticity imposed by external factors. In a society which devalues a woman's experiences, it is often difficult to evolve a sense of self that accurately reflects her own thoughts and feelings.

Myth 2: "The medical model of psychopathology"—This is the notion that a person's current psychological symptoms can be traced back to some flaw in her internal structure that appeared in her early life.

Along with the "it's all in your head" mythology, the traditional psychoanalytic model assumed "it's all in your childhood." A person's current emotional distress was believed to be determined by the events of her early childhood and her reaction to them. Primary emphasis was placed upon her early personal, family, social, and sexual history. If there were any deviations from the assumed norm, this abnormal developmental pattern was "diagnosed" as the explanation for her current problems. Therapeutic interpretations and interventions were aimed at "curing" her individual pathology.

Debunking Myth 2: "Psychological growth occurs within the context of relationships"—Certainly diagnostic labels may sometimes aid us by serving as a kind of shorthand to communicate about the kinds of adaptive strategies an individual has created in order to survive and cope with troubling relationships throughout her life. However, all too often these diagnostic labels have been used pejoratively to define the individual as being psychologically "diseased." For example, the recent creation of a diagnosis called *masochistic personality disorder* implies that a woman has a problem when she stays in a relationship in which she is treated as less important and valued than her partner. Assigning this "disease" to a woman, as if society has not trained her to live in this manner, holds the victim responsible for a situation that is almost inevitable in a society that fosters inequality between women and men. When a woman conducts her life in a fashion that does not appear psychologically healthy, we must look at the historical and current relationship factors that have contributed to this situation, as well as the choices she has made that have brought her to this point.

Myth 3: "The neutral expert"—The traditional model of therapy fosters an emotional distance between the person in pain and the person they have sought out for help. It is argued that this distance is more professional and scientific than therapy that offers emotional connection and nurturance. The relative silence and lack of interaction in the traditional model is more reflective of a male style of personal interaction and is assumed to be "neutral." It helps the authority to establish and maintain a position that is "clinically" removed and intellectually superior to the person in therapy.

Debunking Myth 3: "The greatest healing power is in experiencing the sense of being heard and responded to in a consistently empathic and supportive way"—A therapy relationship, like all other relationships, has the potential to enhance or detract from our sense of self. People usually come to therapy because they hurt. If their legitimate adult need for support and reassurance is interpreted as only an expression of early unmet needs and desires, and if the therapist remains cool and detached, the person's loneliness and emotional isolation is reenacted. It is very common for new patients to ask me what kind of therapy I do and to tell me about previous experiences with therapy where the therapist just sat there, seldom saying a word. Patients rarely find this helpful. It does not feel like neutrality. It feels as if nobody is there. In a neutral therapy relationship, the therapist is recapitulating the male-developmental sequence—the absence of a connection and the lonely experience of feeling deprived of genuine human contact.

A female-oriented model is far less neutral. A patient can almost feel the room warm as the therapist communicates, often nonverbally, that she understands how bad the patient has been feeling and how anyone in that situation might be upset. Women are trained to nurture, and a female-influenced psychology reflects this strength. Interestingly, there is now considerable evidence that the change-producing potential of psychotherapy is directly related to the empathic and supportive attitudes of the therapist. The distant, disease-oriented style of the "expert role" may actually be destructive to the helping relationship.[9]

Many critics—both inside and outside the psychoanalytic profession—have interpreted Freud's glorification of the penis as a thinly veiled projection of his belief in the innate superiority of the male. They have taken him to task for basing his theories solely on biology and ignoring the profound influence of the social environment. However, defenders of Freud remind us that critics rarely acknowledge the caveats Freud placed on his conclusions.[10] They argue that he was aware that his opinions were based on a tiny number of cases and would require additional validation before they could be viewed as universal. They also insist that Freud was well aware of social influences, even though he chose not to emphasize them in his work.

Even avowed feminists have come to Freud's defense. Juliet Mitchell[11] argues that the Freudian model does describe female psychology in a culture where men are dominant and hold more positions of power. She points out that in a culture where women are subordinate, this model does describe how little girls move psychologically into their position of subordination and how little boys disengage psychologically from their mothers via the Oedipus complex and prepare to assume the male role.

Psychoanalysis: The Most Influential Psychological Theory

Psychoanalysis has had an enormous influence on Western culture. Each of us has been exposed to its teachings. Think of how many times someone has teased you about making a Freudian slip when something rolled off your tongue that was not what you intended to say but was somehow revealing. Psychoanalysis has had an even greater influence on mental-health professionals. Because of its pervasive influence, it is important to understand how Freud's theories about women came to be developed.

Freud's view of women grew out of his clinical experience with a very limited number of psychologically distressed women during the years he was in practice (1890–1939) as well as his personal experience with female friends and family.[12] His personal views have had a significant effect upon how our culture has viewed women and how women have come to view themselves.

Even today, psychoanalytic theory, including its perspectives about women, maintains a stronghold in many therapeutic circles.[13] Whenever an outsider, someone not trained as an analyst, raises criticisms, they are often dismissed on the grounds that the person does not fully understand the theory. Many therapists claim that psychoanalytic theory is the only comprehensive psychological theory as an argument for their reluctance to give credibility to other ideas. A comprehensive theory is not necessarily an accurate theory. However, these defenses have served to prevent a radical and complete revision of psychaoanalytic theory.[14]

Early Psychoanalytic Revisions of the Psychology of Women

Psychoanalysis grew out of—and ultimately defended—a culture that was dominated by men. Interestingly, Freudianism and feminism were evolving side-by-side during the early 1900s. In many respects, they were countervailing forces. Feminism argued that women deserved equal freedoms, equal pay, and equal social status. Freudianism held that women were inferior to men in virtually all spheres—intellectual, practical, social, emotional, and political.[15]

For the first five decades of the twentieth century, Freudian thought prevailed. However, there were challenges to Freud's beliefs from the very beginning. While some theorists made only minor alterations in Freudian theory, others differed considerably.

The less radical revisionists, such as Helene Deutsch, were welcomed by Freud. Their perspectives were integrated into his own work. However, several female analysts—and a few men—believed that Freud had very idiosyncratic understanding of female psychology. They immediately began contradicting and revising classical Freudian theory. Some of the women pointed out that their own perspectives and experiences might add to the understanding of women in general. They would certainly provide a point of view that was different than that available to their male colleagues.

Those who challenged Freud's basic tenets, Alfred Adler, Karen Horney, and others, were considered heretics. Most of them left the inner circle of Freud's closest colleagues and their contributions were never integrated into mainstream psychoanalytic thought. Indeed, much of what contradicted orthodox Freudian theory was simply overlooked.[16]

Helene Deutsch published her two-volume *Psychology of Women* in 1944 and 1945. She agreed with many Freudian theories but challenged others. Deutsch shared Freud's belief that sexuality was less important for women than for men. She also agreed that child rearing and home management were the acceptable channels for women's ambition. She considered women who participated in intellectual and nondomestic activities as unfeminine and abnormal.

She also accepted the notion of penis envy as real but did not think that it played a major role in female development. Instead, she argued that feelings of envy were experiences of both women and men. She pointed out, for example, that envy may arise when a new sibling claims a portion of our parents' love and attention or when another child has something of value that we would like to have.

Deutsch also disagreed with Freud's belief that daughters reject their mothers in favor of an attachment to their fathers. She believed that the mother-daughter tie was a strong one that would change but not break as the daughter matured.

One of Deutsch's specific contributions to the psychology of women was her definitions of three personality characteristics as central to femininity: narcissism, passivity, and masochism.

Deutsch believed that narcissism—loving and valuing of the self—had both positive and negative aspects. She saw healthy narcissism as an inherent part of self-esteem—that is, self-respect and caring about oneself independently of other's opinions. She saw unhealthy narcissism as an immature concern and preoccupation with oneself to the point where one requires constant affirmation from others.[17]

The notion of passivity—an attitude of receptive waiting and expectancy—was central to Deutsch's concept of femininity. A woman could be active to the degree that it did not interfere with her role as a wife and mother. However, while a man was expected to have an independent identity, to be objective and rational, a woman was expected to be more subjective, to adapt her opinion and tastes to those of her husband and to use her intuition as a way of "knowing" in the absence of facts.

When Deutsch spoke of masochism she did not mean that women liked pain. She used the term to imply that in many of women's life experiences, such as childbirth, pain was linked with pleasure. Deutsch believed that this ability to accept pleasure and pain, good times and bad, was a necessary prerequisite for a healthy adaptation as a mother. It allowed women to be more sexually receptive and more maternally nurturing than men.

Alfred Adler was initially a member of Freud's inner circle, but he withdrew as he found himself in increasing disagreement with the Freudian model. In marked contrast to Freud, Adler did not believe that people were driven by sexual and instinctual urges alone or that they were all at the mercy of events that occurred in their early childhood. Instead, Adler emphasized the importance of conscious planning, a desire to cooperate, and the powerful human desire for social contact with others.

Adler believed that, for the most part, adults are aware of why they do what they do. He saw each person as building a unique life for themselves based upon conscious rather than unconscious motives, behaving in ways that reflected these conscious choices. He felt that most of us know what our goals are as well as our strengths and limitations in striving for them. He also believed that we can plan our behavior and our lives knowing what the choices we make mean for the realization of our goals and our own development.

In a more optimistic vein than Freud's, Adler believed that the majority of people wanted to preserve their relationships and because of this were motivated to behave in a cooperative manner that would foster the best for everyone. He proposed that people were less motivated by their past experiences than by their personal belief system, arguing that our beliefs make us behave in a relatively consistent fashion. For example, a woman who believes that honesty is the best policy will return a lost wallet or leave a note if she accidentally damages a parked car. Rather than the past having a deterministic grip on our present and future, as Freud emphasized, Adler believed that we plan for our futures guided by our personal and conscious philosophies.

He also disagreed with Freud on the psychology of women. Adler wrote that "all our institutions, our traditional attitudes, our laws, our morals, our customs, give evidence of the fact that they are determined and maintained by privileged males for the glory of male domination."[18] Adler also predicted that women would not put up with their second-class status for long: "The whole history of civilization . . . shows us that the pressure exerted upon women, and inhibitions to which she must submit today, are not to be borne by any human being; they always give rise to revolt."

Like many contemporary feminists, Adler understood that men were psychologically damaged by their social conditioning for dominance. However, he believed strongly that women were far more damaged because of the prejudices against them. Adler did not see the almost universal female dissatisfaction with the role women were expected to play as some deficiency on the part of women. Rather, he understood that these complaints related to social and cultural factors. Unlike Freud, who viewed biology as destiny, Adler saw women as understandably protesting the privilege and power of men.

Karen Horney was encouraged by her mother to become a physician when this was still an uncommon profession for women. Initially trained in classical Freudian theory, Horney later shifted to a more humanistic approach. She found herself virtually alone as a woman daring to criticize and modify Freud's ideas.[19]

By 1926, Horney was sharply disagreeing with Freud. Horney rejected many Freudian ideas about women, particularly penis envy, female masochism, and female inferiority. She believed that these theories were the fantasies of men projected onto women. She thought it was nothing more than male self-centeredness that led to an emphasis on the penis as pivotal in female development.

As she pointed out, the psychology of women, far from being objective, had evolved from a very biased male perspective. She emphasized that any psychological hypothesis needed to be substantiated by actual observations of behavior. Indeed, she speculated that men actually clung to these inventions of their own making because they envied women's ability to bear and breast-feed children. She speculated that the male overemphasis on achievement was a substitute for the creative childbearing capacity of women.

Horney also questioned whether concepts developed from therapy sessions with psychologically distressed women could be fairly applied to all women. In Horney's time, even more so than ours, most institutions and families were dominated by men. She argued that it was a woman's less-powerful position that was the primary influence on her psychology. A woman was expected to adapt to a man's desires; in doing so, this adaptation would seem to be her true self. Rather than being rooted in a woman's biology or childhood fantasies, Horney believed that the resulting traits of masochism, passivity, narcissism, and penis envy were a part of the false self women developed in response to a male-dominated, patriarchal culture. This was an understandable response to woman's subordinate position but far from the preferred situation for maximum psychological health.

Like Adler, Horney's theories about human nature were more optimistic than Freud's. She believed that the need for security motivated human behavior more than sex and aggression. While Freud saw humankind as doomed to conflict, Horney saw people as striving toward self-development and knowledge. She proposed that a child whose needs were met on a regular and consistent basis would grow up healthy and secure.

If the child sensed that her environment was unresponsive or hostile, she would feel insecure and develop feelings of anxiety, isolation, and helplessness. To cope with these feelings, the child would adopt a variety of strategies for dealing with other people. She would try to decrease her insecurity by moving toward people, moving away from people, or moving against people. In a healthy person, these three strategies are integrated and balanced, but in an insecure person, one or more of these strategies is exaggerated.

Thus, an insecure woman becomes either overcompliant and docile, withdrawn and isolated, or overly aggressive. While these "solutions" provide temporary relief from anxiety, in the long run they restrict a woman's growth by undermining her self-esteem and by interfering with the development of satisfying relationships.

Horney was excluded from orthodox Freudian circles. Insult was added to injury when many of Horney's ideas were incorporated into the works of others without giving her the credit she was due.[20] This "gentle rebel's"[21] pioneering work has not yet been given the acknowledgment it deserves.[22]

The Integration and Evolution of Psychoanalysis

Although the discipline was developed by physicians, nonphysicians were permitted to join some psychoanalytic circles. These so-called lay analysts were trained in and practiced psychoanalysis. The participation of people from outside the medical field reflected a fundamental confusion as to whether psychoanalysis and the clinical practice based on its theories really ought to be considered a component of medicine.[23] This confusion has yet to be resolved.

Certainly many physicians and lay analysts contributed to the development of psychoanalytic theory, but despite his many critics, Freud's perspective— including his rather bizarre collection of theories about women—became most influential. Freud's critics, insightful as they were, had neither the political clout nor a sufficiently receptive professional or lay audience to radically alter the views of orthodox Freudians.

In frustration, some of Freud's critics broke away from his influence. A few established independent and competing training programs.[24] Horney, for example, helped establish the Association for the Advancement of Psychoanalysis in New York in 1941, which provided a viable alternative to the Freudian training at the New York Psychoanalytic Institute.

Although almost every one practicing psychotherapy today has been exposed to the teachings of psychoanalytic theory, few contemporary clinicians consider themselves pure Freudian psychoanalysts. In the years after the early criticisms and revisions, the field of psychoanalysis has become increasingly refined and varied. Several influential schools including ego psychology, object relations theory, and self-psychology have evolved as outgrowths of traditional psychoanalytic theory[25] and have greatly altered psychoanalytic practice.

Heinz Hartman is usually considered the major developer of ego psychology,[26] although Anna Freud, Freud's daughter, probably launched its development with the publication of her 1946 book *The Ego and the Mechanisms of Defense.* Unlike orthodox Freudian theory, ego psychology emphasizes the key role of the ego in psychological development. Proponents of this school view the ego as developing independently from the id, or instinctual feelings. This perspective was much more helpful than orthodox Freudian theory in explaining how people cope with reality by not only controlling their feelings, but by controlling their thinking as well. It shows how people interact with their social environment by adapting to the external reality of their lives.

Object relations theorists[27] see the development of an individual's personality as firmly based within the context of relationships. They consider the first two years of life the most important for the development of the inner core of the person, what might be called the ego. Proponents of this school assume that infants have a primary need for human contact and that the thing that makes each person unique is the particular way that her personality, or ego, develops within the context of her early relationships. The name object relations stems from the belief that the growing infant psychologically internalizes other human beings to make up her own inner world. These theorists thought that therapy should include awareness of and adaptation to the contact and care the individual wants and needs. Unlike the Freudians, followers of the object relations school understand the importance of nurturance within the therapy relationship.

The development of self-psychology is most commonly attributed to Heinz Kohut[28] and Otto Kernberg.[29] Kohut seems to have been strongly influenced by ego psychology. He thought that environmental conditions, rather than inner conflicts, were the key determinants in the development of a sense of self. By the term *self*, Kohut meant a kind of common-sense notion referring to the whole person. Rather than the relatively dehumanizing label of *object*, Kohut's sense of the self included both mind and body with its conscious and unconscious components.

Kohut believed that with optimal early parenting, a child would develop a sense of self that would permit psychological independence. He did not mean that the goal was social isolation or withdrawal. Kohut understood that we have a need for relationships throughout our lives. However, he believed that while we all have an ongoing preference to be in relationships, a person with a solid sense of self can feel content and satisfied when she is alone. For a variety of reasons, many of the people who seek help from a therapist do not possess this solid sense of self. In providing therapeutic care for them, Kohut advocated the use of empathy, in contrast to the strict "neutrality" advocated by earlier psychoanalysts.

Otto Kernberg's work seems to have evolved more from the object relations school than from ego psychology, and his experience particularly emphasized the problems of severely disturbed individuals. As a result, it is unclear how much of theory applies to more psychologically healthy people.

Many of the contemporary theorists engaged in rethinking the psychology of women find these revisions of analytic theory more sensible and accurate reflections of human development than the models originally proposed by Freud. Most of these theories recognize that the social and cultural environment have an impact upon individual development. But none fully acknowledged the way women's subordinate position influences the mother-child relationship and has profound consequences for the development of differing female and male psychologies.

The Parallel Contributions of Academic Circles

The problem with all psychoanalytical theories is that they are virtually impossible to verify. Insights depend not on objective measures but solely upon the subjective opinion of the analyst. In fact, much of psychoanalytical theory is based on a handful of case studies. For example, Helene Deutsch studied eleven lesbian women and concluded that homosexuality in women was due to a regression to an earlier stage of development.

Academic psychologists and researchers were producing their own theories of human nature while Freud and others were developing and refining psychoanalytic theory. These psychologists relied on controlled observation and quantitative measurement rather than clinical observations. As a result, they claimed that their conclusions were more objective. However, as we will show, the interpretations of these theorists were also not immune from bias.

Psychologists began to pay particular attention to women around 1900 when they started to incorporate evolutionary theory into their work. Behavior observed in animals was believed to be biologically based. Beginning with the premise that humans evolved from lower animals, the researchers speculated that behavior in humans that appeared analogous to behavior in animals must be innate.

It comes as no surprise then that psychologists became enchanted with the notion of the maternal instinct. After observing the behavior of animals, it seemed reasonable to these psychologists that women were biologically destined to serve as the exclusive caretakers of children. As a result, it was taken for granted that all women were born to be mothers. They were not encouraged to question whether or not they wanted to have and to raise children. Furthermore, because women were seen as biologically destined for motherhood, it was assumed that every woman instinctively knew how to care for children. Given this assumption, any "failures" in mothering were easily and quickly translated into the woman being labeled a purposefully "bad" mother. This kind of false thinking was only one of many contributions to a long history of mother-blaming and holding women responsible for the psychological ills of others.

The maternal instinct and other old-fashioned notions about women were part of a circular argument that blamed women's lesser contribution to public activities on their innately inferior status. What was ignored were the many obstacles to women's full participation in public activities.

To make matters worse, the scientists of the time began explaining the perceived inferiority of women based upon the biological differences between women and men. They noted, for example, that women had smaller brains than men and therefore concluded that men were more powerful, competent, and successful. As a result, men were obviously better suited for important public work, whereas women should limit themselves to the presumably less challenging tasks of child rearing and home maintenance. The fact that psychological testing contradicted these beliefs was conveniently ignored.

Some scientists even proposed a causal relationship between a woman's reproductive capacities and her intelligence. They argued that the rigors of education would drain energy from her reproductive organs and interfere with her healthy fertility. Again, the utter biological impossibility of this phenomenon did not prevent its rapid incorporation into scientific knowledge.

It was relatively easy for the thinkers of the time to accept the notion that men were naturally and biologically superior to women, because the assumption that men were superior was already widely accepted. These hypotheses were easily integrated into scientific knowledge—even in the face of contradictory data—because people wanted to believe they were true. Male superiority was consistent with the political climate of the day.

This point is extremely important. As we begin to explore some of the most interesting recent contributions to the psychology of women in the next chapter, those who prefer the old views may attempt to reject the newer concepts on the grounds that such theories are political rather than scientific.[30] However, as we have shown, outdated theories of male superiority sprang from blatantly political considerations.

From Instinct to Learning

By the mid-1920s, the behaviorist school of psychology began to challenge mainstream psychiatry and psychology. Behavioral theorists believe that most human behavior is learned rather than driven by instinct. By the 1950s, they had developed a comprehensive and systematic approach to clinical problems that has continued to grow exponentially. When people experience psychological distress, behaviorists are able to offer a selection of techniques that are designed to reduce the individual's anxiety and help them master uncomfortable situations. These strategies have been particularly useful in reducing severe panic disorders and agoraphobia.[31]

According to the behaviorists, women learn how to be mothers. In the early 1900s, few women participated in the public world because they were prevented access to the necessary training and education on the grounds that they neither wanted it nor could use it effectively. In fact, it was a lack of opportunity rather than innate inferiority that led women into motherhood to the exclusion of involvement in other arenas.

Values Influence Knowledge

Obviously, in looking back at earlier sexist beliefs, we might assume that much has changed in recent decades. However, in addition to the obstacles that prevented the full development of women for generations, we must remember that beliefs influence our interpretation of science. Psychology is not value free. It would be unwise to assume that current psychological theories are devoid of similar influence. The best that we can do is to identify the values that do color our perspective.

Physicians, therapists, educators, clergy, and applied scientists like to consider their knowledge objective. But the fact is that our understanding of why people behave the way they do is very much influenced by the social and political values of the era in which we live. Scientific knowledge about humans is always subjectively influenced by the social context in which it is studied.[32,33] Theories of women's intellectual inferiority and innate desire to mother satisfied both laypersons and professionals. Consequently, except for some limited interest in the topic of sex differences, theorists did not engage in a comprehensive, scientific study of women until the late 1960s.

Humanistic Psychology

Before a contemporary psychology of women was initiated, however, both psychoanalysis and experimental psychology were challenged by yet another emerging branch of psychological theory: humanistic psychology. One of the most prominent theorists from this school, Carl Rogers, began publishing his ideas in the 1950s.[34] "No other mode of psychotherapy has been so thoroughly investigated by the methods of empirical research as [his] client-centered therapy."[35]

Humanistic psychology was opposed to the medical model characteristic of both psychoanalysis and clinical psychology.[36] Rather than emphasizing the necessity of establishing the correct diagnosis and interpretation of a person's illness, Rogers argued that the therapeutic relationship was the crucial factor in healing emotional trauma. The humanistic model introduced the idea of personal growth through therapy. Rogers minimized the notion that childhood events were central to a person's adult psychology. His central hypothesis was that each person's potential could be realized in a relationship in which another person (usually called the helping person) offered sensitive and accurately empathic understanding and unconditional positive regard and was herself experiencing and communicating her own realness. Research with people suffering with all forms of psychological distress have tended to substantiate Rogers's beliefs.[37]

This movement away from reliance on "expert" psychiatrists and psychologists toward a belief in people's ability to help one another through compassionate relationships was a new and more optimistic model that placed an emphasis on self-care. However, the unshakable belief in the individual's capacity to create herself and her own life completely ignored social reality. Humanistic psychology, and the multimillion-dollar pop-psychology, growth-therapy industry that grew out of it, argue that you are responsible for your own reality—not society, not the environment, not the past, but you as a person right now. Your personal problems are all in your head. The way you view your life is your problem. You are not sick. You are all-powerful.

In the beginning, it seemed like a reassuring concept. How nice to imagine that all the terrible things that happened to some people as children could be relegated to a completely forgotten past that had absolutely no influence over their current life. How liberating to imagine that all the obstacles to individual freedom, including sexism, racism, and other forms of arbitrary discrimination, were irrelevant.

This psychology was developed with the best of intentions. It moved away from the older model that embraced the more stereotypical male-influenced values of intellectual insight, obedience to a male authority, and rigorous analytic self-discipline. It seemed to move toward more stereotypical female-influenced values by emphasizing the quality of the caretaking relationship and focusing on empathy and honest self-disclosure. However, the absence of a political perspective on woman's problems meant that the model was ultimately distorted to serve the needs of an entire group of people who rejected any notion of collective responsibility for one another's pain. Instead, they embraced the belief of absolute individual responsibility for one's own life. In the end, this model also blames the victim, albeit without diagnosing her as sick.

Neither the traditional theories nor these humanistic revisions recognized the critical role of society in the development of individual psychological distress. The traditional therapies emphasize achieving insight through verbal communication and interpretation, while the humanistic therapies emphasize achieving relief from emotional pain by expressing emotions. But self-awareness alone, no matter what techniques are used to achieve it, is limited unless that knowledge and emotional release is integrated within the context of the reality of the person's situation—including her social environment. Feelings and symptoms of psychological distress do not occur within a social vacuum. Awareness must include a sense of the relationship between these thoughts and feelings and the structure of a woman's life.

Psychological Development Throughout the Life Cycle

In the 1960s, Erik Erikson departed from psychology that centered on childhood and argued that development did not stop there.[38] He presented a model called the eight stages of man. The emphasis on "man" is important. Although the shift to acknowledging the capacity, indeed the necessity, for psychological growth throughout the life cycle was critical and empowering, the male experience was again used as the model for all human development. Applied to woman, it became a standard to which she could not measure up.

Erikson believed that each of us must pass through progressive stages of development on our way to maturity. Each stage is a kind of stepping stone to the next. Our success in resolving the struggles of one stage influenced our progression to the next. Erikson defined the eight stages as follows:[39]

1. Basic trust versus mistrust—learning that the provider of comfort is reliable, consistent, and predictable (oral).
2. Autonomy versus shame and doubt—learning to exercise independence and freedom of choice, along with self-control (anal).
3. Initiative versus guilt—undertaking, planning, and attacking a task for the sake of actively doing it (genital).
4. Industry versus inferiority—developing as a worker and producer (latency).

5. Identity versus role confusion—evolving a sense of self that is reliable and consistent, both for oneself and for others [puberty].
6. Intimacy versus isolation—readying oneself for a commitment to affiliations with others and developing the ethical strength to abide by such commitments [young adulthood].
7. Generativity versus stagnation—using oneself in the establishment and guidance of the next generation [adulthood].
8. Ego integrity versus despair—integrating the earlier stages into an acceptance of one's own life cycle and an assured confidence in one's own life-style [maturity].

Unfortunately, whether Erikson chose American Indians or Caucasians as his subjects, he always studied male-dominated societies. When making his observations, he failed to recognize the developmental impact of these cultures' sharply differentiated sex roles. Erikson seemed to recognize the power of social customs in shaping female psychology and behavior and appeared to value the particular qualities that women were taught to embody—particularly caring, compassion, nurturing, and acceptance. However, he idealized women's roles and denied the limitations that these role expectations placed on women's full and equal participation in society.

Even when Erikson did study women, he did not incorporate these observations into his models. For example, at the time Erikson was developing his life-span theory, he observed that for women, "intimacy" preceded "identity." A woman, whatever her occupation or intellectual skills, was expected to sacrifice her independent aspirations to commit herself to her husband's goals and to the care for him and their children. It was assumed that her identity was dependent upon supporting her husband's and children's development.

The reverse was expected of a man. Erikson accurately perceived that a man would be expected to develop his own identity first and only then proceed to intimacy. It is in this order that Erikson presents these developmental tasks. His eight stages of man model remained firmly grounded in the male role, although he presented it as if it were a theory of human development. He viewed the male as the norm, the prototype of human beings from which women deviated. This model needs major revisions before it will accurately reflect the developmental stages of both sexes.[40]

The paradox of Erikson's work is that while he recognized that society affected psychology, he still insisted that female psychology was driven by biology—not by the social customs that existed alongside particular biological realities. Like Freud, he saw a woman's body and her reproductive capabilities as determining her personality and behavior. He tended to overemphasize a woman's reproductive role as if it were the main determinant of her identity. Even though between 10 and 25 percent of women surveyed have said that they do not want to have children,[41] Erikson persisted in his identification of woman as mother.

In spite of the problems with Erikson's work, his model recognizes that psychological growth and development continues from birth to death. This notion was popularized by Gail Sheehy in her book *Passages,* which was primarily based upon the work of Daniel Levinson. Levinson later covered similar territory for men in his book *The Seasons of a Man's Life.* [42] Another impressive report of adult male development is George Vaillant's *Adaptation to Life.* [43] Both studies greatly expanded our understanding of the adult lives of advantaged men in our society. Unfortunately, neither study included women.[44] Sheehy implied that the data derived from the study of men could be applied to women as well, but many women found that her formulations did not reflect their experiences.

The Fallacy of Applying a Male-influenced Model to Women's Development

In marked contrast to theories about women, there are no theories of male personality resting upon men's role as father. Perhaps this is because a man's role in reproduction is only momentarily important. Certainly, fathers typically have less day-to-day responsibility for nurturing their offspring, but this may be determined more by economics and social expectations than psychology. In our culture, the norm is to exempt men from the daily tasks of childcare and nurturing. Understandably, these functions would therefore have little impact upon male personality development. We are only now beginning to understand the consequences of this role differentiation for developing children and their fathers and mothers. It is certainly not all positive.[45]

Mothers, in contrast to fathers, are never exempt from the role of parent. Since a woman's biology allows her to bring forth young and usually causes her to be assigned the social role of mother, she shares with all women a function and role different from men. This difference is considered to have a profound effect on a woman's sense of self. When all is said and done, a woman's psychological development is seen as a deviation from the norm, that is, a deviation from the psychology of men. This deviation is explained on the basis of a woman's potential or realized ability to have children.

Any psychological theory that portrays a woman's development based primarily on her childbearing capacity or as an exception to the male norm is not a theory of human development. The profound impact of society and the specific experiences of women within society must be incorporated into our understanding of psychology if it is to have any validity or usefulness.

Other Psychological Theories

There may be more than 250 different schools of psychotherapy, which variously involve the work of educators, religious and spiritual counselors, and self-help groups.[46] Although several of these schools have influenced our understanding of psychology, there are far too many variations to describe them in detail here. Suffice it to say that until recently, none has been grounded in a woman's perspective. Within the professional realm, female psychology has never been the standard against which men have been found lacking. No global developmental model has successfully established the realities of women's lives as equal to and as important as the realities of men's lives. Even the once optimistic emphasis on androgyny, a psychological model that assumed that the healthy individual had both "feminine" and "masculine" characteristics, has since been abandoned by its originator, Sandra Bem.[47]

Every psychological model must be examined from a woman-centered perspective to determine if changes are needed. Any psychology that assumes that a woman can gain full emotional health within the context of society as it is currently structured is inaccurate. Simply aiming for internal psychological change through insight, emotional release, and comfort ignores the systematic and institutionalized lack of power and access to power that forms the situation of a substantial number of women. When we look at the realities of women's lives throughout their life cycle, particularly the lives of women who experience psychological distress, we see a legacy of events that interfere with the development of a whole and healthy sense of self.

No matter which model we accept, there is no question that psychological development occurs within the context of relationships. A young girl all too often grows up in a family in which her primary caretaker is economically or personally devalued by her husband, where the child is directly exploited or mistreated physically, sexually, or emotionally by her "secondary" parent, and where there is differential treatment, expectations, and support for female and male siblings. True psychological health for women can only be achieved when these family obstacles to development, and all the other obstacles in schools and in the workplace, are removed.

A psychological model that will genuinely serve women must start with an understanding that women's distress is not all in our heads. Such a model must acknowledge the psychological impact of the social, economic, legal, and political realities of women's lives. The most essential feature of a female-influenced psychology acknowledges the relationship between the structure of women's lives and the psychological distress they experience. It recognizes and emphasizes women's strengths as well as their handicaps. Most importantly, it springs from the context of women's life experiences and values rather than men's.

In the next chapter, we will review the contemporary models of the psychology of women that have attempted to eradicate the anti-woman or gender-neutral bias of earlier models. Instead, these emerging models embrace a pro-woman perspective—both in childhood and throughout our lives.

NOTES

1. This was called libido or sexual drives and feelings.

2. Peter Gay, *Freud: A Life for Our Times* (New York: W. W. Norton, 1988).

3. Freud placed considerable emphasis on whether or not one had a penis and what that meant for one's development. He did not seem to appreciate that his emphasis on penises might have arisen because he had one and thus assumed that they were critically important. Female theoreticians of the same era were less enamored of this idea.

4. Two important points can be made here. First, it is significant that the boy who inadvertently killed his father and who expressed great remorse is held accountable for his actions, while the father who purposefully abandoned his son to die is seen as perfectly within his rights. For a further discussion of this see Alice Miller, *Thou Shalt Not Be Aware: Society's Betrayal of the Child* (New York: Farrar, Straus, Giroux, 1984). Second, while the Oedipus complex may be a fairly accurate description of early male development within the context of specific cultural and historical constraints, it cannot be assumed to be an accurate description of early female development. For a comprehensive review of this see Irene P. Stiver, *Beyond the Oedipus Complex: Mothers and Daughters* (Work in Progress, Wellesley, Mass.: Wellesley College, Stone Center for Developmental Services and Studies, 1986).

5. A more sensible explanation, which will be expanded upon in later chapters, is that little girls, through their own experiences and observations, begin to realize that females are treated as inferior to males. Being denied fair treatment understandably and appropriately leads to feelings of resentment. Jealousy is a common response to wanting something that is given to others but withheld or lost to ourselves—in this case, being treated with respect equal to males.

6. Neurosis, as defined in *A Psychiatric Glossary,* published by the American Psychiatric Association, is "an emotional maladaptation arising from an unresolved unconscious conflict. The anxiety is either felt directly or modified by various psychological mechanisms to produce other, subjectively distressing symptoms. The neuroses are usually considered less severe than the psychoses (although not always less disabling) because they manifest neither gross personality disorganization nor gross distortion or misinterpretation of external reality."

7. Narcissus was a mythological young Greek who fell in love with himself when he saw his own image reflected in a pool of water.

8. These myths were elucidated by Miriam Greenspan in *A New Approach to Women and Therapy* (New York: McGraw-Hill, 1983). The debunkings are our own.

9. C. B. Truax and K. M. Mitchell, "Research on Certain Therapist Interpersonal Skills in Relation to Process and Outcome," in *Handbook of Psychotherapy and Behavior Change,* ed. A. E. Bergin and S. L. Garfield (New York: John Wiley, 1971), pp. 328–29.

10. Juanita H. Williams, *Psychology of Women: Behavior in a Biosocial Context* (New York: W. W. Norton, 1977), pp. 27–28.

11. Juliet Mitchell, "On Freud and the Distinction Between the Sexes," in *Women & Analysis: Dialogues on Psychoanalytic Views of Femininity,* ed. Jean Strouse (New York: Laurel Editions, 1974), pp. 39–50.

12. Hannah Lerman, *A Mote in Freud's Eye: From Psychoanalysis to the Psychology of Women* (New York: Springer, 1986). See especially "The Women in Freud's Life," pp. 10–21 and "Who Were Freud's Patients," pp. 39–43.

13. See for example, Shahla Chehrazi, "Female Psychology," *Journal of the American Psychoanalytic Association,* 34 (1986): 111–62.

14. For a summary of the psychoanalytic revisions that have survived but have not necessarily been fully integrated into mainstream analytic theory, see *Psychoanalysis and Women,* ed. Jean Baker Miller (New York: Penguin, 1973).

15. It was not until the 1960s that feminism regained prominence in our society and in the lives of women.

16. Lerman, *A Mote in Freud's Eye,* pp. 112–118. Beside the few theorists who were fortunate enough to be remembered, many of the challengers to Freud became "lost" theorists, including: Beatrice Hinkle, "On the Arbitrary Use of the Terms 'Masculine' and 'Feminine,' " *Psychoanalytic Review* 7 (1920): 15–30; Paul Bousfield, "The Castration Complex in Women," *Psychoanalytic Review* 11 (1924): 121–43; Joan Riviere, "Womanliness as Masquerade," *International Journal of Psycho-Analysis* 10 (1929): 303–13; Ruth Mack Brunswick, "The Pre-oedipal Phase of the Libido Development," *Psychoanalytic Quarterly* 9 (1940): 293–319; Josine Muller, "A Contribution to the Problem of Libidinal Development of the Genital Phase in Girls," *International Journal of Psycho-Analysis* 13 (1932): 361–68; and Carl Muller-Braunsweigh, "The Genesis of the Feminine Super-ego," *International Journal of Psycho-Analysis* 7 (1926): 359–62.

17. People with unhealthy narcissism usually feel quite insecure, although they may cover it up with a great deal of bravado. This is often what we mean when we say someone has a "big ego." Actually, what we are really sensing is that such people feel fragile in some way and are doing their best to cover up their feelings of insecurity.

18. Alfred Adler, *Understanding Human Nature* (New York: Greenberg, 1927), pp. 123, 134.

19. Susan Quinn, *A Mind of Her Own: The Life of Karen Horney* (New York: Summit Books, 1987).

20. Ernest Jones, Freud's biographer and a member of his inner circle, is reported to have used Horney's writing as the basis of his own paper on female sexuality. Quinn, *A Mind of Her Own*, pp. 211–12.

21. Jack L. Rubins, *Karen Horney: Gentle Rebel of Psychoanalysis* (New York: Dial Press, 1978).

22. Marcia Westkoff, *The Feminist Legacy of Karen Horney* (New Haven: Yale University Press, 1986).

23. In its early years, psychoanalysis was frowned upon by the medical establishment, including psychiatrists. The blurring of boundaries concerning whether or not a medical degree was necessary to practice analysis did not help matters. Quinn, *A Mind of Her Own*, p. 138.

24. Carl Jung is another prominent theorist who broke with Freud after an earlier close association. Jung developed a theory of psychology with more spiritual underpinnings. His model is replete with mythological characters and seems to give more equitable weight to both feminine and masculine characteristics in both women and men. A good review of the psychology of women from a Jungian perspective can be found in Jean Shinoda Bolen, *Goddesses in Everywomen: A New Psychology of Women* (New York: Harper & Row, 1984) and Demaris S. Wehr, *Jung and Feminism: Liberating Archetypes* (Boston: Beacon Press, 1987).

25. A French school of psychoanalysis led by Jacques Lacan has been formed, although it has not yet had a major influence in the United States.

26. Heinz Hartmann, *Ego Psychology and the Problem of Adaptation* (New York: International Universities Press, 1939) and *Essays of Ego Psychology* (New York: International Universities Press, 1964).

27. If you want to read the original works of these theorists, they include: Melanie Klein, *Contributions to Psycho-analysis* (London: Hogarth Press, 1948) and *The Psycho-Analysis of Children* (London: Hogarth Press, 1959); W. R. D. Fairbairn, *An Object Relations Theory of Personality* (New York: Basic Books, 1952); Michael Balint, ed., *Primary Love and Psycho-Analytic Technique* (New York: Liveright, 1965); D. W. Winnicott, *The Family and Individual Development* (New York: Basic Books, 1965), *The Maturational Process and the Facilitating Environment* (New York: International Universities Press, 1965), and *Playing and Reality* (London: Tavistock Publications, 1971); Harry Guntrip, *Schizoid Phenomena, Object Relations and the Self* (New York: International Universities Press, 1969); Margaret S. Maler, Fred Pine, and Anni Bergman, *The Psychological Birth of the Human Infant* (New York: Basic Books, 1975); and Margaret S. Mahler, *Separation-Individuation* (New York: Jason Aronson, 1979).

28. Heinz Kohut, *The Analysis of the Self* (New York: International Universities Press, 1971).

29. Otto Kernberg, *Borderline Conditions and Pathological Narcissism* (New York: Jason Aronson, 1975).

30. Political as defined by Margaret Atwood, author of *The Handmaid's Tale,* is "who's got the power and how did they get it, and how do they maintain it, and who is it power over and what is it the power to do?" (*Ms.,* January 1987, p. 90.)

31. For a more detailed review of behaviorism, consider J. Wolpe, *The Practice of Behavior Therapy* (New York: Pergamon Press, 1969) or see chapter 8 of this book.

32. "Science, according to definition, is knowledge based on truth, which appears as fact obtained by systematic study and precise observation. To be scientific is to be unsentimental, rational, straight-thinking, correct, rigorous, exact. Yet in both the nineteenth and twentieth centuries, scientists have made strong statements about the social and political roles of women, claiming all the while to speak the scientific truth. That so many scientists have been able for so long to do such poor research attests to both the unconscious social agendas of many of the researchers and to the theoretical inadequacy of the research framework used in the field as a whole." Anne Fausto-Sterling, *Myths of Gender: Biological Theories About Women and Men* (New York: Basic Books, 1985).

33. Ruth Bleier, *Feminist Approaches to Science* (Elmsford, N.Y.: Pergamon Press, 1986).

34. Carl R. Rogers, *Client-Centered Therapy* (Boston: Houghton Mifflin, 1951).

35. Carl R. Rogers, "Client-centered Psychotherapy," in *Comprehensive Textbook of Psychiatry,* 2nd ed., ed. Alfred M. Freedman, Harold I. Kaplan, and Benjamin J. Sadock (Baltimore: Williams and Wilkins, 1975).

36. Other theorists from the humanistic/growth schools of psychology include Frederick S. Perls (founder of Gestalt therapy with techniques such as double chairing), *Gestalt Therapy Verbatim* (New York: Bantam Books, 1972); Abraham H. Maslow (creator of Maslow's hierarchy of needs), *Toward a Psychology of Being* (New York: D. Van Nostrand, 1968); Alexander Lowen (inventor of the concept of bioenergetics), *Depression and the Body: The Biological Basis of Faith and Reality* (New York: Penguin, 1972).

37. Carl R. Rogers et al., *The Therapeutic Relationship and Its Impact: A Study of Psychotherapy with Schizophrenics* (Madison: University of Wisconsin Press, 1967); Carl R. Rogers, "A Theory of Therapy, Personality and Interpersonal Relationships as Developed in the Client-centered Framework," in *Formulations of the Person and Social Context,* vol. 3 of *Psychology: A Study of Science,* ed. S. Koch (New York:

McGraw-Hill, 1959), p. 184; and Carl R. Rogers and R. F. Dymond, eds., *Psychotherapy and Personality Change* (Chicago: University of Chicago Press, 1954).

38. Erik Erikson, *Identity: Youth and Crisis* (New York: W. W. Norton, 1968).

39. Erikson's label appears first. The Freudian label appears in parentheses, the adult-development-theory label appears in brackets.

40. Tidbits of revisions can be found among the literature on the psychology of women. For example, Victoria Jean Dimidjian, "A Biographical Study of the Psychosocial Developmental Issues in the Lives of Six Female Psychotherapists in Their Thirties," *Women and Therapy* (Spring 1982): 27–44.

41. Earlier research suggested that women who preferred not to have children tended to be urban, white, educated, feminist, and less likely to have positive childhood memories. Margaret W. Matlin, *The Psychology of Women* (New York: Holt, Rinehart, Winston, 1987), pp. 377–79. However, research in progress by Mardy Ireland is challenging this data. Her findings suggest that up to 25 percent of women of every color and class prefer not to have children (personal communication).

42. Daniel J. Levinson, *The Season's of a Man's Life* (New York: Ballantine, 1978).

43. George E. Vaillant, *Adaptation to Life* (Boston: Little, Brown, 1977).

44. Levinson will release a study of forty-five women later this year through Knopf.

45. Michael E. Lamb, ed., *The Role of the Father in Child Development* (New York: John Wiley, 1981).

46. Gerald Amada, *A Guide to Psychotherapy* (Lanham, Md.: University Press of America, 1983).

47. Sandra Lipsitz Bem, "Gender Schema Theory and Its Implications for Child Development: Raising Gender-aschematic Children in a Gender-schematic Society," in *The Psychology of Women: Ongoing Debates*, ed. Mary Roth Walsh (New Haven: Yale University Press, 1987), pp. 226–45.

2 | Contemporary Perspective

By the late 1960s, the mainstream approach to the psychology of women was again being challenged. This time, the objections came from both inside and outside the psychological professions, with the result that the impact proved more powerful and, one hopes, more lasting.

Consciousness Raising

Until the 1960s, attempts to refute psychoanalytic doctrine had primarily taken place behind the closed doors of training institutes. There had been no input from the laywomen who used these professional services. Now, the challenge was coming from actual and potential female patients.

Thousands of women were forming consciousness-raising groups. These informal, leaderless gatherings were safe environments in which women began to share their thoughts and feelings. In the absence of a professional authority, women become their own authorities. They grew to trust their own understanding about themselves rather than to look toward someone else to tell them what was appropriate, correct, or healthy.

At the same time, increasing numbers of professionals, many of whom had been positively influenced by the recent women's movement, were also questioning traditional theory and practice.[1] A 1970 article based on interviews with practicing therapists gave clear evidence that sexism was affecting the psychological care of women.[2] Researchers demonstrated that although therapists used similar terms to describe a mature, healthy, and socially competent adult and a mature, healthy, and socially competent man, they used a very different set of adjectives to describe the well-adjusted woman. Therapists described the psychologically healthy woman as less aggressive, less adventurous, less competitive, and less objective than a healthy adult or man. She was seen as more dependent, more submissive, more emotional, more conceited, more easily influenced, and more excitable in minor crises. These therapists defined mental health in such a way that one could not simultaneously be a healthy adult and a healthy woman.[3] There was no analogous conflict for men.

Therapists' beliefs about what constitutes psychological health are critical to their work.[4] Their beliefs determine how they interpret what patients tell them, how they define the goals the patients and therapists are trying to achieve, and when they consider therapy to have been completed successfully. If practitioners unknowingly rely upon theory that is biased against women, their female patients will be hurt rather than helped. For example, any therapist who misinterprets a woman's competitive strivings as abnormal or leaves unquestioned her willingness to make excuses for an abusive partner is not providing a useful service.

Making Changes

By today's scientific standards, Freud's theories would not meet even minimally acceptable standards of objectivity and precision.[5] Without adequate testing and controls, it is extremely difficult to separate conjecture from fact. This is certainly true when it comes to Freudian beliefs about women.[6]

Although his influence was profound, Freud himself was in many ways a conventional man of his time. Except for Anna, the daughter who became an integral part of his professional life, Freud had relatively limited contact with women in his personal life. He had practically no female friends while growing up and, as was typical of the era, his relationship with his wife, Marthe, was quite distant. His female patients were from the white, upper class of Victorian society, and his purportedly revolutionary theory was used in such a way as to perpetuate and reinforce the authoritarian attitudes of the typical male Viennese physician.

Psychoanalysis was based largely upon Freud's own self-analysis—the self-analysis of a privileged, white, Jewish, male, Victorian physician. When applied to others, his self-analysis was severely limited by the differences between him and his patients—particularly by his position of power in relationship to them. It would seem unreasonable to apply his conclusions to a world broader than the one in which he lived. Yet that is exactly what he and his followers did. Freud's class-bound and male-biased psychological model became the touchstone for the entire world. This theory, based upon a very limited population, was viewed as comprehensive and applicable to everyone.

Recognizing the inappropriateness of Freud's assumptions for women, a few practitioners again began offering alternatives to classical theory.[7] They have fallen into three basic groups: modifications of Freudian theory; gender-sensitive analytically based theory; and female-influenced theory. Several psychoanalysts have made sincere attempts to integrate contemporary research and theory with the more classical Freudian theory.[8] These feminist analysts argue that we should not throw the baby (Freud's insights) out with the bathwater (his anti-woman bias). They believe that the techniques of Freudian analysis have much to offer and that Freud has been greatly misunderstood—by Freudians as well as feminists.[9] Other analytically oriented practitioners are more inclined to apply the principles of ego psychology, self-psychology, and object relations theory than the more classical Freudian thinking, attempting to carve a path that more accurately describes women's experiences.[10] Whether a satisfactory revision can be achieved within a theory so fundamentally affected by male bias remains to be seen.[11] Female-influenced theorists believe that it makes more sense to start anew in constructing a psychology of women rather than attempt to revise earlier models. They have chosen to create new theories of the psychology of women without much commitment to any particular theoretical approach.[12]

Spokeswomen for the New Psychologies of Women
Psychoanalytically-based

In 1966, William Masters and Virginia Johnson demonstrated that the clitoris is the female physiologic and anatomic equivalent to the male penis.[13] Their research made it clear that vaginal penetration alone is less likely to result in orgasm than direct stimulation to the clitoris. It no longer made sense to maintain the Freudian belief that an orgasm achieved through clitoral stimulation was immature.[14]

In an attempt to remain true to Freudian theory while acknowledging the advances that were being made, Mary Jane Sherfey described how this new information might be reconciled with Freudian thinking. She attempted to synthesize Masters and Johnson's findings with the older psychoanalytic theory of female sexuality.[15]

In spite of Sherfey's efforts to support the basic psychoanalytic model, her work was largely dismissed or ignored by orthodox Freudians. Having been rebuffed, she was, not surprisingly, less conciliatory in a 1974 paper. She criticized Freudian psychology for ignoring cultural differences, for failing to recognize the importance of a girl's relationship with her mother, for labeling femininity as passive, and for assuming that women have inferior superegos and suffer from penis envy.[16]

Two years later, Dorothy Dinnerstein wrote *The Mermaid and The Minotaur.* [17] This groundbreaking work set forth what has become a central theme in the revision of psychoanalytic theory: that there are powerful consequences, presumably both conscious and unconscious, of the fact that women are usually the primary caretakers of children of both sexes. Dinnerstein proposes that because of the structure of child rearing, virtually all of us grow up believing—unconsciously, if not consciously—that women are omnipotent. She argues that since virtually all infants and children are cared for by women when they are extremely dependent on that care for survival, women are seen as having awesome power. That power may be used to help or to harm. Dinnerstein suggests that as a result, we all—women and men alike—defend against our fear of women's power by devaluing them. Instead, we behave as if men are the more powerful sex.

Her hypothesis is interesting. However, like many proposed by adherents of psychoanalytic theory, it relies on ideas that are difficult to validate, such as the working of an infant's mind and whether or not there is an unconscious. Nonetheless, the change Dinnerstein proposes does have merit.

Dinnerstein argues that genuine equality between women and men will never be achieved until men assume equal responsibility for the daily care of children. She believes that this is the only way a child's ambivalent feelings about her early caretakers will be distributed equally between men and women.[18] From a practical perspective, mothers who truly share child rearing with the child's other parent are more likely to have quality time for other pursuits. Certainly this kind of arrangement, when possible, would be reasonable, fair, and sensible.

In 1978, a weighty and complicated revision of basic Freudian theory was published by Nancy Chodorow. Chodorow shares Dinnerstein's belief that certain events come to pass because most of us are raised in families in which women are the primary caretakers, but her hypothesis is a radical departure from previous analytic theory. Put simply, Chodorow argues that because women raise children with little regular assistance from men, girls' and boys' earliest identification is female. Eventually, in order to develop a masculine identity, boys must make a sharp psychological separation from their mothers.

Boys must break, perhaps prematurely, their profound attachment to the adult female to whom they are so intimately connected. In the absence of an equally nurturing male, this process is necessary to permit the development of the boy's core identity as male. Girls, on the other hand, do not have to make this psychological break. They can develop their identity as female within the existing identification with and attachment to their mothers.

Thus boys experience significant psychological separation as part of their normal development. The consequence of this is that, at least on the surface, boys appear to function more independently than girls. They seem to have clearer ego boundaries.

It is believed that all psychologically healthy people develop ego boundaries. These boundaries are supposed to give us a sense of where we stop and other people start, allowing us to accurately differentiate between our own thoughts and feelings and someone else's. It appears that these boundaries are more rigid in boys, more fluid in girls. Chodorow proposes that it is in the premature breaking away from the caretaker that leads boys to develop such rigid ego boundaries.

Orthodox theory holds that firm ego boundaries are essential to high-level psychological functioning. Chodorow suggests that an equally good sign of psychological health is the ability to maintain close connections and that this is more manageable when the boundaries are more fluid. She states that females rarely get as psychologically distant from others as males do. Girls seem to remain more connected to their actual or substitute mothers even when these relationships are profoundly troubled. Both as adolescents and adults, women characteristically maintain a variety of supportive relationships with female friends. Chodorow believes that it is through such bonds that women reproduce the mothering relationship for one another.

Chodorow observes that men, on the other hand, are much less likely to maintain mutually nurturing relationships. As a result, they have trouble "mothering" because they have become so "independent" and emotionally disconnected from other people. In breaking away from their caretaker, men fail to achieve the same high level of empathic responsiveness that is developed through the mother-daughter relationship and maintained by women through their friendships with one another.

Thus, in their roles as husbands, lovers, fathers, or colleagues, most men are much less responsive to the needs of others, and they do not usually conceive of giving up as much of themselves to meet the needs of other people. As a result of this inability, men have trouble being truly intimate.

Chodorow suggests that intimacy is particularly threatening to men because it reminds them of their earliest years of utter dependency and the time when they were female-identified rather than male-identified. If there is one thing our culture disdains, it is any evidence of stereotypically female behavior in men. It should come as no surprise that it is the rare man who can acknowledge and enjoy his impulses to be caring, nurturing, receptive, and accommodating.

By weaving psychoanalytic theory into her own perspective, Chodorow has contributed to a reacceptance of the psychoanalytic model by many therapists who otherwise consider themselves feminists. This is a confusing and disturbing phenomenon, since most psychoanalytic theory and practice is not congruent with a nonsexist, let alone a feminist, stance.[19]

Luise Eichenbaum and Susie Orbach (who may be better known in England than in the United States) have written extensively on their work with women.[20] Cofounders of the Women's Therapy Centre Institute in London, they blend knowledge about gender identity and feminism with the object relations branch of psychoanalytic theory. They place particular emphasis on the mother-daughter relationship, arguing that daughters are raised to be like their mothers, learning to attend to the needs of others and restraining their own desires. Taking issue with the popular concept that women are "too dependent,"[21] they point out that women are trained to be emotionally depended upon.[22]

Unfortunately, Eichenbaum and Orbach focus primarily on a woman's internal experience, minimizing the effect of social forces that mold that experience. Mothers are held almost exclusively responsible for their daughters' development. There is no exploration of the ways social influences impinge on mothers and influence the ways mothers prepare younger females to enter the social world. No attention is given to the positive aspects of the mother-daughter relationship or to the healing and supportive qualities of other types of female-female relationships such as those with friends, aunts, and teachers. Most importantly, they do not deal with issues of male power.

Moving Away from an Analytic Base

Jean Baker Miller was originally trained in psychoanalysis, but she has since departed from that camp. In 1976, Miller proposed what has come to be thought of as a female-influenced theory.[23] Indeed, she and her colleagues at the Stone Center at Wellesley College may come closest to creating a comprehensive pro-female psychological theory that rivals Freud's pro-male perspective.[24] Central to their theory is the notion that empathy is an organizing principle in women's lives and that girls' and women's self-esteem is enhanced when they are able to participate in relationships. As Christina Robb has commented, "Their idea is that girls and women thrive in relationships and that for women the apex of development is to weave themselves zestfully into a web of strong relationships that they experience as empowering, activating, honest, and close."[25]

Even Miller's style of leadership stands in contrast to Freud's and eloquently demonstrates the very theory she postulates. Unlike Freud, who battled vigorously with the colleagues and students who challenged him, Miller encourages others to refine the theory she has been developing. She values their perspectives as expanding and adding to her work rather than detracting from it.

This capacity to empower others is central to Miller's understanding of the usual role played by women in relationships. It represents one of several strengths women commonly demonstrate—strengths that have been misinterpreted in classical analytic theory as weaknesses. As Miller sees it, our culture encourages men to develop the qualities of separateness, achievement, and aggression while encouraging women to develop the qualities of connection, caring, and accommodation. In truth, all of these characteristics are essential to the healthy growth and development of every individual. Unfortunately, our culture has until recently overvalued the characteristics encouraged in men and undervalued those encouraged in women. Indeed, the common standard for mental health has been the achievement of "separation and individuation,"[26] a style encouraged in male development and discouraged in female development.

The Stone Center group proposes that female development occurs in a manner that is different from, but equal to, that of males. This model is described as "self-in-relation,"[27] in which women come to create a sense of themselves through their relationships with other people. While men are encouraged to attain psychological maturity by moving away from their most important emotional bonds, women are encouraged to grow within their relationships.

Recognizing the merit of the developmental style exhibited most frequently (but by no means exclusively) by women is critically important.[28] The Stone Center group suggests that dividing the essential elements of psychological health between men and women is the cause of much human suffering. To make matters worse, they maintain, the inequality of status and power inherent in this arrangement can only be maintained through violence.[29] This violence, and the inevitable mistrust between women and men that it fosters, is played out within the family and within the culture at large. It has a profound impact on the psychology of us all.

One outcome of a successful women's movement would be an equitable distribution of human characteristics among both women and men. Efforts to achieve this often place women in the position of challenging institutions and individuals to examine the male bias inherent in many of their most basic assumptions. Since such introspection is not particularly appealing when suggested or demanded by someone else, women often find themselves in conflict with powerful institutions and people to whom they are deeply attached. As the director of the Federal Executive Board in San Francisco, who happens to be a middle-aged black male, stated very bluntly, "Power is never relinquished without a struggle."[30] This conflict between the more powerful and the less powerful often feels profoundly threatening because we have few models for conflict that are nonviolent and growth enhancing.[31] Yet it is only by confronting these issues that both women and men can enlarge the definition of psychological health to include both the ability to feel personally effective and the capacity to nurture fulfilling connections with others.

It is hard for people in power to recognize that it is to their advantage to appreciate the strengths exemplified by women. While the present arrangement almost guarantees that women will suffer from a disproportional amount of depression, anxiety, submerged or ineffective anger, lack of sexual fulfillment, and other emotional disturbances, it also assures that men will suffer from a limited capacity for genuine intimacy, a higher risk of acting insensitively, inhumanely, or violently, and, ironically, a tendency to feel exploited by the very people who are subordinate to them.

In Miller's view the so-called neurotic conflicts experienced by women are important signals that something serious is wrong and needs attention. The symptoms associated with these conflicts will continue until the basic inequality between women and men is addressed and changed. The solution will come not from encouraging women to adapt, but from encouraging society to accommodate women's needs and women's values. Integrating the strengths commonly held by each sex will lead us to a world in which affiliation is prized as highly as self-enhancement and affection is as valued as assertiveness.

The work of the Stone Center has sometimes been misunderstood as ennobling women, risking being as lopsided on the side of women as earlier theories were on the side of men. This is not their intention. However, because it is women who most acutely feel the pain of being in a subservient role, they are the ones motivated to insist on a change. To relieve their own pain, women are pointing out the valuable work they have been doing within our society and without which our society literally will not survive.

Other work that has inalterably changed our understanding of human psychology is the research on moral development by Carol Gilligan at Harvard.[32] She was a student of Lawrence Kohlberg, who at the time was undeniably the most prominent theorist of moral development.[33] Some years previously, Kohlberg had developed a 1 to 6 scale of moral values. On this scale, women usually scored 3.[34] At stage 3 morality involves helping and pleasing others rather than subordinating relationships to rule (stage 4) and subordinating rules to universal principles of justice (stages 5 and 6). Kohlberg did not recognize his gender bias. His findings seemed to support Freud's position that women have weaker superegos than men, less of a social conscience, and are, in general, less morally advanced. Gilligan took issue with Kohlberg. She noted that the way in which female and male behavior was interpreted radically influenced how moral that person was deemed to be. She suggested an alternative understanding of Kohlberg's observations.

In laying the groundwork for her position, Gilligan pointed out that all perspectives are colored by the unique vantage point of the observer. Unless carefully screened for bias, observations are very much affected by the gender, color, ethnic and religious background, sexual preference, and socioeconomic status of the viewer. There is no reality unaffected by the lens through which it is seen. Most psychological theory, at least until recently, has been viewed through a white, professional, male lens. With that bias, there is an emphasis on separation-individuation and a tendency to view dependence and autonomy as polar opposites. Gilligan brought a different lens to her research. She proposed that there were at least two ways to approach a moral dilemma. One was what she called justice, the perspective essentially identical to Kohlberg's. When faced with a moral conflict, a person motivated by justice acts in accord to certain standards, including the weighing of individual claims, rights, fairness, and reciprocity. The same standards are applied to oneself as to others. Gilligan called the second approach care, in which a person tries to avoid any act that will be hurtful. Instead, she tries to identify and respond to the needs of all parties, reluctant to act in any manner that will jeopardize human relationships.

Gilligan based her conclusions, in part, on a study of eighty advantaged adolescents and adults, forty females and forty males. She discovered that although each sex could identify the justice approach and the care approach when faced with simulated moral dilemmas, their choices for action were sharply different. In her examples, Gilligan established three categories of response: care only, justice and care, and justice only. One-third of the females fell into each category, while half the males fell into the justice and care category and half fell into the justice only category. None of the males fell into the care only category.

Gilligan used these results to explain how Kohlberg's system of classification minimized an important dimension of moral choice. Women are not less moral than men, they simply define morality in a different way. A scale of moral development constructed using a male lens would not be tempered by a care only response, and the results would be skewed in favor of justice. A model that included a female perspective would more fully incorporate both care and justice. Neither perspective is necessarily better than the other; however, each needs to be recognized as valuable.

There are profound ramifications in Gilligan's work. Not only does it provide support for the Stone Center theory, but it also has a broader social impact. The most striking and potentially far-reaching effect is the change being proposed within our legal system. We currently have a legal system that is essentially "devoid of care and responsiveness to the safety of others."[35] Rethinking the law to include the value of care as well as justice, as identified by Gilligan, could mean accepting personal responsibility for causing harm to another person. According to Leslie Bender, a law professor at Syracuse University, "The masculine voice of rights, autonomy and abstraction has led to a standard that protects efficiency and profit. The feminine voice can design a tort system that encourages behavior that is caring about others' safety and responsive to others' needs or hurts and that attends to human contexts and consequences."[36]

Nonpsychoanalytic Theories

Many practitioners have shied away from psychoanalytic theory because the clinician is asked to take the theory on faith.[37] Miriam Greenspan offers a nonpsychoanalytic perspective in her understanding of women. She acknowledges that the diversity and complexity of women's lives make it difficult to develop one comprehensive theory, but she believes it is important to try to articulate what is common to most women.

Greenspan suggests that there is a connection between women's internal lives and the external conditions in which they live. She has identified three psychological themes that she believes dominate women's lives as a result of this connection: woman as victim; woman as body; and woman and the labor of relatedness. She believes that these are the inevitable result of women's subservient status in a male-dominated society.[38]

By woman as victim, Greenspan refers to society's expectation that women will become and remain psychologically subservient to men. In this position of lesser power, women adapt to their inferior role. As part of this role, women are frequently victimized. In the process of being frequently victimized, women often come to participate in their own victimization. Greenspan sees many of women's symptoms as unconscious attempts to simultaneously adapt to and rebel against the expectation that they put their own needs, views, and values after those of men.

By woman as body, Greenspan means that the rule for women in society is that, above all, they are expected to be attractive and physically available to men. The standard of attractiveness against which women are measured is defined by others, especially men, rather than by themselves. The current standard calls for a woman to be white, slender, blond, and wrinkle free. Any woman who does not measure up is devalued. In addition to the pressure to be attractive, a woman's body is not really considered her own. It continues to be a matter of public debate as to if a woman should be free to choose whether or not she will bear a child. In many situations, men feel free to make comments about a woman's body and to touch it—whenever and wherever they please. Greenspan predicts that women will continue their symptomatic rebellion until they have the power to truly define the shape, size, and use of their bodies.

Women and the labor of relatedness refers to the fact that the majority of women are trained for intimacy rather than self-advancement. Because this training results in most women thinking of other people first rather than focusing primarily or exclusively on their own self-interests, they are punished by having their psychological style considered immature and masochistic. Yet this style, which is reinforced in women from childhood on, is critical to the making and maintaining of relationships. The capacity for empathy and the fluid ego boundaries developed and maintained by women are essential in their role as caregivers. Every woman knows what remarkable flexibility is required to effectively accommodate to the need of others, but it is often this very focus on connectedness, at the price of self-enhancement, that keeps women in a subservient position.[39]

Greenspan feels that women face a terrible choice: focus on your own goals and end up alone, or focus on other people's goals and lose your sense of your self. Men are not asked to make a choice between their relationships and themselves. It is tacitly assumed that they can and will have both.

These are not just theoretical issues. Practicing therapists see the results of these dilemmas every day. Women arrive suffering with depression, anxiety, recurrent aches and pains of unknown origins, problems enjoying their sexuality, trouble in their relationships, a dislike of their bodies, low self-esteem, and feeling as if they lack a clear sense of themselves. They are asking Who am I and What do I want? Greenspan believes that the psychological symptoms that women experience will continue until the basic problem of women's inequality is corrected.

Essayist and poet Adrienne Rich adds a valuable perspective. She points to the "institutional and random terrorism men have practiced on women . . . throughout history" and asks us to question the cultural expectation that all women are heterosexual.[40] She argues that heterosexuality is the "beachhead of male dominance" and criticizes authors who ignore lesbian relationships or minimize the impact of economics on the psychology of women.

Rich challenges even heterosexual women to imagine a world in which they do not automatically assume that they will try to establish primary relationships with men or that they will bear and nurture children. She startles the reader into recognizing the profound social and cultural forces that encourage and "enforce women's total emotional, erotic loyalty and subservience to men."[41] She is brutal in her assessment of the impact of the way men use power against women and suggests that the pervasiveness of that misuse may reflect men's underlying concern that if they do not control women, women may eventually become indifferent to them.

Rich reminds us that any theory or research that ignores or minimizes lesbians works against a genuine understanding and empowerment of all women. It is lesbian women who have directly and repeatedly challenged the stereotypical notions about women and who even in the face of profound discrimination have created lives based on female values and experiences. Her argument is important not only because she so persuasively asks us to consider the particularly rich experiences of women whose lives are woman-defined, but because she also alerts us to a critical flaw in any unidimensional theory, which cannot possibly encompass the enormous diversity to be found in the lives of women. Any individual woman's psychological structure is just as influenced by the color of her skin, the socioeconomic group to which she belongs, the religion in which she is raised, and so on as it is by her gender. Because of this, there are probably many psychologies of women rather than just one.

Educational psychologist Helen Collier has attempted to recognize this diversity.[42] In her work she acknowledges minority women,[43] women in poverty, lesbians, older women, victims of abuse, working women, and female offenders as well as the population of educated, middle-class white women that is the common subject of psychological theory and practice. She also addresses the unique biological concerns of women such as menstruation, fertility control, childbirth, and menopause without making them the central focus of a woman's life.

Collier attempts to teach therapists how to translate sex-fair theory into action. Sex-fair or feminist therapy is aimed at "counteracting the inequality with which therapists have been trained to view women."[44] Instead of encouraging women to adapt to the current ideal of womanhood, Collier suggests that therapists help them "to deal actively with the world and to make choices rather than to force themselves into a traditional mold."

Successful therapy aids a woman in achieving mental health. According to Collier, the mentally healthy woman demonstrates the following characteristics:[45]

1. She values herself as an individual and as a female rather than depreciating herself as a woman.
2. She chooses behaviors according to their suitability to her and to the situation, perhaps deliberately resisting conforming to female sex stereotypes but certainly not conforming to them unwittingly.
3. She consistently tends toward emotional, social, and economic self-sufficiency, striving for separateness and autonomy before seeking interdependence.

4. She blends autonomy with interdependence in the form of a selected number of deep relationships with others in personal and social activities.
5. She orients herself toward reality and realism, avoiding overreaction in favor of accepting herself, others, and the world for what they are.
6. She appreciates differences as much as similarities, preferring variety in herself and others to stereotypes.
7. She does not victimize herself, does not let herself be victimized, and does not present herself as a victim.
8. She enjoys the power of her emotions and her self and displays this power through vivacity and energy.
9. She takes risks and extends herself without placing too much emphasis on success or failure.

Where Does This Leave Us?

We've given you only a sampling of the many practitioners and theoreticians who are creating, revising, and refining our understanding of the psychology of women. Margaret Matlin estimates that close to one hundred thousand articles and books relevant to the psychology of women have been published since 1967.[46]

As a result of their efforts, several of the basic tenets of female psychology have been profoundly altered:

- Penis envy is now understood to be a completely inadequate explanation for the deep feelings of powerlessness that many women feel when faced with obstacles to achieving personal and professional satisfaction.[47] A woman's desire to achieve satisfaction through work or other activities, as well as or instead of motherhood, is now considered normal and healthy.[48]
- The idea that women are masochistic, that they enjoy pain, has been brought into question. Much of traditional female behavior is actually based on attempts to avoid pain. Furthermore, describing women as masochistic means that such laudable traits as nurturing, patience, and self-denial are mistakenly seen as pathological.[49]
- While the Oedipus theory may adequately explain the relationship of fathers and sons,[50] it does not as satisfactorily explain the seemingly contradictory feelings that occur in the relationships between mothers and daughters. Many women are very critical of their mothers and yet simultaneously have very strong bonds with them.[51]
- Practitioners who have examined the ways families contribute to psychological health and distress have forcefully argued against making the mother-child dyad the central unit of attention. Mother and child are embedded in a network of powerful and significant relationships that have a profound impact upon everyone's emotional well-being.[52] It is time to stop blaming mother.

Resisting New Ideas

These new concepts are only slowly being integrated into general clinical practice. Many practitioners insist that since the bias against women in psychological theory and practice has been inescapably identified, the necessary changes have been made.[53] They believe that the theories they learned during training and rely on in their work are no longer biased against women. They insist that gender stereotypes have been identified and corrected.

Unfortunately, there is compelling evidence that much less progress has been made than one would have hoped. In 1974, researchers conducted a study of gender stereotypes. They found fifty-four characteristics in which the typical male was seen as different from the typical female.[54] The characteristics associated more often with men included forcefulness, adventurousness, aggression, self-confidence, rudeness, independence, ambition, dominance, and inventiveness. The characteristics associated more often with women included affection, emotionality, gentleness, submission, weakness, appreciativeness, fickleness, sensitivity, naggingness, and sentimentality.[55] When the research was repeated in 1983, there was only one change. Respondents no longer claimed that there was a significant difference between women and men when it came to being intellectual.[56] All other characteristics remained unchanged.

In spite of the prevalent fantasy that we are now in a postmodern feminist era where equal rights are unquestioned, the stereotypes about women and men remain essentially the same. Progress is indeed very slow. Conventional practitioners like to think of feminist therapy as a school practiced by a minority group.[57] It has not yet been fully appreciated that a feminist perspective is a specific vantage point from which every psychological theory should be critically examined for its bias against women.

Many members of the caretaking professions have been only minimally affected by the women's movement and are still locked in an outdated psychoanalytic mode. Others have taken these criticisms seriously and are attempting to reconstruct analytic theory to accommodate these new understandings. Yet Freud's ideas and the ideas of those who have followed him have become so pervasive that even practitioners aware of its biases and limitations are reluctant to abandon the model. They seem to fear that they will have nothing equivalent with which to replace it.

A recent surge of interest in trying to use object relations theory and self-psychology to explain women's experience may be a worrisome rebound to a male-influenced model, much the same way that previous attempts to adapt Freudian theory to women were. Both object relations theory (the belief that people develop their core personality in the first two years of life within the framework of their earliest relationships) and self-psychology (the belief that a person's core sense of self is determined more by early environmental conditions than inner conflicts) are improvements over traditional Freudian theory. However, these revisions neither spring from women's experiences nor do they satisfactorily incorporate the particular social, economic, and political realities that so profoundly influence a woman's individual psychological structure.[58] It cannot be denied that each woman must look at her own contribution to her unhappiness and must exercise what power she does have to make personal changes. But an exclusive reliance on theories that only consider internal psychology or do not recognize the impact of pervasive subordination risk pushing the problems back on the individual without recognizing the substantive external changes that must take place if relief from emotional distress is to be achieved.

While it is certainly true that a known theory provides security, it is security achieved at the cost of an inability to provide useful guidelines for the great majority of people. Women, nonwhites, lesbians and gays, the poor—virtually anyone who is not a white male of the middle or upper class—are held to standards that are neither accurate nor appropriate for their life situation.[59] An accurate and comprehensive theory from a woman's perspective, while initiated at the same time as the current male-influenced models, has not been equally nurtured or incorporated into our understanding of human psychology.[60] Because of the obstacles to its development, a female-influenced psychology is still in its infancy.

Considerable effort will be needed to develop a theory grounded in women's experiences rather than men's observations of those experiences. A period of temporary separatism may be necessary until women's views and voices can be fully articulated and validated. As women's perspectives are clarified, they must be incorporated into our understanding of human psychology just as thoroughly as the presently accepted male-oriented models. The goal is to not to completely displace theories and practices that accurately reflect the psychology of men but simply to make equal room for models that more accurately reflect the psychology of women. Integrating this valuable material into male-influenced perspectives will ultimately lead to a more useful theory for us all.

Of course, in addition to a more accurate understanding of women's and men's psychological functioning, real change is also necessary. Family and work structure must be adapted to accommodate the developmental needs of all people—children, women, and men. Infants and children do thrive within the context of empathic, reliable, and competent caretaking by people who have a solid sense of themselves. It is not necessary, or even wise, for only women to perform this role. Simultaneously, institutions and the culture at large must make radical changes if we are to meet the needs of all human beings effectively and compassionately. For maximum psychological health, all adults must have the opportunity to participate both in supportive and satisfying relationships and in public life. We must begin to structure our world in such a way as to recognize that this is a need of all people. The current division between women and men leaves each feeling deprived and results in unpleasant and unnecessary misery.

Toward a Psychology of Women

No theory can be of real use to women unless it takes into account both a woman's very individual story of growing up to be herself and the shared experience of living in a male-dominated society.[61] It might seem ideal to end this chapter with a theory of female psychology that accurately reflects the developmental sequence of woman across her life span. Unfortunately, that theory does not yet exist.[62]

What is emerging are important pieces of what seems at times like a psychological patchwork quilt. As progress in this area continues, it will, we hope, not be long until what now seems only a beguiling collection of separate pieces will come together as a lovely, intricate pattern that binds old knowledge with new and includes the work of both professionals and laywomen.

Of course, the reality is that the quilt is never really done. Society changes. What appeared "true" in the 1950s, the 1960s, and the 1970s no longer rings true for a new generation of women—and a growing number of men—as we move into the 1990s. Knowledge is not fixed, and no authority has all the answers. Their opinions and guidance can be useful, but in the end, each woman must develop and trust her own way of looking at things. The task for all of us is to keep an open mind, ask questions, and continue the search for new understanding.

NOTES

1. Examples include Phyllis Chesler, *Women & Madness* (New York: Doubleday, 1972); Anica Vesel Mander and Anne Kent Rush, *Feminism as Therapy* (New York: Random House, 1974); Dorothy E. Smith and Sara J. David, *Women Look at Psychiatry* (Vancouver: Press Gang Publishers, 1975); and Elizabeth Friar Williams, *Notes of a Feminist Therapist* (New York: Dell, 1976).

2. I. K. Broverman, et al., "Sex-role Stereotypes and Clinical Judgements of Mental Health," *Journal of Consulting and Clinical Psychology* 34 (1970): 1–7.

3. Simone de Beauvoir (*The Second Sex*, tr. H. M. Parshley [New York: Knopf, 1953]) without benefit of research, made a much earlier observation on this: "It is among the psychoanalysts in particular that man is defined as a human being and woman as female—whenever she behaves as a human being she is said to imitate the male."

4. According to Firestone, psychoanalytic theory also had an influence on society's treatment of women. Shulamith Firestone, *The Dialectic of Sex: The Case for Feminist Revolution* (New York: Morrow, 1970).

5. Edwin G. Boring, *A History of Experimental Psychology,* 2nd ed. (New York: Appleton-Century-Crofts, 1950).

6. "Psychoanalysis as a theory that is relevant to the psychology of women is partially validated, partially disconfirmed and, as far as we know now, partially unconfirmable.

That is what has to be concluded from the research evidence available." Hannah Lerman, *A Mote in Freud's Eye: From Psychoanalysis to the Psychology of Women* (New York: Springer, 1986), p. 148.

7. This had been attempted previously. See chapter 1.

8. Shahla Chehrazi, "Female Psychology," *Journal of the American Psychoanalytic Association* 34 (1986): 111–62.

9. Juliet Mitchell, "On Freud and the Distinction Between the Sexes," in *Women and Analysis: Dialogues on Psychoanalytic Views of Femininity*, ed. Jean Strouse (New York: Dell, 1974).

10. See for example Karen Peoples, "The Trauma of Incest: Threats to the Consolidation of the Female Self" (Paper presented at the American Psychological Association Meeting, San Francisco, February 1988); and Jessica Benjamin, *The Bonds of Love: Psychoanalysis, Feminism, and the Problem of Domination* (New York: Pantheon, 1988).

11. Many therapists who might otherwise question the use of psychoanalytic theory argue that even with its flaws, it is the only theory that offers a systematic and comprehensive explanation of human behavior. Whatever credit Freud might be due for popularizing psychological theory, I am not comforted by the use of a greatly flawed and at times damaging theory (to anyone other than advantaged white men) simply because there is not yet an equally comprehensive nonsexist replacement.

12. Christina Robb, "A Theory of Empathy: The Quiet Revolution in Psychiatry," *Boston Globe Magazine*, October 16, 1988.

13. William H. Masters and Virginia E. Johnson, *Human Sexual Response* (New York: Little, Brown, 1966).

14. See chapter 1, p. 9.

15. Mary Jane Sherfey, "The Evolution and Nature of Female Sexuality in Relation to Psychoanalytic Theory," *Journal of the American Psychoanalytic Association* 14 (1966):28–128.

16. Mary Jane Sherfey, "Some Biology of Sexuality," *Journal of Sex and Marital Therapy* 1 (1974):97–109.

17. Dorothy Dinnerstein, *The Mermaid and The Minotaur: Sexual Arrangements and Human Malaise* (New York: Harper & Row, 1976).

18. Whatever the theoretical validity of this argument, women would undoubtedly have much to contribute to society's development if they could be liberated from the

full-time task of raising youngsters. And since women and men exhibit varying parenting styles, the child might benefit by being cared for by both parents.

19. Hannah Lerman, "From Freud to Feminist Personality Theory: Getting Here From There," in *The Psychology of Women: Ongoing Debates,* ed. Mary Roth Walsh (New Haven: Yale University Press, 1987), p. 53.

20. Luise Eichenbaum and Susie Orbach, *Outside In, Inside Out* (Middlesex, England: Penguin Books, 1982); published in an expanded version as *Understanding Women: A Feminist Psychoanalytic Approach* (New York: Basic Books, 1983).

21. Colette Dowling, *The Cinderella Complex* (New York: Pocket Books, 1981).

22. Luise Eichenbaum and Susie Orbach, *What Do Women Want: Exploding the Myth of Dependency* (New York: Coward-McCann, 1983).

23. Jean Baker Miller, *Toward a New Psychology of Women* (Boston: Beacon Press, 1976).

24. The Robert S. and Grace W. Stone Center for Developmental Services and Studies publishes the Work in Progress series, which includes the writings of Jean Baker Miller and others with whom she works. These admirably jargon-free papers do not presume an extensive knowledge of psychoanalytic theory and may be obtained by writing to: Editor, Work in Progress, Stone Center, Wellesley College, Wellesley, MA 02181.

25. Christina Robb, "A Theory of Empathy: The Quiet Revolution in Psychiatry," *Boston Globe Magazine,* October 16, 1988.

26. Margaret S. Mahler, Fred Pine, and Anni Bergman, *The Psychological Birth of the Human Infant* (New York: Basic Books, 1975).

27. Jean Baker Miller, "The Development of Women's Sense of Self," Work in Progress (Wellesley, Mass.: Wellesley College, 1984); Janet L. Surrey, "Self-in-relation: A Theory of Women's Development," Work in Progress (Wellesley, Mass.: Wellesley College, 1985); and Alexandra G. Kaplan, "The 'Self-in-relations': Implications for Depression in Women," Work in Progress (Wellesley, Mass.: Wellesley College, 1984).

28. Philip Slater, *The Pursuit of Loneliness: American Culture at the Breaking Point* (Boston: Beacon Press, 1976).

29. Because we have structured a world in which the values fostered in men are given more weight than the values fostered in women, a dangerous inequality of status and power has evolved. A world in which part of the population (in this case, men) retains a dominant position and the other part of the population (in this case, women)

retains a subordinate position can only be maintained—and has been maintained—through violence.

30. Marvin O'Rear (Opening remarks, speech before the Federal Women's Program Managers Council, Oakland, Calif., August 25, 1988).

31. The civil rights movement and the peace movement are two arenas that we might look to for models of nonviolent conflict.

32. Carol Gilligan, *In A Different Voice: Psychological Theory and Women's Development* (Cambridge, Mass.: Harvard University Press, 1982).

33. Lawrence Kohlberg, "The Development of Modes of Thinking and Choices in Years 10 to 16," Ph.D. diss., University of Chicago, 1958; see also *Philosophy of Moral Development* (New York: Harper & Row, 1981).

34. L. Kohlberg and R. Kramer, "Continuities and Discontinuities in Child and Adult Moral Development," *Human Development* 12 (1969):93–120.

35. Tamar Lewin, "For Feminist Scholars, Second Thoughts On Law and Order," *New York Times*, November 30, 1988, p. 17.

36. Lewin, "For Feminist Scholars, Second Thoughts On Law and Order," p. 17 and 24.

37. C. S. Hall and G. Lindzey, *Theories of Personality*, 2nd ed. (New York: John Wiley, 1970).

38. Although her language is more political, Greenspan essentially agrees with Miller in viewing women's subordinate position as primary in the development of their psychology. Like Miller and others, Greenspan believes that to change the psychology of women, with its high incidence of emotional distress, will require a fundamental change in women's socioeconomic and political position.

39. During a recent interview aired on National Public Radio Mary Ann Gelden, Harvard professor and attorney, reported that she does not think Americans realize what they are doing in this regard with current legal and social policies. The United States is the only industrialized country where divorce is taken to mean that fathers are essentially liberated from their economic responsibility for their children—leaving women, who already earn less money on average than men, with the full burden. Nor does the state, as it does in many other countries, pick up the slack in a meaningful manner if fathers are unable to provide adequate support. In the long run, it is the children who suffer the most from these policies and this has far-reaching consequences for the future of this country. Also, see chapter 12, "Abuse and Violence."

40. Adrienne Rich, "Compulsory Heterosexuality and Lesbian Existence," *Signs: Journal of Women in Culture and Society*, 5 (Summer 1980):631–60.

41. Rich, "Compulsory Heterosexuality and Lesbian Existence," p. 637.

42. Helen V. Collier, *Counseling Women: A Guide for Therapists* (New York: Free Press, 1983).

43. For a more radical perspective, see *This Bridge Called My Back: Writings by Radical Women of Color,* ed. Cherrie Moraga and Glorai Anzaldua (Watertown, Mass.: Persephone Press, 1981).

44. Collier, *Counseling Women: A Guide for Therapists,* p. 3.

45. Collier, *Counseling Women: A Guide for Therapists,* p. 273.

46. Margaret Matlin, *The Psychology of Women* (New York: Holt, Rinehart & Winston, 1987).

47. "While the literal meaning of the interpretation [penis envy] is outlandish, there is plenty of support, not only in psychoanalytic case material but in mythology, anthropology, art, and literature for the theory that a woman's unconscious life is beset by a profound sense of powerlessness, a gnawing dissatisfaction—a feeling for which the term 'penis envy' is thoroughly inadequate, not to say extremely irritating to women." Janet Malcolm, "The Patient Is Always Right," *The New York Review of Books* 31 no. 20 (1984): 13–15, 18.

48. Harriet Goldhor Lerner, "Penis Envy: Alternatives in Conceptualization," *Bulletin of the Menniger Clinic* 44 no. 1 (1980): 39–48.

49. Paula Caplan, *The Myth of Women's Masochism* (New York: Dutton, 1985).

50. Although that too must be open to debate. See note 4 chapter 1.

51. Irene P. Stiver, "Beyond the Oedipus Complex: Mothers and Daughters," Work in Progress (Wellesley, Mass.: Wellesley College, 1986).

52. For additional information on this topic see Harriet Goldhor Lerner, "A Critique of the Feminist Psychoanalytic Contribution," in *Women in Therapy* (Northvale, N.J.: Jason Aronson, 1988); Thelma Jean Goodrich et al., *Feminist Family Therapy* (New York: W. W. Norton, 1988); Marianne Walters et al., *The Invisible Web: Gender Patterns in Family Relationships* (New York: Guilford Press, 1988); and Monica McGoldrick, Carol Anderson, and Froma Walsh, eds., *Women in Families: A Framework for Family Therapy* (New York: W. W. Norton, 1989).

53. R. Wallerstein, "Changing Psychoanalytic Perspectives on Women." Paper delivered at Women and Psychoanalysis: Historical and Clinical Perspective. Symposium conducted by the San Francisco Psychiatric Institute and the University of California, Berkeley, CA, March 1984.

54. J. T. Spense, R. L. Helmreich, and J. Stapp, "The Personal Attributes Question-naire: A Measure of Sex Role Stereotypes and Masculinity-Femininity." *JSAS Catalog of Selected Documents in Psychology,* 4 no. 43 (1974): ms. 617.

55. M. L. Cowan and B. J. Stewart, "A Methodological Study of Sex Stereotypes," *Sex Roles* 3 (1977): 205–16 and J. E. Williams and S. M. Bennett, "The Definition of Sex Stereotypes via the Adjective Check List," *Sex Roles* 1 (1975): 327–37.

56. T. L. Ruble, "Sex Stereotypes: Issues of Change in the 1970s," *Sex Roles* 9(1983):397–402.

57. Gerald Amada, *A Guide to Psychotherapy* (Lanham, Md.: Madison Books, 1985), p. 13.

58. For an example of how theories that do not accurately reflect women's lives result in fundamental errors in the diagnosis and treatment of women patients, see Jeffrey B. Bryer et al., "Childhood Sexual and Physical Abuse as Factors in Adult Psychiatric Illness," *American Journal of Psychiatry* 144 no. 11 (November 1987): 1426–30.

59. Alternative models are presented in Frank X. Acosta, Joe Yamamoto, and Leon-ard A. Evans, *Effective Psychotherapy for Low-Income and Minority Patients* (New York: Plenum, 1982) and Clevonne W. Turner, "Clinical Applications of the Stone Center Theoretical Approach To Minority Women," Work in Progress (Wellesley, Mass.: Wellesley College, 1987).

60. For example, Marcia Westkoff, *The Feminist Legacy of Karen Horney* (New Haven: Yale University Press, 1986).

61. Lerman, *A Mote in Freud's Eye,* pp. 161–94.

62. Most funding institutions have not yet recognized the importance of research into the life stages of women. Even the most prominent researchers in the field have trou-ble garnering funds. Contrast this with a well-endowed, long-term prospective Grant study at Harvard conceived in 1937 and still active today, which examines male devel-opment. George Vaillant reported and continues to report on this study. George E. Vaillant, *Adaptation to Life: How the Best and the Brightest Came of Age* (Boston: Little, Brown, 1977).

PART 2 | Relationships: The Fulcrum of Women's Psychology

Freud argued that the keys to a successful life are love and work. I believe that the quality of our relationships is the single most important factor in determining our psychological well-being. As important as work is, even at this time in our history, relationships play the primary role. Our interactions with coworkers, bosses, employees, customers, or students greatly influence how we experience our work. The work itself can be boring or rewarding, satisfying or mundane, but it almost always takes place within the context of relationships, which can make or break our workday pleasure.

We are born or adopted into our earliest relationships. Parents, siblings, and extended families form the relationship net into which we fall at birth. These families are the context in which we learn about love, conflict, trust, safety, and predictability. We also bring our own personality to these relationships, but our dependency and vulnerability require that we adapt to the circumstances of life created by others and the emotional climate, practical support, and caring that they provide. Years of experience in our first family unit, whatever its character, establish the internal guidelines by which we measure other people and future relationships.

As we move beyond our first family, finding playmates and developing relationships with other adults, we automatically assume that our experiences will be similar to those we had with people in our family. If we have had healthy family relationships, we will have an internal guide that directs us to select healthy friendships among our peers and to participate in those relationships in healthy ways. If we have come from a dysfunctional family, we will tend to gravitate to others who behave in familiar and dysfunctional ways. An almost accidental relationship with a healthy friend or caring adult can actually provide a corrective emotional experience that can begin the process of revising the dysfunctional relationship map we've internalized.

We usually select the people with whom to have more intimate relationships from within our friendship network. From this group, we pick the people we date. From this smaller group, we select the person with whom we eventually form a long-term or permanent primary relationship.

Each relationship leads logically to the next. Yet as critical as relationships are to our overall contentment, the skills necessary to select and keep good relationships are acquired arbitrarily. In our schools, we try to teach every child how to read, write, and do math. We try to prepare every adult for gainful work, but we have no systematic training program to help all people acquire the competency necessary for the most important task in their life: the making and keeping of quality relationships.

The next chapter is a crash course in understanding the most important early relationships in our life and how they influence our expectations of relationships in general. We'll then review the kinds of relationships we go on to develop for ourselves as we begin to move beyond the confines of our biological or adopted family and finish up with a brief training program designed to help you improve your relationship skills.

3 | Family of Origin: Our Parents

No matter our age, whether we are an adopted or biological child, whether we come from a family with a single parent, two parents together after all these years or long since separated, or whether we have had the benefit (or burden) of growing up in a multigenerational or complex remarried family, we remain our parents' child. We are always a daughter.

Always a Daughter

The permanence of our position as daughter first struck me during my medical training. I had been invited to visit the home of an instructor, Patricia. Patricia, aged forty-nine, was twenty years my senior; her father, who lived with her, was in his early seventies. Because she was considerably older and presumably wiser than me, I had the mistaken assumption that Patricia had a lovely, nonangry, worked-through relationship with her father. As a young psychiatry resident, I was still obsessing about my relationships with all of my parents (I have a mother, a stepmother, a father, and a stepfather). Was I in for a surprise! As I watched Patricia and her father interact, I saw an amazing transformation. Patricia seemed to regress before my very eyes. She played daughter to her elderly father, while he willingly assumed his authoritarian and superior role. What a contrast to the woman I had seen run professional meetings, teach sophisticated medical courses, and advise me on handling similar situations with my family.

After my medical training came to an end, I had more time for a personal life. I developed friendships with both older and younger women. I listened as they described their own parents and, occasionally, I was able to observe a visit. A remarkably similar theme emerged. No matter the age of the "child," the attachment to her parents remained powerfully important. The emotions between parent and "child" were sometimes positive and sometimes negative, but they were always colored by the fact that one was the parent and one was the daughter—no matter their ages at the time of the encounter.

What Constitutes a Family?

Our experience of being a daughter is very much influenced by the type of family we have. When we think of family, a very specific model usually pops into our mind—Mom, Dad, and their kids. In psychological jargon, this is called a heterosexual, dyadic nuclear family. In this stereotypical family, the usual roles are:

Woman	Man
Primary parent.	Secondary parent.
Culturally lower status.	Culturally higher status.

Mothering	Fathering
By definition, parent role assigned to woman.	By definition, parent role assigned to man.
• Emphasis on caretaking.	• Emphasis on economic support.
• Nurturing assumed; if less than ideal, seen as inadequate.	• If nurturing, seen as special.
• Increasing economic role along with above responsibilities.	• Increasing but still limited direct caretaking role. Economic role unchanged or decreasing.
• Many women and their families are struggling with the woman's increased role outside of the family while she retains much of her previous role within the family.	• Many men and their families have not dealt with the economic, career advancement, and psychological consequences of men increasing direct caretaking.

This kind of family is assumed to be the commonest and "healthiest" one. It is true that all children begin with an egg from a woman and sperm from a man. And in many cases, these donors participate in raising the child they create. But beyond these unique biologically determined original contributions, the roles and responsibilities parents play in their child's life are influenced more by the culture than biology. Furthermore, our stereotype of the American family does not take into account divorce, single parenthood, extended families, gay and lesbian families, "complex" families with stepparents. Together, these and other variant families now outnumber the "typical" family.[1]

Gender-specific expectations of the female parent as mother and the male parent as father have an enormous impact upon our relationships with them as daughters. In most families, no matter how creative the structure, the child's legal mother (not necessarily biological mother) usually assumes primary responsibility for emotional and practical care. Fathers and stepfathers are expected to provide economic support, but they do not always do so.

Planned "atypical" families are more likely to have given careful thought to the individuals' responsibilities for children. There is often more acknowledgment of the role as primary or secondary parent. Communal families may construct elaborate and explicit guidelines concerning the economic support and nurturance of children. Lesbian families often articulate their precise expectations about raising children. Stepfamilies are guided by legal rules as well as personal beliefs.

Families of Origin

These family bonds are different from any others. They are automatic and involuntary and come with being born or adopted into a particular family. Sometimes there is a pleasant and easy fit. Other times, there is an unfortunate mismatch that contributes to unhappiness and discomfort for everyone. All too often, especially for those who end up in a therapist's office, these connections seem not only unsatisfying, but almost a mistake—like being switched at birth. We did not freely select our parents, and they did not know exactly what kind of daughter they would have. Yet we are bound together emotionally for the rest of our lives—even after family members have long since died.

Most parents anticipate loving their children, even if the circumstances of pregnancy and birth are not ideal. It is a major disappointment when this expectation of love is not transformed into a deep and honestly felt emotion. The reality of raising a child may be far different from what the expectant parent imagined. Sometimes a child is colicky or seems to be rejecting the parent. A parent may have few emotional resources or be overburdened by other commitments. Psychological handicaps, too many other children, an unexpected dislike of parenting, limited financial resources, or the commitment to work outside the home may interfere with the attachment to a particular child. Sometimes this missed connection is corrected in later years as the child and parent mature. Sometimes a loving and satisfactory connection never develops, and the parent and child remain emotionally detached.

At the opposite end of the spectrum, parents—loving or unloving—may have had a child who cannot form an attachment to her parents, even as an adult. Fantasies (or perhaps wishes) of having been adopted flow freely in adolescence as these unhappy teenage girls wonder how they ever ended up with this particular set of parents. As adults, these women may continue to report wondering how they were ever born to these particular people, but to no avail. These are her parents—this mother, this father. Stepparents, adopted parents, grandparents, aunts and uncles, cousins, brothers, sisters—she is stuck with them all. They are stuck with her. We cannot deny the existence of our relatives, and it greatly improves our sense of identity if we come to accept our unique ancestral history.[2]

Families come in many versions. Indeed, we have now reached a time in American history when more children will grow up in "atypical" families than "traditional" ones. Our experiences as daughters and our expectations of our parents are embedded in our unique family configuration and in the larger cultural context. Who our parents were and are is reflected through a complex matrix that includes

- each of their personalities,
- their psychological maturity,
- their "fit" into traditional and/or contemporary gender roles,
- their age,
- our family's socioeconomic, ethnic, and racial background,
- the historical period of our family's life cycle, and
- our unique family circumstances.

To understand the influence of family on our development, each of these variables must be considered. These family relationships are our first relationships. They serve as the foundation for our later relationships of choice and are our models (or antimodels) for how people relate to one another. We see how children are treated and how children are expected to treat adults or other authority figures. We see how men treat women and women treat men.

Many qualities, values, and expectations are communicated subtly or forcefully within our family unit. There might be an emphasis on learning and education, reinforcement through tenderness and affection or manipulation and force, an abundance or a deficiency of affection, the use of drugs or alcohol to cope with problems, enjoyment of family activities, relationships as a burden, the acquisition of money as critical and important, or an enjoyment of the outdoors and physical activity. Whether communicated verbally or nonverbally, these values, experiences, and expectations are played against and complement our own natural gifts, interests, talents, and handicaps. We take them in and weave them together with our individual propensities to build the inner structure of our lives—our sense of self.

Sense of Self: The Inner Structure

Whatever the configuration, our family of origin is the site of our first experience with relationships. It is the context in which our psychological structure—our sense of our self—begins to develop. There is a new building being constructed on the corner across from my office. Watching its progress has served as a metaphor for the way a child's personality develops within her family of origin.

Before the work began, the corner had been the site of a small parking lot and neighboring prefab structure that housed the city's mental-health center. To make room for a new building, the center was to be moved. I remember hearing this news with disbelief. The structure was fragile; I was not confident it would survive the change. Furthermore, patients were attached to the building and the move would be disruptive for them. Nonetheless, the prefab building was picked up by a crane and moved across the lot to the opposite corner. It settled in, walls slightly askew, desks and files requiring rearranging—but adjusting to its new spot.

First with resistance, then with acceptance, the patients and staff adapted and the new building beside it began to take form. A hole was dug, concrete was poured, and girders were welded in place as the steel interior came together. This internal frame would serve as the skeleton for the facade. It was the core upon which the remaining structure would rest. Walls, windows, and various decorations would be added. The exterior would be aesthetically pleasing and visually impressive, but if this inner structure was flawed, even a small earthquake could send the whole thing tumbling.

People seem a little like this. Older siblings—still shaky on their own foundation—may need to be moved aside to make room for a new child. As the new infant grows and develops, the interactions with parents and other caretakers are like the skeleton of a new building. If all the angles are adjusted correctly, if the concrete foundation is well made, if the materials are of good quality, the core structure will be sturdy and endure. The facade may be damaged by insults, but it can be easily repaired if the inner frame is solid.

Dysfunctional versus Functional Families of Origin

Families range from healthy and functional through mildly or moderately dysfunctional to severely dysfunctional.[3] This quality has nothing to do with whether our family fits the stereotype or not. Healthy or dysfunctional families can occur whether our parents are younger or older, a one mother–one father family, or something other than a heterosexual, dyadic nuclear family.

Just like individuals, families go through specific developmental stages. If separation, divorce, or death does not intervene, couples usually start their families with a commitment to each other and children are added later. Eventually, these children are launched as adults, and the parents live their final years again as a couple.

The family life-cycle model is a tool with which to think about our family over time. Within this framework, we can examine who our parents were and are as people, the constraints upon them as they raised their family, and the ways in which we experienced and interpreted our life with them. However, given the remarkable variability among family structures and the uncertainty of fate, the standard model of the daughter-parent relationship can serve only as a guide. You must modify it to include the unique characteristics of your family.

In healthy families, there is a sense of commitment, satisfaction, and pleasure. All members are treated with respect and experience their attachments positively even in the face of differences. Conflicts, which inevitably occur in all close relationships, are dealt with through respectful give and take. Because parents and other caregivers are the senior family members, there is a sense of inequality in parent-child relationships. The parents have more power and also more responsibility than the children.

As Miller has noted, in the best family situations, this is a kind of temporary inequality.[4] Parents see themselves as being of service to their children, providing them with a safe, supportive, and loving environment in which certain limits are set. Simultaneously, they see the child as having intrinsic worth. The child experiences being of value, being liked, being loved—even when certain behaviors may meet with disapproval. Parents communicate their disapproval in ways that are clear but not damaging. They do not abuse their children or deprive them of their basic rights. They do make sure that their children understand that certain behaviors are not acceptable in this family (what is considered unacceptable behavior will vary among different families). These healthy relationships reflect the specific and unique character of each family. If created with love and respect, these relationships lay the foundation for future trusting and respectful relationships between growing children and their parents—even when the children as adults adopt some values and behaviors that are different from their parents'.

These healthy families strive to minimize, if not end, the parent-child inequality. There is a gradual giving over to the children of the rights and responsibilities for conducting their own lives and making their own choices. Ironically, through the very act of viewing their relationships to their children as one of service and temporary inequality, many of these parents end up with the warmest and most respectful relationships with their adult children. People raised in families of this type often voice great admiration for their parents, especially as the children mature and discover that many other people do not have such loving and respectful experiences. As they see the realities of the stresses and strains within which their parents are operating—money troubles, job uncertainty, limited educations, and poor relationships with their own parents—they often develop even greater admiration. This can increase again when these adult children experience first-hand the challenges and pleasures of raising their own children.

At the other end of the spectrum are dysfunctional families in which one or more of the caregivers is psychologically handicapped. Parents suffering from addictions and significant emotional problems are not able to provide their children with the healthy home environment that facilitates development of a sturdy core psychological structure. The parents may physically and psychologically abuse their children or use permanent inequality[5]—a family structure in which children are always viewed as inferior to parents and females are always inferior to males.

At the extreme, children in dysfunctional families may be forced to endure terrible episodes of violence either against themselves or against others in the family. This may take the form of being victims of incest or beatings or watching a parent being assaulted. In more moderate cases, parents may simply be unavailable because they are frequently drunk or emotionally ungiving. Psychological abuse can occur when the pervasive attitude in the family is critical and hostile; constant demeaning comments undermine a child's self-esteem. Families where boys and men are valued more highly than girls and women reinforce rigid roles that interfere with the development of individual talents and interests.

The more blatant the abuse, the higher the risk to the growing child. Extreme defense mechanisms may develop, especially denial—acting as if it did not matter, it did not really hurt, or it did not happen. However, once the abuse is acknowledged, their is little question about the damage that has resulted. Fortunately, Adult Children of Alcoholics (ACOA), Survivors of Incest Anonymous (SIA),[6] and similar organizations provide havens and help many people deal with the impact of growing up in such families.

Moderate or mild abuse can be harder to acknowledge or validate. It seems less intentional, more easily understood, and does not usually cause such obvious damage. Adaptation is often more successful—in some cases, it might not even seem as if a handicap has developed. But it usually has, and it too will benefit from "re-pairing."[7]

Aging Parents

Parents are responsible for their children until the adult children become responsible for themselves at some point. While continuity of parental responsibility—symbolically and emotionally—continues throughout the life span, many adult children also feel responsible for their parents.[8] As parents become frail, the parent-child hierarchy seems to reverse. It is unclear how many parents and their adult children ever truly function as peers. Adult children seem to judge their parents on the quality of parenting they felt they received,[9] which implies seeing them as parents, not as peers. Adult children seem to remain interested in receiving their parents' support or approval long after they are actually dependent upon them, and they often express discomfort with their parents' dependency.[10]

The way adult children react to the increasing dependency of their mothers may be different from the way they react to the increasing dependency of their fathers. Adult children may make an easier transition in becoming the caretakers for their mothers because many mothers and daughters have always been involved in mutual daily nurturance to one degree or another.[11] On the other hand, some daughters may find the transition easier with fathers than with mothers, particularly if the adult daughters still feel disappointed with their mothers' care of them. If Dad played the role of family boss, it may be difficult for both daughter and father to handle the shift in power as the daughter assumes more responsibility for her father than he has for her. Their relationship must be totally restructured.

In our connection with our parents, we are both child and adult. We, as well as they, must struggle with this tension. While we see ourselves as grownups making independent decisions, they remember the kid in diapers struggling to stand on her own two feet. We wanted and needed our parents to support us then, to encourage us to try our wings, to be there when we fell. To some degree, we may even want that support as adults. Many parents have their own struggles providing support to or withdrawing it from their adult children.

Yet as our parents age, the tables are turned. We struggle with encouraging as much independence as they are capable of while being there, ready to catch them in a loving and respectful way when they can no longer do everything themselves. This loving support coupled with respect for autonomy seems to be the goal of caretaking throughout the life span. It is not an easy thing for any of us to offer another human being, but women have been trying. Their real or presumed failures have been well documented. It is not an easy job under the best of circumstances, yet we often have not recognized the intensity of demands until we are in those roles ourselves.

The Powerful Influence of Family Relationships

Relationships come in two basic types: those we are handed, the family in which we are born; and those we create, the friends whom we select and the family we establish. If our family of origin was healthy and warm, we use it as a guide for selecting and maintaining quality relationships of choice. If our family was emotionally troubled, we are at risk to replicate similarly disturbing relationships when we choose friends and lovers. If we recognize the handicaps that we have developed growing up in a dysfunctional family, and if we are committed to learning new relationship skills, we can slowly correct even significant problems.

But we cannot do this alone. It requires placing ourselves in healthier relationships. Often these will involve good friends with whom we share mutual value and respect. Sometimes we are wise to obtain the services of a professional who can understand the consequences of surviving a difficult family situation, who can nurture and coach us as we explore our earlier experiences and their impact on our lives today. This ally can encourage us to try new ways of being with people and help us make sense of the interactions that satisfy and those that hurt or confuse. We will learn to sort through our part in the trouble we have in our lives now, experiment with making changes, and recognize when to hold others responsible for their contributions. With time, risk taking, and hard work, we can turn the legacy of dysfunctional relationships into a resource that helps us trust new and healthier attachments.

NOTES

1. G. Masnick and M. J. Bane, *The Nation's Families: 1960–1990* (Boston: Auburn House, 1980).

2. Marybelle Cochran, "The Mother-Daughter Dyad Throughout the Life Cycle," *Women and Therapy* 4 no. 2 (Summer 1985): pp. 3–8.

3. The continuum might look like this: ← Healthy—Mild dysfunction—Moderate dysfunction—Severe Dysfunction →

4. Jean Baker Miller, *Toward A New Psychology of Women*, 2nd ed. (Boston: Beacon Press, 1986), pp. 4–5.

5. Miller, *Toward A New Psychology of Women*, pp. 6–12.

6. For more information write to Survivors of Incest Anonymous (SIA), c/o S.E. Regional Mental Health Center, 7702 Dunman Way, Baltimore, MD 21222.

7. I use the concept of "re-pairing" to indicate how psychological handicaps can be corrected. To explain the idea, I compare people's lives to roads. Whether due to poor building materials, bad weather, or continued use, roads often develop potholes that need to be repaired. People sometimes have potholes, too. The language of re-pairing is especially useful because people's potholes occurred in the context of relationships, and it is only by pairing with a new person who offers a quality relationship that the problem can be corrected. Thus, the task is to re-pair, to develop a relationship, to form a new pairing with another human being, to fill the pothole.

8. Marvin Sussman and Lee Burchinal, "Kin Family Network: Unheralded Structure and Current Conceptualizations of Family Functioning," *Marriage and Family Living* 24 (1962): 231–40.

9. Sylvia Weishaus, "Aging Is a Family Affair," in Pauline Ragan, ed., *Aging Parents* (Los Angeles: University of Southern California Press, 1979), pp. 154–74.

10. Betsy Robinson and Majda Thurnher, "Taking Care of Aged Parents," *The Gerontologist* 19 (1979): 586–93.

11. Joan Aldous, *Family Careers: Developmental Change in Families* (New York: Wiley, 1978).

Daughters and Mothers

Mother-daughter relationships are sometimes maligned, sometimes idealized, but there is little doubt that women's preoccupation with their mothers borders on obsession. And women's feelings about their mothers are rarely neutral.

Historically, the mother-daughter bond has been the primary attachment holding the family together.[1] Most parents and adult children want to retain their connection, and they rely on women to do it. In middle-class families, where adult children often live significant distances from their parents, daughters more than sons maintain regular contact with relatives. Much of this contact is through the mother. If an adult woman places a phone call to her parents and her father happens to pick up the phone, he usually transfers the line rather quickly to his wife because he is awkward and inexperienced in verbal communication.

While accepting the role of family communicator may seem to serve the family, it is not always in the best interests of mother and daughter. Mothers and adult daughters are left striving to maintain relationships that adequately balance the human need for emotional closeness and distance—not only for themselves, but for the entire family.

Maintaining intimacy through verbal communication is characteristic of almost all close relationships between women. However, mother-daughter relationships are somewhat different. Relationships with our women friends often serve as a place where we can safely complain and solve problems about our relationships with men. The mother-daughter relationship rarely provides such an arena, and neither mother nor daughter is likely to be neutral. An adult daughter is unlikely to complain too much about her husband to her mother. In a conflict, the daughter expects her mother to side with her rather than with her husband. Similarly, a mother will not have an unbiased listener if she wants to discuss concerns about her relationship with her husband. A daughter often has a strong attachment to her father. She is rarely able to hear her mother's concerns without feeling uncomfortable or conflicted.

Yet because they are both female, there is a "natural" identification between mothers and daughters. Their shared female identity sustains the mother-daughter attachment. Unfortunately, one problem with this identification is that daughters have their most powerful tie with the less powerful parent.[2] Daughters see their mothers as having less status in families and in society than they wish for themselves. This cultural devaluing of the role played by women as mothers undermines the mother-daughter relationship and contributes to daughters' conscious efforts to be different from their mothers. For the most part, daughters *do* see their lives, present and future, as different from their mothers'—even those daughters with children of their own. This difference emerges very clearly in expectations about relationships with men.

Adult daughters actually know very little about their mothers' private relationships with men; what they do "know," they often perceive negatively. For the most part, contemporary daughters seek more egalitarian relationships with men than did their mothers. And unlike their mothers, daughters expect to work outside of the home for most of their adult lives.[3] These changes may separate mother and daughter. There may be undercurrents of envy, competition, and anger if a mother resents her daughter's opportunities or a daughter feels guilty about being able to create a life for herself that was denied her mother.[4] There may be overt conflict if a mother believes her daughter should be at home rather than working when her children are young.

Paid employment does alter the daughter's life. Even though working fathers usually make more money than working mothers, wives who work outside the home do have greater power in their marriages than nonworking wives.[5] Yet even in contemporary couples, family jobs continue to be divided along gender lines.[6] While many women can now envision having more work and life-style options than their mothers, and even if male partners share equitably in household maintenance,[7] once children are born, mother and daughter share essentially the same role in motherhood.

If mothers and daughters have a special bond, it is this shared role as mother. The social arrangement of motherhood has changed relatively little in recent decades. Women are still expected to want children, to have children, and to be the primary caretakers of children.[8] All women, even women without children, are expected to behave in "maternal" ways toward others. This expectation encompasses some global notion that women should always be kind to other people, take care of them, wait on them, and not hurt them.

The pressure of this role is most strongly felt in our expectations of our own mothers. Recent social changes stimulated by the women's movement have barely altered this situation. We all have some idealized notion of what a mother should be, and we measure our own mother against this unrealistic stereotype. The more disappointed we are that she has not lived up to our expectations, the more angry we are with her for not giving us what we believe we needed or deserved. Instead of valuing and appreciating our mothers for doing the best they could at an almost impossible job,[9] we judge our mothers harshly. Mother becomes a negative rather than a positive role model.

We have constructed a cultural notion of motherhood that functions as if mothers have no interests or needs of their own. The child is completely dependent on the caretaking adult, and we have tended to view this relationship as being best when the caretaker is all-giving. We have even extended this notion into the later years of childhood and adulthood. We long for a mother who is selfless, who will always put our needs first. We want her always to be totally supportive of our needs and interests as we define them. She must also do this in such a way as to simultaneously not be intrusive.

This model of mothering is unachievable. It is not particularly healthy for a daughter to maintain a lifelong relationship in which she remains excessively dependent on her mother. Nor is it healthy for a mother to remain in a position where she continues to delay her own development separate from her role as mother. In healthier mother-daughter relationships, the stereotype of the all-giving mother is revised. It comes to be understood by both daughter and mother that this is an unreasonable expectation. The all-giving, self-sacrificing mother is a dream.

Theory suggests that it is easier to abandon this dream if one has received "good enough" mothering. This means that the daughter's needs have been met to a reasonable degree, although, understandably, they were frustrated at times. The child learned that her mother had needs of her own that were sometimes contrary to what the child wanted. Sometimes her mother purposefully "deprived" the child out of a more mature awareness that the child's requests or demands were developmentally inappropriate, excessive, or downright unsafe. As the child grew and developed, she learned to defer gratification, to share, and to recognize the rights of others—including her mother's.[10]

In the more disturbed mother-daughter relationship, this growth and development is difficult. For example, if the mother is psychologically immature, her own internal resources will be limited and she will be unable to provide sufficient care for her daughter. This may result in the child becoming prematurely self-sufficient or remaining excessively dependent.

As the adult, the mother must take primary responsibility for any early problems in the mother-daughter relationship. However, both professionals and laypeople are prone to engage in mother blaming[11] without examining the duress under which the mother is operating. The mother herself may have had inadequate parenting, leaving her with substantial developmental deficiencies that will prevent her from providing the best care for her daughter unless she receives help and support. She may be living under difficult or untenable life circumstances such as poverty or abuse. Even mothers in decent family settings are expected to have more control over their child's development than is humanly possible.[12]

We blame the mother when a child does not reach the level of psychological maturity that we expect. We do this even though we know little about genetically linked developmental handicaps that may interfere with healthy development—even when the child is cared for by the most loving and responsible adults. We do this even though growing children begin to exercise increasing free will over which friends they choose, what activities they like, and how disciplined they are in school. All these choices made by the child have a significant influence upon her development.

The pressure women feel to always behave "maternally" means that having anything other than unambivalently loving feelings is complicated and confusing—for both mothers and daughters. It is "wrong" to be directly angry at our mother. We fear the intensity of our anger and are not anxious to take up our complaints with her directly. When we do, our anger is often ineffectual because neither mother nor daughter has much experience understanding and processing unpleasant feelings.

Harriet's experience with her mother demonstrates this conflict. Harriet's seventy-nine-year-old widowed mother, Orah, recently moved from Tampa to Chicago, which has been Harriet's home for over thirty years. Harriet and Orah had not lived in the same town since Harriet left home for college thirty-seven years ago, and they had had a smooth and comfortable relationship during the intervening years. Free from conflict, Harriet enjoyed annual visits to her parents' home, where she spent much of her time helping her father with household repairs.

After her husband died, and without consulting her daughter, Orah moved to be near Harriet. While a little startled by her mother's move, Harriet helped her mother find a small apartment just five minutes from Harriet's office. Harriet thought that the convenience would make it easy to stop at her mother's for short daily visits and to handle any chores her mother needed done. Harriet was surprised when she discovered that after two months of this dutiful activity, she resented visiting her mother every day. Usually happy to close up shop and head for home at the end of a long day, Harriet would procrastinate—always finding one more task to do before leaving the office. As she would drive over to her mother's apartment, her shoulders would begin to ache, her stomach would churn, and her head would start to pound. Walking through the front door of the apartment building, she would feel as if she was going to explode. Her hands would shake, and she would want to run away.

Harriet came to see me because she wanted to understand what was going on. What seemed evident to me, but would take Harriet a long time to face, was that she was angry with her mother. In fact, she had been angry with her mother for a very long time, but she had avoided confronting these feelings by living far away and controlling her visits. The proximity, and her mother's increasing dependence, prevented Harriet from ignoring her feelings any longer. The physical symptoms were signals of feelings that Harriet was trying to keep under wraps. Those feelings had to be given voice—if only in the privacy of Harriet's own mind and my office. Once she understood them better and allowed herself the full range of feelings toward her mother, she could decide how she wanted to handle them.

In all our obsessing about what Mother should or should not have done for us—or do for us now—we overburden her and underburden our other parent, Dad.[13] He is let off the hook much more easily. In families where Dad has left and the young children are in the care of their mother alone, Dad is easily forgiven or forgotten by the children. Adult children may develop a relationship with him later in life or appear to feel little internal strife over the loss. I have listened to adopted adult children who wondered why their mothers (not fathers) gave them away and adult children whose father's left them when they were almost too young to remember. They say that they just do not think about him. But while their relationship with Dad seems easily resolved, their attachment to their mother— the parent who did not abandon them—may remain intensely ambivalent or riddled with sadness and pain. It hardly seems fair.

Of course, if sexually active human beings bear children, someone does have to take responsibility for raising them. The curious thing is how this responsibility came to be the province of women.

Responsible Women

"Being responsible" is one generalization we can make about the nature of the attachment between adult women and their mothers. The nature of that responsibility varies with the structure of the family, the economic and educational opportunities, the personalities of each woman, and the historical period in which they live. In addition, the mother-daughter relationship changes over time as each member develops along her own life path. The intersections and distances will vary for each unique dyad—every mother-daughter relationship is different. But without a doubt, responsibility for care[14] is a theme in virtually every one.

This theme can be described in terms of a hierarchy of responsibility—how much one woman is responsible for the other.[15] When the daughter is an infant, the responsibility goes one way. The infant girl is totally dependent upon her caretaker. As the years pass, the daughter's responsibility to the mother in terms of the exchange of goods and services increases. These exchanges define the unique interaction between mother and daughter and determine who is the giver and who is the receiver at any point in time. Depending upon the type of responsibility each assumes, one or the other may try to supervise or control the other's behavior, will see the well-being of the other as a focus of concern, or will talk or think about the relationship.[16]

This hierarchy of responsibility includes five distinct types of mother-daughter relationships:

1. Responsible mothers/dependent daughters. The mother continues to view herself as responsible for her daughter, and the daughter, at least implicitly, acknowledges that the relationship is asymmetrical.
2. Responsible daughters/dependent mothers. In families with emotional instability in either the mother or the father, daughters often develop highly protective relationships with their mothers. As adults, these daughters may live at some distance from their mothers, creating a boundary on their feelings of responsibility for their mothers.
3. Peerlike friendships. A genuine peerlike friendship between mother and daughter appears to be uncommon. When it does occur, the relationship is marked by two characteristics: high involvement in each others' lives and a strong independent streak in both women. They minimize their debt to each other and support each other's autonomy.
4. Mutual mothering. These symmetrical relationships are characterized by mutual dependence rather than independence. There is a sense of mutual protectiveness that is qualitatively different from a sense of mutuality or balance of responsibility. They develop a set of commitments to each other and supervise each other's lives. They are highly attuned to each other's feelings and tend to become entangled in each other's needs and emotions. They are very responsible to each other but do not necessarily have harmonious or loving relationships.

5. Noninvolved. These daughters and mothers see each other rarely and seem to have little emotional involvement in each other's lives. They have a long history of emotional distance. In most cases, daughters wish they could have been closer and seem to be searching for some kind of "mothering." Even in these extremely limited relationships, when the mothers do have contact with their daughters, they may still behave momentarily in conventionally "mothering" ways—giving a kiss on the cheek, brushing a lock of hair from her daughter's eyes, showing a sensitive concern on her face when she sees her daughter's pain. These moments of intimacy and supervision may cause pain and confusion for both daughter and mother as they see for a moment what could be, and is not, between them.[17]

Dual Development

The hierarchy of responsibility model describes the mother-daughter relationship at one point in time. What do we know about the evolution of mother-daughter relationships over many years?

Because Mom is usually the primary parent, a daughter's (and probably a son's) relationship with her mother across the life cycle is more intimate than with her father. It is not that fathers are necessarily more strict; they may or may not be.

Time spent alone with someone provides an opportunity to develop a unique understanding. At home, a father is likely to guard "his" time much more than Mother guards "hers"—even when both parents are employed. There are usually more limits to a father's availability. Father's status as a family member is, therefore, more peripheral even as it is also more powerful.[18] In our culture, which values men above women, Father's position as a man makes him someone to be feared or idolized *and* loved, sometimes by virtue of his position alone.

Mothers, on the other hand, are always on call. Fathers are not expected to be, nor do they expect to be, as readily available. Because Mother is always there, emotionally if not literally, her time is often considered of lesser value. The less time can be spent with Dad, the more valued that time becomes. The primary parent, usually Mom, has most of the drudgery of daily care. The secondary parent, usually Dad, is freer to play. It is this sense of play that marks the father-daughter relationship as more pleasurable and less conflicted than the mother-daughter relationship.

Female Infants and Their Mothers

The mother-daughter relationship is strongly affected by the cultural norm by which women provide primary parenting for their children. For female infants, this means that the person with whom they have their first, most intense, and probably longest intimate relationship is also female. Because their child is like them (female) rather than unlike them (male), mothers assume they understand their daughters. At each stage of development, the mother can easily imagine what her little girl is experiencing by relying on her own core identity and life experience. This results in a kind of closeness between mother and daughter that is unlikely to occur with a son.

This ease has often been described rather pejoratively by psychological theorists as blurred boundaries. More recently, researchers have suggested that this ease is instead a strength that permits a warm and empathic connection. In healthy mother-daughter relationships, the latter is probably the more accurate description. But some mothers do project their own feelings and thoughts upon their tiny infant daughters and assume that the child is experiencing exactly what the mother is projecting. When these projections do not accurately match the child's experience, the child feels intruded upon and devalued, not empathized with.[19] A realistic description of the quality and character of the mother-daughter relationship needs to take into account the psychological maturity of the mother, the personality of the daughter, and the context or life circumstances in which mother and daughter find themselves. Concepts like blurred boundaries do not always aid in this process.

Adolescent Daughters and Their Mothers

If it is true that the daughter's easier attachment to her mother means that she has more difficulty obtaining some distance,[20] it would explain the stress of the adolescent years. Daughters often remember this as the worst age with their mothers, the period of the greatest direct conflict and hostility.

There is a dynamic shift in the mother-daughter relationship when the daughter enters adolescence. As she moves with stops and starts into womanhood, physiological changes herald her biological capacity for childbearing. The mother has her own reaction to these changes. Her daughter's budding sexuality cannot simply be enjoyed and celebrated. If acted on prematurely or without contraceptive protection, an unwanted pregnancy could follow. If carried to term, this infant could easily—and most probably will—alter the daughter's life permanently, and perhaps the older woman's as well.

The mother, more experienced in the world, knows that women are more vulnerable than men to particular forms of violence. Incest and rape contaminate sexuality with violence and may distort the daughter's development and the mother-daughter relationship. Even before knowledge of these risks was public, many mothers, victims themselves, were aware of the risks their daughters faced. Often these mothers were unable to talk openly about their worries. With the true reasons for their mothers' concern shrouded in secrecy, daughters are left feeling that their mothers are arbitrarily curtailing their freedom.

Even in the safest and healthiest of situations, a mother coping with her first developing adolescent daughter may feel overwhelmed by the demands of the changes in their relationship. One day the adolescent, flooded with hormones, is moody and unavailable, impossible to console. Another day she may be a clinging youngster wanting the advice and protection of a loving mother. The mother's empathic skills are challenged as she tries to read her daughter's fluctuating needs and respond accordingly. Mistakes will be made on both sides. The damage to the quality of the relationship done by these inevitable blunders will depend on the underlying trust and care that marked the earlier attachment between mother and daughter. Some mothers and daughters sail through this new phase of development with relative ease, while others have more difficulty.

For mothers and daughters, the adolescent years are characterized by holding on and letting go. As the mother prepares her daughter for domestic tasks and the demanding responsibilities of adulthood, daughters often feel that their mothers have become more critical. Mother may expect her adolescent daughter to do more household chores and spend more time taking care of younger siblings. She may fret about her daughter's developing sexuality. During this same period, mothers also may feel that their daughters are more critical, sullen, argumentative, or distant. Clearly, both mother and daughter play active roles in altering their attachment.[21]

During these years, mother and daughter develop a variety of ways to maintain their attachment and to establish greater separation. In this they are trying to adjust the hierarchy of responsibility, and the strategies they use affect the quality of their relationship. Some relationships are highly involved, with the daughters spending a lot of time with their mothers and receiving considerable praise from them. Other relationships are somewhat involved, with the daughters either spending time alone with their mothers or receiving praise from them. A minority of relationships are remote, with the daughters spending little time alone with their mothers and receiving little praise from them.

A daughter usually initiates some shift in the mother-daughter relationship by limiting her mother's access to her life. Spending less time together becomes one avenue for generating some separation and decreasing the intimacy in the relationship.[22] About one-third of daughters create this separation by simply censoring their communication with their mother. The remaining two-thirds generate separation more explicitly through overt conflict or emotional withdrawal—often in addition to censorship.

As a daughter pulls away from her mother, she usually transfers her intimacy to peers—girlfriends and boyfriends. In most cases, though, the daughter is invested in keeping her mother in her life. By pulling away, she is simply aiming to change the structure of the attachment.[23] Unfortunately, some mothers take the change personally and feel rejected by their daughters. If these mothers are not fully mature themselves, they may respond in unhelpful ways to their daughters' distancing. A troubled mother who is hurt and angry may abandon her daughter emotionally, if not literally. Other mothers may deny that a change is necessary and press back intrusively, trying to regain the previous level of intimacy. Unfortunately, this is no longer appropriate or healthy for either mother or daughter.

In responding negatively to the young woman's push forward into adulthood, the emotionally distraught mother often obtains a temporary regression from her anxious daughter. However, this state cannot be maintained indefinitely, for it is not in the best interest of either female or their relationship. The daughter fears that if she continues her development as an adult, she will lose her mother as a nurturing presence in her life. If the mother has punished her daughter because the younger woman cannot remain forever an adoring child or if the mother insists upon clinging, the daughter must pull the relationship farther apart in the interest of her own healthy development. If, because of her own unresolved developmental disabilities, the mother cannot bear to be attached to a less dependent daughter, the daughter may have to set up artificial barriers to protect her budding sense of self. While she may do this in the service of her own psychological health, she pays a high price, which leaves its own kind of damage. It takes great courage for a daughter to test this possibility. If she does and the worst happens, the daughter must process the pain, sadness, grief, anger, and loneliness that follows this deep loss.

Rather than withdrawing or clinging, some mothers and daughters establish invested relationships in which they appear to "mother" each other. These mothers and daughters have a high degree of mutual involvement without censorship. More often than not, the mother-father bond in these families has been disrupted. While the mother usually has not experienced widowhood or divorce prior to her daughter's adolescence, the parents are often locked in conflict.

In these mother-daughter pairs, the females form an alliance against the father. In half of these families, the father is quite traditional—an economic provider who has little emotional involvement with his wife or his daughter. In the remaining half, the father is an alcoholic or otherwise irrational. These mother-daughter alliances form some protection from a distant, yet culturally powerful, father, but they also maintain Dad in his traditional role.

When the father is a substantial problem, the mother and daughter tend to keep private and secret information between each other and away from him. In these mother-daughter relationships, there seems to be almost too much of an alliance. The daughter becomes a peer to her mother prematurely, crossing generational boundaries and attenuating her own adolescence. While this is an adaptive and understandable strategy when mother and daughter are coping with a dysfunctional husband and father, both women are denied a rich and enjoyable relationship with him as well as with each other. Huddled together against a common enemy, the mother does not have a full-fledged adult partner with whom to share parental responsibilities, and the daughter does not have two parents upon whom she can depend.

In contrast to these close, although less than ideal, mother-daughter relationships, almost one-fifth of mothers and daughters are strikingly uninvolved in each other's lives. In these relationships there does not seem to be a sense of warmth and pleasure in the mother-daughter relationship. Unlike invested relationships, there appears to be no alliance. These mothers spend virtually no time alone with their teenage daughters and tend not to give their daughters any praise. There seems to be minimal emotional involvement, and both seem to suffer with low self-esteem.

These limited mother-daughter relationships are in marked contrast to the kind of relationships we have come to expect. Their remoteness seems to predict the future of their connection; these mothers and daughters usually remain distant throughout their adult lives. The daughters experience a particular kind of emotional trauma that may interfere with the formation of other relationships. When a healthy father is available, the daughter often grows closer to him than to her mother, and this intimacy may compensate for the remoteness in the mother and daughter relationship. If so, it allows the daughter to develop useful relationship skills that she can then transfer outside the family training ground.

We have little information about what happens to mothers who behave so distantly. There is some evidence that they may have suffered considerable emotional trauma in their own lives that they have never resolved. We do know that these mothers tend to be responsible for large families, often having three or more children. Researchers need to investigate the impact on the mother of having to care for so many youngsters. It seems conceivable that the mother-daughter bond is affected by this larger family unit. In addition, these mothers have often experienced significant marital disruption. Almost half have been widowed or divorced before their daughters reached adolescence. Mothers without adult companions have little relief from their parental responsibility. As solo parents, they have little economic or emotional support and often feel overloaded.

Remote and involved mother-daughter relationships are found throughout society, among the rich as well as in working- and middle-class families. Neither economic resources nor level of education seems to predict the nature of these ties. A healthy mother recognizes that her adolescent daughter is going through an age-appropriate stage and sees her as having some right to establish boundaries. Attached mothers seem to have a sense of joy in their relationship that is missing in relationships where mother and daughter are remote. However, if either mother or daughter (or as more commonly happens, both) is psychologically handicapped, the transition is unlikely to go smoothly.

The adolescent years seem to predict the type of relationship mother and daughter will have as the daughter moves into adulthood. In the best of all possible worlds, there will be an easy flow between dependency, interdependency, and independency. Moving back and forth among these states is necessary and appropriate. While it takes some thought and effort, the healthiest of mothers and daughters are able to manage these transitions reasonably well.

Adult Daughters and Their Mothers

An adult daughter's life circumstances affect the quality of her relationship with her mother. One of the most important factors is whether or not she is "settled." Being settled means having a sense of doing and having done what she wants, having concrete plans for the future, and being able to imagine what her life will be like. Mothers of settled daughters may not be in agreement with their choices, but at least they can feel that important life hurdles have been achieved. If a woman wants to be in a primary love relationship and is not, to have children and cannot, or to work at a satisfying job and does not, she may report feeling quite unsettled. Similarly, her mother sees her in this light. This can be quite distressing to the mother who still worries about her adult "child."

Single daughters under the age of thirty are more likely to have responsible mother/dependent daughter relationships. As the daughter ages, her dependency often diminishes. Older daughters, whether themselves parents or not, appear to have more symmetrical relationships with their mothers, at least until the mothers reach a very old age and must depend more upon their daughters.

Developmental changes often occur in the relationship if the daughter marries and especially if she becomes a mother. For most mothers and daughters, the birth of a grandchild marks the daughter's final transition into adulthood. Motherhood transforms a woman's life even more than a committed relationship or marriage. It is a permanent obligation. By and large, mothers cannot and do not "divorce" their children. They rarely give up custody even when there is a divorce.[24]

Responsibility for a dependent child means that an adult daughter's life becomes more child-centered, a situation that resonates with her mother's own experience. The role of grandparent also creates an emotional tie between grandmother, new mother, and grandchild that serves to tighten the family bond.

In becoming a mother, the daughter often becomes involved with her own mother in new ways. She may be temporarily more dependent upon her for nurturance and support, particularly during the early postpartum period. The older woman may feel unwillingly forced back into a parenting role, or she may feel that it is a normal extension of their mutual exchange of loving services. In any case, mother and daughter may now reinvest time in their relationship around shared experiences and concerns as mothers.

We do not know why women become the primary parent in most families.[25] Contemporary psychological theory suggests that women reproduce mothering across generations because daughters' continuing identification with their mothers leads them to play out the same role in their families that was performed by their mothers.[26] Male children develop their identity and personality structure by denying their similarity to their mothers. They are not groomed to stand in their mothers' shoes when they form their own families.

Social structure, economics, and historical precedence play their part as well. American women in every social class seem to have primary responsibility for children.[27] Even in heterosexual families where both parents work, mothers continue in this role.[28] Most often, women provide this care directly; sometimes, they arrange for others to provide it.[29] Yet mothers still carry the responsibility for childcare and household management even when they are away from home.

It is curious that women continue to have so much home-based responsibility. There are many tasks associated with childcare that need not be done exclusively by one gender. Popular culture is replete with fathers who take their parenting role seriously[30] and, at least in theory, our society no longer assumes that a woman should accept primary responsibility for parenting and domestic chores simply because she can give birth to and breast-feed children. Yet even though these old assumptions have been challenged, it is still Mother who assumes the greatest responsibility for these duties. Theory has not been translated into practice.

Parenting need not preclude an active work life when environmental conditions are favorable. But our society has not come to validate the complicated and demanding tasks of parenthood. We deride mothers who stay home to care for their children full time, and we rarely alter the workplace to incorporate the responsibility of parenting. The primary or exclusive parent must bear the stress of trying to be in several places at once—available to her child, available for her paid work, and available for herself.

For the time being, gender *does* seem to determine who will care for children. As a result, when daughters have children of their own, their relationship with their own mothers takes on a different meaning. Daughters come to realize the immensity of their new role, and thus often see their mothers more benevolently than women who have not had children. Old feelings about their mothers and their relationships with them are stirred up as they raise their own children. As their own young children progress through familiar stages, old memories resurface. Women reexperience and often rework old hurts and misunderstandings or relive positive memories of love and support. The pleasure and the disappointments bubble up, providing new opportunities for growth—for themselves and for their relationship with their mothers.

What happens to the mother-daughter relationship if the daughter does not become a mother? When women become mothers, they experience two perspectives: having been the person mothered as well as the person who mothers. In sharing the role of mother, it is as if the older and younger women become colleagues. Without that shared role, mothers and daughters may not develop the same intensity of attachment. However, given the constraints upon women who mother, some mothers may actually prefer that their daughters not have children. These women often obtain significant vicarious pleasure from their daughters' nonmothering achievements.

Whether a daughter does or does not become a mother herself does not predict the nature of the mother-daughter relationship. For one thing, motherhood is only one form of caring. Most women, even those who never become biological mothers, still demonstrate caring for others as a central theme in their lives. Even if an adult daughter does not have children herself, she still has been trained to behave in a maternal fashion. Single daughters are particularly likely to be the caretaker of their mothers—presumably because they do not have to juggle the competing needs of a spouse and young children.

As with earlier stages of development, we must look at each individual mother-daughter relationship to see how they manage their attachment. There is often as much variability as there is commonality.

Adult Daughters and Their Elderly Mothers

Care of elderly parents is essentially a women's issue. Wives, daughters, and daughters-in-law are more likely to be direct caregivers; men are usually excused from this responsibility.[31] As parents age and grow frail, it is women who usually take over their care.

While not all parents live long enough to require significant care, many mothers do. For the elderly mother, health problems may seem to be a private concern, but the responsibility shifted to her daughter may cause a major disruption. A previously well-functioning parent may experience depression or severe changes in mental function. Parents who suffer a severe medical illness late in life often find their lives transformed. Whether their incapacitation is temporary or permanent, it brings the idea of death much closer. At the same time, their social world is shrinking as many of their friends become ill and die. These changes alter their subjective sense of themselves. In the face of her mother's illness, a daughter may suddenly have increased contact, involvement, and responsibilities for her mother. As a result, the parent-child hierarchy will need to be renegotiated, not just reversed.

Many adults feel disappointed when their parents give up their parental role. For many adult children, a parent's dependency is difficult to accept. It is the clearest statement that they are no longer a "child." If they never received the kind of care and protection they expected or desired, this can be an extremely difficult transition.

An explicit role reversal seems specific to the mother-daughter relationship. Daughters care for their elderly fathers as much as their mothers but do not see their fathers as becoming a "child." Sons report having a protective relationship with their parents but do not see themselves becoming the family "father." Perhaps a reversal of parent-child roles is more difficult in relationships that involve males because *father* has a different meaning than *mother*. In most families, Father has greater status than Mother. For a son to take on a "fathering" role with his parents is a much more radical reversal of the parental hierarchy than for a daughter to take on a "mothering," or nurturing, role. The most threatening challenge is posed by the daughter who insists upon reversing roles with her father, undermining his position as the family patriarch.

Adult daughters with elderly parents have been called women in the middle. Responsibility for both their children and aging parents causes considerable stress as these women balance what may feel like competing commitments. However, while such care is demanding, many women report they do not feel overly burdened by supporting their mothers. These midlife women seem to experience this caretaking as a continuation of their attachment to their mothers, made easier by the fact that the transition into "mothering" an elderly mother usually comes slowly. For the mother-daughter relationships characterized by a mutual give and take of services, this stage of life can seem like a natural extension of their long history together.

Responsibility for Care: The Central Theme in the Mother-Daughter Relationship

Although research in adult development suggests that individual personalities are relatively stable over time,[32] changes in family structure lead to changes in the mother-daughter relationship. There is considerable diversity among family relationships across cultures, societies, and historical periods. Even within the same family, mothers may have different relationships with each of their daughters. Yet gender assures some kind of bond between mothers and daughters.

Women and men have different and unequal status in society and in virtually all families. The status of women is bound up in their biological and social role as mothers. It is only the most recent generation of daughters that has been able to envision lives that are markedly different from their mothers.[33] The ability and legal right to control reproduction and the legal right to work at any job have created more opportunities than ever before. More women work, cohabit before marriage, marry at a later age, have fewer children, often later in life, and divorce in greater numbers. But one thing has not changed. Women remain the primary caretakers of children and dependent adults.

It is hard to shunt the task of daily caretaking outside the family even when financial resources are available. The nature of caretaking means always being ready, on call, all the time. Professional caregivers can be hired, but their care, while often good, is not based on personal commitment and attachment.[34] Caring for young children and for aging parents creates a level of intimacy that women share across generations. It is the role that links their lives.[35]

In the early years of the mother-daughter relationship, the daughter's dependency colors their attachment. In healthy relationships, this is a period when the young girl can rely wholeheartedly on her mother to provide security and daily care. The little girl adores and cherishes her loving mother. Their closeness and pleasure in each other's company has been mislabeled by some as symbiotic, which implies pathology. Contemporary theorists have suggested instead that this female-female attachment is the essence of healthy female development and the context in which the capacity for mutual empathy is nourished.[36]

During adolescence and young adulthood, the daughter often goes through a stage of significant anger directed toward her mother. This may be an age-appropriate rebellion characterized by censorship, conflict, or withdrawal. In searching for her own identity, the younger woman often questions and rejects her mother's values. This period proceeds more smoothly if the older woman has goals of her own that are separate from her role as mother. The emotional availability of an extended family and the psychological maturity of the mother usually allow this period to proceed with relative ease for both parties. The two females remain connected but grow more differentiated as each develops new interests and activities.

Unfortunately, some mothers and daughters become stuck at this developmental phase. Some adult daughters remain angry at their mothers for real or perceived injustices, and they often organize their feelings toward their mothers around mother-blaming. For the mother and daughter to extricate themselves from this battle, both must be willing to change. If only one desires to change the quality of their attachment, she finds it almost impossible. It is like trying to dance with a partner who refuses to cooperate. However, it is possible for either woman to change her *internal* experience of their relationship—even if her partner does not participate. Acknowledging and eventually resolving past hurts and disappointments can liberate both daughter and mother.

As both women grow older, the mother-daughter relationship acquires more equality. Whether or not the daughter marries or has children of her own, the healthiest mother-daughter relationships reach a stage of mature appreciation and acceptance characterized by mutual interdependence and respect. This has been called the era of good feelings.[37]

As the older woman ages, a shift occurs again as the mother becomes more dependent on her adult daughter. Older women may feel abandoned and angry if their daughters are distant and aloof, while their daughters struggle with feelings of guilt and anger if they are not prepared for their mothers' increasing dependence.[38] Daughters who have moved away from their mothers when they were younger may desire greater proximity when their aging mothers need more daily caretaking. The adult daughter may arrange for her ill mother to move near her home so that regular contact can be arranged more easily. Active older mothers may move on their own to be closer to their daughters, particularly if grandchildren are involved. Ultimately, it is flexibility that marks the healthy mother-daughter relationship and allows each woman to adjust to this final exchange of services.

Summary

The mother-daughter relationship undergoes a process of continuous change. Throughout their lives, mothers and daughters adjust the amount of closeness and separateness between them. Dyads that remain close may be either healthy or dysfunctional. Neither geographical distance nor frequency of contact tells us much about the quality of the relationship. To assess quality, we must look directly at the interactions between the women.

Most mother-daughter relationships are close and distant at the same time. Only occasionally is there a complete break between mother and daughter. The successful resolution of each developmental stage of the mother-daughter relationship is characterized by increasing differentiation within the context of an ongoing connection. The healthiest relationships are characterized by an intimacy that includes mutual trust, support, understanding, and a shared view of family history and traits.[39]

Mother and daughter, even when the relationship is troubled, have a long and intimate history. Father has not usually been as regular a presence in his daughter's day-to-day life. The difference in gender between daughter and father also has a significant impact upon their relationship—even if he is loving and involved.

This history of two females living in each other's company for many years, one dependent on the other for a very long time, makes the mother-daughter relationship unique, even when it is dysfunctional. Our shared history as women and our shared role of being responsible for care has a powerful impact on both of our lives. It is the capacity for flexibility and mutual interdependence within the context of this history that marks the best mother-daughter relationships.

Tasks for Women
To Enrich Our Understanding of Dual Development

Mothers have a sense of the historical, cultural, and family context in which the mother-daughter relationship developed, but the daughter's perspective is usually more limited. A daughter can better understand how external factors influenced her mother's life, and consequently her own, if she acquires more information about her mother's history.

Mother and daughter have parallel histories. One way to picture this is to construct a time line that includes your mother's and your own development. Start the first time line with your mother's birth and proceed with circumstances of her life as you know them. Fill in as much detail as you can. As you proceed you will probably discover how little you know about her life. You will probably need to talk with her and/or other family members to fill in many details.

Start the second line parallel to hers. Begin with your birth and proceed with your own life. You may want to vary the spacing of the lines as a visual representation of the quality of the connection between you and your mother over time.

Here are a few questions to stimulate your thinking:[40]

- How old were your grandparents when your mother was born? What was her life like with them?

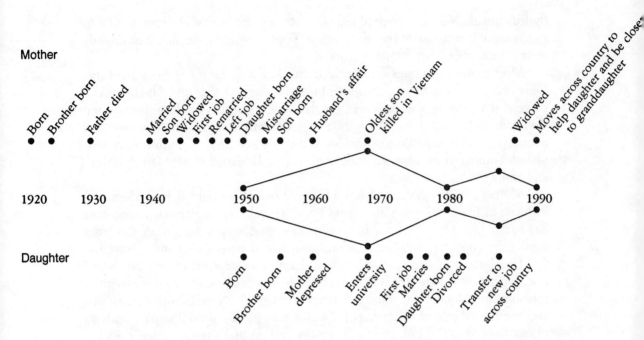

- What was life like economically, politically, and socially as your mother was growing up?
- What were the circumstances of your mother's pregnancy with you?
- How did you relate to your mother when you were a girl?
- If you had given birth to a daughter just like you, how would you have raised her?
- How do you treat your mother? How does your mother treat you?
- If your mother is still alive, how would you like your relationship to be in the last period of her life?
- If your mother is deceased, what memories of her do you carry with you?
- What characteristics do you share with your mother?
- In what ways are you different from her?
- Overall, how did your relationship with your mother influence you?

Many feelings are likely to emerge as you construct this shared life history. Strive to distance yourself intermittently from these emotions by placing yourself in your mother's shoes or in the position of an impartial third party. Imagine how it must have been for her to handle her own life. Try to see her as a new woman, someone you are just getting to know, without making judgments about how she was or should have been in the role of mother. Later you can integrate your increased understanding of her into your own experiences with her. This process will help you better understand your relationship with her.

Reinventing Motherhood: Freeing Our Mothers and Freeing Ourselves

Motherhood is an institution. We have very specific culturally defined rules about how a mother should be. In addition, each of us has internalized images of how mothers should look and how they should behave. To demonstrate how rigid most of us are when it comes to mothers, consider the following story.

> Lisa is a tall, strikingly attractive mother of two young adult children, a son and a daughter. After twenty-four years of marriage her husband, David, left this family to marry a much younger woman. Their children have accepted his new life with remarkable equanimity, but they strongly resist any movement their mother makes to create an equivalent life for herself.
>
> Lisa is a world traveler and independent entrepreneur. She is aching to test her own wings after years of tending to her family, yet her children want her to re-main in the role of mother as they define it. Lisa and I talk about how much she loves to dance, meet new people, visit exotic countries and how she longs to shed this image of a mother as a sexless, self-sacrificing, boring child-centered creature. One day as we are talking, images of Tina Turner keep popping into my mind, a midlife singer and dancer with a terrific body who lives her life with incredible gusto and courage. She has made amazing changes in her life after separating from her cruel and disturbed husband. I share my fantasy with Lisa. She loves the comparison.
>
> A few days later, Lisa and her daughter are watching television when Tina Turner appears in a commercial. With pleasure, curiosity, and interest, Lisa says to her daughter, "Can you imagine having Tina Turner as a mother?" Her daughter looks at her with complete disbelief: "Oh, mother, how awful!"

Make a list of all your shoulds and should nots about the ideal mother. For example,

- Mothers should be pretty.
- Mothers should be nice.
- Mothers should be supportive.
- Mothers should always understand.
- Mothers should not be sexy.
- Mothers should not get angry.
- And so on.

Now ask yourself the following questions:

- Which of these shoulds and should nots do you apply to your mother?
- Which do you apply to yourself if you are a mother or plan to become a mother?
- Describe how your mother really is rather than how the ideal mother is or should be. Include both her strengths and her weaknesses.
- Describe how you really are or will be as a mother rather than how the

ideal mother is or should be. Include both your strengths and your weaknesses.

- If a woman was free to be a whole person who just happened to be a mother, invent an image for how such a person would look and behave. How would she feel about herself? How would others feel about her? What would her life be like? What would be hard and what would be easy?

Women need to take charge of the definition of motherhood. They need to question the source of burdensome and unrealistic expectations of their own mothers as well as similar expectations of themselves. There must be room to be a whole person—not simply a stereotype.

ADDITIONAL READING

Consider reading a novel, rather than a work of nonfiction, as a way of looking at the mother-daughter relationship. You might try

Michael Dorris, *A Yellow Raft in Blue Water* (New York: Warner Books, 1987).

Many nonfiction authors have taken up the issue of the mother-daughter relationship. You might find their perspectives of interest as you examine your own relationship as a mother or daughter.

Paula J. Caplan, *Don't Blame Mother: Mending the Mother-Daughter Relationship* (New York: Harper & Row, 1989).

Jane Lazarre, *The Mother Knot* (Boston: Beacon Press, 1986).

Christine Park and Caroline Heaton, eds., *Close Company: Stories of Mothers and Daughters* (New York: Ticknor & Fields, 1989).

Louise Rafkin, *Different Daughters: A Book by Mothers of Lesbians* (Pittsburg, Pa.: Cleis Press, 1987).

Adrienne Rich, *Of Women Born: Motherhood as Experience and Institution* (New York: W. W. Norton, 1976).

NOTES

1. Peter Willmott and Michael Young, *Family and Class in a London Society* (London: Routledge & Kegan Paul, 1960) and Bert Adams, *Kinship in an Urban Setting* (Chicago: Markham Publishing Co., 1968).

2. Nancy Chodorow, *The Reproduction of Mothering: Psychoanalysis and the Sociology of Gender* (Berkeley, Calif.: University of California Press, 1978).

3. This may be a bond some daughters share with their mothers. Many working-class and black women have had to do paid work as well as raise their children, but this was usually viewed as an economic necessity rather than a preference or choice.

4. Luise Eichenbaum and Susie Orbach, *Between Women: Love, Envy, and Competition in Women's Friendships* (New York: Viking, 1988).

5. Robert Blood and Donald Wolfe, *Husbands and Wives* (New York: Free Press of Glencoe, 1960).

6. Lucy Rose Fischer, *Linked Lives: Adult Daughters and Their Mothers* (New York: Harper & Row, 1986), p. 94.

7. And the evidence does not support that they do, although there has been some slight increase in participation.

8. Mardy Ireland is currently conducting research to better understand the lives of women who cannot or do not want to become mothers. Her work will be titled *The Invisible Women*. This title accurately reflects our expectation that any woman who does not want children or does not have children does not exist in our culture. Yet at least 20 percent or more of adult women never have or raise children. This is a sizable number of women.

9. Paula Caplan asks us to think about what we would do if someone offered us an unpaid full-time job in which we would be accountable for anything that went wrong even sixty years in the future. You may giggle, but that's motherhood. (Paula Caplan, "Mother as the Scapegoat in the Mental Health System," Audio Archives of Canada, Ontario, 1987.)

10. It annoys me that the burden of raising healthy children is almost exclusively placed upon Mother. Why isn't it "good enough" parenting?

11. Paula Caplan and I. Hall-McCorquodale, "Mother-blaming in Major Clinical Journals," *American Journal of Orthopsychiatry* 55 (1985): 345–53.

12. Fathers are good fathers if they do not physically or sexually abuse their children, if they provide reasonable economic support, and if they do not abandon their families. They do not have to do much else to be considered good fathers. If in addition they are playful, warm, and/or nurturing, they are special fathers.

13. Assuming that this is a family in which both genders are represented in the parental generation.

14. Carol Gilligan, *In A Different Voice: Psychological Theory and Women's Development* (Cambridge, Mass.: Harvard University Press, 1982).

16. Except in the case of a remote relationship where little may pass between them.

17. Even in these remote relationships, a sudden illness or unanticipated trauma may bring them back into each other's lives. An unexpected sense of responsibility for the mother or daughter in need can take them by surprise and may just as quickly fade as the crisis passes.

18. Thelma Jean Goodrich et al., *Feminist Family Therapy: A Casebook* (New York: W. W. Norton, 1988), p. 5.

19. Perhaps this is one reason some daughters insist so strongly that they are not like their mothers. They may be warding off a long history of projections.

20. Vern Bengston and Joseph A. Kuypers, "Generational Difference and the Developmental Stake," *Aging and Human Development* 46 (1964): 1–25.

21. While daughter and father may have their own difficulty with these changes, Dad is usually more of an adjunct parent. Having been more distant all along, daughters do not usually have the level of intimacy with their fathers that they have with their mothers. Although mothers have usually been the much more active disciplinarians in daughters' lives, teenage daughters tend to confide in their mothers much more than their fathers. Mother-daughter contact is simply more frequent, more intense, and more complex. John Scanzoni, *Sexual Bargaining: Power Politics in the American Marriage* (Chicago: University of Chicago Press, 1973).

22. Daughters engage in a form of self-censorship—confiding less in their mothers. It is an implicit way of separating. Almost a third will rebel overtly, mostly through arguing. They are disrupting the intimacy in their relationship with their mothers as well as challenging their mothers' authority over them. The argument may vary around topic and intensity. Another form of separation is withdrawal. Some adolescents push their mothers away by withdrawing emotionally, appearing to their mothers as either shy, private, or stubborn.

23. Eighty percent of mother-daughter relationships have some ongoing involvement with some degree of censorship.

24. Alice Rossi, "Transition to Parenthood," *Journal of Marriage and the Family* 30 (1968): 26–39.

25. A colleague, Nancy Kaltreider, M.D., has speculated that some biochemical change may occur in women stimulated by the birth of a child that draws her into the role of primary parent. A biological draw would help us understand the pull many women feel to care for their children and why many women feel torn when returning to work after childbirth. It may not be simply psychological guilt—of which there is plenty—or genuine and often surprising pleasure in the role of mother. To my knowledge, this has not been scientifically studied or documented. Even if it does occur

and can be scientifically verified, I am sure my colleague, an active professional woman, would never want this discovery to be used as a rationalization for women being the *only* parent tending to childcare during their youngster's early years.

26. Chodorow, *The Reproduction of Mothering*, pp. 205–09.

27. M. G. Boulton, *On Being a Mother* (London: Tavistock Publications, 1983), p. 207.

28. Diane Ehrensaft, "When Women and Men Mother," in J. Trebilcot, ed., *Mothering* (Totowa, N.J.: Rowman and Allanheld, 1984) and Alice Rossi, "Gender and Parenthood," *American Sociological Review* 49 (1984) 1–18.

29. Poorer women and wealthier women have always turned over the care of their children to others while remaining the responsible parent. Economic necessity requires that most poorer women work, and they often depend on family to care for younger children. Professional women increasingly rely upon day-care services and live-in helpers to tend to children while they are at work. Wealthier women have always used governesses and full-time employees to raise children while the women fulfilled a wide range of social obligations.

30. Bob Greene, *Good Morning, Merry Sunshine: A Father's Journal of His Child's First Year* (New York: Penguin, 1985).

31. Elaine Brody, "Women in the Middle and Family Help to Older People," *The Gerontologist* 21 (1981): 471–80.

32. Howard Moss and Elizabeth Susman, "Longitudinal Study of Personality," in Orville Brim and Jerome Kagan, ed., *Constancy and Change in Human Development* (Cambridge, Mass.: Harvard University Press, 1980), pp. 530–95.

33. Bonnie S. Anderson and Judith P. Zinsser, *A History of Their Own: Women in Europe From Prehistory to the Present* (New York: Harper & Row, 1988).

34. Eugene Litwak, *Helping Networks of Older People: From Health to Institutionalization* (New York: Guilford Press, 1985).

35. Leonard Perlan is interviewing the caretakers—all women—of parents who have Alzheimer's disease. He has been impressed with the remarkable grace demonstrated by these women. He also notes that while men do not provide direct caretaking for these ill parents, they may take up more of the duties customarily done in their own homes by their female partners. This is a kind of indirect caretaking and perhaps the kind more characteristic of men in general: many will take up the slack when their female partners are absent or overstretched. Personal conversation, 1988.

36. Judith Jordan, "The Meaning of Mutuality," Work in Progress (Wellesley, Mass.: Wellesley College, 1986).

37. G. Baruch and R. C. Barnett, "Adult Daughters' Relationships with Their Mothers: The Era of Good Feelings," Working Paper no. 74, Wellesley College Center for Research on Women, 1981.

38. Elaine Levin and Lynn Thaxton, "Mothers and Daughters: Southern Style," *Women and Therapy* 4 no. 4 (Winter 1985/1986), pp. 81–89.

39. Marybelle Cochran, "The Mother-Daughter Dyad Throughout the Life Cycle," *Women and Therapy* 4 no. 2 (Summer 1985), pp. 3–8.

40. Some of these questions were adapted from Natalie Rogers, "Emerging Woman: A Decade of Midlife Transitions," *Women and Therapy,* 1 no. 1 (Spring 1982), pp. 67–81.

Daughters and Fathers

The first question that must be asked as we begin to explore the father-daughter relationship is why have women written so little on this subject?

For each chapter in this book, I spent an enormous amount of time researching the professional literature. It was usually an overwhelming task. The primary job was to select the best of what is available, summarize it, and integrate it with my own experience as a clinician, researcher, and woman. This chapter was different.

Walk into any bookstore and scan the women's section. You will find a number of books written by women about their relationships with their mothers. Continue scanning and look for the books by women about their relationships with their fathers.[1] There is no paucity of literature on the obviously dysfunctional father—the alcoholic father or the father who sexually or physically abused his daughter.[2] But there is strikingly little written by women describing the healthy father-daughter relationship.

As women, we have inspected our mothers at length. We have blamed them, praised them, rebelled against them, and embraced them. We have placed our relationships with our mothers under psychological, sociological, historical, and anthropological microscopes. But where is Dad? Have we done the very thing that we now chafe against in our own lives? Have we made women (in this case our mothers) exclusively responsible for the well-being of others?

We can ease our conscience somewhat with the notion that it is natural for us to focus on Mother because we are both female. Our identification with Mother is stronger than our identification with Father. Sorting through this complicated female-female connection may seem most difficult and urgent. Furthermore, for most of us, Mom has been the primary parent. She is the person with whom we have our first relationship as an infant, and our dependence on her is profound and lasts many years. Other people are important, but they are likely to have been more peripheral to our developing sense of self. Our first love-hate relationship is with our same-gender parent.[3]

For most of us, Father is noteworthy by his absence. Dad has the culturally defined responsibility of sustaining the family economically. This often means long hours, which over a lifetime can translate into many years away from his family. When Dad is home, strict boundaries are defined between him and his children. Children are cautioned not to bother Dad while he recuperates from a hard day at work—until he gives them permission to do so. With his blessing, time with Dad is often playtime—not the day-to-day grind left to the primary caretaker. Dad's being home might mean twelve minutes of toss the ball, a ride on a toboggan down a nearby hill, or a family outing. In some families, Dad's arrival signals time to dish out punishment. Dad is the authoritarian. What kid does not hear "Wait until your father comes home!"? But Dad is not usually there day in, day out the way Mom is.

Certainly we must continue to define, prevent, and heal the wounds of troubled father-daughter relationships. However, it is equally important for us to identify the impact of healthy fathering.

Dad: Caretaker or Provider?

Ancient images of fathers have more to do with power than tenderness. Father is the stern lawmaker, the source of authority and wisdom. In the post-Freudian era, Dad has tended to be a peripheral figure in families. The mother-child relationship is assumed to be the most significant. Society does not prepare Dad practically or psychologically to have active and comprehensive involvement with his children at all stages of their development. As noted by Caryl Rivers, Rosalind Barnett, and Grace Baruch, authors of *Beyond Sugar and Spice*, "For many men, the first step may be to realize that men can be parents in the true sense, they can care for and nurture their children from infancy on. This first step may be the big one. The old stereotypes about the father have roots that go very deep."[4]

Dad has been called the Lamont Cranston of the American family. (For those too young to remember the early days of radio, Cranston is the alter ego of the Shadow, the crime-fighter who had the ability to make himself invisible whenever he chose.) As the Shadow, Dad expresses his love through his work, which is usually unseen and mysterious to his family. The more money he earns, the more approval he gains. The workaholic father who is rarely home is still considered a good father. Actually, he is considered a good provider. Even national experts like T. Berry Brazelton see a man's work life as "the very core of his position in the family." His absence from the family is to be regarded as a sign of love for them—or at least it has been until recently.

Over the years, father absence has became the standard in the "typical"

American family. Mom tends the children even if she works. Dad's primary responsibility is out of the home and in the workplace. This has not always been the arrangement. Prior to the eighteenth century, home was where both men and women worked. Multiple families lived together in a conglomeration that was part factory, part workshop, and part subsistence farm. Women's work included working on the farm and managing laborers and apprentices who lived in the house. Children came in contact with many adults, male and female. The industrial revolution marked the rise of cities, the creation of a middle class, the beginning of the concept of home as a single-family dwelling, and the notion of a special mother-child bond. The "good mother" as we know her today is more the result of these economic influences than it is the natural state of affairs. Father was directed toward work outside the home, and the "typical" American family was born.

Over the years, behavioral scientists, psychologists, and psychiatrists have reinforced this standard. They have not only assumed the existence of a special mother-child relationship but also the absence of any comparable relationship between father and child. Scientists observing the animal kingdom focused upon maternal rather than paternal behavior and added fuel to these assumptions.

It took a shift in focus to discover that even in the animal world, fathering behavior is often quite prominent. Male marmosets, for example, live in monogamous family units, assist during the birth of infants, and chew up food for the infants to eat. They carry the infants throughout the day, except when the infant is returned to the mother to nurse. Siamang gibbon infants are dependent on their mothers for the first twelve months of life, but from then on, they are carried by their fathers until they are old enough to survive on their own. Siamang mothers groom and sleep with babies; the fathers groom and sleep with juveniles. In the Nairobi National Park, a male macaque was observed patiently teaching an infant to walk, chattering encouragement all the while. Biologists studying male rhesus monkeys, which had previously been considered hostile to their young, have discovered that in the absence of the mother, the male will care for the infant much as a mother would. When the mother is present, she will preempt the male. This work suggests that at least among rhesus monkeys, if not human males, nurturing fathering behavior, just like mothering behavior, might emerge quite naturally if the opportunity was provided.

In cross-cultural studies among human males, there is evidence that a wide range of fathering behavior exists, ranging from remoteness to intimate involvement. Among the Bushmen of northern Botswana, children are indulged and pampered. Each sex works about half of the week for food, allowing a great deal of time for leisure. Families are generally monogamous, and while mothers provide routine care for the infants, the fathers hold and fondle even the youngest babies. Young children often approach the men to ask for food or ask questions. They are never rebuffed. Preparation for fighting does not occupy the men and boys at all. War is rare, and it is not considered important that boys learn to fight.

Halfway across the world, in Lesu village in New Ireland, Melanesia, the population survives by fishing and small-scale gardening. The household is usually a monogamous, nuclear family. The husband frequently cares for the baby while the wife is cooking or gardening, and even men in groups play with and fondle babies. Warfare is almost nonexistent.

In contrast, the Rwala Bedouin of the north Arabian desert live in a society of herders where the men are warriors and the women work hard at domestic chores. In this patriarchal society, there is a strong emphasis on male authority. Fierceness is cultivated in boys, and warfare with other groups is frequent. The fathers remain distant from young children. Children live with their mothers in the women's tent, approaching their fathers only for an occasional talk or for punishment. Older boys are punished for disobedience.

Among the Thonga, a tribal people living on the east coast of South Africa, the women grow grain and vegetables and the men herd animals. The society is polygamous and patriarchal. The men do not involve themselves with infants or young children. Though the men have a substantial amount of leisure, strong taboos prevent them from any contact with infants younger than three months old. Fathers demand absolute obedience from their children, and they are the ones who thrash and punish them. The tribe has an army numbering about two thousand and an elaborate structure of war costumes and weapons.

Obviously, there is no one "natural" way to father. The father-child bond is strongest in cultures that are monogamous. In polygamous cultures, the men have to spend a considerable amount of time accumulating the resources to maintain their many wives. Women's contribution to society can also have an effect on the father-child relationship. Where women's work other than childcare is considered essential and important, men's investment in parenting increases. And in cultures where men are closely involved with young children, there is little warfare. In societies where warfare is important, fathers tend to be distant. And, in societies where war is an important occupation for men, women's role is generally not considered to be of high importance.[5]

Studies investigating the father-child relationship always reflect cultural values. They are not scientifically impartial. As recently as World War II, studies of children without parents referred to "maternal deprivation," even though the father was also absent. The few studies that did consider father absence focused mainly on boys. Researchers assumed the most damaging impact of father absence would be on males and the development of the skills that they would need to function successfully in the world. As far as girls were concerned, studies examined the effect of father absence on their sex-role development. Researchers thought that such females might be handicapped in their ability to form heterosexual relationships later in life. Clearly what mattered for a girl was her ability to marry successfully; what mattered for a boy was the acquisition of skills.

In the 1950s and 1960s, there was an explosion of behavioral research, but little was done on fathering. Much of the recent research on fathering has been done by younger men who have experienced the recent women's movement and the questioning of a traditional male role. These researchers look at the father-child relationship from a different vantage point than their predecessors. Some have investigated the *attachment behavior* of young infants in their homes—not a laboratory—and have discovered that infants show no preference for the mother over the father. In fact, they showed a definite preference for the fathers when it comes to playing.[6]

Other male researchers have challenged the cultural assumptions of the father's unimportance by observing the infant's reaction to its mother, its father, and a stranger.[7] Previous studies have had only the mother and a stranger present when investigating stranger anxiety. This lead them to the erroneous conclusion that stranger anxiety is related to a special mother-child bond. Nonsexist research has shown that an infant interacts with both its mother and father and not with strangers. Infants show equal dismay when either parent leaves the room.[8] There is a minimum level of "fathering" that has to take place before a child can relate closely to its father, but the crude amount of caretaking or playing is not the critical variable. If there is sufficient quality time for the parent-child relationship to develop, a child will feel comfortable with and relate to both parents.

Feelings about Having a Daughter

Fathers often react differently to the birth of a daughter than to the birth of a son. What happens when a father hears the words "It's a girl!"? For reasons they often cannot identify, many fathers feel disappointed, deprived, or even ashamed. If these feelings are transitory, they will have little impact upon the father-daughter relationship, but if a father's dissatisfaction continues, a daughter comes to understand very acutely that she is not what her father wants her to be. If what her father wants is something she cannot possibly be—a boy—the damage to her self-esteem and development is considerable.

Studies in the 1950s found that fathers had different expectations for daughters than for sons. Daughters were expected to be pretty, sweet, fragile, and delicate, while sons were expected to be aggressive and athletic. In one study, adults were shown videotapes of two seventeen-month-old children, each of whom was sometimes described as a boy, sometimes as a girl. Adult males were more likely to rate the children in a stereotypical fashion, attributing qualities of independence, activity, and alertness to babies they thought were boys—even when the "boys" were really girls. If the same baby was presented as a girl, the men described the baby as cuddly and delicate. The responses obviously had more to do with the fathers' preconceived ideas about boys and girls than with reality.

In 1974, researchers at Tufts reproduced this phenomenon. Male babies and female babies of equal weight, length, muscle tone, heart and respiratory rates were evaluated by their parents on a number of qualities such as firm or soft, strong or weak, hardy or delicate, large-featured or fine-featured. Sons, who were objectively exactly the same as daughters, were described by their fathers as firmer, larger-featured, better-coordinated, and hardier. Daughters, who were objectively exactly the same as sons, were described by their fathers as softer, finer-featured, and more delicate. Even though there was no real, measurable difference, fathers saw what they wanted to see—based upon gender.

Fathering Styles

Traditional models of fathering are based on the myth that women will be protected from the outside world by some kindly and omnipotent male. These models are also based on a division of power. Females are trained to entice others to act for them, to be manipulative. They are to use charm and the caretaking of others as an indirect path to their goals. In these father-daughter relationships, fathers play one or more of a number of roles:[9]

1. The White Knight. Father is magical and his daughter is a princess. All of a woman's admiration is reserved for her father, even if he is rarely around. This is a convenient role for busy men.
2. Big Daddy. Father is the one who solves all of his little girl's problems. When Dad is no longer around, these women discover that the world is not as benign as they thought. Many have never outgrown the belief that the world owes them something special. Often, they are in for some tough times.
3. Pygmalion. Father sculpts his daughter to his own needs expecting that she will always remain his pupil, never his equal.
4. The Patriarch. Father is uncomfortable with feelings and separates himself emotionally from his daughter as well as from the rest of the family. He steps in only rarely to settle disputes or deliver the paycheck. His apparent need for authority may obscure his need to withdraw. At the same time, he may feel isolated and exploited by his family.
5. The Invisible Man. These men simply dematerialize. They may be physically present, but emotionally they are just not there.

Fortunately, some fathers may be just as pleased to have daughters as sons. While the experts of the 1940s and 1950s believed that the primary responsibility of a father was to facilitate his daughter's "femininity," a good many fathers ignored the experts and used their common sense. Instead of rewarding dependent, flirtatious, and similarly "feminine" behavior and discouraging "masculine" behavior, these fathers raised daughters to be self-reliant and self-trusting individuals.

These fathers were able to promote a woman's positive regard for men by being warm, loving, and available. A supportive father can also encourage his daughter's ability to function in the public world as a fully developed human. Women are more likely to be self-determining individuals when their fathers treat them as interesting people, worthy and deserving of respect.[10] A father can encourage the same qualities in a daughter that he would in a son. He can teach her to be competent and to take her accomplishments seriously. There is considerable evidence that women who identify with their father (or with the male role as society presents it) and are also able to relate to their mothers have high self-esteem. These women demonstrate the ability to act independently in a caring fashion.

The "New" Father

As more women enter the work force and families become increasingly dependent on two incomes, it appears that the role of father is changing. Increasingly, contemporary fathers are recognizing that their active participation is important in the mental health of their daughters. Two studies done in Boston, one in the 1950s and the other in the 1970s, give an idea of the changes fathers have made.

A 1952 study demonstrated that fathers had different and distinct ambitions for their sons and for their daughters. Half the fathers interviewed would accept the possibility—but only the possibility—that their daughters might have careers. They preferred that their daughters marry. Half of the fathers rejected the idea of a career completely. These same fathers worried if their sons were not doing well in school, if they were acting childish, or if they were too fearful or too docile. The fathers were not as worried about what their daughters did. Their satisfactions focused on the girls being nice, sweet, pretty, affectionate, and well liked. Fathers were not concerned when their daughters were less athletic or aggressive than others. Some of the fathers were troubled if their daughters were "bossy." The researchers observed that the fathers were not concerned by their sons' aggressive behavior and actually interpreted it as a bit of benign devilishness. They were ambivalent about their sons being labelled "bad boys," but indicated that using equivalent language to describe their daughters would carry a much more negative connotation. Obviously, these fathers held to the traditional sex-role stereotypes for their children. (So, I suspect, did their mothers.)

The same study was repeated in 1976. There was a marked change in the attitude of at least some fathers. Unlike the fathers of the 1950s, worried about their sons' careers and wishing some vague sort of marital bliss for their daughters, the fathers in this second study were concerned with their daughters' full human potential. They were also concerned that they were providing good models of identification for their daughters. It was a significant shift.

When we look at earlier generations, women who defied conventional notions about what they could do almost always had strong encouragement from their fathers. If these young girls also had affectionate relationships with their mothers, they developed "masculine" traits without ever questioning their identity as females. As youngsters, these women did not experience sex-role conflicts at home, even if they did in other arenas. Outside their childhood homes, these women found the role of girlhood confining and fought for more freedoms. They were often jealous of the perceived lack of constraints on boys. The support and pride of their fathers allowed them to be comfortable with their drive for success, task orientation, desire to be respected for their abilities, and love of competition.

Dual Development

People change throughout their adult lives. Fathers develop and so do daughters. To understand her father's influence, a woman needs to gather a full picture of him, to broaden her view of the years with her male parent. The relationship between a father and daughter can be viewed as two evolving life cycles, sometimes meshing and sometimes clashing. A double life-cycle approach using thirty years as an arbitrary guide is the sample model used in this chapter, but your own double life-cycle may span a different time frame.[11]

The First Decade

This first stage includes the girl's childhood and her father's twenties or thirties. It is a time of attachment. For the child, there is a preference to be close to specific people who seem to be stronger and wiser. These are the people the child depends on to meet her basic needs and to provide love, affection, and warmth. Margaret Mead has pointed out that forming attachments to more than one person has clear survival value by insuring that the infant is protected if one parent is lost. Contemporary research has clearly established that infants develop attachments to both parents during the first nine months of life. Intense emotions arise during the formation, maintenance, and disruption of these attachments. Maintenance of the bond is a source of security. Adult attachments are influenced by the experiences one has had with similar figures in childhood. There seems to be a strong causal relationship between an individual's experiences with her parents and her later capacity to develop affectionate bonds.

For the middle-class father, his third decade is usually a time when he is preoccupied with building his career.[12] Often he does this at the expense of his marriage, his leisure, his friendships, and his time for introspection. It is the period during which he strives for the position he will achieve in his forties and fifties. While his daughter acquires skills, he gains job status. During this time in their lives, his daughter is unlikely to see much of her father. In most cases, she does see enough of him to form an attachment; by virtue of their far less frequent contact, the father-daughter relationship is markedly different from the mother-daughter relationship. In middle-class families, it is usually the mother who is more involved in daily caretaking and discipline, while father is often a playmate. Throughout the first six years of her life, a daughter provides her father with a happy respite from the rigors of his daily work life. This special "holiday" often continues as one aspect of their lifelong attachment. From age six to puberty, the father becomes more involved in his daughter's intellectual development. He begins to be interested in her schoolwork and to teach her.

The infrequency of their contact may heighten the quality of the time they do spend together. Time with Father can have a specialness that is different from time with her mother. The more frequent contact with Mother often creates a more genuinely intimate, but also more complex, attachment. Unless he is overly committed elsewhere, the emotionally involved father may find that his time with his daughter is one of the few pleasures he allows himself.

The way a father treats his daughter during this period makes an indelible impression on her. By overdoing it, he may cause her to long all her life for this time when she was the center of his attention. If there is little or no happiness with her father in this period, the little girl is left "longing for the father."[13]

The first decade of the father-daughter relationship lays the groundwork for future female-male relationships. Too little or no childhood closeness to an accepting and supportive father can leave a woman with severe emotional scars. An emotionally absent father leaves his daughter feeling devalued, invalidated, and invisible. If the father is absent or angry and rejecting, he leaves his daughter discouraged in her beginning efforts with men. She has no experience of flirting with, gaining attention from, being worshipped by, being validated by, or delighting the man who means the most to her at the most impressionable time in her life. Anger is the inevitable consequence, but the daughter may feel guilty about being angry and hide these emotions under a blanket of insecurity, depression, and anxiety. If the most important man in her life has not given her the love and attention she needed, a woman protects herself by detaching. This detachment from her father is later transferred to other men. She feels cut off and does not know how to be close to men. Her anger, even if it is disguised, may also keep men at a distance.

This unhappy legacy from her relationship with her father leaves her handicapped in selecting men of quality. She may repeatedly opt to be with men who are unavailable and uncommitted, thus causing her familiar, but painful, feelings. To others and perhaps to herself, she appears to be addicted to men.[14] Actually, her tolerance for being treated poorly by men is her inheritance from her relationship with her father. In her heart of hearts, she imagines that if only she were somehow different, her father and other men would find her lovable. She also imagines that through her healing love, Dad and other men will be repaired in their limited capacity to love and they will then be able to give her the love she so deeply desires and deserves.

The effect of a disturbed first decade need not be permanent. A woman may recover from the emotional damage if she does at least three things:

1. recognizes what her father was truly like,
2. identifies how her relationship with him currently affects her, and
3. tries to change that pattern.

Childhood unhappiness is harder to overcome than that of adolescence or the twenties, but self-knowledge, determination to change, and the courage to try different behavior can make an enormous difference. Early childhood trauma can be corrected. Many people are incredibly resilient and can adopt new ways if they want to. Fortunately, older brothers, uncles, or other males present on a continuing basis can counter some of the damage caused by the absent, withdrawn, or rejecting father.

The Second Decade

During this time Daughter is in her teens and Father is in midlife, usually his forties. For both, it is a time of asking Who am I? She rebels against authority and convention. He wonders who he will continue to be. Each may be concerned with the great existential questions of life and death, the brevity of time, and the physical changes of age. Both may be moody, restless, and discontent.

The adolescent girl now begins to establish a more realistic view of her father. Her growing maturity enables her to see that her father, like all human beings, has some real weaknesses. In addition, he may behave badly. These two factors combine to ensure a father's fall from grace. If the fall is too far or too abrupt, it can cause lasting damage. The father who suddenly deserts his family never to see them again can leave a daughter afraid of becoming vulnerable with any man, afraid that other men will leave her. If the fall from grace is not excessive *and* if the father accepts the anger and criticism arising from her disappointment in him, then two good things can happen: the experience can help her readjust her relationship with her father to include a more realistic perspective and it will encourage her to develop reasonable adult expectations of her male partners.

Fathers who are too preoccupied with their own midlife problems are short on patience and lack the willingness to negotiate delicately and respectfully with their teenage daughters. These fathers often issue angry orders. A daughter may respond by becoming withdrawn and absent or engaging in stormy battles with her father. Either way, the daughter is likely to feel let down and abandoned. If there is repetitive anger, rebellion, excessive fighting, or excessive distancing, this second decade can leave lifelong scars that harm her future attempts at relationships with men. Still longing for a healthy relationship with her father, these women are handicapped by perfectly normal, but unmet, needs left over from this period of their lives.

If a father takes pleasure in his adolescent daughter and includes her in his life, sharing the growth, ideas, sensitivities, and intelligence of her youth can bring joy to them both. Good memories from this era allow a woman to enjoy the company of men. She is able to select her male partners well. She develops healthy relationships, selecting men with whom she can be close and who treat her with respect. She can forgive a man his human faults and enjoy a collaborative partnership.

The Third Decade

The process of developing a sense of oneself within the context of relationships begins in infancy. Parents have a powerful influence on this process. Fathers can cling to their daughters at every stage and resist the healthy changes in their attachment, or they can encourage their daughters' differentiation while remaining emotionally attached.

When a woman reaches her twenties, she is ready to accept primary responsibility for her own life. She usually remains emotionally attached while making more of her own decisions. The geographical step of living separately from her family may be much easier than the psychological separation. In every adult, there is a child anxious about being alone.

Separation causes everyone anxiety. No daughter leaves home without fear, ambivalence, and mourning. The process takes varying amounts of time depending on the woman's personality, her maturity, and her support system. In the process of changing her relationship with her father, a daughter modifies her needs and emotions. Her mood swings, characteristic of the adolescent, become less extreme. She is less inclined to get upset about events and more willing to do something about them. She is becoming the mistress of her feelings rather than their slave. Her anger matures. She is neither excessively meek nor does she explode in rage. Rather than impulsive adolescent anger, she is able to feel her wrath, control it, and express it at the appropriate time, when it is in her own interest.

The resolution of her feelings about her father's fall from grace helps a woman feel connected to yet independent from her father. She leaves behind her chronic feelings of anger and disappointment. This process allows a reconciliation between them. If her anger continues unresolved, her emotions (in spite of being negative) will continue to be tied up with him. By forgiving him and accepting him as he is with all his faults and imperfections, she gains energy that will be liberated for other relationships.

If a woman is lucky, her father will help her get on with her life by gently pushing her out of the nest. He will calm her fears and encourage her to make her own choices while remaining available to her should she need him. He will accept her as another adult, not as a little girl.

Father is usually in midlife as his daughter is going through this stage. If his work and marriage are going well, he will be able to handle the changes much better. He will, of course, be sad. However, psychologically healthy men accept the pain and integrate it into the next phase of their lives. Unstable or dysfunctional fathers attempt to hold on to their daughters; they may create emotional scenes of anger and despair.

Whether healthy or dysfunctional, all this adjusting takes time. It rarely proceeds smoothly, even in the best of relationships. Emotions are strong, and few fathers and daughters behave perfectly. There may be tears, anger, and attempts to cling. It takes fathers years to adjust to the adult status of their daughters, just as it takes daughters a long time to see their fathers through a realistic lens.

Intellectually, a young woman knows that her parents are no longer necessary for her survival; emotionally, she is not always quite certain. If Father has been an emotionally reliable protector, she is both excited and anxious about distancing herself from the man who relieved her fears. Daughters who have trouble with this transition may become paralyzed by anxiety or pick a fight that enables them to depart in anger.

Once physically out of the home, a daughter must work on her part of the emotional change in her relationship with her father. If she relies on him too much, turning to him with every problem, she will interfere with the necessary work of mourning and detachment. Some women go to the opposite extreme and have nothing to do with their fathers, assuming that any movement toward their father represents total surrender. Instead, they tightly close off their normal wishes to be attached to their father. Rather than working through their feelings of dependence, they avoid experiencing the perfectly natural feelings of sadness and loss that go hand in hand with their changing relationship. They subvert the emotional process of redefining the nature of that relationship, and they are unable to freely interact with their fathers as adults. As a result, their feelings are not truly available for relationships with other men.

The woman who recognizes the loss and tolerates the pain of changing her attachment with her father becomes a true adult. If theirs is a healthy and mutually respectful relationship, she is no longer afraid of being childlike in his presence. She is not afraid of being overwhelmed by her father's care or her desire for it. She is able to share her life generously with him. They enjoy each other's company, and their relationship is a source of continuing pleasure to them both.

If there has been a history of her father abusing her, a daughter will have a much more difficult time resolving her feelings of anger, hurt, and betrayal. Yet if she is truly to get on with her own life, she must work through this legacy of emotional pain.

Summary

The central theme in the father-daughter relationship is that Dad is often more or less invisible—emotionally, if not in fact. Many fathers seem to relinquish the entire job of raising their daughters to the mothers—perhaps out of a fear that it is a subject about which they know little. Instead of developing a close connection with their daughters, these fathers seem separate, unknown, and often unavailable. It comes then as no surprise that this is the kind of man many women are attracted to in their adult lives. This is what they have come to expect in their relationships with men. This father deprivation accounts for the obsessional concern some heterosexual women have about finding and keeping a significant man in their lives—even when these relationships lack significant mutuality, commitment, concern, respect, and care.

To foster a healthy father-daughter relationship, it is important that a girl's father be accessible. It is also important for fathers. Otherwise, father and daughter are strangers in the same house. Father may be the head of the family but never really a part of it. Loneliness and alienation are the price he pays for letting his wife be the heart of the home. Indeed, men may be more vulnerable to the empty-nest syndrome than women, to the feelings of loss and depression that arise when the children leave home. Now the father has time for the children—but they no longer have time for him.

Through identification, women incorporate a composite of both of their parents into their psychological lives. From their fathers, women have traditionally learned career strengths and assertiveness. In the future, this will undoubtedly be less sex-linked and mothers will contribute much more to their daughters' worldly capacities for thinking and self-respect. Whatever the future holds, mutual respect, affection, and commonality of interest between daughters and their fathers—as well as their mothers—will allow the maintenance of meaningful ties.

A Note to Fathers: A Guide to New Roles and Expectations

There are no easy step-by-step guidelines for fathers raising daughters. However, here are some suggestions:[15]

- First of all, the father-infant bond is very important, despite the fact that until now it has received far less attention than the mother-infant bond. This bond ought to be taken into consideration as a couple thinks about having a baby. Just as mothers, especially mothers with careers, give serious consideration to having a baby, men should do some serious thinking and planning before they and their partners decide when and if to have a baby.
- Fathers may have to assert themselves in stepping into a nurturing role with their newborns. Fathers need not be ashamed or retreat if they are at first clumsy with infants. Most men have not had much or any experience with babies, but they can learn quickly. There is evidence that boys are just as comfortable as girls caring for children younger than themselves if they are not dissuaded from doing so.
- It is important for a father to spend time alone with his daughter, caring for her—and not just in infancy. Studies have shown that the more a fa-

ther takes over childcare tasks, the less stereotyped are his daughter's views of adults. The important factor is not the specific things the father does, but the fact that he is the sole parent in charge, the one who is caring for the girl, not just functioning as Mommy's helper. A father can devise ways to be the primary caretaker often enough so that he can have an important impact on his daughter's life.

- Fathers should avoid encouraging the princess fantasy. It is very easy to let a pretty little girl charm Dad, and it is almost a reflex for fathers to want to protect their little girls. Fathers may also have a reflex to protect their little boys, but they override it. They remember that it is a tough world out there and that their boy has to start growing some protective covering. A girl needs the opportunity to develop the same tough skin. She especially needs to know that she had better count on her own actions rather than charm to get along in the world.

- Fathers should think about the jobs they assign to their girls. It is a good idea to get girls involved in tasks where they can see a lasting result. Consider something like painting the fence. Every time she looks in the yard, she can see the permanent result of her work. Girls below the age of puberty are just as physically strong as boys—often stronger, because they mature earlier—and can do any of the tasks that boys are expected to do.

- Fathers often have more trouble disciplining daughters than sons. A daughter can do an awfully good imitation of the wounded fawn—the quivering lip, the tear sliding out of the eye, the look of woe on the angelic little face. But if little girls consistently get away with this routine, they receive the dangerous message that they do not have to face the consequences of their actions.

- A father can help his daughter feel she is a person of consequence by taking her seriously, by not automatically turning over decisions about her life to her mother. Fathers can go to parent-teacher meetings or girls' club activities. A father may feel embarrassed when he attends his daughter's Brownie event and finds himself standing in line to have a gardenia corsage pinned on him. Organizers rarely expect a father to be there, and fathers may find that they have to take the initiative in pointing out that a nonsexist approach is necessary and expected. Fathers can easily find plenty of activities to share with their daughters—cooking, jogging, spring cleaning, woodworking, and crafts, to mention just a few.

- It is not helpful for girls to grow up thinking that men are the special people and women are ordinary. One way for a father to get around this trap is to let his daughter accompany him doing ordinary things—getting the car filled with gas, shopping at the supermarket, going to the hardware store. This is especially important if he is only rarely home. A father can also demystify his workplace by taking his daughter there to see it.

Tasks for Daughters

Holding Our Fathers Responsible

We have grown up in a culture that encourages women to be primary, if not exclusive, parents. Even the mental-health profession has perpetuated the notion that women alone are responsible for the health and well-being of children.[16] We have gone along with this concept without asking ourselves about its validity. It is important that we shift responsibility equitably away from Mother and toward our other parent. Our father is also extremely important in our development, and we need to understand the direct and indirect contributions he has made. These questions might begin to stimulate your thinking:

1. If your mother was your primary parent, how did your father support or interfere with her caring for you?
2. How active was your father in day-to-day care?
3. If your father was an absent parent, what impact did that deprivation have on your development as a woman?
4. What kind of model did your father provide for your relationships with other men?
5. Does he value and respect your mother? Does he value and respect you?

Father and Daughter over Time

Construct a dual-development time line for your own relationship with your father. Imagine that you are an investigative journalist standing outside constructing a history of two people—a father and his daughter. Obtain as much information about each of them as you can. Then imagine yourself in the shoes of each person. What impact do they have upon each other? What are the good times? What are the bad times? Who are they to each other today?

As our father becomes more dependent, our relationship with him changes. What are or were your thoughts and feelings about this phase of your life with your father? How did his caring for you when you were dependent on him affect your caring for him as he grows increasingly dependent? What will it be like (or is it like) after he is gone? Are there any changes that you might wish to see made? How might you go about initiating them?

Reinventing Fatherhood

Imagine if fathers shared some of the deep emotional care for children that is usually assigned to mothers. How would the daily life of a daughter and father appear? What impact would that have on the father-daughter relationship? How would this new style of interacting influence the daughter's mental health?

Be inventive and specific to your own life. In your imagination, you have total control over all the players. Build a relationship that would be the best for everyone involved and think about how you can translate some of your creative ideas into real-world options.

ADDITIONAL READING

If you would like to explore this topic further, consider:

Linda Schierse Leonard, *Wounded Woman: Healing the Father-Daughter Relationship* (Boston: Shambhala, 1982).

Ursula Owen, ed., *Fathers: Reflections by Daughters* (New York: Pantheon, 1985).

NOTES

1. You will find a few autobiographical pieces where daughters talk about their relationships with their well-known fathers. There is Susan Cheever's book about her famous author father, John Cheever, or Candice Bergen's story of feeling upstaged by her father's dummy, Charlie McCarthy. There is *Imaginary Crimes* by Sheila Ballantyne and *Like Father, Like Daughter* by Suzanne Fields. There are two chapters in *Beyond Sugar and Spice* by Caryl Rivers, Rosalind Barnett, and Grace Baruch.

There are two books written by men. *Fathers and Daughters* by William Appleton suggests a dual-development perspective to help women understand the impact their fathers had on their development. However, the author is a man and a father. He makes a case for understanding the father while minimizing a daughter's disappointment, hurt, or anger with him. It would be enlightening to hear from his daughter. *The Role of the Father in Child Development* by Michael Lamb offers an excellent presentation of the scientific literature. Written for a professional audience, it is intended to be a textbook rather than a resource for laywomen. However, no one covers the topic more comprehensively and his material is valuable.

There are older texts available, such as Levine's *Men Who Care for Children*. *Ms.* magazine has done a few pieces on fathers. It is noteworthy, however, that even in her book *Outrageous Acts*, Gloria Steinem focuses upon her relationship with her mother and remarks little on the impact of her abandoning father.

2. Several books are available describing the impact of profoundly damaging father-daughter relationships such as those that cover the problems of physical and sexual abuse and drug and alcohol addiction. See, for example, Judith Herman *Father-Daughter Incest* (Cambridge: Harvard University Press, 1981).

3. Dorothy Dinnerstein, *The Mermaid and The Minotaur: Sexual Arrangements and Human Malaise* (New York: Harper Colophon Books, 1976).

4. Caryl Rivers, Rosalind Barnett, and Grace Baruch, *Beyond Sugar and Spice* (New York: G. P. Putnam's Sons, 1979), p. 29.

5. M. M. Katz and M. Konner, "The Role of the Father: An Anthropological Perspective," in M. Lamb, ed., *The Role of the Father in Child Development* (New York: John Wiley, 1981), pp. 166–180.

6. Michael Lamb, "Fathers and Child Development: An Integrative Overview," in *The Role of the Father in Child Development* (New York: John Wiley, 1981).

7. M. Kotelchuck et al., "Infant Reaction to Parental Separations when Left with Familiar and Unfamiliar Adults," *Journal of Genetic Psychology* 126 (1975): 255–62.

8. These were middle-class families where mothers did the primary caretaking, demonstrating that infants displayed a clear attachment to their fathers despite the fact that their fathers were rarely available on the same basis as their mothers.

9. Rivers, Barnett, and Baruch, *Beyond Sugar and Spice*, pp. 45–56.

10. Marjorie Lozoff, "Fathers and Autonomy in Women," in R. B. Kundsin, ed., *Women and Success* (New York: William Morrow, 1974).

11. The thirty-year double life cycle is suggested by William Appleton. He acknowledges that any model is by definition artificial. His stated purpose is to simplify and clarify, but he recognizes that his model cannot fit every instance. He believes, however, that the majority of white, middle-class daughters with relatively nonpathological fathers do fit into this model. He states that it orders the complexity of thirty years and encourages a woman to think systematically about those years. His argument is that this perspective stimulates memories and fosters greater understanding of these periods in our life as a daughter. He proposes that if all goes well, by the age of thirty a woman becomes mature and capable of lasting intimacy and gratifying work.

12. This is an example of a concept specific to the middle and professional classes. Working-class fathers are unlikely to be building careers. They may be gaining time toward seniority or establishing a pension. However, a great many find themselves in a much less secure economic position. Lillian Breslow Rubin, *Worlds of Pain: Life in the Working-Class Family* (New York: Basic Books, 1976).

13. Rosemary Dunn Dalton, "The Psychology of Fathers and Daughters: A Feminist Approach and Methodology," *Women and Therapy: A Feminist Quarterly* 5 no. 2/3 (Summer/Fall 1986): 207–18.

14. Robin Norwood, *Women Who Love Too Much: When You Keep Wishing and Hoping He'll Change* (Los Angeles: Jeremy P. Tarcher, 1985).

15. Rivers, Barnett, and Baruch, *Beyond Sugar and Spice*, pp. 64–69.

16. Paula Caplan, "Mother as the Scapegoat in the Mental Health System," Audio Archives of Canada, Ontario, 1987.

4 | Family of Choice: Our Partners

Our family of choice is the group of people we choose to have in our life. In contrast to members of our biological or adoptive family, these are the people with whom we associate voluntarily. If there is emotional or geographic distance from our family of origin, these voluntary relationships often come to form the landscape of our day-to-day lives in ways that are very reminiscent of a family.

If our family of origin was healthy, there is a greater likelihood that we will select equally healthy people as our family of choice. If our family was dysfunctional, we are likely to replicate some variant of this in our voluntary relationships.[1] We do not do this on purpose; rather, it is as if we have special antenna for finding companions who are emotionally familiar.[2] In the earliest stages of a new relationship, this match may not seem apparent.[3] However, once the bond is established, the pattern becomes unmistakable.[4]

Whether this pattern is healthy or dysfunctional, we tend to assume that a woman will "naturally" select a male partner as she creates her family of choice. However, 10 to 20 percent of women prefer to maintain their primary alliances with women. While this has been true throughout history, it has only been with the recent gay- and lesbian-rights movement that primary relationships between women have received greater public acceptance. This change has been beneficial to both lesbian and heterosexual women. For lesbian women, relief from the need to be so secretive lifts a heavy burden off their relationships. For heterosexual women, visible lesbian relationships serve as role models for constructing heterosexual relationships free of role expectations based solely upon gender. These female-influenced primary relationships can serve as useful guides to reforming heterosexual relationships in a manner that enhances the possibility for genuine equality. Therefore, even if your primary partnership is with a man, you are strongly encouraged to read the section "Primary Relationships with Women."

NOTES

1. A few remarkable people seem to demonstrate a miraculous ability to form healthy peer relationships even if their family of origin was highly disturbed. These psychologically resilient people seem to have been born with the capacity to resist integrating the potentially destructive influences of family members.

2. Ray Helfer, *Childhood Comes First: A Crash Course in Childhood for Adults* (East Lansing, Mich.: First Evaluation Edition, 1978).

3. David Klimek, *Beneath Mate Selection and Marriage: The Unconscious Motives in Human Pairing* (New York: Van Nostrand Reinhold, 1979).

4. Jürg Willi, *Couples in Collusion* (New York: Jason Aronson, 1982).

Primary Relationships with Men

My friend Lynne and I were recently hanging around the office talking about a dinner party we had attended the night before with our married women friends and their husbands. We commented on what a pleasure it had been to be in the company of these couples. It struck us because a decade or two back, spending time with our woman friends usually meant tolerating their male partners. We rarely genuinely liked the men, and we certainly would not have chosen to spend time alone with them. In fact, at times we honestly wondered *what* our women friends saw in those guys. Heaven knows, they probably thought the same thing about the men we were seeing. But we all kept our mouths shut. We do remember thinking a lot of terrific women were with very uninteresting men, men who hardly seemed the women's equals.

It wasn't as if these men had no redeeming virtues. They did have their good points, and they weren't physically or psychologically abusive to our friends, which we would have found intolerable. They just weren't the social equals of their partners.

Lo and behold, as we looked around our social lives today, we saw a great change. We liked the men our friends were with—we would even enjoy spending time with them privately. A lot had changed. Some of our long-term women friends had ended earlier relationships and established new ones with very egalitarian and interesting men. Some were with the same men, but the men had changed a great deal. Our newer women friends had male partners we really liked. Maybe that was part of their attraction to us. We were also coupled and enjoyed finding other twosomes who fit into our friendship network.

This chapter is dedicated to those couples.[1] Varying in age from twenty-eight to seventy-four, these women and men have shown me that intimate and enduring quality relationships between women and men are possible. Having seen their examples, I have moved from pessimism about female-male relationships to cautious optimism. It took me a long time to come to this new perspective, because it is not easy for the average woman and the average man to have a mutually satisfying relationship. To understand why, we need to look beyond blaming women for loving too much. How are women and men raised to have different expectations of a life partner? What are the role traps that can cause conflicts? How can women and men learn to communicate their needs and differences in a healthy way?

Four Reasons Why Women and Men Seem to Mix like Oil and Water

First, women and men are raised almost as if they are two different species sharing the same planet. Their socialization is complementary but not necessarily compatible. Women are trained to be "feminine" and psychologically close. Men are trained to be "masculine" and psychologically distant.

Second, both stereotypical "feminine" and stereotypical "masculine" characteristics are needed to sustain a quality relationship. However, when a woman or man is single, psychological health is more closely correlated with traditional "masculine" characteristics than traditional "feminine" characteristics.

Third, we live in a culture in which men generally have more economic, social, political, and physical power than women. Therefore, in heterosexual relationships, women are assigned a subordinate position, which results in a basic power inequality between the partners.

Fourth, many people, women and men, have personality traits that interfere with quality interpersonal relationships. We do not know whether these psychological handicaps arise from a genetic propensity or are a result of being raised within a dysfunctional family. Either way, they make developing and maintaining quality intimate relationships difficult.

Although our society implies that we value families, we do nothing to systematically assure that women and men know how to evaluate the characteristics in themselves and others that will increase the likelihood of a successful relationship; that both women and men develop good communication skills; and that all people are trained in nondamaging, nonviolent conflict resolution. All of these skills are absolutely necessary for a successful, long-term relationship. Given these obstacles, it is surprising that women and men keep trying to connect with one another as much as they do.

Female and Male Socialization:
Two Different Psychologies

There are at least three important psychological differences between women and men, which stem from differences in their socialization:

1. There is a marked difference in the experience of their ego boundaries (the intangible psychological barriers between one person and another).[2]
2. There is a significant difference in the roles they are expected to fulfill.
3. There is a *subjective* difference in how they experience power and an *objective* difference in how much power they actually have.

We need to review the socialization process of early childhood to understand why there are different psychologies for women and men.

In spite of recent efforts to move toward a more egalitarian society, the vast majority of females and males have been raised differently.[3] From the time parents know that they have a female or male child, they begin planning different scenarios of development.[4] Little boys are expected to be bigger, fussier, and more independent. Little girls are expected to be smaller, more compliant, and more dependent.[5] From infancy on, we are exposed to these expectations and the pressure to integrate them as a part of ourselves.[6]

Psychoanalytically-oriented theorists believe that as children we internalize the characteristics of the people with whom we come in contact. Their characteristics then become a part of ourselves. They argue that our primary caretaker, in most cases our mother, becomes an internalized image. This image is the developing sense of self with which we interact with the external world.

Other theorists suggest that even infants have a sense of self distinct from their caretakers.[7] Rather than simply taking in the caretaker, children experience the attitude and actions of caretakers and offer their own response. Similarly, caretakers have their own unique response to infants. These theorists believe that the infant's sense of self interacts continuously with the caretaker's in a mutually responsive way. Through this process of interaction, each participant has an ever-increasing sense of themselves differentiated from the other person. Both child and caretaker develop new and changing notions of themselves over time. They increasingly know how they are different and separate from each other as well as how they are similar and connected.[8]

Whichever theory is correct, everyone agrees that if children experience "good enough" parenting in the first few years of life, they develop a kind of internal security that tells them that people and life are relatively safe, predictable, and reliable.[9] This is called developing a sense of basic trust, the feeling that another person means well toward you and will not purposefully cause you harm. A child who has successfully negotiated this stage of development is said to have achieved object constancy. This is short-hand for the notion that the people (objects) in her world are relatively constant—at least in her head and heart, if not always in her sight. While the important people in a child's life will not always be in the child's presence, they are sufficiently available, emotionally and practically, for the child to develop a sense that they are trustworthy caretakers. Eventually, this belief in the trustworthiness of our caretakers will be transferred to people in general—and will form the basis of our trusting ourselves.

Since children are raised primarily by women, some contemporary theorists believe that a child's earliest identification is female.[10] This presents a problem for boys. By the age of three, a child's gender identity is firmly fixed.[11] Girls know they are girls, and boys know they are boys.[12] Boys have had to switch gender identities.

To switch an early female identity to a male one, a boy must learn that his gender identity is different from his mother's. How does this happen? In the conventional family, the mother does the bulk of the daily caretaking. The father may be somewhat involved with childcare, but he is usually a more distant and less available person. In order to achieve identification as male, a little boy must increasingly identify with this person who is rarely present, infrequently nurturing, and quite separate from his day-to-day life—a person who is often neither physically nor emotionally available. In order to become male as our society has defined it, this little fellow has to give up being emotionally close to the most important person in his short life. He is trained to disengage psychologically from his mother (or substitute female caretaker) at a very early age. As a reaction to this process of loss and aloneness and to protect himself from the pain of being so disconnected from the people upon whom he depends, the little boy puts up a wall in defense. He has to learn to live without the mutually empathic attachment that is fostered between mothers and daughters because they share the same gender identity.

This early psychological separation from mother and increasing identification with a physically and emotionally distant father appear to result in the development of relatively impermeable ego boundaries. While these boundaries serve to distance the little boy from an earlier identification as female, they are as fragile and rigid as glass. Behind them lies a young and tender ego. The process of separating from his primary caretaker allows the little boy to acquire a male identity, but it leaves him vulnerable to other problems later in life. Behind a man's seemingly impermeable boundaries is a longing for intimacy and closeness, along with handicaps that prevent him from achieving it.[13]

The psychological separation of males from their identification with their mothers occurs before language has developed. It has been suggested that this may account for men's tendency to equate intimacy with nonverbal closeness,[14] since physical closeness and nonverbal activity with mother were what constituted intimacy before the psychological break.

Girls are held more closely to their mothers, both literally and psychologically. They do not have to separate in the way boys do to develop their female gender identity. Consequently, girls do not need the same rigid ego boundaries, and they develop more fluid boundaries instead. This makes it easier, indeed preferable, for girls to be emotional *and* verbally close to others. Since a male model has been used as a standard for health, there has been a tendency to assume that girls are handicapped because they do not develop the same psychological distance from other people that boys do. This obvious error is only now being corrected.

Because many theorists still believe that separation of the type experienced by males is a necessary prerequisite for maturity, it appears to them that females are delayed in their psychological development.[15] Changes in the healthy mother-daughter relationship do not require a major psychological disruption. Rather than separating, most women maintain a psychological connection with their mothers (albeit one sometimes fraught with ambivalence). This sequence seems to allow daughters to develop more flexible and permeable boundaries. Rather than considering this a failure to separate, specialists in the psychology of women view this normal female development as differentiation within the context of a relationship. The daughter becomes increasingly clear about who she is and who her mother is *because* the two females have a close relationship with each other. They spend a lot of time together and learn a great deal about each other.

In the healthy mother-daughter relationship, the little girl experiences her mother as a supportive and nurturing person of the same gender. The mother and daughter enjoy their connection with each other and quickly learn how to respond to each other in a caring and empathic manner.[16] As a girl continues to mature, her ego is not forced to remain a young and fragile embryo hidden behind a rigid boundary. Instead, a young girl exhibits an ever-increasing ability to be both in touch with her developing sense of self *and* in touch with a sense of the other person. Her flexible boundaries allow her to develop and refine a capacity for empathy[17] and "mothering"[18] but leave her vulnerable to difficulties with staying clear about who she is and what she wants.

For females, psychological development and language acquisition occur together. No break in the connection with mother is required for females to develop their gender identity. The closeness of the mother-daughter relationship can continue as the daughter learns to add language as a vehicle of intimacy. With the mother-daughter emotional connection intact, this relationship serves as a model for the daughter's future intimacy with other women. Women connect easily through language and the sharing of thoughts and feelings. However, while women remain emotionally attached to other women, they usually switch their erotic attachment to men.[19]

Heterosexual women try to have the same kind of intimacy with men that they have with women, but it is usually difficult. Women do not have to make the same split between words and actions that men do. Women are comfortable with verbal intimacy as the channel through which closeness occurs, and conversation becomes the context within which a woman learns something about her potential male sexual partner. She discovers what his values are, how he regards women, and what role sexuality plays in his relationships. This information helps a woman to decide whether or not this is a man with whom she wishes to be voluntarily sexual.

In the early stage of a relationship, this verbal intimacy precedes erotic intimacy. If a man segregates verbal and physical intimacy, something he learned to do as a central part of his development, a woman is often left feeling invaded rather than seduced.

The traditional and contemporary expectation of "mothering" by women (and socializing all females to "mother") serves as the model of how women and men are to behave as adults. There has been some speculation that the origins of much of our tendency to blame mother when we did not receive the kind of parenting we feel we deserved is rooted in a deep fear of female authority. It is the kind of authority we felt mother had when we were totally dependent infants. Girls, at least, can imagine at some point experiencing this kind of authority in their own lives, but boys never see themselves as moving into this position.

Perhaps to compensate, males have reacted defensively. If females have control of the emotional and private lives of human beings, males will control the intellectual and public life. While there have been some changes since the recent women's movement, the identities and activities of females and males are not interchangeable. Girls and women are more likely than men to focus on the private world of relationships and families even if they are also employed. Boys and men are more likely to put their greatest efforts in the public world of education, work, and achievement even if they also have families. This division of labor by gender is established in the earliest stages of childhood. The maintenance of this division continues through current child-rearing practices and the expectation that women and men will fulfill different roles in the family and in society. With conscious and considerable effort, these expectations are being altered within a few families, but their numbers remain relatively small.

The fact that women do most of the parenting of young children has long-term consequences for women and men when it comes to adult relationships. Intimacy, in the form of verbal communication as well as sexuality, differs greatly between women and men as a result of primary parenting by women. Men's relatively impermeable and rigid ego boundaries make it difficult for them to permit the kind of intimacy that women take for granted. Men often find it easier to talk about personal thoughts and feelings after they have been close to their partner through sex, while women usually find it easier to be sexually close to their partner after they have shared personal thoughts and feelings.

In many relationships, men have greater power than their female partners. As a result, the male style of equating sexuality with intimacy has gained prominence in our society. In addition, women's flexible and fluid ego boundaries contribute to their tendency to comply with the psychological experience of males rather than insisting that males accommodate or at least give equal weight to women's psychological experience. Women are expected to be intimate in a form most comfortable to men; in fact, they even expect themselves to behave in this way.[20]

In recent years, much attention has been paid to sexual technique and women's inability to separate the physical act of sex from their "need" for emotional involvement. While it is certainly important to teach both women and men about the activities needed for orgasms and the sexual pleasure of women, less attention has been paid to the merit of establishing an emotional connection before a sexual connection. The sharing of thoughts and feelings can lead a woman into an erotic attachment; this process would better fit her psychology. Since men define intimacy and sexuality, women who want to delay sexual involvement may be accused of being moralistic. While this may be true for some women (even if it is, there is nothing wrong with having these moral values), many women are simply trying to voice their preferences in developing heterosexual relationships. Men, however, seem to find this form of connection extremely difficult.[21] As a result, while heterosexual women learn to establish their erotic attachment with men, they often turn to other women to fulfill their needs for emotional and verbal intimacy.[22]

In the balance of closeness and separateness, women have come to be the carriers of closeness. Their psychological development lends itself to this, and it is reinforced in our society, which assigns women that task of nurturing and caring for others. Men have come to be the carriers of separateness. Their psychological boundaries allow them to distance themselves from others in a way that is almost impossible for women. This does not mean that a woman is completely unable to be separate or that a man is unable to be close. It simply means that women, as a rule, are raised to be much more in tune with the thoughts and feelings of others and to take those thoughts and feelings into consideration when conducting their own lives. Men, as a rule, have been raised to focus much more on their own development rather than accommodating the needs of others.

Both qualities, the capacity for closeness and for separateness, are necessary to sustain a relationship. There must be enough closeness to permit growth within the context of the relationship and to keep the sense of being a couple alive. There must be enough distance to permit independent functioning outside the context of the relationship. Couples do best when each brings these characteristics to the relationship rather than when one quality is assigned to the woman and the other to the man.

Separateness and independence allow movement in the world apart from the couple. New activities, ideas, and friends are woven into the fabric of the relationship. When balanced with a sense of attachment and concern for the depth and uniqueness of their primary relationship, the sharing of individual experiences, thoughts, and feelings with a partner provides excitement, energy, and opportunities for growth. If the couple is too close, each member has trouble functioning as an individual with a separate identity. If the couple is too distant, the quality of the attachment can be dangerously eroded.

"Feminine" and "Masculine" Characteristics in Relationships

In the 1970s, psychologist Sandra Bem developed a scale to measure the level of "femininity" and "masculinity" present in both women and men.[23] Femininity includes characteristics such as being affectionate, gentle, shy, and understanding. Masculinity includes characteristics such as being assertive, ambitious, forceful, competitive, and self-reliant.

Verbal communication is primarily a feminine characteristic. It is also a key component of a successful and satisfying relationship. While a high degree of masculinity may bode well for an individual's mental health,[24] it turns out that relationships thrive if a couple's femininity score is greater than their masculinity score. This means that if a woman scores exclusively feminine (which no functioning woman does), a man would still have to have some feminine characteristics for the relationship to work.

Types of Female-Male Relationships

In "traditional" relationships, women are the primary carriers of femininity and men are the primary carriers of masculinity.[25] If there is enough femininity, the couple will probably report that the relationship is satisfying. In these couples, the woman remains responsible for home and family. Whether or not there are children, a middle-class woman often does little or no paid work outside of the home, although she may provide a substantial amount of volunteer work for her community. She moves where her partner's work requires, making all the arrangements for transferring their belongings and family to a new place. Her individual aspirations are far less attended to than the aspirations and interests of her male partner. She is expected to obtain most of her rewards and achievements through her husband and children.

Men in these relationships are supposed to provide for their families economically. The family's entire socioeconomic status is dependent upon his work success. He plays with his children briefly in the evenings or on weekends, but the long, demanding hours of work make spending any substantial amount of time with them virtually impossible. Nor does he have much private time with his wife. He is the primary initiator of sex in their relationship, which is about all the time for intimacy he feels that he has. In working-class families, tasks remain rigidly divided by gender. Although many women work, their jobs pay less and the families are often economically strapped.[26]

In "contemporary" relationships, there is a somewhat higher component of masculinity carried by the woman and a somewhat higher component of femininity carried by the man. Problems can occur if the woman's masculinity is high and there is no equivalent increase in the man's femininity. The woman usually has paid work of her own, but this is reduced or temporarily suspended when children are born. She retains the primary responsibility for the home and raising the children. She and her partner are pragmatic. Middle-class men usually earn significantly more than their wives, so if compromises or moves are needed for work, it is usually the woman who adapts to her male partner's requirements. She is likely to resume more independent interests during midlife when the children are older and her husband's work has reached a plateau.

Men in these relationships tend to understand and support their female partners' needs and rights to independent interests and activities. However, they still expect to be the primary, although not necessarily exclusive, financial support for their intact families. Unlike their own fathers, they want to spend more time with their children and expect to do more around the house. But there is no question in their mind that their wives will be more responsible for home and family.[27] Men are concerned about their female partners having satisfactory sexual experiences and know that it is important to reserve enough time for verbal communication. However, they sometimes get frustrated with their wives' "obsession" with wanting to talk about things.

In egalitarian relationships, feminine and masculine characteristics are carried by both the woman and man. Each expects to have paid work throughout most of their adult years, although there may be periods of temporary unemployment or changes in jobs. Decisions about who adapts to which person's work situation are made on an individual basis. If the man accommodates one time, both partners expect that the woman will probably accommodate the next. Household chores are shared equally and are not necessarily divided by gender. Children are coparented. Both parents expect to make adjustments in their work. Each may reduce time at work and increase responsibilities at home, or one may be the primary parent for a while while the other works full time. Later, the scenario can be reversed. Both recognize that verbal communication is the bedrock of a good, long-term relationship. They make time for it, as well as private time together for companionship and sex. Sex is initiated by either partner, and both are interested in their partner's pleasure. These are the most balanced relationships.

When Relationships Change

No matter how the relationship was when it started, there will be conflict and discord if one partner makes changes that the other cannot accommodate. A *relationship balance model*[28] explains what happens in relationships where explicit or implicit agreements about the character of the relationship shift. Adaptations must be made if the relationship is to regain stability.

For a relationship to be harmonious, both expressive (or "feminine") and instrumental (or "masculine") qualities are needed. People who score high on tests of femininity are described as sympathetic, compassionate, and sensitive to the needs of others. People who score high on tests of masculinity are described as dominant, assertive, and competitive.

All of these expressive and instrumental characteristics are valued in our culture; however, they are assigned to women and men in a stereotypical fashion. In traditional relationships, and somewhat less so in contemporary relationships, the woman usually accepts responsibility for the feminine or expressive character-istics. These enhance the life of the couple and family. By seeing her role as including concern for others and focusing on maintaining group harmony, a woman empowers the people in her family through their relationships with one another. Her male partner carries the masculine or instrumental component for the couple and family. His role permits the enhancement of the self through (apparent)[29] autonomy and self-assertion. This benefits the couple indirectly through the elevated status of one member, but it is of greatest benefit to the individual and may be acquired at the expense of the couple.[30]

Balance within the relationship depends on how feminine and masculine characteristics are distributed and can be divided into three major components: positivity, satisfaction, and leadership.

The *positivity balance* depends on how many of the positively valued expres-sive and instrumental personality traits each woman and man possess. The balance will be skewed if each member does not possess an approximately equal number.

The *satisfaction balance* is the degree to which each partner is happy or unhappy with the relationship. The level of satisfaction depends to a considerable degree on the balance between instrumental and expressive traits. Research has shown that when there is a high number of feminine or expressive traits in the relationship, the happiness level is high. When the masculine or instrumental traits exceed the feminine ones, the happiness level is low.

The *leadership balance* describes relative power within the relationship. Lead-ership is dependent both on self-assertion and the willingness of others to accom-modate. Estimating the power of each member of the relationship determines whether the woman or man holds the leadership position or whether they are equal. The man's power is calculated by assessing the presence of stereotypic traits in each member of the couple: the level of the man's masculinity (self-assertion) and the level of the woman's femininity (willingness to accommodate). Let's call this value M. The woman's power is calculated by assessing the presence of nonstereotypic traits in each member of the couple: the woman's masculinity (self-assertion) and the man's femininity (willingness to accommodate). Let's call this value F. When M is greater than F, the man is the leader. When F is greater than M, the woman is the leader. When $F = M$ the woman and man share leadership equally.

When sex-stereotypical traits are present, power is maintained by the man and male dominance (or patriarchy) continues. The recent women's movement has enabled a large number of women to embrace high levels of the culturally valued aspects of both femininity and masculinity. Some women have had trouble adding masculine characteristics to their personalities. For them, it's uncomfortable to feel masculine. It is equally difficult for some men to incorporate nonstereotypical traits that make them feel feminine, particularly when it also feels like losing power.

The relationship balance model shows that the positivity balance for many female-male relationships has changed. Women have added the positively valued traits of masculinity to the positively valued traits of femininity that they acquired growing up. They now have more socially desirable traits than men. As a consequence, their satisfaction with female-male relationships has decreased. Along the leadership axis, women have increasingly learned how to be self-assertive as well as how to compromise, while men continue to be primarily self-assertive and find compromise more difficult.

In order to assure balance in a relationship, women and men need to ask what defines a person's identity as a woman and as a man. What do we mean when we describe a trait as "feminine" or "masculine"? Does being masculine depend on the ability to exercise greater power? Does being feminine depend on accommodating to that power?

In the absence of a movement for men equivalent to the women's movement, the majority of men score high on the culturally valued aspects of masculinity while remaining at low levels of femininity. If men have not increased their femininity, how have they reacted to this change in women? While there is individual variation, their reactions fall into four categories:

1. Some men, completely unable to compromise and change, simply leave relationships in which their female partners change.
2. Some men remain in their relationships but react by increasing their masculinity in an attempt to reassert their power and restore the stereotypical leadership balance. In these cases, masculinity in the relationship is greatly increased, with both the woman and man contributing. Without a compensatory increase in positive feminine values, satisfaction is decreased.
3. A few men have increased their femininity slightly and want everything to be OK. Having made some changes, they want extraordinary credit for their growth. They want women to quit complaining and to quit blaming men for their problems. These men feel unfairly scapegoated by women and self-righteous in their annoyance with women for not appreciating them enough.[31]
4. A number of men have recognized the fairness of making these changes and have been able to increase their comfort with their own femininity. These men may not get or expect much credit for the changes they have made, but they are committed to these changes regardless. For some of these men, it is a relief to have support for a more gentle style of maleness that in the past might have earned them the disrespect of many men—and even of some women.

In an egalitarian relationship, the woman and man would each carry an equivalent number of culturally valued feminine and masculine traits. Having improved their psychological health, in part through the support of the women's movement, women are unlikely to revert to previous stereotypical patterns. This means that if relationships are to be balanced, men must increase their feminine traits so that women's increased masculinity (and established femininity) will then be balanced by men's increased femininity (and established masculinity). With this change, a man's ability to express feminine feelings of concern and empathy will not be a threat to his masculine identity. Relationships in general will become more satisfactory, because both women and men will have equivalent numbers of socially desirable traits. Leadership and power will be shared equally.

The Power Differential and Inequality

Most problems that plague female-male relationships are problems of inequality.[32] To create healthy relationships, we must find ways for a person's sense of femininity or masculinity to be separate from the issue of relative power. Currently maintaining equal power in female-male relationships is no easy task because:

1. We have all grown up and been socialized in a patriarchal society. This has resulted in a basic inequality between women and men. Patriarchy is oppressive to both women and men, but it is more oppressive to women.[33] This oppression and the thoughts, feelings, and behaviors that result cause serious problems in female-male relationships.
2. All psychological development occurs within the context of this external oppression. It shapes the individual psychology of women and men.

We have all been encouraged to believe that a patriarch is a benevolent father. However, while patriarchy assures that men retain greater power than women, it also assures that some men have greater power than other men.[34] Patriarchy assumes that all men will play on the team, even though they know that only a few will rise to the top. Men's value to themselves, to their families, to society is primarily economic. Their task is to work and to gain their self-esteem through this work. Psychologically, they are trained to be emotionally neutral (except for anger and sexuality, which unfortunately often became mixed together). Sentimentality, fear, anxiety, and sadness are taboo.

Patriarchy assigns men specific tasks and roles, many of which they dislike as much as women have disliked many of theirs. But along with men's tasks comes the perk of power, especially power over women. Women are denied the opportunity to earn equal money because their chance for equivalent work is blocked, their pay is less than men for equivalent work, and employed women are also expected to do the unpaid work of the family.

Of course, relationships between women and men are not a simple matter of men having more power and women having less. Women, men, and the families they create are connected by more than power, economics, and role assignments. Besides making money, keeping house, and raising children, women and men are also held together by the intangible but extremely powerful emotional forces of family loyalty, intimacy, responsibility, cross-generational ties, understanding, and love. These emotional connectors must be respected and valued during the process of correcting any power imbalance.

If women are to gain more power individually and within their relationships, they must do more than simply acquire the traits stereotypically associated with men. If women and men are to have good-quality, mutually respectful relationships, the tasks and interests typically carried by women must be valued by all adults and men must voluntarily sacrifice their illegitimate rights over women. There have always been men willing to do so, and their numbers may be increasing. It is with these men that women must affiliate if they wish to have satisfying relationships. Unfortunately, these men are probably not typical and are thus not to be found in great abundance.[35]

"New" Men

The women's movement challenged the rightness of patriarchy, and we know that this has been good for women's mental health. It might also be good for the mental health of men. Patriarchy may give men power, but it does not give them happiness. It encourages a rigid division of labor that leaves many men alienated and estranged from their children, with little or no intimacy with their wives, and vulnerable to many illnesses.[36] Men are struggling with these issues while there is still time to salvage their relationships, reconnect with their children, and enrich their personal lives. There are men who are trying to make changes and create new self-definitions, but they are often conflicted.

Many men come from homes in which a dysfunctional or alcoholic parent left them with low self-esteem and inadequate skills. These men find it hard to relate maturely to a female partner. They may feel ambivalent about their wife's aspirations when they have their own questions about having fulfilled the American Dream. Their anger may leave them baffled and embarrassed. Even though this may have been a common pattern in his own family, the "new" man is ashamed to find himself resorting to similar tactics. He wants to understand his anger and gain control of it rather than have it control him.

To make changes, a man must resolve many internalized social, cultural, and class conflicts. He must look at his relationship with his parents and the impact their parenting style had on his development. He must also take responsibility for the direct care of his own children. This is no easy task when our work structure does not facilitate or value this kind of family involvement for either employed men or women.

Men who have been influenced by the women's movement are coming to

terms with the problems stemming from their privileged position. They understand that simply by virtue of their gender they have been given power over
women and more opportunities for self-advancement. At the same time, they
recognize the price they have paid in terms of being less able to participate fully
in intimate relationships, experience and express a broad range of emotions,
permit healthy dependency in their lives, and have the freedom to live their lives
according to their personal values and interests when these conflict with the
stereotypical male model.

These men have chosen and are choosing to give up the power they inherited
simply by virtue of being male. They are more accepting, less judgmental, less
threatened, and less threatening than the stereotypical male. They do not need
to compete with other men or pretend to be strong when they feel weak and
vulnerable. They adhere to nonviolent solutions to conflict. They desire greater
equality and are supportive to the women in their lives.

These men are not taking the "easier" traditional road offered by society or
their social class but are instead traveling an unfamiliar path. At times they will
feel lonely, frightened, and as if their sense of themselves as men is at risk. Like
women who are trying new roles, these men may get temporarily stuck blaming
others, using denial, passivity, and avoidance. They may have to learn how to
channel anger in constructive ways as their values and life-styles change.

Many, but not all, of these men are from the middle class. They are assessing
their work lives from a new perspective. Some are establishing different priorities
and new expectations—not just in terms of money, but also in terms of finding
meaningful work and creating quality relationships with partners and children.
The trade-off for them is that they must be willing to reduce their emphasis on
achievement and success in work and make the material sacrifices required to
attain their new goals and interests.[37]

For many of these men, their fathers are negative role models—people from
whom they want to be different. My friend John, an ardent feminist, reacts this
way to his own father. While he loves both of his parents, he remembers his father
as being almost nonverbal, while his mother clearly longed for more communication. He vowed that when he was in a relationship himself, he would strive to
behave differently. It takes a conscious effort for him to talk more about his
feelings and to listen to those of his female partner, but it is a characteristic of
his that she values highly.

These "new" men may not subscribe to society's notion of masculinity or
macho, but they are understandably and wisely reluctant to reject all masculine
values. Brian, a close friend who has been greatly influenced by the women's
movement, speaks adamantly about it taking him years to feel OK about being
a man. Like many of his close male friends, Brian takes fathering seriously, but
he also enjoys his work. He invests considerable time and energy in both. Men
like Brian are more comfortable with their emotions and do not expect to offer
women status, financial security, and protection through their own achievements.

They are striving to develop new self-definitions for being a man that include both traditional feminine and masculine characteristics.

The number of men who fit this model is still quite small. To grow, change, and transform old self-definitions into new ones requires time, commitment, and the latitude to make errors and feel confused or conflicted. This is much easier to do if a person has support.[38] Women have used self-help—or perhaps what might more aptly be called mutual empowerment—groups for much of this kind of support. In these gatherings, they share feeling, thoughts, and perceptions that have previously been forbidden, hidden, or misunderstood. A small, but nevertheless significant, number of men have started similar groups. These pioneers may provide the leadership that is necessary for men to have a liberation movement comparable to that of their female companions.

Women who want egalitarian relationships will do best by partnering with men like these who have been deeply influenced by the women's movement. These men are not simply making adjustments because they are altruistic. They live according to these values because they believe in them. It is with these men that women have the best chance for healthy female-male relationships. The best relationships are between decent, caring, and committed men and women who share power comfortably and do not expect stereotypical behavior from themselves or from their partners.[39]

Dysfunctional and Functional Female-Male Relationships

Even with the best of intentions, a woman and a man may have trouble creating a healthy relationship if they came from dysfunctional families. If insensitivity, disrespect, violence, or other significant problems were a part of their lives during their early development, these experiences will color how they see themselves and their expectations for female-male relationships. The differing psychologies of women and men make effective communication difficult enough. Add psychological damage to this situation, and we have a sadly pessimistic scenario.

A man's physical, social, political, and economic power over his female partner means that physical, sexual, or psychological abuse are the most unhealthy legacies of having been raised in a dysfunctional family. Men and women from these kinds of families can however create quality adult relationships if each is willing to do a fair amount of individual work. It cannot be done alone and it cannot usually be accomplished within a relationship between lovers. It is a kind of healing that takes place best within the context of a healthier relationship in which one person is there primarily to support the other. This can be a long-term relationship with a teacher, a surrogate parent, or a therapist. That person's support and trustworthiness will allow the damaged person to develop a more optimistic and realistic notion of what it means to be in a healthy relationship. They will learn that the world is not universally dangerous and that there are some people upon whom they can safely depend.

Sometimes people try to achieve this healing in the context of a female-male relationship. This is extremely difficult. The damaged person is not very good at identifying a healthy partner and has unrealistic expectations of the relationship. Most often, the attachment deteriorates and both individuals become miserable. At this point, the relationship either needs professional assistance or it needs to be ended.

To assure a quality relationship, each partner must be a psychologically healthy and mature individual. In addition, if a woman and man expect to have a satisfying long-term relationship, there must be no power differential between them. However, even healthy women and men may find it difficult to sustain a long-term commitment if diverging or incompatible interests and responsibilities cut into the time needed to maintain a quality attachment. If the couple has children, the responsibilities of raising them may interfere with adequate time for the couple. Working-class couples often find that just trying to earn enough money for the family's basic needs puts incredible stress on their relationship. All these factors affect the quality and longevity of a couple's relationship.

What's a Woman (Man) to Do?

Relationships work if there is respect and reciprocal compromise by both the woman and the man instead of the one-way accommodation that marks more traditional female-male relationships.

While it clearly takes two to make a relationship work, in the past few years there have been a rash of books telling women about *their* problems with men. Some of these books have had spectacular sales. Almost without exception, they place the cause for dissatisfying relationships in the hands of women. One of the most unnerving is *Women Who Love Too Much*. [40] Even with the best of intentions (I have no doubt that the author was trying to help women discontinue destructive patterns), this book, like many others of this ilk, blames women when they cannot achieve a quality relationship. The author goes so far as to describe a woman's inability to find a healthy relationship with a man as an illness akin to alcoholism.

Women's willingness to accept this "diagnosis" is reflective of a long-standing tendency on their part (reinforced by others) to accept responsibility for trouble in relationships. What Norwood and other authors have skirted in their analyses are the facts that many of the so-called symptoms in women are the predictable consequences of a hierarchal relationship and the results of the differing psychologies of women and men that inevitably develop in the conventional family structure.

Female-male relationships are part of a larger social context in which women and men are not equals. Twenty-five years of drawing attention to this fact has helped to reduce the inequality, but it has by no means corrected it.[41] Male-defined standards of mental health continue to devalue women's psychological strengths. Pop psychology books align themselves with this bias when they place problems achieving quality relationships firmly in women's laps. Authors who blame women for not being able to create healthy female-male relationships fail to ask what part men have played in all of this.

The stereotypical feminine qualities carried by women are not deficiencies. If women defined the standards for relationships, the criteria would probably emphasize the capacity for intimacy and interdependence. Indeed, we believe that these are in fact the very qualities needed for healthy and satisfying heterosexual relationships.

Making Changes

Relationships that require women and men to adhere to restrictive gender-defined behaviors are unhealthy because they depend on the continuing devaluing of women's contributions to relationships and ultimately on the subordination of women. Because women's and men's lives are so intertwined (in contrast to many other relationships of inequality such as between persons of color and Caucasians or the middle class and the homeless), the power differential can be altered immediately. Without an act of Congress, without additional funding, without further ado, the person in greater power can demonstrate a clear and unambiguous commitment to equality. The female-male relationship is the primary interpersonal context that can either perpetuate or change the basic inequality between women and men.

Good-quality female-male relationships require equality in both our public and private lives. Neither a woman's nor a man's tendency to conform to traditional scripts are in their long-term self-interest if they wish to have enjoyable and rewarding heterosexual relationships.

To summarize the specifics:

- Relationships between women and men can be placed upon a continuum of dysfunctional to functional. People raised in dysfunctional families need to heal that legacy within themselves through healthier relationships with someone other than a sexual partner before they can have a successful and functional female-male relationship.
- Women and men must master nondamaging and nonviolent forms of conflict resolution. Any relationship in which disrespect, violence, or psychological abuse occurs is not healthy. People survive these relationships by creating defenses that provide some limited protection from the pain of being treated badly. However, when these strategies are applied in other relationships, they eventually prove to be interpersonal handicaps.

- As a society, we must develop alternative child-rearing arrangements both within the public arena and in our private lives. Fathers need to become more involved in the day-to-day lives of their children. It is neither wise nor fair for women to provide most of the primary care for children. Such a change in child rearing can be expected to have a profound and valuable impact on the individual psychological structures of both women and men.

- There has been an increase in instrumental functioning or masculinity among women to complement their expressiveness or femininity. There must be an equivalent increase in expressiveness and femininity among men. It will proceed more quickly and smoothly if men create a supportive movement for themselves analogous and complementary to the women's movement.

- Men must enter environments previously dominated by women. Women, at least middle-class and educated women and a limited number of working-class women, have made inroads into previously male-dominated workplaces. Interestingly, men have not moved equally into territory previously dominated by women. In other words, men have not become equal to women.[42] Men still have the power to choose between work and some efforts at home. Women no longer do. Men need to make these changes.

- Men as a group must voluntarily abandon their unfair authority in relation to women as a group. They must demonstrate their commitment to equality without expecting a great deal of special credit for doing so. They must change simply because they believe it is the right thing to do. Ultimately, a man must recognize that the quality of his own life, as well that of his female partner, is improved through this action. If men *really* love women, they will gladly and immediately make these changes.[43]

Conclusions

Although intellectually we support new roles and new rules for relationships between women and men, we have actually found them difficult to implement. This is in part because early life experiences color our present lives in significant ways. Real and substantial changes in female-male relationships will take several generations, as increasingly larger numbers of couples try to do things differently. It is a disturbingly slow evolution for those of us who would like to see major changes in our own lifetimes.

Both women and men desire the security, companionship, and continuity of a committed relationship. In light of the power differential inherent in many traditional and contemporary female-male relationships, women need to ask themselves honestly what they need and want in a relationship with a man.[44]

We have a culturally dominant notion about female-male relationships and the proper roles of women and men within them. We now know that the role stereotypically assigned to women is not conducive to their mental health. Having discovered this, many women have made changes. We also know that the feminine qualities historically carried by women are essential to the survival of long-term female-male relationships. Women need to stop looking so much to themselves alone for a way to correct relationship problems.

Both women and men will have to take responsibility for making such relationships happen—if they want them badly enough. And for the most part, the next move is up to the guys. If men are willing to work at relationships in such a way as to provide real emotional support as well as share economic responsibility, they will find no scarcity of interested women.

NOTES

1. This section is dedicated to my friends who have enduring heterosexual relationships of quality, including Alice and David, Lillian and Hank, Myra and Burt, Diane and Bill, Irv and Zola, Linda and Barry, Marilyn and Danny, Helene and Mark, Betsy and Richard, Jean and Jack, and Laurel and Chris.

2. When you touch someone, there is a physical boundary (skin) between the two of you. You know where your body stops and where the other person's body begins. Ego boundaries are the psychological equivalent of skin. For example, someone may tell you a story about a situation in her life that is very upsetting. You may feel sad as you listen, but not to the extent that she feels her own pain. This is because your ego boundaries permit you to sense where your psychological experience stops and hers starts.

3. Theorists who have examined the socialization of females and males argue that it is within the structure of the family that females and males begin to develop distinctly different personalities. Lillian Rubin, *Intimate Strangers: Men and Women Together* (New York: Harper & Row, 1983); Dorothy Dinnerstein, *The Mermaid and the Minotaur* (New York: Harper Colophon Books, 1976); and Nancy Chodorow, *The Reproduction of Mothering* (Berkeley, Calif.: University of California Press, 1978).

4. Our socialization for little girls to fill the role of femininity and little boys to fill the role of masculinity is entirely arbitrary. As Sandra Lipsitz Bem has pointed out in a reexamination of her own work on androgyny "the best sex-role identity is no sex-role identity . . . psychological health must necessarily include having a healthy sense of one's maleness and femaleness, a 'gender identity' if you like . . . but I would argue that a healthy sense of maleness or femaleness involves little more than being able to look into the mirror and to be perfectly comfortable with the body that one sees there . . . beyond being comfortable with one's body, one's gender need have no other influence on one's behavior or on one's life style." Sandra Lipsitz Bem, "Probing the Promise of Androgyny," in *The Psychology of Women: Ongoing Debates*, ed. Mary Roth Walsh (New Haven: Yale University Press, 1987), pp. 222–23.

5. It is important for parents to recognize the limitations of their power to influence their children's development when it comes to gender-biased behaviors. A friend, a prominent academician who has written extensively on the sociology of women, has two children, a girl and a boy in their early teens. She reminds me that as children grow and move out of the home, TV, school, peers, and other adults have an increasing impact on the children's values and beliefs. While she was never able to keep dolls from her daughter or hammers and nails from her son, in adolescence her children were displaying even more stereotypical behavior. Another professional woman reports that even though her three-year-old son has been raised in an exclusively female household, he adamantly agreed with a radio commentator's (hopefully facetious) report that boys are smarter than girls!

6. In addition, a parent is often more comfortable with a child of the same gender. An informal survey among my students suggests that each potential parent had an easier time imagining raising a child of the same sex than of the opposite sex. Each woman and man said that she or he could imagine what their same-sex child was feeling by reflecting back upon their own experience at the child's age. Men were a little baffled about what to do with a girl, and women were equally uncertain about how they would interact with a boy. The women also indicated that it was important for the female and male children to feel that they were equals. They wanted both girls and boys to feel free to choose the life-style they preferred rather than feeling compelled to behave in stereotypical ways according to gender. The women expressed concern that their sons might display sexist behavior, and they were not sure how they would handle that. The men did not mention this concern.

7. Daniel Stern, *The Interpersonal World of the Infant* (New York: Basic Books, 1986).

8. Judith Jordan, "The Meaning of Mutuality," Work in Progress no. 23 (Wellesley, Mass.: Wellesley College, 1986).

9. Clearly, both parents are involved in this process. A loving, safe mother cannot compensate for an abusive father or vice versa.

10. In psychological terms, identification is an unconscious process by which a person patterns themselves after another. It is believed to play a major role in the development of one's personality.

11. John Money and A. Ehrhardt, *Man and Woman, Boy and Girl* (Baltimore: Johns Hopkins University Press, 1972).

12. It is difficult to prove that an infant has any internal identity as female or male. In all probability a child simply *is*. It is only through repeated interaction with significant others that a child learns that she or he is of the same or different gender.

13. One of my patients calls this a developmental disability. I think she makes a good point. When we consider the capacity to form and maintain healthy, mutually gratify-

ing relationships as essential to the psychological well-being of people, conventional male development does not permit full and adequate functioning in this regard. It seems that women have had to compensate for this disability. They do this by training educable men and providing direct service for those who are uneducable—unfortunately, often at the price of the woman's own development.

14. Rubin, *Intimate Strangers,* pp. 98–119.

15. If it occurs at all, anything resembling the kind of separation that occurs in male development seems to come later in the lives of women. Since a woman's role has been to assume responsibility for the direct care of men and children, it makes good sense that she would remain connected rather than separated from them.

16. For those who question the young girl's capacity for empathy, Judith Jordan describes a touching mother-daughter interaction. A mother had accidently caught her hand in a door and was obviously experiencing considerable pain. Her eighteen-month-old daughter brought her soft cuddly toy with which she had been comforting herself and rubbed it against her mother's cheek. The child's worried face lit up when her mother reassured her that she was OK and smiled at her loving daughter. Jordan, "The Meaning of Mutuality," p. 6.

17. Judith Jordan, "Empathy and Self Boundaries," Work in Progress no. 16 (Wellesley, Mass.: Wellesley College, 1984).

18. Women tend to behave in ways that are described as "maternal" even if they do not actually have biological children.

19. While we have a tendency to assume that all little girls will grow up and fall in love with males rather than females, we have not actually clarified how this process happens. The little girl's first love is usually a female, Mother. At some point, the daughter is expected to have her primary love and certainly her erotic attachment be with a man. Nonsexual love between women is OK, but having sex with them is taboo. Having sex with men is OK. We can only speculate as to how this happens and why. For a particularly powerful analysis of the assumption that women will have their primary adult relationships with men, see Adrienne Rich, "Compulsory Heterosexuality and Lesbian Existence," *Signs: Journal of Women in Culture and Society* 5 no. 4 (1980): 631–60.

20. It is probably no accident that in long-term relationships, men report that they have less sexual contact with their wives than they would prefer and women report having more than they would prefer. If men would increase their verbal intimacy, their wives might feel more interested in being sexual.

21. There is some evidence that a man does not feel masculine unless he has some regular sexual activity, even if it is only masturbation. A woman does not require sexual activity in order to feel female. Mentally healthy women can go their entire lives

without sexual activity. This is almost unheard of in psychologically healthy men. It has been speculated that current child-rearing arrangements may contribute to men's obsessive concern with their genitals as a way of reminding themselves that they are different from their primary and earliest identification as female.

22. In a recent survey among German women, the majority said that if they had to choose between maintaining a relationship with their best woman friend and their husband, they would choose their friend.

23. At the time, Dr. Bem assumed that virtually everyone was androgynous to some degree. She has since come to question whether we should even use the concepts of "masculinity" and "femininity." She now argues that human behaviors and personality attributes should not be linked to gender, since "masculinity" is not dependent upon having a penis and testicles and "femininity" is not dependent upon having a clitoris and ovaries. Sandra Lipsitz Bem, "Gender Schema Theory and Child Development," in *The Psychology of Women: Ongoing Debates,* ed. Mary Roth Walsh (New Haven: Yale University Press, 1987).

24. Research suggests that for women, high self-esteem and self-acceptance are correlated more closely with a high "masculinity" score than with either occupation or educational level. Vonda Olson Long, "Relationship of Masculinity to Self-Esteem and Self-Acceptance in Female Professionals, College Students, Clients, and Victims of Domestic Violence," *Journal of Consulting and Clinical Psychology* 54 no. 3 (1986): 323–327.

25. This is also congruent with Jean Baker Miller's perspective in *Toward A New Psychology of Women* (Boston: Beacon Press, 1986).

26. Lillian Rubin, *Worlds of Pain: Life in the Working-Class Family* (New York: Basic Books, 1976).

27. A nationwide survey shows that women still do 91 percent of the shopping and 90 percent of the cooking for their families. As Ann Weber, a social psychologist and associate professor at the University of North Carolina in Asheville, said, "Women feel bad if they don't do what is expected of them, and men think they have a right to expect it. It will take longer than a couple of decades to see changes." "Women: Out of the House, But Not Out of the Kitchen," *New York Times,* February, 24, 1988.

28. Gwendolyn L. Gerber, "The Relationship Balance Model and Its Implications for Individual and Couples Therapy," *Women and Therapy* 5 no. 2/3 (Summer/Fall 1986): 19–27.

29. It is only "apparent" because he has the invisible but critical support of his wife.

30. Plus, if the husband leaves the family, he takes his status and usually higher income with him. His exwife and children usually experience a marked decrease in both

status and income. One year after a divorce, a woman's standard of living declines on average 73 percent while a man's increases an average of 42 percent. "Feminization of Poverty," *News for Women in Psychiatry* 7 no. 3 (April 1989): 9.

31. This reaction has almost become a cultural norm. Many men and a substantial number of women think that women and men have achieved equality in spite of considerable evidence to the contrary. These people sometimes consider themselves to be postfeminist. I find this particularly humorous in light of an important, but little-known, piece of historical data. In 1919, a group of female literary radicals in Greenwich Village founded a new journal that, they declared, would be "pro-woman without being anti-man." They called their stance "postfeminist." Ruth Rosen, "A Serious Case of Déjà Vu," *The Women's Review of Books* 5 no. 3 (December 1987): 1, 3. It seems that those who do not remember history *are* doomed to repeat it. It does make me wonder how much progress we have made!

32. Michele Bograd, "A Feminist Examination of Family Therapy: What Is Women's Place?" *Women and Therapy* 5 no. 2/3 (Summer/Fall 1986): 95–106.

33. Jessie Bernard reminded us of how this works years ago. There are layers of power in our culture. Some women are higher than some men, but no women are higher than all men, while some men (currently white males) are above everyone else.

34. These are the power divisions that are created by discrimination based upon differences in socioeconomic, racial, and ethnic backgrounds.

35. One of my acquaintances asked if these men had some obvious identifying feature so that she could recognize one when she saw one.

36. Cardiovascular disease, alcoholism, and a variety of cancers are particularly prevalent in men.

37. The problems for female-male relationships will not be resolved if this reassessment of the man's desires and goals is done without considering his spouse. I remember a dinner conversation with a well-known "new age" man of my own generation who traveled with a female companion while his wife stayed on their northern California farm with their young children. We were discussing women's place in the world, and he replied that he was happy to have women take over the responsibility of running the world because he had "more important things to do with his time."

38. Some of these men are genuinely interested in eradicating their illegitimate power over women and integrating traditionally "feminine" values into their identity. Other pseudo-liberated men are actually attempting to benefit directly from the women's movement. Under the guise of supporting women's rights, these men are attempting to retain most of their power while decreasing the economic responsibility for women and children that they previously accepted in exchange. Barbara Ehrenreich, *Hearts of Men: American Dream and the Flight from Commitment* (New York: Doubleday, 1984).

39. Men can be feminists, but it must be women who define whether or not a man is a feminist. Men who do not truly believe in the values of feminism are prone to exploit language for their own ends.

40. Robin Norwood, *Women Who Love Too Much* (Los Angeles: Jeremy P. Tarcher, 1985).

41. If inequality *had* been corrected, we would see an equal number of women and men as primary parents and an equal number of women and men in Congress, as CEOs of corporations, as domestic workers, as members of fire departments, as nurses, and as elementary-school teachers.

42. Zoya S. Slive, "The Feminist Therapist and the Male Client," *Women and Therapy* 5 no. 2/3 (Summer/Fall 1986): 81–87.

43. Often when I ask women in therapy why they tolerate certain "bad" behaviors from men, they say, "Because I love him." I always wonder (sometimes out loud), "And does he love you? If so, is this the way to show it?"

44. Where are the self-help books for men who love too little?

Primary Relationships with Women

For a woman, the most difficult part of being in a primary relationship with another woman is that people in our culture usually have trouble acknowledging, let alone accepting, deep and intimate love between women.[1] Most of us assume that women are somehow innately sexually attracted to men. Many of us actually disapprove of or are afraid of primary relationships between women. This fear and loathing (homophobia) means that lesbians experience profound discrimination in both their personal and professional lives.

It is difficult to measure the quality of a lesbian relationship independent of this bias. However, when homophobia is suspended, it is possible to pose a very intriguing idea about female partnerships: that healthy lesbian relationships exemplify how two loving adults can share power and provide mutual love and support in the context of a committed attachment.[2] This is precisely the kind of relationship that many heterosexual women have been aiming for, and have found so difficult to achieve, with men.

In spite of the recent women's movement, only a limited number of men have voluntarily relinquished the benefits society affords them simply because of their gender. Consequently, it is still the exception when heterosexual women and men establish relationships of genuine mutuality. The status of most heterosexual women remains subordinate to that of their male partner.[3] The power differential between partners is rarely equalized as it is in same-sex relationships. With this in mind, it is useful for all women to learn more about and understand healthy lesbian relationships.[4]

What Is a Lesbian Couple?

"Lesbians are in a couple relationship when they say they are. Generally, a couple is two women who are committed to being with each other more often, more intensely, or for a longer continuous period than with others. The partners usually profess love for each other and the desire for intimate contact. The two may live together or not; they may have other sexual involvements or not; they may have a formal contract or commitment ceremony or not."[5]

Whether a lesbian has one long-term relationship or a number of short-term relationships depends on her values, choices, and opportunities.[6] A lesbian couple is similar to any other couple in this regard. Some lesbians have chosen to spend all their years in monogamous partnership, while others opt for serial monogamy. Some prefer not to be tied down to one person, while others choose to be celibate or simply decline to have a primary partnership with anyone, enjoying instead the freedom of remaining single.

If a lesbian does enter a primary relationship, she will experience many of the same pleasures and heartaches that are familiar to anyone who has been in an intimate relationship. All couples must negotiate around three major issues: the balance of power, the pulls toward and away from dependency, and the roles involved in nurturing.[7] These issues look somewhat different in lesbian relationships than they do in heterosexual ones, but all quality relationships are the same in their requirements for time, patience, and motivation. Successful lesbian relationships require additional effort because the couple must work to create a bond strong enough to weather other people's negative reaction to their attachment.[8]

Becoming a Couple

All couples—lesbian and heterosexual—progress through fairly predictable stages of development: prerelationship, romance, conflict, acceptance, commitment, and collaboration. Beyond the usual events that mark each of these stages, female partners may have some unique experiences.[9]

Prerelationship

Women have been trained to be especially sensitive to subtle and nonverbal cues. Thus, in the prerelationship stage, lesbians may assume that they can or should be able to read each other's minds.[10] While this kind of heightened awareness or intuition can be a positive aspect of women's relationships, it is also an indirect communication. As a result, interpretations may be unreliable or inaccurate. If uncorrected, misunderstandings at this stage can lead to later disappointments. (Of course, this can also happen in heterosexual relationships. However, intuition is usually more highly refined in women than in men. Consequently, there are often more expectations that it will be used successfully in lesbian relationships than in heterosexual ones.)

Women in the prerelationship stage are also vulnerable to giving too much or of being too understanding. The capacity to be empathic, to imagine how another person might feel, is a valuable strength.[11] As long as a woman does not diminish her own thoughts, feelings, needs, and desires as she takes those of the other woman into account, this strength enhances the two women's attachment. However, if a woman gives without receiving or offers understanding without experiencing or receiving it in return, feelings of resentment—no matter how disguised—will gradually develop. The longer she allows this situation to go on, the more she is likely to feel disappointed and hurt. Chronic unreciprocated giving eventually leads to feelings of betrayal and burnout.

To avoid these potential problems, women must work on verbalizing their needs, wants, desires, expectations, hopes, and dreams early in their relationships. This is difficult, because women have been socialized not to do this, but straight-forward communication allows potential partners to really get to know each other and to assess honestly whether or not they are a good match. If the women do not take the time for this communication, they may jump prematurely into a relationship, only to discover later that they made a mistake. The breakup will be painful; it would have been much better had they simply communicated more clearly in the first place.

Romance

The romance stage of any relationship is usually quite intense, but it may be particularly so between women. All women are encouraged and trained to be intimate, so closeness can feel especially strong in a lesbian relationship.[12] In the glow of an intensely close romance, it is easy for a lesbian couple to assume that they are just alike. They can erroneously imagine that virtually all their interests, values, beliefs, needs, and expectations are the same. This may encourage them to fantasize that they have found the perfect partner rather than scrutinize the relationship more closely. If lesbians move too quickly based upon these feelings and try to form a committed relationship prematurely, they are likely to be setting themselves up for serious problems later.

For a relationship to have a substantial chance of enduring, it requires time. A couple needs to really get to know each other and to be clear with themselves and each other about their wants and expectations. Again, each woman must make a commitment to being as honest as she can. This is not always easy, but unless a woman is true to herself and to her partner, the integrity of their relationship will be compromised.

Conflict

Any intimate relationship is a voluntary agreement between two separate individuals. Each partner has grown up in a unique family with a unique set of "rules" about how couples ought to behave. We all absorb some of these rules, even if we have fought consciously to reject them. Although we may have successfully altered some of the rules we learned in our family, we have just as surely substituted new ones of our own choosing.

When two lesbians join their lives in partnership, they discover that some of these inherited and individual rules are in conflict. Partners must be able to integrate their rules if the relationship is to weather this stressful stage. Unless each woman has had the good luck to be born into a healthy family where collaboration, cooperation, and accommodation were practiced on a regular basis, developing an integrated set of rules will be no small task.

Even if partners have been scrupulously honest and have good communication skills, each is likely to discover unarticulated, even previously unformed or unimagined, wants, needs, and expectations that only emerge after the couple has been together for a while. Following the romance phase, couples begin to face the task of acknowledging and adapting to these new discoveries. In addition, they must achieve a balance between their needs for closeness and intimacy and their needs for individuality and freedom. At some point, each woman may find herself asking How can I retain a sense of myself as my own person and remain close to my partner? How can I make sure my own needs and interests are adequately met without denying those of my partner? How can we really share power and control? How do we assure adequate nurturing for each other and for our relationship? To add to these stresses, people change. What might have been true at the beginning of a relationship may not remain true as time passes. Change in one or both partners can easily lead to conflict.

Conflict is inevitable in any long-term intimate relationship. Every couple will inevitably collide over these and other issues. These struggles are not in and of themselves good or bad. What matters is what the partners do with them. If a relationship is to survive and grow in a healthy way, partners must be able to negotiate and collaborate without compromising on anything that either holds truly dear and nonnegotiable.

It can be difficult to deal with conflict in a constructive way. Few women have had much practice in the effective use of anger,[13] and even fewer couples know how to handle conflict in a mutually respectful manner. Yet these are precisely the skills that must be practiced if a couple is to negotiate through the tumultuous conflict stage of any intimate relationship.

Acceptance and Commitment

The acceptance stage rarely presents problems for lesbian couples, but trouble may arise again when they consider the possibility of commitment. Some women have a personal difficulty in making a firm commitment to another human being, but in many situations, a woman's anxiety about making a commitment is the result of a lack of social support for lesbian couples.

Heterosexual couples have rituals to mark the transitions in their relationship. A heterosexual pair may go steady, become engaged, or get married. Lesbian couples are denied these signposts. Not only are there no socially nor legally sanctioned acknowledgments of their union, but the decision to become committed to each other is often made at the expense of being rejected by other important people in their lives. If partners announce their commitment to judgmental friends, family, or coworkers, they may encounter rejection and loss rather than joy and celebration. It comes as no surprise that some lesbian women find it extremely difficult to make a solid and unambivalent commitment to the person whom they care about the most.

Collaboration

During the collaboration stage, many couples reexperience all the earlier phases in rapid succession, with many of the attendant problems. If the collaboration centers around whether or not to have a child, issues related to parenting will have to be discussed in detail.[14] The issues of who gets pregnant, how pregnancy is achieved, who provides childcare, and so forth will provide hours of fruitful exploration and potential conflict. The couple faces further exposure to people who behave in nonsupportive ways as their youngster enters school and makes friends outside the immediate family.[15] Whatever the nature of the collaboration, whether it is to start a business together, develop a social-service program, or raise a family, this stage often requires a reworking of earlier stages as the couple makes forays into new territory. This kind of adventure can be both exciting and scary. It tests the couple's capacity for respectful and mutual care while mastering new challenges—both individually and together.

Dealing with Family and Friends

When it comes to acceptance and support from people outside a primary relationship, it is often harder to be in a lesbian relationship than a heterosexual one. While we tend to think of the ideal family as a place where we will be accepted and respected for who we really are, many lesbians experience dismay, if not outright rejection, when they come out to their families. Most lesbians have grown up with heterosexual parents who expect their daughter to be heterosexual; they are usually not prepared to learn that she is a lesbian. Similarly, old friends who simply assume that a woman is heterosexual may become cold, withdrawn, hostile, or unavailable when their mistaken beliefs are corrected. Others may take the new information in stride, quickly adjusting their erroneous earlier beliefs.

Disclosure or coming out is an ongoing process in which many lesbians struggle to balance their needs to share their lesbian identity with the needs of the other people for whom they care. When a lesbian does choose to come out to parents and friends, the primary motivation is often a desire to share her life and her identity. She hopes that in risking self-disclosure she will be able to feel closer to them, rather than self-conscious and secretive.[16]

Keeping a lesbian identity secret is a two-edged sword. Secrecy may seem to prevent the problems associated with discrimination, but leading a double life takes its toll. It uses up energy that could go elsewhere and keeps lesbians constantly balancing the truth with lies. There is a level of internalized self-hate that accompanies every act of secrecy,[17] and secrecy also prevents truly intimate relationships with people from whom the information is hidden. Holidays, birthdays, weddings, funerals, and other family gatherings can be particularly difficult if a lesbian couple feels compelled to keep their relationship hidden. Attending separate events with their families of origin is alienating. The desire to lead authentic lives while remaining close to family and old friends leads some lesbians to risk coming out.

It can be psychologically very healthy to come out,[18] and most lesbians invest a great deal of care and responsibility in the process. To disclose means potentially to hurt others and to cause conflict within important relationships, yet disclosure is an act of love. For lesbians, it represents a desire to share their lives and in doing so to affirm the positive aspects of their relationships with their families and friends.

When parents learn of their daughter's lesbian identity, their responses vary from total rejection and acting as if she had died to full acceptance of her and her partner, if she is in a relationship. Some old friends may easily integrate a lesbian's partner into their existing friendship network, while others will have much more difficulty.

Lisa and Carol

Lisa and Carol had been friends for almost seven years. They had gone to law school together during the 1970s and were now practicing in the same town, but with different firms. They got together about once a month for dinner and long conversations, primarily focused on work, until Lisa decided to move to another town. Because they now lived almost two hundred miles apart and had very busy schedules, their visits were reduced to irregular phone calls. However, on their next summer vacation, Carol and her family were camping near Lisa's town and decided to stop by her new home.

Lisa was a bit surprised by the unexpected visit but was delighted to see Carol and her family. Lisa invited them in and introduced them to her "roommate" Bess. Carol had not realized that Lisa had a roommate. She had never mentioned Bess during their phone conversations, but Bess seemed lovely. She was an elementary-school teacher, and Carol's kids took to her like fish to water. Carol's husband, Ben, who taught high-school chemistry, enjoyed having another teacher in their friendship network. He had sometimes found Carol and Lisa's obsession with their legal work boring.

The visit went so well that Carol suggested they figure out some way to arrange more frequent contact in spite of the distance. That winter, Bess proposed a weekend ski outing for the entire group. They rented a chalet with a big sleeping loft. Exhausted after hours of skiing, eating, and playing games in front of the fireplace, everyone just camped out in sleeping bags. At the end of the weekend, they all agreed that they had had an enormously good time.

Some months later, Lisa drove down to her old community to attend a legal conference, and she arranged to have dinner with Carol. The friends seemed closer than ever before. For the first time, they were really sharing personal lives as well as professional ones. Over coffee at the end of the meal, Lisa said, "Carol, I want to tell you something." There was an edge to Lisa's voice that made Carol anxious. She did not know what her friend was going to tell her, but there seemed to be something ominous about it—as if either she or Lisa had done something wrong. "Bess and I are not just roommates. We are lovers."

Carol was genuinely surprised. She quickly searched her memory to see if she had ever said anything unkind or unaccepting that might have hurt or offended her friend. She might have, because she certainly had assumed that Lisa's sexual partners were male, not female. Lisa had been married twice before she and Carol met, and Lisa had never talked about having sexual relationships with women.

Lisa did not know how to interpret Carol's silence and apparent confusion. The next several minutes seemed to stretch for hours as each woman reacted to and digested the change in their relationship. Both felt awkward, vulnerable, and off-center. Finally Carol said, "Well, I would never have guessed. I'm sorry I acted so weird. I thought you were going to yell at me about something. I thought I had done something wrong." That broke the ice. Lisa thought it was funny that Carol had thought she was going to yell at her. Lisa had actually been frightened that Carol would reject her. They both let out an embarrassed laugh and hugged. Their perceptions of each other had changed, and it would take time for everything to settle in, but it felt enormously good to be able to be more honest and intimate than they had been before Lisa came out.

All of us need the support, nurturance, and companionship that fulfilling and close relationships can provide. If family and old friends cannot be trusted to respond in an accepting way, a set of new and accepting friends becomes all the more important. Often these are other lesbians. A community of accepting friends can provide a sense of family when a biological or adopted family is unable to do so. In this way, family is not simply determined by birth or legal status, but by selection.

Lesbian couples also need people in their lives who will be able to affirm their relationship.[19] Other lesbian couples can provide a level of support that compensates for the more formal and legal heterosexual institution of marriage. By treating the pair as a viable couple and assuming that they will continue to be together, other lesbian couples validate their identity.[20]

Rennie and Tina

Rennie and Tina met through their husbands, who worked together at the local community college. The foursome spent many evenings sharing meals, going to concerts, seeing movies, and visiting museums. The women discovered that they had a great deal in common, and when their husbands went out of town for a conference, Rennie and Tina decided to spend the weekend together at a nearby resort.

During hours hiking along trails followed by long soaks in the Jacuzzi, Rennie and Tina shared their life stories. Rennie was a bit surprised and a little titillated to learn that Tina had had female lovers, although she had been married for several years to Len. Rennie had occasionally imagined making love with a woman but had never actually tried it. Tina's openness allowed Rennie to risk flirting with her friend, and before long, the two were immersed in a passionate love affair.

Over the next two years, each woman's marriage unraveled and the friendships that had supported the marriages disintegrated. For some time, Rennie and Tina were alone without the safety of other couples validating their attachment. Finally, Rennie shared her pain and loneliness with a colleague, Chris, whom she knew was an out lesbian.

Chris invited Rennie and Tina to dinner at her home, which she shared with her lover of seventeen years, Elsie. Chris and Elsie remembered how it felt to be so isolated and alone. They had gone through that many years ago themselves, and they tried to help other lesbian couples with this whenever they could. Elsie, almost sixty-five, was delighted to meet this charming young couple and immediately asked them how they had met. The question startled Rennie. She realized that none of her nonlesbian friends had ever asked her that question. It felt wonderful to bask in the emotional warmth of another couple who completely accepted Rennie and Tina's love for each other and were genuinely supportive of their relationship.

Blending Friendship and Sexuality

Lesbians need to have friendships with people with whom they can be honest and open about their love for other women. Yet lesbian friendship networks can be more complex than those of heterosexual women. Lesbians often find friendships turning into love relationships, and couples who break up often remain close.[21] Moving between a sexual and nonsexual attachment requires time and care;

however, it is usually worth the effort. In most places, the lesbian community is relatively small, and maintaining attachments through changes in the types of intimacy is very important. Making these changes, however, can be highly disruptive unless thoughts and feelings are dealt with honestly and openly.[22]

Sally, Debbie, and Anna

Sally and Debbie had been partners for about ten years before different interests and changing life goals caused them to break up. Debbie took a new job in a town about fifty miles away, but the two women still saw each other at least twice a month and talked weekly on the phone. They had made a reasonably smooth transition from lovers to close friends when Sally met Anna.

The romance between Sally and Anna was intense and passionate. Sally's phone calls and visits to Debbie became much less frequent. Debbie was hurt and jealous—not of the couple's sexual relationship, but of their closeness, which seemed to leave Sally with little time or energy for her old friend. But Debbie felt guilty about her feelings. After all, she and Sally had separated by mutual agreement, and it was Debbie who had established even greater distance by moving. Instead of verbalizing her feelings to Sally, Debbie acted crabby and argumentative whenever they were together. To make matters even more difficult, Anna became very anxious when Sally planned visits with her ex-lover. Their meetings often precipitated arguments between the lovers.

Sally found the whole situation frustrating and finally decided to talk it over with another old friend, Beverly. The arguments reminded Beverly of something she had gone through several years before when her primary relationship had changed. Beverly's sharing of her own experience gave Sally some ideas about what might be going on. It also helped Sally realize that she was tired of feeling sandwiched between two women she cared about. She decided that it was time for all three of them to sit down and talk.

The meeting was initially stressful for everyone, but Debbie and Anna each trusted and cared about Sally. Each had enough invested in remaining attached to her that they did their best to communicate as honestly and kindly as possible. Sally began by telling them how much she cared for each of them and how painful it was to be in conflict. She had given the matter considerable thought and wondered if either of them felt upset about her relationship with the other. At first Debbie denied being upset, but when Anna admitted that she felt anxious and threatened by Sally's affection for Debbie, Debbie realized that she had similar feelings about Anna. Debbie was able to reassure Anna that while Sally was very important to her as a friend, neither of them wanted to be involved sexually. Feeling somewhat more secure, Anna indicated that she understood intellectually and that she would work on tempering her emotional reaction.

The clarity between all three women went a long way in reducing each one's distress. It still took time for them to adjust fully to the new arrangement, but since each one's actions matched her words, the threesome eventually became comfortable with one another. With time, Debbie actually grew quite fond of Anna. After a few years, Sally began traveling more for her business. While she was out of town, Debbie and Anna would occasionally get together to share dinner and a movie. The transition was complete.

In addition to romance, lesbians tend to expect and often achieve a high degree of friendship and camaraderie in their primary relationship. This is often the ideal of heterosexual women as well, but is less commonly achieved. Women, rather than men, are trained to nurture relationships. Thus in heterosexual couples, it is usually only the woman who monitors and attends to the health of the relationship.

Heterosexual women may find it relatively easy to have a romantic or sexual relationship with their male partner but find it more difficult to achieve the nonsexual closeness with him that they experience with their women friends.[23] Turning to women friends for their nonsexual intimacy and male partners for their erotic attachment, they end up feeling that their lives are emotionally compartmentalized.

Lesbians find it much easier to integrate these various modes of relating. The erotic is entwined with nonsexual friendship and care. Indeed, in creating an emotional world that seems complete and self-contained, they may find themselves relying on each other to meet all their emotional needs. If this happens, they neglect other friendships and forget to take time for themselves separately from each other. At some point, this leads to its own kind of annoyance and impoverishment.

Iris and Yvonne

Iris and Yvonne had lived in separate apartments for the first three years of their relationship. But the hassles of maintaining two places—packing and unpacking for frequent overnights and constantly finding spoiled milk in the refrigerator— had just gotten to be too much. They decided to find a place together.

Living together had its moments of great relief, ease, and pleasure. It was also sometimes a pain in the neck. Yvonne worked at home and was a very extroverted and social person. The house was always filled with people. Iris commuted to her office at a data-processing firm almost sixty miles away. She relished peace and quiet when she got home after hours on the train and hours in her office with dozens of people—many of whom she did not particularly like. It really annoyed Iris to come home to even more people, and Yvonne disliked having to shoo everyone out of the house when they were enjoying themselves just because Iris might be upset. However, after several tiffs, the couple decided that the way to handle their differences was to keep work hours for individual socializing and off-hours just for the two of them.

For almost seven months, neither woman saw friends outside of business hours, and all their off-duty time was spent together. Initially it seemed to work fine, but after a while they found themselves again becoming irritated with each other. Iris growled that she never had any time for herself, and Yvonne missed the informal gatherings that used to be such a big part of her life.

The couple had to admit that their system did not seem to be working. Iris needed more down time—time when she was with neither Yvonne nor any of her friends. Yvonne needed more time when she could just hang out with whomever happened to be available. Their home did not seem able to accommodate both of their needs, but they did not want to resume living in separate places.

Iris had an idea. She proposed that about once a month or every six weeks, she would arrange for time alone at a nearby bed and breakfast—either for an evening or for the entire weekend. Initially, Yvonne was skeptical, but she changed her mind when the plan worked beautifully. Every other month, Yvonne had the whole house to herself. She often planned roaring parties that went into the wee hours of the morning. Iris, on the other hand, relished her warm bed, a cozy fire, her favorite novel, and silence. Each woman needed time for herself and her own interests as well as time together. Once this was arranged, their bickering all but disappeared, and they could once again enjoy living together.

Lesbian Sexuality

In contrast to most heterosexual women who must deal with male-defined sexuality,[24] lesbians have the opportunity to create sexual styles and patterns of purely female invention. Whether because of biological or social reasons, female sexuality appears to be different from male sexuality. However, we are only beginning to collect accurate information about the sexual component of contemporary lesbian relationships. What we do know is that lesbian couples report having less genital sex than gay or heterosexual couples[25] and that the frequency of sexual contact seems to decrease the longer the couple lives together.[26] Does this mean that inhibited sexual desire is endemic or that it is normal to decrease genital sexual activity after a few years?

Virtually everything about sex is quite subjective. As a result, it is unclear whether lesbians are reporting a real reduction in sexual activity or if these reports are simply an artifact of the way sexuality is usually defined. Most couples limit their definition of sex to genital contact and orgasm. If the definition is broadened to include other sensuous contact like kissing, cuddling, necking, and petting, the frequency of reported sexual activity would not be so low.

Some lesbians do report sexual dysfunction. Occasionally, they are completely unable to experience orgasm (primary anorgasmia). More often they report being orgasmic through self-stimulation but not through lovemaking with another person (secondary anorgasmia). Lesbians rarely complain of pain (dyspareunia) or spasms when an object enters the vagina (vaginismus). If penetration is problematic or uncomfortable, a lesbian can easily eliminate it from her sexual repertoire. Low desire, inhibited sexual desire, and differences in desire between partners are probably the most common reasons lesbians seek sex therapy.[27] It is common to find extraordinarily low levels of genital sexual contact among lesbian couples and even to find relationships in which sexual contact has all but ceased despite an otherwise apparently harmonious relationship.[28]

If low sexual frequency is viewed as a problem, the cause may be:

1. extraordinarily high sexual desire on the part of one partner,
2. relationship problems surfacing via the sexual relationship,
3. erroneous beliefs about how their sexual life should be,
4. sexual frequency problems that are secondary to other sexual problems such as a phobia of oral sex,
5. sexual frequency problems as a result of simple boredom and the need for sexual enhancement in a long-term relationship, or
6. sexual inhibition problems in one or both partners, which often occurs when there has been a history of sexual assault or incest.

Sexual trauma can adversely effect a woman's comfort with sexual activity.[29] An estimated 38 percent of women are sexually abused in childhood,[30] and one or both partners may have been sexually assaulted as adults. These experiences have profound effects on survivors' self-esteem and their ability to trust others, especially in terms of being sexual. Survivors may suffer flashbacks of the abuse during sexual activity and often carry a burden of shame from their experience. An informed partner can respond to these experiences in a much more caring and sensitive way than one from whom these traumas are kept secret.

Every couple develops their own set of sexual signals and rhythms. The type and frequency of sexual contact depends on how much time each partner is willing to spend pleasuring and being pleasured. Indeed, willingness, not desire, is the prerequisite for initiating sexual contact.[31] In many long-standing relationships, sexual desire is no longer some mysterious chemical attraction. It is just as likely to be an emotional and intellectual desire to be close.

Whether a relationship is new or old, it is rare for partners to have identical sexual interests. Each woman needs to be free to explore and honor her own sexual desires rather than superimposing someone else's standard on her own. And these desires must be shared with her partner so that both women can understand what is needed and wanted to make their relationship run smoothly. A quality sexual life depends on each partner identifying and communicating her needs and wants.

There are three elements essential to enhancing sexuality within a primary relationship: time, build-up, and variety. Time means giving attention and forethought to your sexual life just like you did when you were courting. It is important to set aside time to be alone in a sensuous physical way without distractions. In a long-term relationship, it is not easy to move from the state of consciousness in which we conduct our everyday lives to that in which we can feel relaxed and passionate. Many women need build-up time. They find that sex can be facilitated by a transition period, a time when they soak in a hot bath, sit quietly and listen to music, or sip a glass of wine. Interestingly, the more a woman thinks about being sexual, the more she usually chooses to be sexually active. Finally, sex is enlivened by variety. The quality of sexual contact can be enhanced by engaging in activities that increase passion. Consider going on a date, watching a romantic movie, having dinner in front of the fire, delivering flowers, or going away for a weekend together.[32] Create new pleasures and desire is likely to follow. The key is to make sex a priority by thinking about it more, talking about it more, and setting aside time to be together. With care and communication, partners can develop an ongoing process that will allow them to achieve a mutually satisfying sexual relationship.

Monogamy or Nonmonogamy

No matter what their individual histories prior to coming together, every couple has to make a decision about whether or not to be monogamous. While many couples distinguish between having "just sex" outside their primary relationship versus having a "meaningful affair," women in general seem to be less comfortable than men with the idea of casual recreational sex. Most lesbians say they prefer to be monogamous in their committed relationships.

Since they have no legal contract, it is important that a lesbian couple makes a personal agreement about this in good faith. Close friendships may become eroticized, and a trustworthy verbal agreement about monogamy allows partners to feel less vulnerable to outside attractions. While there are no guarantees, monogamy also provides a context in which a couple can deepen their intimacy by dealing with conflicts directly rather than running to another relationship. The couple does not have the ready option of using an affair as a distraction from a troublesome situation with their partner.

Nevertheless, some lesbians do prefer nonmonogamous relationships. They may want the freedom to act on changing sexual attractions and interests or believe that monogamy is a cover for one or both partners' anxiety about being abandoned by her lover. If a couple chooses to be nonmonogamous but still wants a long-term primary relationship, they will have to make sure that they spend enough quality time together to keep their relationship alive and well.

The main drawback to nonmonogamy is that one or more partners may find the concept easier to handle in theory than in reality. Whatever decision a couple makes, it is probably wise to agree to modify it if it is not working.[33] Certainly nonmonogamy dilutes the primary relationship, takes time to coordinate, and is sometimes a cover for fears of being intimate. This may be why there seems to be few long-term nonmonogamous couples. Most enduring relationships seem to need the relative safety of monogamy.

Even with a verbal agreement, a partner who intended to be monogamous may slip into an affair. Whatever the motivation for the affair, it usually precipitates a crisis in the relationship. The woman who had the affair must deal with her feelings, which often range from guilt about her behavior to irritation about her partner's real or perceived reaction. Her partner must deal with feeling hurt, angry, and betrayed. Both women will be unsure what the affair means for the future of their relationship.

As painful as this crisis is, it can be used to face problems within the relationship that may have previously been ignored or minimized. Bringing complaints to the surface may eventually lead to a stronger bond or a decision to break up. The crucial variable in redefining the relationship is communication. Good communication allows the couple to adjust more easily to whatever decision they make about their future.

Not all lesbians are in relationships with women. Some lesbians are married to men and some women prefer to think of themselves as bisexual—enjoying sexual relationships with men as much as those with women. It is probably easiest to think of sexuality as occurring on a continuum with most of us being capable of loving another person independent of her or his gender.[34] A woman can then choose whether to act on those feelings or not. Thinking about sexuality in this way may also make it easier for lesbian women and heterosexual women to understand and accept one another.

Living Arrangements

Once a lesbian couple has decided to make a commitment to each other, they must deal with how public or private they want to be about their relationship. While often more convenient and economical, living together is also a more public statement. Homophobia can make this difficult. Some couples manage by maintaining separate residences either in the same building, the same town, or neighboring communities.

Couples may have other reasons for living separately. Nonmonogamous couples often find their agreement easier to live with if each woman retains her own living space. Even monogamous couples may discover that they cannot agree on day-to-day matters. Conflicts over housekeeping, spending money, and balancing work with socializing, solitude, and time to just be alone as a couple may lead to constant bickering. Living separately may be easier for some couples than dealing with the chronic stress of juggling vastly different needs and desires.

A few couples sustain loving relationships at long distance. Jobs, an obligation to growing children, or even community ties may make a move too disruptive. Air travel and some professional careers make commuting between coasts or even across continents viable options for couples committed to maintaining quality relationships in spite of long distances.

None of these living arrangements is innately preferable. The guiding principle is what works best for the two women. Living with a loved one can be a wonderful experience or a major hassle. The better the women know each other and the more compatible their living habits, the more likely they are to enjoy their arrangement. The key to success is being honest about thoughts and feelings and developing the skills to negotiate differences.

Many lesbian couples do choose to live together. Whenever adults share living quarters, there are many matters that must be discussed and agreed upon. There are no guarantees, of course, but the more two people talk about these issues and their living habits before they share a common household, the more likely they are to enjoy living with each other. In addition to agreements about sexuality questions to ask include

- How will money be managed?
- What are the standards of cleanliness?
- How will domestic responsibilities be divided?
- What agreements will be made regarding time spent together and time spent separately?
- What housing situation is best—renting or buying? And whose house is it anyway?
- How will ownership of possessions be determined?
- What will be done about family and friends?
- What place will children, if any, have in this relationship?

It is wisest for couples to take the time to figure out what they want in their living arrangements, to discuss these wishes in advance, and to identify any potential trouble spots. A couple must look closely at what each partner wants and needs and then design—and redesign—an arrangement that works satisfactorily.

Finances are often particularly touchy. Within a relationship, the way money is managed reflects a number of underlying themes including trust, commitment, and the question of permanence. Within our culture, money raises questions about social roles, power, class, and self-worth. It is often equated with ability, status, power, talent, and goodness. Lesbian couples are not immune from these biases. If they want to assure a truly egalitarian and caring relationship, it is essential that they address these issues directly.

The vast majority of lesbians know that they have to work to survive. Even though women's salaries are typically less than men's, lesbians prefer this to economic dependency. Lesbians tend to have a strong desire to be independent and believe in the notion of fairness; in the majority of lesbian relationships, both partners work.[35]

Some partners pool their resources completely, some divide household expenses proportionally to their income, and others pay equal shares regardless of income. The longer a couple is together, the more likely they are to develop a system based on trust and convenience.

Common arrangements include the one-, two-, and three-pot systems.[36] The one-pot system assumes complete interdependence. The two-pot system assumes each partner will maintain control over her own resources. The three-pot system assumes that partners have both shared and separate money. Most couples arrange their finances so that no one person is the sole provider except under special circumstances such as a partner's illness, pregnancy, unexpected unemployment, or a temporary arrangement while one partner makes a life transition. Whatever system a couple chooses, it is essential that they make a clear and realistic agreement. It is also helpful to write down their understanding to avoid any confusion when memories have faded.

In addition to the usual issues that concern any couple who choose to live together, lesbians may also have to deal with special issues related to coming out. Living together can be difficult if partners have or want to have different degrees of outness. As long as they were living separately, each woman could maintain personal control over how out to be. However, once a couple chooses to live together, it is harder for even the most closeted pair to avoid the speculations of family, friends, neighbors, and colleagues. Each woman and each couple must decide for themselves how to handle this situation. When one partner is more out than the other, it will be less likely to spark conflict if this is simply viewed as differing degrees of outness rather than differing levels of commitment to the relationship.

Values, Attitudes, Beliefs, and Expectations

Psychologically healthy lesbians make certain basic assumptions that contribute to an ethic of equality in their relationships. One is that a lesbian assumes economic responsibility for herself throughout her adult life. She does not expect to be financially dependent on anyone, even if she is a mother. A second is that in the absence of legal and social sanctions supporting her primary relationship, she cannot count on it being there forever. (Heterosexual women cannot either, but sometimes they act as if they can.) At a very fundamental level, a lesbian understands that while her primary relationship may meet her current needs for intimacy, she must still maintain her own life separate from her partner's. She must have her own work, her own friends, and her own interests. She accepts full responsibility for her life.[37]

What does it mean for a woman to approach a relationship with a sense of being responsible for herself? It means that while couples may have small-scale power struggles around issues like who takes out the garbage, cooks the meals, or picks up the kids at day care, they do not have power struggles that always end up with one person feeling subordinate to the other. Economic self-sufficiency and a woman's expectation that she will determine her own identity and create her own life fosters a level of psychological health difficult to match in many heterosexual relationships.[38] When a woman is expected to fit into an identity and life that is primarily determined by someone else's goals, interests, and expectations, she does not feel like an equal, nor can she function as one.

Conventional heterosexual relationships encourage women to view men as more competent in many arenas and allow women to harbor fantasies of taking time off from work and being supported. Not given equal weight are the domestic services implicitly expected in return or the psychological losses in terms of a woman's sense of herself as a whole person. Lesbian women do not expect to compromise in these ways.

When choices are not based on who has the power to make and enforce them, they can be based upon values, attitudes, beliefs, and expectations. Lesbian couples must deal frankly with choices related to domestic chores, child rearing, obligations to other family members, finances, sexuality, where to live, what to do with leisure time, religious preferences, and a myriad of other concerns. These are issues that every couple must address. However, in conventional heterosexual couples, job assignments are often settled by convention or by the man indicating his preference and the woman adapting rather than the two discussing and negotiating a solution.

Sex roles encourage heterosexual couples to make automatic assumptions about themselves and their partners. Lesbian couples do not have such simple solutions. There is no wife. If there are children, there are usually two mothers. "Wifely" chores and "mothering" are much more likely to be evenly distributed than in heterosexual relationships. Lesbian couples have the opportunity to identify exactly what the couple needs done to keep their life together running smoothly and to negotiate these tasks based on talents, skills, and interest. Some tasks are so undesirable that no one really wants to do them. These can be divided fairly to minimize the burden on each partner.

The difference between lesbian and heterosexual couples in these matters is probably most striking in couples where both people work. Among heterosexual couples, women still do the majority of childcare and household work even when they are employed. Among lesbian couples, the burden is not usually foisted on one partner.

Lest lesbian relationships be seen in an idealized light, it must be noted that even relationships between women have their problems. Although lesbians usually accept responsibility for their own financial needs, economic inequality may still occur. One woman may have inherited wealth or have a more lucrative occupation than the other. Such differences can prove to be the battleground upon which power struggles will occur unless money is dealt with honestly and straightforwardly.

Even lesbian couples cannot always escape the sex-role socialization that labels some behaviors feminine and others masculine. Words like *femme* and *butch* reflect these sex-role stereotypes and can pigeonhole lesbians just as much as *feminine* and *masculine* do heterosexual women and men. Falling into behaviors reminiscent of heterosexual couples with life tasks divided along stereotypical lines is not a wise decision. Nurturing the relationship and maintaining the household needs to be the responsibility of both women if neither is to feel inferior to the other.

If values, attitudes, or expectations in any area are too far askew, the couple may have difficulty. It is often hard to accept someone whose thoughts and feelings are vastly different from our own. Our personal beliefs are deeply important to each of us. We truly believe ours are the best, maybe even right. If we thought others were better, we would adopt them. So unless there is some reasonable overlap, too much divergence suggests a poor prognosis for a successful and relatively smooth relationship.[39]

For the most part, however, lesbians run into more trouble bending over backward to please each other than they do hassling about differences. Too many concessions to a partner can leave a woman confused about her own desires. If a couple resists this temptation, they can negotiate based upon individual interests and needs within the context of a nurturing and caring relationship because they are equals—at least as far as sex roles are concerned. This creates a genuine collaboration that plenty of heterosexual women would envy.

Differences

In spite of the commonalties among lesbians, there can also be substantial differences. Women of vastly different classes, ages, and races can join together in an intimate partnership. When this happens, it is important that differences are acknowledged and integrated into their attachments.

Differences in class can have a powerful impact on a couple. Class refers not only to income and education, but also to world view. It says something about how much power you believe you have in your life and in the world. It influences attitudes about work, money, taking risks, and setting goals.

Middle- and upper-class women often feel a sense of entitlement, a sense of their rights, and a sense of optimism about the future. They expect work to be emotionally fulfilling, if not lucrative. Working-class women work to survive. The availability of work and working conditions are usually under someone else's control. This makes work a far less enjoyable experience. If there are class differences in a lesbian relationship, trouble can brew unless these are dealt with constructively and carefully.

Differences in age can be an advantage just as easily as a disadvantage, as long as the partners see it that way. An older woman can bring wisdom and experience to a primary relationship, while a younger woman can offer energy and enthusiasm. As long as both partners feel competent and respected, they are able to develop shared goals and aspirations for a long and healthy life together.[40]

If partners have different cultural backgrounds, this must be acknowledged.[41] Values and attitudes about such matters as family obligations, child rearing, ancestors, food, and spiritual practices vary from culture to culture. Women of color often see themselves as part of a larger group where interdependency and cooperation, rather than individual growth, is valued.

Many women of color learned at an early age to adapt their life-style to the dominant white culture. They figured out how to behave according to white values and expectations while remaining themselves within their own group. Shifting between these different behavioral expectations takes skill, courage, and energy. When they interact with the white culture, women of color must often deal with prejudice and racism. Prejudice refers to preconceived ideas and attitudes based on a person being from a particular race or ethnic background, practicing a specific religion, having a particular occupation, or belonging to some other maligned group. Racism involves prejudice toward people of a different race. To protect themselves from the feelings associated with prejudice and racism, women of color build a protective psychological shell that prevents these experiences from causing too much damage. For some women of color, racism becomes internalized, and they come to believe the myths of the dominant culture. Like internalized homophobia, the self-hate of internalized racism is profoundly damaging to a woman's self-esteem.

Couples need to be aware of their differences, acknowledge their importance to each individual, and negotiate or incorporate them into their lives together. If the couple has a child, it is crucial that the child has positive role models from both parents' groups and traditions. If not dealt with openly, these issues can destroy a relationship. Ignoring them only leads to mistrust, misunderstanding, and the erosion of intimacy. Working through them together helps a couple become closer.

Legacies of Pain

Not all lesbians are able to move easily into healthy relationships. Like their heterosexual sisters, many lesbians come from dysfunctional families. An alcoholic parent may have left a legacy of low self-esteem and limited skills with which to develop a healthy partnership. Growing up in an alcoholic family (or other poorly functioning family) means a childhood filled with broken promises, episodes of violence, crisis followed by crisis, or just plain neglect, inattention, and unavailability. Women from these families often have little or no idea what constitutes "normal" behavior. Instead of having reasonable expectations or developing positive relationships, they make excuses for "crazy" behavior.

They also apply the same adaptive strategies in their current relationships that allowed them to survive in their dysfunctional families.[42] Some become caretakers—super-responsible, serious, capable, and old beyond their years. Others become pleasers and try to keep the peace by keeping everyone else happy. Adapters soak up tension but show none of it themselves; problem adults often develop addictions themselves. Without realizing it, all of these women re-create the same kind of misery in their adult lives that they disliked so much during childhood.[43]

A history of family violence may leave a woman resorting to the above strategies when she is frustrated in her primary relationship. Alternatively, she may shy away from the legitimate and constructive expression of anger when it would be appropriate. While conflict is inevitable in any intimate relationship, violence is not. Except for self-protection in extreme and life-threatening situations, violence is a sign of a serious psychological problem. However, lesbians in violent relationships often minimize this disturbing phenomenon. Sometimes the women do not even identify the behavior as abusive when it clearly is.

Women who grew up in abusive families may fail to label their own or their partner's behavior as violent. They see this unacceptable behavior as "normal." Even a woman who knows that she or her partner is abusive may keep that knowledge secret. She may feel afraid or ashamed and worry about whether she can find support and assistance to correct the situation.

Until recently, violence in lesbian relationships had not been well documented, but we know that physically abusive relationships do exist among lesbian couples. The dynamics are similar to those in abusive heterosexual relationships.[44] The eruption of violence is followed by apologies and a promise never to do it again. A honeymoon period of closeness is followed by another incident of violence.

Which partner is abused does not depend on size, role, or physical abilities. The person who abuses has low self-esteem, few anger-management skills, is afraid of losing control over her partner and over herself, and believes that violence is permissible. The woman who is abused has little sense of personal power, confidence, or control. Frequently, alcohol or drugs are contributing factors.

Although some abusive behaviors are more dangerous than others, most are potentially dangerous. Milder forms of abuse are usually emotional—name-calling, verbal threats, and insults. More severe forms of abuse are physical—slapping, pushing, choking, beating, hitting with objects like sticks, belts, or cords, or forced sex. All show a lack of respect and an attempt to intimidate and control one's partner.[45]

Both partners in an abusive relationship tend to minimize the frequency, intensity, seriousness, and impact of the abuse. Yet even the mildest forms of abuse are worrisome because any abuse can escalate into something worse. If you are involved in an abusive relationship, change is possible. Psychological and physical abuse is always unhealthy—to give or to receive. The ability to resolve conflict in constructive rather than destructive ways is a skill that can be learned. However, support and assistance from a knowledgeable professional is essential. With practice and a high degree of motivation and commitment, partners can eliminate all forms of violence from their interactions.[46]

Incest and sexual abuse interfere with the development of a healthy sexual life and often prevent a woman from feeling safe in even a loving intimate relationship. It is estimated that one woman in four[47] is an incest survivor and almost two in five has been sexually molested before the age of eighteen.[48] The impact of sexual abuse varies depending on the child's age when the abuse occurred, how long it went on, who the abuser was, whether physical violence was involved, and how adults responded if the child told. Incest survivors often feel as if no place is safe after they have been used as a sexual object by a trusted adult.

Rape by a stranger,[49] date rape,[50] and sexual assault within the context of a primary relationship[51] leave a woman feeling fearful, ashamed, confused, and guilty. This is made worse by the tendency to blame women for sexual assaults perpetrated by others. This cruel and insensitive response causes many women to keep these violent experiences a secret.

Incest and sexual assault are emotional as well as physical violations. Intimate relationships become associated with violation, betrayal, and abandonment rather than warmth, security, and affection. It becomes difficult to trust a lover. No relationship feels wholly safe—physically or emotionally. Healing from incest and sexual abuse is difficult. To aid the process, a lesbian who has been hurt in this way would do well to seek competent professional assistance. Unless properly attended to, these open wounds can have damaging effects on other intimate relationships.

Regardless of the type or combinations of abuse a woman has survived, the experience has aftereffects. If the abuse occurred when she was a child, she may be left with a fundamental sense of being unworthy and unlovable. Even abuse in later years can damage a woman's self-esteem and leave her unclear about what is or is not healthy and appropriate behavior. Any abusive experience damages a woman's sense that the world is a relatively safe place where she can assume that most people can be trusted. Undoing this damage can take considerable care and time.

Relationships That End

Heterosexual marriages are legal contracts. We have statistics describing how many are started, how long they last, and how many end in divorce. Lesbian relationships are informal, and we have little solid data about them. They are neither socially nor legally validated. The absence of this kind of structure also means that lesbian couples must weather the inevitable stresses in any long-term relationship with little external support.

A primary lesbian relationship ends when a partner dies or when the couple dissolves their commitment. In either case, there will be a period of grief and mourning. If a couple ends their relationship voluntarily and with grace, they can feel proud about their success in parting with integrity and kindness.[52] This can be achieved if both partners commit themselves to the process. To do this, the women must define what kind of future relationship they want to have with each other. They need to talk about how to communicate their breakup to friends. It is especially helpful if they can let their friends know how to handle future gatherings. Some women need a cooling-off period where they do not have to run into each other. They can ask friends not to invite them to the same parties and may agree to divide territory to avoid accidental meetings.

None of this, of course, actually happens in such a logical and pragmatic fashion. Few of us have experienced ending relationships in a caring way. Furthermore, each woman is usually feeling quite stressed and at times may behave very emotionally or erratically. However, if this can be tolerated as a temporary disturbance, the passage of time will allow the lovers to eventually feel comfortable in their new roles as "just friends."

More often, when a relationship ends, one or both women feel bad. Our cultural expectation is that primary relationships should last for life. When they do not—as many do not—the partners often feel as if they have failed. This attitude deals a powerful blow to a woman's self-esteem, and recovery may be a very slow process. A woman questions her ability to be a good partner or her judgment in selecting an intimate companion.

The death of a lifetime partner is an even more painful event. It is particularly heartbreaking if the couple has had to keep their importance to each other a secret. A faithful lover may be denied access to her partner in the final days or hours of her life by ignorant or unkind health-care providers or the family of the dying person. Upon death, unless the couple has made meticulous plans, the surviving member may be denied the benefits that a heterosexual partner receives automatically.[53] These experiences are devastating. It is absolutely unfair to deny a loving lesbian partner the same respect and understanding that is afforded a heterosexual partner who loses the most important person in her life.

Whether a loss occurs by choice, by tragedy, or by illness, grieving takes time.[54] It will be at least a year and often longer before a woman recovers from the inevitable shock, denial, anger, and depression that follows the ending of such a significant attachment.[55] The day will come, though, when a woman can think about her partner without experiencing excruciating pain. When that time comes, she can safely begin reinvesting energy in a new primary relationship if she wishes.

Final Comments

All couples bring their personal histories into their primary relationships. Many struggle to improve their communication and enhance their intimacy. All go through a variety of developmental stages as their relationships age and mature. Lesbian couples face certain unique challenges in this process.

Lesbians must cope with both external and internalized homophobia. They must decide how to define themselves as a family and whether or not to have children as part of that family. If they want to have biological children, they must decide who will get pregnant and how she will get pregnant. If they want to adopt, they will have to decide how to deal with adoption agencies or arrange for private adoptions. In either case, they will have to discuss how to manage childcare. They must design their own rituals to celebrate and affirm their relationships, and they must do it all without social encouragement or recognition.

What is most impressive is how creative many lesbian couples have been in maintaining and nurturing positive, loving, and healthy relationships in spite of all the obstacles they have to face and overcome. It makes no sense for heterosexual women to deny the lessons that can be learned from their lesbian sisters, and it makes an enormous amount of sense for all of us to accept and celebrate the lives of women in all their diversity. In doing so, we take the life choices of women seriously and enhance the lives of women everywhere.

ADDITIONAL READING

Betty Berzon, *Permanent Partners: Building Gay and Lesbian Relationships That Last* (New York: E. P. Dutton, 1988).

Lesbian Psychologies: Explorations and Challenges, ed. Boston Lesbian Psychologies Collective (Urbana and Chicago: University of Illinois Press, 1987).

D. Merilee Clunis and G. Dorsey Green, *Lesbian Couples* (Seattle: Seal Press, 1988).

JoAnn Loulan, *Lesbian Sex* (San Francisco: Spinsters Ink, 1984).

JoAnn Loulan, *Lesbian Passion: Loving Ourselves and Each Other* (San Francisco: Spinsters Ink, Aunt Lute, 1987).

NOTES

1. Adrienne Rich, "Compulsory Heterosexuality and Lesbian Existence," *Signs: Journal of Women in Culture and Society* 5 no. 4 (Summer 1980): 631–60.

2. I am especially indebted to three women friends—Lori, Diane, and Nanette—who have healthy and long-standing primary relationships with women. My relationship with each of them has allowed me to learn about the powerful love that is possible between women.

3. Jean Baker Miller, *Toward a New Psychology of Women* (Boston: Beacon Press, 1986).

4. Just because a relationship is between women, and therefore without the gender-based power differential, does not mean that it is automatically healthy—any more than with a relationship between a woman and man. The health of any relationship is dependent on the health of each individual, which is influenced by experiences in our family of origin and by social, political, and economic factors. If people have been raised in loving families where every member is treated with respect, they have a better chance of achieving psychological health. If a person's healthy development is short-circuited by experiences such as physical abuse, sexual abuse, or having to "parent" her parents, the probability of achieving full psychological health is reduced. Furthermore, we cannot talk about psychological health isolated from issues of race, class, and gender. Individuals from dysfunctional families and people who have experienced discrimination often need professional assistance to achieve psychological health. This assistance must be from someone who believes in a nonracist, nonsexist, nonclassist, and nonhomophobic theory. It is best to repair emotional handicaps before establishing a primary relationship, but many adults enter relationships before these issues have been resolved. If this is the case, couple therapy as well as individual work may prove beneficial.

5. Merilee D. Clunis and G. Dorsey Green, *Lesbian Couples* (Seattle: Seal Press, 1988).

6. She is also influenced by how much she has internalized the hatred (internalized homophobia or self-hate) she has experienced from the culture at large. If she is still carrying negative feelings about herself as a lesbian, this affects her self-esteem and influences her ability to function in a healthy way within a relationship. Another influential factor is whether or not she has come out. If she has the support of a lesbian feminist community, her options will be much different than if she is still in the closet.

7. Beverly Burch, "Barriers to Intimacy: Conflicts over Power, Dependency, and Nurturing in Lesbian Relationships," in *Lesbian Psychologies: Explorations and Challenges*, ed. Boston Lesbian Psychologies Collective (Urbana and Chicago: University of Illinois Press, 1987), pp. 126–41.

8. Sue Vargo, "The Effects of Women's Socialization on Lesbian Couples," in *Lesbian Psychologies: Explorations and Challenges*, ed. Boston Lesbian Psychologies Collective (Urbana and Chicago: University of Illinois Press, 1987), pp. 161–73.

9. Lee Zevy with Sahli A. Cavallo, "Invisibility, Fantasy, and Intimacy: Princess Charming Is Not a Prince," in *Lesbian Psychologies: Explorations and Challenges*, ed. Boston Lesbian Psychologies Collective (Urbana and Chicago: University of Illinois Press, 1987), pp. 83–94.

10. This characteristic is also prevalent in the romance and conflict stages.

11. Judith Jordan, Janet Surrey, and Alexandra Kaplan, "Women and Empathy: Implications for Psychological Development and Psychotherapy," Work in Progress

(Wellesley, Mass.: Wellesley College, 1983) and Judith Jordan, "Empathy and Self Boundaries," Work in Progress (Wellesley, Mass.: Wellesley College, 1984).

12. Many authors have described this as merging—losing the sense of what's me and what's you. In a healthy romance, it can be the delicious feeling of temporarily losing ourselves in love or lust. In an unhealthy interaction, it is a fundamental and relatively permanent psychological confusion between partners that leaves them feeling like extensions of each other rather than like two separate individuals. It occurs in both heterosexual and lesbian relationships.

13. Teresa Bernardez, "Women and Anger: Cultural Prohibitions and the Feminine Ideal," Work in Progress (Wellesley, Mass.: Wellesley College, 1987).

14. Sally Crawford, "Lesbian Families: Psychosocial Stress and the Family-Building Process," in *Lesbian Psychologies: Explorations and Challenges,* ed. Boston Lesbian Psychologies Collective (Urbana and Chicago: University of Illinois Press, 1987), pp. 195–214.

15. Unfortunately, there are often many other complicated issues that arise for lesbian parents. A woman with children from a previous heterosexual relationship may have to deal with the threat of custody battles from an angry ex-husband. She will have to struggle with hiding her relationship from her child and/or teaching her child to lie. The children of lesbian mothers will have their own coming out experiences, too. They will have to decide when it is safe to reveal their mother's life-style. It takes a special kind of parenting to handle these complex and painful dilemmas.

16. Lennie Kleinberg, "Coming Home to Self, Going Home to Parents: Lesbian Identity Disclosure," Work in Progress (Wellesley, Mass.: Wellesley College, 1986).

17. Nanette Gartrell, "Issues in the Psychotherapy of Lesbian Women," Work in Progress (Wellesley, Mass.: Wellesley College, 1984).

18. Edna I. Rawlings and Dee L. R. Graham, "Are Closets Healthy?" (Paper presented to the Association of Women in Psychology Conference, Boston, March 9–11, 1984).

19. Larry Ulrig, *The Two of Us: Affirming, Celebrating, and Symbolizing Gay and Lesbian Relationships* (Boston: Alyson Publications, 1984).

20. Lesbians need mirror images of their relationships because they are not an everyday item in popular culture. They are not prominent on billboards, TV commercials, magazine covers, or in the movies. Sometimes it is a shock for a new lesbian couple to look at themselves in the mirror. To counteract their surprise and invisibility, lesbian couples need to value their own relationships and others like theirs.

21. Thelma Jean Goodrich et al., "The Lesbian Couple," in *Feminist Family Therapy: A Casebook* (New York: W. W. Norton, 1988).

22. Lesbian couples who have struggled with these issues can serve as models for heterosexual women and men who wish to maintain friendships after they are no longer lovers. Such ongoing relationships between women and men are often not tolerated well by new partners who do not make an effort to work through their feelings of jealousy. Lesbian couples have had considerable experience in tackling these difficult, but frequently rewarding, transitions.

23. Lillian B. Rubin, *Intimate Strangers: Men and Women Together* (New York: Harper & Row, 1983).

24. Ann Snitow, Christine Stansell, and Sandra Thompson, eds., *Powers of Desire: The Politics of Sexuality* (New York: Monthly Review Press, 1984).

25. Philip Blumstein and Pepper Schwartz, *American Couples* (New York: William Morrow, 1983) p. 196.

26. JoAnn Loulan, *Lesbian Sex* (San Francisco: Spinsters Ink, 1984).

27. Margaret Nichols, "The Treatment of Inhibited Sexual Desire (ISD) in Lesbian Couples," *Women and Therapy* 1 no. 4 (Winter 1982): 49–66.

28. Blumstein and Schwartz, *American Couples*, p. 201.

29. Since women are more often the victims of sexual abuse than men, the consequences of sexual abuse are twice as likely to be present in lesbian relationships as in heterosexual relationships.

30. Diana H. Russell, *The Secret Trauma: Incest in the Lives of Girls and Women* (New York: Basic Books, 1986).

31. Clunis and Green, *Lesbian Couples*, p. 76.

32. Clunis and Green, *Lesbian Couples*, pp. 73–74.

33. In establishing or modifying an agreement, issues of power are critical. Problems arise when one partner has greater power in the relationship than the other and uses that power in the decision-making process. Power plays do not allow for the kind of true collaboration that characterizes healthy relationships.

34. Rebecca Schuster, "Sexuality as a Continuum: The Bisexual Identity," in *Lesbian Psychologies: Explorations and Challenges*, ed. Boston Lesbian Psychologies Collective (Urbana and Chicago: University of Illinois Press, 1987).

35. Blumstein and Schwartz, *American Couples*, p. 118.

36. Richard B. Stuart and Barbara Jacobsen, *Second Marriage* (New York: W. W. Norton, 1985).

37. Nanette Gartrell, personal conversation with the author, May, 1989.

38. There is evidence that lesbians are healthier than heterosexual women on a variety of standard psychological variables such as self-esteem. Andrea V. Oberstone and Harriet Sukoneck, "Psychological Adjustment and Lifestyle of Single Lesbians and Single Heterosexual Women," *Psychology of Women Quarterly* 1 (Winter 1976):172–88.

39. Letitia Anne Peplau, "Research of Homosexual Couples: An Overview," *Journal of Homosexuality* 8 (Winter 1982):3–8.

40. Buffy Dunker, "Aging Lesbians: Observations and Speculations," in *Lesbian Psychologies: Explorations and Challenges,* ed. Boston Lesbian Psychologies Collective (Urbana and Chicago: University of Illinois Press, 1987), pp. 72–82.

41. Norma Garcia et al., "The Impact of Race and Culture Differences: Challenges to Intimacy in Lesbian Relationships," in *Lesbian Psychologies: Explorations and Challenges,* ed. Boston Lesbian Psychologies Collective (Urbana and Chicago: University of Illinois Press, 1987).

42. Claudia Black, *It Will Never Happen to Me* (Denver: M.A.C. Printing and Publications, 1981).

43. Lesbians from alcoholic families (or other dysfunctional families) might consider attending a local meeting of Adult Children of Alcoholics (ACOA). Recovering ACOAs acquire basic life skills that they missed in childhood. They discover what qualifies as appropriate and healthy behavior for themselves and for others. They relearn how to think, how to feel, and how to trust.

44. Althea Smith, "Lesbian Battering" (Paper presented at the Second National Lesbian Physicians Conference, Provincetown, Mass., 1985).

45. Barbara Hart, "Lesbian Battering: An Examination," in *Naming the Violence: Speaking Out about Lesbian Battering,* ed. Kerry Lobel (Seattle: Seal Press, 1986).

46. Ginny NiCarthy, *Getting Free: A Handbook for Women in Abusive Relationships* (Seattle: Seal Press, 1982).

47. J. Densen-Gerber, "Sexual Abuse of Children: Emerging Issues," *New York Pediatrician* 2 (1984): 3–6 and J. Herman, *Father-Daughter Incest* (Cambridge, Mass.: Harvard University Press, 1981).

48. Diana H. Russell, *The Secret Trauma: Incest in the Lives of Girls and Women* (New York: Basic Books, 1986).

49. It has been estimated that about one in four women is raped at some time in her life. D. Russell and N. Howell, "The Prevalence of Rape in the United States Revis-

ited," *Signs* 8 (1983): 688–95. However, only about one-third to one-half of these are reported. A. G. Johnson, "On the Prevalence of Rape in the United States," *Signs* 6 (1980): 136–46; D. G. Kilpatrick, P. Resick, and L. Veronen, "Effects of a Rape Experience: A Longitudinal Study," *Journal of Social Issues* 37 (1981): 105–22; M. P. Koss and C. J. Oros, "Sexual Experiences Survey: A Research Instrument Investigating Sexual Aggression and Victimization," *Journal of Consulting and Clinical Psychology* 50 (1982): 455–57; and C. A. Martin, M. C. Warfield, and G. R. Braen, "Physician's Management of the Psychological Aspects of Rape," *Journal of the American Medical Association* 249 (1983): 501–3.

50. Sexual aggression is a common experience for college women. Fifty percent of the women in one survey reported being offended in a dating relationship during the previous year, with experiences ranging from undesired kissing and fondling of breasts and genitals to forced intercourse. E. J. Kanin and S. Parcell, "Sexual Aggression: A Second Look at the Offended Female," in L. H. Bowker, ed., *Women and Crime in America* (New York: Macmillan, 1981), pp. 223–33.

51. About ten percent of married women report having experienced marital rape. Many women may actually have been raped by their husbands, but they may not use the word *rape*. In a survey of battered women, 34 percent reported being raped by their husbands and 73 percent reported being pressured into having sex with their husbands. I. Frieze, "Investigating the Causes and Consequences of Marital Rape," *Signs* 8 (1983): 532–53.

52. Emily Coleman and Betty Edwards, *Brief Encounters: How To Make the Most of Relationships That May Not Last Forever* (Garden City, N.Y.: Bantam Books, 1976).

53. A lesbian partner can be granted power of attorney should the other become incapacitated due to accident or illness. Lesbian couples should be especially careful to consult a competent attorney to arrange for the appropriate legal protection should they share children or property.

54. John Schneider, *Stress, Loss, and Grief* (Rockville, Md.: Aspen Systems, 1984).

55. William Worden, *Grief Counseling and Grief Therapy* (New York: Springer, 1982).

5 | Creating Healthy Intimate Relationships

Most of us desire closeness and sharing, and we want to feel loved, appreciated, and understood. This yearning for intimacy is basic to human experience. Yet even though we desire intimacy, we often do not know how to create lasting, high-quality intimate relationships.

Intimacy does not happen by magic. It comes about as the result of effort and ongoing care. To create a healthy intimate relationship, both partners must be willing and able to be open, honest, and vulnerable. They must also make the effort to get to know each other. This all requires trust, and developing trust takes time.

Our ability to trust and achieve intimacy are associated with many life experiences. One of the most influential is our experience in our family of origin.[1] The healthier our family, the more likely we are to trust ourselves and others and to have acquired the skills needed for successful relationships. The more dysfunctional our family, the more likely we are to feel mistrustful of ourselves and others and to have developed coping strategies that interfere with our ability to develop healthy intimate relationships.

Fortunately, even if we were raised in a dysfunctional family, we can learn the capacity to develop trust and the skills needed for building good relationships. Old patterns that once provided protection from childhood fears can be revised and replaced with more effective patterns that will allow us to choose healthy companions and to achieve fulfilling intimate relationships.

NOTES

1. Other factors include our individual personality, especially the way we experience and interpret our life experiences, and our experiences as the member of a specific race, class, or other minority group.

Basic Ingredients

Although every family is unique, healthy and dysfunctional families fall at opposite ends of a continuum. Healthy families facilitate the growth and development of each member. Family rules and behaviors are appropriate to the ages and abilities of each person. The family is close but members respect individuality. Dysfunctional families usually have inflexible rules and behaviors without regard to the ages and abilities of family members. These rigid patterns evolve in an attempt to bring order to chaos and instability. While they serve as survival techniques, they also create and reinforce patterns that stifle healthy emotional development.

Assessing the Health of Your Family of Origin

You can estimate the level of dysfunction in your family of origin by ranking each of the items below on a scale of 0 to 10, with 0 indicating totally dysfunctional and 10 totally healthy. Add the results to determine your family's score.

Since families do not stay constant, you may find it useful to repeat this test for several different decades of your family's life together. In addition, if you have a complex family structure, with stepparents or other parent figures, you may find it useful to make separate assessments for each family unit. The score at the time you officially exited from your family—usually sometime between the ages of sixteen and twenty-four—is also the approximate level of dysfunction you carried with you into the world.

Evaluating Your Family's Health[1]
The Family System Continuum

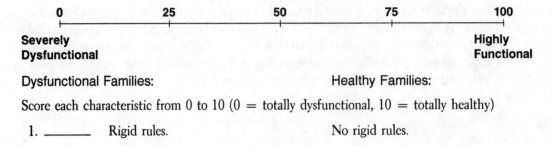

| 0 | 25 | 50 | 75 | 100 |

Severely Dysfunctional   **Highly Functional**

Dysfunctional Families: Healthy Families:

Score each characteristic from 0 to 10 (0 = totally dysfunctional, 10 = totally healthy)

1. _____   Rigid rules.   No rigid rules.

2. _____   Rigid roles.   No rigid roles.

3. _____   Family secrets.   No family secrets.

4. _____   Resist outsiders entering.   Allow outsiders into the family
                                                       system.

5. _____   Great seriousness.   A sense of humor.

6. _____   No personal privacy and unclear   Personal privacy and members
             personal boundaries.   develop an individual sense of
                                                       themselves.

7. _____   A false loyalty to the family;   Members have a sense of family and
             members are never free to leave.   are permitted to leave the family
                                                       system.

8. _____   Conflict between members is denied   Conflict between members is allowed
             and ignored.   and resolved.

9. _____   The family resists change.   The family continually changes.

10. _____ There is no unity; the family is   There is a sense of family wholeness.
             fragmented.

   Total _____

76 to 100–No family is functional all the time. If you scored in this range, there is a possibility
         that you have idealized your family and created an unduly optimistic picture of its health.
51 to 75–Most healthy families fall into this range. During times of intense stress they may exhibit
         dysfunctional patterns, but they do not remain that way for long. These families soon
         reassert their health and return to their normal state.
21 to 50–Most dysfunctional families fall in this range. They exhibit mild to moderate patterns
         of dysfunction. Children from these families may not have experienced direct abuse, but
         they have often been affected by other stresses such as a psychologically fragile parent,
         an extremely authoritarian parent, constant verbal abuse, a parent's moderate alcoholism,
         or a caregiver's prolonged depression.
0 to 20—These families are severely dysfunctional. They usually exhibit entrenched patterns of
         alcoholism, drug abuse, frequent and cruel verbal abuse, physical abuse, and/or sexual
         abuse.

Dysfunctional Family Patterns

Children are especially vulnerable to damage in dysfunctional families because
they are so dependent. They have far fewer options and resources with which to
protect themselves from the family trouble. The younger the child, the more
disturbing the dysfunctional behavior, the greater its frequency, and the longer
it continues, the greater the damage to the child.

In some families, the most blatant forms of abuse may be absent, but there is an underlying level of chronic stress. Children and less powerful adults are deprived of regular healthy human interactions and may even live in fear of being abandoned. This level of dysfunction may be hard to identify because of its subtlety. While there is nothing that actually threatens family members physically, the silent emotional damage can still be very harmful.

In physically abusive families, direct verbal or physical violence may be limited to the adults; however, just being exposed to this violence can have damaging effects on children. More commonly, violence is also directed toward the children by one or both parents. In some families, siblings pattern themselves after their parents and treat one another abusively. Abuse at the hands of a stronger or more frightening sibling can be just as damaging as parental abuse.

Sexual abuse includes inappropriate sexual comments, sexual teasing, single or repeated sexual incidents such as fondling or sexual intercourse. There is a profound power differential between a parent and child or between a larger, older sibling and a younger, smaller one. A vulnerable young child cannot be expected to stand up to someone who is being exploitive or threatening; thus, she cannot truly consent to this activity. Even if the sexually abused child received some pleasure from the contact, she was subjected to experiences before she was developmentally capable of integrating them in a healthy fashion.

An alcohol- or drug-dependent parent is unable to provide the consistency and availability that a growing child needs. They are often too absorbed in their own needs and interests to provide sensitive care and supervision for their youngsters.

Whether moderate or severe, these abusive, traumatic experiences interfere with a child's healthy development. She is less able to trust that she will be treated with respect and adequately cared for by others. She is less likely to see herself as a whole and healthy person who can care for others as well as herself without feeling depleted. Her inner sense of herself feels fragile and underdeveloped. This inner fragility interferes with her ability to connect with others while also remaining clear about her own wishes and desires. Instead, she tries to protect herself by either keeping people at a distance (the Distancer) or by getting too close too quickly (the Fuser).

The Distancer

The individual with a fragile internal sense of herself may develop rigid emotional boundaries to protect herself from feeling too vulnerable to the expectations, requests, and demands of friends and lovers. These protective emotional walls allow her to feel safe by keeping people at a distance, but they also interfere with her capacity for intimacy. Immunity against intrusion is paid for at the price of isolation and loneliness.

Sylvia was entertaining the idea suicide when I first met with her. At forty, she had achieved very high standing in her profession. The only woman in a prestigious architectural firm, she had battled many obstacles to get to the top. Her work was rich and rewarding, but her personal life was almost nonexistent.

Sylvia had had several lovers over the years, but none could compete with her passion for architecture. After a year or two, Sylvia would end even the most promising relationship, exhausted by her lover's complaints about her emotional unavailability. The most recent breakup, however, had been more disturbing because her lover had left Sylvia. Her partner had grown tired of Sylvia's constant attention to details at the office and almost total inattention to their relationship. Usually the first one to distance from an attachment, Sylvia had no resources with which to manage her feelings of abandonment. The emotional pain was so intense that she could see almost no reason to continue to live.

Inside the Distancer is a needy and emotionally undernourished human being who wants to love and be loved but who is terrified of her own desires and the desires of others. Letting anyone inside her protective walls leaves her feeling vulnerable and exposed. As long as she can control the distance in a relationship, she is able to maintain her equilibrium. If the other person pushes for more intimacy and tries to get closer than the Distancer can manage, she simply finds a reason to end the attachment. Unfortunately, she has usually developed genuine feelings for the other person in spite of herself, and if they leave before she has been able to adequately distance herself from them, she is likely to experience enormous pain. This is the kind of distress that often motivates the Distancer to do something about her habit of keeping people at bay.

The Fuser

Some emotionally undernourished women respond to their fragile sense of self by moving too quickly and uncritically to form intimate bonds. Hungry for love and acceptance, they use a friendship or love relationship to feel more whole, but the wholeness is an illusion. The Fuser only feels steady when she is in a relationship. Alone, she is desperate and terrified. Her fear makes her extremely vulnerable to emotional distress when her companion functions as a separate individual—as will inevitably be the case.

Leslie had just been assigned as a nurse to the hospital's new pediatric wing. No sooner had she arrived than Dr. Bert Milner asked her to help him change the burn dressing on one of the children. He was extremely patient and kind with the frightened little girl; Leslie had never seen a man behave so sensitively. Before she could bat an eye, she realized that she was falling in love.

Later that evening during their break, he saw her sitting alone in the cafeteria and asked if he could join her. She was immensely flattered. They talked about this, that, and the other thing, and somehow during their conversation, she got up the courage to ask him to a party she and her roommate were giving the following weekend.

Bert accepted, and it was the first of a series of regular dates. Leslie was on cloud nine. She had never felt so happy and fulfilled in her life. Bert was warm, compassionate, supportive, and friendly. She found herself fantasizing about a long and idyllic future at his side.

Two months later, when Bert told her that he had accepted a job on the other side of the state and would be leaving soon to join a large pediatric practice, Leslie was devastated. Even though he had never talked about a future together, she had just assumed that he felt as strongly about their relationship as she did. Discovering that he could leave with such ease tore her apart.

Leslie was inconsolable. Bert tried again and again to explain his position. Nothing seemed to get through. She felt that he was abandoning her, and she did not know how she could live without him. During the next few weeks, Leslie was on an emotional roller coaster. When she was with Bert, she felt relatively calm. When he was unavailable, she felt utter despair. How could he do this to her? What could she do to make him understand? She loved him so much. She could not bear the thought of losing him.

This kind of intense, irrational, and often unrealistic need for a significant other is characteristic of many people who have been deprived of basic emotional nurturance. They see love in any human being who treats them decently—even if only temporarily. Their very sense of well-being becomes excessively dependent on the availability of that person, even if the degree of interest is not reciprocated. When the loved companion expresses wishes or engages in activities that are different, the Fuser loses all sense of being able to function effectively on her own.

After Leaving Home

Even if an adult is no longer living with her dysfunctional family, she carries her experience with them into other relationships. Learning to live within a dysfunctional family of origin virtually assures that she will have an emotional handicap, through no fault of her own. Her tendency will be to connect with other people who understand and feel familiar because they are also behaving in dysfunctional ways. Specialists in helping people overcome addiction call this behavior co-dependency.[2]

Unless she actively works to heal old wounds and evolve new and more healthy patterns of interaction, she will find herself repeatedly entering into unhealthy relationships. The best way to change these habits is to actively participate in a twelve-step program[3] or obtain good professional care.

What is a Healthy Intimate Relationship?

If you grew up in a dysfunctional family, you may not have a clear idea about what constitutes a healthy intimate relationship. Even if your family was fairly healthy, the qualities that contributed to that level of healthy intimacy may be difficult to identify.

In a healthy intimate relationship, each partner has a commitment to care about the other partner, the relationship, and themselves.[4] Each works at developing good communications skills, maintaining goodwill, and fostering the flexibility to change and grow while remaining connected. Each person is respected and valued for who they truly are—not what we imagine they are or who we think they should be. While this acceptance does not mean liking everything about their behavior, it does mean that the behaviors we do not like are tolerable and nondestructive. In intimate relationships, we offer and are offered validation, understanding, and a sense of being appreciated—intellectually, emotionally, and physically. Through this process of sharing, mutual vulnerability, and care, each couple creates their own unique sense of "we-ness."

Many of us have difficulty developing this kind of intimate relationship in spite of our desire for it because of two major fears: the fear of being close and the fear of being alone.[5] These fears about intimacy do not necessarily mean that we are afraid of intimacy itself. Rather, we are often afraid of being hurt, of not doing it right, of the price we think we have to pay for being close, or of not being able to choose how close or how far away we want to be at any particular time.

Many of us also have inaccurate beliefs about what being intimate means. We may think that we have to be close all the time or that we will hurt our partner if we pull back even a little bit. We may think that being close means we always have to do what our partner wants, even when it conflicts with what we want for ourselves. We may believe that we must always take care of our partner or that our partner must always take care of us. We may worry that the price of intimacy is never wanting what our partner does not provide, or we may have the equally unrealistic idea that our partner should never want what we cannot provide.

These fears often cause us to put up barriers against closeness. Yet intimacy requires sharing all parts of ourselves—our strengths as well as our weaknesses. If you would like to increase the level of intimacy in your relationship, what can you do?

First, risk being open. Intimacy requires that you reveal your thoughts and feelings and that you be fully open to hearing your partner's. You both need to say what you feel and think, honestly yet diplomatically.

Any openness that creates even a little bit of vulnerability is a risk. It is easier to take these risks if you trust that your partner will not hurt you on purpose, that they will keep your confidences, and that they will try to understand rather than judge. If you feel judged or punished when you disclose your thoughts and feelings, you will probably withdraw.

Second, you need to offer and receive signs of caring. Feeling close is enhanced by showing we care—often and in a variety of ways, including cherishing behaviors or small, inexpensive gifts. In quality relationships, these signs of caring are personal, frequent, and go both ways.

When it comes to showing we care, the Golden Rule is reversed. Rather than treating our partner as we wish to be treated, we need to treat them the way they want to be treated. To do this, we need to listen respectfully to their requests and to notice which of our behaviors please or displease them. If we are not sure, we need to ask. And since no one is a mind reader, we also need to ask clearly for what we want.

Third, we must make opportunities for quality time together, no matter how hectic our lives are. Couples must make time for entertainment and relaxation as well as for communicating deeper thoughts, feelings, and concerns. This can be as simple as a daily thirty-minute ritual in which both partners sit down for a private talk or as formal as establishing weekly dates. One couple put a bolt on their bedroom door and trained their children that early weekend mornings were Mom and Dad's time alone. A VCR and a supply of children's programs kept the youngsters entertained while their parents had some very important private time to be together as a couple.

Fourth, intimacy requires that a couple share important values, interests, and goals. Shared goals are a sign of commitment, and they provide a feeling of stability and the sense of a future together. When we know that our efforts are directed toward mutually agreed upon goals, it is easier to tolerate occasional neglect or differences of opinion. Each investment of time, money, and energy that benefits the relationship is a contribution to the future of "we." This is the glue that gives the relationship continuity and purpose.

Finally, a relationship needs to provide space for individuality as well as mutuality. A couple begin to feel smothered if they overdose on togetherness. In order to feel good about being connected, partners must also be able to feel whole as individuals. Both need to be separate people with their own interests and identities. Too much togetherness can be as destructive to healthy intimacy as too little.

Heterosexual couples often allow enough time for the man to have privacy or time with his male friends, but women, especially working women, may find that they have little or no time for adult companionship outside their primary relationship. Lesbian couples are especially vulnerable to seeing themselves as each other's entire emotional support system.

Women must allow time for themselves and time for relationships outside their primary attachment. If they do not, resentments build up. Successful partners learn to strike a balance between couple time and adequate individual time without feeling excessively selfish. They know that ultimately, their relationships benefit from this arrangement.

A quality relationship is not a random affair, and it cannot be achieved through the efforts of only one partner. Healthy intimate relationships take both individual and combined efforts. They are built through a cohesive series of events and interchanges that are determined by each of the partners. A couple's mutual choices determine whether their relationship will be good or bad.

Which Personal Characteristics Are Needed?

Whether you grew up in a dysfunctional or healthy family, you may not have a clear checklist of the qualities to look for in a potential partner. There are twelve essential characteristics each person must bring to an intimate relationship if it is to be healthy and mutually satisfying.[6] A close relationship can be attempted if one or more is missing, but it cannot be sustained in a healthy fashion. In successful intimate relationships, the partners are committed to work at each of these to assure that their relationship is enriched to its fullest.

1. Acceptance—Am I OK the way I am? Is my partner?
2. Communication—Are we able to talk about issues that are important to us? Are we able to share our feelings with each other? Do we know how to do this in such a manner that we are understood? Does the relationship go forward because of the sharing?
3. Compassion—Do I have a genuine concern for the issues that cause the other person concern and vice versa?
4. Compatibility—To what degree do we like and dislike the same things? To what degree does it matter if we differ in certain attitudes and beliefs?
5. Consideration—Am I mindful of the other person's needs as well as my own? Are they equally mindful of mine?
6. Empathy—To what degree am I able to allow myself to feel what they feel? To what degree do they allow themselves to feel what I feel?
7. Honesty—Is this relationship built on truth or are there games involved?
8. Personal Integrity—To what degree am I able to maintain my sense of myself as well as offer myself comfortably to the other person?
9. Respect—Am I treated as if I am of value? Do I treat the other person as if they are of value?
10. Trust—To what degree and on what levels am I willing to let the other person gain access to the things about me that I do not want everybody to know? To what degree is this trust reciprocated?
11. Understanding—Do I understand the other person? Do I understand what they mean by what they say or do? Do they understand me in the same way?
12. Vulnerability—To what degree am I willing to let down my barriers? To what degree am I willing to allow the other person to affect my feelings? Is the vulnerability reciprocated?

If any of these are missing, you have identified a major obstacle to establishing a healthy intimate relationship. This is what I call a red flag. Slow down. Take it seriously. You have discovered an important reason to exercise caution about this relationship.

Sometimes one or more of these characteristics is missing because the person is unable to or uninterested in offering it. If this is the case and you have just started to explore this relationship, ask yourself how much you wish to invest in it. Perhaps you might want to consider a limited affiliation but nothing very intimate. If you are already deeply involved when you discover that something is missing, the situation is much more difficult. Perhaps the person has a psychological handicap. If this is the case and the person is willing to work on their problem, there is cause for optimism. If the person does not see that they have any difficulty, there is cause for concern.

Whenever one of these essential ingredients is missing, you have a choice. If the relationship is important, you must take the personal risk of sharing your discovery with your partner. While this may feel awkward or uncomfortable, it is important. The more the two of you invest in maintaining your relationship, the more likely you are to view this information as ultimately helpful.

The way the two of you address these problem areas will have lasting consequences for the quality of your attachment. Problems do not go away when we ignore them. It is best to tackle these problems before you have gone too far in your commitment. If improvements cannot be made, you cannot build a truly healthy intimate relationship.

To reiterate, a healthy and deeply intimate relationship is only possible when all of these characteristics are present. Do not fool yourself into believing otherwise. It is wisest to look for the presence or absence of the twelve personal characteristics needed for a healthy relationship in the earliest stages of getting to know someone. If problems are identified and you are not willing to raise them or your partner is not willing to discuss them, you would be wise to consider ending this relationship or setting limits on the amount of time and energy you put into it.

Relationships: Six Stages of Development[7]

Although every relationship is unique, relationships in general are relatively predictable. Most couples go through six stages in developing a primary relationship.[8] Knowing about these stages can help us better understand ourselves and our relationships.

Stage 1: Prerelationship

Investigating a potential relationship is a series of choices. Your first choice after meeting someone is deciding whether the two of you want to invest the time and energy to learn more about each other. This is the "getting to know you" stage of any new relationship.

You and your potential partner must decide how often to see each other and how much time to spend together. You may also need to decide whether or when to begin relating to each other sexually. The best way to handle this choice is for each person to be clear about their own values about sex and to follow these. If the couple does decide to pursue a sexual relationship, it is wise for them to discuss whether or not they will be monogamous, how they will protect themselves from the risks of sexually transmitted diseases, and, if birth control is needed, what kind will be used.

Often these choices do not feel like choices because one or both partners may just slide into a relationship without being clear about what they want and expect. At least three things can get in the way of this clarity: making assumptions, mind reading, and being unsure or inaccurate about what is reasonable.

Making assumptions—Often a woman makes assumptions about what a new relationship will be like. Unfortunately, she neglects to share these assumptions with her new companion and then feels hurt and betrayed when the other person violates them.

Mind reading—Women have been taught that mind reading is a loving communication. However, mind reading instead of good verbal communication often leads to misunderstanding, disappointment, and resentment. In heterosexual relationships, women attempt to read the minds of their partners, hoping the men will reciprocate. In lesbian relationships, both women try to mind read and expect it of their companion. Women in either type of relationship are terribly disappointed when they have tried their best to take care of their partner but feel that their own needs have gone unmet.

Am I being reasonable?—There are no objective rules to guide you when it comes to this question. Whether you are being reasonable or not is simply a matter of opinion. The best strategy is to be clear about what you want and to share that information.

Most women have been taught to believe that instead of asking for what we want, if we just give enough, we will get what we want in return. As a result, women frequently deplete their energies by giving without receiving enough nurturance. Because women are very anxious about being selfish, they allow themselves to become burned out instead. They just keep waiting and hoping for more—and carrying on.

It is much wiser to acknowledge your needs and wants as early as possible in any new relationship. Unfortunately, the desire to look good to your new partner frequently gets in the way of this.

"Looking good" means different things to different people. Since men are usually valued for their power and economic value, they are trained to advertise how much status and money they have. "Looking good" for heterosexual women usually includes listening attentively to their male partner's conversation. It also literally means looking good physically—in a very specific and culturally determined way. Lesbian couples are also not immune from trying to look their best for each other. What is best is usually defined by what they think their partner will find attractive or what is expected in their particular lesbian community. Whatever it entails, "looking good" at the expense of hiding our true selves is almost always counterproductive.

Our genuine desires will not go away simply because we do not acknowledge or communicate them. Of course, wanting is not the same as getting, but it is our right and responsibility to communicate honestly and directly. And it gives us a better chance of establishing the kind of relationship we really want.

It is only after stating what they want that both partners can begin to negotiate their differences. They may be able to arrive at an agreement that works for them both, or they may realize that their wants and needs are too divergent. Discovering this allows them to change their expectations of the relationship and frees them to pursue other relationships that will better meet their needs.

Stage 2: Romance

The romance stage of any relationship is a gift. It gives a couple a sense of what is possible in their relationship. During this blissful period, the partners create a shared vision of what they can be as a couple. There are intense feelings of oneness and, not infrequently, lots of exciting sex. As both partners put their best foot forward, potential irritations are overlooked or minimized as lovers bask in the glow of perfect harmony.

This stage is often particularly intense for lesbians.[9] As women, both partners have had many similar life experiences. As a result, they have a kinship, shared history, and mutual understanding that is almost impossible to achieve between women and men in our society.

In heterosexual relationships, the physical differences between men and women and their different cultural conditioning often sets limits on their emotional connection. Men are trained to appear independent and self-directed, while women are encouraged to emphasize intimacy and other-directedness. Women are encouraged to view love, sex, and commitment as linked, while men are not. Being sexual may catapult a women into a deeper intimacy than it does a man. She may long for commitment while her partner seeks nothing more than an enjoyable weekend. These differences can create tension and distance.

Our culture provides heterosexual couples with a path to follow in establishing the seriousness of their commitment—courting, going steady, living together, or getting married. However, sometimes couples ignore these stages or move through them too quickly.[10] Certainly part of the legacy of the 1960s and 1970s was the dismantling of the social guidelines for courtship.[11] In addition, if partners are insecure or emotionally handicapped, they may commit prematurely to a primary relationship. The best protection against making an error in judgment at this rosy-eyed stage is to slow down the process and take time to really get to know the other person. Slowing down is important for all couples. It is especially important for those who come from dysfunctional families.

Women are in the best position to go slow when they are earning their own livings. Training or education for a decent job is the ideal protection against stepping into a relationship too soon. Money literally buys a woman the time to understand her expectations of a relationship while also taking care of herself.

Stage 3: Conflict

The romance stage comes to an end when each partner realizes that the other person is not what they thought them to be. The relationship enters a difficult time in which neither partner believes they are getting what they wanted or expected from the other. Each sees the other as flawed and imperfect. Both feel hurt, disappointed, and resentful.

A woman may try to cope with this stage by using methods that do not really work. She may try to ignore the fact that her partner is irritating or disappointing her, but the resentment that builds will eventually boil over into sudden fights over trivial issues. She may mention her disappointment or grievance, discuss it a bit, decide that it is not really that important (when it is), and smooth over the conflict. When differences are minimized in this way, they are bound to resurface again and again.

Sometimes partners will decide jointly or unilaterally that the relationship is just not working and end it abruptly with little or no discussion. Such endings are often premature. Unless partners clarify what they want and expect of each other, they do not really know whether or not their relationship could be successful.

The most helpful response is for both partners to acknowledge that they have disparate needs and expectations and that these are just differences and not a case of right versus wrong. In doing their best to negotiate, a couple may find they are able to agree on ways to address each person's desires.

Having wants, needs, desires, and expectations that the other person does not or cannot meet is normal. It happens to everyone. It is also normal for conflicts about these to recur over the course of a relationship. By identifying and resolving these issues as they arise, the couple sets up the basic ground rules and communication patterns that will sustain them through the life of their relationship.

Some relationships do not survive this stage. If the couple did not spend enough time getting to know each other at the beginning of the relationship, differences in temperament, values, goals, and life-styles that emerge at the conflict stage may be beyond the couple's skills to resolve.

Stage 4: Acceptance

This is the calm after the storm. During this stage, the couple has a sense of stability, contentment, and deep affection. Disagreements and discomforts are seen as opportunities to learn about themselves and each other rather than as an opportunity to keep score. The couple starts to recognize patterns and learns to resolve the issues faster. The experience of negotiating and resolving problems builds their confidence and helps them to feel successful as a couple.

In the acceptance stage, each partner acknowledges their contribution to the couple's power struggles. They accept the attitudes, expectations, and behavior patterns that their early family situations and their own life experiences are contributing to their current relationship. They also give up the illusion of peace, the notion that once they have learned to take responsibility for themselves and their own history, they will no longer need to confront differences.

Through ongoing dialogue and experience, the couple can develop an understanding of the ways their individual past experiences now influence their pattern as a couple. As their understanding deepens, it becomes easier for them to change old patterns and create the kind of partnership they want, based on the here and now.

Stage 5: Commitment

Commitment means accepting responsibility for our choices. It implies a positive expectation about the future while accepting that life presents insoluble dilemmas and paradoxes. It means letting go of the search for the perfect partner, for the guaranteed future, for the happy ever after.

A full commitment to the relationship cannot be made before the power struggle of the conflict stage or before the understanding of the "me" in the "we" patterns of the acceptance stage. In the commitment stage, partners view each other as basically trustworthy. While there are still occasional rough spots, they are not nearly as frightening as they used to be.

The couple accepts the reality of change and the need for intermittent renegotiations. They come to terms with individual desires by creating solutions that balance the opposing needs of freedom versus security and familiarity versus variety. They learn to rely on their agreement with each other even though they know that it can be changed and may even be broken.[12]

It is during this stage that many couples decide to have a ceremony of commitment or marriage to celebrate their relationship. Even with this, they continue throughout their life together to deal with differences in their needs and figuring out ways to meet them. The fact that they intend to stay on the train until the end of the line does not prevent them from experiencing a few bumps along the way.

Stage 6: Collaboration

Here the couple focuses on something bigger than the two of them to share with the world. This can be something like sharing a cause, having a baby, or opening a business together. As they shift from an exclusively "us" focus to collaboration, they reexperience romance, conflict, acceptance, and commitment. In this way, collaboration can feel like starting the relationship anew. However, this renewed relationship has a history of survival. It is usually more resilient and stable than it was the first time around.

The danger at this stage is that the couple will have a tendency to focus too much attention on their co-creation and too little on the care and feeding of their relationship and themselves. For their long-term health and well-being, it is important that they find ways to cooperate while also attending to their relationship and personal needs.

The Secrets of Happy Couples

What do couples who have maintained lengthy and healthy relationships through all six stages of development tell us about their relationships? Here are some of their ingredients for success:[13]

1. Shared power—In their relationship, leadership is shared. One person may have greater power under specific circumstances or in areas of special expertise, but each person is equally powerful when all factors are considered.
2. Enjoying coupleness—They view themselves as sturdy individuals but believe that being part of a couple gives them even more happiness and allows them to be even stronger.
3. Some quarreling is OK—They do not become overly anxious if there is an occasional conflict. They have the confidence to know that their relationship can endure an outburst now and again.
4. Positive fighting—They recognize that conflict is inevitable. They trust that when their needs or interests differ or clash, their commitment to good communication will allow them to negotiate a solution that is beneficial to them as a couple. They do not take the attitude that one person is giving up something for the sake of the other. Rather, their positive attitude toward conflict allows them to use it as an opportunity for greater mutual understanding. It allows them to practice creative problem solving as a couple.
5. Accepting differences—Being two self-sufficient individuals, they anticipate that they will have some differences that are not open to negotiation. Their goal is to work around these areas of disagreement even if they are sometimes annoying.
6. Personal time—They recognize that each partner needs some independence and privacy. They are comfortable with each person having friendships and activities outside their primary relationship without feeling jealous or intimidated.

7. Curiosity—They take an interest in their partner's job and activities. They care about the quality of each other's life outside the context of their primary commitment to each other.
8. Embracing change—They believe that personal change helps make their relationship interesting, and they are not afraid to incorporate change into their attachment.
9. "That something special"—They always remember that their connection is independent of their relationships with their parents, children, and friends. They do not allow feelings, thoughts, and perspectives from these other relationships to govern their attachment to their partner.
10. Sharing emotions—They recognize the necessity of sharing all their emotions, sadness and grief as well as pleasure and happiness.
11. The limits of closeness—While they relish their attachment, they do not aim to be close all the time.
12. A variety of lenses—Neither partner expects to always see life or their relationship through rose-colored glasses. They have the maturity to endure short periods of distance, irritation, or trouble.

Couples who incorporate these principles into their relationships report that they feel content to be together, share a confidence in their love and care for each other, enjoy doing things to please each other, and find it easy to look out for each other. Their intimacy provides a kind of loving protection without isolating them from others. Without ignoring the realistic troubles of others or the challenges in their own lives, they seem to enjoy life and their place in it. When partners have all the characteristics necessary for a healthy relationship and continue developing better communication skills, they have the material for a lasting and mutually gratifying life together.

NOTES

1. Adapted from Wayne Kristsberg, *The Adult Children of Alcoholics Syndrome: A Step-By-Step Guide to Discovery and Recovery* (New York: Bantam Books, 1988), p. 14. (Previously published by Health Communications, Inc., 1721 Blount Road, Suite 1, Pompano Beach, FL 33069.)

2. Co-dependency is the condition of a person who is emotionally dependent on an outside source to get feelings of self-esteem and who focuses on external stimuli in order not to feel his or her own pain. (Kristsberg, *The Adult Children of Alcoholics Syndrome*, p. 30.) We live in a society that encourages co-dependent behavior in all women by pressuring women to remain dependent on external validation for the measure of their attractiveness, by failing to provide equivalent pay for employed work, and by fostering affiliation with male partners who are permitted to treat women disrespectfully or abusively.

3. There are many twelve-step programs including Alcoholics Anonymous, Al-Anon, and Adult Children of Alcoholics. They are all free. The number of your local chapter can be found in the telephone book.

4. Lewis Smedes, *Commitment and Caring: Learning to Live the Love We Promise* (San Francisco: Harper & Row, 1988).

5. Luise Eichenbaum and Susie Orbach, in their book *What Do Women Want: Exploring the Myth of Dependency* (New York: Coward, McCann, 1983), describe this as fear of engulfment and fear of abandonment.

6. This list is adapted from Janet Geringer Woititz, *Adult Children of Alcoholics* (Pompano Beach, Fla.: Health Communications, Inc., 1983).

7. This is adapted from Susan Campbell, *The Couples' Journey: Intimacy As a Path to Wholeness* (San Luis Obispo, Calif.: Impact Publishers, 1980).

8. Remember that these stages are simply guidelines. The development of a relationship is always an ongoing process and the stages blend into one another. Furthermore:
- no couple moves through all these stages without hitches,
- not every couple starts with the first stage,
- some couples never go through all the stages, and
- certainly not in the order they are presented.
- There is no rule about how long a couple is supposed to stay in a stage.
- There is no rule about how many times a couple reexperiences any of the stages.
- While the emphasis is on primary relationships, much of what happens in intimate couples also occurs in close friendships.

9. Historically, this intensity has been viewed as a component of homosexual "pathology." In reality any couple, heterosexual or homosexual, may bring "pathological" or emotionally handicapped selves to a relationship. The intensity of this stage does not really tell much about the health or dysfunction of any particular individual or couple.

10. Lesbian couples do not have the same socially approved rituals, and this contributes to a greater risk of moving into a relationship too quickly.

11. It is one of the tragedies of our times that the lethal disease AIDS may be the primary factor in bringing back the social rituals of courtship.

12. Many relationships grow stronger in the process of dealing with these broken agreements. Others do not survive even one violation of an important understanding. If an agreement is broken over and over again, there are serious consequences for a relationship. The person who does not abide by their agreement loses self-respect, and their partner may cease to trust at all.

13. Adapted from "Secrets of a Happy Couple," *Wellness Letter* (Berkeley, Calif.: University of California, October 1985).

Upgrading Your Relationship

By now you realize that good relationships do not just happen, they are created, and that "good communication is to a relationship what breathing is to life."[1] Virtually any relationship can be improved if both partners commit themselves to developing better communication skills, and even the best of relationships can benefit from a refresher course.

Blocks to Communication

Communication is complex. It includes not only the spoken word but tone of voice, eye contact, body posture, and gestures. Your actions (or lack of actions) are sometimes even more powerful than your words.

We communicate for many purposes—to ask for help, to pass the time, to negotiate for something we want, and, especially in intimate relationships, to get approval, recognition, or agreement from our partner. Often we are not aware that this is part of the reason for our communication until it does not happen. When we do not receive the approval, recognition, or agreement we want, we feel slighted, unappreciated, hurt, or rejected. Our self-esteem becomes the real topic, and we respond to a trivial matter as if our core identity is on the line. This kind of overreaction is just one of many blocks to good communication.

Another block is filtering. It is not possible to attend to everything that is going on at any one time. Out of necessity, we filter information. When we filter out some details and fill in others without checking them out, we operate on incomplete and biased information. Sometimes this works to our advantage, but it often leads to misunderstandings and hurt or angry feelings.

In addition to filtering, we also classify. In any new situation, we pay attention long enough to decide if this experience is similar to one we have had in the past. We then classify our impressions into a familiar category and fill in the details. Unfortunately, as soon as we classify the experience (or person or situation) as similar to a previous one, we often act as if they are actually the same—whether they are or not. This is one way we help the past repeat itself.

Another block to good communication is making assumptions. Because life moves at a fast pace, we tend to treat assumptions as facts when they really are not. If a couple confuses assumptions with facts and treats their individual realities as if they are the truth, it will be impossible for them to understand each other's point of view. We need to remember that other people really do see things differently than we do and that their view is as true for them as ours is for us. There are many truths.

We also need to remember that language is a very inexact tool for communicating and that many words have soft rather than hard meanings.[2] Hard meanings are concrete and can be measured objectively. The word *table* has a hard meaning. Soft meanings involve personal and subjective judgments and are much more difficult to define. Words like *trust, respect,* and *control* have soft meanings. They mean different things to different people, depending on their values, attitudes, and experiences.

Finally, if you are stressed or if the topic is sensitive, you may listen poorly and interpret incorrectly. Good communication becomes much more difficult under these conditions.

Improving Your Communication Skills

In any communication, there are two real messages—what the speaker thinks she said and what the listener thinks she heard. Good communication means the speaker's intent equals the impact on the listener. This is most likely to happen when the speaker states exactly what she is thinking, feeling, or wanting. She tries to be clear and precise. She does not assume that her listener is a mind reader or that her listener will not understand. The listener does her best to understand what the speaker intends. She does not fill in the gaps with assumptions or guesses. Any couple can improve their communication by improving their speaking and listening skills.

Listening Skills

It is easy to confuse listening with hearing, but they are not the same. Good listening is active, not passive. We have to resist tendencies to mind read, to judge without asking for more information, or to concentrate on our own response rather than on understanding what our partner has said. When we truly listen to our partner, we make a commitment to try to understand how she or he feels and sees things. As much as possible, we put aside our own judgments, assumptions, attitudes, and feelings while we try to look at things from her or his perspective. We are saying to our partner, "You are important to me. I care about your feelings and your experiences."

The only way to find out if we understand what our partner means is to ask. In gathering information, we try to clarify what our partner is saying. Then we can check our interpretations by giving feedback, which allows us to see if what we think we hear is what she or he intended to communicate. In this give-and-take process, we get a fuller appreciation of what is being said.

Often the situations in which it is hardest to use good listening skills are those where they are needed most. One of these situations occurs when we are being criticized or when our partner is upset with us. Rather than becoming defensive and counterattacking, try acknowledging that your partner is correct about some things. As a result, she or he is likely to be reassured that you have really been listening.

Another useful listening technique is the two-question rule.[3] According to this rule, the answer to a question is followed by a second question based on that answer. This helps us to stay focused on our partner rather than slipping back into our own concerns. In a relationship of genuine mutuality, when we show our partner that we care about her or his thoughts and feelings by truly listening, she or he is likely to reciprocate.

Expressing Skills

Expressing ourselves clearly and precisely requires us to be aware, to be self-disclosing, and to make sure our body language is consistent with our message. There are four kinds of expressing skills:[4]

1. Observations. When we express our observations we are reporting just the facts—no inferences, no opinions, and no conclusions. We stick to what we have seen, heard, or personally experienced.
2. Thoughts. Our thoughts depart from the facts. They involve coming to conclusions, developing opinions, creating beliefs, and generating theories. We frequently express these thoughts as if they were facts rather than our ideas. It is important to remember that our thoughts are just our thoughts—not The Truth.
3. Feelings. Many of us find it difficult to express our feelings clearly. Part of the difficulty is determining what we really are feeling. This takes practice, but it is worth the effort, because once we understand our own feelings, we become able to share them with our partner, and shared feelings are the building blocks of intimacy.

    When we share feelings, we are not making observations, judgments, or giving opinions. "I feel hurt" communicates a feeling. "I feel that you are trying to hurt me" is an opinion and a judgment about the other person's behavior. It is not a statement about our own feelings.

    There is a simple way to tell whether a statement clearly expresses a feeling or an observation, judgment, or opinion. Look at the words that come after "I feel." "Hurt" describes a feeling, but "that you are trying to hurt me" describe the speaker's thoughts. To clearly identify these as thoughts (not feelings), the statement should be "I *think* that you are trying to hurt me." Since we may have thoughts as well as feelings, the complete message might be something like this: "I *think* you are trying to hurt me and I *feel* upset about it."
4. Wants and needs. Trying to have an intimate relationship without expressing your wants and needs is like driving a car without a steering wheel. You can do it, but you cannot change directions or steer around potholes. Relationships work best when both partners can express their wants and needs clearly. Unfortunately, this is often especially hard for women to do.

Despite the fact that a woman is the only expert on her own wants and needs and despite the fact that no one can read her mind, she may still have a hard time being clear. Perhaps she fears being selfish. Perhaps she wants her partner to figure out what she wants and needs so that she will not have to ask for it directly. Whatever the obstacle, her lack of clarity greatly reduces her likelihood of getting what she wants.

Even announcing what we want and need is not the same as making a specific request of our partner. Our chances of getting what we desire are better if we add our request to our announcement. If we are afraid to ask, if we believe we should not ask, or if we believe that we should not have to ask, we are likely to express our needs in indirect ways such as withdrawing, behaving passively, or acting crabby.

We are much more likely to have our desires met if we express them. In expressing our needs, we are not blaming or finding fault. We are simply describing what would help or please us. We are making a request of our partner. Our partner can then decide how to proceed with our clear request.

Not every situation requires all four types of expressing skills. However, if we leave something out or mix up different kinds of expressions, our intent will probably not equal the impact on our listener. To minimize confusion, keep the following guidelines in mind:[5]

1. Be aware. When you decide to express something, you first need to be clear within yourself about the content of your message and about your intent in delivering it. Sometimes this requires preparation, perhaps even rehearsal. You also need to be aware of the state your partner is in. If she or he has just come home from a difficult mediation session with their ex-spouse, it is not the time to raise a sensitive issue.

2. Be clear and straightforward. Clear and straightforward messages can feel risky. You may be afraid of being criticized, hurting your partner's feelings, or not getting what you ask for. In fact, it is usually indirect or unclear messages that usually produce the very upset and anger that you are trying to avoid. In addition, you cannot get the understanding and intimacy you want unless you are honest about your feelings and thoughts. Some suggestions for clear and straightforward communication are:

   • Do not ask questions when you want to make a statement.
   • Use "I" messages when expressing your thoughts, feelings, and needs.
   • Focus on one thing at a time.

3. Be honest. Are you afraid of hurting the other person's feelings by being honest? If so, ask yourself if this thought or feeling has been persistent. If it has, then it is probably important that you share it with your partner. Remember, you can be honest while still using tact and consideration.

4. Be respectful and supportive. Name calling, sarcasm, threats, and unwillingness to listen to or consider your partner's opinions are all ways of communicating disrespect. You can respect your partner's opinion whether you agree or not. You can show your support by acknowledging your partner's feelings, whether or not her or his reactions make sense to you.

Applying These Listening and Expressing Skills[6]

There are entire books and courses designed to teach better communication skills (you will find a few listed at the end of this chapter). The model that follows is not meant to be a substitute, but it will give you a glimpse of the skills you can acquire by focusing on improving your listening and expressing skills.

Step 1. Self-Awareness

Good communication depends on understanding yourself and sharing that understanding with your partner. As a general rule, women are more skilled at responding to the experience of others than they are at clarifying their own. This section is aimed at helping women more accurately clarify their own experience.

First, how do you *interpret* a situation or interaction? Interpretations are the biases through which you view something. They are based on your unique past, present, and anticipated future experience. People sometimes believe that interpretations are facts when they are actually only one way of looking at something. Because of this, two people can participate in the same conversation and interpret it differently. It would be better to think of an interpretation as a tentative possibility rather than a confirmed reality.

Second, what information do your *senses* provide? Touch, smell, sight, taste, and sound all provide raw data. They are the tools a good scientist or journalist uses to observe and describe something. Your senses provide objective facts ("You're smiling") into which you fold your subjective interpretations ("You're happy" or "You think I'm being silly").

Third, how do you *feel?* Feelings are your spontaneous and uncensored emotional responses. They are often associated with a physical response in your body. They run the gamut from feeling scared (with associated symptoms of rapid breathing, sweaty palms, racing heart, and churning stomach) to feeling embarrassed (blushing) to feeling content (relaxed face and shoulders, regular breathing).

Feelings are sometimes difficult to identify because you often feel several ways at once, and the intensity may vary. You also tend to push away many of your feelings. Rather than simply acknowledge them, you judge them as inappropriate, confusing, or unacceptable. You may not realize how you really feel about something for days or even years.

Your feelings are valuable indicators of your unique emotional response. You can enhance your recognition of your feelings by paying particular attention to how you are responding to someone, especially your physical response. For example, your boss has just told you that your 10 percent raise has been approved by higher management. A smile comes to your face as she tells you about it. You notice that you appreciate the raise and feel pleased. However, no sooner has she given you this information than she starts complaining that you do not show her sufficient loyalty. As she starts, a sourness develops in your stomach. You feel your body tighten, and you want to run out of the room. You feel angry, guarded, frightened, and anxious. Because she is your boss, there is little you can do directly about this second set of feelings, but it is important to acknowledge them to yourself. Thank her for the news about the raise and acknowledge how pleased you are to receive it. After you are in a safer environment, deal with your other feelings.

Fourth, what are your *intentions?* Your intentions are what you want or how you would like things to be. Intentions can be pleasant (to praise) or unpleasant (to exploit), be long range ("I want to save enough to buy a home in five years") or short range ("I want to take a ten-minute coffee break now"), and have broad goals ("I want economic security") or narrow goals ("I want to walk two miles a day within three months").

Women have not always been encouraged to identify their own intentions, and it may be difficult to be clear about your intentions when you want several things that are in conflict. For example: "Part of me wants to be with you and part of me wants to be alone right now." You can increase your awareness of your intentions by asking yourself "What do I want right now?" Believe your behavior. Whatever you are saying with your mouth, your actions reflect a stronger intention. You are doing what you want.

Finally, what are your *actions?* Actions are patterns of behavior that include what you did in the past ("I spent all day Saturday doing chores for the family"), what you are doing now ("I am wrapping my sister's birthday gift"), or what you plan to do in the future ("Next Sunday we are having a party to celebrate our ten-year anniversary"). Future actions are different than intentions in that actions are what you definitely *will* do. They reflect a commitment, not something more tentative that you want to do but may or may not accomplish.

Step 2. Other-Awareness

Good communication also depends upon empathic attention to your partner's experience. This means that your partner must be self-disclosing. They need to let you know what they are thinking and feeling rather than expecting you to guess. Women are usually better at other-awareness than self-awareness; for men, it is often the reverse. (There are, of course, exceptions.) Nevertheless, even the most intuitive partner can enhance her understanding of her companion by following these six principles.

First, learning to understand your companion better begins with *attentive listening and observing.* Start by giving your undivided attention. This includes listening very consciously without making judgments or formulating your response. Pay attention to all communication—verbal and nonverbal. Use all the sensory data available. Notice your partner's posture, body movements, and facial expressions. The tone of their voice and its volume and tempo are also useful information. Collecting as much information as possible will increase the likelihood of interpreting your partner correctly.

Second, when you listen more attentively, you will usually be rewarded by discovering that your partner will find it easier to self-disclose. You can *invite even more self-disclosure* by giving your partner encouragement through the judicious use of nonverbal cues and verbal acknowledgment. Nonverbal cues can be a nod of the head, a smile, keeping direct eye contact, or murmuring "uh-huh." Verbal acknowledgments include comments like "That's interesting" or "I can't understand what you're saying. Could you repeat it for me?" It also means putting aside anything else you might be doing to give your partner your undivided attention.

Third, *do not assume that you immediately understand* what your partner is saying. *Check it out.* Because your partner may offer only partial information, you will need to ask specific questions. For example, your partner may have told you what she or he thinks about something but not how she or he feels or what she or he would like to have happen. You can ask. You can also ask if an interpretation you have arrived at is correct. By being tentative, you are able to gain more information and show respect for your partner's integrity. Sometimes this is also a very good way to clear the air when there has been a misunderstanding.

When checking things out, there are at least two cautions to keep in mind.

- Avoid asking why questions. These almost always stimulate a defensive response in the listener. Do your best to change a why question to a what, where, how, who, or when question. For example, "What prompted you to buy a new car instead of having the old one repaired?" rather than "Why did you buy a new car?"
- Be careful not to ask leading questions under the guise of checking something out. These kinds of questions are meant to persuade your partner rather than understand what they want. Be as direct as possible and don't attempt to disguise your communication. For example, "I'm disappointed, hurt, and angry that you did not remember our anniversary. What happened?" as opposed to "Aren't you glad we're together? You forgot our anniversary!"

Learning to check things out greatly enhances understanding between partners. Rather than assuming you have understood your partner's communication, checking things out effectively and honestly allows you to affirm accurate interpretations and correct misunderstandings. As you increase your understanding of each other, you have a better sense of what to expect from each other. This kind of predictability makes it possible to increase your sense of trust and being connected.

Fourth, communication is so complex that *it is common to discover that what you thought you heard was not what I thought I said.* Good communication means working toward a shared meaning. You have a shared meaning when the message sent by you is the message received by me. You can arrive at a shared meaning by going through a logical, straightforward process of

1. stating your intention to share a meaning,
2. giving your message,
3. having your partner report the message back in her or his own words, and
4. confirming or clarifying the accuracy of your partner's understanding.

You need to repeat steps 3 and 4 until the message sent and the message received are the same. Affirming that you have arrived at a shared message is decided by the sender, because only the sender knows what was really meant.

Here is a conflict between a couple who do not use this process:

"I don't like it when your family comes to visit."

"Well, I can't tell them not to come."

"I never said you should."

Here is the same conflict between a couple who work toward a shared meaning[7]:

"I don't like it when your family comes to visit." (You have given a message.)

"Hey, wait a minute. I'd like to be sure I'm reading you right. OK?" (Your partner is stating her or his intention to work toward a shared meaning.)

"OK."

"What I understand you to mean is that you wish my family weren't coming. Is that it?" (Your partner is reporting the message you gave in their own words.)

"That's part of it. I just feel annoyed that they will be with us for two weeks. I'm afraid that I won't get much time with you alone while they are here." (You are clarifying your original message.)

"The main thing is that we don't get enough time alone together when they are here." (Your partner is reporting back a second time working on getting closer to a shared meaning.)

"Right. That's what I am really upset about. Now, what would you think about . . ." (As the sender of the original message, you have just confirmed that you and your partner have arrived at a shared meaning. You are now ready to work together to solve this problem.)

You know you have arrived at a shared meaning when the partners feel good about the communication even if they have different points of views. They are likely to be nodding their heads in agreement and making direct and comfortable eye contact. Often, they will be smiling.

Fifth, all of these skills will help you and your partner discover that *you differ on many things.* In fact, being two unique individuals, you will inevitably discover that you sometimes disagree strongly on issues. It is perfectly natural to discover that you agree and disagree about a large number of things. Each person has their own perspective of reality.

These differences can be viewed either as a threat or an opportunity. Viewed as a threat, the partners assume that one person is right and the other is wrong. Viewed as an opportunity to learn, discussing differences can lead to greater intimacy. Each couple must have enough agreement to live with comfort and trust, but many differences and disagreements can be perfectly acceptable, provided they are seen as opportunities for growth—both personally and for the relationship. Growth is much more dependent on understanding than agreement.

Finally *one area where agreement is necessary is on the rules you and your partner use when discussing issues.* These rules help keep your discussions constructive. Here are the key factors to be taken into consideration:

1. What to talk about.
   Start a discussion by agreeing on the issue under consideration.
2. Whose issue it is.
   It is important to determine if the issue is yours, your partner's, or both. This is especially important if the issue belongs only to you and you want your partner to function as your consultant.
3. Who is included.
   Will the discussion include just the partners or will children or other people be included?
4. Where to talk.
   Selecting a comfortable place to talk is important and prevents distractions.
5. When to talk.
   Deciding the best time to talk about a sensitive issue is very important. It is better to select a time when you will both feel like talking and can give the matter your full attention.
6. How to talk.
   If the problem belongs to only one partner, will the other person act as a facilitator? Do you want to work toward a mutually satisfying decision or will this likely be a win/lose debate?
7. Energy available to deal with this issue.
   Sometimes a concern takes more energy to address than you have at the moment. If this is the case, it is better to delay until you both feel up to it.

8. Length.

Rather than allowing a discussion to drag on for hours and hours, exhausting you physically and emotionally, it may be wise to set a limit ahead of time. You can decide that you will end your discussion, at least temporarily, at a pre–agreed upon time and come back to it later when you are both refreshed.

9. Stopping the discussion.

Akin to having a preset time agreement about stopping, it is helpful to have some common rule that allows you to stop a discussion if one or both of you wishes to. This allows either of you to call a time out if further discussion at that time would be unproductive. Of course, the implied agreement is that you will come back to the discussion at a later time.

You will not need this list every time you discuss something. For the most part, just agreeing on the rules for handling concerns is half the job. "The spirit of willingness to work together and support each other is a powerful force in a relationship."[8]

Step 3. Styles of Talking

There are at least four styles of communicating. Each style matches certain intentions and is reflected by complementary behaviors. Good communication requires flexibility and the ability to use all styles effectively at the appropriate time.

First, the *sociable style* is friendly, light, and playful. People are communicating in a comfortable way. Their intention is to be pleasant and they are not interested in changing anything: "Lily and Harry said they really enjoyed vegetarian food. I hope this Mediterranean stew strikes their fancy."

Second, the *control style* is used when you want to be in charge. Your intention is to get something done your way. It can be brief and efficient, but as a result, it leaves open the opportunity for misunderstanding. People can use *light control* when they are giving orders, providing instruction, offering advice, or trying to sell something. The intention is to obtain agreement or compliance through persuasion. Their voice may be a little loud and authoritative: "We're supposed to meet Jim and Betty at the restaurant at 7:30. We need to be dressed and ready to leave the house by 7:10!"

People use *heavy control* when their feelings are very strong and they are trying to force the issue. This style is aggressive. It is a threat to a relationship because it is directed at a person. It can undermine a partner's self-esteem by questioning or attacking her or his motives or competence: "This wouldn't happen if you weren't so irresponsible."

Heavy control can also be exercised in a very powerful, but passive and quiet way. By keeping score, not answering a partner's questions, changing the subject, or refusing to talk, the communicator is manipulating her or his partner through the indirect expression of her or his intentions.

All of us have a lot of experience with this heavy-handed style, so it is easy to find ourselves using it. It is a signal that a very sensitive area has been touched upon. In and of itself, this need not be an overwhelming problem if the couple view its appearance as a clue that something needs to be addressed between them. However, little useful communication can occur if the speaker stays in this style. Because of the power differential between women and men, this style frequently crops up when a heterosexual couple is engaged in a power struggle. They must move beyond this controlling style if they wish to address their conflict in a constructive way.

Third, a *searching style* is used when you are reflecting on a situation or issue. While the purpose of a social style is to keep things going smoothly and that of a controlling style is to change things, a searching style allows you to step back from the action and explore the situation: "I'd like to talk about what makes sense to do after the baby is born. Is it best to have one of us be the primary parent and have the other be a backup or would it work better if we shared working and parenting more or less equally?"

This style is an intellectual activity with little emotional involvement or commitment to take action, although there is almost always an issue being discussed. The value of this style is in opening up ideas and expanding options. It is very helpful when dealing with important and potentially sensitive issues because it permits a great deal of tentative exploration and discussion prior to making a decision.

Finally, a *centered style* is used when your communication is direct and action-oriented. Focused on the present, you acknowledge and accept your experience and act on this awareness. A centered style of communication incorporates a spirit of sharing and valuing both yourself and your partner.

The capacity to communicate in a centered style is critical for women and men who want healthy relationships. It is a cooperative style that reflects caring and mutual support, and it is the style we use to share our private feelings and thoughts. Honest, clear, responsive, and responsible, it is the style that builds true intimacy between partners.

This dialogue between Carol and Matthew provides a good example of this kind of communication:

Carol: I get annoyed and frustrated with you when I'm really anxious about something and you just keep saying "Relax." I hear this as a discounting of my feelings. It doesn't comfort me or make me feel relaxed. I just get more upset because I start thinking that you don't understand how disturbed I am.

Matthew: Uh-huh. Can you give me an example?

Carol: OK. Last night when we were driving home from the movie in the new car, the turn signal wasn't working properly. Every time I tried to signal a right turn, the bright lights came on along with the flasher. It was dark, I couldn't figure out what the problem was, there was a lot of traffic, and you kept reaching over trying to do it yourself.

Matthew: As I remember it, I was just trying to help. You seemed to be getting upset, and I just wanted to try to do what I could to help out.

Carol: Well, it didn't feel helpful.

Matthew: You know, when you get anxious, I start getting a little anxious, too. Saying "Relax" is as much for me as for you. I'm just trying to calm us both down. But it doesn't work. That seems obvious. I just haven't been able to think of anything else to do.

Carol: This gets to the core of the problem, I think. When I'm tired, it is much easier for me to become overly anxious. Yesterday I was feeling overwhelmed by that new project at work that has to be done before we leave on vacation in two weeks. I set the alarm for six A.M.—on a Saturday, no less—to finish the first part of the report before I started running around doing all the things necessary to sell the old car. Once I finally did get to the dealership in the afternoon, it took a lot longer to negotiate the price for the new car than I thought it would *and* when I pay $10,000 for something, I expect it to work. But what really bugs me the most is that you don't seem to take these things seriously. You'll accept something not working just right—even if you've paid a lot of money for it. So last night I started thinking if I wanted the car fixed I'd have to arrange it and I didn't know how I was going to find the time to do that. If I waited for you, it might never get done because you just don't care enough.

Matthew: It's true that these things don't upset me as much as you, but it's not because I don't care about them. It's just that I don't think they have to be fixed right away. Look, honey, it's a new car and everything is under warranty. They'll fix it whenever we have a chance to take it in. Even if we don't have time to do it before we come back from vacation, it will be OK. We don't drive that much at night anyway.

Carol: (Laughing) It didn't even occur to me to think about it that way.

Matthew: Is there something else I can do when you're feeling anxious to help make the situation better instead of worse?

Carol: Well, maybe we could create some kind of signal that we've agreed upon ahead of time. How about something like: "Let's take ten minutes to cool out about this and then talk about how to deal with it?" Do you think you could say that instead of "Relax! Just relax!"

Matthew: I'll sure try. It's hard for me to change on this. I'm not sure I'll
   be able to do it right away, but I'll do my best, OK?"
Carol: I'd really appreciate that. And I'll make more of an effort to calm
   myself down. Now that I know it's not your intention to discount my
   concerns, I might be able to see your comments more as attempts to
   soothe my feelings rather than minimize them. OK, I feel much
   better about this now. I think we'll both handle it better next time."

This style of communication in female-male relationships can be difficult to
master. Fortunately, this is not because of any intrinsic deficiency on the part of
women or men. It is primarily caused by lack of experience. Women—both
individually and as a group—have been actively discouraged from accurately
identifying, valuing, and acting upon their own experiences. They have been
encouraged to identify with the experience of others, especially children and men,
and accommodate to their needs rather than be direct about their own. Men have
been trained to focus upon their own needs and have been socialized to expect
to be catered to. They often have had little experience in valuing their partners'
needs as much as their own. Both women and men have some learning to do if
they want to add this essential ingredient to their relationship.

Although essential for long-term relationships, a centered style is too heavy
for ordinary conversations, where a social style makes more sense. It is inefficient
for handling everyday decisions where a blend of light control and searching would
work better. It is also not wise to use with people you do not trust. If you share
your vulnerabilities with people who are not trustworthy, they may use this
information to hurt you.

Step 4. Enhancing Self-esteem: Yours and Your Partner's

The emphasis here is on what you do—not what your partner does. The essential
attitude is valuing—valuing yourself and your partner. Valuing yourself means
being clear about what you are feeling and what you want for yourself. Valuing
your partner means listening attentively and working to interpret your partner's
communications until you arrive at a shared meaning.

If you value a person—whether yourself or another person—you make a
specific set of assumptions:

- you have faith in your intention to treat each person as important,
- you have confidence in your ability to handle a situation, and you are
  comfortable recognizing what help is needed,
- you trust in the willingness of your partner to follow through on promises,
  and
- you are committed to each other's well-being.

If you discount or devalue a person—whether yourself or someone else—you
make just the opposite set of assumptions:

- little or no faith,
- little or no confidence,
- little or no trust, and
- little or no commitment to each other's well-being.

The foundation of your relationship depends on these attitudes. You can measure how much you value or devalue yourself and how much you value or devalue your partner by considering specific behaviors.

You value yourself

- when you allow yourself to acknowledge you own experience in all its dimensions,
- when you permit self-awareness, including thoughts, feelings, actions, and intentions that you find unpleasant,
- when you share this self-awareness with others when it is appropriate, and
- when you accept responsibility for your own decisions and actions.

You devalue yourself

- when you disregard your self-awareness,
- when you do not fully accept your own experience,
- when you fail to self-disclose when it is appropriate to do so, and
- when you do not accept responsibility for your own decisions and actions.

You value your partner

- when you pay attention to her or him and the expression of her or his own self-awarenesses,
- when you respect and acknowledge your partner's thoughts, feelings, and intentions as much as your own even when you disagree with them or find them unpleasant,
- when you invite or encourage your partner to express self-awareness when it is appropriate,
- when you act in ways that demonstrate caring for and enjoyment of your partner,
- when you leave room for your partner to express differences from you and even appreciate the differences between you, and
- when you provide useful feedback.

You devalue your partner

- when you ignore or refuse to accept and acknowledge your partner's experience as her or his own,
- when you deny real differences between the two of you or insist that your partner be just like you,
- when you try to take responsibility for your partner's decisions and actions,

- when you act in ways that demonstrate a failure to care for your partner, and
- when you avoid giving your partner useful feedback.

When feelings are strong, you can choose to respond in a way that

1. Devalues yourself and devalues your partner. (This implies that neither person can take charge. There is an air of hopelessness and despair as you leave the destiny of your relationship to chance.)
2. Devalues yourself but values your partner. (In this case, you are acting the martyr or attempting to placate your partner. In a situation of unequal power, as is all too common in female-male relationships, this may be adaptive. However, it does not reflect a healthy relationship.)
3. Values yourself but devalues your partner. (This is a win/lose situation in which you are assuming that you are right. Many unresolved fights are due to partners trading this position back and forth. Often they do not even know what they are fighting about. But *you are choosing to fight!*)
4. Values yourself and values your partner. (This is the healthiest option!)

The best relationships are those in which no one is devalued. By exercising this choice, you are demonstrating your commitment to your own well-being and your partner's. You are also initiating a sequence of communications that can create a context for developing understanding and mutual satisfaction. When reciprocated by your partner, you are assured a communication that will not only enhance your self-esteem and your partner's, but will also enhance the quality of your relationship.

When you and your partner are disagreeing, communicating this attitude can be a real challenge. But remember, every communication is a choice. Even in the face of a devaluing statement from your partner, you can choose to respond with a valuing statement.

Tasks for Couples Who Want to Improve Their Relationship[9]

There are specific behavioral strategies a couple can learn to use if they want to enhance their ability to communicate in ways that value them both. Their efforts will allow them to improve their ability to deal with individual differences while remaining emotionally close. These strategies encourage each person to be clear about him- or herself while learning what their partner wants and needs.

Partners may discover that some of their desires are nonnegotiable while others are only preferences and are thus open to negotiation.[10] Some of the information will be new and, perhaps, even upsetting. However, persevering will permit partners to enhance their capacity for collaboration, mutual negotiation, and problem solving. Couples who participate in these tasks with the intention of genuinely learning about themselves and each other will be well on their way to improving the quality of their relationship.

Task 1: Listening and Talking

Purpose: This task is a kind of sorting through. The agreement for this task is that one person is committed to speak and the other person is committed to listen.

It allows each individual to separate who they really are from who their partner thinks they are.

Instructions: A couple agrees on a regular time to meet each week for one hour without interruption. During that hour, each partner is going to listen for a half hour while the other speaks, and then they will switch roles. No other action is required or permitted.

Decide who goes first by flipping a coin. The first speaker is to talk about themselves for a half hour. Their partner is to listen attentively without making any verbal response. When the time is up, the second partner is to speak. Again, the topic is to be only things about themselves. Each partner may talk about their own needs, desires, wishes, frustrations, fantasies, joys, or hurts. They may not talk about their partner or the relationship—only about themselves.

Once both partners have spoken and listened attentively, the assignment is complete. The partners are to have no further discussion of what was shared, and at no time may they respond to each other. If they wish to discuss any of the communications shared, they must wait at least three days to do so. For example, the couple might set aside an evening later in the week, say Wednesday after dinner, to discuss the comments made by either partner the previous Saturday.

Comments: By structuring the time so that one person talks about themselves while the other person listens, the usual continuous flowing together of one person's ideas and thoughts with the other person's is broken. This is important because unproductive arguments often involve preparing to respond to what our partner has said rather than really listening to what our partner is saying.

By setting up an agreement simply to listen, we have a much better chance of actually understanding our partner. It also allows us to recognize the ways in which we are different from our partner. For some people, facing differences can be profoundly upsetting. These couples live with the mistaken belief that there cannot be, nor should there be, any differences between them.

This exercise makes it clear that there is a distinction between partners. If one person listens and cannot speak, she or he is respecting the other partner's individuality. Each person is also dealing with the reality of human aloneness. Ironically, as each partner listens to the other with full attention as they talk about themselves, the couple ends up feeling more intimate. For people who come from dysfunctional families, it is often an entirely foreign experience to feel connected and separate at the same time. They have rarely had the opportunity to learn that remaining empathic yet separate actually promotes a sense of closeness.

Task 2: Intimacy Requests

Purpose: People who are in troubled relationships mistakenly believe that there is only one way to be in an intimate relationship: control or be controlled. Intimacy requests allow a couple to actively experience sharing control, power, and nurturing and to learn to circumvent power struggles.

Instructions: This second task is added to the first listening and talking exercise. It is aimed at training the partners in how to nurture each other and, through this process, to nurture their relationship. For this task, the days are divided between them. One takes half the days of the week, perhaps Monday, Wednesday, and Friday. The other takes three of the remaining days, Tuesday, Thursday, and Saturday. Sunday is a free day. On his or her assigned day, each partner makes one intimacy request. The other partner promises to meet that request.

Certain rules must be followed to assure success:

1. Requests need to be specific and relatively modest. The requesting partner must make a request that the other partner can clearly do. By giving simple directions of easily achievable behaviors, the partner can readily respond. For example, "I would like you to take a walk with me this afternoon—just the two of us" as opposed to "I would like you to love me forever," which does not describe a behavior and cannot be achieved in one day.
2. Every effort needs to be made to avoid requests that place your partner in a conflictual situation. For example, if your partner is expected to be at the school that evening to meet with your daughter's teacher, it is not wise to ask her or him to go to a movie with you.
3. Avoid requests in areas that usually precipitate arguments. Rather than making and responding to intimacy requests, you will find yourselves again in a power struggle. Sex, money, and any other topic that is especially sensitive in your relationship is off limits.

Comments: Unlike the typical power struggle, agreeing ahead of time to distribute the requests and responses equally over the course of a week allows each partner to safely "give in" to the other without inordinate fear or anxiety that the requests will become insatiable and unending. If one or both partners secretly desires to maintain the power differential, they will behave in a manner that assures this outcome. For example, if the more powerful partner does not want to alter her or his status, she or he may simply refuse to participate in these tasks or sabotage them. If this behavior continues for any length of time, the less powerful person may abandon all hope of having his or her needs met.

If there is a power differential and the couple agrees that they want a healthier relationship, each will have to make changes to equalize the balance of power. When practiced regularly, these two tasks will prove to be subtle, yet powerful, tools in initiating this change. The couple will discover that each is able to be increasingly close while retaining a solid sense of self. They will grow more comfortable with intimacy while assuring that no individuality is lost in the process. Each partner becomes empowered rather than remaining locked in a painful and ultimately destructive conflict.

A Starting Point

This section provides only the bare bones of what it takes to develop good communication skills. Please do not expect yourself to improve simply by reading this section. Few of us have been thoughtfully and carefully trained to communicate in a respectful and positive manner. Many of us have grown up in families, been educated in schools, and worked at jobs where power differentials are prevalent and permanent. In these settings, we have had little opportunity to emulate and practice flexible and effective communication skills. Nevertheless, we are all capable of learning better ones—no matter our age, gender, ethnic background, intelligence, education, or economic status. The quickest improvement takes place within the context of a relationship with someone else who also wants to learn. Attend a workshop together, share a self-help book, listen to a training tape, or set aside regular time to do relationship work. If both partners work at improving their skills, they can increase their understanding of each other. The rewards will be immediate and noticeable. Clearer understanding builds more satisfying, secure, and intimate relationships. Those who have made this challenging journey report that it is well worth the effort.

NOTES

1. Virginia Satir, *Making Contact* (Millbrae, Calif.: Celestial Arts, 1976).

2. Richard B. Stuart and Barbara Jacobson, *Second Marriage* (New York: W. W. Norton, 1985), pp. 94–95.

3. Stuart and Jacobson, *Second Marriage*, p. 103.

4. D. Merilee Clunis and G. Dorsey Green, *Lesbian Couples* (Seattle: Seal Press, 1988), pp. 166–171.

5. Adapted from Clunis and Green, *Lesbian Couples*, pp. 171–173.

6. Sherod Miller, Elam Nunnally, and Daniel Wackman, *Couple Communication I: Talking Together* (Minneapolis, Minn.: Interpersonal Communications Program, Inc., 1979).

7. Adapted from Miller, Nunnally, and Wackman, *Couple Communication I,* p. 76.

8. Miller, Nunnally, and Wackman, *Couple Communication I.*

9. Tasks 1 and 2 are adapted from chapter 10 of *Intimate Partners* by Maggie Scarf (New York: Random House, 1987).

10. A partner with greater power can override the desires of a less powerful partner, even those that are actually nonnegotiable. However, getting what is wanted in this way does not lead to a healthy relationship.

Constructive Conflict

Conflict is inevitable. It is a part of life. Healthy and loving couples with good communication skills have conflicts. Dysfunctional families with limited communication skills have conflicts. If we are in a relationship, at some point we are going to come in conflict. It is as simple as that. But few women—or men—have learned how to manage conflict constructively.

Conflict is built on wanting. Women are taught early in life that wanting is greedy, selfish, demanding, and not nice. Good little girls wait until something is offered, share what they have, and do not ask directly for what they want. Through this training, women come to believe that other people's needs are more important than their own. Getting something for themselves means that someone else is deprived. Thus for many women, conflict has strongly negative associations.

Misuses of power within relationships have contributed to the belief that conflict is almost always a power struggle in which one person wins and the other person loses. From this perspective, conflict is perceived as uncomfortable, painful, and to be avoided. This avoidance is often so complete that a woman does not even know what she wants. Unfortunately, ignoring, minimizing, or negating her own desires does not make them go away.

The ability to recognize and express wants is linked to self-esteem, a healthy sense of one's self as a valued and valuable person. In order to use conflict constructively, a woman needs to believe it's okay to want; I deserve to have my needs met; I have a right to ask directly for what I want. When a woman has low self-esteem, she is likely to be unclear about what she wants. She may feel disappointed, hurt, deprived, angry, betrayed, or cheated when her desires are repeatedly unmet. Her feelings often remain unidentified or unexpressed because she is fearful, anxious, or inexperienced in constructive conflict. When conflicts are not dealt with openly and directly, indirect communication begins to emerge. The woman becomes depressed, anxious, or physically ill.

For many women, it is hard to undo their cultural training and come to believe that they have the right to have their own desires acknowledged. Depending on their experiences in their families, adult women may believe that there should either be no disagreements in intimate relationships, that disagreements are best resolved by bowing to the person with greater power, or that disagreements inevitably lead to violence. These beliefs encourage women to placate rather than negotiate.

Everyone has the right to want things. Indeed, some of the things we want will be essential if we are to remain in a particular relationship. In any relationship, however, there are things we want that we do not get. Wanting is not the same as getting. While we may not like this reality, we can live with it if what we do get is good enough.

Before we assume that what we want is impossible to achieve, we must bring it up with our partner. This may lead to conflict, but conflict is a normal and predictable part of any relationship. It is not the presence or absence of conflict that determines the health of a relationship, it is how partners deal with this conflict. Negotiating differences, making compromises, acknowledging genuine but temporary power differences, and learning to function cooperatively are all healthy ways to deal with conflict.

The Role of Power in a Relationship

Two individuals choose to form a partnership because they each give something to the other that makes them feel better being together than apart. During the romance stage of their relationship, each feels nurtured and connected to the other in some important way. However, after the glow of romance has worn off, it is what they do with conflict and power that really determines the quality of their relationship. The ability to share power is the number-one "secret" of successful partnerships; the way a couple handles conflict is critically dependent on how power is perceived and used in their relationship.

Power can be defined in a variety of ways. Historically, we have come to think of power as "power over." That is, the authority, privilege, or capacity to compel a less powerful person to do what a more powerful person wants. When power is used in this way, it maintains relationships of permanent inequality in which one person is of lesser value by virtue of some arbitrary factor such as gender, race, class, nationality, or religion. There is no notion that the person with more power and status aims to end the inequality. Indeed, this type of power enforces continuing inequality instead of teaching us how to move from unequal to equal.

We can just as easily think of power as "the capacity to make things happen."[1] This kind of power is evident in relationships of temporary inequality in which the person of lower power or status is not expected to remain unequal. In these relationships, the more powerful person has some ability or quality that they aim to impart to the less powerful person. Examples of these kinds of relationships are those between parents and children, teachers and students, and therapists and clients. In each case, one person has something that when shared with the other person will work toward equalizing the relationship. This something may be more emotional maturity, more experience in the world, a body of knowledge, or techniques for acquiring certain expertise or some physical skill.

In any intimate relationship, power must be equal if the relationship is to be healthy. When the power balance is not equitable, resentments build and emotional distress is inevitable.[2] Yet in spite of the recent women's movement, equal power in female-male relationships is the exception rather than the rule. It is true that working women, regardless of social class, do have more power than unpaid homemakers, but a woman's power is reduced following the birth of her first child unless the child's father shares equal responsibility for childcare. In relationships where this does not occur, a woman's position is progressively undermined by successive births. The younger the wife, the shorter the time before the birth of the first child, and the closer the children are spaced, the less power she has. The disadvantages are greatest for the wife who was pregnant at the time of her marriage and for wives who carry the entire burden of household tasks.

Equality can occur in heterosexual relationships only when the man views any gender-based power differential as an injustice. These men see their female partner as having intrinsic worth equal to their own in spite of what their culture proclaims.[3] In these companionship relationships, satisfaction rather than longevity is the couple's basis for evaluating the success of their relationship. The division of labor is based on preference and agreement rather than gender. It is not expected that men will do "men's work" and women will do "women's work." The couple emphasizes personal happiness rather than duty and respect, self-expression rather than subordination, and assimilation rather than accommodation as a means of resolving conflict. Each person is sustained and nurtured by internal feelings, especially love and growing mutual identification, rather than external legal constraints. The chief objective is a relationship between two people rather than two roles.[4]

No woman can safely entrust her heart and well-being to a man who does not live by these beliefs. Genuine intimacy is impossible in any relationship unless each partner feels equally important and equally valuable. But, even when a couple creates a companionship relationship and shares power, they will still experience conflict.

No Relationship Is Conflict Free

Often conflict arises between partners as they strive to sustain a sense of themselves as individuals while they remain attached to each other. Most of us desire both to maintain our individuality and to be in a close relationship. Sometimes it can feel as if these two are in conflict. We want to do what we want when we want to do it. Yet if doing what we want jeopardizes our relationship, we are likely to feel inhibited, worried, guilty, angry, sad, or threatened. We are faced with deciding which is more important to us—getting our own way while displeasing our partner or placing our relationship first while denying our individual desires.

Unless each partner is able to balance her or his internal desires for individuality and connectedness, the couple may find themselves in confusing and upsetting arguments. Instead of containing their personal struggles, they play it out in their relationship. Since this conflict can take many forms, the underlying individual effort to strike a balance between freedom and intimacy can be difficult to recognize—and difficult to resolve. Trying to establish the balance becomes a problem *between* the partners rather than a problem for each of them as individuals.

Among married couples, this struggle is most commonly expressed as the woman wanting more closeness and the man wanting more freedom.[5] The woman complains that she cannot get enough warmth and intimacy, while the man complains that he cannot get enough privacy and space. She describes him as undemonstrative, superlogical, and emotionally unreachable. He describes her as hysterical, clinging, and demanding.

Among unmarried heterosexual couples, the man may insist that he does not want to marry, while the woman insists that she does. Actually, each is understandably ambivalent and anxious about making this degree of commitment to another person. Instead of acknowledging their personal and individual concerns, he carries the argument for freedom while she carries the argument for closeness. They hassle it out between them rather than sorting through their own mixed feelings.

Among lesbian couples, this conflict is most commonly expressed as terminal kindness. Female couples can easily slip into excessive togetherness and have more difficulty sustaining their individuality. When they touch on differences, they try to smooth them over. They act as if neither has any needs or interests that are different from or at odds with the other's. Yet if a woman denies that she is separate and different from her partner, the relationship will only appear to be intimate. Unable to fully acknowledge individual desires, needs, and interests, the couple get stuck in a quiet, but troublesome, conflict. Their peace at any price erodes intimacy just as surely as more openly volatile battles.

Any intimate relationship is a voluntary arrangement between two separate individuals who want to be close and attached. Every couple must determine how to balance their needs for closeness with their needs for individuality and freedom. If you and your partner find yourselves avoiding touchy subjects or locking horns in fights that never seem to be resolved, consider the possibility that you are dealing with this most common conflict in any intimate relationship.

Balancing Needs

How do couples learn to balance these needs? The training actually begins in the earliest years of life. Healthy development requires that infants are raised in one or more emotional relationships with loving and protective caretakers. These caretakers can be thought of as attachment figures. Researchers believe that children experience these caretakers as special and loving partners with whom the child can form intense emotional bonds. The quality of these early emotional bonds are believed to have a significant impact upon later psychological health. They also serve as the child's models for future loving relationships.

In healthy parent-child relationships, the developing child experiences a measure of relative safety, care, and concern over a long period of time. The growing mutual attachment between child and caretaker motivates each to view the other's nearness and well-being as emotionally essential.[6] Yet even in the earliest period of life, we have evidence that infants recognize their caretakers are separate human beings.

Even very young children quickly realize that the human beings upon whom they depend can also leave. If children have adequate substitute care during these periodic separations from their attachment figures, they will grow assured that relationships can allow for both intimacy and freedom. Periodic age-appropriate separations from primary caretakers allow children to discover that they can master their fears of separation, that they can transfer their trust to substitute caretakers, and that they can rely on their loved ones to return. These experiences allow children to develop a solid foundation and realistic expectations for future adult relationships.

When we fall in love as adults, the old feelings and experiences from these early years can become reactivated. Couples who enter relationships with a legacy of inner security and emotional health from early childhood relationships find it relatively easy to adapt to loving but separate partners. They can also adapt in healthy ways to the changes and growth that inevitably occur in any adult relationship. The healthy couple's attachment becomes stronger and more intimate as each partner is able to expand, flourish, and attain their full potential within the context of their connection.

Inadequate parenting, poor substitute care, or lengthy separations can prevent the development of a secure emotional foundation. An adult with this early history may be fortunate enough to pair with someone from a healthier background. If so, the healthier person may be able to offset the anxiety of the more insecure partner. More often than not, an insecure adult enters a primary relationship with an equally insecure partner. In these relationships, there is less trust, less closeness, and less mutual attentiveness to each other's needs and wishes. Feeling inadequately nurtured and valued, these partners try to extract what they want from each other by manipulation or force rather than by a process of mutually satisfying collaboration and negotiation. This inevitably leads to a struggle for control.

Neither they nor their relationship is adequately nurtured, and their capacity for intimacy is severely undermined.

Achieving a balance between individuality and attachment in an adult relationship is especially problematic if there is a power imbalance. If the more powerful member exercises excessive authority, the less powerful person is at a disadvantage. In an argument, the conflict may be temporarily "resolved" by the less powerful person accommodating to the desires of the more powerful. Because the couple has not really negotiated around their differences, the relationship is marred by simmering resentment, ongoing emotional distress, or continual outright warfare. If the more powerful partner repeatedly insists on getting his or her way, negotiation and collaborative behavior is impossible. Even in relationships between partners of relatively equal power, conflicts still arise around the issue of balancing the needs of the individuals and the needs of the relationship.

Making Changes

We live in a highly competitive society that has indoctrinated many of us in believing that for one partner to win, the other must lose. This is not true for relationships. In relationships, there is never a winner and a loser. If a couple engages in unhealthy conflict, both lose. If the conflict is productive, both win and the health of the relationship is improved.

Resolving conflict requires some kind of change, and it is rarely easy or simple. There are five major obstacles to making behavioral changes:[7]

1. Inertia. In any relationship, there is an inherent resistance to change. Once a pattern is established, it tends to stay in a rather steady state.
2. Pride. Frequently, both partners feel as if they have been victimized in their relationship. There is a reluctance to be the "I will change first" person. She or he may be concerned that the other partner might respond with arrogance or increasing demands or misinterpret the new generosity as a lack of stability or even weakness. Each expects the other to initiate compensation for what has been suffered, hesitating to be the first to offer small favors or positive steps that might improve the relationship. To do so might feel like giving in or imply that she or he has been stupid or inferior in the past.
3. The inability to visualize a better relationship. To move ahead in a relationship, both partners must imagine and specifically define what a happier relationship would be like. If the couple has trouble visualizing and defining this new kind of relationship, they will not know in what direction to move or they may choose goals for change that are inappropriate or impossible.
4. Lack of skill. A couple may have the courage to change but lack the skills

to change in the desired way. Instead, they may end up fighting over how to improve the relationship.

5. Anxiety about change. Even change for the better produces anxiety. Any change risks failure and movement into the new and still unknown. We may be miserable, but our misery is predictable. We cannot predict what a new situation will be like, and this can be upsetting. Going slowly and talking through mixed feelings about changing can minimize fear and anxiety. This is especially important if change will alter the power hierarchy in the relationship.

Exchanged Behaviors[8]

In any good relationship, the partners may not be getting all of what they want, but they are getting *most* of what they want. They are also aware that it is their *exchanged behaviors*—how they treat each other on a daily basis—that determine the quality of their relationship.

Behavior is every observable action. It can be sitting still, throwing a temper tantrum, sleeping, smiling, smoking, washing dishes, flirting, or not answering a partner's questions. It is from these repeated behaviors that we become known to others.

There are three forms of behavior: molecular, performance, and authority. Molecular behaviors determine the tone of the relationship. These are small, transitory behaviors such as a cheerful greeting, a blank stare, a frown, a small favor done, or a small request neglected. These fleeting behaviors govern the relationship from moment to moment and serve as its red and green traffic signals. They alert us to come closer or keep our distance, communicating "I like you at this moment" or "I dislike you and distrust you right now." These second-to-second behavioral exchanges clearly and unceasingly display the way each partner feels about the relationship. While individually they may appear inconsequential, they come in endless succession. If the preponderance are negative, they can destroy a relationship. If the preponderance are positive, they nourish it.

Performance behaviors are the somewhat larger-scale repeated behaviors that concern the way partners perform activities together, such as mowing the lawn, going to the theater, painting a room, cooking a meal, taking a trip, putting out the garbage, changing a flat tire, playing tennis, or listening to a concert. On a day-to-day basis, they determine the way partners think and feel about each other.

Authority behaviors indicate who has the power in various areas of the relationship. These major behaviors largely concern making important decisions such as buying a home, deciding where to send the children to school, determining what jobs partners will have inside the home, and when and how to have sex. In general, these major behaviors involve decision making. They determine who does what and when and how he or she does it.

Successful couples have learned that when there is a conflict in their relationship, it is easiest to change molecular behaviors but it is more important to change authority behaviors. They also know that to truly improve a relationship, each partner must accept equal responsibility for this change.

Fair Fighting

For some couples, making changes requires developing skills in fair fighting.[9] These skills provide the structure within which the couple can address conflicts and renegotiate previous agreements.

Eight-Step Model for Constructive Conflict[10]

Step 1. Warm-up—This is the solo part. You need to ask yourself what you are upset about and what you would like to do about it. For women, this means becoming acutely aware of your wants, needs, and desires.

Step 2. Set the time—Agree on a specific time to resolve the conflict.

Step 3. State the problem—Stick to the facts.

Step 4. State feelings—Use "I" messages. Resist the temptation to place blame. If you do, your partner is likely to become defensive, and it will be harder to keep the fight on a constructive tack.

Step 5. Make a specific request—Keep it simple, clear, and direct. For women, this means taking the big step of asking clearly and directly for what will satisfy you. (Or, if you do not have a specific request, brainstorm possible solutions. All ideas can be shared—both practical and impractical.)

Step 6. Respond and negotiate—Now the listening partner gets to talk. Appropriate responses are:

- Yes, I'll do it.
- Yes, I agree, with the following conditions.
- No, I won't do it.
- No, I don't want to do that, but I would be willing to do this.
- Or, if you have been brainstorming, pick a solution together.

Step 7. Reach resolution.

Step 8. Clarify the agreement.

Here's an example of a fair fight. David arrives home from an evening meeting. Margie, his wife, is cleaning up the kitchen. She asks him to help. He agrees, but instead of beginning immediately, he sits down at the kitchen table and begins going through the day's mail. This goes on for several minutes. (Warm-up.) Margie realizes that she is beginning to feel ignored. She would like David to stop what he is doing and start helping as he said he would.

Margie knows that one of her own bad communication patterns is that she tends to jump to conclusions and become judgmental and vindictive. In the old days, she might have said something like, "You are so damned inconsiderate, I just can't believe it. You can forget about helping me. I'll God damned well do it myself. And you are a selfish, inconsiderate jerk." Instead, Margie chooses to use the new communications skills she has just learned. (Set the time.) She turns to David and says, "I would like you to put down that mail so I can talk with you now."

(State the problem.) "David," she begins, "you said you'd help, but you've gotten all involved with the mail." (State feelings.) "I'm feeling ignored and irritated." (Make a specific request.) "I would like you to help me as you agreed to." (Respond and negotiate.) "Oh, sweetie. I'm sorry," David replies. "I guess my mind's still back at the school-board meeting. They're raising our taxes and the assessments have just gone out. I was looking to see if ours had come. I really do intend to help. In fact, I was hoping that maybe if we got things done early we could have some quiet time ourselves in front of the fireplace after the kids are in bed."

"I can understand your preoccupation, David, but if you could put it aside for now and finish loading the dishwasher, I can go give the kids their baths." David replies, "Sounds fine to me." (A resolution is reached.) As Margie hands him the dishrag she has been using, she notices that David is still looking at the mail. (Clarify the agreement.) "David, do we have an understanding about you finishing up in the kitchen?" David looks up from the letter he is reading. A smile comes across his face as he realizes that he has not yet switched gears and that Margie will continue to be upset unless he does what he said he would. He puts the mail down and heads for the kitchen sink. "Don't worry, honey. I'll get everything cleaned up while you're getting the kids ready for bed and meet you in front of the fireplace." Margie smiles in return and heads out the door.

If you run into difficulty using this model, here are some suggestions for troubleshooting:

- If you are too angry to continue or if the process is going off track, use the time-out technique. A time-out means that you agree to temporarily stop trying to resolve the conflict. The time-out needs to be longer than five minutes and shorter than twenty-four hours. It can be communicated with an agreed-upon nonverbal cue like a simple T made with two index fingers. The partner who asks for the time-out has the responsibility to resume the process as soon as possible.
- If you have a tendency to blame, practice the "I" message technique and remember to include feeling, not just thinking, statements.
- If you have trouble listening, or if either of you feels unheard or not listened to, give the message back.
- If you have stored up old resentments and throw them into each fight,

list them for yourself. Cross off those you can, and go through the eight steps for constructive conflict with those that still need to be resolved.

- If you find that you are just not able to fight fair or that your fighting styles are creating worse problems than the issues you started off fighting about, obtain good professional help.

NOTES

1. These concepts have been eloquently articulated by Jean Baker Miller in *Toward a New Psychology of Women* (Boston: Beacon Press, 1986).

2. An observation made by Margaret Mead forty years ago still rings true for many people: "The more successful a man is in his job, the more certain everyone is that he will make a desirable husband; the more successful a woman is, the more most people are afraid she may not be a successful wife." Margaret Mead, *Male and Female* (New York: New American Library, 1949), p. 240.

3. In this regard, heterosexual couples could learn a thing or two from how most lesbians construct their primary partnerships. These partnerships have a significant advantage over heterosexual couples when it comes to managing issues of power. Because both partners are female, the division of labor within the relationship cannot be arbitrarily established along gender lines. Although a few couples do create their relationships by assigning some tasks to one as if she is the "feminine" partner and to the other as if she is the "masculine" partner, most negotiate based upon preference, agreement, and a commitment to fairness and equality.

4. Judith Long Laws, "A Feminist View of Marital Adjustment," *Journal of Marriage and the Family* 33 (August 1971): 483–516.

5. Lillian B. Rubin, *Intimate Strangers: Men and Women Together* (New York: Harper & Row, 1983).

6. If, for some reason, good attachments do not occur by the end of the first year of life, the infant is observed to have significant psychological handicaps.

7. Adapted from William Lederer, *Creating a Good Relationship* (New York: W. W. Norton, 1984), pp. 44–46.

8. Lederer, *Creating a Good Relationship*, pp. 51–53.

9. George R. Bach and Peter Wyden, *The Intimate Enemy: How to Fight Fair in Love and Marriage* (New York: Avon, 1968).

10. Adapted from Jetta Bernard, *Self Care* (Berkeley, Calif.: Celestial Arts, 1975) and Thomas Gordon, *P.E.T.: Parent Effectiveness Training* (New York: Peter H. Wyden, 1970).

Changing Partners

Sometimes even with their best efforts, a relationship does not work out as partners intended and the couple breaks up. Since women are trained to define themselves by their relationships, they often feel a deep sense of failure when a relationship ends. Their ability to choose a good partner and maintain a successful relationship is called into question.

Why Relationships End

A relationship may end because the couple jumped into it too quickly. With more time, they discover that they have little basis for a long-term partnership. This can often be prevented by slowing down the early stages of a relationship. Taking the time to really get to know each other leads to a clearer assessment of compatibility and a more realistic prediction for the future of the relationship.

Getting to know each other involves receiving and giving information. Each partner needs to inform the other about who they are and what they want in a relationship. Then each person can decide whether to pursue the relationship based on clear information, rather than on assumptions, hopes, and illusions. A woman who sees this as the prerelationship stage will feel less sense of failure if she can realistically say, "I decided that I didn't want to get involved with Dick (or Jane); we just didn't want the same things from our relationship."

Sometimes it appears that lesbian couples do not stay together as long as heterosexual couples. This may be caused by the relative invisibility of long-term lesbian couples rather than less actual stability. Successful long-term primary relationships between women are often a very private matter. Many lesbians experience so much hostility from the nonlesbian culture that they do not expose their relationship to public scrutiny. Some lesbians also tend to create capital-R Relationships prematurely. Within two months or even two weeks of meeting, the women may feel that they are a couple in a Relationship and start talking long-term commitment. They may even begin living together only to discover that their relationship is based on the desire to be in a relationship or physical attraction rather than on genuine understanding and acceptance.

Moving too quickly into a new relationship is not the only reason for a breakup. Even a long-term attachment may come to an end. Since tradition has it that our primary relationship will be a lifetime commitment, we are often poorly prepared for breaking up. We often feel helpless, disappointed, guilty, angry, and panicky. It is a profound loss, and it takes time to recover from our grief.

There are at least three phases in the grieving process:[1]

1. Shock and denial—"I cannot believe this is happening."
2. Anger and depression—Experiencing the pain of the loss.
3. Moving on—Reinvesting energy in other activities and relationships.

There is no set duration for the grieving process.[2] Usually, our recovery proceeds by degree. Recovering from the loss of an especially important relationship may take years. One sign of progress is the ability to think of the person without intense pain. It usually takes at least four full seasons of the year, if not more, before the grief over the loss of a close relationship begins to abate. If you try to start a new relationship before enough time has passed to process this loss, you are less likely to be successful the next time around. A relationship started on the rebound stands on a very fragile foundation.

To understand your past, try writing a short history of your relationship.[3]

- What did you like and/or admire in your previous partner when you first met?
- What were the most significant positive experiences in that relationship?
- What did each of you do to make the relationship work?
- What were your greatest sadnesses? Your feelings of failure?
- How did your partner contribute to these? How did you?
- In what ways has this relationship added to your life?
- What did this relationship teach you about yourself? About relationships in general? How will this knowledge and experience help you with your next relationship?

Finishing old business from a previous primary relationship is important before you begin a new one. Success in a new relationship depends in part on understanding your previous ones. If you ignore the past or fail to understand it, you run the risk of repeating earlier mistakes.

Beginning Again

When you are ready for a new relationship, finding a potential partner takes a combination of imagination, planning, thought, the willingness to extend yourself, and good luck. You cannot count on stumbling onto opportunities—you have to help create them. You can take three good steps toward choosing a new partner: define the kind of potential partner who interests you, figure out where they are likely to spend their time, and arrange to be there to meet them. The people you meet are the ones you arrange to find, whether or not you are aware of making the arrangement.

Many women complain that it is difficult to find a compatible partner. When I ask what they have done to locate a suitable companion, they seem quite surprised. Women who have no trouble finding a decent, if not exciting, job often seem to be completely inept when it comes to recruiting an acceptable partner into their life. Yet the skills are quite similar. Setting goals, going on interviews, reviewing job descriptions, investigating benefits, and selecting among employment alternatives is a familiar process to anyone who has changed jobs.

Analogous strategies apply to finding a good partner:

1. Setting goals—Carefully define what you are looking for in a partner and in a relationship instead of waiting for that special someone to appear in your life and adapting yourself to who he or she is and what he or she wants.
2. Going on interviews—Initially, dating is simply interviewing. You are getting to know a new person. That person is getting to know you. Be prepared to ask about things that are important to you and to reciprocate. Not all interviews go well, but you will get better with practice.
3. Reviewing "job descriptions"—What is his or her idea of a relationship? What is yours? Are they compatible or do you disagree? Are differences close enough to be negotiated, or are you simply too far apart in your expectations and desires?
4. Investigating benefits—We tend to think of dating as a romantic event. However, choosing a partner for a primary intimate relationship is a serious life decision. We need to make our choice based on pragmatic and practical considerations as well as emotional satisfaction. For example, do you want children while your companion does not? Do you live far apart with little likelihood that either of you could move easily? Is there a big difference in your ages? If so, is that a major problem or minor annoyance?
5. Selecting among alternatives—It is important to remember that being in a primary relationship is only one life-style choice. Some women are not really suited to this option. However, if you do decide that you would prefer a committed long-term relationship, spend time getting to know a variety of people before you settle down. Whom you select as a life partner is one of the most important decisions you will ever make. Getting to know a number of people will give you a clearer perspective on your options.

The Partner Project

An active stance puts a woman in charge of the dating process. Kaitlin took this position when she started looking for a partner at the age of thirty-seven. During her twenties and early thirties, she had dated a number of men, some for a rather long time, but none seemed to be just right. Indeed, for the previous thirteen years, her art career had been the primary focus of her life with relationships in a close, but clearly second, place.

Kaitlin had treasured those years and the opportunity they provided to pursue her work without compromise. With her career and professional identity now secure, she felt ready to invest more time and energy in a primary relationship. With my encouragement she started what we good-humoredly dubbed "the man project." She told several friends, colleagues, and neighbors that she was interested in finding a partner of quality and enticed them to work on the project with her.

Kaitlin had a wonderful time. A neighbor introduced her to six of his friends, a businesswoman introduced her to her best male friend, a colleague called her about the lovely graduate student who was renting a room in her home, and she put an ad in the local newspaper:

INVESTIGATING OPTIONS

37-year-old single professional woman. Ready to settle down within 1–2 years. Looking for A MAN OF SUBSTANCE. Goal: supportive and satisfying partnership of committed equals—eventually, perhaps, a kid. Interested? Tell me about yourself.

The ad prompted a great many responses. Kaitlin had enormous fun contacting the men who answered. They came in all shapes and sizes—younger and older, taller and shorter, attractive and downright homely. The most intriguing response came from a fellow who wrote that he got "along best with intelligent women and men who call themselves feminists." Bingo!

After an exchange of letters and phone calls, Kaitlin and Matt arranged a meeting. It was hardly love at first sight, but they did share a number of interests, values, and goals. They took two years to see if they were truly compatible before deciding to make a commitment. That was four years ago. They continue to be satisfied with their choice and feel that their relationship only grows better with time.

If you would like to try your own partner project, begin by deciding on at least three characteristics that are essential in a partner. Kaitlin had decided that her partner had to be a feminist, had to be bright, and had to be kind.

Now, look for people who meet your three criteria. Put some effort into your search. Give parties, initiate a conversation with a stranger at a museum, join the singles group at your local church or synagogue, take an interesting adult-education course, volunteer for a political campaign, sign up with a mating service. Give yourself an opportunity to get to know any candidate who meets your criteria. Risk the chance of rejection—or success.

Assessing a Potential Partner

When you meet someone who interests you, keep the following guidelines in mind as you assess this person as a potential partner:

Guideline 1. *If there is anything that you very much want in a partner, look for someone who has it already.* The power of love cannot create what is not already there.

Guideline 2. *Remember, love is not enough.* Love is essential for a good intimate relationship, but it is not enough in itself.[4] If two people are not compatible in the way they handle the details of daily life or if their goals, interests, and values are very different, love is not enough to create a satisfying and healthy committed relationship.

Guideline 3. *Similarities and differences are both important.* Some of us believe that opposites attract. While there may be some truth to this, those who bring very different values and goals to a relationship have the making of irreconcilable conflict. While similarity provides comfort, a sense of understanding and of being understood, too much similarity can be boring. We need someone who shares our important values and goals but who is different enough to broaden our perspective and who can make life interesting. Similarities may make life easier, but differences make it stimulating. The trick is to find the right balance.

Guideline 4. *In starting a new relationship, we bring together the past, the present, and the future.* By coming to terms with our past relationships, we can understand ourselves better and avoid making the same mistakes again. By getting clear in the present about what we want in a partner, we increase our chances of recognizing that person when they appear. By taking an active role in arranging to meet potential partners and realistically assessing our compatibility with them, we are much more likely to build a satisfying relationship for the future.

Selecting Men of Quality[5]

Before making a commitment to any man, a woman would be wise to give careful consideration to her decision. We still live in a society in which women are rarely considered the true equals of men. Therefore, it is important that heterosexual women be highly selective about the men they choose as life partners.

If you are considering a relationship with a man, here is a list of questions to ask yourself. The best answer follows each question.

1. a. Does he think he knows what's best for you? (No)
       The interests and values of women and men are not the same.[6] Men seldom know what is best for women.

    b. Do you think he knows what's best for you? (No)
       No one else can possibly know what is best for you, yet some women are not aware of their own needs. Personal awareness of your own needs is essential if you are to have a healthy relationship.

2. a. Does he translate or explain your feelings, thoughts, and/or behaviors for you? (No)

Only you can do this for yourself. If someone else tries to do this, they are discounting you.

b. Do you need him to translate or explain your feelings, thoughts, and/or behaviors for you? (No)

You may try to avoid conflict by allowing him to discount you.

3. a. Does he confuse sexual activity with nurturance and/or love? (No)

Many men have learned to have sex but do not know how to nurture or show love. Does he nurture you when sex is not on the agenda?

b. Do you confuse sexual activity with nurturance? (No)

Have you learned to accept sex without nurturance or love because you think that is all you can realistically expect?

4. a. Does he really like women? (Yes)

Men who really like women have genuine friendships with them. They do not just associate with women when they are being sexually active with them.

b. Do you really like women? (Yes)

Women who do not really like women are unable to truly like themselves. This makes it impossible for them to expect good treatment in an intimate relationship with a man.

5. a. Does he validate your existence apart from his? (Yes)

Does he recognize that you are your own person with perspectives that may well be different from his and that are just as valid?

b. Do you see yourself only in relation to his existence? (No)

Are you able to trust that you may see things differently from him and that your perspectives are equally valid? Are you going to be able to realize your full potential in the context of a relationship with this man?

6. a. How committed is he to traditional concepts of masculinity and femininity? (Not at all)

Traditional roles are a hindrance to full development. Every human deserves the opportunity to develop independently of gender roles. Additional questions to ask are:

i. Does he read *Playboy,* watch porno movies, and/or go to topless bars? (No)

In these arenas, women are sexual objects, not people.

ii. Does violence, especially violence against women, play any role in his life? (No)

Viewing movies and listening to music that depicts violence increase the likelihood of the person becoming aroused by violence.[7] Violence is not natural or normal.

iii. If he lost his job, money, or status, what kind of relationship would you have? (The same)

Some women only value men to the degree that they provide money, status, or a source of identity.

iv. Does he value your strengths and adult qualities? (Yes)

Some men can only be with women who are needy or dependent. They find it difficult to be with women who have the qualities that convey power and status in our culture such as being educated, strong, tall, old,

financially secure, or sophisticated. Do you have to devalue any of your
strengths to prevent him from feeling threatened?

    v. Is he comfortable saying things like "I don't know," "I made a mistake,"
or "I'm sorry"? (Yes)

       A man must be able to grasp that he may not always be right.
Otherwise, when you are dealing with a conflict, he will be unable to
see how he has contributed to the problem and may need to do
something differently.

  b. How committed are you to traditional concepts of masculinity and femininity?
(Not at all)

    Traditional masculinity allows a man to be more powerful than you.
Traditional femininity assigns you a role of economic dependence and limited
competency.

7. a. Is he a biological or cultural sexist? (No)

    Biological sexists do not like women's bodies just the way they are. Instead,
they emphasize looking great and smelling great (by society's standards) no
matter what changes in her natural beauty a woman must make. Cultural
sexists think women are unsuited for things usually reserved for men. They
use excuses like the work is too hard, women are too emotional, or women
are unreliable.

  b. Are you a biological sexist? (No)

    Are you trying to meet the cultural standard of women's attractiveness
through crazy diets, wearing uncomfortable clothes, or submitting to surgery?

8. a. How well does his verbal behavior correlate with his other behaviors? (Very
well)

    If he says he really cares about you and your feelings, do his actions match
his words? If there is any discrepancy, believe his actions rather than his
words.

  b. How well do you want his verbal behaviors to correlate with his other
behaviors? (Very well)

    If he behaves "badly," do you continually forgive him or rationalize it away?
Do you think this is the best you or any woman can expect from a man?

9. a. How does he feel about his mother? (He likes her)

    Men who have angry, unfinished business with their mothers may transfer
some of these feelings to you.

  b. How do you feel about his mother? (I like her)

    We are taught to view mother-in-laws as intrusive and controlling women.
Are you able to see his mother clearly for who she really is?

10. a. How committed is he to personal and partner self-awareness and growth?
(Very)

    Does he accept equal responsibility for making your relationship run
smoothly?

  b. How much do you need for him to be committed to personal and partner
self-awareness and growth? (Very much)

    If you allow only yourself to be responsible for the health of your
relationship, you are imagining that you have more power than you actually

have. You can no more make a relationship work by yourself than you can play a game of tennis alone.

We have a mythology in our culture that a heterosexual woman is incomplete unless she has a primary relationship with a man. The perpetuation of this myth encourages women to affiliate with men who are "developmentally disabled."[8] These men are either unable or unwilling to participate fully in the development and maintenance of egalitarian and mutually respectful relationships.

It is critical that women question this mythology. If your male partner does not meet the above criteria, you are asking for trouble. It may come later rather than sooner, but it will come. Do you need a relationship more than you need to be treated with respect, encouragement, caring, and love? Think carefully about this. The person you choose as your life partner has a profound impact on your psychological health and the quality of your life.

ADDITIONAL READING

John Schneider, *Stress, Loss and Grief: Understanding Their Origins and Growth Potential* (Baltimore: University Park Press, 1984). If you have trouble finding this book, contact Dr. Schneider directly at the Department of Psychiatry, Michigan State University, A-232 E. Fee Hall, East Lansing, MI 48824. Dr. Schneider offers workshops to assist people in the grieving process. He may be planning one in your area.

Diane Vaughan, *Uncoupling: How Relationships Come Apart* (New York: Oxford University Press, 1986). A well-researched description of the process of breaking-up.

NOTES

1. William Worden, *Grief Counseling and Grief Therapy* (New York: Springer, 1982).

2. John Schneider, *Stress, Loss and Grief: Understanding Their Origins and Growth Potential* (Baltimore: University Park Press, 1984).

3. Adapted from D. Merilee Clunis and G. Dorsey Green, *Lesbian Couples* (Seattle: Seal Press, 1988).

4. Love is a deeper emotion than infatuation. It is based on accurate knowledge of ourselves and our partner. Though love is not as intense as infatuation, it has a better chance of resulting in long-term satisfaction. One definition of love is that the security and well-being of another person becomes as significant as (not more significant than) your own security and well-being. This kind of love is seldom spontaneous or instant. It results from promoting equality, from being able to cope and adapt, and from work. It also takes time to create. Excerpted with editing from William Lederer,

Creating a Good Relationship (New York: W. W. Norton, 1984). Lederer attributed these ideas to Harry Stack Sullivan, an early American psychiatrist.

5. Adapted from Doris C. DeHardt, "Can a Feminist Therapist Facilitate Clients' Heterosexual Relationships?" in *Handbook of Feminist Therapy: Women's Issues in Psychotherapy,* ed. Lynne Bravo Rosewater and Lenore E. A. Walker (New York: Springer, 1985).

6. Jessie Bernard, *The Female World* (New York: Free Press, 1981).

7. R. G. Green, "Behavioral and Physiological Reactions to Observed Violence: Effects of Prior Exposure to Aggressive Stimuli," *Journal of Personality and Social Psychology* 40 (1981): 868–75, and G. W. Russell, "Spectator Moods at an Aggressive Sports Event," *Journal of Sport Psychology* 3 (1981): 217–27.

8. I am indebted to one of my patients for this description. Unfortunately, due to confidentiality, her contribution must remain anonymous.

Conclusion

As women, we learn to place special emphasis on developing and maintaining intimate relationships. This cultural training has both advantages and disadvantages. One advantage is that in virtually any relationship between two women, both feel responsible for making it work. Whether this is a close friendship or loving partnership, the impact of two emotionally healthy adults nurturing their attachment is almost certain to guarantee its success. One disadvantage is that women tend to care for their relationships at the expense of themselves. In a primary relationship between two women, one or both may neglect herself by overfocusing on their attachment. In a conventional heterosexual partnership, the woman may discover that she is alone in tending to the relationship. Few men have been trained to share equal responsibility for the health of their intimate attachments.

There is nothing intrinsically wrong with accepting responsibility for attending to a relationship if this contribution is valued, respected, and acknowledged. Caring for others and putting their needs above or equal to a woman's own does not give her partner the right to undermine her self-esteem by exploiting her efforts or minimizing her worth. Women would be wise to avoid partners who behave in this way if they wish to have satisfying relationships.

Designing the Relationship You Want

You are the key factor in determining the health of your most intimate relationship—not because you can determine the quality yourself, but because you choose your partner. In healthy intimate relationships, the ongoing message is "I like you. I am committed to this relationship, and I treasure it." This internal message is carried even, and perhaps most importantly, when the couple is angry with each other. At these times, the internal message is "Even though we disagree and I appear annoyed, I approve and am supportive of you."

Partners in high-quality intimate relationships have the sense that they are different but equal. They have the ability and willingness to adapt to the never-ending changes and circumstances that affect every relationship. They feel content and emotionally secure. They have discovered that there are a remarkable number of creative ways to achieve a high-quality intimate attachment. Some may seem quite unconventional, if not downright bizarre, to other people, but as long as the choices serve their needs, what anyone else thinks is irrelevant. These couples report a feeling of zest that comes from coping with the endless problems and pleasures that are a part of everyday life. If you share their feelings, then you too have achieved the best possible in any human connection.

ADDITIONAL READING

Don Dinkmeyer and Jon Carlson, *Time for a Better Marriage* (Circle Pines, Minn.: American Guidance Service, 1984). It is unfortunate that this book is designed only for heterosexual married couples. If you and your partner do not fall into this category, you may still consider using it. With some creativity, you can transpose the assumptions into descriptions of any couple or any significant relationship, for the ideas presented are universal and clear. With adaptations, this book can be of great use in improving the quality of any relationship between committed and willing partners.

Sherod Miller, Elam Nunnally, and Daniel Wackman, *Couple Communication I: Talking Together* (Minneapolis, Minn.: Interpersonal Communications Programs, Inc., 1979). This group has developed a specific model of communication that serves as a good educational tool to help people begin to identify styles of communication. Their book is complemented by audio tapes that the disciplined couple may find a useful adjuvant. The authors and their colleagues have applied their techniques to a variety of groups, including abusive families and people who suffer with alcoholism. The goal is to build stronger relationships that can prevent crises from developing. This book has less of a heterosexist bias.

Joseph Strayhorn, *Talking It Out: A Guide to Effective Communication and Problem Solving* (Champaign, Ill.: Research Press Co., 1977). Tedious but comprehensive. I like the way genders are sometimes switched—almost as if the universal "he" is occasionally assumed to be "she."

PART 3 | **S**igns and **S**ymptoms: **C**ommon **P**sychological **C**oncerns

When women experience psychological distress, they usually describe it in terms of their signs and symptoms: "I feel worthless," "I'm depressed," "I'm anxious all the time," "I've never had an orgasm," "I'm worried that I might be drinking too much," "I hate my body," or "My husband hit me last night." In spite of being able to identify what is upsetting them, many women express confusion about the best way to reduce their distress. They want to feel better, but they are not sure where to start or how to judge if the option they have selected is truly beneficial.

The next seven chapters describe the common psychological concerns of women, our current understanding of what seems to cause these difficulties, and how a woman might successfully respond to them—either on her own or with assistance.

6 | **S**elf-esteem

Self-esteem is a measure of how much we value ourself, what we think of ourself, and how much we like ourself—just the way we are. The characteristics a woman is born with do not in themselves lead to higher or lower levels of self-esteem, it is the value she is taught to place on these traits.

Self-esteem is not inborn, it is learned. We first learn self-esteem through the relationships we have with the important people during our early years, our family. As an infant, the seeds of self-esteem are planted and nourished in the context of interactions with parents, siblings, and other caretakers. The experiences and feelings associated with these relationships are the foundation of a child's sense and value of self.

If a child has the good fortune to be born into a psychologically healthy family, she will experience being loved and valued by those on whom she depends. If her family is excited and happy to have a new little girl in their lives, their pleasure will enhance her self-esteem. If the family is psychologically handicapped or dysfunctional, the child is more likely to feel that she is a burden. If those on whom she depends believe that girls are not very important, her self-esteem will be diminished even further.

However, our sense of self—the notion of who we are and are not—is not static. It develops and changes over time. As a girl grows, experiences with people outside her family can also enhance or detract from her self-esteem. Positive relationships can counter negative family messages. Later, success at school and competence at work can all enhance lagging self-esteem. On the other hand, ongoing and repeated negative experiences will continue to undermine her self-esteem and leave her feeling defective, inadequate or unlovable.

What Does a Woman with Healthy Self-esteem Look Like?

An adult woman with healthy self-esteem does not consider herself the center of the universe, but she does focus on the positive. While she is not vain, arrogant, or narcissistic, she does enjoy a reasonable degree of self-assurance. Like all human beings, she sometimes experiences self-doubt and may, on occasion, become discouraged or disappointed, but such feelings are not incapacitating, and they generally do not last long.

When a woman with high self-esteem fails at a task, she can comfort herself with memories of past successes and vow to do better next time. If she feels disliked by one person, she can assure herself that there are many who like her. She reminds herself that she can't please everyone. The woman with high self-esteem has a variety of quality human relationships with people of many ages. She has a diversity of skills and interests. She has a realistic idea of her own strengths and weaknesses. When she becomes upset or depressed, she has a variety of ways of restoring her emotional equilibrium.

The woman with high self-esteem has a sense of her innate worth. She feels comfortable and content with who she is. She is not overly self-critical. She can be open and direct with her anger when she feels it is appropriate, but she does not use anger to intimidate or control others. She is equally generous in showing her affection and appreciation of others. She is free to love and be loved. She learns and grows with a sense of pleasure, not pain. She does not believe that there is anything fundamentally wrong with her. She likes herself.

A Woman with Low Self-esteem?

This woman sees herself as a helpless victim of fate. Her life is something beyond her control. She frequently finds herself unable to act in her own interest. If she fails to achieve a goal, she may quite unjustifiably feel that others are critical and rejecting. Her basic sense of self-worth and her confidence in her own abilities are shaky. A loss, a slight, or some other blow to her self-esteem may trigger a prolonged period of despondency. She has few skills or resources for coping with such "assaults." A succession of blows to her self-esteem may throw her into a state of prolonged despair and depression.

Women with low self-esteem often have trouble modulating their anger and using it effectively. They find themselves unable to become angry, even in situations where anger would be quite appropriate. Or if they do become angry, it is in hostile, destructive, or indirect ways that may only make things worse.

The woman with low self-esteem frequently turns to others for emotional support and reassurance because she feels she lacks inner resources. She may repeatedly demonstrate poor judgment in her selection of friends and partners because she is often acting out of extreme neediness rather than mature interest and care. She almost expects, and certainly tolerates, troubled and dysfunctional relationships. Since she tends to depend on the support others provide to maintain her psychological equilibrium, people may perceive her as manipulative and overly dependent. As a result, many of the friendships she forms tend to be fragile and fraught with turmoil and difficulties.

There may be only a very few people on whom she feels she can rely. It often happens that there is only a single, highly important person on whom she feels she can depend. For heterosexual women, this is usually a male partner—a partner who expects to receive, but not necessarily give, emotional support. Nevertheless, a woman with low self-esteem will experience the disruption of such a highly important relationship as the loss of her most vital supply of psychological support. Furthermore, she will have to bear the grief of this loss with few alternative emotional resources.

In a family or a society where a female's experience is frequently one of being devalued, unappreciated, or abused, low self-esteem is an inevitable consequence. Women who through no fault of their own have not received adequate nurturing and care frequently grow up to feel that they do not really deserve to be happy or successful. They often describe feeling inadequate or worthless, and they spend more time worrying about their deficiencies than appreciating their good qualities. They typically dislike their bodies for being less than physically perfect as defined by some arbitrary and changing cultural standard. When things go wrong, they blame themselves, and they tend to be extremely harsh in their self-criticisms.

It is no surprise that women with low self-esteem are extremely vulnerable to depression and that their periods of depression may linger for weeks, months, or even years.[1] Unless a woman with low self-esteem is able to take steps to improve her feelings about herself, she will have little chance of living to her full potential and experiencing happiness.

Understandings about Self-esteem: A Historical Perspective

There have been a number of professional books and articles published on the topic of self-esteem, but until recently, few authors made any distinction between the self-esteem of women and men.[2] Exceptions are Linda Tschirhart Sanford and Mary Ellen Donovan, who have written specifically about women and self-esteem.[3] The other authors wrote about "students," "children," and "adolescents" when their subjects were actually *male* students, *male* children, and *male* adolescents. In those few instances where they did consider women separately, the women were compared with men in a way that implied that the male experience was the standard against which women were to be measured.

Thus, the model for the development of self-esteem based upon the male experience became the norm. It was accepted without criticism by later generations because it reflected the experience of most of the people in the field.[4] These male theorists and clinicians did not seem to consider the possibility that their assumptions might be affected by their common experience of growing up male.

How does each girl and boy in our society develop a sense of themselves and through that their self-esteem? During the period when children are establishing a sense of being female or male (birth to age three), most of the day-to-day caretaking is provided by women, which seems to have a significant effect on psychological development. In order to develop a male identity different from the person with whom they spend most of their time, boys push and are pushed off (separation-individuation) from their primary caretakers. Girls can remain close to their primary caretakers while developing a female identity. This continuing process of separation-individuation is viewed as a series of psychological events through which a youngster establishes her or his own identity separate from other significant people.

A well-established sense of psychological separateness has long been considered a hallmark of the psychologically healthy adult. Given the tendency to describe psychological development from a male perspective, it is not too surprising to find that the process of maturation has been described as a long process of increasing psychological separation.[5] Once this male-oriented model of psychological health became the accepted norm, it was very difficult to challenge. Indeed, it was simply taken for granted that this model was accurate. Women are measured against this standard. Unfortunately, it is a standard that often leaves women feeling inadequate, troubled, or "sick." Yet until recently, it was taken for granted that the problem was with women, not with the model.

Redefining the Meaning of a Sense of Self and Self-esteem

Recently, theorists who work with infants[6] and specialists in the psychology of women[7] have begun to question the assumption that a sense of separation is necessary for good mental health. These observers of human development have suggested that a sense of self develops as a part of an interactive process in which both infant and caretaker participate. Developing a sense of self while remaining psychologically close is an equally valid—if not more accurate—description of healthy development.

From the moment of birth, each individual seems to influence her interactions and relationships with other people. Researchers who have studied infant-caretaker interactions believe that the development of the self is much more complex than the separation model would suggest. It is not simply a matter of a passive infant receiving care from an active caretaker. As every sensitive parent recognizes, the relationship is more like a dance between the participants, an active two-way process in which both infant and caretaker influence the nature of the relationship. Each is aware of and responds to the other. An infant may "reward" a nurturing and empathic caretaker with a variety of nonverbal cues that help to keep the adult engaged in a warm and positive way. An adult may communicate a sense of deep enjoyment and concern for a fussy baby that comforts and reassures the frightened and tired tot. Both caretaker and child show a remarkable ability to perceive and respond to each other's mental states and emotions.

Because of this process of mutual interaction, the infant simultaneously becomes aware not only of her own thoughts and feelings, but of the caretaker's thoughts and feelings as well. In this way, the infant develops a sense of self that incorporates both her own feelings and mental processes and those of her caretakers. From the earliest days of life, the infant learns to perceive herself not as a separated being, receiving care from another, but as a participant in a mutually interactive relationship.

Growing Up Female

This mutually interactive process may be the beginning of what we call empathy—the ability to be closely in touch with another's emotional and mental state.[8] The potential for empathy exists in infants of both sexes, but in our culture, empathy is, for the most part, encouraged in girls and discouraged in boys. Girls are trained to develop their potential for empathy, while boys are actually trained to receive and expect an empathic response. Because a girl's human capacity for empathy is allowed to flourish, emotional connections form the very basis of a woman's continuing psychological growth.

The caretaker who recognizes and supports this growth and development for the younger female does not become more distant—nor does the child. Indeed, the caretaker is changed by her very participation in adapting and accommodating to the growth of the younger person. The pair does not experience separation—rather, their attachment is changed and enriched.

As a girl matures into womanhood, she develops a more complex sense of self within a growing and ever-changing network of increasingly "differentiated" relationships. Adolescent boys, on the other hand, are seen as striving to develop a separate and more isolated sense of self. Rather than pushing toward separation, a developing female expands her image of herself by incorporating an increasing sense of her own new abilities and a sense of her greater capability to express her views and to put her wishes into effect. She begins to think in terms of a larger scope of action—but she does so within the context of remaining connected to the important people in her life. This requires a change in her initial experience of herself and others' experience of her, but it does not require separation.

Healthy women do not experience themselves as benefiting by separating from others. From a woman's perspective, tuning into the feelings of others and enjoying mutual interactions seems very natural, satisfying, and empowering. Most women view these involvements as vehicles of their own development, rather than detractions. Close relationships are enhancing and enriching rather than threatening to their personhood.

The opportunity to take part in meaningful relationships is vital to a woman's self-esteem. Healthy relationships are a source of involvement, pleasure, and mutual empowerment. Women are at their best when they can grow within the context of a life rich in important relationships.

This process is at odds with the established, male-oriented model of psychological health, which emphasizes separation and individuation. The overemphasis on separation and individuation has resulted in many mental-health professionals—women and men alike—underemphasizing the legitimate and healthy need for connection. Because men have been discouraged from consciously acknowledging their needs for healthy dependency, connectedness, and intimacy, women have accepted an extra burden. Heterosexual women often appear overly dependent or overly concerned about developing and maintaining connections and intimacy because they are caring for their needs plus the unacknowledged needs of men. Thus a woman behaving in a perfectly normal and healthy way—indeed, in the way society has trained her to behave—frequently finds herself described as psychologically immature or overly dependent.

Once men come to accept their own need for connection and work to develop and sustain relationships in a manner equal to women's, women will probably not have to overemphasize connecting. But until men take up this responsibility, women are left doing it for them. I call this picking up the emotional socks. In the days before the women's movement, women would complain that their male partners never picked up their own socks. These women wanted the men to pick up after themselves, yet while they complained, they still picked up after their men. It was not until the women literally stopped doing this that men realized they either had to do it for themselves or it was not going to get done. It works the same way in tending to relationships. Women complain about men not doing their fair share, but as long as women continue to do it for them, there is little motivation for men to play an equal role.

A New Model of Women's Psychological Development

In our understanding of self-esteem, as in many other areas of psychological theory, we are faced with the task of revising the commonly accepted description of human experience to include women's perspectives. Thus, the older male-oriented model of separation-individuation based on the breaking of early emo-tional ties is complemented and enriched by the female-oriented relationship-differentiation or self-in-relation model.[9] This model makes it clear that there need be no conflict between development of the individual and growth of the relationship.

Proponents of the self-in-relation model propose that women reach psycholog-ical maturity not by separating from others, but by developing a greater capacity for forming emotional connections with family and friends. These theoreticians believe that while men are encouraged toward psychological separation, women develop a strong and healthy psychological drive to establish intimacy. The capac-ity to remain connected to others while maturing psychologically allows for in-creasing clarity and enrichment of a woman's own sense of herself within the context of relationships.

If the principal benchmark of good mental health really was a highly devel-oped sense of separation, then we would all value "doing our own thing" or "becoming our own person" above all else. This would result in a society made up of highly self-focused individuals with few strong social connections. But this is clearly unworkable, unwise, and indeed unhealthy.

Most psychologically healthy people live in a rich network of social relation-ships. For heterosexual men, it is usually the women with whom they are affili-ated who take the responsibility for keeping these interpersonal links alive. Women tend to value contributing to interchange between people and playing a part in the growth of others—often more than they value their own individual psychological development. As a result, it is primarily wives, mothers, and daughters who establish and maintain enriching, nurturing, and mutually in-teractive family and friendship ties. For example, when adult children call home, Mom usually spends most of the time on the phone with them. Dad often seems awkward and uncomfortable. Mom is also the one who is likely to arrange the family social calendar, buy gifts for family and friends, and remem-ber special occasions. Dad often ends up participating in a social world that is arranged for him.

The self-in-relation model describes how the healthy development of the individual and the growth of relationships can proceed together. For example, most teenagers do not want to separate from their parents, they simply want to change the form and content of their relationship. They are trying to find a way to affirm their own development while allowing new relationships to be incorpo-rated into their lives.

For the parent of an adolescent, this may mean increasingly moving from a relationship of direct caretaking and control to one of increasing consideration, caring, and empowerment. The adolescent takes over greater responsibility for her own life while the parent gradually moves into the role of guide, adviser, and support person. The nature of the connection is altered, but the attachment endures. Ideally, a similar process happens in therapy with an adult woman.

Rather than overemphasizing psychological separation or independence, the therapist assists her client in altering her role in relationships.[10]

Developmental Milestones in the Formation of Self-esteem

When we look at development across a woman's lifetime, we can identify a number of key events that lead to either enhanced or lowered self-esteem.

Family of Origin: Feeling Valued, Loved, and Wanted in Your Family

The roots of our self-esteem lie in our early relationships with our family. The way our parents treated us is especially important, but siblings, grandparents, and other members of our extended family can also have an impact on self-esteem. Children who receive verbal and nonverbal messages that communicate "You are very special; you belong to me; you are precious; you are a delight to have in my life" are being offered the foundation that will help them in the task of developing healthy self-esteem. Girls who receive messages like "Girls aren't very important; the fact that you were a girl was always a disappointment to me; I wish you'd been a boy" will incorporate the idea that there is something wrong with them.

The infant girl will not understand what it is that her parents find wrong with her. Even if she does eventually figure it out as she matures, there is not a darn thing she can do about it. She did not choose to be a girl. Being devalued for something over which she has no control leaves a young girl feeling powerless, which in turn may lead to low self-esteem, depression, anxiety, and ineffectual or chronic anger.

Sad to say, even recent surveys suggest that many parents still prefer male children over female children. Such preferences may be totally unconscious, and the parents may not even realize the subtle and unintentional messages they are communicating to their daughter. As a result, a woman who has grown up in such a family may not consciously realize why she felt so badly about herself growing up. Unless measures are taken to repair this early experience of feeling rejected, a woman will be left with a significant psychological handicap that will continue to influence her comfort and pleasure in life.

Growing Up: Childhood

Experiences during childhood and adolescence also affect self-esteem. A girl's family continues to have the strongest influence, but as she has more contact with other people, they also color her sense of herself. Anyone with whom a child has a relationship—grandparents, aunts and uncles, teachers and coaches—can play an important role in the development of her self-esteem. The treatment she receives from adults outside her family and even from other youngsters can add to or detract from how much she values herself.

Some messages are communicated in words: "You're wonderful." "You're worthless." "We're so proud of you." "You'll never amount to anything." Some are communicated physically: by a tender touch, a spanking, or a hug. Other messages are communicated indirectly: by a tone of voice, a forgotten promise, or by nonverbal body language.

A child who receives a high and consistent level of respect and affection from the adults and others around her is well on the way to developing healthy self-esteem. Such a child grows up feeling that even on those occasions when one of the key adults in her life disapproves of something she has done, the love that adult has for her remains continuous and dependable.

Adolescence: What to Do about Sexuality

Adolescence marks a physical and psychological transition. Until puberty, the differences between girls and boys can often be fairly subtle. Tomboys are free to play alongside their male companions and no one seems concerned, but when a girl begins to menstruate and develops breasts, the differences in the experiences of girls and boys become marked. The young girl's unmistakable sexual and reproductive development must be integrated into her own sense of herself. The way she and the other important people in her life react to these changes will have a profound influence on her self-esteem.

Historically, it is during this period when the family, school, and society begin to send the strongest messages about what is appropriate behavior for girls versus boys. While this is a time of expansion for boys, it's a time of constriction for many girls. During this stage, boys are expected to be adventuresome, to take risks, to try different things. When it comes to sex, it is perfectly OK for a boy to sow his wild oats. Girls on the other hand are often held to tighter curfews, criticism from parents if boyfriends cause concern, and clinical discussions of their capacity to menstruate and bear children rather than education about enjoying their bodies while protecting against unwanted pregnancies.

As a society, we have trouble untangling women's sexuality from their re-productivity. The cultural messages a young woman receives about female sexuality are complicated and confusing. The stereotype of the sexually attractive female is used to sell everything from automobiles to cigarettes. The communication is "be sexy." At the same time, many young girls are sent the unmistakable message that their own sexual feelings are dangerous, taboo, or bad. Parents, much more knowledgeable about the risks of being sexually active for a girl than for a boy, are understandably concerned about teenagers acting on sexual thoughts, feelings, and pressure. The potential to become pregnant and our culture's tendency to hold women rather than women *and* men responsible for a pregnancy have a major impact upon female development.

It has been easier for men to separate sexuality from reproductivity. It need not be so difficult for women. It would mean respecting and celebrating female sexuality for a woman's own pleasure rather than superimposing society's tendency to use female sexuality for its own purposes. It would also mean educating young women and men about female sexuality as well as female reproductivity. It would require the availability of contraceptives and promoting their use by both young women and young men.

Currently, girls are not encouraged to explore or fully understand their own bodies. Boys regularly handle their genitals during urination, and the pleasurable sensations associated with touch become very familiar. Later, in groups and alone, boys learn how to bring themselves to orgasm through masturbation. A girl's equivalent organ of sexual pleasure, the clitoris, is less visible and not routinely handled in nonsexual activities. Few adolescents know that women can have orgasms as easily as men, provided there is adequate manual stimulation to the appropriate organ. There is little support for girls and young women to explore their sexuality and to develop their capacity for sexual pleasure. As a result, for many women, sexual activity precedes orgasm by years or even decades.

Sexuality and reproductivity are not the only differences in female and male development at this stage. The pressure to perform different roles within the family and society at large heats up during adolescence. Parents often assign different household chores to girls and boys. These are frequently divided along stereotypical gender lines and often include a discrepancy in pay. A 1987 survey of the parents of youngsters at a northern California school selected for its nontraditional environment showed that girls' weekly allowances averaged 14¢ less than boys' $1.09. At the top of the pay scale, the difference was even more striking: $6.50 for girls and $7.50 for boys.[11] Even odd jobs done outside the home to earn extra money fall along these same gender lines. Girls are more often able to find work as baby-sitters and housecleaners, while boys move into the more public arena of paper routes and yard work.

The school system also plays a major role in directing girls along one path and boys along another. While there has been some overlap, segregation along gender lines becomes quite evident in junior and senior high school. Different classes and recreational activities are often encouraged for girls and boys. It is still the rare girl who is accepted on the football team and the rare boy who participates in home economics.

Any girl who does not fit comfortably into her gender-defined niche is vulnerable to a disruption in self-esteem. Fortunately, if a family is sensitive to and supportive of her individuality, even in the face of external pressure a young girl is more likely to be able to remain true to her own interests and choices. Without this family support, she must search for it elsewhere. She may be lucky enough to find someone who encourages her unique dreams and aspirations, but it will require considerable strength and tenacity to proceed under these circumstances. She may ultimately achieve her goal, only to discover that an underlying low self-esteem interferes with her contentment.

Adults: In the Family and in the Workplace

Through late adolescence and into early adulthood, young men and women receive very different messages about relationships and work. Young men are raised with little expectation that they will be responsible for the emotional nurturance of other people. Rather than expecting that their primary efforts will be directed at maintaining intimate relationships, young men are taught that their most important task is their own individual development and that they should have only passing regard for its effects on others.

Many decent men do not view this as a matter of selfishness. Instead, they see their self-focus as temporary and, indeed, often a matter of sacrifice. After all, they are behaving responsibly when they might like to just fool around. They believe that they are doing what is expected of them in preparation for their anticipated economic responsibilities in a family. Often without really thinking about it, these young men assume that the women in their lives will adapt in whatever ways are necessary to support their advancement. Mothers, girlfriends, and wives are expected to accommodate the man's preferences, allowing his interests to supersede theirs.

In contrast, most young women have been taught that the needs and desires of other people are just as important as their own. At the extreme, women feel that they are expected to put the needs of other people *before* their own needs. And they are expected to do this gladly, without ambivalence, hesitation, or irritation. Thus young women are taught to foster other people's development. When this support is given willingly, it can be a source of pleasure and enhanced self-esteem for the giver; when this nurturing activity is taken for granted, as it is by some heterosexual men, a woman gives to others at the price of diminishing what she has for herself.

> Ruth was fifty-two when she first called me. A stunningly attractive woman who was uncannily perceptive when it came to assessing other people's difficulties, she could not figure out the cause of the severe depression she was experiencing. In our first session, it became clear to me that Ruth's marriage was, for all intents and purposes, dead. However, she was either unwilling or unable to face this reality. Instead, she spoke of feeling deeply guilty because she had been a selfish wife and mother. "I never gave my all to my family. I always saved 5 percent for myself and only gave 95 percent to them. If I had given more, this might never have happened." It was no easy task helping Ruth to see that saving 5 percent for herself had also saved her life. In fact, she had saved too little for herself. Receiving little emotional nurturance from either her husband or her now adult children, she was almost completely depleted. It was with this tiny bit of self-

esteem she had reserved that she would have to begin rebuilding her psychological health.

Allison's generosity had not left her quite so empty, but at age fifty-six she was finally contemplating leaving her psychologically abusive husband after thirty-two years of marriage. Allison and her professional husband had raised four bright and loving children. The last had recently left for college. Like the other three, he was encouraging his mother to separate from her husband. All four children had pleasurable and mutually supportive relationships with their mother, which attested to her ability to enable their development even when receiving little emotional support from her husband. Ironically, because of her success in nurturing healthy development in her children, she continued to believe that she could heal her husband's psychological wounds. She had stayed in the marriage, giving far more emotionally than she received, hoping that her care would eventually help her husband feel better about himself. With all the children gone, she had to face the fact that her attentiveness had not made him better. To add to her distress, she was now berating herself for staying in the relationship so long. "What is wrong with me? Why did I stay so long?" she asked me between her sobs. It was difficult for her to credit her strength in enduring her husband's unpredictable outbursts of temper. While he had never struck her, he had repeatedly humiliated her. By emphasizing his handicap and struggling to care for his self-esteem over her own, she had allowed him to erode her own psychological health. It was time to be more "selfish" and place her own well-being as a higher priority than trying to understand what caused her husband's loss of control and immature temper tantrums. He needed to take responsibility for controlling his own emotions. She could not fix it for him, no matter how much care she provided.

The contributions of the many women who provide this kind of support are only rarely acknowledged and fully appreciated. These women put out a great deal of nurturing energy but get little in return. Because their important "person-enhancing" work is performed without external validation or reward, women miss a great deal that could otherwise provide the basis of increased self-esteem. Being a good facilitator of other people's development—if it is publicly acknowledged and rewarded—can be a source of self-esteem for women and men equal to achievement in other arenas. And if it were expected of men as well as women, men who did not facilitate the growth and development of others would have lower self-esteem. A "successful" man who got there by crawling over other people would feel guilty and badly about doing something that was hurtful to others, while a "successful" man who got there by supporting others in their own development along with his own would feel satisfied and pleased with everyone's success.

This is one of the important differences between many female-male relationships and female-female relationships. Few heterosexual men have provided the kind of emotional and practical support for their female partners that women have often provided for men. In lesbian relationships, women often exchange emotional and practical support. Many women, both heterosexuals and lesbians, share a level of intimacy with other women that they long to achieve—but rarely do—with men.

Sometimes women who are not in egalitarian and respectful relationships come to the awareness that they are disappointed, hurt, tired, and angry about the lack of support for their own dreams. After years of erosion to their own self-esteem, many decide that they would like to receive more support for their own growth and development, but they are reluctant to make these demands or requests if it seems that these changes will be detrimental to important relationships. Having been taught to value and maintain relationships, it is very frightening for a woman to entertain doing anything that might threaten her closest connections. On the other hand, men who are taught to put their own self-development above all else tend to be more threatened by the notion that they are under pressure to compromise their personal ambitions in order to nurture a relationship. To adapt in this way feels unmanly.

Today, most households continue gender-based division of labor. This becomes most obvious in contemporary relationships with the addition of children to the family. When both partners work, a couple often discover that the previously shared responsibilities for finances and home maintenance are not translated into equal responsibility for childcare. The woman usually struggles to balance work and family or is more likely to make substantial compromises in her work life for the sake of quality childcare. Almost 50 percent of paid working women spend at least 3.5 hours a day with their children, compared to only 13 percent of paid working men. Working women average 29 hours per week of family care; men average 9 hours per week.[12]

Earning her own living is an important source of self-esteem for a woman. Ideally, it should be work she enjoys, but even a routine and mundane job provides a woman with a sense of being able to make her own way in the world. This is essential if she is single, but even women in relationships report feeling more powerful if they contribute directly to the family's economic resources.

Unfortunately, women still confront many barriers in the workplace. They have a harder time obtaining high-prestige jobs,[13] and when they do get the job, they are almost always paid less than their male counterparts. In the blue-collar work world, a woman's place has barely changed. "While about 49 percent of the professional work force is now female, only 8.6 percent of precision, production, crafts, and repair jobs are held by women. While middle-class women have made dramatic inroads into management—a 77 percent increase from 1975—working-class women represent only 3 percent of mechanics, 1.5 percent of construction workers."[14]

According to the U.S. Department of Labor, in 1980, women doing work comparable to men's made less than sixty cents for every dollar made by a man.[15] More education was no help. An employed man who was an elementary-school dropout earned more ($10,474) than the average full-time, year-round employed female night-school graduate ($9,769). By 1987, the gap had been narrowed, with women working full-time making 70 percent as much as men.[16] Why should there be any discrepancy? Even more disturbing is the continuing problem that the majority of adults living in poverty are women.[17] Many of these women are raising small children alone.

The women's movement has encouraged more women to pursue self-development in a manner that was previously reserved for men; however, women are expected and expect themselves to integrate this with the maintenance and nurturance of relationships. A woman's self-esteem is threatened if she is performing below her standards in either her work or her relationships, yet neither the workplace nor most contemporary families are structured in such a way as to make this easily achievable.

It seems clear that men and women have very different approaches to the notion of "self." For women, a sense of self and consequently of self-esteem is deeply entwined with interpersonal relationships. More recently, success at work has been added as a source of self-esteem and identity. For men, a sense of self has been more intimately connected to an identity as a working person, with a later overlay of emotional attachments. We now recognize that half of the culture's population has been able to behave in this apparently separate fashion only because the other half has provided the necessary support and has attended to the relationships that hold society together. Perhaps we can now expand our understanding of the notion of self and self-esteem to include the whole range of human behavior. To be a fully functioning human being, one must have a fully developed individualized self *and* a self that connects with others. Any human being with only one of these two attributes is psychologically impoverished.

Midlife and Elderly Women: Aging and Decreasing Value

As women age, they find their self-esteem again undermined. Our culture is extremely youth oriented, and women are punished more severely than men for normal aging. Facial lines and gray hair give a man character. They make a woman just plain old. The discrepancy between how aging affects a man's self-esteem and a woman's is evident in the cosmetic and anti-aging surgical industry. These products and services are directed primarily at women. The message is that a woman's value decreases as she grows older. She ought to do whatever she can to prevent these natural changes.

On the other hand, a man in his forties, fifties, or sixties is still a good catch—physically, sexually, and economically. If he seeks a second wife following a divorce or widowerhood, she is frequently several years his junior. A heterosexual woman of the same age generally has a much more difficult time finding a suitable companion. Fewer older women enter second or late marriages, even when they might like to. An acquaintance recently told me that heterosexual women who indicate that they are forty or older on the questionnaire for a local computer dating service will not receive a single match.

During this age, a woman enters menopause. Menopause could—and should—be considered a normal life transition. Instead, it has often become a focus of worry and concern. It has been used by both professionals and laypeople as a wastebasket term to explain any kind of psychological distress a woman experiences between her early forties and her late fifties.

In reality, menopause is rarely the actual reason for a woman to become emotionally distraught during this time of life. Rather, it is the meaning of menopause to her and others that is responsible. For example, some people believe that a woman who is no longer able to bear children is less of a woman. This is like the mirror image of adolescence. Reproductivity is again being confused with sexuality. Linking a woman's value to reproductivity rather than to who she is as a person forces her to be judged by events over which she has no control. An older woman is perfectly capable of enjoying an active and rewarding emotional and sexual life if an acceptable partner is available. Yet we tend to deromanticize and desexualize aging women.

Our culture is obsessed with youth. Menopause is the most concrete marker of growing old. This dreaded reality is more easily established in the lives of women than men. If the distress a woman experiences as a result of her decrease in value is wrongly attributed to menopause, the actual cause of her discontent will not be identified, reducing the probability that she will initiate the changes necessary to improve the quality of her life. An opportunity to enhance her self-esteem is missed.

Women as Second-Class Citizens

In addition to the individual developmental milestones of a woman's life that lead to enhanced or diminished self-esteem, the generally held value of women in the culture influences how much an individual woman values herself. No person is completely immune from these cultural messages. Many young girls grow up seeing women being treated as second-class citizens and mothering deemed a second-rate adult activity. As the young girl's identity evolves—first through the relationship with her primary caretaker, usually her mother, and later through her relationships with other important people—she receives a succession of messages indicating that women are the inferior sex. These messages may be as subtle as a mother's preoccupation with dieting and appearance—or as blatant as a father's physical abuse of his wife. The family and community valuation of women will become incorporated into the growing girl's sense of herself even when she consciously fights against them.

In case you are skeptical about my premise that women are still viewed as second-class citizens, consider this recent University of Colorado study. It vividly demonstrates the degree to which women in our culture really are devalued. Two thousand children in grades three through twelve were asked to imagine what it would be like if they found themselves transformed into the opposite sex. Boys were asked to think of what life would be like if they were girls. Girls were asked to imagine themselves as boys.

Boys reported that the experience would be very difficult for them. They used words like *nightmare* and *disaster*. One third grade boy told the researchers, "If I were a girl, everybody would be better than me—because boys are better than girls." Most of the girls, on the other hand, felt that their lives would improve if they became boys. They felt they would gain freedom, social status, self-worth, and value in their parents' eyes.

Women in therapy frequently speak of their conviction that they must do everything possible not to be like their mothers. These women have observed the long devaluation and humiliation of their own mothers as well as their mothers' adaptive, albeit sometimes unhealthy and unhelpful, responses to these experiences. Adult daughters want to avoid a similar fate at almost any cost.[18]

This is easier said than done. For most women, Mother was the primary caretaker. It is almost inevitable that a girl raised primarily by her mother will incorporate many of her qualities. The very awareness that a daughter is in some ways like her mother—who was devalued within the family and within the society—is often enough to substantially lower a woman's self-esteem.

Rebuilding Self-esteem

Children need five basic things in order to have a solid foundation of self-esteem:[19]

1. A sense of significance—The feeling that they matter as people, that they are worth paying attention to and giving love to.
2. A sense of competence—The confidence that they can accomplish their goals and make things happen.
3. A sense of individuality—The knowledge that they are uniquely themselves and that this uniqueness is valued.
4. A sense of realism—The ability to be realistic in their perception of themselves, their abilities, and where they fit in the world.
5. A coherent set of values and ethics—What is right? What is wrong? What is important in life? What do I personally value? High self-esteem rests on the ability to answer these questions with certainty and security.

Most women with high self-esteem have had the good fortune to be born into a psychologically healthy family that provided this kind of foundation. These women received solid support and positive messages from their parents.

If a woman's parents did not provide such support, it was not necessarily because they were bad or intentionally unkind people. As Donovan and Sanford have written, "It's hard to imagine parents leaning over their infant's crib and saying, 'If we play our cards right, this kid will really hate herself when she grows up.' " Most parents grew up in a culture that devalued women. Many parents also suffer from low self-esteem themselves because of the messages they received from *their* parents and the society in which they grew up. They may be trapped in the negative parenting patterns they observed and experienced as children. Other parents were so overwhelmed with their own problems—alcoholism, depression, money worries—that it was simply beyond them to give their children the support they needed. With all these obstacles to achieving high self-esteem, it is almost more surprising when a woman does value herself than when she doesn't.

If you have problems with low self-esteem, all is not lost. There is much you can do—both alone and with the help of others—to bolster your feelings of self-worth. The four guidelines[20] and the exercises that follow suggest some ways to get started in the right direction. The additional resources listed at the end of the chapter provide more details and methods a woman can use to upgrade her self-esteem. It is encouraging to note that these same steps can also help women prevent or deal with depression.

Accepting Your Own Feelings as Rational and Valid

Strong feelings do not necessarily mean that you are out of control. If you are emotionally upset, it is important to trust your gut reaction. This does not mean, of course, that you will act on everything you feel. But your emotions are a barometer of what is going on for you internally. The message may be a little obscure—something like Morse code, but that does not mean it is any less valid. Allow yourself to have your feelings, and then use your brain to figure out what they are trying to communicate. With that information about yourself, you can decide what you want to do with your feelings.

You have a right to express your feelings and thoughts, even if someone else disagrees or sees it differently. Each person in a relationship has an equal right to her or his own opinions and perspectives. I often hear women with low self-esteem speak of others, particularly their husbands, discounting what they have to say. These critics tell the women that they have it all wrong. That they don't know what they are talking about. That that wasn't how it was. This is very disrespectful treatment, since no one person has a monopoly on accuracy. However, because these women are already vulnerable to questioning themselves *and* because they do want to give serious consideration to the other person's perspective, they often end up doubting their own ideas and feelings rather than trusting themselves.

It is important to make and keep close relationships only with people who treat you and your thoughts, feelings, and opinions with respect equal to theirs. To the best of your ability, do not allow yourself to be abused—physically or psychologically—by your partner, husband, boyfriend, or lover. Women with low self-esteem are at risk for becoming involved in abusive relationships. This is often because they haven't the foggiest idea of what a healthy relationship looks like, let alone how to help create one.

If you are currently in an abusive relationship, you must make every attempt to commit yourself to the abuse being stopped. Note that I did not say that you should stop the abuse (unless, of course, you are doing the abusing). The person who is being abusive is the one who should stop! You will need to make it clear that you will not tolerate being abused and that the abusing person is responsible for discontinuing this behavior. Occasionally, if the abuse has not been going on for long and the abusing person feels badly about behaving this way, simply taking an unambivalently self-protective position will stop the abuse. If it continues, the abuser has a serious problem for which she or he needs help. You cannot provide this help. You can only take care of yourself. If the abuse does not stop, consult a battered-women's shelter, a woman's program, a counselor, a lawyer, or the police. And be prepared to leave if the abuse continues.

Short of abuse, you may believe that a disrespectful relationship must be maintained or endured. If this is true, for whatever reason, develop strategies for minimizing the impact of this person on your self-esteem. Using self-encouragement or the informal support of good friends, joining an all-women's support group, or seeking therapy are all reasonable methods for protecting your self-esteem.

Being Able to Please Yourself

Your needs and wants are important, too. It is important that you establish what you like, need, and want. These will come in two categories: your negotiables and your nonnegotiables. Negotiables are desires that are preferred but not absolutely necessary. You can make compromises around them. For example, your sister's family with whom your family vacations every year may want to go to Disneyland, while your family would like to spend time camping. There are several ways that these different desires can be negotiated and the conflict resolved. Perhaps you will make a deal to go one place this year if everyone agrees to go to the other next year. Or perhaps you agree to go to the amusement park providing that you camp at a state park nearby rather than staying at a hotel.

Nonnegotiables are the matters on which you stand firm. There is no room for compromise. It is important to be really clear with yourself about these, because if you accidentally compromise on a nonnegotiable matter, you are going to end up very unhappy. For example, your partner may believe in a nonmonogamous relationship, but you may find this absolutely unacceptable. It is essential that you state your position and make it clear that this is a matter over which there is no compromise.

If a couple disagrees on important nonnegotiable matters, the relationship is up for question. However, there are some nonnegotiables that can be easily accepted within the relationship. Perhaps a reciprocal compromise can be negotiated elsewhere. In our family, we have developed something we call the point system. If one person wants something, perhaps something that is nonnegotiable for them, and the other person would rather not compromise on this matter, but can, an arbitrary number of points are given to the compromising partner. These points can then be used for the "purchase" of a negotiable compromise from the other person at a later date. For example, my partner is an absolute urbanite. I prefer the more open spaces of suburban or rural living. Michael is so clear about his desire to live in a city that he reverse-commutes three hours a day round-trip on the train from home to his full-time job in the suburbs many miles away. I could not tolerate that kind of commute added to a full day's work, but it obviously indicates how important it is for him to live in a city. Indeed, for him it is nonnegotiable. I left a lovely small community north of the city where I was quite content in order to respond to Michael's nonnegotiable desire. It was a significant compromise for me, and I was granted sixty-seven points for making the change. Some of these points were cashed in over time for favors I wanted that Michael would have preferred not doing. The remainder were depleted when I pushed for the purchase of our first home—an investment Michael would have happily declined.

Our point system makes concrete what practically every family does anyway. We all keep score—even if we are not fully aware of doing so. Good relationships are based on mutuality—a give and take that comes out about equal in the long run. However, acknowledging significant sacrifices for the sake of the relationship or pleasing the other person prevents a sense of being taken for granted. The point system is a creative strategy for doing this; I am sure you have, or can invent, others.

To assure that you are pleasing yourself at least as frequently as you aim to please others, you will need to learn to make requests. People cannot read your mind. If you do not tell them what you need or want, they will not know. We have a tendency sometimes to think that what someone does for us is of less value if we have had to ask for it. Sure, something might feel very special if it is done as a surprise or without us having to make our desires known. But if you sit around simply waiting, you greatly reduce the likelihood of getting what you like and need. It is important to take action on your own behalf. Don't wait for someone else to do it for you.

In line with this, it is important that you are prepared to earn your own living. It is perfectly conceivable that there may be periods in your life when you are able to rely on someone else to provide economic support, for example, if you become the full-time caretaker of young children. However, you are likely to feel excessively dependent and less powerful if you are unable to earn a living wage on your own should that be needed or desired. A work identity in this day and age can be just as important to women as it is to men. Research also shows that married women who earn a part of the family income feel that they have more power in their relationships with their husbands than women who do not make an economic contribution.

Pleasing yourself also means making sure that you take time for yourself and

activities, friends, and events that please and interest you. If your life is full with
work, partner, and children, finding time for yourself may seem almost impossible,
but it is essential. Burnout is not simply a problem for presidents of corporations.
You will get very burned-out if you do not reserve opportunities to replenish
yourself.

Most women spend a great deal of energy attending to the needs of others.
Even when a woman works full time outside the home, it is often assumed that
she will continue to provide the traditional female services—cooking, cleaning
house, and dealing with the children. All too often when time runs short, one of
the first things to go (after sleep) is time for herself. It is important for your own
self-worth that you set aside the time to do something "selfish"—something for
yourself. This may mean an hour a day to jog or walk, time in the evening for a
long relaxing bath, or the freedom to spend uninterrupted time with a friend.
Many women living in couples or families will have a difficult time finding such
time for themselves unless they recruit other family members to perform a fair
share of the domestic tasks that used to be considered woman's work.

In pleasing yourself, it is important not to put all your eggs in one basket.
Participate in a variety of cultural, physical, and community activities. Expanding
your range of interests is an insurance policy against the possibility that something
might go wrong in the one or two key areas of your life. Besides enjoying these
varied activities, you'll have the opportunity to make friends with others who share
your new interests.

Identifying Your Strengths

Pleasing yourself and being pleased with yourself also mean seeing yourself accurately and realistically. It means valuing who you are as a woman. While a woman
can easily identify the things she likes about her best friend, she often has much
greater trouble identifying her own strengths and likable characteristics. As part
of our move toward equality between the sexes, we have tended to overemphasize
women adopting values that have historically been characteristic of men. We
began taking assertiveness training, dressing for success, and working rather than
staying home with children. This was an understandable developmental phase as
we struggled to gain the status and power that had previously been reserved for
men. Younger women, who are more likely to take equal rights as a given, are
demonstrating special leadership in working to combine the traditionally feminine
skills and qualities of making and maintaining relationships with the traditionally
masculine skills of self-development and mastery in work.

The strengths women have to offer are of equal value to those men offer.
Women, and enlightened men, are aiming toward feeling OK about being successful and capable as defined by the individual rather than heading toward some
externally defined measure of success. Valuing your feminine strengths of care and
nurturance as highly as your masculine strengths of justice and self-sufficiency are

essential to improving self-esteem. Practice becoming comfortable with making as many positive statements about yourself as you are likely to make about others you value.

Knowing and Accepting Your Imperfections and Being Gentle with Yourself

It is important to be able to state your shortcomings without feeling overly apologetic. No one is perfect. If you make an honest error, it is not the end of the world.

Practice giving yourself comforting messages if you are criticized: "Wow, Pam was really annoyed with me for not getting that message from Ted to her before his office closed. She's right that I ought to have thought about how she was going to return his call if she didn't have it before he left for the day. I don't know what I was thinking about. I sure didn't do it on purpose. I'm usually very good about making sure the staff gets those kinds of messages—even if it means that I have to track them down or interrupt them in a meeting—but sometimes I do seem to space out. I bet as soon as she calms down she'll apologize. She's probably just upset because that sale means so much to her. We usually get along really well. I bet this will blow over pretty quickly."

These kinds of self-empathic messages will help you stay relatively calm in the face of negative input. If you have done the best you can, you can be kind to yourself. Undoubtedly you would be quite forgiving of a friend who made an accidental error. Why maintain a double standard? Be as gentle with yourself as you would with your friend. If you set realistic expectations and manageable goals—neither too high nor too low—you will find it easier to accept your limitations with grace.

Planning Your Own Program for Increasing Your Self-esteem

Working on Your Own

Improving self-esteem includes implementing the personal skills we reviewed earlier. Here are the steps to apply.

1. Accepting my feelings as rational and valid.
   - Validating my feelings by tracing their sources; recognizing that strong feelings do not necessarily mean being out of control.
   - Trusting my feeling reactions as genuine and unique responses to something real.
   - Being able to express my feelings to others as I so choose.
   - Establishing and maintaining close friendships only with people who respect me and my feelings.

2. Being able to please myself.

- Knowing what I like, want, and need.
- Clarifying which of these are nonnegotiable and which are negotiable.
- Feeling important and worthy enough to say what it is I want.
- Taking action on my own behalf; making requests.
- Being prepared to earn my own living.
- Participating in a variety of cultural, physical, and community activities.
- Reserving private time for myself.

3. Identifying my strengths.

- Revaluing my feminine skills and qualities.
- Feeling the courage to be as successful and capable as I can be.
- Making positive statements about myself, to myself and others.

4. Knowing and accepting my imperfections and being gentle with myself.

- Having realistic expectations of myself and manageable ideals to inspire me.
- Feeling calm in the face of criticism.
- Being able to state what my shortcomings are.

Here are a couple of exercises you can do now that may help to start you along the right path.

Exercise 1: Seeing Yourself through a Friend's Eyes[21]

1. Find a quiet, private, comfortable place where you will not be interrupted. Take the phone off the hook.
2. Make yourself comfortable, either lying down or in a chair. If it feels right, close your eyes.
3. Picture someone you trust and care for sitting across from you.
4. Tell that person three things you like about her.
5. Now close your eyes and picture yourself in that chair looking back at yourself.
6. Imagine that you are your friend, and, speaking as that friend, tell yourself three things you like about yourself.
7. After you have completed the steps above, ask yourself which part of the exercise was more difficult—complimenting yourself or complimenting your friend? If you're like most women, you found it harder when you had to speak well of yourself. Why do you think this is?
8. You can begin to counteract this difficulty in speaking well of yourself by finishing the sentence, "I like myself because . . ." at regular intervals throughout the day. Try doing it at regular times—as you're brushing your teeth, taking a shower, or driving to or from work. You wouldn't hesitate

to identify such positive qualities in a friend. Practice being as kind to yourself.

Exercise 2 [22]

One contributor to low self-esteem is continually having our thoughts and feelings invalidated or repeatedly failing to have our needs satisfied. In our desire to avoid the conflict and disapproval we expect if we complain about these experiences, we tend to block, minimize, ignore, or "forget" our deepest feelings. Instead, we tend to express the direct opposite of our true feeling as a form of self-protection. While this adaptation is understandable, ultimately it is detrimental to our self-esteem.

How can you assess your tendency to cope in this manner? Think about how you or others might describe your general behavior and demeanor. If you always act in a totally loving and dutiful way toward others, consider the possibility that you are ignoring legitimate feelings of hostility. If you always aim to preserve an ideal of self-reliance and emphasize toughness over tenderness, consider the possibility that you are ignoring your normal and healthy dependency needs—that is, the freedom to rely on and trust others.

To play with this notion, try on the feeling opposite of your usual style—first in small ways, then in increasingly larger ways. For example, if you are always sweet and kind but still feel intermittently depressed, you are undoubtedly refusing to allow yourself reasonable feelings of annoyance, frustration, and irritation.

We all have things that irk us. The next time something bothers you, let yourself acknowledge it, if only in your own mind. A second and more anxiety-provoking step would be to express these feelings out loud. For example, perhaps one of your coworkers promised to have lunch with you. It was a date that you were really looking forward to. But your friend forgot, and you ended up waiting alone in a café. This is not the first time your friend has forgotten. In fact, her obsession with her own work has meant that this "forgetting" happens frequently. She can count on you always understanding. It's one of the things she tells you that she likes about you, but you're tired of being stood up, even though you do understand how much pressure she feels at work.

This time, try something new. Practice in your mind telling her about your disappointment. Once you feel comfortable with what you have to say, tell her how you feel. Pick a time when you are not particularly upset so you will have more control of your emotions. Phrase your concern diplomatically. This will make you feel better about yourself and will enhance the likelihood that your friend will hear your concern.

You may find it easier to practice this new skill if you begin by telling your friend how hard this is for you and ask that she support you in trying to attend to something that is troubling you in your relationship with her. Make it clear that you value her and want to improve your connection. It is in this context that you are letting her know about some atypical feelings that have arisen and that you believe are important—even if difficult to share. Be prepared for your friend to have her own emotional reaction. After all, you are behaving in a new way, and this alone is likely to surprise her. In addition, you are, perhaps for the first time, registering a complaint with her, and she may initially feel defensive. Stick to your guns. In the long run, your self-esteem and the quality of your relationships will be improved when you are freer to communicate your feelings.

On the other hand, perhaps you have no trouble expressing anger, but giving praise or communicating love sticks in your throat. Perhaps you are extremely uncomfortable relying on others. If this is the case, design an exercise that allows you to practice the very thing that you usually avoid—perhaps even disdain. An easily angered woman might try looking at an irritating situation in the most benevolent terms; a woman who has to do everything herself (the socially sanctioned and reinforced Superwoman is a recent variation on this theme) might try asking a friend to accompany her to outpatient surgery while she has a checkup for an atypical Pap smear. As Linda K. Stere noted, "Personal independence is [not defined as] not needing others, but as the ability to find companionship in which one can be most openly and honestly oneself."

Exercise 3 [23]

Identify three women, real or fictitious, and describe what you admire or appreciate about them. What characteristics do you have in common with these women? What do they do that you also aspire to?

As a young woman, I was a great fan of Katharine Hepburn. Seeing her live a life as an unmarried, childless woman who clearly supported herself and contributed to the larger world was a great reassurance to me. Her life-style was in marked contrast to the lives of the women in the working-class suburb where I grew up. It gave me hope that my own natural inclinations, while contrary to the apparent choices or most readily available options for women in my hometown, were viable alternatives.

Who have been your role models? How do these women reflect qualities that you may be denying in yourself? Are you glorifying these women to keep yourself down? Consider picking one or a few friends with whom you can discuss these matters. Talk with one another about what you have in common with these role models. Aim to define realistic ideals and models for inspiration rather than setting yourself up against women who have had extraordinary resources, support, or gifts that gave them a distinct advantage.[24]

Using Supportive Friends Informally

If you did not have the good fortune to be born into a family that fostered healthy self-esteem (no woman was born into a society that values women equally to all men), you will need to create opportunities for this in your adult life. This means participating in relationships where you receive as well as give in loving and growth-enhancing ways. Reaching out to friends and acquaintances for human contact is just as important as depending on members of your immediate family. It is unrealistic to expect that family members will be able to meet all your needs for emotional contact—especially if any of these people also suffer with low self-esteem themselves. Limiting yourself to only a few social contacts leaves you tremendously vulnerable to unexpected changes in your primary relationships.

Build relationships with nurturing people with high self-esteem. I call this "playing up." Improving one's self-esteem is like learning to play tennis—you will benefit the most by playing with people who are good at it. Seek out people—women and men—who are nice and who feel good about themselves. Because these people like themselves and clearly choose to be with you, just spending time with them will begin to make you feel better about yourself. In addition, such friends will be excellent role models. They are likely to have a variety of friends and a diversity of skills. They will be people who care but who also realize that you cannot always please everybody or do everything. They will appreciate their own strengths and will forgive themselves for their weaknesses—and they will do the same for you. This will help you build your own self-esteem, because you will learn that you are lovable just the way you are.

Having a network of supportive women friends is particularly important. Even in the best of marriages, women usually outlive their mates. In their later years, women are much more likely to live out their days surrounded by other women. For young and old women alike, the friendship of women can be a vital source of strength, encouragement, and nurturance.

Using Formal Support Groups

Local organizations frequently sponsor groups for women. The themes may be specific, such as a midlife women's support group, a group for the adult children of alcoholics, a group for first-time mothers, or a general women's support group. If there is nothing to your liking in your own community, consider starting a group. You might recruit members from your existing friendship network or aim to locate new and unfamiliar women by placing an ad in the local newspaper or a notice on a community bulletin board. As the founder, you might set the time and place for the first meeting, but thereafter responsibility can rotate or questions can be decided jointly. An agenda for the first meeting could be just getting to know one another a little bit and discussing how you would all like the group to work. Some groups have a regular schedule of topics; others are more free-floating. Some are simply safe places where women can air their complaints and concerns privately with one another; others are geared toward problem solving. You can design your support group any way you wish.

Using a Therapist

While valuable and useful, self-help plans, friends, and support groups may not be enough to restore your self-esteem. If that is the case, you may wish to hire a competent and concerned therapist. A good therapeutic relationship can be an excellent way to correct damage that was done—either intentionally or unintentionally—at an earlier period of your life. Those past years can never be relived, but a good therapist can help you take charge and enjoy more fully the years that remain.

Activism

You will also need to rebel against and resist society's devaluing of women. It is not easy, but it can be done with knowledge, awareness, and the support of other like-minded people. Activism can occur at a very personal level within your own life or at a larger level in public, social, or political arenas. Rather than conforming to external messages and pressure, activism allows us to aim for authenticity. Achieving psychological health means there is a congruence between who we feel and believe we really are on the inside and how we present ourselves to the world. People who are unable to live authentically expend considerable energy maintaining the discrepancy between their true selves and the false self that shows outside. Many people will not be able to live authentically, however, until we as individuals and as a society dismantle the barriers that discriminate against them. This means tackling the racism, ageism, homophobia, and sexism that continue to plague our culture.

Conclusions

Our self-esteem affects virtually everything we think, say, and do. It influences whom we select as our friends and what we decide to do with our lives, and it has significant impact on how others treat us. It affects our ability to take action and to change conditions that do not suit us—in our personal lives and in the world at large.

Perhaps the two most important things you can do to bolster your own self-esteem are:

1. Surround yourself with nurturing, supportive people who genuinely care for you.
2. Fight for the rights of all women to be treated with love, value, and respect.

It bears repeating. *Contrary to popular belief, self-esteem does not come about by learning to love yourself, nor is it something you can give yourself. Self-esteem comes, at least initially, from other people loving and valuing you. It also comes from how much we are loved, valued, and respected as women in the culture at large.*

Whichever way you choose to approach it, the task of increasing your own self-esteem can yield immense rewards. It can help you find more contentment and satisfaction in your life. It can help improve your ability to attain your goals and to cope with life's inevitable disappointments. It can help you act effectively on your own behalf.

By increasing your self-esteem, you will not only learn to take better care of yourself, you will also be in a much better position to care for those you love. Ultimately, the best way to be good to the other important people in your life is to be equally good to yourself. Having the psychological resources to care for others in a generous way is like having a checking account. You have extra to give others if the amount for your own expenses is covered first. You truly need enough for yourself before you really have enough to give others without feeling depleted, resentful, or angry.

This new view of women's psychology provides a perspective from which the process of rebuilding self-esteem is not nearly as overwhelming as it might seem. Many women feel that in order to increase their self-esteem they need to have a total psychological and physical makeover. In large part this is because women have until recently been measured against inaccurate standards of psychological health.

Women can begin to improve their self-esteem by letting go of the old, obsolete, male-influenced models of psychological health. Rather than changing themselves, women can engage in more self-appreciation and self-acceptance. Learn to accept and acknowledge what you already have and to love the remarkable, capable, and vulnerable person you already are.

Because our culture is not pro-woman, you are swimming upstream. It is important to know and remember that many of the troubles you are experiencing are not of your making. Your difficulty finding a man who treats you like a true peer, your history of having grown up in a dysfunctional family, your experience with career obstacles such as sexual harassment or employment discrimination, the resistance of your employers to adapt to your biological and societal role as primary caretaker and nurturer in the family, the reality of being a woman in the world where few women hold positions of power and authority—these are part of the many forces contributing to your struggle in feeling deeply comfortable with your feelings and values. Having recognized these forces, you can actively begin to take charge of minimizing their current influence on you through active awareness and personal retraining. The task of reclaiming our self-esteem is not to take on the values, attitudes, and behaviors of men. The goal is to accept ourselves as we are and to have the values, perspectives, and attributes of women fully integrated into society at large.

ADDITIONAL READING

Dorothy Corkille Briggs, *Celebrate Yourself* (Garden City, N.Y.: Doubleday, 1977).

Linda Tschirhart Sanford and Mary Ellen Donovan, *Women and Self-esteem* (New York: Anchor/Doubleday, 1984).

NOTES

1. Myrna M. Weissman and Gerald L. Klerman, "Sex Differences and the Epidemiology of Depression," *Archives of General Psychiatry* 34(1977): 98–111.

2. Prominent works include Nathaniel Branden, *The Psychology of Self-esteem* (New York: Bantam Books, 1969); Stanley Coopersmith, *The Antecedents of Self-esteem* (San Francisco: W. H. Freeman & Co., 1967); and Morris Rosenberg, *Conceiving the Self* (New York: Basic Books, 1979). Except for five paragraphs near the end of Rosenberg's book where he specifically discusses women, these authors seem to assume that their material applies equally to women and men.

3. Linda Tschirhart Sanford and Mary Ellen Donovan, *Women and Self-esteem* (New York: Penguin, 1984).

4. According to Helen Collier, except in settings established specifically by and for women, the majority of mental-health-care providers are male even though two-thirds of all patients seeking psychological help are women. Helen V. Collier, *Counseling Women: A Guide for Therapists* (New York: The Free Press, 1982), p. 3.

5. Female-influenced theorists argue that the separation-individuation model may well be an accurate reflection of our culture's approach to raising men, but that it is an inappropriate standard for evaluating female psychological development. Even among men, the notion of separation may be an illusion. Heterosexual men are viewed as separate when, in fact, they are very much connected through their relationships with women. Work with couples in which the female partner is reducing or discontinuing her emotional and domestic support after many years of "marital service" has demonstrated the reality of a man's dependency and interconnectedness. When the woman insists on alterating the balance of power within the relationship or expresses a desire to pursue a separation or divorce, this allegedly separate man often experiences profound psychological distress. This "independent" man, who has presumably achieved a high degree of psychological separation, has actually been receiving a great deal of support and caretaking. Much of this has been provided by women—a mother, a wife, daughters, a lover, a secretary, or a housekeeper. Rather than being separate, these men are highly connected. However, the man's visibility and the women's relatively invisibility as the behind-the-scenes people perpetuates the appearance of male separateness, autonomy, and independence.

6. Daniel N. Stern, *The Interpersonal World of the Infant: A View for Psychoanalysis and Developmental Psychology* (New York: Basic Books, 1985).

7. Including Jean Baker Miller, Carol Gilligan, and others affiliated with the Stone Center for Developmental Services and Studies at Wellesley College.

8. Judith V. Jordan, "Empathy and Self Boundaries," Work in Progress (Wellesley, Mass.: Wellesley College, 1984) and Judith Jordan, Janet L. Surrey, and Alexandra Kaplan, "Women and Empathy: Implications for Psychological Development and Psychotherapy," Work in Progress (Wellesley, Mass.: Wellesley College, 1983).

9. Jean Baker Miller, "What Do We Mean by Relationships?" Work in Progress no. 12 (Wellesley, Mass.: Wellesley College, 1984); Janet L. Surrey, "Self-in-Relation: A Theory of Women's Development," Work in Progress no. 13 (Wellesley, Mass.: Wellesley College, 1984); and Jordan, "Empathy and Self Boundaries," p. 1.

10. An exception, of course, may be abusive relationships, which may involve a relative or complete separation. However, this kind of physical separation ought not to be confused with the kind of internal psychological constructs we are discussing here.

11. "Girls Do More, Get Less: Traditional Sex Roles Reinforced, P.A. Survey Shows," *San Jose Mercury News*, 1987.

12. Michelle Fine, "Reflection of a Feminist Psychology of Women: Paradoxes and Prospects," *Psychology of Women Quarterly* 9 (1985): 174.

13. "A Special Report: The Corporate Woman," *The Wall Street Journal*, March 24, 1986.

14. Susan Faludi, "Diane Joyce," *Ms.*, January 1988, p. 64.

15. Women earned approximately $.59 to the male dollar in 1980, as compared with $.58 in 1939 and $.59 in 1959. U.S. Bureau of Labor Statistics. *Perspectives on Working Women: A Data Book* (Bulletin 2080). Washington, D.C.: U.S. Printing Office, 1980. Women's median earnings as a percentage of men's median earnings, however, have been slowly improving since then. In 1988 women earned approximately $.70 to the male dollar. Alison Leigh Cowan, "Poll Finds Women's Gains Have Been Taking a Personal Toll," *The New York Times*, August 21, 1989, p. 8.

16. "The ratio of women's-to-men's earnings is highest among younger workers 16 to 24 years old—89%. It declines with age to 60% for the over-65 population . . . Men continue to out-earn women in virtually every broad occupation group." From "Paychecks Keep Up With Inflation," *San Francisco Chronicle*, July 31, 1987.

17. Reported by the National Advisory Commission of Economic Opportunity, *Jobs Watch* 1 no. 6 (1981).

18. Irene P. Stiver, "Beyond the Oedipus Complex: Mothers and Daughters," Work in Progress no. 26 (Wellesley, Mass.: Wellesley College, 1986), p. 23.

19. Sanford and Donovan, *Women and Self-esteem,* pp. 38–55.

20. Identified by Linda K. Stere in "Feminist Assertiveness Training: Self-esteem Groups as Skill Training for Women," in *Handbook of Feminist Therapy: Women's Issues in Psychotherapy,* ed. Lynne Bravo Rosewater and Lenore E. A. Walker (New York: Springer, 1985).

21. This section is adapted from Dorothy Corkille Briggs, *Celebrate Yourself* (Garden City, N.Y.: Doubleday, 1977) and Sanford and Donovan, *Women and Self-esteem,* p. 20.

22. Variant of a task described in Stere, "Feminist Assertiveness Training," pp. 56–57.

23. Variant of a task described in Stere, "Feminist Assertiveness Training," p. 58.

24. Miriam Polster in "Women In Therapy—A Gestalt Therapist's View," in Violet Franks and Vasante Burtle, eds., *Women and Therapy: New Psychotherapies for a Changing Society* (New York: Brunner/Mazel, 1974), pp. 247–62 has noted that growing up female in this society would cripple or deform all but the most exceptional.

7 | **D**epression

Depression is overwhelmingly a woman's problem. Over her lifetime, a woman is nearly twice as likely as a man to experience depression.[1] For one in ten women, this depression will be very severe.[2]

In this chapter, we will review what depression is and identify some of the known and suspected causes. We will also suggest corrective measures, because appropriate intervention can prevent or reduce the symptoms of depression.

Depression: Normal or Pathological?

Sad moods and depressed feelings are part of everyone's experience. As a "normal" mood, feeling blue or depressed is a transient phenomenon. When a woman is plagued by persistent and pervasive feelings of hopelessness, helplessness, guilt, self-recrimination, and low self-esteem, she is said to be suffering from pathological depression. Such despair is an indication of an underlying problem that needs attention. Unfortunately, the boundary between this kind of "normal" depression and something more serious can be fuzzy, but there are guidelines to assess a depression's severity.

Of the many schemes used to classify the various types of depression, we have found an integrated approach most useful.[3] In assessing the source of a woman's depression, three categories must be investigated:

1. Biological causes.
2. Internal contributors (interpretation of events, failure to use anger appropriately, always putting others first, etc.).
3. External contributors (loss, trauma, social expectations, etc.).

Each category must be thoroughly evaluated. When more than one factor is involved, each must be addressed to assure complete improvement.

Unfortunately, there is a tendency among mental-health professionals to focus on only one or two of these three key factors. Some look only at the biological aspects of depression; others consider only the internal or intrapsychic factors; and growing numbers now combine a sophisticated understanding of the biological and intrapsychic origins of depression. However, only a limited number of professionals consider all three factors.

Among professional therapists, it is the external social and cultural influences that are most frequently underestimated. This is indeed unfortunate, because *the primary reason most women experience depression is the particularly malignant overlap between external contributors and women's unique internal psychology.* [4]

Biological Depressions: The Affective or Mood Disorders

Biological depression is a medical problem. It may last for a few weeks or many months. Often there are depression-free periods between bouts of major depression, but for some people, biological depressions alternate with periods of mania (extremely elevated and expansive moods). This pattern is called manic-depressive illness or bipolar disorder. Neither major depression nor manic-depressive illness will respond to social support or therapy alone. Treatment with the appropriate medication is necessary.

If you experience five or more of the following symptoms for at least two weeks, you may be suffering from a biological depression:[5]

1. Depressed mood.
2. The inability to feel pleasure, even temporarily, from things that were previously of interest (ahedonia).
3. A loss of appetite with a weight loss (as much as seven pounds in a month)—occasionally excessive eating with weight gain.
4. Consistent trouble going to sleep and staying asleep—or excessive sleeping.
5. Slowness of speech, movement, or thought (psychomotor retardation)—or marked agitation.
6. Loss of energy and interest in activities (fatigue or lethargy) including a decrease in your previous level of sexual interest and/or activity.
7. Feelings of worthlessness and/or excessive guilt.
8. A decreased ability to think or concentrate or marked indecisiveness.
9. Unrelieved sadness and gloom with recurrent thoughts of death or suicide.

What causes this type of depression? Some medical problems—and certain drugs—can produce biological depression. A person who experiences a sudden or unexplained depression should have a thorough physical exam to rule out specific physical illnesses. Cushing's disease, hypothyroidism, and other conditions can produce depressive symptoms. Steroids, thyroid medications, birth-control pills, and other drugs that affect the body's hormone levels can also produce depression. In these situations, treating the medical problem or altering use of the medication is the appropriate intervention and usually results in improvement. Occasionally, additional treatment with therapy and/or antidepressant medication is advised.

In most cases, biological depression is caused by other less obvious changes in the body's functioning. The specific causes of biological depression are still not clearly understood, although researchers have a number of working hypotheses, including:[6]

1. Changes in the brain's neurotransmitters—Neurotransmitters are chemical messengers in the brain that control mood and several body functions. People who are biologically depressed appear to have lower levels of some of these neurotransmitters. They not only feel gloomy, they also experience alterations in appetite, sleep, energy levels, and sexual interest.
2. Changes in the body's endocrine or hormone system—Some people seem to have trouble effectively regulating certain hormone levels, especially levels of cortisol. This hormone, which plays a critical role in a person's response to stress, has been found to be abnormally elevated in many patients suffering with depression. The dexamethazone suppression test (DST)[7] is currently being used at some medical centers to assess flaws in this regulatory system. Unfortunately, the test has not proved sufficiently accurate to be used on a regular basis by general psychiatrists.
3. Changes in the brain due to separation and loss—Some studies have revealed a relationship between the stressful events of separation and loss and biological changes in the brain. These changes seem to be reversible with appropriate intervention.
4. Changes in "natural" body rhythms—Circadian rhythms are the natural twenty-four-hour schedules of our bodies. Some research suggests that these rhythms are disrupted in depression (and mania).

Because depression is more common in women than men, two assumptions have often been made: that women have a greater genetic or hereditary tendency to become more depressed than men or that depression in women is caused by the presence of female hormones. Neither of these hypotheses seem to hold up under critical examination.[8]

There is reasonable evidence that vulnerability to affective disorders does run in families, but not more so for women than for men.[9] The closer you are genetically to a relative who has a history of biological depression (or a bipolar disorder), the greater your risk of developing such a problem. For example, the identical twin of a person with a biological depression has a greater risk of developing the disorder than another sibling. Alcoholism and eating disorders also seem to run in these families. These correlations have led some researchers to speculate that there might be a link between alcoholism, eating disorders, and depression, although this has not been proven.

What about female hormones? For years, it has been believed that depressions were associated with women's reproductive cycle. However, research findings are inconsistent. There is good evidence that premenstrual tension and birth-control pills may cause a small increase in depression but not enough to account for the large number of women who become depressed. There is excellent evidence of an increased risk of depression following the birth of a child, although the mechanism for this is unknown. Even so, this risk does not explain why women are twice as likely to be depressed as men across their lifespans. And, contrary to conventional wisdom, research indicates that a woman is not at greater risk for depression during menopause.[10] If a woman becomes depressed at this time, it is indicative that something else in her life is depressing her. If that problem is neglected and it is assumed that her problem is menopause, appropriate attention to her genuine problem will be neglected.

The few contemporary researchers who specialize in female endocrine physiology have demonstrated that gender differences do matter when assessing the biological causes of depression.[11] They note that the tendency to accept rather than question old myths about women seems to have interfered with rigorous scientific investigations. Careful attention to gender and age reveal striking relationships between these factors and the response to medical treatment of depression, but researchers have rarely included this kind of data in their studies. Obviously, much more work is needed in this area.

The diagnosis of a biological depression is based on a clinical evaluation by a trained psychiatrist. Considerable clinical experience has shown that biological depression can be successfully treated with proper medication.[12] If depression occurs without episodes of mania, the medication of choice is an antidepressant (see the appendix for a list of these medications). If periods of major depression alternate with episodes of mania, the treatment of choice is lithium carbonate.

There are several different kinds or classes of antidepressant medications. As their effects vary from person to person, the process of finding the right drug and the right dose is a one-on-one collaborative endeavor between the patient and the clinician. The challenge is to find the one medication and the proper dose that works for each individual. This may require several trials with medications from a variety of classes. One does not become immediately "undepressed" with the use of these medications. A trial period of two to six weeks is required before it is clear whether or not the medication is working.

Some people have reservations about taking these medications because they do not want to become dependent on them. We have all heard horror stories of people who became addicted to mood-altering medications. Lithium carbonate and antidepressants do not fall into this category. They do have some annoying side effects and must be taken exactly as prescribed, but they are not physically addictive.[13]

These medications must be taken under medical supervision, but they are not a crutch. It is no more a weakness to rely on appropriate medication for the treatment of biological depression than for the treatment of diabetes or any other medical problem. While mild mood changes may be under our conscious control, major mood swings are not. It would be an error to deny ourselves the opportunity for appropriate medical care.

Internal Contributors to Depression: Learning to Be Depressed

The way we are raised in our family and socialized in our culture plays a major role in the development of our internal psychology (or intrapsychic structure). We learn how to be female or male and the different psychological attributes that are expected of women and men. Unfortunately, rather than being seen simply as different psychologies, mental-health professionals have viewed the stereotypical characteristics of men as superior to those of women.[14]

The majority of therapists in a 1970 study equated the characteristics of a healthy person with the characteristics of a healthy man, including being "active, independent, competitive, and logical." However, a "healthy" woman was reported as being "submissive, dependent, subjective, emotional, and easily hurt." When retested in 1983, these stereotypes remained relatively unchanged in spite of the women's movement.[15]

This research implies that it is impossible to be both a healthy woman and a healthy adult. Indeed, the characteristics of the so-called healthy woman are a setup for depression. Learning to be feminine means learning to be depressed.[16] Unfortunately, many women who experience these feelings do not even realize they are depressed. Instead, they accept this mood as a normal way of life.

Interestingly, two authorities in the study of depression, Drs. Arieti and Bemporad, accurately described the depressive-prone personality without recognizing that it was precisely the personality structure expected of women. In 1978, they reported that the person with a placating personality demonstrated "the necessity to please others and to act in accordance with their expectations . . . [which] makes him unable to get really in touch with himself. He does not listen to his own wishes; he does not know what it means to be himself . . . When he experiences feelings of unhappiness, futility, and unfulfillment, he tends to believe that he is to be blamed for them."[17] These authors saw the link between this personality structure and vulnerability to depression. They understood that a *man's* inability to listen to his own wishes, need to please others, and feelings of self-blame were problematic. What they did not seem to appreciate was that these characteristics are far more common among women than men. Indeed, women are encouraged to pay more attention to and support the wishes of others over their own—particularly the wishes of their partners and their children.

Women are trained to please others whom they are expected to serve—

unselfishly. At the same time, women are criticized for being attentive to others and are expected to accept blame for failure when a relationship or a person does not develop in a healthy and satisfying way. Women are then labeled as dependent, masochistic, and smothering. In fact, women are expected to be wholly attentive to others and never to expect reciprocal attention to their own needs and desires. That is quite a dance, if you can do it. Most women try, not recognizing the impossibility of succeeding at the task being asked of them. Even when they become depressed, they see the problem as their weakness rather than as a flawed situation.

For men, a different and complementary role is expected. We tend to admire a man for what he does. His actions may reflect little or no contribution to building relationships, and his self-esteem is not tied up with his capacity to forge these connections. At its simplest (and, of course, neither life nor psychology is that simple), a man becomes depressed if he does not reach his expected goals; a woman becomes depressed if relationships for which she holds herself responsible are not working well. Men seek achievement through their own accomplishments, which is psychologically very different from seeking growth through connection.

As a general rule, relationships do not have the same meaning for men as they do for women. Men definitely want relationships, but what they want, expect, and usually receive in relationships is support. Indeed, there is often a host of women—wives, secretaries, housekeepers—supporting "autonomous" men. For men, relationships mean *receiving* emotional and practical support, sometimes in exchange for providing economic support (although men increasingly carry less of the burden for this). For women, relationships mean *providing* emotional and practical support (and, increasingly, economic support as well).

Male-influenced psychological theories stress the importance of becoming an autonomous and separate person as the healthiest developmental path. Given the expectations and resulting attributes of many women, this hardly seems an accurate model of female development. As an alternative, a self-in-relation model has been proposed to describe more precisely the psychology of women.[18] This model suggests that a woman's core sense of herself and her primary motivation for psychological growth occur within the context of relationships. Thus, while males are encouraged to value independence, females are trained to value social connections.[19]

Mainstream psychological theory proposes that the intrapsychic causes of depression are:

1. the personal interpretation of an emotional loss,
2. the inhibition of anger, aggression, and the avoidance of conflict,
3. the inhibition of action, and finally
4. low self-esteem.

Using the self-in-relation model, we can easily understand why a woman who tries to live up to the expectations of her role as a woman is profoundly vulnerable to depression.

1. The personal interpretation of an emotional loss—An actual loss or trauma that is not fully resolved and grieved for will leave a person vulnerable to depression. Many depressed women have not only experienced such a loss or trauma, but they *have lost the confirmations of a core part of their identity—their sense of self-in-relation.*

   Women seek to maintain empathic connections with others. Women want these connections to be mutual, and they are disappointed when this does not happen. If this disconnection occurs repeatedly, as it often does in heterosexual relationships, a woman feels as if she is in a constant state of loss—a loss of emotional connectedness, a loss of the core sense of herself as a person. If this occurs over a lifetime—first through the rejection of a parent, later from a spouse—the message is that a woman's basic desire for connection and for growth within a relationship is wrong.

2. Inhibition of anger, aggression, and the avoidance of conflict—Women are often reluctant to express or sometimes even experience their own anger for fear that it will disrupt important relationships. It is hard for a woman to express her legitimate anger if she is worried that others will not take her concern seriously or that they will reject her for complaining. If others experience or misinterpret assertiveness in women as anger, or if they label her anger as excessive, inappropriate, or unnecessary, a woman may begin to view her anger as destructive. She may then inhibit thoughts, actions, and feelings that are essential if she is to feel better.[20] Holding back appropriate anger is disempowering. It leaves women with a sense of being constricted, of something being wrong. Unfortunately, women rarely have the opportunity to discover that the diplomatic communication of anger within the context of a mutually empathic relationship can be an affirming and bonding experience.

3. Inhibition of action—If a woman feels that she cannot control the consequences of her behavior, she may grow increasingly reluctant to act on her own behalf. Researchers have described this as learned helplessness.[21] When no amount of accommodation or adaptation on a woman's part seems to make a relationship work successfully, she tends to take responsibility for the problem. If only she was "better," the couple would not have this difficulty. Pained by the disconnection, she tries harder to establish the connection—to reinforce her core sense of self-in-relation. Unfortunately, this action is almost always directed at what is good for someone else, rather than what is best for herself. For example, a woman who spent ten years supporting her husband while he developed his career may have enormous difficulty developing her career when she discovers that he is not as genuinely supportive of her development as she was of his. To continue building her career would mean not only displeasing him but also risking the relationship. Faced with this possibility, many women become paralyzed and cannot act on their own behalf.

4. Low self-esteem—A woman's sense of self-worth rests heavily on her ability to make and build relationships. It is dependent on the freedom to pursue one's other desires, behavior that is strongly encouraged in men. Women, on the other hand, often feel that if they pursue their own interests, their connections will be threatened. A woman who focuses on achievement in much the same way as a man may feel unhappy and dissatisfied if the price she has to pay is the loss of a gratifying primary relationship. Men know that they can have both—women do not (and often cannot), since it takes their partners' cooperation to foster achievement and many male partners are unwilling to provide it.

A key aspect of women's psychology is their capacity to be attuned to the feelings of others. Women learn to value empathizing with others. Beyond the routine and often mundane tasks of daily caretaking, this empathy has a profound impact on other's development. For women, being connected with others in this way is central to healthy development. Women learn to value the process of facilitating and enhancing connectedness; at the same time, their own identity is enriched and clarified through the increasingly complex network of relationships that results.

In the most satisfying relationships, this is a reciprocal process. The capacity to be understanding is balanced by the experience of being understood. This connection does not detract from individual development, nor is it a one-way street where only one person benefits. When there is give and take, both participants feel enhanced and empowered through their empathic connection with each other. Unfortunately, in our culture the focus is on becoming separate, not on development within the context of relationships. Such development is viewed as a weakness rather than a strength.

When heterosexual relationships do not work, women are seen as needy, passive, and "loving too much." When relationships with children are unsatisfactory, the tendency is to blame Mother for her failings.[22] In both situations, the women usually see themselves as failures. What is ignored is that in many relationships women are expected to care for others without requiring nurturance, support, and validation in return; often prevented from fully developing their relational capacities; and frequently punished for expressing themselves in this vein. To make matters worse, what looks on the outside like passivity, dependence, and helplessness actually requires considerable internal activity. A woman is supposed to behave in a selfless way in order to live out the kind of "goodness" that is expected of her. This means that she must actively silence any negative thoughts and feelings that she and society find unacceptable.[23] The lack of respect for women's strengths, the absence of mutuality in heterosexual relationships, and the unending expectation of self-sacrifice make depression understandable and inevitable.

External Contributors to Depression

Loss, trauma, and women's second-place status in society are the three most common external factors that cause depression for women.

Loss

Since making and maintaining relationships are very important to the psychological health of women, separation and loss within a relationship can be a particularly upsetting experience. The intensity of the upset is usually proportional to the importance of the person or thing lost or depth of the trauma.

Sudden or unexpected personal tragedies may be more difficult to deal with than those that can be anticipated. A loss due to an accident or sudden abandonment may cause a much more severe depression than the death of aging parents or a loved one who has been suffering with a prolonged medical illness. In these circumstances, we might be sad and miss the person, but there has been time to prepare. In fact, if the loved one has been in considerable pain or distress, we might actually be relieved that they are no longer suffering. Depression caused by loss can be mild or severe, but it is likely to be relatively short-lived if a woman has other intimate and confiding relationships in her life.

Trauma

Experiences of trauma or abuse, whether subtle or severe, also undermine a woman's psychological health. While men have been the primary victims of violence at the hands of strangers, women are more commonly the victims of violence by loved ones. Whether the trauma is incest, date rape, sexual assault, or battering, many women realize that they are at risk for this kind of abuse.[24] We are only now beginning to recognize the long-term consequences of living under such circumstances. One is that women cannot automatically assume that heterosexual relationships are safe. This undermines many women's ability to trust the person with whom they are most intimate.

Learning to protect yourself physically is one of the most useful psychological protections against violence. A self-defense class specifically designed for women can be particularly empowering. This kind of training affords a woman some protection against larger, threatening people. Preparing for a potential assault by rehearsing options may facilitate a lifesaving response if and when a woman faces an actual assault. Women who are prepared to be "unladylike" have demonstrated that quick and clearheaded thinking is incredibly important in self-protection.[25]

Unresolved childhood losses and traumas also leave a legacy that effects present-day functioning. As children, we feel helpless in the face of overwhelmingly painful events. Whether it is a caregiver's depression, our parents' divorce, or inadequate parenting, we respond protectively with a variety of strategies called defense mechanisms. At the time, these are adaptive and, given our limited resources, enhance our survival. However, these same defense mechanisms may operate as automatic responses later in life when they are no longer necessary or appropriate. What was once helpful now interferes with healthy functioning and development.

Adult depression is often linked to these early childhood experiences—even those that we may not remember. With our resources as adults, we need an opportunity to acknowledge and process these early fears, traumas, and losses. The loving support of close family and friends and, if necessary, the support of a supervised lay counselor or professional therapist can facilitate the healing of these old wounds.

Other kinds of trauma, such as witnessing an accident, surviving a major fire in your home, or experiencing a substantial financial loss, can also precipitate a depression. Ironically, even positive events such as a promotion at work can stimulate depression if they mean a significant change in our life-style or relationships.

Unfortunately, some traumatic experiences are random and not preventable. Women should not hold themselves responsible for events over which they have no control. Acknowledging our feelings about surviving and processing the consequences of experiencing trauma are necessary for recovery and healing.

The best "treatment" for depression caused by loss and trauma is the loving support of family and friends. The broader a woman's social network, the more support she can count on to carry her through a depression. Close friends and intimates serve as an emotional safety net that can support us during these difficult times. If an adult woman is the victim of an assault in spite of her efforts, she may want to file a legal complaint.[26] For some women, participating in social activism allows them to feel that they are exercising some power and influence over would-be assailants.

It is also important that men recognize their role in contributing to women's vulnerability to violence and depression. It is especially important that fathers and the loving partners of women participate in correcting the unnecessary exposure of girls and women to threatened or actual abuse and violence. As the old saying goes, "If you're not part of the solution, you're part of the problem." Men who would never consider abusing their own children, wives, or female friends and yet do nothing to stop abuse by other men are passively colluding in ways that are damaging to all female-male relationships and to women specifically.

We must come to grips with those events over which we have no control and work on those that we can change through our efforts and with the help of others. Eventually, we will regain a sense of relative mastery in our world.

Women's Social Status

The most pervasive external contributor to women's depression is contained within our social structure. We grow up believing that all Americans have equal access to opportunity and that those who excel will naturally rise to the top. But this is not actually the case. Our society has a political and economic power hierarchy. The greatest number of human beings are clustered at the bottom, a substantial but nonetheless smaller number are in the middle, and a very few are at the top. The people at the top have the most power. The people on the bottom have the least and are expected to be subservient to those above them. People in the middle have more power than people on the bottom but less than those higher up. They are to respect the status of their superiors while also exercising power over those below them.

One's place in the power hierarchy is as influenced by socioeconomic class, racial and ethnic background, and gender as it is by talent, initiative, self-discipline, and ambition. The freedom to move between the different levels is restricted to a large extent by these inherent characteristics. It is these restrictions (discriminations) that keep the power gradient relatively unchanged. The base of the pyramid has more poor people, more people of color, and more women. As we move up the pyramid, people become better off financially and there are significantly fewer people of color and women. While women provide two-thirds of the world's work hours and produce 44 percent of the world's food supply, they receive only 10 percent of the world's income and own only 1 percent of the world's property (and much of that ownership is on paper only, for tax purposes).[27] Obviously, the world is run more by men than it is by women.

Our social system needs certain kinds of people to perpetuate this power hierarchy. It needs aggressive, dominant people (usually men) who still respect the power of those above them and passive, subservient people (usually women) to serve the dominants. This system has a profound effect on men's and women's psychology.

For a heterosexual woman, the patriarchal structure of society is usually duplicated in her closest love relationship. Her subordinate status means that she has less power than the man with whom she lives—and often loves. It means that if a woman's inner thoughts or feelings are at odds with her male partner's, she is required to inhibit her internal experiences as well as any actions they might stimulate. She is to appear conforming, compliant, and submissive. To do this, she often tells herself how she *should* feel and think instead of acknowledging how she *does* feel and think. She squelches her authentic self—her real self—but in doing so, she begins to experience resentment and anger.

This anger is complex. She is angry because her perfectly normal needs for intimacy are not being met. Indeed, her desire for intimacy and her needs for a relationship are viewed as weaknesses. She is angry at herself because she has abandoned her own feelings, thoughts, and goals by continually putting others first. She is angry at others (her husband, parents, religion, society) who assign her a morality of care[28] and self-sacrifice that supports the destruction of her authenticity.

Women have learned to repress this anger in order to survive—within their relationships with men and within the society at large. They have turned this anger inward, becoming depressed. Women who do this successfully are seen as having adapted to society. Women who do not successfully repress their anger experience, at the very least, social coercion and ostracism ("She's such a bitch!") and, at the worst, battering and abuse.

Women are often trying—although not consciously—to resolve their conflicting desires to simultaneously preserve and eradicate their dependency on men. Depression is the emotional compromise. Women *want* intimate relationships with men, yet staying in them often means a kind of economic and social dependency that feels like giving themselves away. Being depressed instead of being angry allows a woman to stay dissatisfied or unhappy. Whatever anger women do experience in these situations is often chronic and bitter rather than active and energizing.

Depression is inevitable if a woman sacrifices herself to maintain a relationship.[29] This is not to say that moments of self-loss do not have their pleasure. At the start of a new love affair or during enjoyable sex, temporarily "losing" ourselves can be a natural and healthy process. But a chronic sense of self-loss, the kind of self-sacrifice that is consistent with our culture's definition of being feminine is another matter. A woman may want to be self-confident and self-possessed, to belong to herself, but in our society this is a model for the masculine, not the feminine. Feminine people are suppose to belong to someone else—particularly men. To prize herself means, in a sense, that a woman feels like a man.

The dilemma for a depressed woman is how to improve her situation without losing her most important attachment. Many women in relationships with men fear that if they are directly angry and insist on mutuality and equal power, their male partners will refuse or be incapable of responding. Yet to conquer her depression, a woman must acknowledge and experience these feelings.[30]

When Factors Overlap

Any of the factors that contribute to depression can occur singly, although it is very common for them to occur in combination. For example, a stressful life situation can precipitate a biological depression in a woman who is genetically vulnerable.

> Carol, age forty-two, was referred to me for a medication consultation by her therapist, Susan. Carol had contacted Susan four weeks earlier complaining of uncontrollable crying spells and an inability to get more than a few hours' sleep each night. They met to explore what might be causing Carol so much distress.

> Carol had first seen Susan two years ago following a painful break-up with her lover. The therapy had been short, only six sessions or so, but Carol had found it very helpful. She had not felt the need for any additional psychological care until now, and she was glad to be able to turn to someone she knew.

Susan, a social worker by training, was a very experienced therapist. She had already gained Carol's trust through their earlier contact, so Carol was quite comfortable sharing her thoughts and feelings with her. When Susan asked Carol what she thought the trouble might be, Carol initially said that she had no idea. Work was going well, she had just bought her first home which she liked very much, and she was dating someone she enjoyed enormously. Overall, her life was better than it had ever been. The only thing she could think of seemed terribly far fetched, but she decided to share it with Susan—even if it sounded strange.

The month before had marked the ten-year anniversary of her father's death. In fact, the money from his estate, which had taken many years to settle, was what had allowed her to buy her home. She thought that she should have been happy about this unexpected inheritance. Instead, she found herself feeling guilty, ashamed, and sad.

Susan had seen many patients with similar delayed grief reactions. She reassured Carol that her hypothesis about the source of her distress was probably quite accurate, but Carol's symptoms seemed unresponsive to their weekly meetings. Rather than feeling better, the depression seemed to be getting worse with every passing week. Her sleep was more disrupted, she had lost almost ten pounds, she cried at the slightest provocation, and she felt chronically fatigued. Carol denied using alcohol or any other drugs and insisted that she would never consider suicide, but Susan was aware that Carol's father had been a deeply troubled alcoholic who ultimately ended his own life. This history placed Carol at risk for a severe depression.

Susan referred Carol to my office for a comprehensive psychiatric evaluation. It did appear as if there was a biological component to her depression. We discussed the treatment options, and Carol agreed to a trial of antidepressant medication. During the first two weeks on the medication, Carol did not notice much change in her symptoms, but by the third week there had been a marked improvement. She was sleeping through the night, her appetite had returned, her spirits had lifted considerably, and she felt like going out and doing things again. She was also able to focus her attention on her long-ignored feelings about her father's alcoholism and suicide. This time, therapy would continue for over a year, but Carol successfully tapered off the antidepressant medication after six months without any return of her most severe depressive symptoms.

The most frequent cause of depression for women is when troubling external circumstances impinge upon their intrapsychic experience.

Donna's experience captures this overlap. When their first child was born three years ago, Donna's husband, Stan, had been excited and supportive. However, shortly after Donna discovered that she was pregnant with their second child, Stan began behaving in a very irrational and unpredictable fashion. He began drinking heavily and coming home late. Eventually, he was fired from his job. Donna was worried and anxious—not only for Stan, but for the whole family. She finally decided that the best temporary solution was to leave their son in Stan's care and take a part-time job to tide them over until Stan found new work.

But Stan never did find a job. Instead he spent his days drinking, and as Donna would later discover, using cocaine. She would return from work only to find the baby unfed and the house a mess. As the months passed, she grew discouraged and frightened by Stan's behavior. Her usual strategy of empathy and support did not seem to improve the situation. Finally, exhausted from the pregnancy, her job, and her continuing responsibilities at home, she blew up. She told Stan that he needed to find a job and to take more responsibility for their family life. Stan responded by telling her that she was a nag and a fat slob and that he did not have to put up with her bitching. He left the house in a huff and stayed away for three days.

All the time he was gone, Donna was beside herself with worry. What had she done wrong? When would he come home? Would he come home? How would she ever support two young kids on her own? She loved Stan and she was worried about him. She vowed that if he came back, she would never allow herself to yell at him again.

When Stan finally returned, Donna apologized for losing her temper and promised to be more understanding. Stan agreed that that would make a big difference. He loved her and their son; he was just upset about having been fired. He was glad that she now seemed to appreciate all the pressure he was under. Her depression lifted—temporarily.

After a few peaceful days, the situation began to deteriorate once again. Another outburst was followed by another separation. The scenario repeated itself several times until Donna discovered that Stan had taken all the grocery money. There was no food in the house and no Stan. She was fuming. When he did return at 2:00 A.M., he was high on drugs and incoherent. He insisted on having sex, ignoring Donna's attempts to resist. The next day, Donna noticed some spotting of blood in her underwear. Worried about the pregnancy, she called her doctor. An examination revealed that the baby was fine and the bleeding had been caused by sexual trauma.

Donna was both relieved and angry. She realized that Stan was not as concerned about the well-being of this baby as she was. While she had trouble remaining angry for herself, she found it easier to be angry on behalf of their developing child. Frightened and anxious, Donna gave Stan an ultimatum: quit drugs and get a job or get out.

He did what she most feared—or thought she most feared. He left. As soon as the door slammed behind him, she wondered what she had done. She was terrified. For three days she walked around the house in a daze. How would she ever pay the mortgage and support two small children? What could she have done differently to prevent this? She could not sleep and her appetite disappeared. She asked her employer for more work. She needed the money, but he had nothing else to offer her.

In the weeks and months that followed, Donna had to take many, many risks. She had to find suitable substitute childcare for her son. She had to interview for and find a new job. She had to go through labor accompanied by a close woman friend rather than her husband. She had to hire an attorney and file for divorce. There were days when she was almost paralyzed with grief, depression, and fear. But as each of these steps was accomplished, her strength and self-esteem grew.

After the divorce was final, she found herself ending up in bed with men she did not like and others who did not really like her. She felt lonely, unattractive, unlovable, and unwanted. She decided to avoid men for a while. At the advice of a friend, she joined a women's support group and learned a lot. Most of all, she learned that she was not alone. Many other women have been through similar situations and survived. No, not just survived. They have grown and so had she. She still had moments when she felt really scared and depressed, but they did not last as long or strike as deep.

Through the insights she developed within the group, Donna finally began to accept that she could be angry and still be OK. Ironically, it was only after she had become comfortable with her own anger that she felt free to be close to men again. She felt stronger, better able to speak for herself and her own needs as well as for the needs of her children. Because she was able to stand up for herself, she could risk becoming involved in a relationship without fearing that she might lose herself in the process. She now knew that there were alternatives to being depressed.

Undoing Women's Victim Psychology

In order to feel good about ourselves, we must, like Donna, develop a sense of effectiveness and power, a sense that we can make things happen. Women's subordinate position makes this difficult. Subordinates often feel like powerless victims in the face of events that distress them. Victims internalize the sense of being devalued. They take feelings that are generated outside and incorporate them into their feelings about themselves. The victim turns her sense of powerlessness on herself. She comes to feel that she is "lesser than," and instead of getting angry at the externally imposed dictates, she gets angry at herself for feeling worthless. She sees her problems as being something wrong with her rather than as something being put upon her.

A victim becomes her own oppressor, her own enemy. "It's my fault," she tells herself. "If only I were a better person, things wouldn't be so bad." By seeing herself as exclusively responsible for her own difficulties, she maintains the illusion of having control over things that she actually does not control. She feels bitter, angry, and helpless, but as long as she remains in this victim role, she will be unable to make positive changes.

When Donna saw that empathy and support were not having much impact on the way her husband was acting, the healthy response would have been anger. Initially, Donna was unable to allow herself this feeling because she was still immersed in the role of being a good woman. Because women live in a world that says that it is not possible to feel authentically powerful and feminine at the same time, depression serves as an attempt to resolve this dilemma. At best, victims experience their anger indirectly, then behave in ways that appear manipulative or passive-aggressive. The direct expression of anger is forbidden, especially when it is directed at dominants. As long as Donna was unable to use anger directly and effectively, she remained depressed.

As Donna began to unravel the reasons for her depression and discover the feelings this mood disguised, she felt as if she were climbing an emotional sand dune. She would climb two steps up only to slide one step back. A step in touch with the anger. A step out of the depression. With each step forward, she was plagued by anxiety. Frightened, she pulled back, and the depression reappeared. She was flooded by the sense that she was not getting better. In this zig-zag pattern she slowly but consistently moved from an ingrained, albeit unhealthy, model of femaleness toward a sense of being a strong and whole person.

As she became better at expressing her anger, Donna experienced a backlash from her husband, which is not uncommon. It is one thing for a husband, parents, or friends to want us to feel better, to be less depressed. It is another thing altogether when we really get in touch with why we are depressed and begin to press for change. Our loved ones may not be convinced that we are improving if it seems to them that we have simply exchanged our depression for anger. This is especially true if we are directing that anger toward them. *"I* don't want to change," they lament. *"You* change! You're the one with the problem."[31]

The reality is that it is impossible for a person to change without some change in every other aspect of her life. Friends and family will experience you as different. Don't be surprised if they try—not purposely of course, but nonetheless very intensely—to get you to go back to your old, depressed, nonangry ways. You may even experience a similar backlash in yourself—especially with the anxiety inevitable with change. This backlash is likely to be the most powerful at the times when you are really breaking new ground and becoming aware of old, dysfunctional patterns.

Like other women who have conquered depression, Donna learned to take control of the events of her life. The victim role was a way to protest without taking a risk, of asking for care and resisting it at the same time, of being feminine and at the same time struggling against femininity.

For women, depression may serve to secure a modicum of nurturance from others. This kind of indirect power (crying rather than asking for or arguing for what one wants) seems to work better for women when they are trying to get nurturance from men, but it is only a temporary solution and ultimately self-defeating and self-destructive. Being depressed may well be an understandable accommodation to social reality, but it is not in the best interest of women. A woman does not feel powerful when she is depressed. She has to learn how to stop behaving like a victim and start using her power more directly.

Women must develop an awareness of both the external and internal sources of their distress. Any situation that expects our continued subordination must be protested. We must not only accept responsibility for ourselves, we must also indicate that unacceptable treatment by others must stop. We must continue voicing our complaints until changes are made. If a reasonable period of waiting and working for change does not produce the necessary results, we must be prepared to end the relationship.

Those who emphasize a feminist perspective are sometimes accused of placing the blame for women's difficulties exclusively outside of themselves. But therapists who ignore a feminist perspective often see a woman's problems as lying exclusively within herself. Neither approach is sufficient. Externalizing alone is not helpful because it does not encourage a woman to exercise personal power to change the situation. Internalizing alone is equally limiting because the focus is only upon changing oneself, ignoring the external circumstances that must also be addressed.

The failure to recognize external contributors to a woman's depression accurately will add to her sense of powerlessness. Instead of accepting a realistic sense of responsibility for herself, the victim tries to control forces over which she in reality has no control. She turns her powerlessness into a false sense of power by imagining that she could have controlled the situation. *"If only I were better (nicer, thinner, prettier, smarter) these things would not be happening."* A woman maintains this position by striving toward perfection. She allows others to define how she should be and pretends that someone whom she imagines to be wiser and stronger will solve her problems.

It is an endless cycle. The victim/patient/woman is chronically blaming herself and/or someone else. She feels bitter and helpless. While she complains, she rarely gets angry enough to move herself forward. Instead, her anger is expressed indirectly through her symptoms. Afraid that these years of steaming repressed anger will overwhelm her and everyone in her path, she refuses to let go of the victim position. She is consumed with self-pity and envy rather than liberating annoyance and action.

Summary

As difficult as it is for some people to admit, we live in a culture that permits a great deal of disrespectful treatment of women. Because of this, it becomes almost "normal" for many women to dislike and devalue themselves. Depression becomes a circuitous survival strategy in a society that devalues women while demanding femininity.[32] A woman has nowhere to turn. If she remains feminine, she dislikes herself; if she rebels and becomes masculine, she dislikes herself. Many women feel caught in an intricate, tangled knot of depression.

Women's training for and ultimately their need for connectedness have been misrepresented as excessive dependency. In reality, women have been raised to be depended upon, to place their emotional needs second to those of others, to never be selfish. Deferential behavior like "I can't change my own tire" has been mistaken for the desire to have one's true, healthy, and normal emotional dependency needs met: "I need someone who will love me and understand me."

But most women soon discover that they spend a great deal of time giving to others but much less time is spent by others giving to them. Women are assigned the task of attending to relationships. Heterosexual boys grow up learning to depend on women—first mothers, later wives. We have a tendency to think of men as not having dependency needs because their needs are more successfully and quickly met—often without the man even having to acknowledge that he has them. A girl grows up expecting that she will provide nurturance, caring, and the desire to participate in a mutually supportive emotional environment. Girls become adults who know that others rely on them.

If an adult woman is unable to achieve the kind of intimacy she is trained to seek in her most important relationships, she is unable to feel a solid sense of herself. She is not able to feel that she is whole, alive, and valued; that she contributes; that she matters.

Women are also assigned and accept responsibility for creating quality relationships. Having been assigned the task of sustaining emotional connections, a woman who experiences difficulties in doing this well tends to view herself as responsible for the trouble. Since many women believe that they can only take action when it is in the service of facilitating the growth of others, they have marked difficulty taking action if they feel that they are being selfish or if the action is viewed as potentially destructive to the relationship. All her energy goes into trying to fix a nonworking relationship—alone. When this occurs, the woman experiences a personal sense of worthlessness and powerlessness. This inner sense of incompetency and low self-esteem handicaps a woman from taking any further action on her own behalf to change the situation. A spiral of diminishing returns perpetuates the situation and the woman becomes increasingly depressed.

Seen with a narrow focus, depression appears to be the problem of an individual person. However, the social condition of women is that of subordination to men. Women are relatively powerless in a male-dominated society. Feelings of hopelessness, helplessness, worthlessness, futility, and suppressed rage, the major ingredients of depression, are the emotional responses of anyone in a permanently subordinate position. Under these conditions, depression can serve as a nice, feminine way of getting cared for or protected by men who have power over us—husbands, lovers, and bosses. Of course, this strategy is really no protection at all. Men are not required to support women economically or emotionally. A chronically depressed wife, lover, or employee may find herself divorced, abandoned, or terminated.

In a society that keeps most women as economic, social, political, and emotional subordinates, a state of chronic deprivation is inevitable. In addition, a woman's emphasis on connectedness rather than separateness and her denial of the necessity of having her legitimate emotional dependency needs met leave her extremely vulnerable to depression.

To feel good about herself, a woman must have a sense of effectiveness, a sense of power, a sense that she can make things happen. Instead, as a woman looks around the public world, she only rarely sees herself reflected in any position of power. Women can come to feel that their needs are marginal and unimportant, which in turn is depressing because it is hard to see how a woman's needs can be fully understood and taken into account if they are different from the needs of the people in power.

The healthiest response to this state of affairs is anger, followed by action. Depression is inevitable if a person has difficulty consciously recognizing feelings of anger. Women are not supposed to get angry; to do so is to feel unfeminine. But to fail to get angry is to become and to remain depressed.

Women also experience chronic sadness. A sadness reflecting a conscious or unconscious recognition of loss—loss of status in the world, loss of recognition of one's value, loss of safety and respect, loss of economic security, loss of a sense of self as a full and valued person. These losses cannot be grieved for or resolved until women obtain full parity and representation in the world. This will require the use of effective and diplomatic anger.

In the final analysis, depression that appears in the individual woman is actually a problem for all women. The cure for depression is not in simply attending to the depression of an individual woman. It includes altering the social reality for all women. This means we have to do more than implement self-care strategies or even psychotherapy. We need to make larger changes in the structure of our society, changes that will secure equality and the respectful treatment of all people.

Treating Depression

In the best of all worlds, we would be raised in families and cultures in which everyone was loved and valued. Sadly, this is not the case. Parents, damaged through no fault of their own, do their best to raise their children. In the process, the unresolved pain of one generation is often unintentionally passed to the next. If this is part of your inheritance, you have a choice: either live with the damage as best as you can without attempting to repair it *or* minimize its impact on your life and, indirectly, on those whom you care about. Women who have suffered serious trauma, profound losses, or repeated blows to their self-esteem early in life are likely to experience persistent feelings of depression that interfere with their enjoyment of life in the present. Women who are currently in depressing situations often need support and assistance to change these difficulties. While therapy is demanding, both emotionally and economically, good therapy can speed changes and facilitate the healing process.

What do you do if you find yourself troubled by continuing depression? If you have symptoms associated with a biological depression, contact a psychiatrist for a consultation. Self-care strategies will not help with this kind of depression. If the symptoms of a biological depression are not present, begin with the self-care measures described below.[33] It should come as no surprise that many of the recommendations made here will be directed at improving self-esteem. This is because low self-esteem caused by a woman's treatment in society and her internalization of the devaluation of women and women's values is one of the primary causes of depression in women. If these strategies work for you, you will not need professional help. However, if your depression continues, seek assistance from a well-trained and sensitive therapist.

Self-care and Education

Self-care and education are two strategies you may use without the help of professionals to correct nonbiological depressions. Lasting improvement requires motivation, commitment, and self-discipline, but you will find the effort well worth it.

Do not tolerate physical or psychological abuse—If you are currently in a relationship where you are being subjected to physical or emotional abuse, it is imperative that this stop immediately. Insist that the person who is being abusive stop this behavior. If the abuse does not stop, you must be prepared to remove yourself (and children, if you have them) from this situation. You will need help from friends, family, or professionals to implement this plan. Use all the resources available in your community.

Obtain the training and education you need to earn your own living—All women must be ready, willing, and able to earn their own living. A woman unprepared to do this is much more likely to feel subordinate to anyone on whom she depends for financial support. Economic dependence can cause a woman to be extremely anxious about leaving a bad relationship. For any woman to separate from a person with whom her economic life is entwined, she must be able to support herself.

Control your reproductivity and role as mother—A willingness to delay childbirth until you have trained yourself to earn an adequate living, resolved to the best of your ability any emotional injuries you may have experienced as a child, and solidified a mutually respectful relationship will greatly enhance your chances of having a satisfying life.[34]

Actively seek relationships and build support networks with nurturing, caring people, including men, who value clear, open communication—We cannot pick our families, but we can and do pick our friends. If you are not spending time with people you care for and who make you feel good about yourself, you are perpetuating your own depressive situation. Select and maintain relationships with supportive people who will behave in loving and honest ways. This does not mean that you will never be angry with these friends or that they will never be angry with you. It does mean that any conflict between the two of you will be handled with sensitivity and caring.

Picking good people includes being selective about the men we permit into our lives. We *can* control which men we select, although whom we select is often colored by our past experiences. If a woman views herself as a good catch, she will understandably be highly selective about the men she chooses to be with. Unfortunately, for a woman it is an uphill climb to develop the kind of high self-esteem that is required before she can be this selective.[35]

If you are already in a heterosexual relationship with a decent but uninformed man, develop a program of continuing education for him. Get support and coaching from a male or female support-person who understands the issues involved. This work can be challenging, but it will pay off handsomely. Preserving and improving a long-standing relationship can be a very gratifying experience.

Do not put all your eggs in one basket—If all your positive self-regard is tied up in one relationship, one project, or one career, you will be extremely vulnerable to depression if that single area of your life develops problems. By nurturing a multitude of interests and involvements and by maintaining a wide and diverse variety of friends, you will be more resilient in the face of life's inevitable reverses and misfortunes.

This advice is especially important when it comes to primary relationships. Women prefer to be in relationships. However, even when these relationships are not mutually empathic, some women maintain the illusion that their dependency needs are being met. The maintenance of this illusion is not to our benefit.

A woman can become very anxious when she is unattached. She will be better able to cope with this anxiety if she participates in a number of activities that she defines as worthwhile, meaningful, or enhancing of her self-esteem. Satisfying and rewarding work, interesting hobbies, and a rich network of relationships are our best protections against severe depression.

Attend to your "skin hunger"—Women who are not currently in satisfying relationships frequently speak about a particular kind of pain and sadness that comes from the lack of human touch. People of every age benefit from being touched in affectionate and loving ways. This is something especially missed when we are not part of a couple. We can even experience "skin hunger" while in a relationship if our partner is insensitive to meeting this need. If your need for touch is not being met by family or friends, find other ways to get the tactile stimulation you need. Long, luxurious baths or professional massages are two good options to consider.

Give yourself permission to put yourself first, at least some of the time—Most women are very talented at anticipating the needs of their children, lovers, husbands, and bosses—meeting them often before these individuals even know that they have them. Turn this wonderful talent toward yourself. Indulge yourself. Consider being selfish. Being selfish does not mean denying or ignoring the needs of others—it means valuing your needs as much as theirs. Women in heterosexual relationships are sometimes anxious or frightened by putting their needs first— even occasionally—because they live in a world where that prerogative belongs to men.[36]

Ask yourself what you would like and what you can do to increase the possibility that your needs will be met. This will sometimes include having your emotional and other needs receive priority.

Arrange to be waited on—If your needs are not being adequately met by family or friends, arrange to be waited on by someone else. Eat out even if it is only fast food. Ignore women's magazines that encourage you to do all the work for holiday gatherings. If you can afford it, hire help around the home. Insist the next dinner party for your husband's office be catered. Request an assistant at work. Arrange to have others help in ways that feel good to you.

Make sure that you arrange for regular private time and space—In many middle-class families, the kids have their own rooms and Dad has his study, but women frequently do not have their own private space. Society has reinforced the notion that women should be available to meet the needs of others twenty-four hours a day, seven days a week. This is unacceptably draining. It is important for a woman to maintain some personal privacy and to control her availability to others. Even if it is in only the smallest way, it is imperative that a woman has a place where she can get away from it all. This can be a personal hobby, some private time separate from others, or a room of her own.

Participate in peer counseling or co-counseling—This is a kind of therapy without money. It is a structured format that allows two nonprofessionals to provide a therapeutic relationship for each other. If you and I were to engage in a co-counseling session, I would work on my material with your support for forty-five minutes. We would then take a short break. Then it would be your turn to work on your material with my support. No money would change hands.

A wide variety of local centers offer classes in peer counseling. There is also a nationwide group, the Re-evaluation Counseling Network, that trains interested laypeople in co-counseling skills. Originally developed by Harvey Jackins,[37] the Re-evaluation Counseling Network has teachers in most cities. The same guidelines for selecting a professional therapist apply when selecting a co-counselor. For women this must include being knowledgeable about the unique psychology of women and the relationship between a woman's psychological state and her position in society.

Join or form a support group—The purpose of a support group is to have a safe forum in which to discuss personal and shared concerns. While any individual woman may be uncertain about how to handle a specific problem, another woman may have already faced a similar issue. Sharing resources, ideas, and active problem solving among peers can be a reassuring and empowering process. The women who help benefit as much as the women who are helped.

This low-cost alternative to professional group therapy should meet on a rotating basis at various people's homes or on neutral territory. If you always hold it at one woman's home, she will become the group caretaker waiting on you rather than getting her own needs met. Leadership can be shared among members, and topics for discussion may be planned in advance or permitted to emerge as needs arise.

Continue to educate yourself about women's place in society—Subscribing to pro-woman magazines, reading books by pro-woman authors, listening to pro-woman specialists on radio and television, in films and at the theater will provide a much-needed perspective as you struggle to understand intermittent waves of depression, anger, anxiety, sadness, and other distressing moods. Women's groups and women's media form a national and international network that can help us through a tough and confusing time.

Support organizations that support women—Do this in any way you can. It may be through volunteer work or donating money. Doing what we can to help women means helping ourselves as well as others. Doing good works enhances self-esteem and enhances our sense of empowerment. Most importantly, it provides a sense that what happens to women—including ourselves—really matters.

Exercise, eat well, and do all the other things we know are good for health—Maintaining your physical well-being can boost your psychological health. Exercise can actually improve mood through the release of the body's natural antidepressants, endorphins. A healthy diet can sharpen your thinking and raise your energy level. Avoid alcohol and other drugs used to self-medicate depression. They can interfere with the motivation to change the situation and, eventually, may become problems of their own. The mind and body are intimately connected. Good health means caring for both.

Working with a Therapist

If the self-care steps outlined above are not enough to lighten your mood, you may wish to consider therapy. Be selective. Make sure your therapist is informed about the issues raised in this book. Your therapist will most likely be a woman, but it can be an enlightened man.

The women's division of the American Psychological Association has published guidelines for selecting a therapist. They have also included the rights and responsibilities of both prospective client and therapist. I recommend that you look at this brochure as well as chapter 14 in this book as you interview potential therapists.[38] Your local women's center is a good place to begin when looking for therapists. The staff of a woman's studies program is likely to know a few therapists who are well-regarded and informed about the psychological concerns of women. Or ask a trusted woman friend who has had a good therapy experience whom she might recommend.

Given the impact of culture, therapy alone will not improve the psychological health of women. So what *can* therapy do for women? The therapeutic process can help a woman identify, acknowledge, understand, and trust her own feelings and thoughts. It can also help her see how some of these are caused by her status as a woman. This can encourage her to examine and change the process by which she may be internalizing the anti-woman attitudes of the culture in which she lives.

For a woman who is depressed, the essence of therapy is to help her identify the anger and sadness beneath her depression. These underlying feelings must be given voice if she is to get beyond feeling like a passive victim and become more active and alive.

She must learn to tolerate more direct experiences and communications of her own anger if she is to use it on her own behalf. To paraphrase Miriam Greenspan,[39] the primary goal of therapy that is in the best interests of women is to help women redefine and reexperience their authentic power as people. This means developing women-identified definitions of femininity rather than accepting the definition we currently have. It means helping transform the victim in women into the fighter—the fighter for her own true self.

It is not enough for a woman to replace her depression with either sadness or anger. To move beyond a position of powerlessness, helplessness, and hopelessness, women must get in touch with the power they already possess—both individually and collectively. Women are not simply people who have been assigned a second-class position in families or in society. Nor are women people who simply react to their social reality. Each woman is also a unique human being with her own dreams, values, ideas, interests, and life experiences. Even within the constraints of the society in which she grew up and in which she now lives, *a woman is still the most active player in constructing her own life.*

The goal of successful therapy is to help us value ourselves as individuals, to be who we are as fully as we can, and to replace our unconscious rebellion with conscious and playful challenges to the conditions that had been depressing us. For a woman, becoming undepressed is not a matter of keeping her mood on an even keel. In the end, it is learning to love herself—as a person and as a woman.

RESOURCES

National Depressive and Manic Depressive Association (MDDA)

A self-help organization offering services to members, public education, and advocacy for people with depression and manic-depressive illness.

Recovery, Inc.

A self-help group for people who have experienced mental-health problems.

MAGAZINES AND NEWSPAPERS

Ms.

One Times Square, New York, New York 10036.

Available by subscription or at your local newsstand, a monthly magazine that covers basic issues of concern to women.

New Directions for Women

108 West Palisade Avenue, Englewood, N.J. 07631

Published bimonthly, *New Directions* brings you all the news that's fit to print—for women. Excellent national coverage with thoughtful attention to minority women.

ADDITIONAL READING

Luise Eichenbaum and Susie Orbach, *What Do Women Want: Exploding the Myth of Dependency* (New York: Coward, McCann, 1983).

Demitri Papolos and Janice Papolos, *Overcoming Depression* (New York: Harper & Row, 1987).

Maggie Scarf, *Unfinished Business: Pressure Points in the Lives of Women* (New York: Doubleday, 1980).

NOTES

1. Myra Weissman and Gerald Klerman, "Gender and Depression," in *Women and Depression: A Life Span Perspective* (New York: Springer, 1987).

2. These are not simply women who see health-care professionals. Researchers conducting community studies interviewed women who had never sought medical or psychological care for their depression. The same frequency of depression remained true even among women who never sought professional help. (Men have their own set of problems. The research suggests that men experience more alcohol abuse and evi-

dence more violent behavior. It has been hypothesized, but not proven, that these are the equivalents of depression in men.)

3. This is based upon Engel's biopsychosocial model. For more information see G. L. Engel, "The Need for a New Medical Model: A Challenge for Biomedicine," *Science* 196 (1977): 129–35 and G. L. Engel, "Resolving the Conflict Between Medicine and Psychiatry," *Resident Staff Physician* 25 (1979): 70–4.

4. For more information see Miriam Greenspan, *A New Approach to Women and Therapy* (New York: McGraw-Hill, 1983) and Jean Baker Miller, *Toward a New Psychology of Women* (Boston: Beacon Press, 1986).

5. *Diagnostic and Statistical Manual of Mental Disorders* (DSM-III-R) (Washington, D.C.: American Psychiatric Association Press, 1987), pp. 222–23.

6. Demitri Papolos and Janice Papolos, *Overcoming Depression* (New York: Harper & Row, 1987).

7. In recent years, a variety of tests have been developed in an effort to establish a laboratory test for biochemical depression. Scientists have been looking for something like the blood sugar test commonly used to diagnose and monitor diabetes. In measuring the blood sugar of a diabetic, a person's response to diet, oral medication, or insulin injections can be measured. None of the tests currently used to diagnose biological depression is equally accurate. The tests that are available are often used by researchers working with patients who have tried a variety of antidepressant medications with only limited success. These researchers have considerable experience assessing "challenging cases." However, the laboratory tests currently available to assess biological depressions are not particularly useful or necessary for routine assessment, although this situation may change with more experience and greater test accuracy.

8. Myra Weissman and Gerald Klerman, "Sex Differences and the Epidemiology of Depression," *Archives of General Psychiatry* 34 (1977): 98–111.

9. Janice A. Egeland, "Genetic Studies of Affective Disorders among Amish," National Institute of Mental Health Grant Application, February 1986; John I. Nurnberger and Elliot S. Gerson, "Genetics of Affective Disorders," in *The Neurobiology of Mood Disorders* (Baltimore: Williams and Wilkins, 1984); and Paul H. Wender and Donald F. Klein, *Mind, Mood, and Medicine* (New York: Farrar, Straus, Giroux, 1981).

10. Myra Weissman, "The Myth of Involutional Melancholia," *Journal of the American Medical Association* 242 (1979): 742–44.

11. J. A. Hamilton and R. M. A. Hirschfeld, "Letter to the Editor: An Additional Recommendation on Reporting Depression," *American Journal of Psychiatry* 141 (1984): 1134–35.

12. There is evidence that biological depressions that only occur in winter, called seasonal affective disorder (SAD), may respond to phototherapy, daily treatment with bright white light, in lieu of medication. Michael Freeman, "Don't Be SAD," *Medical Self Care,* January/February 1989.

13. Potentially addictive medications are the antianxiety medications such as Valium, Librium, and Xanax when taken over long periods of time. Even these medications are safe for people without a history of substance abuse when taken as prescribed for specific problems over relatively short periods of time under a physician's supervision.

14. I. K. Broverman et al., "Sex-role Stereotypes and Clinical Judgments of Mental Health," *Journal of Consulting and Clinical Psychology* 34 no. 1 (1970): 1–7.

15. T. L. Ruble, "Sex Stereotypes: Issues of Change in the 1970s," *Sex Roles* 9 (1983): 397–401.

16. Miriam Greenspan has named the intrapsychic structure that develops under these circumstances "victim psychology." She argues that such a psychological structure is inevitable because of women's virtually universal second-class status.

17. S. Arieti and J. Bemporad, *Severe and Mild Depression: The Psychotherapeutic Approach* (New York: Basic Books, 1978).

18. Miller, *Toward a New Psychology of Women;* Jean Baker Miller, "The Development of Women's Sense of Self," Work in Progress no. 12 (Wellesley, Mass.: Wellesley College, 1984); and Janet Surrey, "The 'Self-in-Relation': A Theory of Women's Development," Work in Progress no. 13 (Wellesley, Mass.: Wellesley College, 1985).

19. One result of this is that ending relationships is particularly difficult for women. Now that women are speaking in their own voices about their own experiences, we have a better understanding of why this is so, and why it is not all bad—although it can cause women serious trouble when they find it hard to disconnect from unhealthy relationships.

20. One of the most unpleasant criticisms a woman must endure if she is to experience and express her anger is the commentary from others that she is an angry woman. Less diplomatically, she is called a bitch. Few people recognize the hostility directed at a woman in this name calling. Labels like this are extremely critical and devaluing and are used to discount the woman's complaints. Enduring these hostile statements from others is extremely painful although sometimes necessary if a woman is to validate her own legitimate, yet confusing, anger. Around our office, we have defused the potential of these words to harm by inventing new definitions. For example, "A bitch is a woman who is not doing what you want her to" or "A bitch is a woman who gets things done."

21. This concept was first developed when researchers observed that animals who were exposed to inescapable shocks had more difficulty learning to avoid an escapable

shock than did animals who had never before been exposed. The researchers felt that the previously exposed animals had learned that they had no control over the situation and had given up. They exhibited behaviors that were similar to those seen in people who become depressed. M. Seligman, "Depression and Learned Helplessness," in F. Friedman and M. Katz, eds., *The Psychology of Depression* (Washington, D.C.: Winston, 1974). Interestingly, a medical student who was working with the animals conducted a clever study to test the possibility of unlearning helplessness. The student knitted tiny sweaters for the depressed animals with strings attached to the sleeves. By pulling on the animals' paws, marionette fashion, the animals could be trained to stop the shock. No longer helpless, the depression-like symptoms stopped. This suggests that with the appropriate help, people who have learned helplessness can turn their behavior around.

22. Paula Caplan, "Mother as the Scapegoat in the Mental Health System," Audio Archives of Canada, Ontario, 1987.

23. Dana Jack, "Silencing the Self: The Power of Social Imperatives in Female Depression," in *Women and Depression: A Lifespan Perspective* (New York: Springer, 1987), pp. 161–81.

24. Judith Herman, "Sexual Violence," Work in Progress no. 8 (Wellesley, Mass.: Wellesley College, 1984).

25. Pauline Bart and Patricia O'Brien, "Stopping Rape: Effective Avoidance Strategies," *Signs* 10 no. 11 (Autumn 1984): pp. 83–101.

26. Other women are reluctant to do so. It is currently believed that less that 50 percent of all rapes are reported.

27. A concise summary of the present condition of women is provided by these statistics in an International Labor Organization study presented at the United Nations Conference on Women in Copenhagen in 1980 and quoted in Marilyn French, *Beyond Power: On Women, Men and Morals* (New York: Summit Books, 1985), p. 259.

28. Carol Gilligan, *In A Different Voice: Psychological Theory and Women's Development* (Cambridge, Mass.: Harvard University Press, 1982).

29. Harriet Goldhor Lerner, "Female Depression: Self-Sacrifice and Self-Betrayal in Relationships," in *Women and Depression: A Lifespan Perspective* (New York: Springer, 1987), pp. 200–221.

30. One group of researchers believes that *the major contributor to depression in women is marriage.* V. C. Gordon and L. E. Ledray, "Depression in Women: The Challenge of Treatment and Prevention," *Journal of Psychosocial Nursing* 23 no. 1 (1985): 26.

31. Harriet Lerner, *The Dance of Anger: A Woman's Guide to Changing the Pattern of Intimate Relationships* (New York: Harper & Row, 1985).

32. Susan Brownmiller, *Femininity* (New York: Fawcett Columbine, 1984).

33. Self-care does not mean that you do this all by yourself. That would only be perpetuating a significant part of the problem—an overemphasis on independence vs. an emphasis on mutually enhancing and egalitarian relationships. Self-care is what you can do without direct professional assistance.

34. Mindy Bingham and Sandy Styker, *More Choices: A Strategic Planning Guide for Mixing Career and Family,* Advocacy Press, P.O. Box 236, Dept. A, Santa Barbara, Ca., 93102. Other books from the same press include *Choices, Challenges,* and *Changes.* They are all thoughtfully written for persons of different ages, genders, and life situations.

35. "If many feminists are without men, that is in large part because of the heightened sensitivity of feminists to male diminishment and oppressive habits, and women's new economic power, which allows some of them to live comfortably without men." French, *Beyond Power,* p. 470.

36. Sometimes men feel particularly criticized and misunderstood by this statement because many men feel economically responsible for their families. When they put their work first or their advancement in work first, they also sincerely believe they are not only doing this only for themselves, but also for their families. The problem is that if the family breaks up, the man retains what he has achieved in emphasizing his development in the public world, including greater financial resources than the woman and family from whom he is separating. The woman who has dutifully remained primarily concerned with caring for this man and their children, who never or rarely put forth her own needs for advancement, finds herself with limited economic resources and limited skills for surviving in a style equal to that of her now-absent provider.

37. Harvey Jackins, *Fundamentals of Co-Counseling Manual: Elementary Counselor's Manual for Beginning Classes in Re-Evaluation Co-Counseling,* Rational Island Publishers, P.O. Box 2081, Main Office, Seattle, Washington, 98111.

38. *Women and Psychotherapy: A Consumer Handbook* (Washington, D.C.: Federation of Organizations for Professional Women, 1981).

39. Miriam Greenspan, *A New Approach to Women and Therapy* (New York: McGraw-Hill, 1983).

APPENDIX: ANTIDEPRESSANT MEDICATIONS

Tricyclic antidepressants (TCAs)
Amitriptyline (Elavil)*
Desipramine (Norpramin)
Doxepin (Sinequan)
Imipramine (Tofranil)
Nortriptyline (Pamelor)
Protriptyline (Vivactil)

Newer antidepressants
Amoxapine (Asendin)
Bupropion (Wellbutrin)
Fluoxetine (Prozac)
Maprotiline (Ludiomil)
Trazodone (Desyrel)

Monoamine oxidase inhibitors (MAOIs)
Isocarboxazid (Marplan)
Phenelzine (Nardil)
Tranylcypromine (Parnate)

*Examples of trade names for these psychotropic agents follow their generic names in parentheses. Some of these agents are made by more than one company and have more than one trade name. For simplicity, however, only one example is shown here.

8 | **A**nxiety

Anxiety is second only to depression in prompting women to seek the care of mental-health professionals. Each year, two to three times as many women as men report experiencing the symptoms of anxiety. For 3 to 5 percent of American women, these symptoms will be very severe.[1]

In this chapter, we will review what anxiety is, identify some of the known and suspected causes, and suggest corrective measures to prevent or reduce the symptoms of anxiety.

Anxiety: Normal or Pathological?

Human beings are designed to monitor their physical and emotional environment for threats to their safety and well-being. The ability to be anxious is a kind of human alarm system. Just like a smoke detector, this human alarm system is in place just in case. We hope neither the smoke detector nor the human alarm system ever goes off, but if it does, it needs to be jarring enough to really capture our attention. Its annoying blast warns us of a real or perceived danger. When we experience anxiety, it is our body's way of signaling that something needs attention.

Our almost spontaneous response to this alarm has been called the fight, flight, freeze, and faint response. It has four basic components: physical, cognitive, emotional, and behavioral. The physical symptoms tend to be felt in our heart, lungs, nerves, muscles, stomach, and bowels or through our hormonal system. They include such sensations as a racing heart, rapid breathing, trembling, tense muscles, diarrhea, or flushing. Cognitive aspects are the things we think about. When we're anxious, our thoughts can take on catastrophic proportions. We worry that the worst might happen—whatever "the worst" means to us. Emotionally, we experience profound feelings of fear, doom, or anger as we respond to feelings of overwhelming danger. Finally, we want to flee, but instead we often freeze. With repeated bouts of severe anxiety, we may become reluctant to venture beyond our safe territory.

Anxiety is functional when it facilitates a healthy response to an exciting or threatening situation. Anxiety becomes dysfunctional when it interferes with such a response. If anxiety interrupts clear thinking, good judgment, adequate problem solving, or appropriate action, our alarm system needs an adjustment. If left uncorrected, unremitting and severe anxiety can cause a significant or total disruption of a woman's personal or professional life.

The symptoms of anxiety are virtually indistinguishable from those of fear. In fact, anxiety is most often caused by feeling fearful or nervous. Sometimes the cause will be obvious, but other times it will be quite obscure. Anxiety occurs when we are experiencing something out of the ordinary. All of our attention is focused upon the present event. That event can be invigorating or exciting, frightening or dangerous. Our response in these situations is functional; it is a clear, direct, and appropriate reaction to a specific situation.

For example, it's Career Day at your local high school. Over the last several years, you've developed an interest in natural dyes and have had considerable success creating an unusually wide variety of fabrics. You've been invited to give a talk on your work. You know your topic well, and you love sharing your knowledge with others, but as you stand in the wings waiting to go on, your heart is pounding, your hands grow clammy, and there is an enormous lump in your throat. This performance anxiety gives you that extra edge just before you go onstage. It usually abates within a few minutes of actually addressing your audience, but it has served to get you off to a flying start. A small amount of performance anxiety encourages you to give your full attention to the matter at hand and in this way actually helps you do your best.

After the meeting, you're driving home along a crowded freeway in a light rain, listening to the evening news and thinking about getting your shoes off when the car in front of you hits a slick spot and swerves out of control. You glance in the rearview mirror; you are only inches from disaster. Your pulse quickens. Your hands tighten on the wheel. You can feel the jolt of adrenaline pumping through your veins. You are intensely aware of the colors and sounds of the cars and trucks around you. All systems of your body and mind are on full alert. You pump your brakes and turn your emergency flasher on. The car in front of you is skidding to the right. You veer to the left and guide your car to safety. Once you're clear of the danger, you pull over to the side of the road. You sit there for a few minutes, taking long, slow breaths, your body still shaking. Your anxiety was precipitated by a genuine emergency, and your natural physical and psychological response helped you cope effectively with the danger.

Other times, the cause of a woman's anxiety is not at all obvious. It may even seem to take on a life of its own.

For a month, Joanne had been agitated, easily startled, and chronically worried. She was obsessed with images of failure and despair and terrified that something terrible would happen to her little boy. She could not pinpoint when her symptoms began. In some ways, she saw herself as always having been a somewhat nervous person, but lately her tension had increased. She first noticed it truly interfering with her life when she was on vacation with her family. Air travel had always been a source of considerable stress. She despised getting on planes, would feel anxious throughout most of the flight, and would only settle down after the plane landed and she was out of the airport altogether. During her most recent vacation, she was so reluctant to fly that rail transportation had to be substituted at the last moment. What could have taken four hours by plane expanded to two days by train. She knew the situation had gotten out of hand. Her anxiety had become dysfunctional.

Frieda's anxiety took her more by surprise. She was thirty-four when she experienced her first anxiety attack—or rather, panic attack. She was in the hospital and just about ready to leave with her new baby. The baby, her second child, was healthy, and Frieda expected to return home to her daughter, Loyla, age six and her second husband, Terry, an accountant. Loyla was Terry's stepdaughter, and while he adored her, he was excited to have a child of his own. Terry wanted to be an active father, but his firm did not approve of parental leaves for men, and a flexible work schedule was out of the question. Like it or not, Frieda would do the major share of the childcare. Her company did have a good policy of parental leave for women. Her job was guaranteed when she returned, and she could take up to three months with pay after delivery and an additional three months without pay if she wished.

Frieda was aware that she was slightly worried about how to manage and frustrated that Terry was unable to participate more, but she understood the reasons and was prepared to work around them. So she was confused and frightened her last night in the hospital when she woke up suddenly from a sound sleep feeling terrified. She had an impending sense of doom. She was afraid that she was going crazy or that she might die. She had a tingling sensation in her hands, her feet, and around her mouth—much like her foot would feel when it fell asleep after she sat cross-legged too long. Desperate, she yelled for the nurse who arrived quickly, assessed the situation, and told Frieda that she was having a panic attack.

The nurse brought a brown paper bag and told Frieda to breathe into it. Frieda was hyperventilating—breathing too shallow and too fast. She followed the nurse's advice and in a few minutes felt remarkably calm—and embarrassed. When a second attack occurred as she was packing her bags to leave, Frieda remained frightened even as the worst of the symptoms subsided. The attack seemed to come out of thin air with no rhyme, reason, or predictability. What if the next one came while she was driving or alone with the children? She mentioned her concerns to her physician. Normally the doctor would have prescribed tranquilizers, but since Frieda was breast-feeding, the drug would be passed on to the baby. Any unnecessary medication was out of the question.

Without medication to alleviate her symptoms, Frieda sought alternatives. At a friend's recommendation, she called me, and I saw her for an evaluation. We reviewed Frieda's current situation and her past history. I concurred with the nurse's evaluation. Frieda was having panic attacks—intermittent episodes of extreme anxiety. Fortunately, she was addressing the problem before it escalated or became an entrenched and long-standing pattern. Many women have these symptoms for years before seeking professional care. As a consequence, simple, intermittent panic attacks grow into phobias—the desire to avoid something or some situation in order to avoid having a panic attack. These phobias can be quite challenging to alter. Nevertheless, in spite of seeking early treatment, Frieda's panic attacks were interfering with her life. They were dysfunctional and needed her attention.

Types of Anxiety

Problems with anxiety are classified into seven types:[2]

1. generalized anxiety
2. panic attacks
3. simple phobias
4. social phobias
5. agoraphobia
6. obsessive-compulsive disorder
7. post-traumatic stress disorder

The essential feature of *generalized anxiety* is unrealistic or excessive worry about more than one life circumstance on an almost daily basis for six months or longer. For example, you are experiencing generalized anxiety if you worry about the safety of a loved one when there is no particular reason to be overly worried at the same time you worry about your finances when your income is stable, adequate, and shows no signs of changing.

Panic attacks are discrete, unexpected, and recurrent episodes of intense fear or discomfort. They typically begin with the sudden onset of apprehension or terror. Associated physical symptoms often include shortness of breath, dizziness, choking, an increased heart rate, trembling or shaking, sweating, nausea, numbness or tingling, chills or flushing, and chest pain or tightness. There may be a fear of dying, of going crazy, or of being out of control.

A *simple phobia* is fear of one specific thing. Common simple phobias involve animals, especially dogs, snakes, insects, and mice. Other simple phobias involve discrete places or events such as a fear of heights (acrophobia) or a fear of closed spaces (claustrophobia). Whether or not a simple phobia interferes with life depends upon the form it takes. A snake phobia is hardly a serious problem for a city dweller, but if claustrophobia prevents them from using elevators, then their phobia becomes a significant handicap.

A *social phobia* is a fear of being embarrassed or humiliated in front of other people. It can be as mild as a trembling hand when writing in front of another person or as severe as a complete inability to talk with someone for fear of saying something foolish.

Agoraphobia is the most disabling of the phobias. A person suffering with agoraphobia fears being away from her safe place, usually home, or her safe person, usually a parent or spouse. She also fears being in any place where she is confined—either physically or by social convention. If she cannot get away easily, she becomes very anxious. Agoraphobia can include a fear of driving—especially on expressways, through tunnels, or over bridges. It can also include a fear of using public transportation, eating in restaurants, going to church, attending entertainment programs, or being alone. Going to a dinner party may be anxiety-provoking because a woman cannot leave midcourse if she starts to feel anxious. An elevator may be frightening because she fears being stuck between floors. Driving away from home becomes virtually impossible unless she is sure that she can immediately turn around toward the safety of home if anxiety strikes. This may mean avoiding freeways and other limited-access highways for fear of feeling trapped.

Recurrent obsessions or compulsions can become so time-consuming as to significantly interfere with a woman's normal routine. If this is the case, she is said to have an *obsessive-compulsive disorder*, which is characterized by persistent and unwanted thoughts or impulses. A common obsession is an unrealistic preoccupation with dirt, contamination, or germs that drives her to perform repetitive cleaning behaviors, such as washing her hands or taking a shower many times in a single day, when there is obviously nothing to be cleaned.

Finally, *post-traumatic stress disorder* is the long-term adverse psychological consequences of severe stress such as active military duty, a natural disaster, physical abuse, or sexual abuse. The evidence is clear that previously mentally healthy women can and do develop this disorder in response to highly stressful life events.[3] These women have suffered some kind of traumatic event that caused intense fear and helplessness. It was an event that would have been distressing to almost anyone. Afterwards, the women often have recurrent, intrusive, and distressing memories of the event, difficulty sleeping, an exaggerated startle response, and a number of other behavioral changes that signify that their world no longer feels safe.

Women appear to be susceptible to some forms of anxiety more than others.[4] For example, it seems that women and men are equally vulnerable to generalized anxiety, simple phobias, social phobias, and obsessive-compulsive disorder, but panic attacks, agoraphobia, and post-traumatic stress disorder are far more prevalent in women than in men. The reason for these variations is unclear. However, research suggests that physical differences in brain structure as well as divergent life experiences and life stress may account for many of the differences in symptoms observed.

Causes of Anxiety

Whatever the type of anxiety, there are three potential causes, any or all of which may be in operation: a biological or inherited propensity toward anxiety; external contributing causes; or internally generated psychological responses. We will discuss each of these in turn, although they can, and frequently do, overlap.

Biological Causes of Anxiety

Low levels of anxiety alert us to the possibility of a threat or the need to prepare for a potential threat. Our alarm goes off if the threat is perceived as great enough to warrant our immediate and undivided attention. The key word here is *perceived,* because what seems like a threat to us may not seem like a threat to someone else. Indeed, at times the threat to ourselves is so obscure that even we cannot figure out what we are reacting to. In these situations, it can appear as if we have hit the panic button when there is no real need.

A biological or inherited vulnerability toward anxiety has been clearly demonstrated in studies of families.[5] However, this vulnerability may be expressed differently among women and men. Women seem more prone toward *feeling* anxious, while men seem more prone to *expressing* their anxiety through action. In nondestructive ways, the latter can include sports and exercise. At the extreme, it includes destructive behavior such as alcohol and drug abuse and violence directed toward others.

We do not know the exact cause of biologically based anxiety, and the cause may in fact be different in different people. Current research suggests that it may include some alteration in the neurotransmitters, the substances in the brain that regulate feelings and mood. Neurotransmitters form the chemical messenger systems that relay information between the nerves in the brain. Three of these systems seem to be particularly important in the experience of anxiety: the noradrenergic system, the serotonergic system, and the GABA system. The first two are the same systems that are involved in biological depressions. The GABA system is unique to the experience of anxiety and is regulated by benzodiazepines, the antianxiety agents.[6]

It is believed that anxiety usually originates within structures deep in the brain, as do feelings of fear. These structures have esoteric names such as the limbic system, the thalamus, the locus ceruleus, and the reticular activating system. However, some researchers believe that it is the psychological sensation of anxiety that leads to apprehension and fear followed by hyperventilation. The hyperventilation exacerbates the sensation of anxiety, increasing the apprehension and fear even further. This vicious cycle can then take on a life of its own, resulting in a panic attack.[7]

Very few researchers have looked at the biological variables resulting in a reportedly higher incidence of some kinds of anxiety in women than men. Those who have propose two potential physical sources for the disparity: differences in sex hormones and differences in central nervous systems. For the time being, evidence that differences are due to fluctuations in sex hormones remains quite minimal.[8] On the other hand, evidence that differences between women's and men's central nervous systems may account for the variation in anxiety is quite compelling. Behavioral differences between women and men start at birth and seem to coincide with known differences in the development of certain parts of the brain, including those areas that regulate anxiety.[9] It is speculated that these differences may be mediated by sex hormones, thus drawing the two variables together.[10] However, much more research will be needed before we have a clear understanding of this phenomenon.

As more sophisticated technology is developed, it will become possible to determine the specific cause of various types of anxiety and to target interventions more accurately. For the time being, biologically mediated anxiety is usually treated with one of a number of antianxiety medications or (interestingly) one of the antidepressant medications. These medications will be discussed in the section on treatment.

Anxiety is also associated with a number of medical problems as well as some prescription and/or recreational drugs. Symptoms of anxiety can result from certain problems with a woman's heart, lungs, hormonal and nervous systems, including congestive heart failure, asthma, hyperthyroidism, premenstrual syndrome, and epilepsy. If any of these are suspected, a thorough medical evaluation is essential.[11] Legal as well as illegal drugs, including over-the-counter diet pills, oral steroids, sedatives, alcohol, and cocaine, are frequent causes of anxiety. Even caffeine, when consumed in high enough quantities, causes anxiety. Some people are more sensitive to these drugs than others, but any of them taken in large enough doses over a sufficiently long period of time can cause trouble. Some, such as alcohol, may initially be used to self-medicate anxiety and then lead to a second problem of substance abuse.

External or Social Contributors to Anxiety

An awareness and acknowledgment of the external contributors to anxiety is essential. Without this perspective, there can be a tendency to blame the victim for dysfunctional levels of distress. These external contributors range from mild to dangerous. Mild factors include virtually any life change, particularly when the change includes increased responsibility. New responsibilities at work or at home almost always result in some degree of anxiety. Mastering the skills needed to respond effectively to these changes usually results in a reduction in anxiety.

More destructive causes of anxiety are, unfortunately, all too common in many women's lives. An incest survivor, a battered wife, a rape victim, or a woman who experiences sexual discrimination or harassment at work may be particularly prone to anxiety. If and when she is finally able to get away from these situations, the severest symptoms of anxiety usually abate in six to twelve months. However, some traumas are so profound that a significant degree of anxiety or hypervigilance remains indefinitely.

In the absence of a purely biological cause, anxiety is a clear signal that something is amiss in a woman's life. Perhaps she is simply trying to do too much. For instance, most working mothers have two full-time jobs, one at the office and a second one at home. They find there is not enough time for sleep, let alone leisure. In these circumstances, anxiety signals a need for change. At home, it may mean altering her standard of orderliness and recruiting children, partners, or husbands to do more of the work. At work, it may mean taking some time off, arranging for more flexible hours, or restructuring her work space to provide some modicum of privacy and personal control.

For some women, the source of the anxiety runs much deeper. Profound violations of trust in early childhood, adolescence, or adulthood contribute to the development of a personality that is particularly vulnerable to anxiety.[12] Women with generalized anxiety, panic attacks, agoraphobia, or social phobias often report an usually high incidence of trauma, the most frequent being physical or sexual abuse. In some cases, this type of anxiety might be more accurately diagnosed as post-traumatic stress disorder, since the woman has often survived an unusually frightening and threatening life experience. Repairing these wounds is a difficult and long-term process. It usually requires the assistance of a sensitive and well-trained mental-health professional who is knowledgeable about the damaging legacy of trauma that occurs within significant relationships.

Internal Contributors to Anxiety

Internally generated causes of anxiety include the way a woman interprets her experiences in the world—right here and right now—whatever her experiences at an earlier time in her life. Does she see change as an exciting or frightening event? Is she generally optimistic about the world and the people in it, or is she pessimistic? Does she view herself as helpless and dependent, or does she feel most often that she has the ability to cope with what life doles out?

If a woman feels relatively safe within her world, her internal experience is likely to reflect this. However, if her world feels unsafe—either because of violations of trust or worry about potential abuse—her psychological development will leave her hypervigilant to the risk of danger and the need to protect and defend herself. If she comes to believe that all her efforts at self-protection will come to naught, she may eventually give up all hope and her anxiety will become inappropriately low, leaving her particularly vulnerable to further mistreatment.

Attitudes, beliefs, and self-talk, all of which make up a woman's ongoing internal dialogue with herself, all influence the amount of anxiety she feels in a particular situation. Fortunately, these are in her control. She can change them by acknowledging them, questioning their validity, and revising them to reflect more helpful internal communications. Here are some questions a woman can ask herself: "What is my self-talk? What kinds of thoughts go through my head? Do I build myself up or undermine my self-worth?" For example, in a relatively benign situation, a single heterosexual woman may think: "I'm so fat that that good-looking guy across the hall would *never* be interested in dating me! I couldn't possibly talk to him." This kind of self-talk erodes her self-esteem and contributes to her anxiety about meeting new men. In a more malignant situation, an abused woman may think: "He was treated so badly by his own father. That's why he gets so frustrated. If I just give him more love and affection, he will eventually feel better about himself and he won't have to behave so badly." This kind of self-talk keeps a woman in a dangerous position. It leaves her with the kind of anticipatory anxiety that is inevitable when one waits for an assault that can come at any time. It's like living in a guerrilla war zone.

A self-care program may prove to be adequate for reducing mild to moderate anxiety in relatively benign situations where anxiety is interfering with what should be a reasonable and manageable situation. Often, a relaxation training program that facilitates integration of mind and body can be very helpful for reducing anxiety. Changing our internal self-talk can also be a valuable tool. Therapists who specialize in the former approach are called behaviorists; those with special training in the latter approach are called cognitive-behaviorists. These professionals can be recruited if efforts at self-care are unsuccessful.

If the cause of the anxiety is a genuinely threatening situation, changing internal self-talk or learning relaxation techniques is not only inadequate, it is counterproductive. Sometimes, the psychological experience of anxiety is a strong and clear message that a life change is essential. To focus exclusively on anxiety management in these situations may be both unhealthy and unsafe.

Evaluating and Treating Anxiety

Assessing an individual woman's experience with anxiety requires a comprehensive review of all three potential contributors: biological, psychological, and social. The successful reduction or elimination of a woman's symptoms depends on the accuracy of this evaluation. The type of anxiety mandates the specific intervention—medication, behavioral training, psychotherapy, or something else. Identifying all contributors points to the approach most likely to lead to the fullest recovery. All three potential contributors must be considered. When more than one is involved, each must be addressed. An incomplete evaluation or inappropriate intervention not only wastes precious time, it may actually lead to a worsening of the situation.

If Biological Factors Are Prominent

Physicians often prescribe tranquilizers or antianxiety agents for women who report the physical symptoms of anxiety such as chronic fatigue, headache, or an upset stomach without first trying drugless interventions. Women have become justifiably cautious about the use of these drugs since there is the risk of dependence if they are used in high doses for long periods of time. However, in spite of occasional misuse by both physicians and patients, it is important to be cautious about throwing out the baby with the bathwater. When used carefully and thoughtfully, antianxiety medications do have a place in the management of severe anxiety, and it is unwise and unnecessary to avoid them altogether for fear of their potential misuse.[13] Any medication has risks and when used inappropriately, these risks increase. Nevertheless, if we shy away from using a medication appropriately because we are concerned about potential misuse, we deny women access to genuinely helpful interventions.

Antianxiety medications effectively break the spiralling cycle of anxiety; when they are taken judiciously under the supervision of a well-trained professional, the potential for abuse and addiction is greatly reduced. These medications are not under any circumstances recommended for long-term use, and they are virtually contraindicated for anyone who already has a history of addiction to any other substance. Furthermore, when there are clearly psychosocial factors contributing to a woman's distress, these medications will not, in and of themselves, solve the real source of her difficulty. But if her anxiety is so severe that she is unable to do any effective problem solving, it must be reduced before she will be able to deal with the real source of her distress.

In most cases, a physician will recommend the use of a benzodiazepine for the short-term (less than four months) treatment of uncomplicated anxiety.[14] You are undoubtedly familiar with many of these drugs. They include chlordiazepoxide (Librium), diazepam (Valium), and alprazolam (Xanax). There are a number of other benzodiazepines, but these are the ones most frequently prescribed. The medication should be chosen specifically for your life and health status. For example, some of the antianxiety medications are processed through the body much more quickly than others. This will have advantages for some women and disadvantages for others depending on the severity of their anxiety, the tasks they must accomplish while on these medications, and other individual factors.

While these drugs are relatively safe when used as prescribed, they do have side effects. Perhaps the greatest problem is a reduced ability to control voluntary movements and coordinate our hands, arms, and legs. This presents a special risk in driving. Drivers using benzodiazepines are nearly five times more likely to be involved in a serious accident than those not using these medications.[15] Memory and attention can also be impaired, and thinking can be dulled. Some people have been known to develop depression while on these medications, and a few actually become agitated rather than relaxed. None of these medications should be mixed with alcohol, and they should be discontinued gradually rather than suddenly to avoid withdrawal symptoms.

A new antianxiety agent, buspirone (BuSpar), is a promising addition to the treatment options for biological anxiety. Unlike the benzodiazepines, buspirone does not seem to pose the risk of addiction. It is also far less sedating, does not cause memory loss or impaired coordination, and does not interact dangerously with alcohol. And, most importantly, when the medication is no longer needed, it can simply be stopped without any apparent ill effects. Unfortunately, buspirone does not have the rapid onset of the traditional antianxiety agents. It takes one to two weeks of regular use as prescribed to reduce anxiety. Furthermore, it is a relatively new drug and more time and study will be needed to determine its long-term safety and effectiveness.

Some physicians prefer to prescribe an antihistamine for the treatment of anxiety. In this case, the patient usually responds to the sedative effect of the medication rather than a genuine antianxiety effect. While this medication does not run the risk of addiction, it is unclear how helpful it is in reducing anxiety. Some physicians prescribe a beta blocker (such as Inderal) to reduce the physical manifestations of performance anxiety. If an increased heart rate, excessive sweating, or nervous stomach are interfering with the competency of a public performer, beta blockers can prove to be very useful in controlling these symptoms.

Interestingly, the most effective medications for panic disorders are antidepressants. Imipramine (Tofranil) is the most widely studied antipanic medication, but almost all of the commonly used antidepressants appear to be effective in reducing the frequency and duration of panic attacks. These medications have no addictive potential but still must be taken precisely as prescribed. Because they take two to six weeks to achieve full effectiveness,[16] I sometimes recommend adding an antianxiety agent during the time the patient waits for the antidepressant to take effect. The antianxiety drug breaks the cycle of anxiety immediately, and a few weeks on these medications will not result in addiction. The antianxiety medications can be tapered off and discontinued after two to six weeks of use, at which time the antidepressants should be providing adequate protection against the worst of the anxiety.

Some clinicians prefer using a monoamine oxidase inhibitor (MAOI) for the treatment of anxiety. Like antidepressants, MAOIs are also used to treat biological depressions. Unlike more conventional antidepressant medications, MAOIs require strict dietary regulation.[17] Patients taking these medications must avoid all foods and beverages containing tyramine, a natural by-product of fermentation. This includes many cheeses, alcoholic beverages, and certain fruits, nuts, and vegetables. Some other medications must also be avoided or used cautiously, especially many cold and sinus preparations.

A new drug, clomipramine (Anafranil), widely available in other countries but not yet in the United States, seems to be very effective in the treatment of obsessive-compulsive disorder. This drug does not seem to eliminate the obsessions or compulsions, but it does make it easier for the patient to resist them. Thus they spend far less time on nonproductive thoughts and activities. Behavioral therapy has also proven to be helpful in treating this problem.[18]

Actually, treatment with medication works best if it is used in conjunction with a therapy program. Medication may alleviate the symptoms of anxiety, but only a therapy program provides an opportunity to acquire new strategies for coping with the anxiety when it occurs at a future time when the woman is not taking any medication.

A Behavioral Approach: If Medication Appears Unnecessary or Inappropriate

People often self-treat simple phobias by avoiding the thing or situation that causes their anxiety. When this is impractical or impossible, a therapist with behavioral training can help design a program of systematic desensitization in which a woman learns to relax actively while imagining or "imaging" the source of her phobia. The patient and therapist develop a program where the patient imagines increasingly anxiety-provoking situations in her mind. In most cases, her anxiety will generally pass within twenty or thirty minutes and she will feel more relaxed even while imagining the previously distressing situation. She eventually links the previously frightening thing or situation with a relaxed rather than anxious response. By enduring or "surviving" her anxiety, she will gradually overcome her phobia—at least in her mind. Eventually, her visual mastery can then be translated into real-life circumstances. Again, she and her therapist develop a program of increasingly anxiety-provoking situations that she gradually enters. Her anxiety is slowly replaced with a sense of mastery. This transformation, while requiring commitment and perseverance, can be very gratifying.

Agoraphobia is a more severe form of phobic anxiety. It has often been portrayed as the housewives' syndrome—something that keeps a woman housebound.[19] This is far from an accurate picture. Agoraphobia is just as common among employed women as women who are exclusively homemakers. Treatment usually requires the intervention of a professional, although considerable progress can be made by a woman who is motivated to design and carry out her own program of change.

> Beverly and I met at a political gathering. She was an attractive, intense, competent, and clearly powerful woman. I liked her immediately and greatly admired her achievements as an independent consultant for nonprofit agencies. I did not know anything about her personal life until she called my office one morning so

upset that she was almost unable to speak. We made an appointment to try to figure out why she was so frightened and what could be done about it.

Beverly had grown up in a rather poor Polish family where girls were expected only to become mothers and homemakers—not professionals. Her parents had refused to subsidize her college education, although they paid for her brothers. She put herself through college working nights and weekends and sometimes taking terms off to work full-time. It took six years in all to get through. Beverly met her husband, Larry, toward the end of college. They dated for two years and had been married for almost fourteen. Both were ambivalent about having children, but as Beverly approached her fortieth birthday, she became more and more aware of her "biological clock." She was almost as afraid of giving up the idea of having a child as she was of actually becoming a parent. She began "forgetting" to use birth control, something she had previously been fastidious about. When she discovered that she was pregnant, she was terrified.

In addition to her present distress, I learned that Beverly suffered severe anxiety attacks whenever her husband was out of town. Since Larry's job required frequent travel, this had become a major problem. When he was away, Beverly would begin feeling anxious as soon as dusk fell. She would spend the night chain-smoking and watching television. Occasionally she became so frightened that she would spend the night at a friend's home—although this was always an embarrassing last resort. She never had these attacks when Larry was home.

Beverly loved Larry and she knew that he valued his job, so she hid her fears from him. Consequently, he was quite unprepared for the severity of her present distress. Unfortunately, Beverly had been far too ashamed to acknowledge the anxiety she experienced when she was separated from him, but the pregnancy unleashed a level of anxiety that even she could not hide. It also gave her a "reason" to contact me.

Since Beverly was pregnant, she could not take antianxiety medication. Instead, I gave her a lesson in using relaxation techniques and advised her to begin using them three times a day. In weekly therapy sessions, we explored her ambivalence about being pregnant. Although she was a strong prochoice advocate, her Catholic upbringing left her reluctant to have an abortion. She decided to continue the pregnancy and to learn more about why she became so anxious and what to do about it.

Admitting that she was anxious freed Beverly to discuss her experience with others. Much to her surprise, she discovered that her sister, Tina, had experienced agoraphobia some years before. With Tina's help, Beverly created her own behavioral treatment program.[20] She made a list of all the people she could call and talk to no matter what time of the night and included the numbers of several hot lines for times when she did not want to disturb a friend. She used her telephone to keep connected to other people when she felt disconnected from her husband. She trained herself to go to bed when her husband was out of town instead of sitting up in the living room. She read heavy, almost boring, books at bedtime rather than watching action-packed shows on television. She stopped smoking and instead kept her fingers busy with cross-stitching and making outfits for the baby. She learned to replace her anxiety-provoking thoughts with soothing ones. Instead of worrying that he might not return, she reminded herself that he loved her and planned to be home the following evening.

After almost six months of her own treatment program, Beverly's new skills were put to the test. Her sister accepted a job out of state. In the past, this kind of separation would almost certainly have caused Beverly extreme anxiety. This time she acknowledged her desire to remain connected to her sister in spite of the separation. She made plans to help Tina find a new place to live and to visit in person and by phone on a regular basis.

By the time Beverly went into labor, her ability to manage her anxiety was very sophisticated, and she delivered a healthy seven-pound baby without any extraordinary difficulty. At our last visit, two months after the birth, she was doing just fine and was very pleased with the changes she had made in her life.

If this treatment plan had been unsuccessful, it might have been helpful to add a program of exposure therapy. A trained therapist goes with the woman into the situation(s) she fears. They start with the least anxiety-provoking situations and graduate, step-by-step, to ones that cause increasingly greater fear. As they work together, the therapist educates the woman about the various aspects of her response to anxiety, such as hyperventilation. The therapist teaches the woman to take slow, deep breaths rather than the shallow, rapid breaths that commonly accompany and contribute to anxiety. The exposure therapist sticks with the woman until her anxiety subsides. After the woman masters the anxiety in the presence of the therapist, the therapist gradually withdraws and the woman learns to master the anxiety on her own.

Although this type of intervention is effective, it is time-consuming and expensive. Furthermore, well-trained therapists may be hard to find in smaller communities. An equally effective alternative can be group training. In this setting, a woman experiencing anxiety discovers that she is not alone with her symptoms. A group of women at different levels of improvement can share support and helpful strategies with newcomers.

As you can see, agoraphobia is not usually a problem that comes on all at once. It normally develops in stages:[21]

Stage 1 is the experience of a spontaneous panic attack.

Stage 2 is the anticipatory anxiety phase. The person begins to anticipate the occurrence of the next attack with dread.

Stage 3 is when the person decides to try to cope with panic by avoiding the situations where they have occurred or are likely to occur.

Stage 4 is when the avoidance has progressed so far that the person's self-esteem has been significantly eroded in the process of becoming so dependent on others. The person is often depressed as well at this stage.

The earlier the problem is accurately identified and corrective measures are implemented, the easier it will be to turn the problem around—whether through self-care or professional assistance.

A Self-in-Relation Perspective

Neither biology, trauma nor irrational self-talk are the only precipitants of a woman's anxiety and neither medication or behavioral therapy are the only methods for treating such symptoms. I am not a behaviorally oriented therapist and I see many women with symptoms of anxiety who make significant progress in our work together. What do we do together that proves to be helpful?

We begin by exploring her experience. I ask the woman to tell me about herself and her symptoms. When did the anxiety start? Why does she think she became anxious at that particular time? What has she tried to relieve the anxiety? What worked and what didn't? Many women report that anxiety emerges when they are getting ready to alter a significant relationship. In the past, this has been called separation anxiety. It was presumed that in distancing herself from a significant other, a woman became anxious as she became more autonomous. This belief derives from the notion that the woman was moving away from a position of dependence to a position of independence.

While it is true that in many instances the woman is making some major shift in her emotional positioning with a significant other, often her deepest desire is to remain connected to that person, but in a different kind of way.[22] She wants to change something about herself—or for herself. Sometimes she also wants the other person to change or something to be changed in the nature of their relationship. But she is not separating. She is trying to become more true to herself while also remaining attached.[23] She is anxious because she is uncertain whether or not the relationship can tolerate and survive her need for change.

> Celeste is a successful thirty-five-year-old banker. She and her husband, Matthew, had been married for three years after dating for over five. Since the beginning, their relationship had been marked by conflict—often over what seemed to be petty issues. Nonetheless, they also felt a considerable amount of love and affection for each other and sought therapy to help them deal with their conflicts. They tried hard, but nothing seemed to make much of a difference. With much pain and turmoil, they decided to separate.
>
> Although it was a mutual agreement, it was Matthew who actually left the couple's home. Celeste was shocked to discover how abandoned and upset she felt. Intermittently sad and angry, she ruminated about what she had done wrong in the relationship. Her anxiety took many forms. She snapped at the bank's customers—behavior quite unusual for her and worrisome to her colleagues. She had trouble sleeping, and she relied frequently on sleeping medication, which left her feeling groggy in the morning. She demanded to talk with Matthew at all hours of the day and night, and she became extremely agitated when she discovered

that he was dating. She realized that she might really lose him. A separation was one thing—a permanent loss was something else.

Fortunately, Celeste was already in therapy with a very competent therapist, and she had a large network of loving and concerned friends—all of whom she relied on extensively to help her cope with her feelings. In therapy, Celeste discovered that her conflictual relationship with Matthew was very reminiscent of her relationship with her parents, who had been intermittently loving and judgmental. She had learned to put up with being treated in a critical and hostile manner because the people who treated her this way were also the people she relied on for love and caretaking. It seemed to her familiar and natural that the two were tied up with each other—even if they didn't really feel very good. She thought it was unrealistic to expect something else. Her therapist offered her an alternative experience—clear, occasionally confrontive, information in the context of a nurturing and empathic relationship.

This was an eye-opening experience for Celeste. She realized that in the past she had selected friends who were more like her parents and Matthew; now she was gravitating toward people who were more consistently supportive, although certainly not pushovers. (She was picking friends more like her therapist than her parents.) She was now understanding her anxiety, recognizing that if she wanted to make some change in her relationship with another person, that individual might resist the change by being hostile and argumentative.[24] She had previously felt as if she either had to give in to their demands, which she was very reluctant to do, or hold her own ground. When she did the latter, she became very fearful that the other person would not support her position and might terminate the relationship altogether. She had had little experience with relationships in which each member of the pair grew and changed in harmony. To be different meant to risk being totally alone.

Celeste began to think in terms of the little girl inside her getting anxious and needing loving support from the competent parent/adult she also carried around inside. Gradually, Celeste discovered that when she became anxious she could think about strategies to soothe that worried little girl. She developed a whole collection of options. Sometimes she went to a movie or to a friend's house. Sometimes she read a book in the comfort of her own home. Sometimes she called her therapist or a caring friend. She made a commitment to learn how to master her anxiety because it was a good thing to do for herself, rather than because it might bring Matthew back or bind other friends to her. The self-understanding Celeste gained came in the context of a therapy based on self-in-relation theory, although the program Celeste designed for herself certainly required behavioral changes. She did not just experience empathy and gain insight—she actually made satisfying life changes.

Even though Matthew eventually decided that he wanted out of the relationship permanently, Celeste had made enough progress in her own emotional work that she could tolerate the end of her marriage and still feel OK about herself—and Matthew. She was disappointed and hurt but not devastated, and she was able to negotiate the details of their divorce settlement with relative equanimity. Two years later, Celeste remains single, but she enjoys a rich social life and her work is going fine.

A self-in-relation perspective is equally useful in understanding more severe forms of anxiety such as panic attacks and agoraphobia.

Betty was thirty-seven. Over the course of seven months, she had become so incapacitated by episodes of anxiety that she rarely left her house. She was no longer able to go to work, visit her elderly mother who lived in a neighboring town, participate in her son's cooperative day care, do the household shopping, pick her husband up at the airport when he returned from his frequent business trips, or enjoy having sex with him. The episodes of anxiety were punctuated by an inability to catch her breath, pounding of her heart, profuse sweating, and an intense fear that she was going to die. She had talked about these symptoms with her family physician who did a brief physical exam. He found nothing wrong physically and told her it was just her nerves.

Her physician wrote a prescription for one of the well-known tranquilizers and told her to take one whenever she felt an episode coming on. But Betty was afraid to use the drugs. Her father had died of alcoholism, and she was frightened of her own risk of addiction—with good cause, since it is a problem that tends to run in families. She talked about her worries with her best friend, Sharon, who lived next door. Sharon had heard me speak on the subject of anxiety and recommended that Betty call me.

Betty and I set a time for a consultation, but she missed that first appointment. Her home was in a town north of San Francisco. The Golden Gate Bridge separated her from my office and from the many urban activities that had previously been a regular part of her life. Sometimes she could not bring herself to drive across the span, fearing that she would panic midway. She called me to apologize and described feeling profoundly embarrassed and guilty. We talked about what might make it possible for her to come in and see me. She thought that she could do it if Sharon would be kind enough to drive her and wait with her twenty-two-month-old daughter in my waiting room while Betty and I had our meeting. This was arranged. Betty's friend was happy to help and actually ended up escorting Betty to my office for several sessions until our plan began to work.

At the end of our initial meeting, I explained to Betty that she was having panic attacks, that they were biologically mediated and could best be managed with antidepressant medication. Betty was just as wary about this proposal as she had been about the recommendation to use tranquilizers. I explained that antidepressant medications are very different from tranquilizers and that she could not become physically addicted to them. I described our current understanding of what happens in the body when we have a panic attack and why these particular medications are superior to tranquilizers in reducing the worst of these symptoms.

I added that I thought she would feel much more in control of her own recovery if we included some deep-breathing and relaxation exercises in her treatment program. She could use these skills even after the medication was no longer necessary, and they would allow her to feel much more mastery over her own body.

Finally, I suggested that these two interventions, the medication and the behavioral training, would only help her control her symptoms. Neither addressed the problem that had triggered her episodes.

Betty told me that she had never been a particularly anxious person until recently, and her episodes did not seem to reflect a long-standing biological vulnerability to anxiety. They were, I suspected, directly related to an event seven months earlier that Betty had been afraid to tell anyone about—until I asked specifically if she had been subjected to any physical or sexual abuse.

Seven months earlier, Betty had come home early from her office to discover her trusted baby-sitter sexually molesting her fifteen-month-old daughter. She immediately dismissed the sitter but was flooded with guilt over leaving her daughter vulnerable to such abuse. Betty had shared her distress with no one. She called her office the next morning and simply said that she was not coming in and did not know when she would return. Her boss was startled and confused. Although Betty only worked part-time, she had always been an extremely reliable and conscientious employee on whom he depended enormously. It made no sense to him, but Betty refused to offer any explanation.

Previously, Betty had comfortably left her daughter in the sitter's care whenever she had to be away from home and her husband was not available. Now she would not allow her daughter out of her sight and she was terrified of leaving her in the care of anyone except Sharon. Sharon, a friend since childhood, was the only person Betty had ever told about being sexually abused by her often drunk father. Betty had always been afraid to tell her husband about what had happened, fearful that he might somehow hold her responsible or feel she had been tainted by the abuse. Betty had never had much interest in sex, and her husband sometimes commented about this, but now the situation had become more problematic. She did not want to have sex at all, and her husband was, understandably, confused and annoyed.

Betty and I agreed to work together, starting first with medication and behavioral techniques. As her anxiety subsided, we started to talk about what had happened to her as a child. I tried to help her realize that she was not to blame for what had happened to either her or her daughter and that her relationship with her husband might actually be improved if she could start to share what had happened—both to herself and to their daughter. I also suggested that she and her husband might want to decide together if they wanted to bring charges against the sitter, who continued to care for other children in the neighborhood. Betty had been feeling guilty about keeping quiet, but she was also anxious about blowing the whistle. What if she had overreacted because of her own experiences? What if this would not be seen as that big of a deal to other parents or to the authorities?

Therapy was a very painful process, but ever so slowly Betty started to feel better about herself and closer to her husband. She eventually talked with her mother about what had happened to her when she was a child. Bringing up this secret and clearing the air allowed these two women to resolve some misunderstandings and resentments that had plagued their relationship for years. Betty's employer had readily agreed to a brief disability leave after I had written him a letter, and her job was ready and waiting when she returned. Her neighbor, Sharon, agreed to care for Betty's daughter along with her own son until the young girl could join her own brother in day care. Betty and her husband eventually contacted an attorney to investigate what they might do about the abusive sitter.

Betty is now symptom free and no longer on medication. She still does her relaxation exercises twice a day and finds them a safe and healthy alternative to the two glasses of wine she use to drink almost every night after work. Asking about abuse had been critical to our work. If we had simply used medication and behavioral techniques to treat Betty's symptoms while leaving the actual trigger event unaddressed, her recovery would have been incomplete and she would have been vulnerable to recurring symptoms at a later date.

Because Betty wanted to forget her own painful history and the recent abuse to her daughter, only a therapist who asks about these experiences and is prepared to hear about it in an empathic way would be permitted into her confidence. Often, even when a therapist asks, a patient may not be prepared to discuss painful episodes at that time or may have pushed them so far out of her memory that even she denies her own experience. However, since the therapist has asked about them, it may be easier for the patient to reveal them when she feels safer or when her memories return. We now know that up to 20 percent of all women have been sexually abused and we suspect that the percent is even higher among women who enter therapy.[25] Yet, although this is a trauma that has colored the lives of many women, only therapists who ask their patients about these experiences and are prepared to deal with the emotional fallout are likely to learn about them. Only in sharing these experiences and working through the pain will the patient's emotional wounds have an opportunity to heal.

Reducing Anxiety

In order to successfully reduce excessive anxiety, it is essential that the causes be accurately determined. It is not reasonable to hold a woman responsible for distress caused by external factors, nor is it fair for her to blame others when the cause is simply the way she is interpreting certain experiences. All the revised thinking in the world and behavioral changes will not help if she has a biological propensity toward anxiety that is left untreated.

A woman has no control over her genetic heritage or the traumatic events of early childhood. As an adolescent or adult, she can refrain from using anxiety-provoking drugs like cocaine, alcohol, and excessive amounts of caffeine that only make matters worse. She can seek treatment for any medical illnesses that cause anxiety. She can also do her best to avoid people who treat her disrespectfully. Nevertheless, her position as a second-class citizen makes it highly probable that she will face numerous episodes of discrimination, if not outright abuse, for which anxiety is an understandable response.[26] How can she best reduce her distress?

Anxiety, although at times extremely unpleasant, is not usually life-threatening (which is not to say that some circumstances that cause anxiety, such as abuse, are not life-threatening). You have time to find the best program for you. If money or your desire to be self-reliant is an issue, consider beginning with a self-help program. There are numerous books and tapes specifically geared toward motivated self-care, and self-help groups are available in many communities.

Through education and self-care, a woman can sometimes do a great deal to reduce and control her anxiety. She can change beliefs and attitudes that sustain unnecessary anxiety. She can use relaxation techniques to control her anxiety. She can desensitize herself to anxiety-provoking situations. And she can work toward making healthy changes in important relationships without terminating them altogether.

Basic Education

- Not all types of anxiety are the same.
- Sometimes anxiety is a healthy and appropriate response to a real problem. In this case, the genuine problem needs to be identified and addressed. While reducing excessively high levels of anxiety may be necessary to assure effective problem solving, covering up anxiety symptoms with alcohol, tranquilizers, or other mind-altering substances is not a solution.
- Panic attacks and obsessive-compulsive disorders may have a biological basis that requires the appropriate medical treatment.
- Most phobias can be reduced with active nondrug interventions. Occasionally, medication is a useful adjuvant to behavioral changes.
- Agoraphobia develops in stages. It is most easily treated early on.
- Post-traumatic stress disorder can cause severe anxiety symptoms in even previously healthy individuals. Intervention is best handled in conjunction with a knowledgeable and supportive professional.
- When making changes, remember that we all have good days and bad days. Some are simply harder than others. Give yourself a breather if things just seem too hard one day, but don't slack off for so long that you slip back into avoiding making necessary changes.
- When you are working on a self-designed program of change, schedule regular practice sessions into your daily routine. Make it a time when you are not too fatigued. Retraining is demanding. You're working hard, so don't schedule your training sessions when you're totally exhausted.

Self-care

The Relaxation Response[27]

1. Once or twice a day, sit comfortably in a quiet place with your eyes closed.
2. Deeply relax all your muscles, beginning with your toes and working all the way up to your face to the top of your head. (If you have a tape recorder with earphones, you may find it useful to make a tape of your own voice leading you through this exercise, or you can use one of the tapes listed in the resource section.)
3. Focus on your breathing. Use your diaphragm to take nice deep breaths rather than relying on your chest and your lungs alone. As you exhale through your mouth, silently say to yourself the word "one." As you inhale through your nose, silently say to yourself the word "two."
4. If thoughts enter your mind, just let them pass through. Keep a passive attitude. Don't focus on anything other than your breathing and relaxing your muscles.
5. Each session should last ten to twenty minutes. When you're finished, sit quietly with your eyes closed for a few moments. Then open them and rest a few minutes more before you stand and go about your business in your newly relaxed state.

Self-talk (Also Called Cognitive Restructuring)[28]

Self-talk is the way you think about any event or situation. If you think positively about something, it is likely to reduce your anxiety. If you think negatively, it is likely to increase it.

Obviously, thoughts alone do not create bad feelings, but they can go a long way to make us feel better or worse. Fortunately, the way we think about something is completely in our control. For example, if you assume that every time your boss wants to talk with you it is because you've done something wrong, you will be anxious whenever she asks you to come into her office. On the other hand, if you do not jump to conclusions and wait to hear what she has to say, you will not make yourself unnecessarily anxious. What if it turns out that she really values your perspective and wants to seek your advice about a delicate matter in private? If you had made a negative assumption about her request, you would have created your own distress.

How do people make themselves unhappy by thinking alone and what can they do about it?

1. All-or-nothing thinking—You see something as completely one way or another with nothing in between. In real life, things are usually partly good and partly bad. Try looking for the good part rather than focusing on the bad.

2. Jumping to conclusions—You get a tiny bit of information and immediately jump to the most disastrous conclusion. Try collecting more information before you make a judgment.

3. Mind reading—You think you know what another person is thinking about you—without any real evidence. Usually you assume their thoughts are negative. Try checking your beliefs before assuming you are clairvoyant.

4. "Catastrophizing"—You blow things way out of proportion. Try assuming that the problem, whatever it is, is really a small one that can be easily corrected.

5. "Awfulizing"—You assume that something will be awful even before it happens. Try waiting to see how the situation actually goes instead of imagining the worst.

6. Mental filtering—You filter out the positive and absorb only the negative in any situation. Try the reverse for a change and see what happens.

7. The "fallacy of fairness"—Life is not fair, although many of us think it should be. Try assuming that things will go right at least half the time. You will probably get less upset the rest of the time when things do not work out the way you had hoped they would.

8. Overgeneralizing—Just because something is true some of the time does not mean it is true all of the time. Try to isolate a negative event within its situation rather than projecting it into every similar one.

9. "Crystal-balling"—Unless you are truly psychic, you cannot possibly know the future. You will upset yourself unnecessarily if you assume that you can and if your assumptions are negative. Try living in the present and trust more that you will deal successfully with events in the future when they present themselves.

Sometimes your negative thoughts prove to be realistic. OK, put them in perspective. Things occasionally do not work out the way we would like them to. That's life. You still have a choice about whether to dwell on the negative or focus on the positive. It's all up to you!

Designing Your Own Exposure-Therapy Program[29]

If your anxiety is related to a specific situation, you may want to try creating your own therapy program before turning to a professional. There are seven principles to follow:

1. Confront the feared situation by venturing into situations that cause anxiety. Learn to deal with your fear of fear.

2. Let the anxiety peak and pass. Anxiety will not increase indefinitely. If you stay in the anxiety-provoking situation until the anxiety subsides, your

anxiety will be less the next time. Leaving an anxiety-provoking situation reinforces avoidance. Staying leads to recovery.

3. Accept the panic—even bring it on. This is a critical change in attitude. While panic is uncomfortable, it is not dangerous. It is simply an exaggeration of the body's response to stress. It takes energy to push it down or avoid it. If you stop fearing the anxiety and allow it to happen, you can begin to learn how to deal with it more effectively.

4. Develop and use a graduated hierarchy of exposure. List those situations that cause you anxiety and rank them from the least anxiety provoking to the greatest. Managing anxiety effectively means beginning with situations that only cause mild to moderate anxiety, not full-blown panic attacks. As you have success at each level, move up your hierarchy of anxiety. If you move in small steps, you will find that you can gradually master even the most challenging situations.

5. Use a safe person or a safe object. Don't make learning harder than it need be. You will find it easier to start your program if you practice with a person or object that helps you feel safer. (Remember Linus's blanket? We all need our own security blanket, no matter how old we get!) After you have mastered your anxiety with their help, you can gradually phase them out.

6. Use SUDS. SUDS (Subjective Units of Distress Scale) is a tool to measure anxiety. Zero is no anxiety; 1–3 is mild anxiety; 4–6 is moderate anxiety; 7–9 is severe anxiety; 10 is PANIC! Keep returning to each new situation on the next level of your anxiety hierarchy until your anxiety begins to drop down. For example, if entering an elevator causes you severe anxiety (say an 8 on your SUDS), keep doing it until it only causes moderate anxiety (say a 5). We call this habituation. It is your body's signal that you are successfully reducing your reaction to an anxiety-provoking situation. As you keep repeating the same steps over and over again, your anxiety will continue to go lower and lower. Perhaps it will eventually disappear altogether!

7. Focus on behavior, not feelings. Concentrate on what you do, not how you feel. Remember that whether you leave the house alone or get through that tunnel is more important than whether you feel scared and sweaty.

Time for Play and Leisure[30]

Play and leisure are not really optional, even if we imagine they are. Without them, our life gets out of whack and, ultimately, so do we—either physically or psychologically.

I was reminded of the importance of making time for play and leisure while

I was writing this book. Through a series of events outside my control, work had gradually taken over most of my time and energy, while my financial obligations more than tripled. To meet all my commitments, I had reduced my sleep to six hours a night, was working every Saturday and Sunday in addition to twelve to fourteen hours each weekday, and had gone without any vacation for almost an entire year.

One frightening morning at 5:15 A.M., I passed out as my heart suddenly started racing at 180 beats per minute. It was not my first symptom of anxiety. Two months earlier, I had developed a constant lump in my throat, promptly and accurately diagnosed by me as globus hystericus—a purely psychological phenomenon that feels as if something is closing your throat. I ignored it and continued working. One month later, my body added two more anxiety symptoms—shortness of breath and tightness in my chest. With these I saw my doctor. She diagnosed anxiety and reminded me to do daily ten-minute relaxation sessions. I thanked her for her reassurance that it was psychological, not physical, and promptly ignored her advice. That's when my body pulled out all the stops and insisted that I pay attention.

A comprehensive physical evaluation revealed no medical explanation for the sudden increase in my heart rate. This was anxiety pure and simple, and only a life-style change was going to bring an end to the symptoms. It didn't take a genius to figure out that unless I made more time in my life for play and leisure, I wasn't going to be around much longer to make a choice. I hope you don't wait until your anxiety level gets as high as mine did before you integrate regular time for play and leisure into your life!

Make Your World as Safe as Possible

Many women find that anxiety stems from a basic concern about their physical safety. To reduce your worry about being home alone, have good locks installed on your windows and doors and consider purchasing an alarm system to deter intruders.

If you worry about your ability to protect yourself, sign up for a self-defense class. Many of the standard programs do not take a woman's smaller body size or reluctance to behave in an "unfeminine" way into consideration, so be sure to take a class designed specifically for women.

It goes without saying that any woman who is being treated disrespectfully by another person, either psychologically or physically, will feel anxious in their company. If the situation is alterable, take the appropriate action to effect change in the relationship as soon as possible. If this proves to be too difficult or downright impossible, extricate yourself as quickly as you can. While making this kind of change may temporarily increase your anxiety, you will eventually find that it yields a greater sense of safety and peace.

Good Health Practices

If you suspect the source of your anxiety is medical, have a complete physical exam. Treat any problems that seem to be causing or contributing to your symptoms of anxiety. It certainly helps to reduce or discontinue your use of caffeine, alcohol, and/or other anxiety-inducing drugs. Regular, moderate exercise is a good antianxiety strategy, and a nutritious diet is always a bonus.

Professional Assistance

If you have been unable to determine the cause of your anxiety or to effectively reduce it, you may decide to seek the assistance of a competent professional. You will need a consultation with someone who can perform an accurate assessment and recommend the best program or intervention for you.

Select a clinician who is knowledgeable about all three causes of anxiety rather than someone who specializes in just one approach. Interview several clinicians. Ask about their credentials, method of treatment, and track record. Do not work with someone who fails to assess all three areas of potential difficulty. A clinician who treats your anxiety with pills without exploring your past or present life experiences is ignoring or minimizing other contributors to your anxiety. You also have a responsibility to give your health-care provider a full accounting of contributing factors.

Decreasing your anxiety requires a collaborative effort and shared responsibility. Although life is never anxiety free, anxiety does not have to control your existence. It is possible to establish a manageable level of anxiety rather than struggle with it in overwhelming amounts. With wisdom and hard work, you can gain more control over your own life.

RESOURCES

Self-help Organizations:

CHAANGE: Free from Fears
2915 Providence Road, Charlotte, NC 28211, (704) 365-0140

This group offers a number of pamphlets and audio tapes specifically for individuals who wish to implement a program of change without using professional assistance.

Phobia Society of America
Department R, 133 Rollins Avenue, Suite 4B, Rockville, MD 20852-4004

Send a business-size, self-addressed envelope with two first-class stamps. You will receive general information about phobias and panic disorders, information about the society's services and activities, and recommendations on how to find effective treatment should you eventually seek it.

Self-help Tapes:

"Deep Relaxation"
Effective Learning Systems, Inc., 5221 Edina Industrial Boulevard, Edina, MN 55435, (612) 893-1680

This tape offers two strategies for progressive relaxation. On one side you are guided into a relaxed state by simply relaxing parts of your body. On the other, you are led through a process of tensing then relaxing your muscles. The latter style is commonly used by behavioral therapists who wish to help people overcome phobias. The former is useful for daily relaxation sessions and can easily be used at the office or home.

"Overcoming Anxiety: A Program of Self-management" by Gary Emery, Ph.D.
BMA Audiocassettes, 72 Spring Street, New York, NY 10012

This is an audiocassette program that details proven, effective strategies for the management and maintenance of anxiety reduction. It helps individuals deal with immediate difficulties caused by anxiety and reinforces easy-to-master techniques for long-term coping. It explains the link between self-trust, a sense of mastery, and lower level of anxiety and provides an abundance of mastery exercises.

"Ten-Minute Stress Manager" by Emmett E. Miller, M.D.
Software for the Mind Cassettes, Source Cassettes, Inc., P.O. Box W, Stanford, CA 94305, (800) 528-2737

This tape begins by guiding you through relaxation using music and the sounds of waves and birds. It then leads you into an energizing pep talk. A good tape to use before you start a new activity. Not for bedtime use!

Books:

Each of these books takes a slightly different perspective in explaining the causes of anxiety and what to do to reduce it. Some focus more on professional assistance, while others lean toward a self-care approach. You might look at several of them and select one or more that seem to be most helpful for you.

Stewart Agras, *Panic, Facing Your Fears, Phobias, and Anxiety* (New York: W. H. Freeman and Sons, 1985).

Herbert Benson, *The Relaxation Response* (New York: Avon, 1976).

Joan Borysenko, *Minding the Body, Mending the Mind* (New York: Addison-Wesley, 1987).

Carin Chambless, "Fears and Anxiety," in *Everywoman's Guide to Emotional Well-Being,* ed. C. Tavris (Garden City, NY: Doubleday, 1986).

Martha Davis, Matthew McKay, and Elizabeth Tobbins Eshelman, *The Relaxation and Stress Reduction Workbook* (Oakland: New Harbinger Publications, 2200 Adeline, Suite 305, Oakland CA 94607, 1982).

J. H. Greist, J. W. Jefferson, and I. M. Marks, *Anxiety and Its Treatment* (Washington, D.C.: American Psychiatric Press, 1986).

David Sheehan, *The Anxiety Diseases* (New York: Charles Scribner's Sons, 1983).

NOTES

1. *The Psychiatric Times,* November 1988, p. 1.

2. *Diagnostic and Statistical Manual of Mental Disorders* (DSM-III-R) (Washington, D.C.: American Psychiatric Association Press, 1987).

3. R. K. Pitman, "Post-Traumatic Stress Disorder, Conditioning, and Network Theory," *Psychiatric Annals* 18 no.3 (March 1988): 182.

4. Oliver G. Cameron and Elizabeth M. Hill, "Women and Anxiety," *Psychiatric Clinics of North America* 12 no. 1 (March 1989): 176.

5. R. Shader, "Epidemiologic and Family Studies," *Psychosomatics* 25 no. 10 suppl. (October 1984): 12–13.

6. C. Barr Taylor and Bruce Arnow, *The Nature and Treatment of Anxiety Disorders* (New York: Free Press, 1988).

7. D. M. Clark et al., "Respiratory Control as a Treatment for Panic Attack," *Journal of Behavioral Therapy and Experimental Psychiatry* 16 (1985): 23–30.

8. Oliver G. Cameron et al., "Menstrual Fluctuation in the Symptoms of Anxiety," *Journal of Affective Disorders* 15 (1988): 169–74.

9. D. F. Swaab and M. A. Horman, "Sexual Differentiation of the Human Brain: A Historical Perspective," *Progressive Brain Research* 61 (1984): 361–74.

10. Cameron and Hill, "Women and Anxiety," pp. 175–86.

11. A. B. Raj and D. V. Sheehan, "Medical Evaluation of the Anxious Patient," *Psychiatric Annals* 18 no. 3 (March 1988): 176–81.

12. Jean Baker Miller, "Connections, Disconnections, and Violations," Work in Progress (Wellesley, Mass.: Wellesley College, 1988).

13. Norman Sussman and James Chou, "Current Issues in Benzodiazepine Use for Anxiety Disorder," *Psychiatric Annals* 18 no. 3 (March 1988): 139–45.

14. R. O. Pasnau, "Consequences of Anxiety," in *Consequences of Anxiety: Question and Answer Booklet* (Chicago: Pragmaton, 1988).

15. D. C. G. Skegg, S. M. Richards, and R. Doll, "Minor Tranquilizers and Road Accidents," *British Medical Journal* 1 (1979): 917–19.

16. For further information on the particular medications, see chapter 7, "Depression."

17. R. J. Baldessarini, *Chemotherapy in Psychiatry: Principles and Practice* (Cambridge, Mass.: Harvard University Press, 1985).

18. M. A. Jenike and L. Baer, "Behavior Therapy Techniques Effective in Treating OCD," *The Psychiatric Times*, August 1988, p. 15.

19. Robert Seidenberg and Karen DeCrow, *Women Who Marry Houses: Panic and Protest in Agoraphobia* (New York: McGraw-Hill, 1983).

20. Isaac Marks, "Self-exposure Treatment Effective in Helping Patients with Anxiety Disorders," *The Psychiatric Times*, September 1988, p. 32.

21. Taylor and Arnow, *The Nature and Treatment of Anxiety Disorders*, p. 345.

22. Miller, "The Development of Women's Sense of Self," p. 10.

23. Harriet Goldhor Lerner, *The Dance of Intimacy: A Woman's Guide to Courageous Acts of Change in Key Relationships* (New York: Harper & Row, 1989).

24. Harriet Goldhor Lerner, *The Dance of Anger: A Woman's Guide to Changing Patterns of Intimate Relationships* (New York: Harper & Row, 1985).

25. Christine A. Courtois, *Healing the Incest Wound: Adult Survivors in Therapy* (New York: W. W. Norton, 1988), p. 5.

26. Simone de Beauvoir, *The Second Sex* (New York: Alfred A. Knopf, 1952).

27. Adapted from Herbert Benson, *The Relaxation Response* (New York: Avon, 1976).

28. Adapted from Aaron T. Beck and Gary Emery, *Anxiety Disorders and Phobias: A Cognitive Perspective* (New York: Basic, 1985), pp. 190–209.

29. Adapted from Taylor, *The Nature and Treatment of Anxiety Disorders*, p. 346.

30. Robert Eliot and Dennis Breo, *Is It Worth Dying For?: Self-Assessment Program to Make Stress Work for You, Not Against You* (New York: Bantam, 1984).

9 | **S**exuality

A woman's sexuality develops within the context of specific cultural, familial, and personal realities. Great variations exist within economic, religious, and ethnic groups and between women of different generations. Even geography seems to make a difference.[1]

Her capacity to feel comfortable with her own sexuality depends on a woman's past and current sexual experiences. This includes how a woman is introduced to sexuality as well as the messages she receives throughout her life.

For the most part, sex is defined in terms of the male experience and is usually thought of as intercourse. However, when sex is viewed from a woman's perspective, the emphasis is more likely to be on the emotional and physical closeness that can come with being sexual.

Historical Overview

Sex may be grounded in biology, but its expression is very much mediated by culture.[2] Most of us focus on fairly recent history when we think about sexual values and practices. Our own knowledge encompasses a generation or two, but even ancient values and beliefs can have a powerful influence on a woman's sexuality.[3]

Although some historians disagree, folklore has it that the early Christians taught that there were two types of women: mothers and prostitutes. Mothers had no sexual desires of their own; they only had sex to bear children. Prostitutes were debased individuals driven by lust to ravage men's bodies and souls. They were viewed as unpleasant necessities who served to uphold the morality of the family.

The story of Eve is a graphic portrayal of the way women are held responsible for men's sexual activity. Adam is pure. It is only Eve's temptation that leads him out of grace. This double standard for sexuality has persisted throughout history. It was certainly a basic tenet in the 1800s and played a significant role in psychoanalytic assumptions about female sexuality.

Freud's work allowed sexuality to be discussed more openly, but his theories about female sexuality were greatly biased by Victorian values. Female sexual development was defined as a reaction to the absence of a penis. Without this particular piece of sexual equipment, a woman was considered biologically inferior to a man and, as a rule, never quite recovered from her sense of deficiency. This early trauma caused her to become narcissistic. To compensate, she gave excessive attention to her appearance. She was also likely to be perceived as masochistic, perpetually reenacting the symbolic loss of her penis. To resolve her penis envy, she had a baby as a substitute. If her strategy was unsuccessful, she became neurotic or developed a masculinity complex, attempting to deny that she lacked anything.

Healthy adult women were presumed to have no spontaneous sexual feelings and to require introduction to sex by their husbands. Any substantial knowledge about sex or sexual experience outside of marriage tainted a woman's reputation. If an unmarried woman became pregnant, she had either tempted the man or failed to resist his advances. Either signified some moral weakness on her part. She, not the father, was responsible for her fall from grace.

After the slaughter of over ten million men in Europe during World War I, there was a radical change in the expression of female sexuality. Many women regularly practiced masturbation, participated in transitory and serial relationships, and turned to other women for sex.[4] In America, the flapper of the 1920s wanted more autonomy and sexual openness.

However, being sexually active still carried a higher risk for women than for men. In 1916, Margaret Sanger was thrown in jail for attempting to provide birth-control information to women. Since many men were reluctant to use condoms, withdrawal and dangerous illegal abortions were often the only alternatives to unwanted pregnancies. It was not until 1923 that Sanger and her staff were able to legally establish a birth-control clinic for women.

Better control over their fertility allowed women to be sexual with much more safety. Indeed, Kinsey's 1953 report on female sexuality verified that many women had become very sexually active.[5] He also documented enormous variations in sexual behavior. Masturbation, oral sex, and lesbian sex were much more common than was previously considered normal. However, it was the availability of birth-control pills and IUDs in the 1960s that marked the beginning of the greatest public sexual revolution. Now women, like men, could genuinely separate sex from reproduction.

Ideally, this would have been an opportunity for women to learn more about their own sexuality without fear of an unwanted pregnancy. Certainly, new information about the female sexual response did make it possible for more women to enjoy sex. Researchers verified that the basic theories of sexual arousal and orgasm were the same for women and men. They also determined that the clitoris, not the vagina, was the source and transmitter of genital arousal for women.[6] With adequate clitoral stimulation, women could stop faking orgasms and actually start having them.

However, while the sexual revolution implied the liberation of women as well as men, it was actually the projection of male-defined sexuality on women. Disentangling sexuality from reproductivity meant that women could no longer "legitimately" decline to be sexually active. Even among peace-loving flower children, expectations were based on gender stereotypes. Women were to do the grunt work—washing dishes, stuffing envelopes, cooking meals, and being sexually available. What a woman was not supposed to do was say no.[7]

As usual, it was heterosexual women, rather than their male partners, who carried the burden of reproductive protection. The pill and the IUD were hardly risk free. Beyond the minor annoyances of nausea, weight gain, and breakthrough bleeding, they were associated with infection, infertility, and cancer. Some women paid a very high price for their so-called sexual freedom.[8]

The 1970s was the decade of the most blatant sexual experimentation. There was strong social belief that people did not grow unless they were sexually active. The implication was that this growth was unlikely to occur within the context of a monogamous relationship.[9] Some women felt that they benefited from this loosening of sexual mores, but others felt coerced into having casual sex when they would have preferred a more committed relationship.

Redefining Female Sexuality

Nevertheless, some of the greatest obstacles to the development of a female-defined sexuality did begin to erode during this period. Women in consciousness-raising groups made sexuality just one of the many topics to be discussed. They shared with each other how they *really* felt about sex rather than how they were supposed to feel. Some said they felt rejected by their partners; others complained that their husbands never left them alone sexually. Some said they were afraid to tell their lovers what pleased them; others said their partners resented being told. Some spoke about passes they had to contend with at work and on the streets; others felt bereft because men ignored them. Some felt that men found them intimidating, but that it was taboo for them to make advances themselves. Some spoke about the reprisals they feared or suffered as lesbians; others spoke of their fear of lesbians. Some shamefacedly confessed to having masturbated all their lives; others declared, in anguish, that they could not masturbate. Many complained bitterly that men rarely took responsibility for birth control, for children, or for the progress of their relationships.

We do not know how women might express their sexuality if they did not live in a male-dominated environment. For some women at least, the focus seems to be on the tactile and psychological rewards of intimacy more than the actual act of intercourse. However, since none of us exists in a cultural vacuum, it is difficult to know what might be uniquely female instead of a reaction to a predominantly male-defined sexuality.

Lynda Barry's irreverent *Naked Ladies Coloring Book*[10] suggests that adolescent girls may be sneaking more than a casual peek at their fathers' girlie magazines. Except for this pornographic and erotic material designed by and for men, most women have turned to romantic novels for their vicarious sexual pleasure. While pornography packages sex with violence, possession, and promiscuity, romance packages sex with love, fidelity, and marriage—and often a healthy dose of victimization. Girls and boys come away from their readings with very different ideas of what being sexual means.

Few men view sex in the same way as their female partners. Certainly, women's tendency to define sex as tenderness as well as, or instead of, erotic pleasure has been undervalued. Women have been made to feel that their reticence to engage in lustful genital contact in the absence of emotional closeness is somehow a deficiency. Cuddling is for kids. Adults have *sex*—meaning intercourse.

In many circumstances, sexuality is determined more by the exercise of power than by mutual pleasure and respect.[11] A good deal of what passes for sexuality is actually an expression of male dominance. Prostitution remains a lucrative, albeit dangerous, profession for women because men can and do exchange sex for money. Far too many people confuse pornography with erotica and healthy sexuality. Sexualized violence in the form of incest and rape has the potential to contaminate even the most benevolent heterosexual relationships. This abuse of power plus the risk of an unwanted pregnancy with no assurance of a safe abortion entwine with a woman's sexual development in such an intricate and complex pattern that identifying sexuality independent of these harsh realities is extraordinarily difficult.

The Development of Healthy Sexuality

There has been only a limited amount of research on human sexuality from a woman's point of view. Consequently, it is wisest to assume that our current understanding of female sexuality is incomplete. Nevertheless, research suggests that in the absence of personal trauma, most women's sexual development follows certain predictable patterns.

Most women appear to have the potential to feel sexually attracted toward both women and men. This capacity for bisexuality suggests that the line between heterosexuality and homosexuality is more fluid than we might previously have believed.[12] Eventually most women seem to develop a preference for partners of one gender. Whether this preference is determined by biology or culture remains a matter of considerable debate.

Loving and erotic feelings toward other females are part of many women's early life experience. Women who later come to identify themselves as heterosexuals often minimize, ignore, or forgot these feelings or think of them as preparation for an adult sexual relationship with a man. Women who come to identify themselves as lesbians often interpret remarkably similar histories in a very different way. They see their childhood and adolescent feelings as preludes to their adult preference for women as sexual partners. There is a continuity in their attraction for women that contains little or no room for men. Some women come to identify themselves as bisexuals. In describing their sexual interests, they say things like "It's the person, not their gender, that matters to me," "I might fall in love with a man or I might fall in love with a woman." These women are able to enjoy sex with someone they are attracted to regardless of that person's gender.

However, acknowledging the presence of a sexual attraction does not require that a woman actually have a sexual relationship. A woman does not have to act upon a feeling simply because she experiences it. Sexual feelings and sexual attractions do not mandate sexual behavior. Celibacy is a perfectly viable option.

Choosing Celibacy

We live in a very sex-oriented society. Women in particular have often been defined by others through their sexuality. Theoretically at least, a woman could obtain economic support, a home, children, and security by offering herself to a man. Indeed, until recently society allowed women few viable alternatives to this life-style. Consequently, many women have been preoccupied with their physical appearance, especially the shape of their bodies. For these women, self-worth comes from being considered attractive to men. Their sexual appeal is tied to their very survival. And, while being sexually active might not always be personally satisfying, it does provide an indirect source of security and power. This is not healthy sexuality, but it is the sexual life that many women feel is inevitable.

This has made it difficult for women to feel good about choosing not to be sexually active. For many men, and for some women, it is difficult to fathom that some women do not need or want sex. Historically, the only identities for such a woman were spinsterhood or a religious calling. It is, however, perfectly possible for a woman to live a whole, satisfying, and creative life with love but without sex. Sex is not obligatory.

Celibacy may be a way for a woman to create and manage her own life. The confidence that comes with knowing that she can stand on her own two feet and does not have to be one-half of a partnership can lead to a surprising sense of personal freedom and power. There are many advantages to choosing to be celibate: freedom from the risk of sexually transmitted diseases, freedom from the hassles and health risks of using contraceptives, freedom from unwanted pregnancies, and, perhaps most importantly, freedom to pursue other interests. Celibacy also reduces a woman's risk of experiencing sexual violence.

Choosing Sex

Although celibacy is a perfectly legitimate alternative to sexual activity, the majority of women will engage in sexual activity at some time in their life with either male or female partners.

Sexual relationships between women—As one lesbian wrote, "Lesbianism is not about sex, not about having orgasms. It's about how you want to live your life, and I want to live my life surrounded by women and knowing women closely, and getting all my sexual and emotional pleasure and comfort from women. I think probably the core of lesbianism is a strong *emotional* attachment to women."[13]

Some people believe that lesbians are significantly different from heterosexual women. Except for feeling sexually attracted to women instead of men, they are not. Lesbians do not have different family backgrounds, upbringings, relationships with parents, childhood experiences, or psychological makeups than heterosexual women. They are not biologically different from heterosexual women in terms of genes, chromosomes, hormones, genitals, or general body shape. In fact, there is no ready explanation why some women are lesbians and others are not. Unfortunately, for women who feel sexually attracted to other women, their sexual feelings cannot be acted on with impunity.

Each of us experiences our sexuality in the context of societal norms. Our cultural norm for sexual expression is heterosexuality.[14] Our lives and the media are full of practicing heterosexuals. As small girls, we learn that we are expected to grow up and fall in love with a man. This massive social conditioning means that most heterosexual women experience their preference as "natural." If we step outside this norm, we face the possibility of societal retaliation. Thus, a woman living a lesbian life-style risks profound punishment.

At one point in American history, so-called Boston marriages, romantic friendships between women, were considered quite acceptable,[15] perhaps because many people denied the sexual component of these relationships. We now live in a society that discriminates against people with same-sex partners. Our culture's homophobic response to lesbians overemphasizes the sexual component of these relationships and minimizes the broader issues of friendship, companionship, intimacy, support, and concern that we all strive for in our loving relationships.

Given the risk of discrimination and the reality of social conditioning, some lesbians live a heterosexual life-style but maintain important and loving relationships with women friends. Some, in spite of the relative absence of visible role models, amazingly and courageously identify themselves as lesbians. However, they often remain highly selective about who they share this information with, because the negative consequences of coming out can be excruciatingly painful.

Given the prejudices against lesbianism, coming out can feel like an enormous risk. Parents may be profoundly rejecting, a current spouse may attempt to interfere with parental rights—even housing and employment may be threatened. But keeping secrets has its own risks. It can be exhausting and damaging to a woman's identity and self-esteem to pretend that she is something she is not. Because of the risks involved, each woman must decide for herself whether or not to tell others about her life-style until our society makes it safe to be honest about lesbianism.[16]

It is important to note that a relationship with another woman is no guarantee of a happy or healthy sex life. Sex between women can be intense, passionate, loving, warm, caring, and friendly. It can also be disappointing. Sexual inhibitions and desire discrepancies are no less common in lesbian relationships than in heterosexual partnerships.[17] It is not unusual to find low levels of genital contact among lesbian couples and even to find relationships in which sexual contact has ceased completely despite an otherwise healthy and harmonious attachment.

Just as in heterosexual relationships, some lesbian relationships can be destructive, particularly if there is inequality and misuse of power. Healthy sex always requires a mutually respectful and supportive relationship—whatever the partners' genders.

Sexual relationships between women and men—In our culture, it is assumed that most women will fall in love with a man or a series of men, that they prefer a monogamous life-style, and that they eventually hope to marry. But given today's economic and political realities, just being a heterosexual adult and wishing to be sexually active is no reason to commit to one man or to choose marriage. If a woman is to take these steps, she needs to have very good reasons for doing so. Just being in love is not good enough.

In traditional relationships, women are expected to adapt to their partner's world. With marriage, women often lose many of their individual rights. In many marriages, the woman is treated as if she has no separate identity, as if she is her husband's property. As a result, she is denied economic equity and physical safety. In addition, there is a covert agreement that the woman will accept primary responsibility for household management and childcare, that she will circulate among her husband's associates, and that she will engage in or support his interests without expecting reciprocation.

In contemporary relationships, women are not expected to be so self-sacrificing, and this change is reflected in many couples' sexual lives. Research suggests that women and men view sex differently. Women see intimacy as the pathway to sex, while men see sex as the pathway to intimacy.[18] Feminism has helped women feel more comfortable insisting that emotional intimacy proceed genital activity, and many women now report that their sexual lives are quite gratifying.[19]

Female Sexual Development

Although every embryo is either genetically male with XY sex chromosomes or female with XX sex chromosomes, in the absence of a burst of male hormones at the appropriate time during fetal development, the infant will be born anatomically female. After birth, the child's parents begin the gender training that also molds her sexual development. Whether a child is socialized into passivity or activity, subordination or domination decides the way she experiences sexuality. By the end of the first year of life, a child already seems to have a sense of her identity as female. By the age of three, this self-concept is essentially unchangeable.[20]

A young girl usually learns the name for her clitoris much later than a boy learns the name of his penis. In addition, she is often taught to misname her vulva as her vagina.[21] The clitoris is such a tiny organ that a child may have a difficult time actually seeing it. When a young girl wants to talk about what it feels like to touch her clitoris, she finds few words to describe the sensations. Enlightened parents may turn to drawings or picture books to help the little girl better understand and visualize her genitals only to discover that many drawings do not include the clitoris or identify the vulva. Instead, there are pictures of the uterus, ovaries, and fallopian tubes, all organs of reproduction rather than sexuality. Thus females are characteristically presented a reproductive rather than sexual view of themselves.

By adolescence, hormones are operating as powerful factors in female sexual development. The hormonal shifts of puberty cause bodily changes that draw attention to the teenager's developing sexuality. In contrast to males, sexual expression does not seem to be critical to a woman's personality development. Masturbation is erratic. Only 20 percent of girls have masturbated to orgasm by age fifteen.[22] By age twenty, only about 65 percent of perfectly healthy women have ever masturbated to orgasm, and half of these women discovered masturbation within the context of a sexual relationship. A woman's sense of being female seems to evolve in nonsexual ways. It certainly does not depend on experiencing orgasms. Indeed, many women have the capacity to abstain from sex altogether without negative consequences. For those women who do incorporate sexuality as a significant component of their identity, it is not usually limited to genital expression.

Nevertheless, the way a young woman experiences her emerging adolescent sexuality depends very much on cultural standards and expectations. In the not-too-distant past, girls were taught to control themselves and not let the boys go too far. With the sexual revolution, some young girls are having sex much earlier,[23] but most are still expected to exercise more self-control than boys in their sexual behavior.

Limited knowledge and lack of attention to her pleasure is one of the major reasons that a woman reaches her sexual prime later than a man. In addition to adequate information and experience, good sex requires time, energy, and privacy. If a woman is drained by financial worries or serving the needs of others, she is unlikely to have much interest in sex. Furthermore, while the romantic version of sexuality is not as harmful to a couple's sex life as violence masquerading as sex, it is not a realistic reflection of most couples' ongoing sex lives. Few relationships can sustain the erotic charge of earlier sexual encounters.

In the passion of courtship, time is set aside to prepare for being sexual. While there is no reason that this cannot be integrated into long-term relationships, it is more challenging when a couple is balancing other responsibilities. If a couple wants an enduring, high-quality sex life, each will have to make a conscious effort. Good sex requires creativity and commitment. It does not just happen spontaneously.

Love, romance, intimacy, and sexuality are not really very different at age eighty than they are at eighteen.[24] Given the availability of an acceptable partner, many elderly women enjoy remaining sexually active. They may have sex less often, but the quality of that sex may actually be enhanced.[25] Many midlife women have more time now that child rearing is behind them. Others are delighted to be free of worries about pregnancy.

Some women prefer not to be sexually active in their later years, and that is a perfectly legitimate option. However, while voluntary celibacy may reflect the choice to use one's limited energy and time in other arenas, forced celibacy is another matter.[26] Finding alternatives such as male escorts or eligible men of the same or different generation undesirable, distasteful, or unavailable can leave an older woman who wishes to be sexually active despondent. If no appropriate partners can be found, older women might consider other forms of sensuous pleasure including masturbation, massage, personal adornment, dancing, and exercise. Greater socialization with an open and active search for a suitable companion are also recommended.[27]

Getting to Know Your Own Body

Ironically, many women know more about male genital anatomy than they do about their own. A great deal of a woman's ability to enjoy her own sexuality depends on how she feels about her body and how much she knows about her sexual organs. Unfortunately, few women feel completely satisfied with the appearance of their bodies. This lack of self-acceptance certainly has negative effects on their sexual pleasure.

To make matters worse, women rarely know much about their own genitals, partly because much of the female sexual anatomy is hidden from view, but mostly because of inadequate information and discouragements to learning. The way a woman feels about her vulva—the appearance of her inner and outer labia and the natural scent of her vaginal fluids—is especially important to her sexual comfort. Lack of information greatly contributes to a woman's sexual inhibitions.[28]

Anatomy and Physiology[29]

There are enormous variations in the size, shape, and color of women's vulvas. If you have not already seen yours, you can examine it using a small flashlight and a mirror. At the opening to the vagina, you will see the labia. The labia consists of outer and inner lips. The outer lips are not neat and tidy as they often appear in drawings. Instead, they are irregular—like the thick, fleshy petals of tropical flowers. The colors of the outer lips range from shades of blue, violet, pink, crimson, gold, tawny or deep brown to black. The inner lips are thinner, smoother and more silky. Sometimes they curve out and over the outer lips. These inner lips are usually pink to deep red, their color becoming more dramatic during pregnancy. During menopause, their color usually mutes to a soft rosy gray.

The glans of the clitoris, the part you can see outside the body, is about the size of a pea. It is often hidden by a hood. By pulling your lips aside, you pull back the hood and can see the clitoris more easily. From an embryological and anatomical point of view, the clitoris is the equivalent of the male penis. Like the penis, it is highly sensitive to touch.

Reach inside your vagina and feel the front and back surfaces. You will be able to locate the urethral and perineal sponges. These become engorged when you are sexually excited. You will know that you have touched the root of the clitoris when you see the glans plump up in response. The clitoris stretches out during sexual excitement. At its full length, it becomes very similar in shape and size to a small erect penis.[30] However, only the tip of the clitoris is visible on the exterior of the body. The remainder is in the interior of the body and not available for visual inspection.

The vagina undergoes dramatic changes during sexual arousal. It is supplied with an extensive network of blood vessels, which causes the shape and length to change as a woman becomes aroused. While you have your fingers inside your vagina, squeeze the muscles surrounding the vaginal walls. These are some of the muscles you feel contracting during orgasm.

Strengthening these muscles through regular exercises will improve their ability to support the organs of the lower pelvis. It will also increase your muscle tone, permitting more intense orgasms. The easiest exercises are called Kegel's exercises. You can learn how to do these by stopping and starting your stream of urine during urination. Once you get the hang of it, you can replicate this exercise anyplace. It becomes an easy way to pass the time standing in line at the grocery store, waiting for a red light to change, or watching a boring TV show.

If you reach far back into your vagina, you will feel your cervix. This is the lower end of the uterus. Its texture feels a bit like the tip of your nose. If you insert a plastic speculum into your vagina, you can easily examine your own cervix with the aid of a mirror.

You cannot actually feel the main part of the uterus above the cervix. Its small pear shape is determined by a set of overlapping muscle fibers. These muscles are richly supplied with nerves and blood vessels and are very responsive to hormonal changes. They tighten during menstruation, often causing painful cramps.[31] Milder, and usually more pleasurable, contractions can occur with stimulation of the nipples and breasts and during orgasm.

Masturbation or Self-pleasuring

Masturbation, erotic self-stimulation, usually begins at a very young age. In the process of urinating, a boy handles his penis on a frequent and regular basis. A little girl has less reason to handle her clitoris, but children of both genders find it pleasurable to touch their sensitive genitals.

Children do not necessarily associate these pleasurable feelings with sex. Sexuality is an adult concept projected onto children. A little girl knows only that it feels good to touch her vulva and clitoris, to squeeze her pillow between her legs, to ride a rocking horse, to shinny down a pole or slide down a banister. Depending on parental response to these pleasures, children learn when and where these activities are acceptable—if they are acceptable at all.

By adolescence, most of a young woman's information about sex is coming from her peers, which can lead to some remarkable misunderstandings. My friend Annie talks about studying one of her parents' sex books when she was twelve years old. She read the section on the penis and how its size increased during sex. She misread the sentence that said the penis became twice its flaccid size when erect. Instead, she shocked the neighborhood children when she informed them that an erect penis became twice the size of the human body.

Given that most literature describes the arousal of men much more clearly than that of women, it should come as no surprise that men's perspective on female sexuality is more widely known than women's. Many young girls read and reread the sexy parts of novels, which only serves to reinforce the male point of view. Literature targeted directly to a female audience usually provides an excessively romanticized version of female sexuality, which is not much of an improvement.

Where are girls to find clear and accurate descriptions of their own genitals and how they and their partners might stimulate them? Young boys may have plenty of opportunity to practice ejaculating with their buddies, but I wonder how many girls show each other how to masturbate. Can you imagine eight little girls in flannel nightgowns hiked up around their waists giggling "Let's see who can come first!" "How does this feel?" "What do I look like?" "Let's see what you look like!"

Orgasm

Women's inexperience with their genitals and masturbation is unfortunate, because most women who learn to masturbate do experience orgasms. If sufficiently stimulated, some women can experience multiple orgasms.[32] Female orgasms have four stages:[33]

1. The *excitement stage* lasts from several minutes to several hours. A woman's heart and breathing rates increase, her nipples harden and become erect, and a natural lubrication is produced by the blood vessels in her vagina as extra blood is shunted to the muscles of the pelvic floor.
2. The *plateau phase* comes just before an orgasm. A woman's body becomes hot and flushed, her muscle tone increases, and there may be involuntary shuddering. Her heart and breathing rates increase even more, her uterus lifts off the pelvic floor, and the hood of the clitoris swells, as do the lips surrounding it. The clitoris usually disappears from view, and the woman usually feels a sense of tension in her pelvic muscles.
3. *Climax* is a series of involuntary muscle contractions that are rhythmic and very fast. Her blood pressure, heart and breathing rates are at their highest. The uterus contracts in a squeezing motion starting at the top and moving down into the vagina. If stimulation continues, some women can often have additional orgasms of greater or lesser intensity.
4. During *resolution,* the clitoris goes back to its usual position, and breathing and heart rate slow down.

Some women can have orgasms through vaginal penetration alone, but most require direct stimulation of the clitoris or vulva. If you are not sure whether or not you have had an orgasm, you probably have not. Fortunately, there are a number of good resources for learning how to have an orgasm if you wish to educate yourself. *For Yourself* by Lonnie Barbach, which is listed in the readings section at the end of this chapter, is especially recommended.

Self-pleasuring or masturbation need not be limited to genital stimulation. It can be a whole series of sensual and erotic self-pleasures simply for pure enjoyment.

Sex with a Partner

Good sex with a partner requires trust, touch, time, and talk. The attitude that "boys lie about love to get sex and girls lie about sex to get love"[34] is the beginning of what is sometimes a set of lifelong sex and intimacy problems for women and men. Lesbians may actually be able to provide each other with more consistently satisfying sexual experiences. As women, both partners more easily understand a woman's sexual responses. They are much more likely to include verbal and nongenital intimacy as a regular component of their sexual expression.

In heterosexual relationships, if a male partner has not learned how to stimulate his female companion properly, she can teach him. While the "standard" missionary position may easily lead to orgasms for men, it is not very conducive to orgasms for women. Training an uninformed partner may not be part of the early stages of a sexual relationship when the couple is charged by the passion of a new encounter. However, as they settle down, they can begin to learn more about each other's bodies and to incorporate these discoveries into their lovemaking.

The female orgasm always starts in the clitoris. With sufficient indirect stimulation by the thrusting penis or direct stimulation from a hand or tongue on the clitoris or surrounding vulva, most women will experience orgasm. This stimulation can occur before, after, or in place of her partner's orgasm. Even women who have orgasms only with manual or oral stimulation may still like vaginal penetration. Some of this desire is related to the arousal of the anatomical structures at the entrance of the vagina; some is purely psychological. A heterosexual woman may like the notion or feeling of her lover's penis inside her. She may enjoy participating vicariously in his pleasure.

Sexual pleasuring with a partner need not be limited to genital stimulation. Women often like many other areas of their bodies to be touched and stroked as a part of sexual stimulation. In addition, the brain is the most active sexual organ. Our thinking determines how we feel about sex and our bodies. Within loving relationships, these beliefs are the most powerful determinants of our sexuality.

Sexual Interest

The initial stage of any sexual encounter is willingness.[35] Pleasure is the goal. Willingness is not something passive. It is the active position of wanting to be sexual. You may be willing because you want to have a fuller sex life, because you know that once you start sex, you enjoy it, or because you simply want the pleasure sex may bring.

Once a woman is more familiar with her own sexuality, she begins to identify variations in her sexual drive or libido. For many women, sexual interest peaks immediately before and during menstruation with a second, less pronounced, peak at ovulation. If a woman experiences severe premenstrual tension (PMT), her libido may be lower during this phase of her cycle. However, mild PMT may have just the opposite effect. Some women have pain during ovulation and are too tender for sexual activity. If a woman is using certain brands of birth-control pills, she may not notice variations in her libido at all. The important thing to remember is that there is no standard. Each woman has her own sexual rhythm. As she becomes aware of these variations, she can communicate this information to her partner.

Common Sexual Problems

Until we provide better sexual education for both women and men, they will learn about sex by trial and error. Until all women feel protected against sexualized violence, it will take a long time for many women to overcome their sexual inhibitions. In the meantime, is it any wonder that many women find it difficult to feel valued as sexual persons and that inhibition of sexual desire may be the norm rather than the exception for many women?[36]

How can women focus on having fun in heterosexual sexual relationships when their very safety may be in question or if they are overburdened with rearing children, tending the sick, caring for the elderly, and sustaining men? Healthy sex with a partner can only occur in the context of a relationship built upon trust and mutual respect where there is some time, energy, and space for the expression of genuine care and reciprocal pleasure.

Many of women's sexual problems are a result of our cultural acceptance of uninvited sexual attention and sexualized violence against women. Because of this, women need to be exceedingly careful about who defines what is a sexual problem or dysfunction, for what reasons, and by what criterion.[37] Pornography, sexual harassment, exploitation, coercion, incest, rape, and other abuses of power are the source of many of women's sexual difficulties.[38] Unfortunately, turning to a professional for treatment of these problems is no guarantee of help, since some providers ignore ethical codes forbidding sexual relations with patients. This kind of exploitation is rarely helpful in correcting a woman's sexual problems and often contributes to further difficulties.[39]

It is no surprise that many of the victims and survivors of abusive treatment report inhibited sexual desire. For many heterosexual women, sexual activity is actually deference to a male partner. What looks like masochism is actually a fear of displeasing. Masochism is not intrinsic to female sexual development; it exists because there is often a profound power differential in a heterosexual relationship. This results in women faking orgasms, not insisting on or expecting adequate stimulation for herself, assuming that the male orgasm terminates a sexual encounter, and paying excessive attention to pleasing rather than to being pleasured. At the extreme, men are able to treat women in abusive ways and misname this sex rather than violence.

Even in the absence of these traumatic events, many women still report sexual problems. The most common are listed below.[40]

1. *Lack of interest* may be caused by the absence of an acceptable partner, no longer being attracted to your present partner, boredom, a recent pregnancy, normal monthly variation, depression, anxiety, side effects of

some medications, heavy drinking, endocrine problems, or a desire to be celibate.

2. *Negative feelings about sex* may be caused by feeling that sex is inappropriate or that it might be painful, worries that you might not be a good lover, concerns about the messiness of sex with its secretions and odors, anxiety about becoming pregnant, or fears that you might appear undignified or ugly during sex.

3. Many women report that their first sexual experience does not fulfill their expectations, but even women who have been sexually active for years may still report *unfulfilled expectations.* Their sex life may have become tedious or dull, they may not be orgasmic, their partner may suffer with a sexual dysfunction, sex may be too genitally focused, they may imagine that their partner should know how to please them without their telling him how, or they find that their partner is not as caring, loving, or responsive as they would like.

4. *Lack of arousal* may occur because of an inexperienced partner, the stress associated with trying to live the life of a superwoman, failure to create the right mood, focusing only on a partner's pleasure, feeling guilty or ashamed about sex, or a complete lack of interest in being sexual.

5. High, medium, and low sex drives are all within the range of normal. Sexual relationships work most easily when a couple has compatible sex drives, but even those with *incompatible sex drives* can have a perfectly satisfactory relationship if they can communicate effectively and negotiate a solution that allows them to bridge the gap.

6. *Penetration problems* are often caused by fear, but they may have a medical cause. Intercourse may be painful because a woman is unaccustomed to sexual activity, recovering from a pregnancy, suffering from some medical problem, or is inadequately aroused.

7. *Failure to reach orgasm* is usually caused by anxiety, inexperience, or inadequate stimulation.

8. *Vaginal irritation* and *vaginal discharge* are medical problems that almost always respond to the appropriate medical treatment.

All of these symptoms are responsive to the proper physical or psychological care.

Developing a New Model for Heterosexual Sex

Are the differences between the female and male versions of sexuality determined by biology or culture? The answer is unknown. People do not live in cultural vacuums, so we are never able to see how a person might be if they were not influenced by the society in which they live. However, we do know that sexual development is not uniform in all cultures. Some cultures foster openness in both genders, while others are more repressive. This suggests that within the constraints of biological limits, much sexual behavior is influenced by social learning.

For an adolescent boy, frequent spontaneous ejaculations, his regular handling of his genitals, and his unambiguous experiences with masturbation virtually guarantee the integration of genital sexuality into his sense of himself. The failure to define a girl's spontaneous vaginal sensations in the same way, the less reason she has to handle her genitals regularly, and a delayed or ambiguous experience with masturbation may contribute to less emphasis on genital sexuality as a prominent aspect of a young woman's sense of herself.

Researchers studying sexuality from a woman's perspective are questioning the central role of orgasm in sexual experience.[41] Without denying the pleasure a woman can feel when she does experience orgasm, many women find that other forms of sensual and erotic pleasure are of equal importance. Women can have orgasms without feeling fully satisfied if they are not also emotionally satisfied. For women, sex seems to be about relationships—not just intercourse.

For a woman, sex is more than having orgasms. It is how she feels about herself and how her lover feels about her. It is certainly more than something that just happens to her genitals. It is something that happens with her mind, her body, and her heart. For many women, sex is inextricably linked with the way she gives and receives love. At its best, female sexuality can be "exciting and alive with longing, tenderness, passion, and strength."[42] In fact, from a female perspective, what is considered normal male sexuality might easily be viewed as hypersexuality or some other form of sexual dysfunction. It is time to reassess the assumption that genital sex is of overriding importance in everyone's sexual life.

An overemphasis on genital sex has only occurred because men are the ones who have been able to define what is "normal" sexual behavior. Books on sexuality too often focus on technique and ignore the power imbalance in relationships. Sexual liberation must include the freedom to reject or enter into sexual relationships fearing neither exploitation nor punishment. But sexual exploitation and punishment still threaten every woman. The denial of complete reproductive freedom and the often total economic and emotional responsibility for child rearing are punishments for being a sexually active woman. The threat of job loss, ridicule, rejection, isolation, and even the psychological intimidation of rape are punishments used to threaten women who refuse sex.

Improving a Woman's Sex Life

Until recently, we have too readily assumed that the male model of sexuality is freer, more beneficial, and more desirable. By now, it should be obvious that we need a model of sexuality that includes a female perspective. Fortunately, some women have been attempting to determine what female sexuality might look like if it were independent of male-influenced values.

As women have gained more control over their bodies and their economic lives, they have had a chance to define sexuality through their own minds and own experiences.[43,44] While our understanding of a female-influenced model of sexuality is far from complete, it seems to embrace at least some of the following characteristics:

- Voluntary, nonexploitive, and violence-free activity.
- Emotional pleasuring and caretaking integrated with, or instead of, genital expression.
- An emphasis on process versus performance.
- Feelings of mutual respect, fun, and romance.
- Shared contraceptive and health protection.
- Erotica versus pornography. Erotica is sensual and nonexploitive material that is titillating and arousing. Pornography is any sexualized material that treats people in a dehumanizing fashion, is abusive or degrading in any way, and/or results in the victimization of any individual.

Efforts to improve women's sexual experiences must be both personal and public. At a personal level, each and every female child deserves an accurate and comprehensive education about her own body, including her genitals. She needs to know what they look like and how they work. She needs information about how her sexuality changes throughout her life, including during such uniquely female events such as menstruation, pregnancy, and menopause. This very important knowledge, *which every human being acquires one way or another,* should not be left to chance. This education could occur in all the usual places of learning: schools, churches, through the media, and at home.

As adults, we can embrace and enjoy the use of erotica and humor and reject pornography.[45] We can enjoy our own bodies and focus on what pleases us. As we identify new areas of pleasure, we can share this new-found information with our partners. Our sexual development is an ongoing process. We are all learning together.

At a public level, as long as sexuality is entwined with violence, we will all be at risk of confusing "normal" sexuality with sexual abuse. We must be especially protective of those people who are at risk for or have been victims of childhood sexual violence.[46] We must also make every effort to stop rape. Until all forms of sexualized violence are aggressively challenged and discontinued, being sexual with even the gentlest of lovers can sometimes feel dangerous.

We must continue to question cultural beliefs that permit a double standard of sexual morality and then use that double standard to justify male mistreatment of women. The 1986 assault and murder of a young woman in a New York park vividly demonstrates that if a woman is sexual, she is responsible for a male's sexual and violent misconduct. Stories of this victim's sexual history were prominently displayed in the media as if by being sexually active, she relinquished all rights to equal and full protection under the law. The assailant's equally active sex life was not considered abnormal in any way or subject to as much public disclosure. This case vividly demonstrates the continuing and unacceptable belief that men have the right to dominate women and that women, not men, are responsible for the negative consequences of this domination.

This injustice can only be altered through corrective social and political action. To accomplish this:

1. The sexual abuse of all children and all adults—and this has been and continues to be primarily abuse by men against female children and female adults—must not be tolerated.[47] All people, even those who have not been victims or perpetrators themselves, must act to stop this abuse. A failure to act is colluding with those who actually commit these heinous crimes.

2. We need to continue to examine the ways in which we socialize the sexes from early childhood on to fit narrow and rigid sex-role stereotypes. We must then work toward changing attitudes and practices that contribute to inequality and discrimination.

3. Girls, boys, women, and men all need to be taught accurate information about their bodies and to be encouraged in the safe, respectful, and loving expression of their sexuality.

4. Women must exercise extreme caution about accepting current knowledge as accurately portraying female sexuality. There has never been a long-term prospective study of female sexuality that accurately determines how a woman's sexuality develops and changes over time. We need more research to continue the investigation of sexuality from a female perspective.

Safe Sex

In this day and age, it would be irresponsible to discuss sexuality without acknowledging the risk of sexually transmitted diseases, especially AIDS (acquired immune deficiency syndrome). There are many sexual activities a couple can enjoy that are not known to place them at risk, even if one or both partners tests positive for antibodies to HIV, the virus believed to cause AIDS. There is little or no known risk associated with sensuous bathing or feeding, erotic reading and viewing of movies and videos, sexual fantasies, flirting, hugging, kissing, phone sex, body massage, nongenital oral contact like licking and nibbling, smelling, consensual exhibitionism or voyeurism, caressing, using your own sex toys, body rubbing, masturbation, and viewing respectful live sexual entertainment.

The key in safe sex is to never exchange body fluids. This means semen, blood, vaginal secretions, urine, and fecal matter should not touch an open cut, the vaginal area, the tip of the penis, the mouth, or the rectum. Heterosexual women can lower their chances of acquiring AIDS by only having sex with men who use condoms and nonoxynol-9 spermicide. Both heterosexual and lesbian women should use a latex barrier or rubber dam for oral sex. The dam is placed over a woman's genitals to trap all secretions.

Conclusions

Remember, virtually everything there is to say about sex is subjective. The fact is that we know very little about what sex from a woman's perspective looks like. Even our language reflects this deficiency. A man with a healthy and vigorous sexual appetite is called virile. There is no word to describe a woman who functions in an analogous way. To correct this and other problems with our understanding of so-called human sexuality, we are trying to learn about the *real* experiences of women and how they feel about them—not men's descriptions and explanations of women's desires, behavior, and feelings.

A review of the history of sexual expression reveals that it is strongly determined by culture. There was a time when masturbation was thought to cause insanity. Now, anyone who does not masturbate or cannot masturbate to orgasm is considered to have a sexual dysfunction. In recent years, at least until the AIDS epidemic, sexual activity of virtually every conceivable type was being encouraged and acted on. Group sex, sadomasochism, various fetishes and obsessions were all considered within the range of normal adult sexuality. The line between acceptable and unacceptable was, and still is, difficult to determine. Yet the so-called sexual revolution was essentially a *male* revolution. It gave men more access to women's bodies, it legitimatized multiple partners, and it made the sexual norm a male-identified model that separated sex from caring and isolated body sensations from emotions.

There does appear to be a lag between women and men when it comes to learning about their respective genital responsiveness. Men report the greatest sexual prowess in their teens and twenties while women report enjoying sex more in their thirties and forties. It may be that women enjoy sex more in their later years because they have finally gained enough knowledge to obtain sexual satisfaction or because they have finally acquiesced to a male emphasis on genitals. We simply do not know.

The ideology of sex as romance that is fed to women hardly suffices if a woman feels as if she has given up her identity, personal power, and the freedom to control her own destiny. It also makes it difficult for a woman who does not wish to be monogamous to freely admit this preference. Instead, women tell themselves that they are looking for the right person or that they are in love when they actually are in lust. Both lesbians and heterosexual women sometimes have difficulty viewing sex as separate from love in a way that does not violate trust or, conversely, as an extension of a close friendship. Instead, they imagine that sex must be connected to a lifetime of undying devotion or that it will cause damage to a friendship.

As women, we need to look at ourselves and clarify who we really are and what we really want. It may well be that we have to break through our own inhibitions before we can clarify what sexuality means to us. What passes as sexuality in our culture is often the desire to dominate. Certainly, women need to feel powerful in respect to men. We cannot afford to feel dominated by men in our sexual lives or in any other arena. To do so prevents us from being truly free.

In relationships of equality, sexual expression becomes an extension of the care shown within the relationship.[48] Neither partner is dominant or subordinate. The emphasis is on the capacity to give and receive pleasure in the context of a mutually respectful attachment. In a solid love relationship of some duration, sex can be "a reliable glue . . . a powerful means of touching back to a depth of intimacy and pleasure in one another that is not always as easily accessible as some taking-for-grantedness becomes a part of the daily relationship."[49]

For each woman, being sexual must include the right to make her own decisions. It involves what she wants to give and receive, when and with whom. Every woman must have the right to define her own sexual life.

RESOURCES

Good Vibrations
3492 22nd Street, San Francisco, CA 94110.
A sensual toy and book service for women.

ADDITIONAL READING

Lonnie Barbach, *For Yourself: The Fulfillment of Female Sexuality* (New York: Doubleday, 1975).

Lonnie Barbach and Linda Levine, *Shared Intimacies: Women's Sexual Experiences* (New York: Doubleday, 1980).

Lonnie Barbach, *For Each Other: Sharing Sexual Intimacy* (New York: Doubleday, 1982).

Lonnie Barbach, *Pleasures: Women Write Erotica* (New York: Doubleday, 1984).

Lynda Barry, *Naked Ladies, Naked Ladies, Naked Ladies: A Coloring Book* (Seattle: The Real Comet Press, 1984).

Joani Blank and Marcia Quackenbush, *A Kid's First Book About Sex* (Burlingame, Calif.: Yes Press, 1983).

Edward M. Brecher, *Love, Sex and Aging* (Boston: Little, Brown, 1986).

Federation of Feminist Women's Health Collectives, *New View of A Woman's Body* (New York: Simon and Schuster, 1981).

Cynthia Heimel, *Sex Tips for Girls* (New York: Simon and Schuster, 1983).

Shere Hite, *The Hite Report: A Nationwide Study of Female Sexuality* (New York: Dell, 1976).

Carmen Kerr, *Sex for Women Who want to have fun and loving relationships with equals* (New York: Grove Press, 1977).

The Kensington Ladies' Erotica Society, *Ladies Home Erotica: Tales, Recipes, and Other Mischiefs by Older Women* (Berkeley, Calif.: Ten Speed Press, 1984).

Martha Kirkpatrick, *Women's Sexual Development: Explorations of Inner Space* (New York: Plenum, 1980).

Shelia Kitzinger, *Women's Experience of Sex* (New York: Putnam, 1983).

JoAnn Loulan, *Lesbian Sex* (San Francisco: Spinsters Ink, 1984).

Eleanor Morrison and Vera Borosage, *Human Sexuality: Contemporary Perspectives* (Mountain View, Calif.: Mayfield Publishing Co., 1977).

Judith Silverstein and Jim Jackson, *Sexual Enhancement for Women* (Cambridge, Mass.: Black and White Publishing, 1978).

Emily Sisley and Bertha Harris, *The Joy of Lesbian Sex* (New York: Fireside, 1978).

Ann Snitow, Christine Stansell, and Sharon Thompson, eds., *Powers of Desire: The Politics of Sexuality* (New York: Monthly Review Press, 1983).

Bernard D. Starr and Marcella Bakur Weiner, *The Starr-Weiner Report on Sex and Sexuality in the Mature Years* (New York: McGraw-Hill).

Catharine Stimpson and Ethel Person, eds, *Women: Sex and Sexuality* (Chicago: University of Chicago Press, 1980).

Maurice Yaffe, Elizabeth Fenwick, and Raymond Rosen, *Sexual Happiness: A Practical Approach* (New York: Henry Holt and Co., 1988).

Yellow Silk: Journal of Erotic Arts, P.O. Box 6374, Albany, CA 94706.

NOTES

1. Helen V. Collier, *Counseling Women: A Guide for Therapists* (New York: Free Press, 1982), p. 188.

2. Page Smith, "Sex in American History," *San Francisco Chronicle*, February 12, 1989, pp. 5–6.

3. Myrna I. Lewis, "The History of Female Sexuality in the United States," in *Women's Sexual Development: Exploration of Inner Space*, ed. Martha Kirkpatrick (New York: Plenum, 1980).

4. Collier, *Counseling Women*, p. 190.

5. A. C. Kinsey et al., *Sexual Behavior in the Human Female* (Philadelphia: W. B. Saunders, 1953).

6. W. H. Masters and V. E. Johnson, *Human Sexual Response* (Boston: Little, Brown, 1966).

7. Margaret W. Matlin, *The Psychology of Women* (New York: Holt, Rinehart & Winston, 1987), p. 341.

8. Even with the very real risk of lethal infection during sexual activity, there are heterosexual men who still refuse to use condoms because it interferes with their pleasure.

9. Nena O'Neill and George O'Neill, *Open Marriage: A New Lifestyle for Couples* (New York: M. Evans, 1972).

10. Lynda Barry, *Naked Ladies, Naked Ladies, Naked Ladies: A Coloring Book* (Seattle: The Real Comet Press, 1984).

11. Pepper Schwartz, "Research on Adult Female Sexuality: The Next Decade," in *Women: A Developmental Perspective*, ed. Phyllis W. Berman and Estelle R. Ramey, U.S. D. H.H.S., NIH Publication No. 82-2298, April 1982.

12. Carla Golden, "Diversity and Variability in Women's Sexual Identities," in *Lesbian Psychologies: Explorations and Challenges*, ed. Boston Lesbian Psychologies Collective (Urbana and Chicago: University of Chicago Press, 1987).

13. Shelia Kitzinger, *Women's Experience of Sex* (New York: Putnam, 1983).

14. Adrienne Rich, "Compulsory Heterosexuality and the Lesbian Experience," *Signs: Journal of Women in Culture and Society* 5 no. 4 (1980): 68.

15. Lillian Faderman, *Surpassing the Love of Men: Romantic Friendship and Love between Women from the Renaissance to the Present* (New York: William Morrow, 1983).

16. My professional preference is that all lesbians come out. I am of the opinion that in trying to pass, closeted lesbians are permitting out lesbians to carry an unnecessarily greater burden. There are enough women living lesbian life-styles (estimates range from 10–20 percent of the female population) that if absolutely every single lesbian was out, they would prove to be a sizable group with which the heterosexual community would have to contend.

17. Philip Blumstein and Pepper Schwartz, *American Couples* (New York: William Morrow, 1983).

18. Lillian B. Rubin, *Intimate Strangers: Men and Women Together* (New York: Harper & Row, 1983).

19. Lillian B. Rubin, Personal communication with the author, April 1987.

20. John Money and Anne A. Ehrhardt, *Man & Woman, Boy & Girl* (Baltimore: Johns Hopkins University Press, 1972).

21. Mildred Ash, "The Misnamed Female Sex Organ," in *Women's Sexual Development: Explorations of Inner Space,* ed. Martha Kirkpatrick (New York: Plenum, 1980).

22. Kinsey et al., *Sexual Behavior in the Human Female,* 1953. This study was repeated twenty years later and the numbers remained relatively unchanged.

23. Lillian B. Rubin, personal communication with the author, April 1987.

24. Bernard Starr and Marcella Baku Weiner, *The Starr-Weiner Report on Sex and Sexuality in the Mature Years* (New York: McGraw-Hill, 1982).

25. Consumer Reports Books, *Love, Sex, and Aging,* ed. Edward M. Breacher (Boston: Little, Brown, 1986).

26. Juanita H. Williams, *Psychology of Women: Behavior in a Biosocial Context* (New York: W. W. Norton, 1977).

27. Collier, *Counseling Women,* p. 19.

28. Recent research by Domeena Renshaw, M.D., Professor of Psychiatry, Loyola University, suggests that overweight women may be less inhibited about their bodies and may enjoy sex more easily and freely because they don't spend as much time worrying and obsessing about whether their bodies will or will not be attractive to and accepted by their partners. Gloria Weiss, LCSW, private practice, Chicago, personal communication with the author, Sept. 1988.

29. Kitzinger, *Women's Experience of Sex*, pp. 41–57.

30. Federation of Feminist Women's Health Collectives, *New View of a Woman's Body* (New York: Simon and Schuster, 1981).

31. Penny W. Budoff, *No More Menstrual Cramps and Other Good News* (New York: Putnam, 1980).

32. Actually, according to JoAnn Loulan, less than 18 percent of women experience multiple orgasms. JoAnn Loulan, *Lesbian Sex* (San Francisco: Spinsters Ink, 1984).

33. Masters and Johnson, *Human Sexual Response*, p. 5.

34. Domeena Renshaw, quoted in *Journal of the American Women Medical Association* 42 no. 1 (January/February 1987): 12.

35. Loulan, *Lesbian Sex*, p. 43.

36. Helen Singer Kaplan, *Disorders of Sexual Desire* (New York: Brunner/Mazel, 1979).

37. Doreen Feller-Seidler, "A Feminist Critique of Sex Therapy," in *Handbook of Feminist Therapy: Women's Issues in Psychotherapy*, ed. Lynne Bravo Rosewater and Lenore E. A. Walker (New York: Springer, 1985).

38. Elizabeth Rave, "Pornography: The Leveler of Women," in *Handbook of Feminist Therapy: Women's Issues in Psychotherapy*, ed. Lynne Bravo Rosewater and Lenore E. A. Walker (New York: Springer, 1985).

39. Nanette Gartrell et al., "Psychiatrist-Patient Sexual Contact: Results of a National Survey I: Prevalence," *American Journal of Psychiatry* 143 (September 1986): 9.

40. For more information, see *Sexual Happiness: A Practical Approach* by Maurice Yaffe and Elizabeth Fenwick with editorial consulting by Raymond Rosen. This is an especially useful book for sexual problem solving.

41. C. Jayne, "A Two Dimensional Model of Female Sexual Response," *Journal of Sex and Marital Therapy* 7 no. 1 (1981): 3–30.

42. Kitzinger, *Women's Experience of Sex.*

43. L. Tiefer, "The Context and Consequences of Contemporary Sex Research: A Feminist Perspective," in S. Cox, ed., *Female Psychology: The Emerging Self,* 2nd ed. (New York: St. Martin's Press, 1981).

44. A. Rossi, "Materialism, Sexuality and the New Feminism," in J. Zubin and J. Money, eds., *Contemporary Sexual Behavior: Critical Issues for the 1970s* (Baltimore: Johns Hopkins University Press, 1973).

45. Wonderfully humorous pieces on sex from a woman's point of view can be found in books like *Sex Tips for Girls* or *Ladies' Home Erotica.* Try some of these to expand your sexual horizons.

46. Current research indicates that as many as 25 percent of all females may have been the victims of some kind of sexual abuse, and this is probably an underestimate. In his early years, Freud began to uncover evidence of this as well. However, for a variety of reasons, either he did not believe or did not have the courage to support the stories of many of his female patients. Only in recent years have many women, at great risk to themselves, had the courage to break silence about the abuse at the hands of family members and friends. Judith Lewis Herman, *Father-Daughter Incest* (Cambridge, Mass.: Harvard University Press, 1981).

47. Judith Herman, "Sexual Violence," Work in Progress (Wellesley, Mass.: Wellesley College, 1984): 5.

48. E. Hatfield et al., "Equity and Sexual Satisfaction in Recently Married Couples," *The Journal of Sex Research* 18 no. 1 (1982): 18–31.

49. Alice Cottingham, letter to the author, Dec. 28, 1987.

10 | **A**lcohol

One-third to one-half of the people in the United States who have trouble with alcohol are women.[1] Although this means that literally millions of American women have serious drinking problems, we know embarrassingly little about women and alcohol.

Alcohol research started in the 1800s, but prior to the 1970s, nearly all the classical studies of alcohol use had been done exclusively with men.[2] It was not until 1976 that the National Council on Alcoholism established the first national Office on Women and Alcoholism and initiated the first Senate hearings on women and alcohol. The paucity of research has contributed to the impression that women rarely have problems with alcohol. In fact, any woman who drinks is at risk for alcoholism.

Why Do Women Drink?

The percentage of women who drink has been steadily increasing since 1939.[3] Today, almost 50 percent of all drinkers are women. Fifty-five percent of these women are moderate drinkers (defined as consuming fewer than fifteen drinks per week) and 5 percent are heavy drinkers (defined as consuming more than fifteen drinks per week).[4]

There are a number of reasons why women drink. Although there is a stigma against heavy drinking, there are now fewer prohibitions against women's social drinking than in the past. Having a drink at home with friends or a quick one after work with colleagues is a commonly accepted social ritual. Local bars serve as comfortable meeting places for people to relax away from home or work. Moderate drinking is considered an easy way to unwind after a hard day. Many women enjoy the mellowing and relaxing effects of this kind of light drinking.

Other women drink to self-medicate distressing feelings of depression, anxiety, anger, and confusion. While many men learn to drink as a part of the ritual of "manliness," a greater number of women seem to drink because they feel inadequate, shy, sexually inhibited, or lacking in confidence. These women are often trying to be the person they think they should be instead of the person they actually are. By drinking, they are attempting to quell the feelings associated with living less than full and authentic lives. Not every woman in this situation turns to alcohol, but some do in an effort to anesthetize their pain.

Men also seem to have a strong influence on the drinking patterns of their female companions. Women often drink in the company of men who encourage them to drink and who may have drinking problems themselves. Unmarried women are usually provided alcohol (and other drugs) by boyfriends and lovers.[5] They rarely purchase it themselves. Yet if a woman allows a man to buy her drinks, she may feel a certain indebtedness, which she then thinks she must pay back by being sexual.

While men most commonly report that they drink to obtain relief from work stress, women most commonly report that they drink to obtain relief from domestic stress. For the busy working woman who does double duty at home, there is always something to do. As a general rule, women do have more to do than men. Either their work at home never ends or it continues at home after they return from paid jobs. These women may feel guilty if they just relax and take time for themselves. Drinking serves as a way not to do other things.

In addition to being responsible for household chores, women's role in society is to attend to other people and to be sensitive to their feelings. While this care of others is valuable, women often find themselves focusing on others' needs without having reciprocal attention paid to their own. Some women have a hard time limiting their caretaking. Instead, they use alcohol to decrease their sensitivity to other people. Alcohol does lower a woman's inhibitions. Feelings of irritation or a desire to have her own needs acknowledged and respected are more likely to emerge when she has been drinking. Alcohol becomes a way to set more rigid boundaries of self-protection against the impulse to always be the caregiver, and lets a woman indulge her desire to be the care receiver.

Lesbian women may also use alcohol to establish more clear boundaries in their attachments. Our society has "rules" about how men and women are to behave with each other. Even if these rules are sometimes hindrances, they do provide external standards to guide the internal boundaries of the relationship. In intimate relationships between women, these boundaries have to be shaped by the women themselves without these external guidelines. This is no easy task. Some women may resort to alcohol as an immediate, albeit eventually unhelpful, strategy for managing these boundaries.

Alcohol also serves as a pacifier. Because of lack of opportunity, talent, or ambition, many women do not feel able to achieve their dreams. Anger and resentment brew under the surface, but a steady supply of alcohol reduces the desire or need for effective expression. Intoxicated people are unlikely to change their life situations. Alcohol seems to make life more bearable by reducing anxiety, lifting spirits, and numbing loneliness and boredom. It also encourages women to suffer rather than to work toward changing their situations.

Cultural factors also affect women's drinking.[6] Increased purchasing power, ease of access, and advertising campaigns have all contributed to an increase in drinking among women. The price of alcohol has been decreasing at the same time that women have more money.[7] Alcohol once required a trip to a specialty store, but it can now be purchased while picking up groceries at the neighborhood market. The alcohol industry has targeted the women's market as highly profitable and has successfully aimed advertising directly at women. When alcohol is cheaper and more accessible, the amount of alcohol consumed increases. In recent decades, women of all ages, ethnic backgrounds, and social classes have become major consumers of alcohol. An increase in drinking has led directly to an increase in alcohol-related illnesses and deaths in women.

What Is Alcoholism?

It is probably wise to view drinking as occurring along a continuum from abstinence through social, moderate, and heavy drinking to alcoholism. If a person drinks at all, they fall somewhere on this continuum. Social drinkers drink to relax, to lower their inhibitions, or to simply enjoy the high. This moderate use can be an enjoyable and relaxing activity for many people. Beyond this, whether or not a person has a drinking problem is a matter of degree. An estimated 10 percent of all drinkers become alcoholics, and no one knows how to predict who they will be.[8]

More than 10 million people in the United States are addicted to alcohol.[9] When we use the word *alcoholic,* it is easy to imagine the most seriously troubled drinkers who live on the streets and have ruined lives, but these drinkers actually represent only 3–5 percent of alcoholics. Most serious problem drinkers hold jobs, have families, and function in the community. The damage to themselves and their families is not always obvious, but it is always significant.

The drinking patterns of alcoholics vary enormously. Some alcoholics only drink expensive white wine, while others limit themselves to beer. Some only drink on the weekends or after work, while others drink every day, all day. The pattern does not matter. Alcoholism is not defined by what you drink, how much you drink, when you drink, or how long you have been drinking. It has to do with how important alcohol is to you and how your dependence on it affects your life. What is moderate for one person may be far too much for someone else.

The exact definition of alcoholism is still being debated.[10] According to the National Council on Alcoholism, alcoholism is repeated drinking that causes trouble in your personal, professional or family life. When alcoholics drink they cannot always predict when they will stop, how much they will drink, or what the consequences of their drinking will be. Denying the negative effects of drinking is common in alcoholics and those close to them.

If alcohol is taking a toll on your health, your emotional well-being, your personal relationships, your work, or your finances, you have a problem. The more drinking interferes with these areas of your life, the more serious your problem. A precise definition is probably less important than the practical implications of problem drinking.

What Causes Problem Drinking?

There is probably no single cause. The prevailing theory is that alcoholism is multidetermined. In other words, there are usually a number of factors that lead to the development of alcoholism in any one individual. These include inherited vulnerability, personal problems and coping strategies, social attitudes, and cultural conditions. It is the interaction among these that results in some drinkers becoming alcoholics.

A person's initial drinking pattern seems to be affected by cultural values. In the United States, drinking is accepted by the majority of people as a sociable adult behavior. Ben Morgan Jones, an alcohol-treatment specialist, says, "The cocktail party may rank as the commonest form of organized drug-taking in the Western world." In low doses, alcohol has a mood-lifting effect. However, in larger doses, alcohol is a depressant that produces anxiety and addiction. Anyone who drinks risks developing dependence.

At the broadest level, alcohol use and abuse is affected by gender roles, social class, racial and ethnic background, age, sexual preference, job status, the emotional climate of a person's early childhood, the part played by alcohol in her family, a person's adolescent personality development, and the way she responds to crises in adult life. We do not know if these experiences cause alcoholism, but they occur frequently enough in the life stories of people who develop drinking problems to be considered potential contributors.

One of the greatest causes of alcohol dependence is lack of information. In spite of the enormous amounts of alcohol consumed in our society, most of us know very little about the risks associated with using this drug. Alcoholism is not a skid row problem. It is a common health problem that can be both subtle and severe. We contribute to the problems associated with heavy drinking if we do not educate ourselves about these risks or if we deny signs of alcohol abuse.

Women and Problem Drinking[11]

Many of the early theories about the psychological causes of alcoholism were based on research with men. In 1960, researchers interviewed 255 men and concluded that their alcoholism was caused by intense longings to have their dependency needs met.[12] By 1972, a new group of researchers had challenged this dependency theory. They argued that alcohol allowed men to experience heightened illusions of power over others.[13] Neither of these studies clarified women's reasons for using alcohol.

In very basic ways, the life experiences of women are significantly different from those of men. Consequently, many of the psychological causes of alcohol abuse for women are obviously different than those for men. Women who develop drinking problems report that they started drinking because of boredom, frustration, and a search for relief from the stress in their lives at home or within relationships. Female alcoholics have a high rate of clinical depression and tend to experience low self-esteem.[14] Some, seeing no way out of their despair, turn to alcohol.

Some of these women report having felt pressured to drink by peers or male companions who would simultaneously disapprove if they became drunk. There is a double standard for women and men when it comes to heavy drinking. We rarely see a contradiction between a good family man and a heavy drinker, but we have a difficult time imagining a good family woman who also drinks heavily.

Another group of women drink alone and in secret. Responsibility for children, limited economic resources, and a sense of being devalued by both men and women may contribute to surreptitious drinking. Men and women think less of a drinking woman who is not caring for her children than they do of a drinking man. A father can use the corner bar to escape his family responsibilities, while a mother is expected to stay behind with the children. Feeling inadequate, shy, depressed, anxious, and sexually inhibited, both groups of women lack the self-confidence to resist these pressures and exercise personal choice. Instead, they harbor feelings of unrecognized or unexpressed anger and fear while using alcohol to quiet their emotions.

The isolated married mother is not the only woman who develops trouble with alcohol. Unemployed women who would rather be working and single working mothers are the women most at risk for developing drinking problems.[15] Economics play a significant role in the drinking patterns of these women. One-third of all households are now headed by women living below the poverty level. Many of these women are in pink-collar clerical jobs with little opportunity for advancement. Ninety-seven percent of typists, 93 percent of telephone operators, 99 percent of secretaries, 91 percent of waitresses/waiters, and 97 percent of private household workers are women. They must cope with the boredom of underemployment, the powerlessness inherent in any low-status job, and job discrimination if they try to advance. They also cannot afford to go out to drink. Drinking at home is far less expensive than drinking at a bar, and the quantity is not tempered by the reactions of anyone else.

The few studies that have been conducted with women suggest that excessive drinking seems to be connected to feelings about being female. Some women experience profound conflicts between who they feel they should be and who they actually are.[16] Some of these women use alcohol to feel more traditionally feminine, while others discover that alcohol "allows" them to be more aggressive. These women are using alcohol to self-medicate the pain and distress associated with the realities of their lives.

Painful life experiences contribute to the development of a psychological state that places a woman at risk for developing alcoholism.

Many women who abuse alcohol report emotionally brutal childhoods. Up to 74 percent of alcohol- and drug-dependent women have been victims of sexual abuse.[17] A large number of women lost parents through divorce, desertion, or death while still children. These women often have damaged self-images stemming from their chaotic early years. In the face of depression, anxiety, and stress, they may turn to alcohol. In limited amounts, alcohol provides temporary relief. In large or more frequent quantities, it makes matters worse. Psychological dependency can develop within months. This reinforces a woman's habit of using the drug when she is distressed and puts her at risk for developing physical dependency.

Having a parent who drinks also increases the chances of developing problems with alcohol. There appears to be a genetic susceptibility toward alcoholism in some families,[18] while other problem drinkers simply learned to drink by patterning themselves after their parents. Parents model how to cope with life's problems, and children tend to emulate their style.

Some researchers have found that women identify a specific traumatic event as triggering their problem drinking. Others are not convinced that a woman's heavy drinking is actually triggered by a trauma, but that it may occur independently and then be linked together by her as an explanation for why she started drinking heavily.[19]

These problems contribute to heavy drinking in all women, including lesbians. Lesbian women carry the additional burdens of severe economic, legal, and psychological oppression above and beyond that experienced by heterosexual women. Lesbians have to worry about being fired from their jobs, expelled from schools, kicked out of apartments, ostracized in neighborhoods, and forcibly separated from their children. Women's bars serve as social gathering and meeting places for lesbian women. In some studies, lesbian women report spending 80 percent of their social time in women's bars or at parties where alcohol is served. What seems on the surface like a safe haven from discrimination may actually put a lesbian at risk of developing problems with alcohol.

Unfortunately, the few available studies related to alcoholism and lesbians are all seriously flawed.[20] There have been no studies of alcohol use in women who do not frequent women's bars or who do not seek care for their drinking. Thus we know little about the majority of lesbian women and alcohol use. What we do know is that in our society, any woman who loves another woman is devalued. Feeling devalued places any woman at risk of using alcohol as an escape. For some lesbians, as for some heterosexual women, this temporary "solution" can become a permanent problem.

For heterosexual women with drinking problems, low self-esteem makes them vulnerable to becoming involved with an alcoholic partner. Alcoholic women are often married to alcoholic men or men with other psychiatric problems. Their marriages tend to be unstable, and they have a high rate of separation and divorce. Alcoholic women are severely condemned for stepping out of their prescribed role of attending primarily to the needs of others: while nine out of ten men leave their alcoholic wives, nine out of ten women remain married to their alcoholic husbands.[21]

To outsiders, the marriage of an alcoholic woman to a nonalcoholic husband is viewed differently than the marriage of an alcoholic man to a nonalcoholic woman. If a man is married to an alcoholic wife, the tendency is to see him as deprived, and he is likely to receive sympathy for his burdens. If a woman is married to an alcoholic man, she tends to be suspected of contributing to his drinking problems.[22] Most of the nonalcoholic women married to alcoholic men are "diagnosed" as co-dependent and are seen as part of the problem. Many of these women are struggling to maintain a family life despite the problems caused by their alcoholic partner. Men married to alcoholic women do not usually stay long enough to be diagnosed with anything.

The price and availability of alcohol also affects our drinking habits. When alcohol is cheaper and more accessible, drinking increases. However, it is the properties of alcohol itself that ultimately cause problem drinking in women. "It is now thought that anybody under certain circumstances could become physically dependent on alcohol."[23] The negative image of a drunken woman decreases the likelihood of her openly acknowledging that she has a problem and obtaining early treatment. Women who have drinking problems are shielded by family, friends, and physicians, which undermines their chances for recovery. Even when women decide that they want treatment, it is often difficult to obtain. For the lesbian alcoholic who does seek help, there are even fewer services geared specifically to her needs.

Case Histories[24]

To understand how these risk factors translate into women's actual lives, a group of English researchers asked women with drinking problems about their alcohol use. Each woman's story had individual variations, but many themes occurred repeatedly.

Jane began drinking because she felt depressed. She thought that she was less competent than other women at work and believed that her husband found other women more attractive. She felt inadequate as a worker, a wife, and a woman. She began taking speed for her depression and gradually added alcohol. About the same time, she lost her job, and her depression grew worse. Out of loneliness and fear, she became increasingly aggressive toward others. She drank even more heavily, convinced that her relationships with her children and her husband were irreparably damaged. In the end, feeling hopeless and helpless, she made several aborted suicide attempts. It was not until she was brought to the hospital and entered therapy that Jane began to receive some care for her problem. She developed a more realistic picture of the conflicts between her needs as an individual and the demands of her role as wife and mother. She went from seeing herself as an inadequate, "bad" mother to seeing herself as a worthwhile and unique person who was a "pretty average and OK" mother. She was able to become more self-accepting. She concluded that "a woman needs to find out what she really is, to be proud of it, to believe it, and to accept it. The most important thing is just to be."

Julie began drinking because she believed she was both intellectually and sexually inadequate. She hated her work and felt anxious around men. In order to decrease her inhibitions before having sex with a man, she would drink herself into a state of deep intoxication. It took years for Julie to face the fact that she was simply not attracted to men. She came to realize that her life would be more satisfying if she allowed herself to accept her emotional and sexual preference for women. The ability to accept herself as she was rather than trying to fit herself into an uncomfortable stereotype permitted Julie to stop her excessive dependence upon alcohol.

Miriam had followed her husband around the countryside as his military career took the family from base to base. As a result, she had no sense of having her own place in the world. She felt constantly uprooted and disconnected from others. To anesthetize these feelings, she began to drink. Eventually she started to have blackouts—periods when she would appear to function normally but of which she would have absolutely no memory later. When she came to, she could not remember what had happened during the period when she was out. It was a frightening loss of part of her own life. She decided to stop drinking. With time, care, and understanding she was able to say, "I realize I must accept more responsibility for my own life now than I used to."

Elly had no independent dreams for herself but rather saw marriage as her goal. She harbored the unrealistic idea that her husband "would be [her] slave for ever more, give [her] freedom and financial security." When reality sunk in, Elly began to use alcohol to erase the feelings of dissatisfaction with her marriage. Rather than face her fantasy world, she drowned her disappointment in compulsive drinking. Unfortunately, her behavior only lead to guilt, embarrassment, and eroding self-esteem. She finally hit bottom with a suicide attempt. "I stopped drinking. I had to learn to live in the real world without props . . . Through AA [Alcoholics Anonymous] meetings, I built up my self-respect. I found the spiritual tone off-putting at first until I learned not to confuse spirituality with religion . . . I do think listening to women at AA meetings, that their drinking has a lot to do with women's expected role in marriage—and questioning these values."

When we listen to the personal stories of women who drink, we begin to empathize. The feelings and experiences they report are similar to those of many women. They talk about feeling compelled to attend to other people's need rather than their own, of feeling powerless, of having low self-esteem, and of being depressed. They talk about their personal conflict over doing what they believe is the "good" and caring thing to do and what they "selfishly" wish to do for themselves.

It is impossible and ultimately unhelpful to separate women's drinking patterns from the context of their lives. A woman's drinking often seems to be connected to something "wrong" with herself. She feels uncomfortable in the role of a woman as wife, mother, worker, or lover. She sees her discomfort as personal inadequacy and blames herself for her trouble. Holding herself responsible for not fitting, she feels guilty. Alcohol provides a temporary escape from her feelings. It does not occur to her to question the expectations as unfair, inappropriate, or constraining.

Each woman must develop strategies for dealing with the lack of affirmation she experiences as a woman in our culture. Each copes in whatever way she can. Why some women chose alcohol and others do not remains to be explained, but clearly a substantial number of women do turn to alcohol, often to excess. Whatever the stimulus for a woman to drink heavily or frequently, it places her at risk of sliding into alcoholism, and her self-esteem drops even lower. Clearly, alcohol is no shortcut to self-confidence, career success, pleasure in a relationship, or sexual sophistication.

How Alcohol Affects a Woman's Body

Biochemically, alcohol is a depressant that slows the activity of the brain. Twelve ounces of beer, five ounces of wine, and one and a half ounces of whiskey all contain about the same amount of alcohol. In low doses, this legal drug for adult use has disinhibiting and consciousness-altering properties. In large enough quantities, it is a lethal poison.

During pregnancy, alcohol passes from a woman's bloodstream through the placenta and umbilical cord into the bloodstream of the fetus. After delivery, a breast-feeding mother who drinks passes alcohol to her child through her breast milk. Drinking during pregnancy and while breast-feeding risks causing alcohol-induced damage to the child.

Considerable attention has been paid to these dangers for children; less has been studied about how alcohol affects women directly. What we do know is that alcohol affects women differently than men and that equivalent doses are more damaging to women than to men. If a woman and a man of the same weight drink the same amount of alcohol, the woman becomes drunker and, over time, is more likely to become dependent on alcohol. Women also develop health problems at a lower level of alcohol consumption than men and have a higher risk of dying once these health problems arise.[25]

As a general rule, as long as you do not consume more than one drink an hour, your blood alcohol level will remain relatively low. However, there is some variability in how an individual woman's body handles alcohol. How much you can "hold" depends on your weight, the stage of your menstrual cycle, how much you have eaten and how recently, your state of mind, your general health, and how used your body is to processing alcohol. For most women, drinking more than one drink per hour causes alcohol to accumulate in the body and results in intoxication. If a person drinks too much too fast, the pylorus valve between the stomach and small intestine goes into spasm, usually causing vomiting. This is the body's way of trying to protect itself against absorbing more alcohol than it can handle.

The more a woman drinks, the more physical tolerance she develops. The bodies of very heavy drinkers learn to metabolize alcohol more quickly than those of light or moderate drinkers. As a result, it takes increasingly larger amounts of alcohol to produce the same level of intoxication. Heavy drinkers learn to drink huge amounts of alcohol without seeming to be drunk, but they do so at great cost to their health. A woman using alcohol to this extent is a problem drinker.

Health Problems Associated with Heavy Drinking

Alcohol is absorbed from the stomach and small intestine into the bloodstream. The blood then carries the alcohol to all the tissues of the body including the brain, heart, lungs, and liver. In high enough doses, alcohol causes damage to practically every body system.

The Liver

The liver has three major jobs. It maintains blood-sugar levels, breaks down proteins and stores fat and vitamins, and purifies the blood by removing toxins and impurities. Ninety percent of alcohol is broken down in the liver. If the liver is repeatedly subjected to alcohol, the fat content rises. A fatty liver can lead to other complications like alcoholic hepatitis (inflammation of the liver).

Either heavy drinking alone or alcoholic hepatitis can lead to cirrhosis (scarring of the liver), which prevents the liver from removing impurities from the blood. Women appear to develop cirrhosis more quickly than men when they drink heavily.[26] Forty percent of all patients with cirrhosis are women. If the disease is caught early and a woman stops drinking, her liver can recover. If she continues drinking, cirrhosis can lead to death from liver failure or uncontrollable bleeding from the gastrointestinal tract.

The Gastrointestinal System: Esophagus, Stomach, and Intestines

In the morning after a bout of heavy drinking, the stomach rebels with queasiness, a reduced or absent appetite, and vomiting or the dry heaves. Heavy drinkers risk developing heartburn, gastritis (inflammation of the stomach lining), and ulcers in the esophagus, stomach, small intestine, or duodenum. Pancreatitis (inflammation of the pancreas) is also associated with the regular consumption of excessive amounts of alcohol and can be fatal; the other problems are all likely to be experienced as a chronic stomachache. Some can result in heavy, life-threatening bleeding.

The Cardiovascular System: Heart and Blood Vessels

The notion that alcohol keeps us warm in the cold is a myth. When we consume alcohol, we feel temporarily warmer because alcohol sends blood rushing to our capillaries. This increased exposure of warmed blood in surface capillaries actually causes a lowering of body temperature from loss of heat.

In people with ischemic heart disease (decreased blood to the heart muscle), even moderate amounts of alcohol can cause an irregularity (arrhythmia) in the heartbeat. If severe enough, this irregularity causes an inefficiency in the circulation of the blood to the brain and other essential body organs that can result in death. In addition, alcohol is a poison that kills heart muscles. A weakened heart dilates, becoming a large, floppy muscle that no longer functions effectively. This condition can eventually lead to heart failure and death.

Menstruation, Pregnancy, and Breasts

Our response to alcohol may vary at different points in our menstrual cycle. During ovulation or right before our periods, we may drink more than usual or become unexpectedly drunk on our usual dose.[27] With heavy drinking, ovulation and menstrual flow become irregular and hormone output decreases. Birth-control pills cause the body to metabolize alcohol more slowly, and a woman stays intoxicated longer on her usual number of drinks. It appears that as little as three drinks a week may increase a woman's risk of breast cancer by 50 percent, but we do not yet know why.[28]

Consuming alcohol during pregnancy can cause fetal alcohol syndrome.[29] Symptoms include intrauterine death, early deliveries, babies who are underweight for their age, various growth deficiencies, and mental retardation. We do not know how much alcohol is required to cause problems with fetal development or at what point in pregnancy the fetus is at risk for damage. Even small amounts of alcohol seem to increase the risk. Because a level of safety is unknown, the current recommendation is that women who are likely to conceive should not drink at all.[30]

Bones: Accelerating Osteoporosis

Alcoholic women seem to be particularly vulnerable to developing osteoporosis (brittle bones).[31] This is partly caused by poor nutritional habits and partly because alcohol interferes with the absorption of whatever calcium is consumed.

Sleep, Headaches, and Sex

Heavy drinking contributes to fatigue by reducing the REM (rapid eye movement) component of the sleep cycle. Allergies to many alcoholic beverages contribute to headaches. Even limited amounts of alcohol interfere with vaginal lubrication by reducing ADH (antidiuretic hormone). ADH allows us to hold on to the fluid our body needs to function in a healthy fashion. When it is reduced, we urinate more than we consume. All the mucosal membranes become excessively dry, and intercourse is uncomfortable. While a limited amount of alcohol may increase sexual interest, chronic drinking actually reduces sexual arousal.[32] After a while, the alcoholic woman simply is not interested in sex at all.

Psychological Effects of Alcohol

The initial effect of alcohol is to partially anesthetize the brain and reduce its control system. A modest amount of alcohol seems to minimize anxiety and reduce depression. We feel less inhibited and slightly euphoric.

This "happy" stage of intoxication corresponds to a blood alcohol level of 0.05 percent or less than two drinks in one hour for most women. At this level, alcohol makes us feel more confident, but we are actually less competent. Our attention span and reaction time is reduced, and driving can be dangerous.

In the next four stages of intoxication, the more negative and frightening aspects of alcohol consumption emerge. Stage 2, the "excited" stage of intoxication, corresponds to a blood alcohol level of 0.1 percent. There is a marked loss of control. Thinking is impaired, reactions are slowed, and judgment is poor. Behavior is emotional and erratic.

Stage 3, the "confused" stage, occurs at a blood alcohol level of 0.2 percent. Staggering, disorientation, moodiness, fearful or angry outbursts, slurred speech, and double vision are prominent. By stage 4, a blood alcohol level of 0.3 percent, the drinker is in a stupor. She can neither stand nor walk. She is probably vomiting and incontinent and is barely conscious. At stage 5, with a blood alcohol level of 0.4 to 0.5 percent, the drinker is in a coma and death can occur rapidly.[33] At least one thousand people die each year because of the direct effects of stage 5 intoxication.[34]

Although social drinkers (people who consume slightly more than two drinks two to three times a week) are not considered to have problems with alcohol, even this amount of consumption can produce anxiety, depression, and mood swings between periods of drinking.[35] These mood changes are often compounded by feelings of guilt, remorse, shame, and self-accusation—especially if a woman behaves in ways while she is drinking that embarrass her when she sobers up.

Beyond the damaging effects of alcohol alone, women are at particular risk for poly-addiction (the addiction to more than one substance).[36] This is often the result of prescription drugs being used with alcohol. It is estimated that 60 to 70 percent of all female alcoholics use tranquilizers and sedatives.[37] The combination of these pills and alcohol is extremely dangerous. The use of two depressant drugs simultaneously greatly increases a woman's risk of physical and psychological damage as well as premature death.[38]

Drinking a substantial amount of alcohol over a long period of time will eventually cause memory problems (amnesia). In the early stages, these are simply "brownouts" such as not remembering where we left our shoes or our purse. Continued heavy drinking causes blackouts, complete loss of recall for a significant period of time. At its most severe, heavy drinking can lead to Wernicke-Korsakoff syndrome, a more crippling and pervasive kind of amnesia caused by a deficiency in vitamin B (thiamine).

If You Drink

The body eliminates alcohol at a constant rate. If you consume too much, you experience the symptoms of a hangover—shakiness, sweating, headache, and tremors. A hangover is the body's way of protesting the ingestion of a noxious poison.

What if you are a safe drinker most of the time, but once in a while you drink very heavily. How can you prevent a hangover?

- Quench your thirst with water or a nonalcoholic beverage rather than one containing alcohol.
- Drink alcohol slowly, sipping rather than gulping your beverage.
- Limit yourself to one drink per hour.
- Do not drink on an empty stomach.
- Stop drinking several hours before you plan to go to sleep.
- If you do stay up late drinking, try to sleep as long as you can. If you are unable to sleep in, make sure the next night is an early one and alcohol free.

If you already have a hangover, the only sensible guide is to drink plenty of nonalcoholic fluids, rest, and wait.

- If you use painkillers, avoid aspirin because it can irritate your stomach.
- Replenish your body with the vitamins and minerals lost through heavy

drinking. Especially important are the B and C vitamins as well as potassium and calcium. Oranges, tomatoes, milk, cheese, and the judicious use of multivitamins will help.

- Get some fresh air and exercise, but avoid too much jostling. Instead of running, consider yoga or gentle swimming.
- Try a soothing drink like herbal tea, hot cocoa, or warmed milk. Avoid strong coffee, which can make you more anxious and jittery.
- Abstain from drinking alcohol for several days to allow your body sufficient time to recuperate.
- And finally, do not take a morning drink. Such a drink will temporarily avert the unpleasant symptoms of withdrawal; however, this behavior is a sure sign that you have an alcohol problem. You are only making the situation worse for yourself if you drink to "cure" a hangover.

Remember, it is not possible to speed the sobering process with black coffee, cold showers, or fresh air. These strategies may make the drinker feel more awake, but only the passage of time and the efforts of the liver to process the alcohol will reduce the level of intoxication. There is no way to speed up your body's metabolism of alcohol.

Even if you are currently drinking at a safe level, do not assume that you are invulnerable to developing a drinking problem. Remember, anyone who drinks is at risk for alcoholism. During stressful life changes, we may inadvertently increase that risk by altering our drinking patterns. Monitor your drinking habits and regularly assess where you are on the drinking continuum. This will help you decide if your present level of drinking is OK, if you need to cut back, or if you need to quit.

What Kind of Drinker Are You?*

The following questions (based on a London Council on Alcoholism questionnaire) are designed to help you assess your drinking pattern in terms of dependency and vulnerability to problems. Check the statements that are true, or closest to the truth for you. Check one for each category, and then add up your score as shown below.

1. If I was advised to give up drinking for the sake of my health—
   a. I could do so easily.
   b. I could do so but I'd miss it.
   c. I could do so but with difficulty.
   d. I could only do so if I had help.
   e. I don't think I could do it.

*This questionnaire is reprinted with permission from Brigid McConville, *Women Under the Influence* (New York: Schocken Books, 1985), pp. 117–19.

2. This time last year my favorite drink was—
   a. stronger than what I drink now.
   b. weaker than what I drink now.
   c. the same as what I drink now.
3. When I am drinking with my friends I notice that—
   a. they seem to drink about the same speed that I do.
   b. they drink faster than I do.
   c. some of them drink slower than I do.
   d. most of them drink slower than I do.

If you answered yes to a or b, also answer the following:
   e. I have changed my friends.
   f. I have kept my old friends.

If you answered yes to e, then also answer the following:
   My new friends—
   g. drink faster than my old friends.
   h. drink slower than my old friends.
4. Where I buy my drink—
   a. I have a credit account.
   b. I do not have a credit account.

If you answered yes to a, then also answer the following:
   The amount that I owe on my credit account is—
   c. generally about what I would expect.
   d. sometimes rather more than I'd expected.
5. I usually first think about drinking—
   a. when I wake up.
   b. some time during the morning.
   c. at lunchtime.
   d. late in the afternoon.
   e. in the evening.

If you answered yes to a, b, or c, then also answer the following:
   When I plan the rest of my day—
   f. drinking is a high priority.
   g. drinking is not particularly important to me.
6. Before going to a social event—
   a. I never have a drink.
   b. I seldom have a drink.
   c. I usually have a drink.
7. When I decide whether to go to a social event—
   a. it doesn't matter to me whether or not alcohol is going to be available there.
   b. I prefer some drink to be available there.
   c. I don't really enjoy it unless some drink is going to be available.
   d. I will only attend if I know drink will be available there.
8. After I have had a few drinks—
   a. I never pretend to have had less than I really have.
   b. I occasionally do pretend that.

c. I often do pretend that.

d. I sometimes declare I had one more drink than I've actually had.

9. When it gets toward closing time—

a. I find I've had enough to drink.

b. I tend to double my final order or buy some to take home with me.

10. In the course of everyday conversation my friends—

a. seldom talk about drinking.

b. quite often talk about drinking.

If you answered yes to b, then also answer the following—

I have noticed that my friends usually—

c. joke about it.

d. offer some kind of advice to me.

e. talk about drinking much more than me.

Add up your score as follows and then assess yourself according to the following categories:

1. a = 1, b = 1, c = 2, d = 3, e = 4
2. a = 1, b = 3, c = 2
3. a = 1, b = 1, c = 2, d = 3, e = 2, f = 1, g = 4, h = 2
4. a = 2, b = 1, c = 1, d = 2
5. a = 4, b = 3, c = 2, d = 1, e = 1, f = 3, g = 1
6. a = 1, b = 2, c = 3
7. a = 1, b = 2, c = 3, d = 4
8. a = 1, b = 3, c = 4, d = 2
9. a = 1, b = 3
10. a = 1, b = 2, c = 3, d = 4, e = 1

Relax—If you scored 17 or under you are not a dependent drinker and have no need to worry at present about your drinking habits. But don't forget that drinking habits can change, particularly in times of stress, and you may not *stay* a non-dependent drinker.

Be wary—If you scored from 18 to 24 you are likely to be a regular, but moderate, drinker. You may feel a "need" to drink now and then and may be causing yourself harm—or causing others difficulties—from time to time.

You are in the area of mildly vulnerable drinking and should watch your consumption carefully for signs of drinking more, or more often. If your friends say that you are starting to drink more, take heed: remember that it is easy to move along the continuum toward the problem end of drinking.

Cut down—If you scored 25 to 30, you are probably drinking regularly and drinking too much for the good of your health and relationships. You may not notice the "need" to drink—because you are rarely going without it. You are now running a very high risk of developing more serious drinking problems, so try to cut down the amount you drink and to drink less often.

Seek help—If you scored over 31 you are probably dependent, physically and psychologically, on alcohol. You are certainly harming yourself and could be causing suffering to others.

If you stop drinking or try to cut down you may experience unpleasant withdrawal symptoms (trembling, sweating, feelings of panic) and may feel confused, moody, or depressed. As time goes on you will need more and more alcohol to reach the same level of intoxication. You should seek help from one of the organizations listed at the end of this chapter.

If you have not developed a drinking problem but are concerned about your risk, controlled drinking may prevent alcoholism from developing. A number of studies have shown that even the early stage problem drinker may be able to successfully control her drinking if she commits herself to the appropriate self-help program.[39] One of the best guides to responsible drinking is outlined in William Miller and Ricardo Muñoz's book *How to Control Your Drinking,* which is listed in the reference section at the end of this chapter.

Self-Help Groups for Women Who Drink

If you are not an alcoholic but want to alter your drinking pattern, a self-help plan may work. An all-women's support group designed to help members control their drinking can be especially useful. Look for an existing group or organize one among your friends, through a woman's center, or by advertising in the local paper. Talking with other concerned women provides an opportunity to understand how a woman's situation in society contributes to common frustrations and annoyances. While drinking may at first seem like an easy way to deal with some of these feelings, it is better for a woman to learn how to deal with them in more constructive ways. Members of these groups report that they benefit enormously from discussing mutual concerns and from the support they give and receive.

You may or may not recruit a professional leader to assist the group. If you do decide to use a professional, select someone knowledgeable about the special risks alcohol poses to women. Whether you use a leader or not, some structure is essential to keep the group focused. One way to do this is by defining areas of discussion. Four potential topics are listed below:

Why and where do you drink?   Each woman needs to identify the circumstances and situations that make her feel like drinking. She may be drinking for fun or relaxation, but if she is drinking to alter or avoid situations that are upsetting, she can use the group to learn new ways of coping with these difficulties. A woman must learn how to be effectively assertive, to feel comfortable insisting

The Michigan Alcoholism Screening Test*

1. Do you feel you are a normal drinker?	Yes	No
2. Have you ever awakened in the morning after some drinking the night before and found that you could not remember part of the evening?	Yes	No
3. Does your wife/husband or parents ever worry or complain about your drinking?	Yes	No
4. Can you stop drinking without a struggle after one or two drinks?	Yes	No
5. Do you ever feel badly about your drinking?	Yes	No
6. Do you ever try to limit your drinking to certain times of the day or to certain places?	Yes	No
7. Do your friends or relatives think that you are a normal drinker?	Yes	No
8. Are you always able to stop when you want to?	Yes	No
9. Have you ever attended a meeting of Alcoholics Anonymous?	Yes	No
10. Have you gotten into fights when drinking?	Yes	No
11. Has drinking ever created problems with you and your wife (husband)?	Yes	No
12. Has your wife (husband, or other family member) ever gone to anyone for help about your drinking?	Yes	No
13. Have you ever lost friends or girlfriends/boyfriends because of your drinking?	Yes	No
14. Have you ever gotten into trouble at work because of drinking?	Yes	No
15. Have you ever lost a job because of drinking?	Yes	No
16. Have you ever neglected your obligations, your family or work for two days or more in a row because of drinking?	Yes	No
17. Do you ever drink before noon?	Yes	No
18. Have you ever been told you have liver trouble?	Yes	No
19. Have you ever had DTs (delirium tremens), severe shaking, heard voices, or seen things that weren't there after heavy drinking?	Yes	No
20. Have you ever gone to anyone for help about your drinking?	Yes	No
21. Have you ever been in a hospital because of drinking?	Yes	No
22. Have you ever been a patient in a psychiatric hospital or on a psychiatric ward of a general hospital where drinking was part of the problem?	Yes	No
23. Have you ever been seen at a psychiatric or mental-health clinic or gone to a doctor or clergyman for help with an emotional problem in which drinking has played a part?	Yes	No
24. Have you ever been arrested, even for a few hours, because of drunken behavior?	Yes	No
25. Have you ever been arrested for drunken driving or driving after drinking?	Yes	No

Scoring
0–2—Social Drinking
3–4—Heavy Drinking
5 or above—Alcoholism

*Reprinted by permission from the *American Journal of Psychiatry* 127 (1971): 1653–58. Copyright 1971 by the American Psychiatric Association.

that her own needs be met, and to select situations where she is treated with respect. If she develops and maintains healthy self-esteem, she can reduce her risk of problem drinking.

How much are you in the habit of drinking? Keep a log for a typical week. Even if your self-report shows that your consumption is alarmingly high, do not despair. Cutting down is a slow process. Begin with smaller, weaker drinks. Next, reduce the number of drinks. Finally, take days off without consuming any alcohol. This allows your body to recover and replenish itself. Give yourself credit for every bit of progress you make. Reducing your risk of alcoholism deserves a big reward. Be generous with yourself.

What kind of drinker are you? You have already taken one test to assess your drinking pattern. You may also want to try one of the standard tests, like the Michigan Alcoholism Screening Test, used by professionals in assessing the risk of alcoholism. Again, the purpose of taking any test is to give you a better idea of where you are on the drinking continuum and whether you should cut down or quit.

What are some strategies for cutting down? These are changes that you can implement right now to reduce your drinking.

- Set a specific time of the day, preferably with or following your evening meal, where you permit yourself to drink modestly. Do not drink at any other time of the day.
- Decide how many drinks you will allow yourself each week and stick to it. If you drink heavily one evening, reduce or abstain the next to keep within your self-defined limit.
- Do not drink at lunch. Ever. Period.
- In social situations, follow every alcoholic drink with a nonalcoholic beverage. Club soda or seltzer with a twist of lemon is a good alternative and no one will be the wiser—except you.
- Do not allow anyone to top off your drink. It is easier to go over your limit if someone else fills your glass.
- Make a list of alternative activities that can substitute for drinking such as yoga, dancing, tennis, or swimming. If you choose more vigorous sports, refrain from quenching your thirst with a few beers. Fruit juice, one of the electrolyte replenishing beverages designed for athletes, or even plain water is a much wiser option.
- Make an agreement with one of your friends that the two of you will not drink on specific nights during the week. Use the money you save to do something new and exciting together.
- Commit yourself to two nondrinking days each week. Tell your close friends about this plan. Social support helps us keep our agreements.

- Do not drink alone and do not drink with anyone who pressures you to drink beyond your self-defined limits.
- Never drink more than two drinks per hour.
- At a bar or restaurant, always order only one drink at a time. Ordering doubles or two drinks to get under the wire at happy hour increases the risk of excessive drinking.
- Make a list of the number of calories in each drink. When you realize that you have a choice between two hundred calories in a second drink before dinner or a piece of chocolate cake after dinner, you may decline that second drink to save your calories for the cake.
- If you find yourself craving a drink at some time other than your self-designed program allows, consider satisfying your craving with a particularly delicious snack instead. These tasty morsels can be a good way to protect your commitment to yourself and are likely to contain no more calories than the drink you might otherwise have taken.

Other Groups: Drinkwatchers

Drinkwatchers is a British organization designed to help people drink sensibly. Their program is not for alcoholics, but for people who can and do drink. Members choose to have alcohol as a part of their life-style, but they want to cut down or maintain moderate use. They meet for two hours a week to learn more about alcohol use and abuse. After meeting, they socialize at a local bar where they practice their new skills.

The goal of this group is to learn to relax, to say no to excessive drinking, to be aware of drinking patterns, to cope with difficult situations without using alcohol, and to develop a healthier way of life. I am unaware of any groups like this in the United States, but there is no reason you cannot start one. Many people develop a drinking problem out of ignorance rather than informed consent. This kind of free or low-cost program provides education and prevents abuse by helping women alter risky behavior before it gets out of hand.

If You Have a Drinking Problem

Alcoholism does not usually develop with the first drink. There is a common sequence in its development.[40]

Stage 1: Asymptomatic Phase—During this phase, a drinker uses alcohol to cope with stress. Her drinking is not usually viewed as a problem either to herself or to others, although after a time she does begin to develop an increased tolerance to alcohol. Here is where the problem begins. Everything that follows spells trouble.

Stage 2: Prodromal Phase—At this point, a drinker's behavior is beginning to reveal that alcohol is more than a social beverage. She is preoccupied with alcohol, drinking on the sly and protecting her supply. She begins gulping the first few drinks, concerned that she will not get enough. She may start experiencing blackouts. She feels guilty about her drinking yet denies the seriousness of her problem.

Stage 3: Acute Phase—The drinker has a noticeable loss of control over her drinking, yet she is still trying to pretend that she is in control. She begins to feel almost a physical demand for alcohol. Any tension leads to a desire to drink, and any drinking leads to more drinking. She tries rationalizing her drinking by saying to herself, and perhaps to others, that she would not be drinking if this or that were not happening. As her life revolves more and more around drinking, she starts having serious trouble in all areas—at work, at home, and in friendships.

Stage 4: Chronic Alcoholism—This stage is marked by prolonged periods of drunkenness, or benders. Life has now deteriorated tremendously. She can rarely hold a steady job, cannot maintain old friendships, and is likely to be estranged from her family.

Don't put the quality of your life and health at risk by drinking to excess. There is no question that you are an alcoholic if you have passed beyond stage 1, you have developed tolerance to alcohol, or you experience withdrawal symptoms. Tolerance means that you must drink more alcohol than before to feel the same effects. Severe withdrawal is characterized by convulsions and hallucinations, but withdrawal also includes much milder symptoms. If you decrease or stop drinking and experience shaky hands, weakness, agitation, a racing or pounding heart, depression, irritability, sweating, anxiety, or insomnia, you are in withdrawal.

Reducing rather than abstaining is a reasonable option for some drinkers. However, if even moderate drinking endangers your physical or psychological health, then controlled drinking is not for you.[41] If you are an alcoholic, the only safe solution is abstinence. Don't kid yourself. Get help immediately. People who drink too much are ill, and any ill person is permitted and encouraged to receive help from others. You are not to blame for your illness, but you are responsible for taking good care of yourself.

Help with a Drinking Problem

There is no single pattern to problem drinking. A drinker's tendency to deny that she has a problem means that her consumption often continues until she becomes very ill. Angry confrontations and desperate pleading seem to have little effect on her drinking. Judgmental accusations often reinforce her guilt and only add to her "reasons" for drinking. Yet colleagues, friends, and loved ones who minimize or ignore the problem are not helping.

It may take a disaster such as a partner leaving, getting fired, or a severe health problem before some seriously ill women seek treatment. There are a limited, but growing, number of resources specifically designed for the woman alcoholic. Fortunately, some women do not have to hit bottom before they seek help. Early interventions can work, and the sooner a woman acknowledges her problem, the easier it will be to obtain effective treatment. If you are worried that a friend or loved one drinks too much, see page 350 for a discussion about talking to someone you care about who has a drinking problem.

What can you do if you already have a drinking problem? Until you acknowledge that you are powerless over alcohol, you share the great obsession of every alcoholic: the fantasy that you can somehow control your drinking. An alcoholic cannot control her drinking. To stop drinking, she needs help and the sooner the better. I am not suggesting that this is an easy thing to do. Turning away from an addictive drug requires enormous courage and determination. To make a change of this magnitude without assistance is almost impossible and, frankly, unnecessary given the resources available today.

Alcoholics Anonymous

Alcoholics Anonymous (AA) is a worldwide network for mutual aid, support, and self-help with over a million members. While the AA style and ideology may not be for everyone, AA has been remarkably successful in helping drinkers stay sober. It is estimated that 91 percent of AA members who attend meetings regularly stay sober. At least one-third of AA members are women.[42]

AA is a twelve-step program that is described as spiritual rather than religious.[43] It offers a structure to replace the one provided by going to the bar or spending leisure time drinking. Instead of relying on alcohol to anesthetize problems, AA members learn to talk about their problems with other people who can offer support.

The Twelve Steps of A.A.*

1. We admitted we were powerless over alcohol—that our lives had become unmanageable.
2. Came to believe that a Power greater than ourselves could restore us to sanity.
3. Made a decision to turn our will and our lives over to the care of God as we understood Him.
4. Made a searching and fearless moral inventory of ourselves.
5. Admitted to God, to ourselves, and to another human being the exact nature of our wrongs.

*The Twelve Steps are taken from *Alcoholics Anonymous,* published by A.A. World Services, New York, N.Y., 1939, 1955, 1976, pp. 59–60. Reprinted with permission.

6. Were entirely ready to have God remove all these defects of character.

7. Humbly asked Him to remove our shortcomings.

8. Made a list of all persons we had harmed, and became willing to make amends to them all.

9. Made direct amends to such people whenever possible, except when to do so would injure them or others.

10. Continued to take personal inventory and when we were wrong promptly admitted it.

11. Sought through prayer and meditation to improve our conscious contact with God as we understood Him, praying only for knowledge of His will for us and the power to carry that out.

12. Having had a spiritual awakening as the result of these Steps, we tried to carry this message to alcoholics, and to practice these principles in all our affairs.

AA has no dues and no membership fees. The only requirement is a desire to quit drinking. There are both open and closed meetings. Anyone is welcome to attend open meetings. Closed meetings are for alcoholics only. Try several open meetings at different locations before deciding which group is right for you. The larger the community, the more likely you are to find a group into which you fit comfortably.

Among women, the main complaint about AA is that it is male-dominated. The AA bible, the so-called Big Book, reflects this bias. There is a chapter called "To Wives," but no comparable chapter called "To Husbands." In addition, AA uses a self-repressive approach. This can be helpful for those who suffer from an unhealthy level of grandiosity and narcissism, but it tends to denigrate personal desires and aspirations as unhealthy egotism. This is less appropriate for women, many of whom suffer from low self-esteem. The impact of this bias can be tempered by careful selection of a group that encourages women to develop a healthy sense of self-respect.

Even with its limitations, I recommend that women with drinking problems attend AA. It is a free service, available regularly and frequently. Its self-help program offers a supportive structure that a clinician working alone with a client is unable to provide. I worry about the woman who does not avail herself of this program during at least some phase of the recovery process. The failure, for whatever reason, to use this readily available program is usually a form of self-sabotage. When a woman has reservations about attending AA, I suggest that she focus on what is helpful about the program rather than emphasizing its drawbacks.

Programs similar to AA have been developed to help families. There is Al-Anon for the spouses of people who drink, Al-Ateen for the adolescent children of people who drink, and Adult Children of Alcoholics (ACOA) for adults who grew up in families where one or both parents drank. These programs are also based on the "twelve-step" model and have been enormously helpful to the many people in our society who have been affected by living with a person who drinks. These programs can help family members, even if the problem drinker does not seek help herself.

More than 28 million American adults have had at least one alcoholic parent.[44] These people have "survived" their childhoods at the price of adapting to a dysfunctional family situation.[45] These adaptations interfere with their creating satisfying lives as adults. People who grew up in alcoholic families seem willing to accept unacceptable behavior. They tend to put other people's needs before their own, suspect that they are driving the person they love to drink, and believe that if only *they* were doing things better, they could control or cure the drinker's behavior.

Growing up in an alcoholic home also increases a woman's risk of becoming an alcoholic[46] or selecting a life partner who is an alcoholic or demonstrates some other form of severe and troubling behavior. These adult children of alcoholics are vulnerable to molding their behavior to the dysfunctional behavior of their troubled partners. This has been called co-dependency.[47] ACA resources listed at the end of this chapter may help you understand more about this phenomenon and, if you wish, help you change your own behavior.

Women for Sobriety

This program was started as an alternative to AA by Dr. Jean Kirkpatrick, a sociologist and recovering alcoholic. She envisioned a place for women with more privacy than AA and where women could help other women. Like AA, the goals of the members of Women for Sobriety are first to stop drinking and then to work on personality handicaps. Some women, especially those who have been physically or sexually abused, may feel safer in these all-women groups.

Professional Assistance

Unfortunately, many physicians are unprepared to help women who have problems with alcohol. Even though alcohol abuse is the third-largest health problem in the United States, the average medical-school student spends less than ten hours studying alcoholism. Alcoholism is often seen as a moral issue rather than a health concern and is often an unpopular illness to treat. To make matters worse, it hits too close to home for many health-care professionals who use and abuse alcohol themselves.[48]

Even when a professional is knowledgeable about alcoholism in general, there is no guarantee of caring and effective treatment for women. Women continue to be underrepresented in most alcoholism treatment programs. Nationally, women constitute less than 20 percent of all clients in alcohol treatment, although estimates indicate that they represent a much higher percentage of the total alcoholic population.[49]

Before committing yourself to any program, investigate what is available. Your local council on alcoholism and nearby women's center should be able to help. You will probably find that there are outpatient counseling services, day treatment centers, alcohol treatment units, residential facilities, private facilities, and programs through general or psychiatric hospitals. If you are or were a member of the armed forces, investigate their treatment programs. A variety of programs is necessary because alcoholism is a complicated illness. No one program works for everyone. Each woman must locate the resource that works best for her at the time she is ready to make a change.

Select a program in which the staff holds positive attitudes about women and fosters egalitarian relationships between women and men. My own recommendation is to look for programs designed and run by women.[50] Even a well-meaning man may fail to recognize fully the impact that sexism has upon the development of alcoholism as well as on its diagnosis and treatment.[51] Male-oriented treatment programs have not fully responded to the special and practical needs of alcoholic women, and women have tended to drop out of them.[52]

Programs designed by women are more likely to recognize the reality of women's lives. They understand the life circumstances that can lead to excessive drinking for women. They communicate respect for a woman as an individual, and they make it clear that while her drinking is understandable, it is not healthy problem solving. They see that women do have the power to make personal changes and choices in spite of their life circumstances.

Women have special problems that must be addressed throughout the recovery process if it is to be successful. These include resources for childcare, vocational counseling and training, attention to the special needs of lesbians, minority women, and the victims of incest and battering, and the option of women's groups and female counselors.

Many alcoholic mothers are supporting their children economically as well as emotionally. Even if a woman is living with a man, he is unlikely or may be unwilling to take primary responsibility for the children. Who cares for the children when a mother enters a treatment program? Any program providing services for women must assist in arranging for childcare.

Alcoholic women often have severe financial difficulties and need job training. Most treatment programs fail to offer this essential service. Even when they do, women are often encouraged to train for low-paying jobs rather than more lucrative occupations. Good programs provide counseling and training for well-paying jobs. Economic independence is often the key to successful recovery.

A staff interested in women and knowledgeable about women's experiences understands that excessive alcohol use is triggered by many different experiences. Many alcoholic women suffered as children from sexual or physical abuse. A substantial number have also been sexually or physically assaulted as adults. Some women have experienced social pressure to drink to excess, especially from male partners.[53] An unwanted pregnancy may follow an episode of excessive drinking and lead to additional guilt and shame. Some women have started drinking heavily to quell the emotional pain of a recently broken relationship. Most feel conflicted about longing to have their personal needs met while behaving in ways expected of them. Alcohol numbs the conflict.

An all-women's therapy group can provide a safe haven for tackling problems. In this environment, women can help other women by offering mutual support and practical advice on handling difficult situations. Successful women's groups are often run by women.[54] On the other hand, an experienced and compassionate male therapist who treats female clients with genuine respect can provide an opportunity to interact with a safe and decent man. For some women, this may be the first time they can really depend on a man who does not take advantage of them. This unique female-male therapy relationship can serve as an emotional bridge to healthier female-male relationships outside the therapy environment. Individual therapy with a knowledgeable clinician can also be useful in recovery as long as the woman is sober. Therapy of any kind cannot be effective if a woman is still drinking.

If a woman requires protection from the symptoms of withdrawal, she may need to enter an inpatient program. There the appropriate medications can prevent the serious physical consequences of detox while her body adjusts to the absence of alcohol. She may also need vitamins and a good, healthy diet. In this environment, treatment can also begin for any alcohol-related medical problems like cirrhosis and gastritis.

If inpatient treatment is needed, a mother's responsibilities for her children cannot resume at full-speed immediately upon discharge. Just as a recently discharged person is expected to resume employment gradually, household duties and responsibility for childcare must also be assumed slowly. The staff needs to be aware of planning for this component of long-term recovery.

Alternatives to inpatient care are residential or halfway houses. These all-female environments can provide for recovery without the immediate pressure to respond to men. A few include housing for children, meeting a serious need for many alcoholic women who are the primary or sole providers for their youngsters. Halfway houses also provide good preventive medicine. Since we know that children who grow up in alcoholic homes are at greater risk for developing alcoholism as adults, early intervention can go a long way to break the family cycle of self-destruction. Six months to one year of living in a protective environment allows both children and mothers to learn healthier adaptive skills that will greatly enhance their chance for continued recovery upon "graduation." Unfortunately, less than 10 percent of residential treatment programs are for women; 90 percent offer services to men only.[55]

Whatever therapeutic option is chosen, it is important for a woman to mourn what she lost during her years of drinking. If she is a mother, she will need to work on feelings of guilt. Dealing with her real or perceived neglect of her children and their justifiable developmental needs will be a difficult struggle. For every woman, there will be the battle to stop hating herself for what she was and who she is. It may be hard for her to forgive herself. Although the therapist's attitude is important, the responsibility and credit for recovery both rest squarely in the woman's lap.

No matter what alcoholism treatment plan is selected, it should include at least the following goals:

- STOP DRINKING.
- Find ways to replace the perceived positive effects of alcohol. Ex-drinkers need to find alternative or renewed satisfactions in family life, hobbies, further education, or other goals now that satisfaction is no longer provided by the bottle.
- Prepare yourself for gainful employment if this has not already been done.
- Process anger about never being able to drink again.
- End isolation. Alcoholic women have often been hiding: hiding from people; hiding from life; hiding from themselves. They need to risk the rewards and dangers inherent in getting involved with other people in intimate and important ways.
- Pursue relationships with friends who do not have drinking problems. Old drinking buddies will have to give way to friends committed to constructive and healthy living.
- Emphasize positive goals. Plan a program for developing your full potential.

While a woman-oriented treatment plan is preferred, neither a talented therapist nor a superb treatment program will assure recovery from an alcohol problem. Most important is the motivation and commitment of the woman herself.

Talking to a Problem Drinker You Care About

If you are concerned about a friend or family member, there is something you can do. A drinker may not be consciously aware that she has a problem or may be terrified of the possibility that she does. While she must decide if she is ready to face her problem, you do not have to stand by helplessly.

An empathic intervention can be a profound and courageously caring act. A loving and supportive confrontation by a friend or family member can sometimes break through a woman's denial about her drinking. Once you are prepared to speak, tell your friend or loved one that you would like to have a private conversation. Offer the information that you want to share in a straightforward and nonjudgmental manner. It is important to select a time when she is sober and when you are both fairly calm. The seriousness of the problem is less likely to be denied if an alcohol-related troublesome event has occurred within the last day or two.

Tell her that you are concerned about her drinking. Provide specific examples of situations that have worried you. Perhaps it is her driving after drinking, trouble completing work assignments, recent bouts of alcohol-related medical problems, or repeated conflicts with you, her partner, or her children. Whatever evidence you present, use it to show your concern rather than to blame. Try to make it clear that you believe by denying the seriousness of her problem, she is hurting more people than she realizes—including herself. Make it clear that you believe she needs help. Have a list of phone numbers and resources readily available. If she does decide to seek help, you may want to volunteer to accompany her to an AA meeting or to investigate professional services for her.

This kind of confrontation is ripe for feelings of guilt on the part of both women. The woman who drinks is vulnerable to feeling guilty about excessive drinking; the woman who lovingly confronts will worry about hurting her friend. You will be better able to manage your own feelings of guilt if you are very clear with yourself as to why you are bringing this up and if you are kind and careful about your style of communication. Sometimes, several people will get together to offer this kind of intervention. This can be even more effective. A professional may be helpful in providing guidance as to how to stage this kind of gathering.

Do not be surprised if your initial intervention is unsuccessful. Denial is a powerful process. However, if you communicate clearly and do not blame the woman, you will be able to return to the subject again. Remember, all you can do is provide information, support, and encouragement.

In the meantime, if you have been rescuing your friend from difficult situations, stop. Let her begin to take the consequences of her own actions. It may be hard to stand by rather than rescue her, but facing the results of her own choices may ultimately give her an opportunity to live a healthier and happier life. She can choose to recover.

Final Comments

Everyone in our society is encouraged to participate in social drinking. It is advertised as a way to unwind and to escape the daily pressures of work and home. Why does society encourage chemical "solutions" to problems? A major reason is money. The sale of alcohol is the fourth-largest source of federal revenues after corporate and individual taxes and windfall profits on oil. Drinking is big business. The more people drink, the greater the profits. Unfortunately, the more people drink, the higher the incidence of physical and psychological damage that is caused.[56]

The alcohol industry has been remarkably successful in its campaign to sell alcohol to the women's market.[57] Along with this "success" has been an increase in drinking problems. More women are becoming ill and dying of alcoholism. Luckily, they are also seeking treatment.

To reduce the damage caused by alcohol, less must be consumed. To achieve this goal, we must reduce availability, ban alcohol advertising, increase taxes to keep the price high, provide better alcohol education programs, and enforce tougher drunk-driving laws. Driving under the influence of alcohol reduces a driver's competency and increases the risk of error. For far too long our legal system has minimized responsibility for causing injury or death to others if the assailant uses a car rather than a gun.[58]

Alcoholism is a complex illness that requires a broad range of therapeutic approaches. Individual responsibility and the power to make personal changes must be balanced with knowledge about the social, political, and economic forces that encourage women to drink. Women are underrepresented in alcohol research and well-funded treatment programs. It seems that women's problems with drinking are viewed as less serious than men's. Although alcoholism is the third most common cause of death among people aged thirty-five to fifty-five, an estimated 70 percent of female alcoholics, or 3.5 *million* women, never receive care for this illness. They go undiagnosed, misdiagnosed, or untreated. This is particularly unfortunate given that alcoholism is a treatable emotional and physical disorder with a potentially high recovery rate when addressed appropriately.

This public denial along with the alcoholic's personal denial is detrimental to early intervention and treatment. This situation must change if we are to successfully improve the situation for women who drink.[59] We must recognize that drinking falls on a continuum. Any drinking puts us at risk of drinking too much. If we have an inherited vulnerability or if we are uninformed about the long-term effects of regular consumption, turning to alcohol in response to personal or social problems may lead to problem drinking. There is no typical alcoholic, and any woman who drinks must consider herself at risk.

Current knowledge suggests that many, albeit certainly not all, women can drink in moderation. If we are going to limit the number of women who develop drinking problems, education and prevention is critical. Using guidelines based upon female anatomy and physiology, some women can develop relatively safe drinking patterns. This reduces a woman's risk for alcohol-related problems—both physical and psychological.

Women who drink to excess often do so in isolation, believing that their problems are unique and self-induced. Women do have individual and personal responsibility for their drinking. However, women's drinking patterns develop within the context of certain social and political realities. These external factors must be recognized and taken into account when designing interventions.

Alcoholism is a women's issue. If you have a drinking problem, get help. The National Council on Alcoholism estimates that 98 percent of the people who stay sober for two years never return to drinking. Staying sober means having a chance for a healthy life on your own terms rather than someone else's. And, in the end, that's what it's all about!

RESOURCES

If you are not now a problem drinker but would like to alter your drinking habits:

How to Control Your Drinking: A Practical Guide to Responsible Drinking by William R. Miller and Ricardo F. Muñoz, 1982.

They also produce various self-help tools to use with this text such as instructions and exercises for calculating one-drink units, individualized blood alcohol concentrations tables, self-monitoring cards, relaxation instructions and audio tapes, and guided imagery tapes for self-hypnosis.

For further information and order forms write to William R. Miller, Ph.D., Department of Psychology, Alcohol Research and Treatment Project, University of New Mexico, Albuquerque, NM 87131.

If you have identified a drinking problem, look under Alcoholism in the white pages of your phone directory. You will discover a number of resources immediately available in your own community such as AA, Al-Anon, and ACOA.

For additional information contact:

National Clearinghouse for Alcohol Information
Box 2345, Rockville, MD 20852.

National Council on Alcoholism
733 Third Avenue, New York, NY 10017.

Alcoholic Anonymous World Services
468 Park Avenue South, New York, NY 10016 (or check your local phone directory).

Women for Sobriety, Inc.
P.O. Box 618, Quakertown, PA 18951.

Al-Anon Family Group Headquarters
P.O. Box 862, Midtown Station, New York, NY 10018.

National Association for Children of Alcoholics
31706 Coast Highway 201, South Laguna, CA 92677, (714) 499-3044. Toll-free number for books: (800) 321-7912; ACA independent groups: (213) 651-1710.

SUGGESTED READING

If you want to do further reading on women and alcohol:

Chaney L. Allen, *I'm Black and I'm Sober* (Minneapolis: CompCare, 1978).

Nancy L. Hall, *A True Story of a Drunken Mother* (Houston: Daughter, Inc., 1974).

Brigid McConville, *Women Under the Influence: Alcohol and Its Impact* (New York: Schocken Books, 1985).

Janice Keeler Phelps and Alan E. Nourse, *The Hidden Addiction and How to Get Free* (Boston: Little, Brown, 1986).

Marian Sandmaier, *The Invisible Alcoholics: Women and Alcohol Abuse in America* (New York: McGraw-Hill, 1980).

Jean Swallow, *Out from Under: Sober Dykes and Our Friends* (San Francisco: Spinster's Ink, 1983).

Geraldine Youcha, *Women and Alcohol: A Dangerous Pleasure* (New York: Crown, 1986).

If you want to read more about women as adult children of alcoholics or about co-dependency:

Melody Beattie, *Codependent No More: How to Stop Controlling Others and Start Caring for Yourself* (New York: Harper/Hazelden, 1987).

Claudia Black, *It Will Never Happen To Me!* (Denver: M.A.C., 1981).

Judith S. Seixas and Geraldine Youcha, *Children of Alcoholism: A Survivors Manual* (New York: Harper & Row, 1985).

Sharon Wegscheider-Cruse, *Another Chance: Hope and Health for the Alcoholic Family* (Palo Alto, Calif.: Science and Behavior Books, 1981).

Charles Whitfield, *Healing the Child Within* (Pompano Beach, Fla.: Health Communications, 1987).

Janet Geringer Woititz, *Adult Children of Alcoholics* (Pompano Beach, Fla.: Health Communications, 1983).

NOTES

1. Nan Robertson, "The Changing World of Alcoholics Anonymous," *The New York Times Magazine,* February 21, 1988.

2. "It is a strange fact," said the *British Journal on Alcohol and Alcoholism*, "that although women constitute at least half of the population, most of the information that we have about alcoholism is related to men and male rodents." Office of Health Economics, "Alcohol: Reducing the Harm," *British Journal on Alcohol and Alcoholism,* April 1981.

3. Between 1939 and 1978, the percentage of women who drank increased from 45 percent to 66 percent. The statistics are even more startling among students. A 1975 study of thirty-four New England colleges indicated that 95 percent of female students were drinkers, and in a 1983 survey, 31 percent of senior girls admitted that they had consumed five or more drinks at least once in the preceding two weeks.

Vasanti Burtle, "Developmental/Learning Correlates of Alcoholism in Women," in *Women Who Drink: Alcoholic Experience and Psychotherapy,* ed. Vasanti Burtle (Springfield, Ill.: Charles C. Thomas, 1979); K. Thompson and R. Wilsnack, "Drinking Problems Among Female Adolescents: Patterns and Influences," in *Alcohol Problems in Women,* ed. S. Wilsnack and L. Beckman (New York: Guilford Press, 1984); and Johnson et al., *Use of Licit and Illicit Drugs by American High School Student, 1975–84* (University of Michigan Institute for Social Research, 1985).

4. W. B. Clark et al., "Alcohol Use and Alcohol Problems among U.S. Adults," in *Working Draft* (Berkeley, Calif.: University of California School of Public Health, 1981).

5. In a survey of college students, 70 percent of the males indicated that they bought their own alcohol while only 11 percent of the females purchased their own. Eighty-nine percent of the women drank alcohol bought for them by their male companions. Marian Sandmaier, *The Invisible Alcoholics: Women and Alcohol Abuse in America* (New York: McGraw-Hill, 1980), p. 165.

6. History demonstrates that changes in the law that affect the price and availability of alcohol can alter social opinions about drinking. This has a direct impact upon drinking habits in either direction. Our consumption of alcohol doubled between 1960 and 1985 as there was a real decrease in the price of alcohol products, a lessening of controls on the distribution and purchase of alcohol, and a relative increase in the standard of living at least through the 1960s and 1970s. In earlier eras when money was needed for military development (such as England in 1915–16), strong licensing and other controls kept alcohol expensive and more difficult to obtain. Alcohol-related illness and deaths remain strikingly low. "Alcohol, Reducing the Harm" (London: Office of Health Economics, April 1981).

7. Between 1958 and 1978, the number of women in the work force has increased from 32 percent to 42 percent. Even though women still only make 73 percent as much as men for equivalent work and even though many women work part-time or at low-paying jobs, wages for the average woman did triple between 1972 and 1977. For some women the increase has been even greater.

8. Geraldine Youcha, ed., *Women and Alcohol: A Dangerous Pleasure* (New York: Crown, 1986), p. 109.

9. "Alcoholism and the Family," *Newsweek,* January 18, 1988.

10. Here are some samples of the definitions offered by various authorities:
An alcoholic person is "one who is unable consistently to choose whether he should drink or not, and who, if he drinks is unable consistently to choose whether he should stop or not." Mark Keller, *The Invisible Alcoholics: Women and Alcohol Abuse in America* (New York: McGraw-Hill, 1980), p. 248.
The World Health Organization defines alcoholics as "those excessive drinkers

whose dependence upon alcohol has attained such a degree that it shows a noticeable mental disturbance or an interference with their bodily and mental health, their inter-personal relations, and their smooth social and economic functioning; or who show the prodromal [warning] signs of such development." Youcha, *Women and Alcohol*, p. 84.

"An alcoholic is someone whose drinking causes a continuing problem in any de-partment of his or her life." Marty Mann, founder, National Council of Alcoholism, quoted in Youcha, *Women and Alcohol*, p. 84.

"In essence, any individual who relies on alcohol to meet the ordinary demands of living and continues to drink after alcohol has caused [her] marital or occupational difficulty is an alcoholic, whether [she] drinks only in the evening, has never taken a drink when alone, or has not touched anything but beer for five years." J. A. Smith, psychiatrist, quoted in Youcha, *Women and Alcohol*, p. 85.

11. Our knowledge about women and alcohol is based primarily on work with Cauca-sian women. We know much less about black, Hispanic, American Indian, and Asian women. There has been little research directed toward their problems and few treat-ment programs explicitly designed to incorporate their cultural backgrounds. An insen-sitivity to their customs and language adds to the psychological toll of living on the margins of society. Some of the information we do have is:

- Black women are half as likely as white women to drink at all. However, if black women do drink, they are almost twice as likely as white women to have a drink-ing problem and six times as likely as white women to develop cirrhosis. J. Lelan, "Alcohol Use and Abuse in Ethnic Minority Women," in *Alcohol Problems in Women* (New York: The Guilford Press, 1984), p. 126.
- The rates of alcoholism in women versus men are higher for black women than for white women. For black women, the female to male ratio is 2:3; for white women, it ranges between 1:4 and 1:5. (*Developing a National Agenda to Address Women's Mental Health Needs* (Washington, D.C.: American Psychological As-sociation, 1985), p. 23.
- Hispanic women are more likely to abstain from drinking than either black or white women. The cultural influences that discourage alcohol use among Hispanic women are reduced as these women become more incorporated into "main-stream" American culture. A. M. Alcocer, "Alcohol Use and Abuse Among the Hispanic American Population," in *Alcohol and Health Monograph* no. 4, DHHS Pub. No. (ADM) 82-1193 (Washington, D.C.: GPO, 1982), pp. 361–82. Among those who do drink, 8 percent drink heavily. Paula Johnson, *Sex Differ-ences in Drinking Practices* (Report to National Institute of Alcohol Abuse and Alcoholism, U.S. Department of Health, Education and Welfare, April 1978), p. 15.
- Alcohol problems among American Indian women appear to be quite serious even though they are rarely mentioned in reports about Native Americans. For exam-ple, between the ages of fifteen and thirty-four, American Indian women die of cirrhosis at a rate thirty-six times the rate of white women. Lelan, "Alcohol Use and Abuse in Ethnic Minority Women," p. 126.
- Asian women do not appear to be included in surveys of alcohol consumption. As

a consequence, we have virtually no information about their experiences with alcohol. Sandmaier, *The Invisible Alcoholics,* p. 146.

12. This widely accepted psychoanalytically based hypothesis was published in 1960 by William and Joan McCord, authors of *The Origins of Alcoholism* (Stanford: Stanford University Press, 1960).

13. D. C. McClelland, W. N. Davis, R. Kalin, and E. Warner, *The Drinking Man* (New York: The Free Press, 1972).

14. *Developing a National Agenda to Address Women's Mental Health Needs* (Washington, D.C.: American Psychological Association, 1985), p. 23.

15. Johnson, *Sex Differences in Drinking Practices,* p. 10.

16. Sharon Wilsnack, "Sex Role Identity in Female Alcoholism," *Journal of Abnormal Psychology* 82 (1973): 253–61. Sharon Wilsnack, "The Impact of Sex Roles on Women's Alcohol Use and Abuse," in *Alcoholism Problems in Women and Children,* ed. Milton Greenblatt and Marc Schuckit (New York: Grune and Stratton, 1976).

17. Sharon Wilsnack, "Drinking, Sexuality and Sexual Dysfunction in Women," in *Alcohol Problems in Women* (New York: The Guilford Press, 1984), p. 33.

18. Max Glatt, *Alcoholism* (Baltimore: Hodder & Stoughton, 1982).

19. Elizabeth Morrissey and Marc Schuckit, "Stressful Life Events and Alcoholism in Women Seen in a Detoxification Center," in Geraldine Youcha, *Women and Alcohol, Dangerous Pleasure* (New York: Crown, 1986) p. 100.

20. Dee Mosbacher, "Lesbian Alcohol and Substance Abuse," *Psychiatric Annals* 18 no. 1 (January 1988): 47–50.

21. Jean Kinney and Gwen Leaton, *Loosening the Grip* (St. Louis: C. V. Mosby, 1978).

22. Brigid McConville, *Women Under the Influence: Alcohol and Its Impact* (New York: Schocken Books, 1985), p. 114.

23. McConville, *Women Under the Influence,* p. 114.

24. McConville, *Women Under the Influence,* p. 5.

25. S. Hill, "Vulnerability to the Biomedical Consequences of Alcoholism and Alcohol-Related Problems," *Alcohol Problems in Women* (New York: The Guilford Press, 1984), p. 126.

26. On average, a woman develops cirrhosis after only thirteen years of excessive drinking, while a man averages twenty-two years. McConville, *Women Under the Influence*, p. 90.

27. B. M. Jones and M. Jones, "Women and Alcohol: Intoxication, Metabolism and the Menstrual Cycle," in *Alcoholism Problems in Women and Children*, ed. M. Greenblatt and M. A. Schuckit (New York: Grune and Stratton, 1976).

28. A. Schatzkin et al., "Alcohol Consumption and Breast Cancer in the Epidemiologic Follow-up Study of the First National Health and Nutrition Examination Survey," *New England Journal of Medicine* 316 (1987): 1169–73 and W. C. Willet et al., "Moderate Alcohol Consumption and Risk of Breast Cancer," *New England Journal of Medicine* 316 (1987): 1174–80.

29. Fetal alcohol syndrome was named by Drs. Kenneth L. Jones and David W. Smith in 1973 (J. W. Hanson, K. L. Jones and D. W. Smith, "Fetal Alcohol Syndrome, Experience with 41 Patients," *Journal of the American Medical Association* 235 (1976): 1458–60), although observations about this phenomenon were made as early as 1736.

30. Dr. David Van Theil of the University of Pittsburgh School of Medicine has raised concerns about whether men with low fertility should drink if they want to father a child. Testosterone is reduced in men who drink for even a short period of time, and alcoholism has resulted in impotence and sterility. Heavy drinking can reduce the production of sperm and result in the production of abnormal sperm. However, we have not studied what contribution this makes to fetal alcohol syndrome. Without this information, there is a tendency for the mother to be assigned and to carry all the guilt if development is not wholly normal. It seems only common sense that both parents ought to be well-nourished and free from toxins if they are to provide the best early start for their child.

31. Autopsy reports have shown that the bone densities of alcoholic women under forty-five resemble the bone densities of nonalcoholic women over age seventy. P. D. Saville, "Alcoholism-Related Skeletal Disorder," *Annals of the New York Academy of Sciences* 252 (1975): 287.

32. Sadja Greenwood, "Alcohol: A Special Problem for Women," *Medical Self-Care*, March/April 1988, p. 16.

33. These descriptive stages were recommended by the National Council on Alcoholism in "What Everyone Should Know About Alcohol," Scriptographic Publications, 1981.

34. L. Van Egeren, "Psychological Aspects of Alcoholism," *Psychiatry Hand-Out* (1973): 8.

35. "Study links women's social drinking with sober-state mood disturbance," *Medical World News*, May 28, 1984, p. 70.

36. In a 1983 AA survey, 40 percent of the women reported addiction to another prescribed or illicit drug. The number increased to 64 percent for women age thirty and younger. General Services Branch of A.A., Inc., 1983 membership survey.

37. *Developing a National Agenda to Address Women's Mental Health Needs*, p. 24.

38. Many common drugs result in an increased depressant effect when taken with alcohol. The symptoms can range from drowsiness to loss of coordination to coma and death. Examples are analgesics (painkillers like aspirin), antihistamines (over-the-counter and prescribed drugs for allergies and cold symptoms), sedatives and tranquilizers (like Valium, Librium, Xanax, and others), hypnotics (sleeping pills like Dalmane and Halcion), and anticonvulsants for epilepsy (like barbiturates and Phenytoin). McConville, *Women Under the Influence*, p. 92.

39. "Specifically the person who tends to succeed at controlled drinking generally:
- has had enough problems with drinking to be concerned about alcoholism, but alcohol has not yet caused *major* life crises such as loss of family or job,
- considers herself to be a problem drinker but not an alcoholic, although she may worry that alcoholism will develop,
- does not have close blood relatives who are alcoholics,
- has had problems related to drinking for less than ten years, and
- has not been physically addicted to alcohol (that is, can go for a week or two without taking alcohol or tranquilizers and not have unpleasant physical symptoms or 'withdrawal.')"

From William R. Miller and Ricardo F. Muñoz, *How to Control Your Drinking: A Practical Guide to Responsible Drinking* (Albuquerque: University of New Mexico Press, 1982).

40. Van Egeren, "Psychological Aspects of Alcoholism," *Psychiatry Hand-Out*, pp. 5–7. These phases have been developed based primarily on the study of male alcoholics. Consequently, they may not be fully applicable to women. However, I have been unable to locate equivalent published long-term studies of female alcoholics.

41. Controlled drinking as a goal ought not to be considered if any of the following is true:
- if you have liver disease, a stomach ulcer, or any other disease of the gastrointestinal system that will be made worse by drinking,
- if you have a type of heart disease that is made worse by drinking,
- if you have had any physical condition in which your health and well-being would be threatened by even moderate drinking,
- if you are pregnant or trying to become pregnant,
- if you lose control of your behavior with even moderate amounts of alcohol,
- if you are or ever have been addicted to alcohol,
- if you are taking tranquilizers, sedatives, sleeping pills, antidepressants, or any other drug or medication that is dangerous when combined with alcohol, or,

- if you are currently abstaining successfully.

Miller and Muñoz, *How to Control Your Drinking,* p. xix.

42. Robertson, "The Changing World of Alcoholics Anonymous," p. 42.

43. Melody Beattie, *Codependent No More* (New York: Harper and Row, 1987), p. 189.

44. "Alcohol and the Family," p. 62.

45. It is now clear that a great number of adults behave in dysfunctional ways as a result of adaptive strategies that allowed them to survive growing up in troubled families. However, these strategies are now a handicap and perpetuate behaviors that are no longer necessary or healthy as adults. I strongly advise that people who grew up in families where there was any form of alcoholism, whether subtle or severe, investigate resources available for adult children of alcoholics.

46. Of children who grew up in alcoholic families, one in four becomes an alcoholic as compared to one in ten out of the general population. "Alcohol and the Family," p. 63.

47. Much has been written lately about the phenomenon of co-dependence, the dysfunctional behavior of people who grew up with and/or associate in adult life with alcoholics. While co-dependent behavior does not cause or facilitate alcoholism in others, it does interfere with recognizing the alcoholic's illness and initiating appropriate interventions.

48. Mary Ann Forney and Paul D. Forney, "Studies Reveal Alcohol and Substance Abuse by Med Students," *The Psychiatric Times,* May 1988, pp. 43–44.

49. "Alcoholism and Alcohol-Related Problems among Women" (Washington, D.C.: National Council on Alcoholism, 1985).

50. Vernelle Fox, M.D., former medical director of the Georgian Clinic for the treatment of alcoholic patients and chief physician in the Alcoholism Service at Long Beach General Hospital, initiated a treatment program for women in the late 1950s. A meticulous research protocol determined that much of the dropping out by women patients was due to environmental conditions. Women were trying to get help in a program designed and primarily staffed by men. Many of the female patients experienced a level of sexism and outright harassment by male staff and residents, which led them, understandably, to leave the program. Once a segregated treatment program for women was established and supervised, the hospital's success rate with women became greater than that with men. Vernelle Fox, "Clinical Experiences in Working with Women with Alcoholism," in *Women Who Drink,* ed. Vasanti Burtle (Springfield, Ill.: Charles C. Thomas Publishers, 1979), pp. 119–26.

51. Sometimes programs may appear to be woman-oriented but the power may still reside with men. For example, in my own community there is an inpatient facility that specializes in the treatment of women. There are many women on the staff at the lower rungs of the hierarchy, but the medical director is a man. When asked why this is the case, concern was expressed that people would shy away from a facility that had only women's names on the letterhead. Odd rationale, I thought. I doubt that these administrators would assume that people would shy away from a facility if there were only men's names on the letterhead.

52. Indeed, the health-care system is a microcosm of the larger society. Behavior and attitudes commonly held in society at large are also found among health-care providers. My premise throughout this book is that sexism accounts for a substantial component of the causes of women's psychological distress. Sexism also exists within the medical community. When damage is caused to an individual undergoing medical care by the treatment itself, it is called iatrogenic damage. The iatrogenic effects of sexism in the health-care system are a major obstacle to recovery for many women.

53. E. S. Gomberg, "Alcoholism in Women," ed. B. Kissin and H. Begleiter in *The Biology of Alcoholism,* vol. 4 (New York: Plenum, 1976).

54. One treatment program discovered that the percentage of women who completed the program increased from 35 to 59 percent when a female therapist ran the group. It dropped to 38 percent when a man resumed responsibility.

55. Youcha, *Women and Alcohol,* p. 188.

56. Perhaps the government and the insurance industry could develop a formula for the cost-benefit ratio of generating *revenue* in the government, alcohol industry, medical profession, and funeral industry by encouraging drinking versus the expense of treating the resultant damage to emotional and physical health.

57. According to *Impact,* a liquor-industry newsletter, women will spend $30 billion on alcoholic beverages in 1994, compared with $20 billion in 1984. "Betty Briefcase Buys More Bottles," *Advertising Age,* September 12, 1985.

58. Grass-root organizations such as Mothers Against Drunk Driving (MADD) have had a significant impact on changing laws related to drinking and driving, but much still needs to be done.

59. L. Beckman and H. Amaro, "Patterns of Women's Use of Alcohol Treatment Agencies," in *Alcohol Problems in Women,* ed. S. Wilsnack and L. Beckman (New York: Guilford Press, 1984).

11 | **B**ody Image and Eating Disorders

It is extremely difficult for women to accept and love their bodies just as they are. Women are trained to measure themselves against the culture's standard of female beauty: young, white, blond, and thin. Since only a few women look this way naturally, most are never quite content with how they look.

Body Anxiety

While women are hardly the victims of a purposeful conspiracy, there is no question that they are bombarded daily by images of how they "should" look. Advertising sells the ideal American woman. These images—in magazines and newspapers, on television and on billboards—function as women's mirrors, yet they rarely reflect the genuine diversity in their size and shape. The promotion of an unrealistic, and often unobtainable, standard causes many women to feel anxious. To reduce their anxiety, they turn to diets and beauty aids.

Women are constantly comparing themselves to one another, to the cultural standard, and, perhaps most repeatedly, to their fantasy of themselves ten pounds lighter. In the pursuit of "beauty," they subject themselves to a vast array of questionable practices. Cosmetics, hair dyes, and vaginal deodorants often contain ingredients to which many women develop allergies. Fashionable shoes distort the natural shape of the foot and hamper freedom of movement. Tanning salons increase the risk of skin cancer. Low-calorie diets deprive women of much-needed nutrients. Procedures like intestinal bypass, collagen injections, face-lifts, liposuction, and body sculpting expose women to the dangers of unnecessary surgery. Yet all of these are marketed to women with one unmistakable message in mind: your body is not OK as it is. Is it any wonder that so many women feel negatively about their physical selves?

Fear of Fat

For most women, fear of fat is a constant preoccupation. This obsession with slimness is a subtle but powerful form of sexism that sets women in a perpetual struggle with their natural bodies. As part of this struggle, many women are permanently—or for long stretches—on a diet.

The recommended dietary allowance (RDA) for a woman is 2,000 calories per day with a range from 1,600 to 2,400, depending on her size. While the common reducing diet recommends a range of 1,200–1,700 calories per day, many women actually consume less than 1,000 calories per day in order to maximize weight loss. The World Health Organization defines starvation as consuming less than 1,000 calories per day. Thus, when dieting, many women place themselves in a state of semistarvation.

The human body reacts one way to starvation—whether it is caused by poverty or self-will. It becomes more efficient. If it is receiving fewer calories than it needs to sustain itself, it adapts and gets by on less. As a general rule, one pound of body fat equals 3,500 calories. But for each month of dieting, the body becomes increasingly efficient. With time, a woman may be eating the same low number of calories but finds that she is losing less and less weight. This plateau is an indication that her body has adapted to a reduced caloric intake. It has learned how to get by on less.[1]

When a woman stops starving herself, her efficient body continues to make the most of every calorie it receives. It will most likely replace or exceed the lost weight—and most of the replaced weight will be in the form of fat. Within the next two to five years, 94–99 percent of dieters will regain all the weight they had lost. Ninety percent will regain more than they lost because their bodies have become so efficient.

Regaining this weight is a physiological adaptation, not a personal failure. Women's bodies are designed to survive under adverse conditions. They do not know that the cultural standard for female attractiveness has changed. They just know that they are being asked to get by on 1,200 calories a day rather than their usual 2,000. They are doing their best to make do while women play "the thin game."

The Thin Game

Whether because of heredity or learned eating patterns, a woman's natural body usually resembles those of her relatives. Consequently, women come in many different shapes and sizes. Yet the image of the ideal woman is thin.

Since few women fit this ideal naturally, many of them play the "thin game":

- The average adult female nonathlete is 23–24 percent fat, while the average male nonathlete is 15–16 percent fat.
- During a given year, 45 percent of all households have someone dieting.
- 76 percent of women are dieting for cosmetic rather than health reasons.
- 80 percent of men are dieting for health reasons.
- Nineteen out of twenty American women think they are fatter than they really are—even when they are at a normal weight.
- The average American woman goes on 2.2 diets a year.
- They are most unhappy with the shape of their buttocks, thighs, stomachs, and breasts—the parts of their bodies most likely to accumulate fat.
- They spend about thirty dollars per pound lost on diet supplements, weight-loss programs, books, and other strategies to lose weight.
- 56 percent of women ages twenty-five to fifty-four are dieting.
- 75 percent of college women are dieting.
- 25 percent of all girls admit to having been on a diet since age thirteen or earlier.
- It is estimated that 13 percent of American teenagers may be practicing some form of binge-purge behavior.
- One in a hundred teens may suffer from anorexia. More and more women over thirty now suffer from bulimia or anorexia.
- The average adult gains about one pound of fat per year after age twenty-five. It is not uncommon to have gained fifteen pounds of fat by age thirty-five and twenty-two pounds by age forty.
- We often predict who will win the Miss America beauty pageant. The thinnest woman usually wins!

In a culture that values thinness in women so highly, many who are not naturally thin long to achieve this coveted state. Dieting, or self-starvation, becomes a logical course of action. After achieving some approximation of their goal through dieting, these women misinterpret the cause of the weight rebound that usually occurs shortly thereafter. They hold themselves responsible for their body size. Because they are able to change their weight *temporarily* through dieting, they assume that they should be able to change it *permanently*. They view it as a personal failure when they are unable to remain unnaturally slender.

For many women, dieting becomes almost a career. Americans spend over $10 billion a year in the hopes of becoming slimmer. Becoming thin is seen as a solution to life's problems. The dieter imagines that being slender will make her a better and more desirable person. By "improving" herself physically, she will become worthy of other people's respect and affection.

This obsession with weight control—which is clearly a losing proposition—undermines a woman's self-esteem. She does not recognize that the prolonged and stringent dieting required to obtain the American ideal is not a matter of choosing to be thin. It is gambling against very long odds.

The High Cost of Gambling

Freud believed that women were innately narcissistic. What he failed to appreciate was that their preoccupation with their appearance is an inevitable consequence of a society that judges women by their bodies rather than other attributes. Under these conditions, it is easy to see how a woman's self-esteem becomes intimately tied to the way she looks. This link between appearance and self-esteem leads to her obsession with weight.

An enormous number of women are obsessed with their weight. When this preoccupation is transformed into dieting behavior, the average woman places herself on a behavioral continuum with those who suffer from anorexia and bulimia, the most extreme forms of weight obsession.

Body Size and Its Relationship to Health

Obese——Sturdy and Substantial——Regular ——— Slim ——— Skin and Bones

Unhealthy ←——————————— Healthy ————————————→ Unhealthy
overweight   underweight

←——— Bulimia ————————————————→ ←——→ Anorexia ——————→

Anorexia

Anorexia is the most severe form of constant dieting. Women with anorexia, like most American women, are clearly convinced that they are fatter than they really are. Yet by any objective measure, women with anorexia weigh well below normal. They can lose up to 25 percent of their body weight and still deny having an eating problem.

No one knows precisely why anyone suffers with anorexia or why its incidence appears to have increased in recent years. Anorexia occurs in people of every age, gender, skin color, level of intelligence, and income bracket. The causes are undoubtedly complex and probably include cultural, family, biological, peer, and social factors.

A study of conscientious objectors during World War II provided startling evidence that anorexia is unlikely to be caused by psychological disturbances alone.[2] Rather, severe chronic dieting may *cause* psychological disturbances. Subjects were selected from a group of conscientious objectors who underwent a battery of tests confirming their physical and psychological health. In lieu of active military duty, they agreed to go on a supervised long-term semistarvation diet.

During the diet, every man became profoundly disturbed. Each developed starvation symptoms that were remarkably similar to those demonstrated by contemporary women with anorexia. There was an increased preoccupation with recipes, cookbooks, menus, and food-related events. Binge eating occurred in some men. Most demonstrated significant social withdrawal. There were changes in their thinking, including decreased concentration and impaired judgment. Emotional changes included depression, anxiety, irritability, anger, and psychotic episodes. There were also a wide range of physical symptoms. Some symptoms, particularly their preoccupation with food and a vulnerability to mood swings, did not abate even after the study was concluded. Starvation dieting changed the lives of these men forever.

Comparing this data with the experiences of women anorectics in the 1980s prompted one eating-disorder specialist to conclude that some people demonstrate certain symptoms not because they are intrinsically unhealthy or because of cultural expectations, but simply because they are starving themselves.[3]

Most researchers believe that at least one component of the rigid monitoring of food intake by women with anorexia is an attempt to feel some control over their lives. Presumably feeling unable to control other areas of their lives and confused about the boundary between normal and abnormal dieting, women with anorexia misinterpret the body cues that advise them their health is in danger.

Far from never being hungry, as has often been claimed, women with anorexia are constantly hungry. They are simply overriding their hunger and stubbornly refusing to respond appropriately. While this behavior may be adaptive in terms of their life situation, it is maladaptive in terms of their health.

After a period of self-imposed starvation, women with anorexia develop a skeleton-like appearance. They frequently cease to menstruate and exhibit a growth of soft fine hair on their bodies. They may have lowered body temperature (hypothermia), lowered blood pressure, excess water in their body tissues (edema), slowed heartbeat (bradycardia), and disturbances in their sleep patterns. If this self-starvation continues unabated, it can lead to death.

Bulimia

Unlike simple overeating, women who suffer with bulimia go on food binges during which they ingest from one to several thousand calories at a sitting. They then purge themselves of that food by vomiting or using laxatives. Many women continue this activity for ten or fifteen years without anyone knowing. Some binge once or twice a week. Others binge and purge up to forty times a day.

A bulimic's grocery bills can easily add up to seventy dollars a day, but the emotional cost is much higher. Those who secretly binge and purge report feeling guilt, shame, embarrassment, and significant depression. Of those women who come to the attention of health-care professionals, 75 percent have experienced negative physical changes, including kidney problems, tooth-enamel erosion, stomach ulcers, involuntary vomiting from ruptures of the esophageal sphincter, and fatigue.

Women with bulimia, like many "normal" women, are obsessed with food, eating, and weight maintenance. Their actual weight may fluctuate, but they tend to keep it close to average levels. In the past, it was believed that bulimics came from middle- and upper-middle-class families.[4] More recent studies suggest that like anorexia, bulimia knows no socioeconomic, racial, or cultural boundaries.[5] As a group, women with bulimia tend to have fewer day-to-day difficulties than women with anorexia, but they do suffer from low self-esteem compounded by a strong drive toward perfection. When confronted with their behavior, most women with bulimia will admit to having a problem.

Fighting Fat

At the other end of the spectrum are women who are genuinely overweight, although the definition of overweight remains highly subjective. Although still controversial, the Metropolitan Life Insurance Company recently revised its optimum-weight charts up by several pounds based upon research that indicates that the "ideal" body weight for a woman is at least ten pounds higher than previously believed.[6]

Still, many medical practitioners and consumers assume that extra weight is unhealthy. If a woman is obese, or 20 percent over her ideal body weight, her health problems are often attributed to her obesity. Yet research suggests that obesity, in and of itself, may not be the problem. Margaret Mackensie, Ph.D., a cultural anthropologist, studied women in Western Samoa where fat is not considered unattractive or unsexy.[7] She learned that these fat women have no more or different health problems than any other members of the community.

Contrasting this with women in the United States, Mackensie proposes that it is not necessarily fat itself that is unhealthy, but rather the cultural interpretation of that fat. The stress and discrimination that a fat woman experiences in our culture may be a greater contributor to her health problems than her excess weight.

At an earlier time in history, and in some present-day societies, women are proud to be large. Being fat is a sign of prosperity. Just the opposite is true for American women. We are a culture obsessed with appearance, and we have a strong prejudice against large people. Normal-weight children rate obese children as less likable than children with a variety of handicaps, disfigurements, and deformities.[8] Chubby children are regarded by their peers as ugly, stupid, mean, sloppy, lazy, and dishonest and are frequently teased. Adults look at a heavy woman and think "She has such a pretty face. It's too bad that she let herself get that fat."[9]

The social stigma and associated psychological stress experienced by the overweight person is very damaging.[10] Beyond the pain of being treated negatively by others, it engenders a level of self-hatred that constantly undermines a woman's self-esteem.

Fat and Health

We are not suggesting that obesity is necessarily healthful for American women, particularly given the psychological distress it seems to cause. However, even when problems are noted in those women who are more than 50 percent overweight (so-called morbid obesity), researchers often do not correct for the complicating factors of smoking, exercise, and stress. Thus it is incorrect to assume that obesity alone causes their health problems.[11]

Many health problems attributed to being overweight have a less clear-cut relationship to weight than was once assumed. New studies indicate that modest losses of only ten to twenty-five pounds may be enough to counter the major health risks of obesity.[12] Furthermore, it is important to assess all the factors that contribute to health problems in overweight women and to provide the appropriate treatment for these associated risks. Interventions for smoking, stress, joint problems, diabetes, or hypertension should not be postponed until a woman loses weight on the assumption that being overweight is the exclusive source of these problems.

Whatever the reasons, there is evidence that morbid obesity may shorten a woman's life span. What remains unclear is whether the incidence of these health problems, and even the risk of death associated with excessive weight, is higher than the incidence of health problems associated with chronic starvation through dieting.

If a woman and her health-care provider do decide that she should try to reduce her body size for medical reasons, research and experience strongly suggest that, in the long run, dieting alone is not successful. Research has demonstrated that the average fat person does not eat more calories than the average thin person.[13] Indeed, when people are fed much more than they need to maintain their current weight, people of normal weight can eat two to three times their normal intake for three to five months and only increase their weight by 10–12 percent. Fat people gain much more weight on the same number of calories.

Repeated low-calorie dieting may be a major cause of ill health. On a very low-calorie diet—that is, a semistarvation diet—the body does not just burn fat. It also burns protein in the form of lean body tissue or muscle. At extremely low calories, this puts a tremendous strain on the body. The brain does not get enough glucose or sugar to think clearly, the kidneys must handle more nitrogen than usual, which risks kidney damage, and the dieter is very likely to become depressed and irritable. On a total fast, as much as two-thirds of the weight lost is lean body tissue. If or when dieting stops, *the lean tissue lost from muscles is usually replaced with fat.* The lost muscle tissue can only be redeveloped through vigorous exercise.

Whom do we believe: the scientists who say lose weight or ruin your health or the researchers who argue that we may equally ruin our health through dieting? The answer is by no means clear cut. However, given the uncertainty about what causes obesity, the dangers associated with dieting compared to the dangers associated with being overweight, and the apparent inadequacy of dieting in controlling body size and shape, we do have to ask if it is ethical to treat obesity with dieting.

Obviously, because the bodies of fat people use food much more effectively than the bodies of thin people, dieting alone will not "cure" obesity in fat adults. For a fat person to lose weight and to maintain that weight loss by dieting, they must remain in a lifelong state of semistarvation.[14] Obesity, and the health problems attributed to it, may be detrimental to health, but it's a mistake to believe that dieting is a reasonable treatment.

Why Now?

How have contemporary American women become so obsessed with controlling their weight? Current efforts to "make women smaller" may be a backlash against the women's movement. Some theorists have even suggested that the mass semi-starvation of women is the modern equivalent of "foot-binding, lip-stretching, and other forms of female mutilation."[15] Certainly, what was considered sexy in the 1950s would be considered soft, if not plump, today. Marilyn Monroe–like curves are out; Jane Fonda–like muscles are in. The generous bodies of post–World War II movie stars have been replaced, first by the adolescent-boy bodies of women like Twiggy and later by hard-muscled women reminiscent of male weight lifters.

It seems that just as Betty Friedan and other feminists stimulated women to ask whether they wanted to spend the rest of their lives sewing curtains, chauffeuring children, and making fancy Jell-O desserts, the arbitrary "standard" for what constituted an attractive female body changed. But body size and shape are not altered as easily as hemlines. Asking women to adjust, rearrange, and accommodate to a new standard of attractiveness every decade or so ties up energy and time that could go elsewhere.

The fear of fat robs women of self-esteem and pride, keeps them preoccupied with their appearance, and, perhaps most disturbingly, keeps them from taking up "too much space" in the world. It is OK for a man to be big. A man has to actually be fat to suffer from fatness. A woman only has to be a woman. The thinnest woman is no less fat-obsessed than women who are truly heavy.[16] In light of this situation, it becomes very important to understand who decides how women should relate to food and their bodies.

Women and Their Relationship to Food[17]

Americans are simultaneously fat avoidant and cuisine obsessed. We are surrounded by plenty, yet we live in a diet culture. Food has particular significance for women.

Food symbolizes nurturance with women as its providers.[18] Women are usually responsible for purchasing and preparing food for their families. A mother often feeds her child with nourishment generated from her own body. Through these responsibilities, women come to develop a special relationship with food, yet they are denied the robust enjoyment of it themselves. Their task is to provide attractive, well-prepared, and nourishing meals for others while keeping a tight rein on their own consumption lest their bodies balloon out of control.

When women do eat, food takes on multiple meanings. For some women, food is nourishment for unmet emotional needs. Others eat instead of expressing anger. When a woman feels blue, she may indulge in her favorite food, which is usually fattening and therefore "forbidden." More often than not, she immediately begins to feel guilty and resolves to resume her diet. At its worst, her compulsion to diet leads to an eating disorder.

A woman's constant quest to control her desire for food connects with our culture's constant fear of women becoming "too big." A ban on eating prevents women from taking up the physical and psychological space reserved for men. Women with dysfunctional eating habits may be acting out the ultimate stereotype of the female role while covertly rebelling against it. These women demonstrate a resistance to the oppressive culture within which they must operate. Recognizing, if only at an unconscious level, that they are not valued for who they are and what they look like naturally, they rebel—albeit indirectly.[19]

By exercising extreme self-denial while simultaneously repressing anger and conflict, the woman with anorexia is conforming to the cultural ideal. She is pleasant, stoic, and rail-thin while defying family and professional efforts to stop her dangerous game. The woman with bulimia is more directly rebellious. She does not completely deny herself the pleasures of food, but she still avoids the increased weight that actually digesting it would cause. Indeed, there is evidence that college women sometimes binge and purge in groups—in effect, transforming bulimic behavior from a disease to a social activity.

Underneath it all, an overweight or obese woman may actually enjoy being big. She may secretly treasure rebelling against cultural expectations and, at the same time, establishing a solid boundary of self-protection. Men simply do not sexually harass fat women as readily as they do women who meet the cultural standard of beauty.

Figure control may be one of the few forms of control that many women feel able to exercise. Indeed, our culture supports pathological eating in women while simultaneously blaming them for behaviors that go beyond women's and medicine's control.

In fact, body size is never exclusively within a woman's control. We have to challenge the belief that thinness in genetically heavy people can be successfully maintained through individual struggle and achievement. A woman's repeated inability to reduce her body size and to keep it reduced over time results in inappropriate self-blame and contributes to low self-esteem. Women who remain thin without dieting need to recognize that this is in large measure an inherited trait.

If women are truly to enjoy food, it must become one of life's freely experienced sensuous pleasures. By eating well, women take care of themselves on the most basic level. Currently, the cultural taboo against the full enjoyment of food is accepted, albeit ambivalently, by most women. It does not serve a woman's purposes to acquiesce to this expectation unquestioningly or to let food become the major outlet for expressing her feelings. By substituting eating—or not eating—for genuine control of her life, a woman is contributing to her own oppression.

Drawing the Line between Normal and Abnormal Weight

Our culture puts women in the position of trying to control something over which they may actually have very little control. In fact, through dieting alone, women have about as much control over their weight as they do of their height. When women attempt to control their body by dieting, they are assuming that this is a successful strategy for altering body size and shape. Yet there is a limit to how much weight a woman can take off and keep off indefinitely while remaining physically and psychologically healthy.[20] This limit seems to be about 10 percent below her set point.

The set point is the weight a person achieves at free-feeding—eating what she wants, when she wants, while maintaining her usual level of physical activity.[21] This weight might be called a woman's natural body weight. It appears that a woman can maintain her weight within a range around that weight, say ten pounds above or below, without serious negative consequences. But she will only be able to maintain it at an altered level *if she institutes a permanent life-style change.* Sustained changes in a woman's set point are determined not only by the number of calories consumed, but also by her level of physical activity.

The average woman needs to understand that she is genetically programmed to be a certain size and shape. Her height, bone structure, even the shape of her buttocks, breasts, and thighs are determined long before she is born. She cannot make radical changes in any of these features without expensive, painful, and sometimes disappointing, if not dangerous, cosmetic surgery.[22]

In addition, a woman will find that it is difficult to get all the nutrients she needs to stay healthy from a low-calorie diet. Many experts now believe that it may actually be healthier to weigh ten to fifteen pounds above your ideal weight for your height than to compromise your health through erratic dieting.

It is far wiser for women to learn to accept what they cannot change about their bodies and to make the best of how they look naturally. Unhealthy and chronic dieting is not good for women's bodies or their psyches.

What Can Women Do?

It takes an incredibly secure woman to resist the profound cultural pressure to be thin. Until our society becomes more accepting of a wider range of human shapes, women will continue to have conflicts about their weight. While dieting alone does not guarantee a successful long-term change, and surgery is a risky and questionable option, the situation is far from hopeless. If a woman feels that she must work toward controlling or altering the natural size and shape of her body, she can do so in a manner that has a better chance of success than dieting and is less radical than surgery. *She can simply increase her level of physical activity.*

The switch from eating less to exercising more is not an easy one for most women to make. Crash diets seem to bring immediate results. Even if the earliest loss is simply water, the quick results are rewarding and reinforcing. It is harder to recognize that the short-term success is far outweighed by the long-term disadvantages.

Every time a woman goes on an extremely low-calorie diet, she is training her body to handle calories more efficiently. When she stops the diet and the weight returns, she will have a more difficult time losing it the next go-around. Her increasingly efficient body necessitates greater and greater caloric reduction to achieve the same weight loss. Furthermore, if a woman could see inside her body, she would discover that fat is replacing muscle as each diet comes to an end and the weight is regained.[23]

The only way to alter this chain of events is to change the method of weight control. A woman must increase her physical activity rather than, or in addition to, decreasing calories. The exercise approach requires a willingness to defer gratification. Visible results are achieved more slowly, but they are more lasting. With an increase in physical activity, a woman not only loses fat, she also gains healthy muscle. She becomes stronger and trimmer.

Exercise Regularly

Exercise seems to play a crucial role in regulating metabolism.[24] In a Stanford study comparing reducing calories versus increasing physical activity as methods of weight control, exercise won hands down. Group 1 reduced their caloric intake by three hundred calories per day. Group 2 ate as usual but walked or ran ten to twelve miles a week. At the end of one year, the average dieter in group 1 had shed fifteen pounds, twelve of it fat. The average exerciser in group 2 had shed only nine pounds, but all of it was fat. The real benefit, however, came at the end of the second year. The dieters had regained half of the lost weight and the exercisers had kept all of theirs off.[25] Thus regular exercise is both the healthiest and most enduring strategy for managing body shape and size.

Aerobic exercise is the best choice. This endurance activity requires a steady supply of oxygen through the heart and lungs. Each aerobic session should last thirty to sixty minutes. It is not possible to burn a significant number of calories in a shorter period of time. At a minimum, these sessions should be done every other day; ideally, five or six times a week.

A complete workout session that includes an aerobic component has four parts:[26]

1. Warm up—Five to ten minutes of moderate exercise such as walking or jogging slowly in place to help loosen tight muscles.
2. Stretching—Ten minutes of slow, gentle stretches without bouncing or jerking.
3. Aerobic exercise—Twenty to thirty minutes of exercise that gets your heart pumping at 80 percent of its maximum rate—220 beats per minute minus your age.
4. Cool down—Ten minutes of the same exercise at a slower pace, followed by ten minutes of stretching.

While a brisk three-mile walk can burn 200 to 250 calories, many busy women find they have little time for regular exercise. Nevertheless, they can still increase their activity by 50 to 100 percent through simple changes in their daily routine. They can take the stairs rather than the elevator, park their car a half-mile from work or at the outer corner of the shopping-center parking lot, walk or ride a bike when they can, or take their family on a hike rather than to a Saturday-afternoon movie.

For long-term success, plan for a slow, steady loss of fat rather than a rapid but short-lived loss of weight. With exercise, muscle is preserved or even increased, and weight loss is caused by real fat loss, not loss of lean tissue. Exercise also increases the density and quantity of muscle. So while losing fat, your weight may not necessarily change, but your shape will. Once you start a program of increased activity, do not weigh yourself more than once a week. The scale is not a good indicator of fat loss. A better guide is to see how your clothes fit after a few months.

It is essential to recognize that *changing a woman's natural size and shape requires a commitment to a permanent life-style change.* Returning to old sedentary habits after reducing body size will only mean having to start all over again in the future.

Physical activity includes all forms of movement, not just what is conventionally thought of as exercise. Give yourself permission to find the type of activity that is right for you. It needs to be something you like enough to stick with. Personally, I cringe at the notion of group exercise. I cannot bear joining a bunch of sweaty humans jostling their respective anatomies with rock music blaring through a loudspeaker. I like the flexibility of exercising when I want to, not when someone else schedules it.

To design your own program, begin by making a list of all the physical activities you either enjoy, must do, or can do. My own list includes regular active walking, morning stretches, canoeing, kayaking, horseback riding, biking, and hiking. I never—well, rarely—drive when I can walk. My elderly neighbor gets most of her exercise working in her garden, a strenuous year-round activity for this agile ninety-two-year-old San Francisco native. My friend up the block has the most incredible upper-body strength from lifting her two young boys up and down all day.

With a little imagination, it is easy to increase physical activity without spending a lot of money. There is no requirement to join a health club, invest in fancy machinery, or purchase special clothes. However, many of my friends and colleagues swear by this approach, so by all means do these things if you can afford them and if they help keep you motivated.

Exercise can have a profound positive effect on a woman's self-esteem and individual well-being. Almost without exception, women who are regularly active report liking and enjoying their bodies. They may not meet the conventional standard for a beautiful woman, but that does not really seem to matter to them. They enjoy being in their own skin, feeling healthy, capable, and strong. They like their bodies.[27]

Use Your Head

Changing the size and shape of your body is not the only way to cope with conflicts about weight. A critical examination of the external pressures a woman must cope with may allow her to resist rather than succumb to these negative messages.

The way a woman feels about her body has been colored by her own personal and family history. If she was fortunate enough to be raised in a consistently loving family with a good, solid appreciation of every member's physical self, she is likely to feel pretty comfortable with her natural body. Yet outside even the most supportive families, girls and women are encouraged to think about themselves in terms of their looks from early childhood on. The message is that you must look a certain way to be considered attractive.

A real eye-opener is scanning the "women's" magazines while standing in line at the grocery store. Here is the ultimate paradox! Almost every magazine contains something about the latest diet advice and the newest makeup recommendations for the woman and recipes for the sweetest dessert for the man in her life. Women are buying food for themselves and their families while being confronted with directives on how to limit their own food consumption. Once a woman appreciates the frequency with which she is bombarded with messages telling her to control her body, she may be able to more effectively resist them.

Every woman can learn to think of her body in a more positive way. Building self-esteem, developing a sense of control over her life, and receiving support from others—for who she really is and what she looks like naturally—are the key factors in counteracting an obsession with weight.

Pick Friends and Partners Who Accept You

Media images and cultural pressures have less impact if family and friends like us as we are. You couldn't pick your family, but you can pick your friends and lovers. Why bother with any who do not appreciate your natural shape and size?

> Katie, quite a slender young woman, was dating a man who constantly nagged her to become even thinner. He urged her to get more exercise. When he cooked, he always served her smaller portions.
>
> One day he told her that he was haunted by fantasies that she might become fat. Initially, Katie felt hurt, frightened, and depressed. Like many women, she was anxious about whether or not her partner found her body attractive. Her boyfriend's comments continued to disturb her until she shared them with her friend Sandra.
>
> Sandra's response was absolute shock. She herself was twenty pounds over her ideal weight. Katie, Sandra reminded her, was downright skinny by comparison. This reality test allowed Katie to feel irritated with her boyfriend's comments. First of all, given her current slender body and genetic inheritance, becoming fat seemed highly improbable. And so what if she did? Did that mean that he would not like her any more?
>
> Katie began her own set of fantasies. She imagined tripling her weight and in doing so dwarfing her boyfriend. Dressed in long, billowing caftans of rich and elegant colors with heavy and stunning jewelry, she became a woman of considerable substance. The image made her feel quite powerful.
>
> Eventually, Katie realized that her boyfriend's lack of acceptance was a source of constant stress in their relationship, and she decided to stop seeing him. It was only in retrospect that she realized he probably had anorexia. As a marathon runner, his obsession with body size and eating habits had served to disguise his eating disorder. Katie is now seeing a man who is delighted to have her in his life and likes her as she is. He does not want her to make any changes just to please him.

Altering Your Role as Feeder

While some women prepare food because they truly enjoy cooking, others only cook because it is expected of them. It is not essential that only women do the cooking in a family. Whatever your body size or shape, consider the possibility of feeding the family as a shared responsibility. If you are in a primary relationship, think about recruiting your partner to accept some or most of the tasks related to feeding you and your family. You could easily reciprocate by doing other chores instead. If calories are your concern, try something that burns calories—like mowing the yard or waxing the car.

The role of feeder does not automatically come with being female. It is assigned by our culture. You can choose not to cook if you wish—or you can do the cooking only a part of the time. For the most part, I gave up cooking years ago. My mother found it boring. I find it boring. For a number of years now, I have either eaten or lived on yuppie food—interesting, tasty, and freshly prepared individual portions from the local deli. I am an enormously appreciative guest when my friends invite me over to their places for dinner, and it is probably no accident that the man I selected as my partner is a superb cook.

Other Options[28]

- Experiment to find the weight that feels comfortable to you rather than trying to be unnaturally thin.
- Think about becoming more accepting of the increase in weight that often comes as a woman ages.
- Shift your focus away from obsessing about your weight to other interests and goals. Take your mind off food and boost your self-esteem by beginning a new course of study, setting goals for improving your job status, or aiming to improve your primary relationship by doing something new together.
- Beyond economic self-sufficiency, one of the best things a woman can do for herself is to stop accepting the notion that her appearance should or can be defined by someone else. Remind yourself that the thin-is-in social pressure on women is sexist. This may help you rise above it.
- Look critically at ads and articles that deal with women and "beauty." Develop an awareness of how much you are being bombarded by media hype that limits your concept of female beauty. Support companies that offer a varied and realistic image of women. Consider boycotting companies that demean them.
- Clarify which health problems are truly associated with being overweight. For example, diabetes and high blood pressure may be, but many others may not. Learn to distinguish between fact and fiction by continuing to learn about these issues and consulting knowledgeable health-care providers.

- Challenge people who judge, choose, and discard women on the basis of a narrow standard of appearance.
- Talk with friends or form a small group to discuss these issues further.

Fat Liberation

If you are truly overweight and are staying that way (by choice or because of genetics), activists in Fat Liberation offer the following advice on living in a discriminatory world:[29]

- No matter what anyone says to you (or what you fear they might say about you), you have the right to go anywhere and do anything you like: to eat whatever you want in restaurants; to dance; to swim; to play; to enjoy life.
- If someone's rude remarks make you feel uncomfortable, you have the right to feel hurt and may choose to respond angrily. Practice a few good withering glances or comebacks.
- If aisles are too narrow or chairs too small in public places, request that the management make changes. You cannot possibly be their only large customer. If they realize that they are losing business because of their insensitive or discriminatory policies, they may be highly motivated to change.
- Whatever the size of your stomach, thighs, or rear end, stop binding them up. You have the right to be comfortable in your own skin. Buy or make clothes that fit easily. Pleated pants with elastic in the waist are less likely to bind. Tight clothes do not make you look thinner. They do make it harder to feel comfortable.
- Take up all of the space your body occupies. Do not try to look smaller. Be big and proud.

Mission Impossible

If, in spite of all the above, you still decide to diet, select a program that emphasizes exercise and healthy eating patterns, not one that requires semistarvation. Do not let fad diets fool you. If they sound too good to be true, they are.[30]

The New Our Bodies, Ourselves offers the following advice:[31]

1. Become much more physically active. This may be the single most important change you can make in your life.
2. Eat a wide variety of healthy foods rather than junk foods. Make every bit count nutritionally.[32]
3. You are more likely to be successful if you lose weight slowly and if you set your goal within twenty pounds of your present weight. Do not restrict your calorie intake more than 500 calories a day under your usual

level. It is virtually impossible to get your major nutrients, let alone trace elements, on fewer than 1,200 calories.

4. There are no magic pills to help you lose weight. Over-the-counter weight-loss pills often contain ingredients similar to amphetamines or speed that can cause agitation, dizziness, high blood pressure, even psychosis.

5. A food diary of what you eat, when you eat it, and why you eat it can help clarify when you eat because you are hungry and when you eat for other reasons. This information is helpful if you want to change undesirable habits.

6. Trust your body signals. Eat when you begin to get hungry rather than waiting until you are starved. If you feel ill, you may have a medical problem that needs treatment. See a doctor.

7. Body water will cause your weight to fluctuate daily. Do not weigh yourself more than once every one or two weeks.

8. Join a group to discuss dieting, feelings about your body, and social pressure to be thin.

Most importantly, "Get it right the first time . . . Don't start a diet unless your motivation is high and you adopt a good program of life-style changes that promote permanent weight loss."[33]

On Going Along with Cultural Norms

Some women go along with cultural expectations, like shaving their legs or using makeup, because not doing so would interfere with their lives. If I stopped shaving my legs, my male colleagues at the hospital might spend more time thinking about them than about the dialogues I need to have with them. I do not want them to be distracted. Other women appear to adhere to the cultural standards of beauty but are actually choosing to do what pleases them. If beautiful colors and elegant fabrics make a woman feel attractive, she has every right to enjoy the pleasure they bring her. Some women do not realize that they have unknowingly internalized the cultural expectations of femininity.[34]

If you suspect that this may be the case for you, step back and reflect on the forces that have shaped your thoughts and feelings about your physical appearance. Try to identify honestly what you really think and feel rather than what you have been trained to think and feel. Reconsider or reconfirm your choices from this vantage point.

There is nothing wrong with wanting to look and feel good. Every woman has the right to make her own decisions about what feels most comfortable, attractive, and fits best with her life-style.

Conclusions

A recent British study of a group of college women chosen at random found that only 2.5 percent were actually overweight (20 percent or more above predicted weight for height) but nearly one-third were attempting to control their weight by dieting, vomiting, or using laxatives. In San Francisco, almost 50 percent of a group of 494 elementary-school girls thought they were overweight when only 15 percent really were. Eighty-one percent of the ten-year-olds were dieters![35]

These girls and women "are pursuing the concept of an ideal weight . . . [and] hold similar attitudes to those who have frank eating disorders . . . The finding that such a high proportion of young women who are not overweight are attempting weight control is a cause for concern."[36]

Although most women benefit from keeping their bodies as healthy and strong as possible, there is little benefit in trying to make them unnaturally smaller. We now recognize that it may be possible to be just as healthy as a fat woman than as a thin one. In any case, diets alone do not work as a long-term solution to reducing body size. Given that diets do not work, that they cause shame and grief to both fat and thin women, that they often have dangerous side effects, and that they may be unnecessary to boot, it makes sense for women to carefully reconsider their attitudes about weight.

Who does it serve to have women disliking their own bodies? The diet and beauty industries are big business. It would be wise for women to question externally imposed standards of how their bodies should look and what they should weigh. Women need to rethink their unquestioning acceptance that thin is good and beautiful and fat is bad and ugly. Girls and women need to resist messages that undermine their self-acceptance. Self-acceptance allows a woman to appreciate the body that she has rather than to obsess about the one she does not have.

Women need to learn to accept their normal body size and to resist the image of the ideal thin woman promoted by the media and our culture. They can use physical exercise to support and nurture their bodies. They may decide that they want to change their thoughts and feelings about their bodies rather than actually change their bodies.

When all is said and done, why should women let any one else decide how they should look? Instead, women can concentrate on loving themselves and one another as they are by deliberately countering the view that only thin, white, blond, young women are lovable and valuable. Once we achieve a deeply self-loving attitude toward our bodies, we can throw away our diets and have much more energy for other purposes. We can take pleasure in eating good, nourishing food, we can enjoy our ability to be physically active in whatever form we choose, and we can treasure women's bodies whatever their size or shape.

Self-care Exercises

Questions to Ask Yourself

- Who in your life thought or thinks your body is terrific?
- Who in your life thought or thinks your body needs changing?
- When did you first start to become self-conscious about the size and shape of your body?
- What or who contributed to your thinking about it as often as you do?
- On average, how much time do you spend concerned with this issue (in terms of days/weeks/months/years)?
- What would be your ideal body?
- What would you have to do to achieve it, if you even can?
- Is it worth it?
- What else could you do with that time?
- Why do you allow our culture to ridicule you and control your size?
- What are the consequences of this continuous emotional unhappiness?

An Exercise to Try[37]

Almost every woman judges some part of her body, feeling that it is not quite right. Ashamed of it, she tries to hide it from view, especially from lovers. See if you can begin to transform these feelings.

Imagine yourself naked in front of a mirror. Turn around slowly. Do you like what you see? Try saying something appreciative to the part of yourself that you usually want to hide. If you can't say much today, try again another day. Keep working at it. Slowly but surely, a change in feelings will follow a change in thinking.

RESOURCES

American Anorexia and Bulimia Association, Inc.
133 Cedar Lane, Teaneck, NJ 07666.

Boston Women's Health Book Collective
Box 192, Somerville, MA 02144, (617) 924-0271.

1. *Food and Fat*
These bibliographies cover seven topics—agribusiness/hunger, curriculum material, eating problems, nutrition, self-help, vegetarianism, and women. Cost: $10.

2. *Women and Weight: An Information Packet*
A collection of information and articles on women and weight, the hazards of dieting, fat oppression and liberation, eating problems, and women's body image. Cost: $15.

Fat Liberation Publications
P.O. Box 5227, Coralville, IA 52241.

National Association to Aid Fat Americans (NAAFA)
P.O. Box 43, Bellerose, New York 11426, (516) 352-3120.

Overeaters Anonymous World Service Office
2190 190 St., Torrance, CA 90504, (213) 320-7941.

Radiance: A Magazine for Large Women
P.O. Box 31703, Oakland, CA 94604 (415) 482-0680.
Subscriptions: $10/year.

ADDITIONAL READINGS

William Bennett and Joel Gurin, *The Dieter's Dilemma* (New York: Basic Books, 1982). An excellent overview with an emphasis on medical information. Discusses setpoint and the virtual impossibility of losing weight through dieting alone.

Kim Chernin, *The Obsession: Reflections on the Tyranny of Slenderness* (New York: Harper & Row, 1981). An analysis of our culture's obsession with weight, the way it affects women's lives, and the eating disorders that result.

Marcia Germaine Hutchinson, *Transforming Body Image: Learning to Love the Body You Have* (Trumansburg, N.Y.: Crossing Press, 1985). A guide to developing respect for your own body.

Pat Lyons and Debby Burgard, *Great Shape: The First Exercise Guide for Large Women* (New York: Arbor House, 1988). The name says it all.

Marcia Millman, *Such a Pretty Face: Being Fat in America* (New York: Norton, 1980). A sociological view of fat women's lives.

Susie Orbach, *Fat is a Feminist Issue* (New York: Berkley Publishing, 1978). This book has some helpful material about accepting your own body weight, but it has an underlying assumption that to be healthy, you must be slim.

Susie Orbach, *Hunger Strike: The Anorectic's Struggle as a Metaphor for Our Age* (New York: W. W. Norton, 1986). Orbach argues that anorexia is the expression of women's confusion about how much space they may take up in the world.

Nancy Roberts, *Breaking All the Rules: Feeling Good and Looking Great, No Matter What Your Size* (New York: Penguin, 1987). A fat-positive book focused on fashion and related self-esteem issues.

Wendy Sanford, "Body Image," in *The New Our Bodies, Ourselves* (New York: Simon & Schuster, 1984). Short but helpful article with good advice.

Lisa Schoenfielder and Barb Wieser, eds., *Shadow On a Tightrope* (Iowa City, Iowa: Aunt Lute, 1983). Writings by fat women.

NOTES

1. Some ballet dancers have maintained their weight on 800 calories a day in spite of the fact that the Department of Labor lists ballet as the most physically demanding occupation.

2. A. Keys, et al., *The Biology of Human Starvation* (Minneapolis: University of Minnesota Press, 1950).

3. D. M. Gardner et al., "Psychoeducational Principles in the Treatment of Bulimia and Anorexia Nervosa," in *Handbook of Psychotherapy for Anorexia and Bulimia,* ed. D. M. Garner and P. E. Garfinkel (New York: Guilford Press, 1985), pp. 513–72.

4. C. Johnson and D. J. Berndt, "Preliminary Investigation of Bulimia and Life Adjustment," *American Journal of Psychiatry* 6 (1983): 774–77.

5. Melanie Katzman, "Understanding Bulimia: A Multidimensional Perspective," *Psychiatry Newsletter* vol. 5, issue 6 (Summit, N.J.: Fair Oaks Hospital, 1987).

6. 1983 Metropolitan Height and Weight Table for Women. Source of basic data: 1979 Build Study, Society of Actuaries and Association of Life Insurance Medical Directors of America, 1980.

7. M. Mackensie, "A Cultural Study of Weight: American vs. Western Samoa," *Radiance* 3 no. 3 (Summer/Fall 1986): 23–25.

8. S. A. Richardson et al., "Cultural Uniformity in Reaction to Physical Disabilities," *American Sociological Review* 90 (1961): 44–51.

9. Marcia Millman, *Such A Pretty Face: Being Fat in America* (New York: Norton, 1980).

10. O. Wooley, S. Wooley, and S. Dyrenforth, "Obesity and Women: A Neglected Feminist Topic," *Women's Studies Institute Quarterly* 2 (1979): 81–92.

11. To determine if obesity alone is the cause of a woman's health problems, all other potential contributing factors must be eliminated.

12. Jane E. Brody, "Research Lifts Blame from Many of the Obese," *New York Times,* March 24, 1987.

13. S. Wooley, O. Wooley, and S. Dyrenforth, "Theoretical, Practical, and Social Issues in Behavioral Treatments of Obesity," *Journal of Applied Behavioral Analysis* 12 no. 1 (Spring 1979): 5.

14. N. C. Kiefer, "Less Than Meets the Eye," *Nutrition Today,* July/August, 1983, p. 24.

15. Mayer Aldebaran, "Fat Liberation," *The Radical Therapist: Journal of Radical Therapy*, vol. 1, no. 3 (Summer 1973): 3–6.

16. Jean Gornick, "Fat Babble," *San Francisco Focus*, June 1986, pp. 100–107.

17. S. Dyrenforth, S. Wooley, and O. Wooley, "A Woman's Body in a Man's World: A Review of Findings on Body Image and Weight Control," in *A Woman's Conflict: The Special Relationship Between Women and Food*, ed. Jane Rachael Kaplan (Englewood Cliffs, N.J.: Prentice-Hall, 1980).

18. Kim Chernin, *The Obsession: Reflections of the Tyranny of Slenderness* (New York: Harper & Row, 1981).

19. Susie Orbach, *Hunger Strike: The Anorectic's Struggle as a Metaphor for Our Age* (New York: W. W. Norton, 1986).

20. Terence Monmaney, a writer for *Newsweek*, suggests that our understanding of people's ability to lose weight and keep it off is biased by studies with people who have had trouble taking and keeping weight off. He argues that we may know very little about people who have successfully taken and kept weight off and have thus never come to the attention of health-care providers, weight-control programs, or researchers studying body size and shape. "Diet Books with No Sugarcoating," *Newsweek*, February 2, 1987, pp. 76–78. His position would seem to be supported by the research of Columbia University psychologist Stanley Schachter who studied 161 adults and found that 57 percent of the women, dieting on their own, had lost substantial weight and kept it off for an average of ten years. Summarized in G. L. Becker and D. A. Hammock, *Eat Well, Be Well Cookbook* (New York: Fireside, 1986).

21. Richard E. Keesey, "A Set-point Theory of Obesity," in *Handbook of Eating Disorders: Physiology, Psychology, and Treatment of Obesity, Anorexia, and Bulimia*, ed. Kelly D. Brownell and John P. Foreyt (New York: Basic Books, 1986).

22. Robin Maranz Henig, "Body and Mind," *New York Times Magazine*, February 29, 1988, pp. 41–42.

23. In a study of dieting rats, Kelly Brownwell, a psychologist at the University of Pennsylvania, showed that on the first diet it took the rats twenty-one days to lose a specific amount of weight and forty-six days to put it back on with their normal caloric intake. On the next diet cycle, it took forty days to accomplish the same weight loss and the animals gained it all back in only fourteen days! They also gained back proportionately more fat than they had lost. Brody, "Research Lifts Blame from Many of the Obese," p. 19.

24. This is stated tentatively because the research on female metabolism and exercise is extremely limited. Most of the studies linking exercise with increased metabolism have been done with men while, not surprisingly, most studies on weight reduction

have been done with women. One exception is Kenneth Cooper and Mildred Cooper, *New Aerobics for Women* (New York: Bantam Books, 1988).

25. Brody, "Research Lifts Blame From Many of the Obese," p. 19.

26. Recommendations from D. W. Edington, M.D., Director, Fitness Research Center, University of Michigan, as reported in "The At-Home Spa," *Women's Health Advisor* 5 no. 1 (1988).

27. Jan Eigner, "Body Image and Self-esteem," *The Melpomene Report,* Fall 1986, p. 10.

28. Wendy Sanford, "Body Image," in *The New Our Bodies, Ourselves* (New York: Simon & Schuster, 1984), p. 8.

29. Los Angeles Radical Feminist Therapy Collective, *A Fat Women's Problem Solving Group: Radical Change* (Sun Valley, Calif.: Fat Liberation Publications, 1974).

30. David L. Engerbreton, "Don't Let Fad Diets Fool You," *The Walking Magazine,* December 1987/January 1988, pp. 25–31.

31. Esther Rome, "Food," in *The New Our Bodies, Ourselves* (New York: Simon & Schuster, 1984), p. 22.

32. The kind of food eaten does make a difference. Fat seems to beat a direct path to the body's fat stores, but starches must be processed first. This processing reduces the calories to the body by 25 percent. Just switching from a high-fat diet to a diet high in carbohydrates without actually lowering the total number of calories will result in a net loss of calories to the body. Research by Elliot Danforth, University of Vermont, Burlington, quoted in Brody, "Research Lifts Blame From Many of the Obese," p. 19.

33. Quote by Kelly Brownell in Brody, "Research Lifts Blame From Many of the Obese," p. 19.

34. Susan Brownmiller, *Femininity* (New York: Fawcett Columbine, 1984).

35. "Dieting, Just Like Mommy," *Newsweek on Health,* Fall 1987, p. 18.

36. A quote by Dr. Paula H. Salmons as reported in *Family Practice News,* October 15–31, 1987, p. 56.

37. Adapted from Marcia Germaine Hutchinson, *Transforming Body Image: Learning to Love the Body You Have* (Trumansburg, N.Y.: The Crossing Press, 1985).

12 | **A**buse and Violence

Abuse is any act of mistreatment or disrespect. Violence is any act that is likely to cause injury. These disturbing and destructive behaviors can occur anywhere—in our homes, on our streets, among our neighbors and friends, even among our professional acquaintances. No racial, cultural, ethnic, religious, social, or education group is exempt.[1]

The prevailing evidence is that abuse and violence are primarily perpetrated by males against females. Ninety-five percent of all assaults by one member of a couple against the other are committed by men.[2] Men are responsible for ninety-seven percent of all incest.[3] All rapists are male. However, it is in the context of their intimate relationships that women are most frequently the victims of abuse and violence.[4] Twenty-five percent of women have been physically abused by a man with whom they have, or have had, an intimate relationship. More frighteningly, hundreds of husbands kill their wives each year.[5]

Nevertheless, women are not simply the victims of abuse and violence. Some are also perpetrators. Mothers are as likely as fathers to physically abuse their children.[6] Indeed, this is one of the few contexts in which women are known to be as violent as men. Most of these mothers are also being battered by their male partners.[7]

Family Violence

Tragically, family violence is the most common form of violence in the United States.[8] Some type of violence occurs in roughly half the homes in the United

States at least once a year.[9] To the outside observer, some of these families appear highly disorganized, but others seem quite ordinary.[10] So what distinguishes a healthy, nonviolent family from a dysfunctional, violent one?

In the healthy, nonviolent family:

- No single member has a disproportionate share of the power. Individuals do not jeopardize the well-being of others in order to meet their own needs.
- Attachment between family members exceeds or balances competitiveness. Family members enjoy and make sacrifices for one another.
- Parents respond to their children's needs. Adult family members have the ability to nurture each other and their children.
- Most of the time, the family is capable of meeting the needs of its members. When it is unable to, the family will use outside resources.

In dysfunctional and violent families:

- There is an imbalance of power.[11] When the most powerful person does not get his or her way, the response is disproportionate anger and aggression.[12]
- Feelings of reciprocity, care giving, altruism, and emotional attachment are reduced. These are the mechanisms that usually insulate family members from competitive and aggressive feelings.[13]
- There are few effective, healthy strategies for responding to frustration.[14]

The one feature that cuts across all violent families is the misuse of power.[15] The most powerful member insists that his or her needs be met first. This starts a chain reaction. The misuse of power runs through the family: husband to wife, wife to child, older child to younger child, youngest child to family pet. No living creature in the home is left unhurt.

Physical Abuse

Americans learn to glamorize rather than question competitiveness and violence. Cops and robbers, cowboy heroes, and other tough guys fill our movie theaters and TV screens. In our lives, whether in Little League or big business, we place a premium on competitive success and winning. We make it clear that climbing to the top is the goal. We are less clear about the cost of getting there—to others and to ourselves. In our failure to provide clear guidelines about what constitutes acceptable and unacceptable behavior, we open the door for the use of aggression, abuse, and violence. Sadly, this extends to the way we treat our children.

Child Abuse

The weather had turned unusually warm for a spring day. The teacher, Ms. Bethers, noticed that seven-year-old Katie was still wearing the same long-sleeved sweater in the playground that she had been wearing in the air-conditioned classroom. Ms. Bethers called Katie to her side and started to lift her sweater over her head while explaining to the child that it was too hot to wear something so warm. Katie started to cry and tried to tug the sweater back down, but by this time it was well off her arms and Ms. Bethers saw that they were covered with dark, ugly bruises. She kneeled down and hugged the little girl while the story spilled out.

Her mother had been drinking. Katie had been playing after school rather than cleaning the kitchen as her mother expected. When the mother realized that Katie had not done her chores, she grabbed her by the arms in an angry grip and dragged her over to the sink, insisting that she was responsible for the mess. Katie struggled to get away, but her mother would not let her go. She started screaming at Katie and shaking her wildly. Katie was so scared. "Mommy, please stop," she cried. "You're hurting me!" The mother threw the child aside and stormed out of the house. That night, Katie cleaned the kitchen and put herself to bed. The next morning, her arms were black-and-blue. Katie felt embarrassed about the bruises and pulled on an old long-sleeved sweater to hide them from view before she headed off to school.

The teacher held Katie in her arms until the sobbing subsided. Once she had calmed down, Ms. Bethers took her inside and contacted the principal. Together they would file a report with child-protective services. Katie's mother would be contacted by a trained worker who would offer strategies for improving her parenting skills as well as providing protection for Katie.

The story of Cain and Abel reminds us that violence against children dates back to biblical times, but it was not until 1970 that states enacted laws requiring mandatory reporting of any suspected child abuse.[16] Yet even with these laws, children are not completely protected. Teachers do not always notice injuries, kids do not always relate their experiences, and childcare agencies do not always have the resources to follow up in a helpful manner.

Our society still gives tacit and legal approval to the corporal punishment of children. Seventy-seven percent of parents say that slapping or spanking children is a "normal" form of discipline. Three percent of children are threatened with knives or guns, and one in a thousand parents actually use these weapons against their children.[17]

Up to 76 percent of mothers report using some form of violence with their children. These women seem to have more difficulty dealing with the stress of parenting than mothers who do not abuse their children.[18] They are more irritable and less responsive to changes in children's subtle signals. They often find a baby's crying annoying and have difficulty playing with their children even when things are going well.[19]

Certain social factors increase the risk of women behaving abusively toward their children. Mothers receive strong sex-role expectations. Even in contemporary families, mothers are held more accountable than fathers for the care of their children. In many families, mothers try to provide this care even when their own resources are limited or exhausted. Furthermore, children usually interfere more with their mother's personal plans than their father's.

A mother can easily feel overwhelmed by it all unless she is receiving emotional sustenance and practical support from her spouse or another reliable adult. If she has little or no help, her own sense of deprivation can lead to an angry sense of unfairness, which she may take out on her children. This is especially true for single, teenage mothers who are barely out of childhood themselves.

Abusive parents, mothers and fathers alike, seem to be immature and to have a limited capacity for empathy. This may be because they did not receive sufficient warmth and caring from their parents.[20] Whatever the reason, abusive and violent parents are prone to feelings of intense anxiety which explode in outbursts of violent anger and they often demonstrate little remorse for the pain they inflict upon their children.[21] By their behavior, these parents are training their children to use violence.

Sibling to Sibling Abuse

Betty heard a crash from the back bedroom followed by a scream from her youngest child, Sandy. She ran into the room and saw her oldest son, Daniel, just as he was hiding his baseball bat in the closet. Sandy was on the floor covering her head with her arms and sobbing. Betty lifted the younger child and checked for injuries. There was no obvious damage. She put the little girl down and told her to stop her crying while she reprimanded both children for interrupting her. She left the room muttering under her breath, "Kids!" A tiny smile came to her face as she shook her head and returned to household chores.

As a society, we are surprisingly tolerant of sibling violence. While families are reluctant to talk about child abuse or wife beating, they readily acknowledge violence between siblings as a common, indeed almost normal, aspect of family life. Four out of five families report at least one violent act between siblings in a typical year. Girls are only slightly less violent than boys. Eighty-three percent of boys and 74 percent of girls use violence. These children are attempting to resolve conflict through physical force.

Terms like *sibling rivalry* imply that sibling violence is more benign than it may actually be. In any one year, 47 percent of siblings try to get their way by kicking, biting, or punching one another. Sixteen percent resort to beating up a sibling. One percent use a gun or a knife and, in the most extreme cases, sibling violence can be fatal.

Partner Abuse

Women are at the greatest risk of being abused in their most intimate relationships.

> Jennifer came to see me for therapy three months ago. She and her husband, Ben, were having marital trouble. Jennifer wanted to return to school to finish a degree she had put on hold when Ben's company transferred him to the West Coast. Ben wanted her to stay home and have a baby. This evening they had had a particularly heated argument about their future plans and Ben had struck Jennifer across the face.
>
> Jennifer left the house and called me from a public telephone. She was afraid to be alone with Ben. We discussed her options and Jennifer decided to spend the night with a friend. She would call Ben in the morning and tell him that she would not return until he arranged to see a therapist. I gave her the names of two people I knew who worked with men who behaved abusively. She would offer them to her husband, but she knew that the next step was up to him.

While physical violence between adults in intimate relationships must, in all fairness, be called partner abuse, most of these assaults are committed by men.[22] Only a very small percentage of wives abuse their husbands, and their behavior is not equivalent to wife battering.[23] Men exhibit a much higher rate of the most dangerous and injurious forms of physical abuse. They use violence more often, and, because of their greater physical strength, their abuse does more damage. Furthermore, many women who use violence do so in self-defense or in response to blows initiated by their male partner.

The traditional view of the man as head of the household has allowed men to use violence against women as they deemed necessary to keep the women in their place.[24] Furthermore, men have had license to behave violently toward women with little or no risk to themselves.[25] In colonial America, the Rule of Thumb law allowed a man to beat his wife with a stick no larger than the circumference of his thumb.[26] As recently as 1970, town ordinances in some communities still permitted a husband to beat his wife—as long as he did not do it after 10 P.M. or on Sundays.[27] In each year between 1978 and 1982, 2.1 million married, divorced, or separated women were assaulted by their partners. Even today, the most common call received by the police is a request to assist with domestic violence between married or live-in partners.[28]

Prior to the opening of the first emergency shelter for battered women in 1973, there were few viable alternatives for American women living within abusive relationships.[29] In 1976 the National Organization of Women made stopping wife abuse a top priority. Since then, many laws have been rewritten, most major cities have shelters for abused women and their children, and numerous programs have been instituted to prevent or treat wife abuse. However, unlike child abuse or even abuse of the elderly, *we still do not have a mandatory reporting act for the abuse of women.* Most of the violence between cohabitating adults continues to be viewed as a private matter.[30]

Elder Abuse
Efforts are increasing to protect the elderly from the risk of abuse.

> Beatrice, almost eighty-two, was brought to the hospital by her youngest daughter, Martha, with whom Beatrice had been living since she was diagnosed with Alzheimer's three years ago. For the first two years, Martha had been able to handle her mother's needs rather well, but in the last several months her mother had become increasingly paranoid and belligerent. Four days ago she had become convinced that her food was poisoned and had stopped eating. This newest accusation was one of a series she had brought against Martha in recent weeks.
>
> The doctor gave Beatrice a quick physical exam. As usual, Beatrice was strong as an ox. However, Dr. Rabin did notice a cut on her cheek and asked Martha about it. She covered her face with her hands and confessed between sobs that she had slapped her mother yesterday morning in frustration. She felt very badly about her behavior and asked the doctor to help. Mother had become more than she could handle alone. Dr. Rabin comforted the middle-aged woman and reassured her that she would make a referral to the elder-care program at the hospital.

Martha was willing to ask for help, but some people will not confess when they are abusing an elderly dependent. Nor will every elderly victim admit to being abused.

Since the introduction of antibiotics in the early 1940s and the major medical, public health, and nutritional advances of the 1950s, the United States has seen a dramatic increase in its elderly population. Many of these older Americans are coping with the hardships of chronic disease and physical disabilities on low fixed incomes with limited health insurance. As a result, they are often compelled to turn to their middle-aged offspring for assistance. While the majority of families in this sandwich generation take these responsibilities in stride, an estimated 500,000 to 1.5 million find the care of an elderly family member to be a burden that leads to neglect, exploitation, and abuse.[31]

Elder abuse most commonly afflicts those over age seventy-five. Since 80 percent of these people are women and since it is middle-aged, or even elderly, women who are most likely to provide the direct care for even older parents, *elder abuse is predominantly a problem faced by women.*

Many stresses contribute to elder abuse. The caretaker often suffers from a profound loss of privacy, time, and personal space. The financial drain and physical efforts can be enormous. For the dependent elderly adult, there is also a loss of privacy as well as a loss of control over her own life. In addition, she may have recently lost a spouse and numerous friends. Caregivers typically become abusive and violent when they feel that they have no physical, psychological, or financial cushion for themselves. Alcoholism, drug addiction, chronic medical or mental-health problems in the caregiver or the dependent can make the situation even more difficult.

Sexual Abuse

Tragically, sexualized violence against girls and women borders on the common-place.[32] It is estimated that one in five children are molested and up to one in four women in the United States are raped at some time in their lives.[33] Until the women's movement drew our attention to this devastating problem, most victims lived in shame, secrecy, and isolation. Yet even today, it is believed that over 90 percent of sexualized violence never comes to the attention of a social agency.

Incest and the Sexual Abuse of Children

Shirley bolted upright in bed. The clock read 3:07 A.M. It was that nightmare again. She could never see his face. It was the sound of his footsteps coming up the stairs that struck terror in her heart. She knew the pattern. First, the light under the door, then the door opening with a creak. The quiet steps across the bedroom rug past the bed where her younger sister slept. Then the rancid smell of his smoky, drunken breath. "Be still, sweet pea," he whispered as she lay frozen under the covers. He lifted her nightgown and began to touch her thighs. The nightmare was always the same. She woke up just in time to stop his hands. If only she had been able to do that at age seven . . . when the terrible nightmare really began.

Mental-health providers have a long and embarrassing history of denying the prevalence of childhood sexual abuse. In 1896, Freud wrote that the basis of every case of hysteria was childhood sexual assault.[34] One year later, he changed his mind and began to interpret his female patients' reports of sexual abuse as fantasies. Because theories like the Oedipus complex were substituted for the real problem of childhood sexual abuse, thousands of victims over the last one hundred plus years have lived in shame and humiliation.

The Kinsey report published in 1953 offered the first scientific challenge to this aspect of Freudian theory. It revealed that one in four women had had sexual contact with an adult male before she reached the age of twelve.[35] Thirty years later, Diana Russell found that thirty-eight percent of women reported having had childhood sexual contact with an adult male. Sixteen percent of these encounters were with relatives. Almost five percent was father-daughter incest.[36] When the molester was someone outside the child's immediate family, they were usually a more distant relative or some other familiar person rather than a stranger. While the rare case of mother-son and mother-daughter incest has been reported,[37] most incest is perpetrated by men.[38]

Sexual abuse of a child includes not only oral and vaginal penetration but also fondling of the child's sexual organs and encouraging the child to fondle the sexual organs of others. It gradually proceeds to masturbation and oral-genital contact. The abuse often begins when the child is between the ages of six and twelve, although the abuse of much younger children has been widely reported. Vaginal intercourse is not usually attempted until the child reaches puberty. Physical violence is rarely employed since the overwhelming authority of an adult or older child is usually sufficient to gain the child's compliance. For the abuser, sexual contact with children often becomes a compulsion.[39]

The incestuous family is hard to recognize. The family is often outwardly stable, and the father is often a highly respected and involved member of the community. But whatever the socioeconomic status, at home the father is a tyrant who rules with an iron hand. He is usually emotionally isolated from his wife, and the daughter he is abusing is usually isolated from her mother.

These male sexual offenders are exquisitely sensitive to the realities of power. In the presence of a medical or legal professional, they will deny, minimize, or rationalize their abusive behavior while simultaneously appearing pathetic, meek, bewildered, or ingratiating. Faced with this performance, the naive or colluding professional will frequently transform the crime into an event perpetrated equally by the mother. The mother may be seen as denying her husband his so-called legitimate sexual access to her or may even be viewed as dominating a relatively powerless father.[40]

In reality, there is a high rate of serious physical and psychological disability among mothers in incestuous families. Often, these women can barely take care of themselves and their children, let alone dominate their male partners. "Economically dependent, socially isolated, battered, ill or encumbered with the care of many small children, mothers in incestuous families are generally not in a position to consider independent survival, and must therefore preserve their marriage at all costs, even if the cost includes the conscious or unconscious sacrifice of a daughter."[41]

As a rule, incestuous fathers do not take over the parenting tasks that these ill mothers are neglecting. Instead, the responsibility is passed to the daughter from whom the father also expects to receive emotional support and nurturance. The father seems to view his daughter's sexual availability as an extension of the wifely role into which she has been placed. And, contrary to popular belief, most offenders continue to have sex with their wives while behaving incestuously with their daughters. Those who do discontinue sex with their wives do so by choice— not because their wives make themselves unavailable.[42]

Sexual contact between siblings is a less frequently discussed form of incest, but it can be equally damaging. A larger and older sibling can use as much force and coercion against a younger, smaller sibling as a sexually abusive adult. The long-term consequences for the victim of sibling incest can be no less traumatic than that of incest perpetrated by a parent.[43]

Rape

Entering adulthood gives a woman no particular protection against sexual assault.

> Sarah was walking along the lake in the park watching the children play on the paddle-wheel boats that could be rented at the concession stand. A family of ducks crossed in front of her. They seemed to say, This path is ours—not yours. She laughed at their antics while waiting for the last little one to reach the other side. Then she turned off the paved route onto a running path that went through a wooded area. She loved the smell of the earth and the crunch of leaves under her feet.
>
> Suddenly, she was grabbed from behind and thrown to the ground. Something oily and damp was stuffed in her mouth. She struggled, but she could not move. A huge man with a ski mask loomed over her. He ripped her pants down her legs. In terror, she doubled her efforts to get free. He pushed a knife against her throat. She froze as he whispered, "Move . . . make a sound . . . and I'll slit your throat."
>
> She could hear a couple laughing nearby as he thrust himself inside her. It hurt so much that she felt as if she was going to pass out. A minute later, he was gone. She pulled the dirty, stained rag out of her mouth and tried to clean herself off. She walked home numb, humiliated, violated beyond anything she had ever experienced. She told no one. She just wanted to forget it had ever happened. She vowed never to go in the park again.

Rape degrades and humiliates a woman more than any other form of physical assault. Not only is her body handled and used against her will, but "short of being killed, there is no greater insult to the self."[44] Rape can also feel life threatening and, often, it is. Eighty-seven percent of rapists either carry a weapon or threaten their victim with death if she resists.[45]

Forty-four percent of women report at least one attempted rape.[46] Up to one-quarter of these assaults occur in their own homes.[47] Interviews with married women suggest that at least one in seven has been raped by her husband.[48] Among college women, 83 percent report having suffered some attempt at forced sexual contact in a dating situation.[49]

Ninety thousand rapes are reported in the United States each year,[50] but hundreds of thousands more go unreported. Some are perpetrated by strangers, but many are committed by men known and trusted by the women. Date rape and marital rape are particularly confusing—and disturbing—because the woman is victimized by a man who she presumes cares about her.[51] Yet 25 percent of college men say that they would be willing to use force to get sex. Fifty-one percent would be willing to attempt rape if they were sure they could get away with it.[52]

An astonishingly high percentage of rapists seem to think that their victims actually enjoy being assaulted. Research suggests that viewing hard-core pornography that shows women tied up, beaten, tortured, and sometimes murdered may increase the risk of a man behaving in a sexually violent fashion.[53] And no female is off-limits. Girls as young as five months and women as old as ninety-one, women of every racial and ethnic background have been the victims of rape, most frequently by a man of their own skin color. Misguidedly, family, friends, the police, and even other women sometimes blame the victims rather than the rapists for these assaults.

Fear of being raped is a part of every woman's heritage.[54] Forty-four percent of women—as contrasted with only 18 percent of men—report being afraid when they go out alone at night.[55] The men are afraid of being robbed or beaten up. The women are afraid of being raped. As Susan Brownmiller writes, "Man's discovery that his genitalia could serve as a weapon to generate fear must rank as one of [his] most important discoveries . . . from prehistoric times to the present . . . rape has played a critical function. It is nothing more or less than a conscious process of intimidation by which *all men* keep *all women* in a state of fear."[56]

Rape is a crime. Yet the impact on the victim is often minimized or distorted. At one rape trial, the judge viewed gang rape as an understandable reaction to a woman wearing tight jeans. In another case, the same judge declared an adult male rapist the innocent victim of a flirtatious five-year-old girl.[57] One judge indicated that on a scale of 1 to 10, with 10 a serious crime, rape rated no more than a 2.[58] Not surprisingly, women judges do not always agree with their male colleagues and often rule more harshly.[59]

Therapist-Patient Abuse

It is alarming that even entering the care of trained professionals offers women no guarantee of protection from sexual exploitation.

> It had taken Erin years to forgive herself for not leaving sooner. She had trusted Dr. Cleaver so much. It had never occurred to her that he would abandon her so callously. When she first began therapy with him, he had seemed so sensitive and caring. When he suggested that having sex with him during their sessions would help her overcome her inhibitions with her husband, she believed him. Besides, she had grown very fond of him. He seemed so much more capable of intimacy than her husband.
>
> They met twice a week for the next three years. Each session involved sensuous conversations and erotic lovemaking after which she paid his usual fee. Nothing had changed in her relationship with her husband, but that did not seem to matter as much. All her affection was directed toward Dr. Cleaver until one day, without warning, he announced that therapy was over. He would not discuss the reasons but simply said that he could not see her anymore.
>
> Erin was stunned. She was in a daze as Dr. Cleaver ushered her out of his office, warning her not to discuss what had gone on between them with anyone else. If she did, he would deny everything. He would claim that she was crazy— completely out of touch with reality—and that her word could not be trusted.

In a nationwide survey of American psychiatrists, 7 percent of the males and 3 percent of the females acknowledged having sexual contact with their own patients during or within six months of ending therapy.[60] In a similar study of psychologists, slightly less than 1 percent of female psychologists reported having sexual contact with their patients during or within three months of ending therapy, and approximately 8 percent of male psychologists reported engaging in this kind of behavior. Eighty percent of these therapists reported having sexual relationships with more than one patient.[61]

The majority of these sexually abusive therapists acknowledge that they have sex with their patients for their own gratification and they deceive themselves into believing that their patients feel the same. In fact, an estimated 90 percent of patients suffered ill effects as a result of their mistreatment. Of this group, 11 percent require hospitalization and 1 percent attempt suicide.[62]

Although the codes of ethics of both the American Psychiatric Association and the American Psychological Association explicitly prohibit sexual contact between therapist and patient, victims often find little comes of reporting abuses to other therapists, ethics committees, and state licensing boards unless they are willing to bring legal charges.[63] Since the victims realize that defending attorneys will try to hold them responsible for their mistreatment, or will at the very least portray them as consenting adults, victims are understandably reluctant to bring charges. As a result, just as in incest and rape, few of these violations ever come to public attention. The consequences for most of the professionals who break these ethical codes are relatively minor and infrequent, while their victims feel deeply ashamed, humiliated, and abused.

Who Abuses and Why?

Physical abuse is most likely to occur in relationships where it is considered an acceptable avenue for exercising authority and getting one's way.

Abusive parents are usually psychologically immature and easily frustrated by the normal misbehavior of children. When overwhelmed, they resort to abuse in an attempt to control their youngsters. Abusive mothers are likely to have been abused as children.[64] As adults, they are subservient to their partners, who are also likely to have been abused as children.[65] Neither parent is well prepared for the realities of raising youngsters.[66]

When faced with the conflicts that inevitably occur in an intimate relationship, healthy couples strive to resolve them through cooperation and compromise. Abusive partners do not have the skills to negotiate these conflicts effectively; instead, they resort to threats and intimidation. An abusive man may offer his female partner some measure of caring, but he is incapable of consistently intimate behavior. The affection he does offer is punctuated by violent outbursts.

An abusive partner tries to prevent his victim from developing outside relationships.[67] In her isolation, their destructive relationship becomes unrealistically important.[68] If she somehow gains the courage to venture out, her partner is likely to employ any means necessary to gain her return.[69] For some women, killing their partners can seem like the only means of escape.[70] For a far greater number of women, the struggle only ends when they are killed.[71]

Elder abuse has more in common with child abuse than abuse between adult companions, although the person who abuses an elderly dependent often engenders somewhat more sympathy. Caretakers who behave abusively are often stretched beyond their emotional, physical, and financial limits. The demands and needs of an elderly dependent can tax the resources of even the most loving and concerned family. However, for families with a long-standing history of family violence, elder abuse may simply be an extension of a pattern that has included child abuse, sibling violence, and wife battering.

The small fraction of rapists who are caught and convicted appear to have quite severe psychiatric disturbances.[72] However, this tells us very little about those men who are never caught or whose behavior is too subtle to cause suspicion.[73] An incestuous father has no identifying characteristics. A date or marital rapist is simply behaving in an exaggerated version of the accepted norms for the expression of male sexuality.[74] The rapist who is unknown to his victim may never be found and brought to justice—even if she files a complaint.

For many years, it was believed that behaving violently was an inevitable consequence of growing up in a violent family. There is undoubtedly some truth to this, but it is not a wholly adequate explanation.[75] Enormous numbers of people manage phenomenally high levels of stress without ever engaging in any form of abuse or violence. In fact, fewer than 15 percent of parents who were abused as children abuse their own children.[76] Furthermore, being molested is not in itself enough to create a molester. If sexual victimization and perpetration were so completely linked, there would be far more female perpetrators. Yet reports of females sexually abusing children are remarkably rare.[77] So we must consider another explanation for the pervasiveness of violence in our personal relationships.

The key to understanding abuse is that it is almost always *an act perpetrated by a dominant to gain or maintain control over a subordinate.* Between strangers, the elements of surprise and threat to life leave the victim little opportunity to protect herself. Within families and other intimate relationships, the subordinate person is, to one degree or another, dependent on the dominant person. This dependency means that the subordinate person has less power to leave or to change the abusive situation. The psychological consequences for such essentially inescapable victimization are profound.

Psychological Ramifications of Abuse

Abuse damages the emotional bond between people. The person who is being hurt copes with their pain through a variety of adaptive, but ultimately dysfunctional, responses. Whatever form of abuse a child or adult experiences, there are a number of consequences.

- Emotional trauma and psychological difficulties—Survivors of physical abuse seem to be the most psychologically resilient of all abuse victims. Many have been known to endure what seem like impossible situations and still behave productively. Others develop significant emotional problems. Sexually abused children appear to have most serious long-term problems.[78]
- Behavioral problems—Some children respond to abuse by becoming mature beyond their years. However, underneath their adaptive exterior is a compliant, painfully compulsive and anxious worrier. Extremes in abuse can result in delinquency, running away, prostitution, substance abuse, suicide attempts, and premature parenthood.
- Social and interpersonal problems—Many victims are unable to develop healthy social skills and, consequently, have difficulty developing satisfying relationships of any kind.[79] Some survivors display a curious mixture of bonding with those who hurt them and finding it difficult to engage with individuals who might truly be trustworthy.[80]
- Acceptance of the victim role—Even in the face of indisputable evidence, it is common for the victims to deny being abused. Many literally do not realize that the behavior they are enduring is mistreatment. For others, surviving pain, fear, and isolation are preferable to abandonment and the unknown. Many are fearful of retaliation and see no real escape.[81]
- Vulnerability to revictimization—Many victims find it hard to protect themselves from repeated experiences of abuse even when they are aware of having been mistreated.[82] To make matters worse, many are victimized in one way or another by the professionals to whom they turn for help. Battered women may be diagnosed as masochistic and, if they finally respond in self-defense, must often go to great lengths to prove why they felt in danger.[83]

In addition to these almost universal reactions to abuse, there may be specific responses depending on the age of the victim, the severity of the abuse, and how long it was endured.

Physical Abuse of Children

When a parent's frustration and anger is transformed into abuse, it has a powerfully negative effect on a child. Abused children minimize or distort their need for care, support, reassurance, or acceptance in order to remain emotionally connected to parents who mistreat them. This adaptation causes these children to develop an intense desire for closeness along with a deep fear of being hurt and abandoned.[84] Repeated abuse interferes with their ability to trust, erodes their self-esteem, and reduces their capacity for empathy—both for themselves and others. These handicaps interfere with their ability to engage in relationships that might offer genuine love and affection.

People abused in childhood are rarely able to form genuinely secure attachments in adult relationships. In their neediness, they are vulnerable to attaching to anyone who is available. Once in a relationship, they often vacillate between fears of separation and abandonment and anxiety about closeness and intimacy.

Physical Abuse of Adults

In an abusive relationship between adults, unhealthy dependency replaces mutual respect. Among women the victim stays because she imagines that she has more to lose by leaving. She denies her victimization and attributes her partner's problems to outside pressure. She convinces herself that the abuse will stop when the pressure abates. She tells herself that her abusive partner is a good person who has certain problems that can be resolved with her help.

The victim's thinking seems particularly bizarre since she envisions helping her partner while simultaneously assuming that she cannot help herself. In doing this, she denies her options. Instead, she relies on a belief in the fundamental "goodness" of marriage to cope with the contradiction between the violence she receives and the love she and her partner purport to feel for each other. In his eyes, violence comes to be seen as the result of her failure to provide adequate nurturance. She is incompetent, unworthy, and unlovable and, therefore, she deserves the abuse.[85]

Sexual Abuse of Children

In childhood sexual abuse, a child's needs for reasonable affection arc ignored or distorted by an insensitive and self-serving adult. Enduring such inescapable, intrusive, and terrifying experiences requires extreme adaptive strategies.[86] In the face of overwhelming feelings and forced silence, the young girl often employs internal escapes by numbing herself to the event.[87] Sometimes she disassociates from the experience completely. This provides some semblance of emotional safety at the time, but it leaves her vulnerable to severe psychological disturbances in the future. While many boys react to being sexually abused by becoming aggressive men,[88] most sexually abused girls become depressed or self-destructive adults.[89] Preoccupied with obtaining the nurturance and affection that was missing in childhood, they find it painful to make peace with the possibility that certain emotional injuries may never be completely repaired.[90]

Sexual Abuse of Adults

A victim's response to rape depends on a number of factors, particularly the brutality of the assault, whether the attacker was familiar or unknown, and how much support she received from those to whom she turned for help. In the period immediately following the rape, the victim may be distraught and agitated or she may present a calm, composed, and subdued external appearance. Almost all rape victims report racing thoughts and feelings of worry, fear, confusion, and anxiety—sometimes long after the rape.[91] Even years later, many victims are not fully recovered.[92] Fear is a persistent problem. Many become averse to any form of sexual activity, and self-blame is disturbingly common.

Psychiatric Disturbances

Survivors of particularly traumatic abuse often behave in highly erratic and self-destructive ways. Some display such severe disturbances that they eventually enter the mental-health system. When this occurs, they may be diagnosed as having a personality disorder, an individual flaw in their character; however, some mental-health professionals have suggested that it is more accurate to identify survivors as suffering from post-traumatic stress syndrome, the same disorder that has been diagnosed in many Vietnam veterans.

Post-traumatic stress syndrome (PTSS) is the physical and psychological response to sudden and emotionally overwhelming events. It occurs in a wide range of extremely stressful situations regardless of the individual's health prior to the event.[93] The trauma model that underlies the PTSS diagnosis has been used for many years to explain the lingering disturbances seen in survivors of natural disasters, terrorist attacks, and war.[94,95,96]

The symptoms of PTSS include being easily startled, agitation and anxiety, chronic apprehension and vigilance, sleep disturbances and nightmares, depression, and listless passivity. Among young children, bed-wetting, social withdrawal, and misbehavior are also common. Many of these symptoms are caused by actual changes in the body's physiology that occur following trauma.[97] Others are psychological adaptations to extraordinary stress. All of them have been reported by the many children and adults who have survived physical and sexual abuse.

How much an individual's long-term psychological health is affected by the trauma depends on the age of the victim, the intensity and duration of the abuse, the relationship of the assailant to the victim, and the presence or absence of other soothing and supportive people. If the victim is young, if the trauma is repetitive or severe, if the perpetrator is a loved one or someone on whom the victim depends, and if there is little or no external emotional support, the traumatized person is vulnerable to developing a significant emotional disability. The most enduring psychological legacy of chronic and severe abuse for the individual is a fragmented identity.[98] This is evidenced by emotional instability, poor control of aggressive impulses, and disturbed relationships. There is a limited capacity to trust and a simultaneous failure to behave in appropriately self-protective ways.[99]

To diagnose and treat these survivors as if their handicaps were purely individual character flaws without understanding their histories would be like diagnosing and treating Vietnam veterans without acknowledging that they had been in a war.[100] Surviving trauma—be it on the battlefield or at the hands of a brutal or self-serving loved one—can have profoundly damaging effects on psychological functioning. The trauma model allows us to approach the victim with understanding and compassion instead of blaming them for the abuse they have endured.

In What Specific Way Is Abuse Damaging to Women?

Until recently, the mother-child dyad was considered the child's central formative relationship, and a child's healthy psychological development was seen as requiring a kind of one-way nurturing from the mother. Within this theory, increasing maturity for the child meant an ever-expanding separation from the mother while she continued to provide age-appropriate support and nurturance. In addition, if the child was male, he was also expected to separate himself from any identification with the kind of nurturing activity his mother offered him. If the child was female, the expectations were different. She was to retain her identification with her mother as a person who offered nurturance and, through this, to remain engaged in relationships.

Unfortunately, a girl's training to remain involved in relationships occurred in a society that equated psychological health with the capacity to be separate rather than connected. This conflict between "normal" female development as connected and so-called healthy psychological development as separate presented the maturing female child with a complex psychological task. She was expected to become increasingly separate from her mother while simultaneously remaining actively engaged in relationships. While complicated, this development pathway would not have been a problem *except* for the fact that she would come to be held responsible for fostering other people's growth, even at the expense of her own. Therein lay the difficulty.

Participating in psychological development through relationships is an essential activity in every society. However, it need not be one-way or assigned primarily or exclusively to women. An emphasis on mutual psychological development could allow everyone to interact in ways that fostered one another's development.[101] Increasing maturity could be seen as the ability to attend to the development of others—as well as oneself. The goal would be an increasing sense of oneself in connection with others, rather than a sense of separation from them.[102]

Unfortunately, most societies do not yet appreciate the value of mutual psychological development. Instead of setting this as a standard for both women and men, "nurturing," "mothering," or "satisfying other's needs" is an activity assigned to women. With this assignment, learning to attend to relationships becomes a large part of many women's lives. Consequently, their sense of self-worth is deeply grounded in their ability to make and maintain relationships.[103]

There is nothing wrong with having one's self-worth dependent on the ability to develop quality relationships. What is wrong is that this trait is encouraged in females rather than in all human beings. The truth is that if a person is not behaving in ways that foster other people's growth, she or he is usually interfering with it. This interference can be viewed as a disconnection in the relationship. Disturbing disconnections occur when someone ignores, invalidates, or minimizes another person's thoughts or feelings about her or his own experience. Devastating disconnections occur when a person is physically or sexually abused. Disconnections of any sort are particularly upsetting to girls and women because they are trained to remain connected *and* to accept responsibility for that connection.

Obviously, life is filled with minor disconnections. As long as these occur in the context of larger connections, they can be endured. In fact, we can even learn from them. But the key to whether learning can take place is whether or not the individual can express her own experience and have it be received by others in a way that ultimately leads to greater understanding and reconnection.

Examples of managing disconnections abound in the women's medical practice of which I am a part. We all work under a lot of stress—caring for patients, tending to the requests of our staff, worrying about paying the bills, and struggling to balance our personal lives with the demands of being physicians. There are times when we feel stretched beyond our ability to cope and we snap at one of our partners, the staff, or (heaven forbid) a patient. After things settle down a bit, the crabby person examines her recent behavior, feels bad, and apologizes. In most cases, the response is acceptance and forgiveness. The relationship can endure difficult feelings. Both members are pleased to maintain their connection and to have the opportunity to be understanding and supportive. A serious disconnection could occur if the crabby person did not catch herself and apologize or if her apology is not accepted. Unrepentant crabbiness or an inability to accept an apology can, and has, resulted in several permanent disconnections and the dissolution of those relationships. The pain for everyone affected by one of these breaks is apparent.

Clearly, these are nonviolent relationships. In abusive relationships, the disconnections are more serious. When the more powerful person creates a dangerous situation, the less powerful person has a much harder time leading the pair back to a healthy connection. If the dominant person makes little or no effort to reconnect in a healthy way, the subordinate may try to make the connection in whatever way she can. If changing the relationship is impossible, she will change herself. Twisting herself inside out, she maintains the relationship at the price of sacrificing the best parts of herself. *She tries to make herself into an acceptable person in an unacceptable relationship.*

Relationships that are not mutually enhancing undermine the sense of connection that is central to women's lives.[104] When these disconnections occur repeatedly without successful reconnection, women begin to feel sad, lonely, and fearful. Indeed, many of the psychological symptoms women experience—including depression and anxiety—are the result of enduring repeated disconnections and violations in important, but unequal, relationships. A more useful response would be anger.

Putting Anger and Abuse in Context

When a woman is unable to participate in a relationship in a mutually empowering way, she has every right to be angry.[105] Anger can be a very valuable resource when used constructively. At a personal level, anger can be used to correct an inequitable situation. At a social level, collective anger in such forms as the peace movement, the civil rights movement, and the women's movement have helped all of us move toward correcting injustices. But the transformation of anger into abuse and violence is not constructive. Abuse and violence are the misuse of power.

Power within a relationship is the ability to define what can and cannot occur.[106] When this power is used to get what we want no matter what it does to someone else, it is destructive. Girls and women are the most frequent victims of this misuse of power.[107] The reasons are complex. They include, but are by no means limited to, the facts that:

- Many victims are simply in no position to effectively resist mistreatment. They are too young, too small, too fragile, or too dependent. They have no place else to turn.
- Childhood experiences of victimization seem to predispose a woman to victimization as an adult.
- The paucity of supportive childcare alternatives adds to the burnout of a beleaguered, and sometimes abused, mother.
- Women are trained to defer to, comply with, and otherwise make themselves subservient to men while at the same time living under a cultural imperative to be in a relationship with a man.
- Economic forces keep women in violent relationships.
- An unresponsive legal system hinders the pursuit of other options.
- The medical system may just as frequently revictimize as help.
- Family violence is only seen as a legitimate social concern if it is children or elderly who are being abused. Society does not feel compelled to provide mandatory protection if the abuse is directed at an adult woman—whose real alternatives may be no greater than those of either the child or the elderly dependent.

Making Changes

Fortunately, abusive and violent behavior can be changed.[108] It is possible to exercise power without misusing it. It is possible to communicate feelings of anger without resorting to violence. It is possible to provide children and adults with nonviolent methods for solving conflicts.[109] It is possible to involve all people in building mutually empowering relationships, but deinstitutionalizing violence and institutionalizing the principle of respect for every human being is a big job.

Reducing abuse and violence means addressing these issues in many different ways. No one knows which will work most effectively, but no person of goodwill and integrity can deny that the work must be done. The Surgeon General's Workshop on Violence and Public Health has already made some recommendations:[110]

1. Institute a complete and universal ban on the sale, manufacture, importation, and possession of handguns except for authorized police and military personnel.
2. Establish criminal penalties for the possession of any weapon where alcohol is served or sold.
3. Develop a full employment policy.
4. Establish an aggressive government policy to reduce sexism and racial discrimination.
5. Decrease the cultural acceptance of violence by discouraging corporal punishment in homes and schools and by abolishing capital punishment.
6. Decrease the portrayal of violence on television and in all media.
7. Increase the public awareness of the association of violence with alcohol consumption and encourage a reduction in alcohol consumption.
8. Fund research to assess the relationship between lack of resources for the mentally ill and the associated rates of assaultive violence.
9. Improve early intervention and treatment of high-risk individuals with communication and cooperation among medical, legal, educational, and social-service organizations.
10. Create multidisciplinary community facilities to address the detection, assessment, and treatment of all forms of interpersonal violence.
11. Develop demonstration projects aimed at decreasing interpersonal violence.
12. Educate health-care professionals in the identification, treatment, and/or referral of victims, perpetrators and persons at high risk for violence.

To assure adequate protection of girls and women, abusive and violent men must be held accountable for their behavior. We must stop looking toward the victim and saying "Why do you put up with that?" and look instead toward the perpetrator and say "Why do you behave like that?" Battered women must no longer be asked what they did to provoke the attack or why they stay with an abusive partner. Instead, their partners must be asked why they behave so badly. We all must ask what keeps women trapped in such awful situations. Rape victims must no longer be interrogated as to what they might or might not have done to provoke the assault. Instead, we must direct our attention toward why men perpetrate this particular form of brutality and why most remain relatively immune from punishment. Incest victims and patients who have been sexually exploited by therapists must never be accused of being seductive or imagining the abuse. Instead, we must ask what was done to them, by whom, and how we can protect them from further mistreatment.

It is time that we all said loudly and clearly that *abuse and violence are unacceptable.* To this end, we need to build a social order in which the more powerful do not abuse the less powerful. We have already made some progress in these areas. In all fifty states, we now have mandatory child mistreatment reporting. In some communities, law-enforcement officials do press charges in situations of violence between intimate adults. Mandatory reporting statutes related to mistreatment of the elderly are increasing. Tragically, current programs of crime prevention, detection, and prosecution have not been sufficient to stop the misuse of power against girls and women.

Protecting the psychological health of girls and women means insisting on human interactions that reflect genuine respect toward all females—no matter their age, skin color, sexual preference, marital or socioeconomic status. To accomplish this we must challenge the notion that violence against women is "normal."

- *We must encourage girls and women to be more active and expressive.* They must gain confidence that their own wants, needs, and feelings are important. They need to believe that they can and should express them, act on them, and expect others to respect and defend them.
- *We must help boys and men to understand and change sexual stereotypes that dehumanize and devalue women.* Within our schools and in public forums we must teach boys and men about the ethical issues related to the use of violence in their relationships with girls and women. We must ask them to examine the role of pornography in the sexual abuse of women. We must educate them about the prevalence of rape and request their participation in rape-prevention programs. We must make it clear that they have a responsibility to treat all girls and women with respect.
- *We must involve our legislators and other policymakers in reforming media coverage, changing the laws and legal system, and encouraging community involvement.* We must encourage outrage, not personal anonymity and effacement, as a coping mechanism to defend against violence toward women.
- *We must institute a personal, family, and global expectation that promotes respect for women.*

At a Personal Level

The process begins with each of us. We do not have to wait for an act of Congress to begin reducing abusive and violent behavior. Each of us can work toward making our lives violence-free zones. Conflicts and disputes are an inevitable part of life, but the use of physical force to resolve them is unnecessary. We can all learn how to engage in constructive conflict and to help others who have not yet learned how to change their destructive behaviors.

By fostering mutual responsibility and caretaking, we all become responsible for one another's safety. Start the process now. Ask yourself, How might I help a frustrated parent who slaps her child in the supermarket? What might I say to a co-worker with unexplained cuts and bruises on her face? What kind of guidance do I want to provide to my son before he starts dating?

These are difficult ethical questions. Americans value individualism and frown on interfering with what is seen as another person's business. But what does our nonintrusive stance mean and who does it really serve? What do we communicate when we allow a stronger person to misuse their power against someone smaller or weaker? Are we respecting someone's rights or colluding with abuse? What *is* our responsibility as individuals in these situations? Where do we want to draw the line between interference and noninterference?

There are no easy or simple answers to these questions, but by raising them we begin the process of questioning our current behavior and considering the possibility of change. As individuals and as a society we need to clarify how much we are prepared to interfere with the harmful or inappropriate behavior of a stranger. The opportunities to help make gentleness a virtue are all around us.[111] We have only to decide if we wish to act on them.

You have the power to play an enormous role in reducing the prevalence of abuse and violence. Education and prudent control for those who cannot control themselves seem in order, but how will we implement these programs? Talk with your family and friends about these tough ethical issues. Bring them up in your church or synagogue, write a letter to your local newspaper, speak to the elected officials in your community, help your child's teacher organize a panel discussion at school. Ask questions. Start a dialogue. You don't have to have the answers. You only need to be sincerely interesting in finding and implementing effective solutions.

If you are currently being abused or abusing someone else, get help immediately. If you are a survivor of abuse or violence and have not yet pursued a program of self-care or professional assistance, you are likely to be carrying the emotional wounds of those experiences. You are *not* responsible for what happened to you at the hands of someone else, but you are responsible for taking charge of how those experiences affect the rest of your life.

Being treated with respect is as basic to our emotional health as food, clothing, and shelter are to our physical well-being. If you have endured physical or sexual abuse, your needs for emotional nurturance have probably not yet been adequately met. If so, it is important that you allow yourself to heal within the context of caring and respectful relationships. With time, trustworthy relationships will permit you to reweave that frayed, threadbare part of your life into a more solid and reliable emotional fabric. You will come to value and trust yourself and, in doing so, you will come to expect others to treat you with respect.

Abuse and violence need not be a part of any person's life. We can—and must—protect ourselves and others from enduring these truly unnecessary and damaging traumatic experiences.

RESOURCES

For men who abuse or wish to stop abuse against women:
Brother to Brother
1660 Broad Street, Providence, RI 02905, (401) 467-3710.

Men Stopping Violence, Inc. (MSV)
1020 Dekalb Avenue, N.E., Atlanta, GA 30307, (404) 688-1376.

For parents who abuse or wish to stop abuse against young girls and boys:
CHILD, Inc.
Box 2604, Sioux City, IA 51106, (712) 948-3295.

Parents Anonymous
The Kentucky Council on Child Abuse, 240 Plaza, Lexington, KY 40503, (606) 276-1299.

For families who abuse or wish to stop family violence:
Domestic Abuse Project
204 W. Franklin, Minneapolis, MN 55404, (612) 874-7063.

National Coalition Against Domestic Violence
2401 Virginia Avenue, N.W., Suite 306, Washington, DC 20037, (202) 293-8860.

For abused women or women who wish to stop spousal abuse:
National Coalition Against Domestic Violence Hotline
24 hours a day, 7 days a week—(800) 333-SAFE.

Spouse Abuse Centers
There are over seven hundred centers in the United States. Look in your telephone directory for the one closest to you.

For abused elders or those who wish to stop elder abuse:
The Institute on Aging's Elder Abuse Prevention Program
1600 Divisadero Street, San Francisco, CA 94115, (415) 885-7850.

Victim Assistance:

National Victim Advocacy Center
307 W. 7th St., Suite 1001, Fort Worth, TX 76102, (817) 877-3355.

National Organization for Victim Assistance
717 D St., N.W., Washington, D.C. 20004, (202) 303-6682.

Self Defense:

Alternative to Fear
2811 East Madison, Suite 208, Seattle, WA 98122, (206) 328-5347

Model Mugging
P.O. Box 291, Monterey, CA 93942-0921. (408) 646-5425

ADDITIONAL READING

Male Batterers:

Aegis: The Magazine on Ending Violence Against Women
National Communications Network, P.O. Box 21033, Washington, D.C. 20009.

Emerge: A Men's Counseling Service on Domestic Violence
25 Huntington Avenue, Room 323, Boston, MA 02116.

Child Abuse:

K. Oates, ed., *Child Abuse: A Community Concern* (New York: Brunner/Mazel, 1984.

What's a Kid to Do About Child Abuse?
Pamphlet available from Cornell University Distribution Center, 7 Research Park, Ithaca, NY 14850. Cost: $2.

Incest and Sexual Abuse:

Ellen Bass and Laura Davis, *The Courage to Heal: A Guide for Women Survivors of Child Sexual Abuse* (New York: Harper & Row, 1988).

D. Finkelhor, *A Sourcebook on Child Sexual Abuse* (Beverly Hills, Calif.: Sage Publications, 1986).

Susan Forward and Craig Buck, *Betrayal of Innocence: Incest and Its Devastation* (New York: Penguin, 1978).

Sister Vera Gallagher, *Speaking Out, Fighting Back: Personal Experiences of Women Who Survived Childhood Sexual Abuse in Home* (Seattle: Madrona Publishers, 1985). To order write to P.O. Box 22667, Seattle, WA 98122.

Judith Herman, *Father-Daughter Incest* (Cambridge, Mass.: Harvard University Press, 1981).

Family Violence:

D. Davis, *Something is Wrong at My House* (Seattle: Parenting Press, 1985).

Mildred Daley Pagelow, *Family Violence* (New York: Praeger, 1984).

M. A. Straus, R. J. Gelles, and S. K. Steinmetz, *Behind Closed Doors: Violence in the American Family* (Garden City, N.Y.: Anchor/Doubleday, 1981).

Battered Women/Spouse Abuse:

M. Bard and D. Sangrey, *The Crime Victim's Book* (New York: Brunner/Mazel, 1985).

L. H. Bowker, *Beating Wife-Beating* (Lexington, Mass.: Lexington Books, 1983).

A. Browne, *When Battered Women Kill* (New York: Free Press, 1987).

Ginny NiCarthy, *Getting Free: A Handbook for Women in Abusive Relationships* (Seattle: Seal Press, 1982).

L. Okun, *Woman Abuse: Facts Replacing Myths* (Albany, N.Y.: SUNY Press, 1987).

Erin Pizzey, *Scream Quietly or the Neighbors Will Hear* (Short Hills, N.J.: Erin Pizzey-Ridley Enslow Publishers, 1977).

Rape:

Pauline Bart and Patricia O'Brien, *Stopping Rape: Successful Strategies* (New York: Pergamon Press, 1985).

Susan Brownmiller, *Against Our Will: Men, Women and Rape* (New York: Simon & Schuster, 1975).

Linda Ledray, *Recovering from Rape* (New York: Henry Holt, 1986).

Sharon L. McCombie, ed., *The Rape Crisis Intervention Handbook* (New York: Plenum Publishers, 1980).

M. T. Gordon and S. Riger, *The Female Fear* (New York: Free Press, 1989).

Elder Abuse:

M. A. Quin and S. K. Tomita, *Elder Abuse and Neglect* (New York: Springer, 1986).

A. Winter, "The Shame of Elder Abuse," *Modern Maturity,* October/November 1986, pp. 50–57.

Prevention:

F. S. Dayee, *Private Zone: A Book Teaching Children Sexual Assault Prevention Skills* (Edmonds, Wash.: Charles Franklin Press, 1982).

Thomas Gordon, *Parent Effectiveness Training* (New York: Wyden, 1970).

B. A. Edelstein and L. Michelson, eds., *Handbook of Prevention* (New York: Plenum, 1986).

NOTES

1. M. A. Straus, R. J. Gelles, and S. K. Steinmetz, *Behind Closed Doors: Violence in the American Family* (New York: Anchor/Doubleday, 1980).

2. Federal Bureau of Investigation Uniform Crime Report, *Crime in the United States* (Washington, D.C.: GPO, 1982).

3. Judith Herman, "Sexual Violence," Work in Progress (Wellesley, Mass.: Wellesley College, 1984).

4. L. J. Dickstein and C. C. Nadelson, *Family Violence: Emerging Issues of a National Crisis* (Washington, D.C.: American Psychiatric Press, 1989).

5. Federal Bureau of Investigation Uniform Crime Report, *Crime in the United States* (Washington, D.C.: GPO, 1984).

6. Straus, Gelles, and Steinmetz, *Behind Closed Doors,* p. 56.

7. Elaine Carmen, "Family Violence and the Victim-to-Patient Process," in L. J. Dickstein and C. C. Nadelson, eds., *Family Violence: Emerging Issues of a National Crisis* (Washington, D.C.: American Psychiatric Press, 1989) p. 18.

8. E. P. Benedek, "Baseball, Apple Pie and Violence: Is It American?" in L. J. Dickstein and C. C. Nadelson, eds., *Family Violence: Emerging Issues of a National Crisis* (Washington, D.C.: American Psychiatric Press, 1989).

9. Dickstein and Nadelson, *Family Violence,* p. 6.

10. E. Carmen, "Family Violence and the Victim-to-Patient Process," p. 18.

11. A. N. Groth, W. Hobson, and T. Gary, "The Child Molester: Clinical Observations," in J. Conte and D. Shore, eds., *Social Work and Child Sexual Abuse* (New York: Haworth Press, 1982).

12. J. P. Deschner, *The Hitting Habit: Anger Control for Battering Couple* (New York: Free Press, 1984).

13. F. G. Bolton, Jr., *When Bonding Fails: Clinical Assessment of the High-Risk Family* (Beverly Hills, Calif.: Sage Publications, 1983).

14. J. Giles-Sims, *Wife-Battering: A Systems Theory Approach* (New York: Guilford Press, 1983).

15. Carolyn F. Swift, "Women and Violence: Breaking the Connection," Work in Progress (Wellesley, Mass.: Wellesley College, 1987).

16. H. C. Kempe et al., "The Battered Child Syndrome," *Journal of the American Medical Association* 181 (July 1962): 17–24.

17. Straus, Gelles, and Steinmetz, *Behind Closed Doors*, p. 61.

18. E. Canick, "An Exploration of the Capacity for Fantasy in Mothers with a History of Abusive Behavior," Ph.D. diss., Massachusetts School of Professional Psychology, 1985.

19. B. Melnick and J. R. Hurley, "Distinctive Personality Attributes of Child Abusing Mothers," *Journal of Consulting and Clinical Psychology* 33 (1969): 746–49.

20. J. Belsky, "Child Maltreatment: an Ecological Integration," *American Psychologist* 35 (1980): 320–35.

21. J. Bowlby, "Violence in the Family as a Disorder of the Attachment and Caregiving Systems," *American Journal of Psychoanalysis* 44 (1984): 9–27.

22. Federal Bureau of Investigation, *Crime in the United States*, 1982.

23. Straus, Gelles, and Steinmetz, *Behind Closed Doors*, p. 44.

24. D. S. Kalmuss and M. A. Straus, "Feminist, Political and Economic Determinants of Wife Abuse Services," in D. Finkelhor et al., eds., *The Dark Side of Families* (Beverly Hills, Calif.: Sage Publications, 1983).

25. L. Walker, *The Battered Woman* (New York: Harper Colophon, 1979).

26. D. Williams-White, "Self-help and Advocacy: An Alternative to Helping Battered Women," in L. J. Dickstein and C. C. Nadelson, eds., *Family Violence: Emerging Issues of a National Crisis* (Washington, D.C.: American Psychiatric Press, 1989).

27. D. Williams-White, "Self-help and Advocacy."

28. P. J. Mancuso, "Domestic Violence and the Police: Theory, Policy, and Practice," in L. J. Dickstein and C. C. Nadelson, eds., *Family Violence: Emerging Issues of a National Crisis* (Washington, D.C.: American Psychiatric Press, 1989).

29. S. Schechter, *Women and Male Violence: The Visions and Struggles of the Battered Women's Movement* (Boston: South End Press, 1982).

30. M. D. Pagelow, *Family Violence* (New York: Praeger Scientific, 1984).

31. U.S. Congress, Joint Hearings before the Special Committee on Aging, U.S. Senate and the Select Committee on Aging, U.S. House of Representatives, *Elder Abuse: Society's Double Dilemma*, 96th Congress, 1980.

32. Caroline H. Sparks, Bat-Ami Bar On, "A Social Change Approach to the Prevention of Sexual Violence toward Women," Work in Progress (Wellesley, Mass.: Wellesley College, 1985).

33. D. Russell and N. Howell, "The Prevalence of Rape in the United States Revisited," *Signs* 8 (1983): 688–95.

34. Sigmund Freud, "The Aetiology of Hysteria," in James Strachey, ed., *The Standard Edition of the Complete Psychological Works of Sigmund Freud*, vol. 3 (London: Hogarth, 1962).

35. Alfred Kinsey et al., *Sexual Behavior in the Human Female* (Philadelphia: Saunders, 1953).

36. Diana Russell, "Incidence and Prevalence of Intrafamilial and Extrafamilial Sexual Abuse of Female Children," *Child Abuse & Neglect* 7 no. 2 (1983): 133–46.

37. Susan Forward and Craig Buck, *Betrayal of Innocence: Incest and Its Devastation* (New York: Penguin, 1978).

38. D. Finkelhor, *A Sourcebook on Child Sexual Abuse* (Beverly Hills, Calif.: Sage Publications, 1986).

39. Judith Herman, "Recognition and Treatment of Incestuous Families," in L. J. Dickstein and C. C. Nadelson, eds., *Family Violence: Emerging Issues of a National Crisis* (Washington, D.C.: American Psychiatric Press, 1989), p. 31.

40. Herman, "Recognition and Treatment of Incestuous Families," p. 34.

41. Herman, "Recognition and Treatment of Incestuous Families," p. 35.

42. N. Groth, *Men Who Rape: The Psychology of the Offender* (New York: Plenum, 1979).

43. R. S. Kempe and C. H. Kempe, *The Common Secret: Sexual Abuse of Children and Adolescents* (New York: W. H. Freeman, 1984).

44. M. Bard and D. Sangrey, *The Crime Victim's Book* (New York: Basic Books, 1979).

45. M. D. Hirsch, *Women and Violence* (New York: Van Nostrand Reinhold, 1981).

46. Diana Russell, *Rape in Marriage* (New York: Macmillan, 1982).

47. S. Katz and M. A. Mazure, *Understanding the Rape Victim* (New York: John Wiley, 1979).

48. Until 1975, every state exempted husbands from rape statutes. As California state senator Bob Wilson said, "If you can't rape your wife, whom can you rape?" Russell, *Rape in Marriage,* p. 18. By 1984, only eight states had revised their laws so that husbands could be prosecuted for rape.

49. Eugene J. Kanin and Stanley B. Parcell, "Sexual Aggression: A Second Look at the Offended Female," *Archives of Sexual Behavior* 6 (1977): 67–76.

50. Alice Sebold, "Speaking of the Unspeakable," *The New York Times Magazine,* February 26, 1989, pp. 16–18.

51. Judith Herman, "Sexual Violence," Work in Progress (Wellesley, Mass.: Wellesley College, 1984).

52. Neil M. Malamuth, "Rape Proclivity Among Males," *Journal of Social Issues* 37 no. 4 (1981): 138–57.

53. Niel M. Malamuth, "Do Sexually Violent Media Indirectly Contribute to Antisocial Behavior?" in Mary Roth Walsh, ed., *The Psychology of Women: Ongoing Debates* (New Haven, Conn.: Yale University Press, 1987).

54. Susan Griffin, *Rape: The Power of Consciousness* (San Francisco: Harper & Row, 1979), p. 3.

55. S. Riger and M. T. Gordon, "The Fear of Rape: A Study in Social Control," *Journal of Social Issues* 37 (1981): 71–92.

56. Susan Brownmiller, *Against Our Will: Men, Women and Rape* (New York: Simon & Schuster, 1975).

57. Margaret W. Matlin, *The Psychology of Women* (New York: Holt, Reinhart & Winston, 1987), p. 431.

58. E. Hailwood, "Unspeakable Practices, Unnatural Facts," *Toronto Life,* December 1984, pp. 54–59.

59. K. L'Armand and A. Pepitone, "Judgements of Rape: A Study of Victim-rapist Relationship and Sexual History," *Personality and Social Psychology Bulletin* 8 (1982): 134–39.

60. N. Gartrell et al., "Psychiatrist-Patient Sexual Contact: Results of a National Survey I: Prevalence," *American Journal of Psychiatry* 143 (September 1986): 1126.

61. J. C. Holroyd and A. M. Brodsky, "Psychologists' Attitudes and Practices Regarding Erotic and Nonerotic Physical Contact with Patients," *American Psychologist* 32 (1977): 843–49.

62. J. Bouhoutsos et al., "Sexual Intimacy between Psychotherapists and Patients," *Professional Psychology: Research and Practice* 14 (1983): 185–96.

63. N. Gartrell et al., "Reporting Practices of Psychiatrists Who Knew of Sexual Misconduct by Colleagues," *American Journal of Orthopsychiatry* 52 no. 2 (April 1987): 287.

64. D. Finkelhor, *Child Sexual Abuse: New Theory and Research* (New York: Free Press, 1984).

65. K. J. Ferraro, "An Existential Approach to Battering" (Paper presented to the Second Family Violence Researchers Conference. Curham, N.H., August 1984).

66. R. L. Burgess et al., "A Social Interactional Approach to the Study of Abusive Families," in J. P. Vincent, ed., *Advances in Family Intervention, Assessment, and Theory: An Annual Compilation of Research,* vol. 2 (Greenwich, Conn.: JAI, 1981); E.C. Herrenkohl et al., "Parent-child Interaction in Abusive and Non-abusive Families," *Journal of the American Academy of Child Psychiatry* 23 no. 6 (1984): 641–48; and A. Kadushin and J. A. Martin, *Child Abuse: An Interactional Event* (New York: Columbia University Press, 1981).

67. R. J. Gelles and M. A. Straus, "Physical Violence in Families," in E. Corfman, ed., *Families Today—A Research Sampler of Families* (Washington, D.C.: GPO, 1980).

68. A. L. Ganley, "Counseling Programs for Men Who Batter: Elements of Effective Programs," *Response* 4 no. 8 (1981): 3–4.

69. D. S. Kalmuss and M. A. Straus, "Feminist, Political and Economic Determinants of Wife Abuse Services," in D. Finkelhor et al., eds., *The Dark Side of Families* (Beverly Hills, Calif.: Sage Publications, 1983).

70. Since 1975, several American women charged with murdering their husbands have been acquitted on grounds of self-defense or temporary insanity after years of abuse.

71. Isabel Wilkerson, "Indianian Uses Prison Furlough to Kill Ex-wife: Women Say Case Shows Gap in Justice System," *The New York Times,* national edition, March 12, 1989, p. 14.

72. G. E. Abel, Chart from Tarrant County Child Abuse Council presentation, Fort Worth, Tex., May 1985. Courtesy of K. Dolan, Texas College of Osteopathic Medicine, 1985.

73. D. Russell, *Sexual Exploitation: Rape, Child Sexual Abuse, and Sexual Harassment* (Beverly Hills, Calif.: Sage Publications, 1984).

74. Herman, 1989.

75. C. Pedrick-Cornell and R. J. Gelles, "Elder Abuse: The Status of Current Knowledge," *Family Relations* 31 (May 1982): 457–65.

76. R. L. Burgess and L. M. Youngblade, "Social Incompetence and the Intergenerational Transmission of Abusive Parental Practices," (information sheet prepared by Pennsylvania State University, Department of Individual and Family Studies, 1985).

77. B. James and M. Nasjleti, *Treating Sexually Abused Children and Their Families* (Palo Alto, Calif.: Consulting Psychologists Press, 1983).

78. C. Adams-Tucker, "Proximate Effects of Sexual Abuse in Childhood: A Report on 28 Children," *American Journal of Psychiatry* 39 (1982): 1252–56.

79. R. S. Kempe and C. H. Kempe, *The Common Secret: Sexual Abuse of Children and Adolescents* (New York: W. H. Freeman, 1984).

80. M. D. Pagelow, *Family Violence* (New York: Praeger Scientific, 1984).

81. M. W. Galbraith and R. T. Zdorkowski, "Teaching the Investigation of Elder Abuse," *Journal of Gerontological Nursing* 10 no. 12 (1984): 21–25.

82. D. Finkelhor, *Sexually Victimized Children* (New York: Free Press, 1979).

83. L. E. Walker, "Battered Women: Psychology and Public Policy," *American Psychologist* 39 no. 10 (1984): 1178–82.

84. B. van der Kolk, *Post-Traumatic Stress Disorder: Psychological and Biological Sequelae* (Washington, D.C.: American Psychiatric Press, 1984).

85. E. Hilberman, "Overview: The 'Wife Beater's Wife' Reconsidered," *American Journal of Psychiatry* 137 no. 11 (1980): 1336–45 and L. B. Rosewater, "The MMPI

and Battered Women" (paper presented at the Second Family Violence Researchers Conference, Durham, N.C., August 1984).

86. J. Bowlby, "On Knowing What You Are Not Supposed to Know and Feeling What You Are Not Supposed to Feel," *Canadian Journal of Psychiatry* 24 (1979): 403–8.

87. J. Herman and L. Hirschman, *Father-Daughter Incest* (Cambridge, Mass.: Harvard University Press, 1981).

88. D. Gelinas, "Persistent Negative Effects of Incest," *Psychiatry* 46 (1983): 312–32.

89. R. Gladstone, "Observations on Children Who Have Been Physically Abused and Their Parents," *American Journal of Psychiatry* 122 (1965): 531–40.

90. A. Browne and D. Finkelhor, "The Impact of Child Sexual Abuse: A Review of the Research," (information sheet prepared by the University of New Hampshire Family Violence Research Program, Durham, N.H., 1984).

91. D. G. Kilpatrick, P. Resnick, and L. Veronen, "Effects of a Rape Experience: A Longitudinal Study," *The Journal of Social Issues* 37 (1981): 105–22.

92. A. W. Burgess and L. L. Holmstrom, "Rape: Sexual Disruption and Recovery," *American Journal of Orthopsychiatry* 49 (1979): 648–57.

93. Van der Kolk, *Post-Traumatic Stress Disorder*, p. 64.

94. J. L. Titchener and F. T. Capp, "Family and Character Change at Buffalo Creek," *American Journal of Psychiatry* 133 (1976): 259–99.

95. F. Ochberg and D. Soskis, *Victims of Terrorism* (Boulder, CO: Westview, 1982).

96. C. Figley, *Stress Response Syndromes* (New York: Brunner/Mazel, 1978).

97. B. van der Kolk and M. S. Greensberg, "The Psychobiology of the Trauma Response: Hyperarousal, Constriction and Addiction to Traumatic Reexposure," in *Psychological Trauma,* ed. Bessel van der Kolk (Washington, D.C.: American Psychiatric Press, 1987).

98. Frances Arnold and Eleanor Saunders, "Borderline Personality Disorder: Conceptualization and Treatment," (paper presented at the Harvard Medical School Department of Continuing Education Workshop Women: Connections, Disconnections and Violations, June 9–10, 1989).

99. P. P. Rieker and E. Carmen, "The Victim-to-Patient Process. The Disconfirmation and Transformation of Abuse," *American Journal of Orthopsychiatry* 56 (1986): 360–70.

100. J. B. Bryer et al., "Childhood Sexual Physical Abuse as Factors in Adult Psychiatric Illness," *American Journal of Psychiatry* 144 (November 1987): 1426.

101. Jean Baker Miller, "Connections, Disconnections, and Violations," Work in Progress (Wellesley, Mass.: Wellesley College, 1988).

102. Harriet Goldhor Lerner, *The Dance of Intimacy: A Woman's Guide to Courageous Acts of Change in Key Relationships* (New York: Harper & Row, 1989).

103. Jean Baker Miller "What Do We Mean By Relationships?" Work in Progress (Wellesley, Mass.: Wellesley College, 1986), p. 9.

104. Jean Baker Miller, "Connection, Disconnection and Violations," p. 5.

105. Jean Baker Miller, "The Struggle for Connection: Threads in Women's Lives," (paper presented at the Harvard Medical School Department of Continuing Education Workshop Women: Connections, Disconnections and Violations, June 9–10, 1989).

106. Miller, "Connection, Disconnection and Violations," p. 10.

107. Carmen, "Family Violence and the Victim-to-Patient Process," p. 17.

108. Sparks and Bat-Ami, "A Social Change Approach to the Prevention of Sexual Violence toward Women," p. 3.

109. Straus, Gelles, and Steinmetz, *Behind Closed Doors,* p. 93.

110. Elissa Benedek, "Baseball, Apple Pie, and Violence: Is It American?" pp. 9–12.

111. Ramsey Clark, "A Modest Proposal to Reduce Violence in America," in *Violence and the Violent Individual,* ed J. R. Hays, T. K. Roberts, and K. S. Solway (New York: SP Medical and Scientific Books, 1981).

PART 4 | **M**aking **C**hanges

If you have never consulted a psychiatrist before, you may be nervous about your first meeting. There are many misconceptions about who sees a psychiatrist and why. It seems that psychiatrists are either idealized ("They're doctors, so they must be the best therapists to see") or anxiously avoided ("Why are you seeing a psychiatrist? You seem so normal?" or "I don't think I need a psychiatrist. There isn't anything seriously wrong with me. I'm not crazy or anything").

It is true that all psychiatrists are medical doctors. By virtue of this training, they are able to diagnose physical problems that manifest themselves as psychological disturbances. They have also had considerable experience with individuals who suffer from the most severe psychological disturbances such as schizophrenia, psychotic depressions, manic-depressive illness, and acute alcohol or drug addiction.

Many psychiatrists go on to specialize in one or more of these areas. However, some psychiatrists prefer to specialize in psychotherapy. Patients* who choose to see this subgroup of psychiatrists might just have easily opted to see a psychologist, a counselor, a social worker, or some other health-care professional who offers "talking" therapy. The main advantage of seeing a psychiatrist, as opposed to a

---

*There is considerable controversy about what kind of language to use when identifying the individual who seeks psychological care. Some professionals prefer the word *client* while others use *consumer.* The word chosen usually reflects the professional training of the health-care provider. Consistent with this tendency, I will refer to the person seeking mental health care as a *patient,* "a person receiving care or treatment; especially, a person under the care of a doctor" (definition from Webster's New World Dictionary).

professional from one of these other disciplines, is that a psychiatrist can determine if any of the patient's symptoms might be caused by a physical problem. If so, this problem should be treated first. A number of psychological symptoms are biologically based and will respond very effectively to the appropriate medication.

Beyond this special expertise, however, the competency of any psychotherapist, whatever her credentials, is determined more by her talent and training than by the initials after her name. Unless there is a biological problem that requires medical treatment, a therapist should be selected for her ability to provide a safe, empathic emotional environment in which a patient feels reasonably comfortable risking being vulnerable. The person seeking help needs to gradually feel willing to share her innermost secrets, worries, anxieties, and experiences—trusting that the therapist will both care about these thoughts and feelings and encourage the patient to try new behaviors to cope with them effectively.

For the patient, the purpose of therapy is to:
- understand themselves better (gain insight), and
- make productive changes in their lives (become empowered).

A good therapist does her best to participate with the patient to achieve these two goals. In my opinion, a therapist provides the best possible service when she evaluates all the potential contributors to a person's psychological distress. Thus it is important to assess biological (medical), psychological (internal), and social or environmental (external) factors. To cover only one or two areas would leave the evaluation incomplete and might delay rapid resolution of the patient's distress.

If you are experiencing psychological distress and choose to consult a psychiatrist, you can expect that they will be interested in collecting a comprehensive history as part of your initial meeting. You might find it easier to participate in this process if you have some idea about what will be covered. The purpose of chapter 13 is to provide a guide for the kind of history you can expect to be asked. Not every psychiatrist asks all of these questions. Indeed, it would be impossible to cover all of this material in the first meeting. However, if you choose to develop an ongoing therapy relationship, over time you can expect to cover most of these topics in detail. Chapter 14 reviews what you can and cannot expect to happen in this combination healing, training, and education process called therapy; the specific characteristics to look for when selecting a therapist; how to judge the progress of your working relationship; and the signs that indicate it is time to bring therapy to an end.

13 | Taking Your Own History

There are many ways you can use this guide. You can easily do parts of this history on your own. You might find that just thinking about the questions posed is enough to help you understand yourself better. Some people find it helpful to actually write their answers down. This strategy is particularly useful if you think you might want to refer to them at a later time. If you have a close and trustworthy friend, you might consider sharing your answers with them. Or, a support group is another resource in which sharing this material might be very productive.

Sometimes people standing outside of a troubling situation can see it a bit more objectively and provide useful feedback. Sometimes just reviewing these questions will help you develop a plan for making changes on your own. Other times, they only point you in the right direction, but you need the assistance of a professional to move things along.

Your Biopsychosocial History

Your Present Concern(s)

First, describe your current difficulties. This list should be as detailed as possible. Start with when you first noticed your distress. Were there any events that seemed to start the whole sequence rolling? What were they and why do you think they upset you so much? For example, did you lose your job, have a major conflict with a lover or partner, experience the death of a loved one, suffer unexpected financial problems, or have trouble with your children?

How has your situation progressed with time? Have things gotten better or worse? Where do things stand right now?

If your current difficulties are similar to any previous ones, how does your current situation relate to those past experiences? You will explore these in more detail later, so you only need to note them briefly here.

Have you noticed any specific symptoms of distress (anxiety, depression, crying jags, angry outbursts, repetitive or unresolved conflicts with others, trouble sleeping, a change in your appetite, a change in your sexual pattern or interest, excessive use of alcohol, cocaine, or other drugs, thoughts of hurting yourself or others, etc.)? If so, describe these in detail. How have you reacted to these symptoms? How have friends and family members reacted?

As you go through this exercise, if you have any trouble reconstructing information, if you feel embarrassed, have difficulty remembering details, or find yourself becoming emotionally upset, make note of these reactions. These responses are often important clues to understanding the cause of your distress and to understanding your personality.

What kinds of things have you already tried to deal with the problem or to make you feel better? What has worked and what hasn't?

What exactly do *you* think is causing your distress? Have you consulted anyone else—friends, colleagues, or professionals? If so, what do they think?

Your History

The goal of this section is to create your own autobiography, to tell your story. As you cover the various sections, you will discover that there are places where you have little or no information about yourself. This may be particularly true about events surrounding your birth and early childhood. Nonetheless, these circumstances may have played a significant part in the development of your personality, your style of handling emotional difficulties, and your general functioning.

You may discover that you have to initiate discussions with people who knew you when you were very small to complete this part of your history. Often this endeavor alone can be quite therapeutic, although it might not be easy. Remember, the goal is to understand yourself better and to understand the sources of your current and past distress. It is not to blame anyone—neither yourself nor the other people in your life.

What you are looking for are historical factors that might have contributed to your current distress. Remember that in looking at your early history, contemporary factors that may also be contributing to your distress must not be ignored or minimized. This is why a comprehensive history that includes your past *and* present life circumstances is so important. Future desires and goals are also important because for many of us they serve as the guides by which we direct our lives. Our view of the past, present, and future all play a part in our current distress.

Let's proceed with the individual elements of your past history.

Your Family Background

Visual images are often very good tools for discovering patterns in families. In this section, draw your family tree. The diagram I use is based on a family-therapy model.[1] A sample and some of the symbols used in making this kind of family tree are given below. Your family tree does not have to be constructed in this manner, but it should be a visual representation of the people in your family. Include something about each of them as individuals and indicate their relationships to one another.

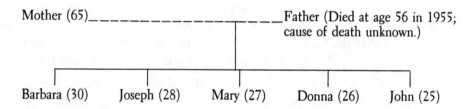

Mother (65)_ _ _ _ _ _ _ _ _ _ _ _ _ _ _Father (Died at age 56 in 1955; cause of death unknown.)

Barbara (30)   Joseph (28)   Mary (27)   Donna (26)   John (25)

Write a brief family history beginning with any information that you know about the oldest family member, whether she or he is dead or alive. You will probably discover that there are many things about your family that you do not know. Look for the gaps. These are spaces that you might be able to fill in by talking with other people in the family. Just communicating with one another can ultimately be very healing even if it is stressful at first.

Here are some of the things you may want to include in your family history:

- The attitudes and outstanding personality traits of family members.
- Your relationship to your mother, father, siblings, lovers, partners, and friends, including your feelings about these people.
- Any medical and psychological problems in your family.
- Any history of alcoholism, drug abuse, physical violence, sexual abuse, or eating disorders.
- The economic, cultural, and social conditions in which you were raised.
- The educational background of each family member.
- Their work histories.
- Their relationship histories.
- Any important financial successes or losses.
- Any trouble with the law.
- Any family disruptions resulting in serious separation including divorce, immigration, jail, child placement, and so on.

The idea is to describe what kind of family was living in what kind of way in what kind of community at what time in history.

Your Developmental History

Begin this section with a description of who you are. Indicate your age, ethnic or racial background, religion, occupation, marital or relationship status, educational level, and any other descriptive information. This anchors your present history and will be a valuable reference point if and when you repeat this process in the future.

Infancy and childhood—This section should include anything you know about the circumstances of your conception, birth, and early childhood. Think of it as if you were viewing a movie of your own life, and report what you observe. Although few people have conscious memories before the age of three, baby pictures and the stories other people tell about you as a young child can be invaluable in reconstructing your history—along with whatever memories you do have. Feelings related to these memories are important and should be included. Here are some of the questions you might use to stimulate your thinking:

- Describe two or three of your earliest and most important childhood memories. Be sure to include your attachments to significant people, places, and things.
- Describe your parents and any other significant caretakers in your life. Include your thoughts and feelings about them.
- What were your parents' attitudes and feelings about your arrival in their lives?
- How did other significant people feel about your birth?
- What were your parents' ages? How was their health, especially your mother's during her pregnancy?
- Were there any medical problems noted—either for you or for her—at your birth?
- How did early childhood go for you? What were your sleeping and eating patterns? Do you know anything about your early play habits?
- Who were your primary caretakers? What was their parenting style? What kind of discipline did they use?
- What were the positive things that happened during this phase of your life? What were the most difficult?
- Who were your main helpers and supporters? What did you receive from them that was most valuable?
- Describe your relationships with your siblings.
- How was it growing up in your neighborhood? Say something about your relationships with neighborhood kids and adults.
- Describe any major disruptions or losses such as moving, changing schools,

the death of a family member, friend, or pet, and so forth along with their impact upon you.

Adolescence—This is a period of your life when you can really begin to rely on your own memories, although those of others may certainly enrich your understanding. (Remember that all people filter memories through their own particular perspective—and no one else's is any more or less accurate than your own. Everyone has their own bias.)

In adolescence, you were able to exercise more free choice than you were as a child. By this age, you were less dependent on your parents or other caretakers for arranging activities or organizing opportunities to be with friends. You began expanding your relationship network beyond relatives and neighbors. As you incorporated new people into your life, you made changes in your former relationships. There was often less time and energy for your immediate family, and they (or you) may have seen this as a mixed blessing. The way you and your family handled this transition pretty much determined whether adolescence was smooth or rocky.

When you reflect on your teen years, explore school, relationships, play, and work. Since education is usually a big part of most American kids' lives, give special attention to this area.

- When did you start school and how did you progress through the various grades?
- Which aspects of school were easy? Which were hard?
- What were your favorite subjects? Your least favorite?
- How were your relationships with teachers? With classmates?
- What kinds of extracurricular activities did you participate in (athletics, music, art, theater, etc.)? How actively were you involved?
- Did you miss much school? Why—illness, skipping classes?
- What were your experiences with smoking, drinking, and other drugs?
- How old were you when you finished or left school?
- Did you obtain additional training or education beyond that? If so, what kind and how did that experience go?
- What has been your highest educational or training level?
- What are your ultimate goals in this area?

The quality of relationships during this period is particularly important to development.

- Describe your important attachments. How did you get along with your parents? Brothers and sisters, if you had any? Other important family members? To whom did you feel closest and why?
- Any losses? How did you cope with these changes?
- Describe how your friendships developed, evolved, and dissolved.

Other important areas to explore include:

- Did you work during this period—either volunteer activities or for money?
- What did you do for fun?
- Overall, what were your ideals and ambitions during this period?

Adolescence is often the age when sexual activity begins. An entire section will be devoted to this later. Don't forget to include your adolescent years. Hormonal changes during puberty often make this an emotionally volatile period. The way your family, friends, and acquaintances responded to your emerging sexuality may have been quite an important influence on your sexual development.

Adulthood—There are two important factors to consider in your adult developmental history: relationships and work and finances.

1. Relationships.[2] A psychology based on male development has overemphasized separation and autonomy and underemphasized attachment, intimacy, and developmentally appropriate dependency and interdependency. A psychology based on female development is grounded in the belief that the healthiest growth and change occurs within the context of mutually enhancing relationships.[3]

The psychological and sociological differences in the meaning of relationships between women and men can cause significant distress for women.[4] Our culture fosters inequality between the sexes that is not simply reflected in economic, political, and power differentials. Instead, it is seen in the very fiber of daily interactions, where there is often an inequality in the time, talent, and valuing of the establishment and maintenance of relationships.

From this perspective, all of the relationships with the significant people in a person's life are important in her development. These relationships also develop and change over a lifetime. Their quality and endurance is a central component of psychological health. Each will most likely have both beneficial and problematic aspects. Healthy new relationships in the adult phase of life can heal wounds left from earlier dysfunctional relationships.[5]

In this section of your history, you will explore your significant relationships.

- What relationships have been or are the solid anchors in your life? Select at least three and describe them in detail.
- What are the ways in which you contribute to relationships with people who are important in your life?
- In what ways do your contributions represent important psychological strengths, and how would you characterize these strengths? Include your mother, father, sister, brother, other family members, friends, lover, husband, children, co-workers, and bosses.
- What do you receive from these relationships?
- Do you have any trouble in any of these relationships? In particular, are any of your relationships affected by feelings of anger, sadness, fear, guilt, shame, or other strong feelings? Describe them in detail.

- Are your current relationships sufficient for you? If not, what can you do to change this situation?
- How do these relationships affect your ability to carry out other important life tasks? For example, your ability to work effectively, to attend school, or to parent.
- Conversely, how would greater effectiveness in other life tasks improve your relationships? For example, if you are married, would having an independent source of income allow you to state your feelings and needs more directly to your husband?
- Disruptions in important relationships can be very upsetting. Describe the disruptions you have experienced and their impact on your psychological well-being. For example, have you ever given a child up for adoption? Or were you adopted? Were your parents divorced? What were the consequences for you in terms of relationships? Are you currently married or in a long-term primary relationship? Describe it in detail, including compatibility, strengths, and weaknesses. Are you having trouble in any of your current relationships? If so, what kind? Have you had other significant primary relationships in the past? How do they work out for you? Describe them in a similar fashion.

2. Work and financial status. Financial security is a key component of psychological health, yet many women have not been trained to aim for economic self-sufficiency.

- What did money mean in your family? For example, was it freely given or was it used as a tool of manipulation? Describe what money currently means to you. What do you want your relationship to money to be in the future?
- Do you have a budget? Do you follow it?
- Do you have a regular savings plan? If so, describe it.
- Have you established credit in your own name?
- How much of your own money could you get your hands on within twenty-four hours if you absolutely needed to?
- If you are living with another person(s), how have you decided to manage money?
- If you have a family, could you support them alone if you needed to?
- What are your financial plans for retirement?
- If you are employed, describe your current and past work experiences. What are the good and bad aspects? Do you feel secure in your present position? Do you feel valued or just another cog in the machine? Does work enhance your self-esteem or detract from it?
- Has the role of work in your life changed over the years? If so, how?
- Is your work easily integrated into your life or are there obstacles? If so, what are they? Describe the stress of coordinating paid work, limited eco-

nomic resources, inadequate childcare options, the strains of commuting and having little time for leisure and adult relationships if any of these are issues for you.

- What special skills do you possess? Do you need any additional training for the kind of work you would like? If so, what kind and how will you get it?
- If you are married and are not presently employed, how have you protected yourself financially? (This is especially important for homemakers who have never worked outside the home or have worked only part-time. Unless precautions are taken, upon divorce, a woman who has been a wife for many years and is now suddenly an ex-wife can find most or all of her "husband's" financial assets going to a new wife. Reliable legal and financial consultations are definitely advised in these matters. Have you contacted the appropriate resource people?)[6]
- What are your work plans and aspirations?

Sexual history—Sexuality can be a source of pleasure or pain.[7]

- How did you first learn about sex and from whom? How old were you? What were your thoughts and feelings on the subject?
- What were your family's attitudes about sexuality?
- Describe your first experience with masturbation.
- With whom did you have sexual experiences? Describe your first sexual experience (if any) with a male partner. Describe your first sexual experience (if any) with a female partner. Were these by choice or coercion? What influence do these experiences—either positive or negative—have on your present sexual functioning?
- Give an overview of any sexual experiences that have not otherwise been covered. Describe pleasurable as well as painful or frightening experiences.

Abuse and trauma history[8]—

- Have you ever been the victim of physical abuse,[9] sexual harassment, or sexual abuse? Include incest, assault, and/or attempted or completed rape as a child (sixteen and under) or as an adult (over sixteen), date rape, marital rape, and professional misconduct.
- Describe these events in detail. What happened, who assaulted you, what kind of help did you get from others, who knows about what happened to you, and how have they responded? How do you feel about it now?
- What safeguards are in place to minimize the possibility of this happening to you again?
- Have you ever been abusive to yourself? Describe the circumstances. What kind of help have you gotten for yourself? Who knows about what you have done and how have they responded? How do you feel now about what happened?

- Have you ever been physically or verbally abusive to others? Describe the circumstances. What kind of help have you gotten for yourself? For the person(s) you hurt? Who knows about what you have done and how have they responded? How do you feel now about what happened?
- What safeguards are in place to protect you from behaving like this again?
- Describe how experiencing or witnessing any of these traumas has affected your life:
  1. a threat or having a close call (such as almost being mugged or almost being hit by a car),
  2. witnessing a close call,
  3. news of the unexpected death or injury of someone close,
  4. robbery or vandalism,
  5. seeing someone hurt or killed,
  6. witnessing a successful or unsuccessful suicide attempt,
  7. knowing someone who attempted or completed suicide,
  8. seeing an accident or injury,
  9. being in a serious accident or sustaining a serious injury, or
  10. being in a disaster such as a major fire, a flood, a chemical spill, the collapse of a building, or any other traumatic or frightening experience.

Other potential problem areas—Describe any excessive, worrisome, or self-destructive behavior not mentioned elsewhere such as:

- gambling (including the stock market),
- impulsive stealing,
- unsafe sexual practices (include sadomasochism and sexual addictions), or
- unsafe sexual intercourse (without contraceptive protection when pregnancy is not desired or when there is a risk of sexually transmitted diseases).
- Have you ever engaged in any upsetting, risky, or dangerous behavior not mentioned above? If so, describe it and the consequences for the quality of your life.

Religious orientation and participation or spiritual practices—

- What is your religious background?
- What kind of changes have you made in your religious affiliations or spiritual beliefs over the years, if any?
- What are your current religious or spiritual activities and affiliations and what is their significance in your life?

Military history—

- Describe your military history, if you have one. Include branch of service, draft or enlistment status, specialties, highest rank attained, disciplinary actions, decorations or citations, dates of entry and exit, and discharge status.
- What are your feelings about being or having been in the military?

Hobbies, recreational and cultural activities—What we do for fun, to relax, or to balance our work lives can have an enormous influence on our psychological health. The stress and strain of work can be countered by dancing, hikes along peaceful country roads, engrossing involvement with photography, or listening to concerts on public radio.

- Describe the things you do for fun, leisure, and rejuvenation. Include your favorite ways to relax and what you do for fun.

Strengths—Even in the face of difficult times and diminished functioning, you do have strengths. It is important to acknowledge them and emphasize them as you work your way through any psychological trouble. If you are having trouble at home, it is often useful to describe the work you do outside the home. You may rediscover strengths that you have been ignoring or minimizing. Conversely, if your distress is related to work, the strengths you demonstrate at home may counterbalance the loss in self-esteem that comes from not performing as well as usual on the job.

- What are your strengths?

Women can be particularly understanding and helpful to others, but they are often unaware that these abilities represent valuable psychological resources. Women's tendency to do things with thoughtfulness and kindness is frequently, unfairly, and inappropriately undervalued. It is taken for granted rather than recognized as a substantial strength. This is particularly true if the woman receives little of the same from others close to her.[10]

- What strengths do you demonstrate in your interactions with other people? Consider such strengths as being loyal, friendly, hardworking, persistent, kind, fighting for what you think is right, trying to see the situation from the other person's perspective, continuing to love even in the face of being mistreated, and so on.

Values—Values are the internal set of rules that guide your behavior and ethical choices. For example, are children a burden or a joy? Is work a necessary evil, an avoidable chore, or an opportunity for satisfaction? Are friends people to exploit, people to share with, or potential enemies?

- What are your values? What really matters to you and why?

Social situation and living arrangements—Over our lifetime, our living arrangements may change dramatically. Initially, we usually live with our biological parents, although some people live with adoptive parents or in foster homes. If we go to college, we usually share housing with peers. The recent economic situation has resulted in more adult children of working-class families returning to their parents' homes. This poses adaptive challenges for both the older parents and the younger adults. As our population ages and more parents are geographically separated from their children, the elderly are either living alone or in retirement communities.[11] Some end their days in nursing homes. At some point, either by choice or circumstance, most of us live alone.

- Describe your living arrangements. With whom do you live and where? Have there been any recent changes or are any planned for the future? If so, what?

Physical health and medical history—This section should include a comprehensive health history, including menstrual and reproductive history. Be sure to include the attitudes and feelings you have about your physical health and elaborate on any current medical problems.

- Describe any operations or accidents.
- What prescription or over-the-counter drugs or medications, including vitamins and minerals, have you taken within the last year?
- Describe any unpleasant or dangerous reactions to these or any other medications that you have taken.
- Describe your use of potentially addictive substances. Include cigarettes, caffeine-containing beverages, alcohol, and drugs.
- Describe your history of dieting, bulimia or anorexia, overeating, overweight, or obesity.
- Describe the kind of physical exercise you do and its frequency. Any injuries?
- How would you describe your usual stress level: high, moderate, or low? What kinds of stress-management strategies do you use and how regularly? Include yoga, biofeedback, relaxation, etc.
- Your reproductive and menstrual history should include when you began menstruating and your experience with this significant life change; whether or not you have used or are currently using birth control and if so, what kind(s). What have been your experiences with birth control? Have you ever been pregnant, had an abortion or a miscarriage? Describe these experiences. Have you ever undergone sterilization? Have you ever considered a hysterectomy or have you already undergone that procedure? Have you begun/completed menopause? If so, what has been your experience?
- Do you have any physical handicaps? If so, what are they and how have they affected your life?

- What kinds of significant illness have you had?
- Describe your present health.

Experiences with therapy or other psychological care—

- Have you ever sought assistance from a therapist, counselor, or other professional for psychological concerns? What was helpful or unhelpful about your experience? Describe each experience in detail.

Mental-Status Evaluation

A complete mental-status evaluation requires professional training, but you will be able to perform parts of it yourself. You can then review the description of the more technical aspects of this evaluation, which will give you some idea of what a mental-health professional will look for.

The best way to conduct a self-administered mental-status exam is to step back from yourself—almost as if you were a separate person observing yourself. With this process in mind, consider the following:

General Appearance, Behavior, and Attitude

Provide a vivid mental image of yourself in words. Include a discussion of the speed and style with which you move and talk, your posture, your voice, the way you dress, something about your grooming, how you behave with people and by yourself. What is your general attitude toward life, yourself, and others? Are you generally optimistic, argumentative, laid-back, organized, suspicious, and so forth?

Consciousness, Orientation, and Memory

Have you had any trouble with your memory, and if so, what kind? Have you ever lost consciousness or had blackouts, blocks of time that you cannot remember? Do you ever find yourself feeling confused? If so, how? Do you ever have trouble remembering where you are or who someone else is? Describe these experiences.

Feelings (Affect)

Your moods are important clues to your psychological state. Describe the range of moods that you feel and their intensity, depth, and duration.

For the professional, affect is more than feelings or mood. It also involves something called vegetative signs. When a professional is assessing whether you might have a disturbance of mood, such as depression or bipolar disorder (manic-depressive disorder), they ask about the associated vegetative symptoms.[12] While on the surface these symptoms might appear to have little to do with feelings, they are in fact significant clues to the type of disturbance a person is experiencing.

From an anatomical point of view, the part of the brain that modulates mood is intimately connected with the areas that control the vegetative signs. If these signs are present, it indicates a biological component to the mood disturbance (which does not, of course, eliminate the additional presence of psychological contributors or depression-inducing external factors). The vegetative signs of depression include:

- a significant change in appetite with a weight gain or loss,
- a significant change in sleep patterns—either sleeping too much or too little,
- a change in bowel functioning, especially constipation,
- a change in sexual interest and activity (libido),
- morning and evening variation in mood,
- a seasonal variation in mood,
- a change in menstrual functioning, and
- suicidal thoughts.

Motor Activity, Retardation, Overactivity, Restlessness

Do you have any tremors, tics, or striking mannerisms? Do you find yourself easily angered or prone to violence? Do you ever worry about hurting yourself or others? Have you ever hurt yourself or others? Do you feel agitated or restless? Do you feel sluggish or lethargic? If so, describe the circumstances in which any of these feelings and behaviors emerge.

Thought Processes

How would you characterize your own thinking? Do you find that thoughts just float in and out of your mind, or do you focus on certain ideas and obsess about them? Do you have negative thoughts about yourself or others, and if so, what are they? Do you have positive thoughts about yourself or others, and if so, what are they? Do you ever have trouble thinking? If so, what kind?

Thought Content

Describe your fantasies, dreams, ambitions, fears, and preoccupations. If you have ever had a severe psychiatric disturbance (a psychosis), you may have experienced hallucinations, for example hearing voices or seeing things that are not really there. Note any other unusual psychological experiences.

Intelligence

It is important that limited education not be mistaken for lack of capacity. A woman's racial, economic, and cultural background may have limited her educational opportunities. This does not necessarily say anything about her intelligence.

Assessing intelligence requires estimating not only a person's present skill, but also her unrealized potential. Most clinicians can estimate whether intelligence is average, below average, or above average. Testing provides more accurate assessment. It can be arranged with the help of a qualified professional, usually a psychologist with special training in psychological and intelligence testing.

Feedback from Friends and Colleagues

Trusted friends and colleagues usually have their own perceptions of us. Requesting honest feedback from them can sometimes be a valuable reference point when you are trying to understand yourself better. You might want to ask one or two for their thoughts and feelings. But remember, their perspectives are no more or less accurate than your own. It is impossible for anyone to be completely objective. Nevertheless, what they say may have some value for you. At the very least, it will be input from a vantage point different from your own.

Insight

Occasionally, other people can provide feedback that will allow you to develop new insights about yourself. Insight, of course, is a very subjective matter. It is hard for any of us to fully understand our motivations all of the time. We may be especially confused when our feelings are intense or seem to be irrational. However, within limits, we can all make some assessment of the reason for our distress. In other words, we can ask ourselves what we think is wrong and why.

Judgment

Judgment is more objective than insight. Good judgment is the ability to compare facts, to relate them to one another, and to draw reasonable conclusions. Poor judgment is the opposite. For example, it is poor judgment to drive while intoxicated, to have unprotected intercourse if pregnancy is not desired, or to chronically and repeatedly spend more money than one earns.

Pulling It All Together

A mental-health professional uses all this information in her assessment of your psychological health. However, even while the clinician is still asking questions, she has already started to piece together some ideas about the source(s) of your difficulty. Biological, psychological, and social factors will all be considered. With this information, the professional develops a formulation and diagnosis—a working hypothesis about what might be contributing to your distress. You can do much the same thing, although you will not necessarily have the sophistication, or for that matter the biases, of the clinician.

Let me show you how this is done.

Working Hypotheses
Formulation

This process aims to bring together all the important elements of the history into an intelligible whole. The significant symptoms and associated historical events are summarized and an attempt is made to identify a potential cause and effect explanation for the patient's distress. Here's a case history that shows how this process works.

Problem: Laurie had been feeling irritable, lethargic, and uninterested in sex.

Possible cause: Laurie and her husband, Sam, have been struggling with each other for almost a year and a half about whether or not to have children.

At the beginning of their marriage eight years ago, neither Laurie nor Sam knew whether or not they wanted children. As the years have passed, Sam has decided that he definitely wants to be a parent, while Laurie remains uncertain. Now every time they have sex, Sam hassles Laurie about using birth control. It has reached the point where Laurie dreads the conflict so much that she has become reluctant to have sex at all.

To make matters worse, in the last few months Laurie and Sam seem to have been snapping at each other over the slightest provocation. They have stopped doing much of anything together just for fun. Laurie spends her evenings lying on the couch in front of the television. She doesn't seem to have energy for anything else. She usually goes to bed before Sam gets home from visiting with his friends after work.

Laurie feels disheartened and discouraged. She dreads the thought of losing Sam. On the other hand, their relationship has become so unpleasant. She thinks that maybe it wouldn't be so bad being single again. But what about the loneliness? Maybe she should have a baby. Sam wants it so much and she does believe that he would make a good father, at least in the traditional sense of the word. But that's part of the problem . . . she loves her work, and having a child, if it means she has to do most of the caretaking, would not be her cup of tea. There doesn't seem to be any good answer.

Distressed by two equally undesirable choices, Laurie sinks deeper into the dumps. And she berates herself for being like this. It's just the way she remembers her mother acting with her father: bitchy, depressed, and cold. She vowed she'd never be like her mother and here she is. Knowing that only makes her feel worse.

In formulating a hypothesis, the clinician considers all possible contributors:

- Biologic predispositions—For example, does Laurie have the vegetative signs of depression? Were other members of her family prone to depression?
- External or social factors—For example, there is a lot of pressure on women these days to both work and have children. In this social context, it may be difficult for Laurie to figure out what she really wants. But the most pressing external contributor is Sam. Their relationship is very important to Laurie. She does not want to deny Sam the right to be a parent, yet she is personally uncertain about having children.
- Internal or psychological factors based on personal history and personality style—For example, Laurie's mother did not seem to like the role she was expected to play. Her father was equally unavailable—working long hours and rarely actively involved in her day-to-day life. Laurie tends to get anxious when people make demands on her. She doubts that she would easily tolerate—let alone enjoy—the demands and interruptions of an infant and growing child.

Differential Diagnosis

The primary purpose of a diagnosis is to guide a woman (and her clinician, if she is using one) toward the most helpful life-style change or treatment. Often, a diagnosis is not absolutely clear. There may be more than one potential explanation for a problem. The differential diagnosis is an attempt to consider all possible causes.

Psychology is a highly subjective field. Consequently, there are many different systems of diagnosis. Within each one, there is room for misuse as well as wisdom. Professionals of good faith and training may take the same information and arrive at very different opinions about the cause of distress and the course of action that should be recommended. Whatever system is used, working toward the most accurate diagnosis within that system minimizes the risk of mistreatment and avoids wasting a patient's valuable time and money.

As a psychiatrist, I am obliged to use the system developed by the American Psychiatric Association, which is contained in the DSM-III-R, *Diagnostic Statistical Manual,* third revision.[13] Therapists with other training and credentials may not necessarily use, or even value, this so-called medical model. Indeed, it may not always be the best or the most useful model for every kind of psychological problem. However, since psychiatrists have the greatest formal power among mental-health providers, understanding something about their assessment tools is important.

Any clinical tool must be used with discretion, caution, and respect. Where women are concerned, every assessment tool and diagnosis must be critically examined for a potential anti-woman bias. A psychiatric diagnosis may not always capture the essence of a woman's life accurately, fairly, or completely. Certain pejorative diagnoses may contribute to some therapists treating patients in a negative or unhelpful manner.

The DSM-III-R system has five components. Describing the problem in these five different ways provides a relatively comprehensive understanding of a woman's psychological status. No one component alone is adequate to do this. The five components are:

1. Axis I—These are acute problems. They are either recent, transient, or biologically based.   People with Axis I problems are likely to experience a considerable level of distress, which may take the form of depression, anxiety, memory loss, irritability, drinking too much, difficulty adjusting to a recent loss or change, and so on. These people feel pretty miserable, both in terms of what they are going through and in terms of what they are putting other people through. They usually want to feel better as soon as possible.

If you are using this chapter as a self-assessment tool, try to weigh all three potential contributors: biological, psychological, and social.

2. Axis II—These are more pervasive, chronic, and long-standing patterns. Everyone has certain character or personality traits. Some people's are so rigid that they are said to have a personality disorder. A personality disorder is a maladaptive pattern that is quite entrenched and difficult, but not impossible, to change. Unfortunately, the behavior of people with personality disorders often provokes the very reaction from others that they are trying to avoid.

> Jane is hungry for close emotional relationships. In order to bring people closer to her, she gives them lovely presents, calls them on the phone a lot, and continually asks them to come visit. Other people think that she is clingy and needy. One acquaintance said, "She feels sticky." Instead of enjoying her company, most people do their best to avoid her. When they do extend an invitation, it is often out of a sense of obligation or guilt. At one level, Jane views these gestures as signs of genuine friendship. At another level, she recognizes that she is being tolerated and feels indignant and hurt.

> Jane's annoying behavior results in her legitimate dependency needs never being adequately met. She is not doing any of this on purpose. We often ask of people like this "Doesn't she understand how she just drives people away with all her clinging behavior?" It seems so obvious to the outsider, but it is far from obvious to the person doing it.

> Her friends feel as if she is a bottomless pit. No matter how much they give, it is never enough. After a while, they start to feel trapped and try to extricate themselves to some degree from the relationship. Jane experiences their distancing as an emotional insult and feels betrayed by yet another person to whom she has been so nice. People are not to be trusted.

One way of understanding what causes a person to behave in ways opposite to what they say they want is to assume that an unconscious motivation is driving their action. The unconscious is believed to be that part of the mind or mental functioning that is only rarely subject to awareness. It is a kind of holding tank for thoughts, experiences, and feeling that have either never been conscious or may have been briefly conscious but were then repressed. They are thought to reappear sometimes in disguised form through other obscure avenues like dreams and Freudian slips.

According to analytic theory, we behave in emotionally maladaptive ways when we have unresolved unconscious conflicts. While I do not fully embrace the notion of an unconscious, I do think that we are not always completely aware of our motives for some of the things we do. Often, our behavior makes more sense to us after the fact than when we are in the middle of it. In any case, people with character problems (Axis II) may feel miserable, but as frequently as not, they also cause misery for other people. Consequently, they often engender little empathy from others when they are in distress.

A person with a character problem is like a slow driver on an expressway. For about two years, I lived in Florida, working as a dental assistant before I went to medical school. I had grown up in the Detroit area where everyone learned certain rules about driving. One clear rule was that the fastest drivers headed over for the left lane while slower drivers stayed on the right.

Well, St. Petersburg drivers clearly had a very different set of rules. Elderly drivers would pull SLOWLY into the right lane as they came on the freeway and then would work their way over to the left lane, where they would stay, poking along at the slowest possible legal speed. They seemed oblivious to the trouble they were causing other drivers. If they noticed at all, they thought the other drivers had the problem. After all, they were observing the speed limit.

I once saw one of these slow drivers actually cause an accident. As the car made its slow way across the expressway to the exit, out of sync with the other drivers, a couple of them did not compensate quickly enough. They had to swerve off the road to prevent hitting the slow driver. The driver of the slow car meandered off the exit totally unaware of the trouble she or he had caused for others.

The implications of an Axis II diagnosis make it important to use it very cautiously.[14] As a therapist who specializes in psychotherapy with women, I have seen women's "personality" problems misunderstood as inflexible character flaws when in fact these women are demonstrating adaptive responses to difficult environmental conditions.[15] The same women might behave very differently under different circumstances. Thus an Axis II diagnosis must be used to facilitate understanding and appropriate change. It should not be used in a destructive or pejorative fashion.

Research suggests that we are all genetically predisposed to a certain personality type. Anyone who comes from a large family is well aware of this. Kids born to the same parents, even those of the same gender and relatively close in age, may have very different personalities. The way any one child develops is the result of an overlap between her personality and predispositions and the events that occur in her life. Different children may experience and interpret the same events quite differently, and this has significant consequences for the development of their personality.

Bessel van der Kolk, M.D., director of the Trauma Center at the Massachusetts Mental Health Center, Harvard Medical School, argues that "people are biological organisms that develop . . . in a social context . . . Studies in a variety of animals have demonstrated that the distress call of an infant . . . and the parental response [are] mediated by endogenous opioids . . . There is animal evidence that social isolation during critical stages of development directly affects the number and sensitivity of brain opiate receptors."

In other words, what happens to an infant during early childhood may have a real impact on their physical development. There is evidence that emotional deprivation in infancy and childhood can cause actual physical damage in the developing brain, and this can have a lifelong effect on psychological development. This early damage caused by emotional distress can sometimes be reversed with sufficient substitute nurturance and care. Two points should be noted here. One is the intricate connection between physical and psychological development. Each clearly can affect the other; they cannot be separated. Second, even severe problems can sometimes be corrected with enough of the right kind of emotional nurturance.

If you do have character troubles, it will be hard for you to see them. That is the very nature of such troubles. However, if you find that there are trails of emotional accidents in your life, it may be useful to consider your contribution.

3. Axis III—These are concurrent medical problems. Describe any current physical condition that may be important in understanding the patient's psychological distress or may affect which action to take to reduce it. For example, if a patient has thyroid disease, it may be causing her psychological symptoms. The thyroid problem should be treated before pursuing other interventions. The symptoms may abate with the appropriate medical treatment.

4. Axis IV—This is where you estimate the severity of stress. A 1 (none) to 6 (catastrophic) scale is used to estimate the severity of the stresses that may be contributing to the patient's psychological distress. For example, a child leaving home is viewed as mild stress (2), a miscarriage as moderate (3), divorce as severe (4), rape as extreme (5), and captivity as a hostage as catastrophic (6).

5. Axis V—Here you describe the highest level of adaptive functioning over the last year. This is an overall judgment of a person's psychological, social, and occupational functioning on a continuum of 1 to 90. On this scale, 81–90 indicates absent or minimal symptoms, good functioning in all areas, interested and involved in a wide range of activities, socially effective, generally satisfied with life, no more than everyday problems or concerns; 41–50 indicates serious symptoms or any serious impairment in social, occupational, or school functioning; and 1–10 indicates persistent danger of severely hurting self or others or persistent inability to maintain personal hygiene or possibility of serious suicidal act with clear expectation of death.

Plan

This is the place where guidelines are developed aimed at altering the patient's level of distress. It is important to consider changes that might be necessary in all areas: physically, socially, and psychologically. For example, the person might benefit from:

- medication,
- participating in an exercise program,
- reducing the number of hours that they work,
- recruiting someone to assist in childcare,
- returning to school,
- attending a marriage-enrichment course,
- learning how to communicate more effectively,
- moving to a battered women's shelter,
- becoming more assertive with the boss,
- joining a self-defense class,
- working toward more equitable wages,
- looking for a new job,
- learning coping strategies for staying in an unpleasant situation for which there is no viable alternative in the foreseeable future, or
- obtaining professional help.

Initial Plan

Describe your specific plan including all three areas—biological, psychological, and social or environmental—and put it in writing. Include your objectives and the way you plan to achieve them.

Your plan will almost certainly include a self-help component such as joining or forming a support group, taking a class, or reading one or more books devoted to your special problem or concern. It may also include a professional consultation with a physician or therapist.

Feedback and Review of Plan

Set a specific time in the future to review your progress—say in three months. Indicate where improvement has occurred and what the obstacles have been to change.

Revised Plan

To maximize your continuing improvement, describe the adjustments you will make in your plan and set a new time frame for assessment.

Conclusions

Whether you work alone with this chapter as a guide or consult a professional, you will probably find it useful to keep a notebook or diary of your thoughts and feelings. Many components of this guide to a comprehensive psychiatric evaluation do not lend themselves to use by the individual in emotional distress. However, if you do choose to seek the assistance of a psychiatrist, you now have a good idea of what to expect in the initial meeting, and you can use the time most productively by having already put together some of your own history.

Outline for Taking Your Own History

I. Your Present Concern(s)

II. Your History
  A. Your Family Background
  B. Your Developmental History
    1. Infancy and Childhood
    2. Adolescence
    3. Adulthood
        a. Relationships
        b. Work and Financial Status
    4. Sexual History
    5. Abuse and Trauma History
    6. Other Potential Problem Areas
    7. Religious Orientation and Participation or Spiritual Practices
    8. Military History
    9. Hobbies, Recreational and Cultural Activities
    10. Strengths
    11. Values
    12. Social Situation and Living Arrangements
    13. Physical Health and Medical History
    14. Experiences with Therapy or Other Psychological Care

III. Mental-Status Evaluation
  A. General Appearance, Behavior, and Attitude
  B. Consciousness, Orientation, and Memory
  C. Feelings (Affect)
  D. Motor Activity, Retardation, Overactivity, Restlessness
  E. Thought Processes
  F. Thought Content
  G. Intelligence
  H. Feedback from Friends and Colleagues

      I. Insight
     J. Judgment
  IV. Working Hypotheses
     A. Formulation
     B. Differential Diagnosis
   V. Plan
     A. Initial Plan
     B. Feedback and Review of Plan
     C. Revised Plan

NOTES

1. M. McGoldrick and R. Gerson, *Genograms in Family Assessment* (New York: W. W. Norton, 1985).

2. In both this section and the later section on strengths, I am endebted to Jean Baker Miller, M.D., and Nicolina Fedele, Ph.D., for sharing their outline *Guideline for Treatment Planning,* which they developed at the Women's Program, Charles River Hospital.

3. Jean Baker Miller, M.D., and her colleagues at the Stone Center at Wellesley College have begun the task of defining psychological development from a woman's perspective. For further information, write for a copy of the most recent in the Work in Progress series, Wellesley College, Stone Center for Developmental Services and Studies, 106 Central Street, Wellesley, MA 02181-8293.

4. Lillian B. Rubin, *Intimate Strangers: Men and Women Together* (New York: Harper & Row, 1983).

5. For a discussion on this topic see Lillian B. Rubin, *Just Friends: The Role of Friendship in Our Lives* (New York: Harper & Row, 1985).

6. For additional consumer information on the law, write for "Access to Law," Nolo Press, 950 Parker Street, Berkeley, CA 94710, (415) 549-1976.

7. See chapter 9 for an overview of sexuality.

8. I am particularly indebted to E. Borins, M.D., at The Women's Clinic, Toronto Western Hospital, for sharing her research protocols and questionnaires, which were used in the development of this component of the history.

9. Physical abuse refers to acts of physical aggression that carry a risk of physical or psychological injury to the victim.

10. A list of strengths from which to choose may be necessary because it is so hard for women to think of themselves as having strengths.

11. Maggie Kuhn of the Grey Panthers has been a pioneer in creating multigenerational living situations. Now in her eighties, she shares her home with other people considerably her junior. They provide one another with practical support and companionship as well as sharing an economically workable housing environment.

12. For more information, see chapter 7, "Depression."

13. This is also the standard required by many insurance companies. If you have mental-health coverage, the insurance carrier will probably ask your therapist to determine a diagnosis according to DSM-III-R. In some cases, insurance companies use another coding system. One such system is called ICD-9-CM. Whatever system they require, you will need a specific diagnosis in order to receive reimbursement.

14. Current Axis II diagnoses include paranoid, schizoid, schizotypal, antisocial, borderline, histrionic, narcissistic, avoidant, dependent, obsessive-compulsive, and passive-aggressive. Recently, three additional diagnoses received great resistance from feminist professionals and the laywomen's community: late luteal phase dysphoric disorder, sadistic personality disorder, and self-defeating personality disorder. It was argued that there was inadequate scientific evidence to support the first diagnosis, that the second diagnosis would allow a person who should be dealt with through the legal system to "escape" into the medical system, and that the third diagnosis could easily be the result of stereotypical female behavior; in effect, making a "normal" woman mentally ill. As a result of considerable resistance, these three diagnoses have been placed in an appendix of DSM-III-R indicating that they need "further study."

15. A character diagnosis is always sticky because there is a tendency to think of the person with this problem as incurable. Indeed, the problems do seem to be more deeply ingrained than the more acute disorders and, particularly in the absence of social and cultural changes, they are much more difficult to alter. However, if both the patient and the therapist are motivated to engage in a long-term process committed to growth, change is often possible. As demanding as this effort is for everyone involved, quality of life can be markedly enhanced. Recent articles describing the risks associated with character diagnosis include J.B. Bryer et al., "Childhood Sexual and Physical Abuse as Factors in Adult Psychiatric Illness," *American Journal of Psychiatry* 144 no. 11 (November 1987): 1426–30 and E. Stark and A. Flitcraft, "Personal Power and Institutional Victimization: Treating the Dual Trauma of Woman Battering," in *Post-Traumatic Therapy and Victims of Violence*, ed. Frank M. Ochber (New York: Brunner/Mazel, 1988), pp. 115–51.

14 | **U**sing Professional Assistance

Much the same way that a general practitioner, family physician, or general internist is a primary-care physician for your physical health, a psychiatrist is a primary-care physician for your mental health. Unless you are absolutely certain there is no biological contribution to your emotional distress, a consultation with a psychiatrist is a very wise investment.

A comprehensive biopsychosocial assessment can usually be completed within one to three meetings. Your psychiatrist will then be able to provide feedback about the probable contributors to your distress and offer specific recommendations. These may focus primarily, or even exclusively, on therapy, or they may include the use of certain medications. Once you have this information, you can decide whether or not to pursue the recommendations. Remember, your psychiatrist is functioning as your adviser and consultant. You remain the ultimate decision maker.

Finding a Psychiatrist

Competent psychiatrists can be found in virtually every setting. Many are in individual or group private practice. Others work for privately or publicly funded agencies, organizations, or institutions. Quality is far more important than place or price.

You may be eligible for free or low-cost psychiatric care through your school if you are a student or through your workplace if you are employed. Clinics and community mental-health centers are another source of low-cost care. These resources may not offer the same level of choice that private practice does, but low cost and ease of access may outweigh this disadvantage.

If you are looking for a psychiatrist in private practice, ask someone you know and trust for a recommendation. Other referral sources include local consumer groups, women's centers, or nearby colleges or universities. Referrals from other physicians can be useful, but remember that these other physicians often know the psychiatrist only as a colleague and may not know about their skills as a biopsychosocial consultant. Only you can judge whether a particular psychiatrist meets your needs.

When selecting a psychiatrist for a consultation, choose someone who:

- indicates that they offer a biopsychosocial approach,
- is willing to offer you a comprehensive assessment in one to three visits, and
- will offer therapy if that is needed, will refer to you a non-M.D. psychotherapist if that is your preference, or will work cooperatively with the non-M.D. psychotherapist of your choice.

Other questions to ask during your consultation include:

- if you decide to use medication, how often you will be expected to return for follow-up appointments and what is the approximate cost for this care,
- whether lab tests are involved and if so, what is the approximate cost,
- what medication is likely to be recommended,
- how soon improvement can be expected,
- what the common side effects are,
- if there are any foods, beverages, or other medications that you should avoid while on this medication,
- how long you will need to use these medications,
- when and how they will be discontinued, and
- if in-patient care is ever needed, whether this psychiatrist provides that kind of care or whether you will need to see someone else.

If medication *is* recommended and you decide to accept this advice, you can either continue working with this psychiatrist or transfer to another one. In some cases, medication is recommended in conjunction with therapy. Some patients decide to see one psychiatrist for both because they want the same person monitoring all aspects of their care. Other patients choose to see a psychiatrist for their medication while seeing a non-M.D. psychotherapist for therapy. This team approach can be very beneficial if the psychiatrist and psychotherapist work collaboratively. If two clinicians are involved in your care, however, you must monitor the risk of viewing one clinician as good and the other as bad. If you find this happening, discuss it with both clinicians as soon as possible. This prevents problems or miscommunications that might interfere with your care.

Selecting a Psychotherapist

If only therapy is recommended, you can choose to continue with your psychiatrist or transfer to a non-M.D. psychotherapist. Some people decide to stay with their psychiatrist because they feel safe and comfortable in her care or because she has special expertise in their area of concern, but it is not necessary to see a psychiatrist to obtain quality psychotherapy.

Many professionals offer psychotherapy, including psychologists, social workers, nurses, pastoral counselors, and others. Each speciality offers some unique aspect of care. For example, many psychologists can provide psychological testing, and ministers usually include a religious perspective in their counseling. Unfortunately, distinguishing the practitioner of one discipline from another is extremely difficult. Indeed, the credentials after a clinician's name are far less important than her skill, training, and competency as a psychotherapist. You will want to consider all these factors when selecting the best therapist for your purposes.

Whatever you do, make sure to choose someone who has experience with your concerns.

What Is Psychotherapy?

The therapy group I practice with gave a presentation on psychotherapy last week for local physicians and their office staffs. After a careful and, we thought, thorough discussion of the many fine points of what therapists do, one of the medical assistants said, "But, I still don't understand. What *is* therapy and how does it make people better?" If that wasn't the $64,000 question! It's amazing that as many people enter therapy as they do, considering how inept we therapists have been at describing it and demonstrating how it works.

In many ways, the process of therapy *is* very difficult to explain. It's almost as if therapy is something you must experience to understand how it works—and even then, you may still not be able to describe it. It's not as if people haven't tried. There are literally hundreds of professional books describing what therapy is and how it works. There are no small number of books directed toward the potential user of therapy. Each has a slightly different slant, but all are intended to help the reader understand what therapy is and how it helps people feel better. Still, the process of therapy remains something of an enigma to those who have not yet tried it.

First and foremost, psychotherapy is a relationship, a very special kind of relationship. The sole purpose of this relationship is to assist the patient in sorting through, understanding, and reducing the distress that she is experiencing. It is a relationship in which the patient discusses and comes to an understanding of problems that are bothering her.[1] There is no expectation of reciprocity or mutuality as there is in a relationship between friends or family members.

The basic tool of psychotherapy is good communication. Language is the primary vehicle for this communication. The therapist listens while the patient shares her deepest personal concerns. She not only listens to what the patient is *actually* saying, she tries to understand what the patient *means* by what she is saying. Because even the same words mean different things to different people, the therapist must listen beyond the words to grasp the intent of the communication.

The overriding purpose of therapy is for the patient to learn to behave in ways that work better. A warm and supportive therapy relationship can provide much-needed support when a woman is frightened about making changes. Sometimes a bit of confrontation or nagging is necessary if she is dragging her feet.

Ultimately, the most valuable outcomes of a successful therapy relationship are increased self-awareness and self-acceptance. For the woman burdened with excessive guilt or low self-esteem, therapy may be the one relationship in which she begins to recognize and acknowledge that she has legitimate needs that deserve to be met—at least some of the time. Self-awareness allows her to identify those needs, and self-acceptance allows her to pursue them.

Almost every patient enters therapy with false expectations. Some imagine that just by coming to therapy and talking, their problems will magically disappear. Others expect their therapist to fix them. Some worry that they will become dependent on their therapist and will never be able to leave. Others hope (or fear) that their therapist will tell them what they should do.

Many of these myths are generated and maintained by the fact that therapy is an unusually private experience. It is impossible to describe exactly what goes on behind the closed doors of every therapist's office. However, if you could be an invisible observer in the office of any number of competent therapists, you would discover that the care each offers is remarkably similar. It doesn't really seem to matter what school a good therapist was trained in or the type of therapy they practice. Experienced and competent therapists have more similarities than differences when it comes to actually doing psychotherapy.

The patient seeking relief from her emotional distress will need to explore all the contributing factors. She will need to consider her own contribution to her difficulties as well as the contributions of others. Because her current situation is likely to have been influenced by past experiences, she may find it productive to explore how these might be influencing her present functioning. This may mean acknowledging, grieving, and resolving old emotional hurts, some of which may have been temporarily forgotten, pushed aside, or ignored, but which are still influencing her life.

However, her exploration must not be limited to the past. It is equally important to investigate present-day circumstances to determine what she and others may be doing that contributes to her distress. And the way she envisions her own future will serve as a guide to the changes she will need to make to improve the quality of her life.

Psychotherapy does not cure psychological distress in the way that antibiotics cure an infection. Rather, psychotherapy is "a collaborative educational process based on [the patient's] active participation."[2] It is more like an individualized tutorial than a conventional doctor-patient relationship. The therapist is a teacher who facilities self-discovery. She assists the patient in becoming aware of the ways in which she and external circumstances interfere with her psychological growth and development. In coming to understand what is causing her distress, the patient can begin to solve her problems more effectively and thus improve her situation.

Psychotherapy is an enormous investment—emotionally, financially, and in terms of time. Success depends as much upon the patient's active involvement as it does on the severity of her problems or the talent of her therapist. To assure that you get the most you can out of your therapy relationship:[3]

- Choose your therapist carefully.
- Be an active partner.
- Formulate goals and keep your attention on your progress.
- Use everything that happens—in therapy and in your life—to learn more about yourself.
- Try out what you are learning—in and out of therapy.
- Plan your leaving in advance with the cooperation and support of your therapist.

Choosing *Your* Psychotherapist

When it comes to titles, psychotherapists usually have two. The first is just that—psychotherapist. The second describes their academic training. In addition to being a psychotherapist, your counselor may also be a psychiatrist (M.D.); a psychologist (Ph.D., Psy.D., Ed.D., or M.A.); a social worker (M.S.W., D.S.W., or Ph.D.); a nurse (R.N. or M.A.); or a pastoral counselor (M.A., M. Div., D. Div., D. Min., or Ph.D.). In California, there are two additional unique degrees: D.M.H., Doctor of Mental Health, and M.F.C.C., Marriage, Family, and Child Counselor.[4]

In many states, anyone can call themselves a therapist without having received any particular training or receiving any official credentials. While credentials certainly do not assure competency, the lack of them can be worrisome. However, as always, the quality of the therapy relationship is by far the most important factor when it comes to good psychotherapy. Good (as well as bad) therapists can be found with or without particular degrees and titles.

There are many factors you will want to consider in selecting a therapist. Beyond training, experience, and credibility, as well as her fees, a good therapist is someone you feel that you can learn to trust. She is a person with whom you can imagine sharing your most intimate thoughts and feelings without worrying about them being abused or misused.

You can begin your search for a therapist at the same place where you looked for a psychiatrist. Try to get at least three referrals and then pick up the telephone. Ask each therapist a few basic questions before making an appointment with any of them. Useful questions include:[5]

1. "How would you describe the kind of therapy you do?"
2. "What kind of clients do you work with?"
3. "What is your background?"

Here's how I usually answer these questions.

1. I tend to be a practical and pragmatic psychotherapist who enjoys working with patients in a collaborative fashion. I provide both short- and long-term therapy. My style is very interactive. I don't just sit there and listen silently. I tend to integrate theories and methods from a variety of different schools and attempt to individualize the approach to each person's needs.
2. I have had training in family and group psychotherapy, but I find I work best with individuals and couples. Most of the people I see are working women, but there are a number of men who choose to consult me. I do not offer inpatient care. Consequently, I do not work with people who are actively psychotic (out of touch with reality and/or hallucinating) or who need antipsychotic medication or with people who are addicts unless they are concurrently in a twelve-step self-help program like AA (or whatever program is appropriate to their problem).
3. I am a board-certified psychiatrist who is affiliated with a multidisciplinary women's health center. My special interest is psychotherapy, and I have had extensive training and experience with women—individually, in groups, in couples, and in families.

During your phone conversation, listen to both *how* your questions are answered and *what* the therapist actually says. If the therapist's answers are satisfactory, set up an appointment for a consultation. Most therapists charge their standard fee for this, but it is well worth the investment when you consider how important a good working relationship is to successful therapy.

Your therapist will probably guide the initial consultation. Each therapist has her own style in this regard. I usually use an abbreviated version of the history process given in chapter 13. In addition to providing information to the therapist, be sure that you have the opportunity to ask your questions as well. Before returning for a second appointment, review these questions:[6]

- Did you feel that your concerns were taken seriously and that you were treated with respect?
- Were you satisfied with the therapist's answers to your questions?
- Were you relatively comfortable with her recommendations?
- Did you feel that you could grow to trust her?

If the answer to each of these is yes, you are probably wise to try a trial of therapy with this psychotherapist. You can always discontinue if your assessment proves to be inaccurate or if circumstances change.

A face-to-face consultation, and sometimes a brief trial of therapy, is the only way to determine if there is a match between you and a particular therapist. A good match is one of the most powerful predictors of a successful therapy relationship.[7] This match is based as much on your respective personalities as it is on the therapist's skill and your motivation.

A good match gives you the feeling that this is a therapist you could grow to trust. You have the sense that she is putting you and your best interests first. She seems genuinely interested in you and your problems. This doesn't mean you'll never feel embarrassed, uncomfortable, misunderstood, or disappointed, but you have the sense that you *could* talk with her about anything and that she would try her best to understand and be helpful. Her explanations of your problems, as she understands them, make sense to you. In short, you feel relatively comfortable with her style and you expect to get good results from your working relationship.

This almost inexplicable chemistry between patient and therapist is not the same as that felt in seduction. Therapists should never allow their own needs, sexual or otherwise, to supersede the needs and rights of their patients. Therapy is not a romantic relationship. It is a professional one. Because the therapist is kind and understanding, it is easy for the patient to get a "crush" on the therapist. However, this "crush" should never be acted upon. Because the therapist has more power than the patient, the burden rests with the therapist to prevent this from happening.

It is the therapist's responsibility to assure that the therapy relationship is a private, safe, and respectful environment in which trust will be offered, never betrayed. Protection from exploitation is assured by one very simple rule. Therapy is for talking—not for touching. On rare, indeed very rare occasions, this rule may be temporarily suspended, but this is only to offer a warm, nonerotic gesture of support, comfort, or encouragement, never to gratify erotic or sexual needs. And it should only occur then at the instigation of the patient.

> Libby was ending therapy after almost three years of hard work. She reflected on how much had changed. When she had first sought care from Dr. Hendricks, Libby had been so depressed that suicide seemed an all-too-real possibility. Dr. Hendricks had helped Libby to see that she could find other ways out of a difficult marriage. Instead of ending her life at age fifty-four, she obtained a divorce, started her first full-time job, and bought her own condominium. She felt content and capable in her new life and she was very appreciative of the support Dr. Hendricks had provided.
>
> Today was their last meeting. Libby knew she could always return to therapy if the need arose, but it was entirely possible she would never see Dr. Hendricks again. As Libby stood to walk out the door for the final time, she felt a wave of warm affection and deep gratitude. She turned to Dr. Hendricks and asked,

"Would you mind if I gave you a good-bye hug?" Her therapist nodded, accepting this gift from Libby as they parted. "Take care, Libby," Dr. Hendricks said. Libby replied, "I will." She stepped back, took one last look around the office, smiled at Dr. Hendricks, and walked out the door.

Assuming competency, there are at least five other key ingredients to consider in selecting a therapist. You may not be able to judge these satisfactorily based on one meeting alone. Continue to monitor them as you work in therapy.

1. Trust—Basic trust is the feeling that another person means you well and will not intentionally harm you.
   Because there are no perfect parents and no perfect society, each of us experiences a certain degree of pain while growing up. The more painful our growing-up experience, the more distrust of others we develop. This distrust is like a thick wall. It is intended to be our protection against getting hurt again. Unfortunately, it also leaves us feeling lonely and isolated.
   A trustworthy therapy relationship is a nonthreatening, secure, and safe place in which the patient risks being vulnerable again with another human being. In being vulnerable, she slowly but surely dismantles her wall of self-protection and replaces it with skills, behaviors, and tools that allow her to protect herself without excluding other people from her life.

2. Honesty—The therapist's behavior matches her words.
   If the therapist makes a mistake, as all people do, she is willing to acknowledge her error and apologize. For the most part, she is genuinely warm, supportive, and kind, but she is willing to admit to negative feelings as well as positive ones when it is appropriate to do so. If she's angry with a patient, she doesn't try to hide it—nor does she behave abusively. This kind of honesty is also called congruence. You have the sense that her inside feelings match her outside behavior and words.

3. Commitment—She is there for you at least 70 percent of the time.
   The 70 percent rule says that another person can only be there for us 70 percent of the time.[8] But that constitutes a pretty strong commitment. If somebody is there for you 70 percent of the time, you've got the best that any ordinary mortal can fairly expect. This includes mothers, teachers, friends, and therapists! They are, after all, only human.

4. Nonjudgmental attitude—The therapist's unique training allows her to suspend judgment while trying to develop some understanding about why the patient thinks, feels, and acts the way she does.
   The therapist's nonjudgmental curiosity encourages the patient to turn inward and examine her motives and actions in a similar fashion. The

self-knowledge gained from this process provides the opportunity to make more informed choices.

5. Empowerment—The therapy relationship is one in which the inequality between therapist and patient is used to empower the patient.

The therapist, by virtue of her training, authority, and experience, has more power than the patient. The task of the therapist is to begin the process of reducing this power differential. As the therapist encourages the patient to examine her history, to process her feelings, to consider other options to her current situation, and to experiment with change, the patient becomes increasingly in charge of her own life. Thus, "the therapy relationship becomes a model of power building, a microcosm that helps the [patient] gather and use power" in more productive ways.[9]

Remember, you are in charge. No matter how distressed you are, the therapist is your employee. You are hiring her to provide a service. The more informed you are about your needs and the better you match these needs with what the therapist has to offer, the more likely you are to achieve your therapy goals.

Selecting a therapist means trusting your own thoughts and feelings. A good therapist will occasionally make you uncomfortable by asking challenging questions or encouraging you to risk new behaviors, but she will not make you feel consistently frightened, anxious, or uncertain about why you are in therapy.

Psychotherapy Options

There are also many types of psychotherapy. The most common ones are individual, group, family, and couple's therapy. They may be used alone or in combination.

Individual therapy is a one-on-one relationship between a patient and a therapist. It is private and highly personal. *Group therapy* involves a collection of patients who make a commitment to try to understand themselves and one another better with the help of one or more therapists. Patients receive less individual attention, but this is compensated for by the opportunity to try new ways of relating to a variety of people. In *family therapy,* the emphasis is on bringing about changes in the relationships between family members rather than in any one individual. Similarly, in *couple's therapy,* the focus is on the relationship rather than the individual partners.

There are no hard and fast rules about which type of therapy works best for any particular problem. If you are uncertain about which option to choose, you might simply start with the one that makes the most sense to you or feels the most comfortable. You can always switch or add another at a later time.

There are more than four hundred different schools of therapy. All profess to lead to the same end—relief from emotional distress.[10] They all have common threads, but there certainly are differences. Selecting the school that is most congruent with your own belief system is no small task.

When interviewing potential therapists, ask them to describe the school of therapy they practice. Many adhere to only one, while others are more flexible. Some therapists actually define themselves as integrative-eclectic therapists.[11] They aim to ignore the ideological barriers that divide the various schools of psychotherapy by focusing more on their commonalities and what is useful in each.

An integrative-eclectic approach acknowledges that no school appears to be consistently superior to any other.[12] Each has its successes and its failures. By combining them, the weaknesses in one are compensated for by the strengths of another, and the therapist is able to tailor the therapy to the specific needs of each patient.[13]

The Therapy Agreement

Once you enter a therapy relationship, you and the therapist implicitly agree to accept certain rights and responsibilities. Many of these may be specifically spelled out in a verbal or written agreement; others are taken for granted unless inadvertently "broken" by either party. As a patient your responsibilities include:

- coming to your appointments on time or compensating the therapist for her time if you are unavoidably delayed,
- paying the agreed-upon fee,
- being honest,
- working toward your goals,
- talking with your therapist about whether or not the therapy relationship is working for you, and
- if it is not, explaining this to your therapist and stopping.

The therapist's responsibilities include:

- being available on time or compensating unavoidable tardiness by adding time to the end of the session, reducing the fee, or rescheduling the appointment at a mutually acceptable time,
- facilitating insurance reimbursement,
- behaving in an ethical and professional fashion,[14]
- assisting the patient in working toward her goals,
- being open to feedback from the patient about her perception of the therapy relationship, and
- assisting the patient in finding another therapy relationship if this one is terminated before she has achieved her goals.

As a patient you also have many rights. Foremost among them is the right to have a safe and trustworthy relationship. This means that *at no time should there be any erotic or sexual contact between you and the therapist.* An erotic or sexual relationship between patient and therapist is both unethical and illegal. It is an abuse of the therapist's greater power within the relationship. It exploits the patient and betrays her trust. Therapists who behave in this fashion should be reported to the licensing board of the state in which they practice and/or the ethics committee of the profession in which they are credentialed. For example, psychiatrists who misuse their power in this way in my community are reported to the Board of Medical Quality Assurance for the State of California and the Ethics Committee of the American Psychiatric Association.

Other rights granted a consumer of psychotherapy have been clearly defined by the Federation of Organizations for Professional Women. According to their guidelines, you have the right:[15]

- To ask questions at any point.
- To know if a therapist is available to see you now, or if not, how long the wait will be.
- To be fully informed of the therapist's qualifications to practice, including training and credentials, years of experience, and so forth.
- To be fully informed about the therapist's therapeutic orientation.
- To be fully informed regarding the therapist's areas of specialization and her limitations.
- To ask questions about issues relevant to your therapy, such as therapist's values, background, and attitudes and to be provided with thoughtful, respectful answers.
- To be fully informed of the limits of confidentiality in the therapy setting, knowing with whom and under what circumstances the therapist may discuss the case.
- To be fully informed of the extent of written or taped records of therapy and their accessibility.
- To be fully informed of your diagnosis (if the therapist uses one).
- To specify or negotiate the therapeutic goals and to renegotiate when necessary.
- To be fully informed regarding the therapist's estimation of approximate length of therapy to meet your agreed-upon goals.
- To be fully informed regarding specific treatment strategies employed by the therapist.
- To be fully informed regarding the format of therapy (individual, couple, family, group).
- To be fully informed regarding fees for therapy and method of payment, including insurance reimbursement.
- To be fully informed regarding the therapist's policies on issues such as missed appointments, emergency coverage, and so forth.

- To get a written contract regarding conditions of therapy.
- To refuse any intervention or treatment strategy.
- To request that the therapist evaluate the progress of therapy.
- To discuss any aspect of your therapy with others outside of the therapy situation, including consulting with another therapist.
- To be provided with summaries of your written files at your request.
- To require the therapist to send a written report regarding services rendered to a qualified therapist or organization on your written authorization.
- To give or refuse to give permission for the therapist to use aspects of your case for a presentation or publication.
- To refuse to answer any question.
- To know the ethical code to which the therapist adheres.
- To solicit help from the ethics committee of the appropriate professional organization in the event of doubt or grievance regarding therapist's conduct.
- To terminate therapy at any time.

Obviously, there are many variables to be considered in establishing and maintaining a helpful and productive therapy relationship. You are wise to do your best to clarify the specific rules of your therapy relationship before you make a full commitment to the process.

Inpatient Care

Historically, inpatient care has been viewed in a very negative light. Certainly, the sexist treatment of women in some institutions and by some clinicians has been well documented.[16] Fortunately, the pioneering work of several contemporary clinicians and administrators has led to the development of more inpatient programs specifically tailored to the needs of women.[17]

Long-term inpatient psychiatric care is virtually a thing of the past, but under sufficient stress, even the healthiest individual may find herself behaving in a highly dysfunctional fashion. For women in this situation, outpatient therapy may not provide sufficient safety, protection, and improvement. A brief hospital stay is often useful or even necessary.

Some of the biological contributors of emotional distress can result in such severe and disturbing symptoms that inpatient care is essential to prevent inappropriate or destructive behavior. Many people prefer to begin recovery from alcohol or drug abuse by entering an inpatient chemical dependency program. Survivors of incest, rape, or battering may appreciate the structure, support, and protection that can only be provided by round-the-clock care in an inpatient setting.

The same principles that guide the choice of outpatient services apply in the selection of inpatient care. However, because a woman temporarily surrenders considerable control over her day-to-day life when she enters an inpatient program, she or those arranging for her care must be especially meticulous about the selection. Look for a facility that has a woman's program or ask for a clinician who has had specific training and experience in the care of women.

The Therapy Process

People usually start thinking about seeking therapy when they are in emotional pain that they have been unable to relieve by any other means. Successful therapy is a process involving four basic components: engagement, pattern search, change, and termination.[18]

Engagement means that the patient and therapist enter a relationship in which the sole purpose is to try to figure out what is upsetting the patient and why. If a person has never sought therapy before, she is usually anxious or frightened by the prospect of starting therapy for the first time. Their anxiety or fear can have many different sources. Some people are afraid that they are "going crazy," and seeing a therapist only confirms their worst fears. Others are worried that the therapist will be able to "read their minds," thereby gaining control over them in some way. Some worry about losing their independence or creativity. Others are just plain scared to look at themselves honestly and directly.

Since almost everyone is anxious and afraid in the face of the unknown, entering therapy for the first time is an act of considerable courage. The person who takes this courageous step is saying, My pain is greater than my anxiety and fear and I am going to take the responsibility to do something about it!

Once a person has made this decision and actually starts therapy, she often feels some degree of immediate relief. Making a commitment to therapy is making a commitment to herself, and this act alone is an important component of the healing process. She is doing something about her problems, and that feels good! However, starting is just that—starting. It may provide some temporary relief, but permanent relief will only come through the hard work of sticking with the process until it is completed.

Sticking with the Process

The hard work of therapy includes pattern search and change. *Pattern search* enables the patient and therapist to identify dysfunctional behaviors. These are usually survival strategies that once served a good purpose but that no longer do. Once these dysfunctional behaviors have been identified, the patient is encouraged to *change* them in some beneficial way. This means the challenging work of giving up old patterns and initiating and maintaining new ones.

In brief, focused, and goal-oriented therapy, this process is relatively straightforward. For example, if you become nervous when you give speeches, as long as you can avoid having to give speeches, you don't really have a problem. But, if giving speeches suddenly becomes a critical part of your recent promotion, your avoidance has become dysfunctional. Your pattern search in this kind of situation is very brief and your emphasis will be on making changes.

If the cause of your distress is less specific, the patterns will be harder to define. Say you come to therapy because you are unhappy. It will take a while to sort out what is contributing to your unhappiness. Pattern search will take more time, and change will proceed more slowly. However, with the assistance of your therapist, you will eventually be able to identify exactly what you want to change, how long it is likely to take, and what will constitute the end point. You may discover that you cannot achieve your intended goal as easily, as quickly, or as thoroughly as you had hoped, but your goal will nevertheless become fairly clear.

In short-term therapy, you usually select one specific goal. For example, you may want to be more comfortable giving speeches. Training in progressive relaxation, visualization, and other behavioral techniques will probably reduce your distress in a dozen sessions or less.

In long-term work (six months or more), lasting change does not come so rapidly. In fact, a patient may at times actually feel worse rather than better. A patient requiring long-term therapy will probably have to make some pretty substantial changes in her life to achieve a greater level of happiness, if that is her goal. It will not be easy. She will experience many ebbs and flows of feeling as she struggles to change.

Change becomes possible when we become aware that there are many different ways of responding to the same situation. Instead of being on automatic pilot, we consider a wide range of options and begin to experiment with some that we have never used before. It is not that we lose our ability to handle a situation in our usual way. It is just that we learn new alternatives from which we can choose the best.

So change "is an adding on rather than a subtracting,"[19] but it is still scary. We are anxious about giving up, or at least altering, behaviors that have helped us survive difficult life situations. Nevertheless, as we become aware of other options and learn how to use them effectively, we develop a sense of mastery and control over a whole range of previously distressing situations.

Sometimes therapy becomes ploddingly slow or doesn't seem to be going well. There seems to be no change taking place. When this happens, one of your biggest challenges is deciding whether you are simply resisting—putting on the brakes to your own growth and development—or whether there is a genuine incompatibility between you and this particular therapist. Negative feelings arise in successful therapy relationships as well as those that prove to be unsuccessful. This is why the slow parts of therapy are so difficult to assess.

Resistance occurs in every therapy relationship, and it is likely to be the strongest just at the point when we realize that we are standing in our own way of feeling better. Faced with this reality, our impulse is to flee rather than accept responsibility for change that now rests squarely on our shoulders. On the other hand, sometimes a therapist is incompetent or just unsuited to your needs. If either of these factors is operating, you might as well leave the relationship and transfer to a new therapist. No matter how small your community is, there is usually no paucity of good therapists. Since your psychological well-being is a very precious commodity, you should certainly work with the best person you can find.

The last stage of therapy is *termination*. In short-term therapy, you terminate as soon as you achieve your specific goal. Long-term therapy, on the other hand, has only achieved its purpose when you feel like a whole and integrated person. Ending this therapy relationship is in order when:

- You have a pretty good sense of what's going on in your life and why.
- You no longer experience the symptoms that brought you into therapy in the first place.
- You know that the world and the people in it are neither all good nor all bad, and you are able to see and accept the positive and negative in yourself and others.
- You have good-quality relationships in which you are neither excessively dependent nor overly independent.
- You can extricate yourself from unhealthy relationships without too much difficulty.
- You have a way to earn your own living or plans to obtain satisfactory work.
- You have easy access to both your thoughts and feelings. When you find yourself "too much in your head," you have strategies for getting in touch with your feelings. When you feel too emotionally charged, you have strategies for calming yourself down.
- You have confidence that your personal strengths outweigh your vulnerabilities.
- You can cope with your life—even when things are not going smoothly.
- You are ready to handle the ups and downs in your life without the sanctuary of a therapy relationship.

Each person has her own characteristic way of ending a relationship, and ending therapy is no exception. Some patterns are obviously more negative than positive. For example:

- Some people avoid saying good-bye. They think this will spare them and others from feeling hurt or uncomfortable.
- Some people use anger as a justification for ending therapy. Their anger seems to protect them from experiencing other painful feelings such as longing, sadness, or even joy.
- Some people linger indefinitely, often settling for crumbs. They are usually either worried they will miss something if they go or fearful that they cannot manage on their own.

- Some people leave by devaluing the therapy relationship. By minimizing its importance they seem to be telling themselves that there is really nothing to miss.
- Some people deny the importance of leaving. They protect themselves from a whole range of feelings by simply refusing to feel anything.

The best way to leave a therapeutic relationship is to plan for it. You may leave because you really are finished or you may end before all your goals are met or before you have achieved the ideal. Sometimes you only want to do part of the hard work and plan to return to therapy at another time to work some more. And a "leave of absence" because of financial or emotional constraints is not unusual.

Whatever the reason, when you feel ready to end, discuss it with your therapist and agree on a date. If the ending is planned between you and your therapist, you will feel more comfortable returning at a later date if you wish. Planning also gives you time to process the thoughts and feelings that arise with your decision to leave. You may want to taper your sessions rather than just quitting. Some people prefer coming every other month, or even once a month, until they are ready to say good-bye. It also gives you time to adjust to the loss of this important relationship and to move on.

If the therapy relationship has been a good one, leaving is usually bittersweet. There is a special closeness that comes with the care and acceptance we feel from our therapist. In no other relationship do we have the same level of undivided concern and attention focused on our thoughts and feelings. It should come as no surprise that even after achieving our goals, we have mixed feelings about leaving. Part of us wants to use our time and money for other people, places, and things. Part of us wants to stay forever in this uniquely warm, secure, and supportive environment.

The longer you have been in therapy, the more time you will probably need to plan for its ending. Ending a successful therapy relationship can stir up unexpectedly strong emotions. This doesn't necessarily mean that ending is a mistake, just that you have feelings about the impending loss of a significant relationship.

To avoid facing the end of this extraordinary relationship, we often fantasize about transforming the therapy relationship into a friendship. Genuine friendship with a former therapist is impossible. The therapist knows more about you than you will ever know about her and, besides, in a *real* relationship, you would have to contend with all of who she is as a person—not just the warm, empathic side she provides during therapy. It is better to deal with your feelings of sadness and pleasure about leaving than to try to turn the therapy relationship into a relationship of peers. Besides, good therapists are harder to find than good friends. If you keep her as your therapist, you can always return if you want to.

The Process Never Ends

Successful therapy does not make life stress free, but it does allow a person to become her own therapist, parent, and teacher. The therapeutic process becomes a permanent part of who she is. The person who successfully completes long-term therapy

- has a better understanding of herself, a greater awareness of her options, and the ability to change,
- is able to apply the principles she learned in therapy to other relationships,
- is not always happy but can deal with trouble when it does appear in her life,
- is able to evaluate herself with relative accuracy and to make decisions based on that evaluation,
- is able to act on these decisions with relative confidence—even when these actions create difficulties in important relationships,
- has caring relationships, has realistic and reachable goals, and avoids self-defeating behavior,
- can deal with the problems in her life and knows how to find help if she needs to, and
- is hopeful and optimistic about her future.

Most importantly, she accepts personal responsibility for what she says, what she does, and what she thinks.

Therapy Is Not Magic, but It Does Work

Now we come back to that $64,000 question: what is therapy and how does it make people feel better? Therapy is a collaborative effort in which language and human presence are the tools of healing and change.

By talking about their thoughts and feelings, people learn things about themselves that they did not previously know or appreciate. This greater self-understanding allows them to make more informed life choices. By sharing these thoughts and feelings in the presence of a caring and concerned person, they experience acceptance and support, which enhances their capacity for basic trust in human relationships and allows them to risk being more vulnerable with others. In risking being more vulnerable, they come to experience greater intimacy, which allows them to feel loved and valued. Feeling loved and valued enhances self-esteem and self-acceptance.

Anyone who believes in psychotherapy believes in the capacity of people to grow and change given the right circumstances. If a person's growth is blocked, they develop emotional symptoms of distress, signals that something is wrong that needs attention. In psychotherapy, that person has the opportunity to explore the ways they or circumstances limit their psychological growth and well-being. By revealing these obstacles, they then have the chance to change those that are within their power to change.

Whatever happened earlier, whatever situation you are in now, you are responsible for the rest of your life. You make your own future. I don't mean to be a Pollyanna about this. There are very real constraints and limitations on each of us, but within that context, we still have enormous choice over who and what we become.

It's your life. And, as far as I know, you only get one shot at it. Psychotherapy helps you make it the best it can be!

ADDITIONAL READING

Pamphlets:

Mental Health Directory
National Institute of Mental Health, Superintendent of Documents, U.S. Government Printing Office, Washington, DC 20402-9325, (202) 783-3238. Lists outpatient clinics and inpatient facilities nationwide.

National Institute of Mental Health Catalogue
NIMH Publications Department, 1021 Prince St., Alexandria, VA 22314-2971, (703) 684-7722. Contains a wide variety of useful listings including informative, low-cost pamphlets.

Women and Psychotherapy: A Consumer Handbook
Federation of Organizations for Professional Women, 2000 P Street, N.W., Suite 403, Washington, DC 20036. An excellent summary of the major issues related to women and therapy. It provides facts, suggestions, and the essential informational tools to be an informed consumer of therapy services. This pamphlet can only be ordered prepaid. Send $3.75 per copy plus $1.00 for postage and handling.

Books:

M. Aftel and Robin Tolmach Lakoff, *When Talk Is Not Cheap or How to Find the Right Therapist When You Don't Know Where to Begin* (New York: Warner, 1985). This book has a number of handy checklists that can help you select a therapist, assess the progress of your own therapy, and determine when to end.

Gerald Amada, *A Guide to Psychotherapy* (Lanham, Md.: University Press of America, 1983; Madison Books, 1985). A good, concise book that covers a lot of the questions people ask about psychotherapy in a very clear and personable way.

Fredda Bruckner-Gordon, Barbara Kuerer Gangi, and Geraldine Urbach Wallman, *Making Therapy Work: Your Guide to Choosing, Using, and Ending Therapy* (New York: Harper & Row, 1988). This is a combination workbook and textbook with handy checklists and exercises for evaluating when to start therapy, how to assess the progress you are making, and when to stop therapy.

Otto Ehrenberg and Miriam Ehrenberg, *The Psychotherapy Maze: A Consumer's Guide to Getting In and Out of Therapy* (New York: Simon & Schuster, 1986). This book is quite densely written and the authors have some biases that are, in my opinion, based more on personal belief than an accurate understanding of every aspect of psychotherapy. However, with these drawbacks, they really cover the waterfront when it comes to describing the various approaches to psychotherapy.

Susan Stanford Friedman, *A Woman's Guide to Therapy* (Englewood Cliffs, N.J.: Prentice-Hall, 1979). This is an "old" book now for anyone familiar with the changes that have occurred in therapy as a result of the women's movement. However, it is one of the few that also addresses the needs of women requiring inpatient care. If this is an option you are considering, you may want to read chapter 9, "Women and Mental Institutions: Some Issues."

Lynne Bravo Rosewater, *Changing Through Therapy* (New York: Dodd, Mead & Co., 1987). This book demystifies therapy by providing a description of what happens at every stage of the process.

RESOURCES

If you are looking for a practitioner who is likely to be familiar with the principles discussed in this book:

- contact your community women's center, rape crisis hotline, department of women's studies, or local chapter of the National Organization for Women (listed in the phone book) and ask for a recommendation, or
- contact one of the professional organizations listed below.

However, remember that a referral is not an endorsement. You will still need to investigate whether or not a practitioner is the right person for you.

Committee on Women
American Psychiatric Association, 1400 K Street, N.W., Washington, D.C. 20005.

Leah J. Dickenstein, M.D., President
Association of Women Psychiatrists, University of Louisville School of Medicine, Louisville, KY 40292.

Michele Harway
Association for Women in Psychology, Feminist Therapy Roster, Social Research Institute, University of Southern California, Los Angeles, CA 90007.

American Psychological Association
1200 17th Street, N.W., Washington, D.C. 20036, (202) 955-7600.

National Association of Social Workers
7981 Eastern Avenue, Silver Spring, MD 20910, (301) 565-03333.

National Association of Marriage and Family Counselors
225 Yale Avenue, Claremont, CA 91711.

National Academy of Certified Clinical Mental Health Counselors
5999 Stevenson Avenue, Alexandria, VA 22304, (703) 823-9800.

American Group Psychotherapy Association
25 East 21st Street, New York, NY 10010, (212) 477-2677.

American Association of Marriage and Family Therapy
1717 K Street, N.W., Suite 407, Washington, D.C. 20006, (202) 429-1825.

American Association of Pastoral Counselors
9508A Lee Highway, Fairfax, VA 22031, (703) 385-6967.

American Nurses Association
2420 Pershing Road, Kansas City, MO 64108, (816) 474-5720.

American Association of Sex Educators, Counselors, and Therapists
11 Dupont Circle, N.W., Suite 220, Washington, D.C. 20036-1207, (202) 462-1171.

Women's Therapy Center Institute
80 East 11th Street, Room 101, New York, NY 10003, (212) 420-1974.

NOTES

1. *Women and Psychotherapy: A Consumer Handbook* (Washington, D.C.: Federation of Professional Women, 1981), p. 31.

2. Otto Ehrenberg and Mariam Ehrenberg, *The Psychotherapy Maze: A Consumer's Guide to Getting In and Out of Therapy* (New York: Simon & Schuster, 1986).

3. Fredda Bruckner-Gordon, Barbara Kuerer Gangi, and Geraldine Urbach Wallman, *Making Therapy Work: Your Guide to Choosing, Using and Ending Therapy* (New York: Harper & Row, 1988).

4. Psychiatrists have had very extensive training (four years of college, four years of medical school, four years of residency training in psychiatry, and often additional training in the specialty of their choice). In addition, their overhead costs (malpractice insurance, professional membership, conference fees, hospital dues, etc.) are higher than those of non-M.D. therapists. Consequently, psychiatrists' fees tend to be higher than those of most other psychotherapists. If money is a factor, a non-M.D. therapist may be less expensive.

5. Lynne Bravo Rosewater, *Changing Through Therapy* (New York: Dodd, Mead, 1987).

6. Adapted from Fredda Bruckner-Gordon, et. al. *Making Therapy Work*, p. 56–58.

7. L. Luborsky, *Principles of Psychoanalytic Psychotherapy* (New York: Basic Books, 1984).

8. M. Wells, "Techniques to Develop Object Constancy with Borderline Clients," *Psychotherapy* 23 (1986): 460–68.

9. Mandy Aftel and Robin Tolmach Lakoff, *When Talk Is Not Cheap: How to Find the Right Therapist When You Don't Know Where to Begin* (New York: Warner, 1985).

10. T. B. Karasu, "The Specificity Versus Nonspecificity Dilemma: Toward Identifying Therapeutic Change Agents," *American Journal of Psychiatry* 143 (1986): 687–95.

11. B. D. Beitman, M. R. Goldfried, and J. C. Norcross, "The Movement toward Integrating the Psychotherapies: An Overview," *American Journal of Psychiatry* 146 no. 2 (February 1989): 139–47.

12. W. B. Stiles, D. A. Shapiro, and R. Elliott, "Are All Psychotherapies Equivalent?" *American Psychologist* 35 (1980): 991–99.

13. A. Frances, J. Clarkin, and S. Perry, *Differential Therapeutics in Psychiatry* (New York: Brunner/Mazel, 1984).

14. Martin Lakin, *Ethical Issues in the Psychotherapies* (New York: Oxford University Press, 1988).

15. *Women and Psychotherapy: A Consumer Handbook,* p. 16–17.

16. Phyllis Chesler, *Women and Madness* (New York: Avon, 1972) and Dorothy E. Smith and J. David Srar, *Women Look at Psychiatry* (Vancouver: Press Gang, 1975).

17. "Women Developing Treatment Programs for Women," symposium presented at the annual meeting of the American Psychiatric Association, Washington, D.C., 1986. Co-directors: Jean Baker Miller and Karen Johnson.

18. Bernard D. Beitman, *The Structure of Individual Psychotherapy* (New York: Guilford Press, 1987).

19. Rosewater, *Changing Through Therapy*, p. 3.

Epilogue.
Combining Love and Power:
The Resourcefulness of Women

Integrating women's perceptions and experiences into psychological theory and practice alters the definition of psychological health. Emotional well-being must now be viewed as including the ability to sustain and nurture relationships along with the capacity to function as a separate individual. Independence is no longer an overrated virtue nor dependence a weakness. Caring as well as a judicious approach to conflict changes the standard by which behavior can be judged acceptable or unacceptable.

In taking a high degree of responsibility for relationships and for the well-being of the individuals within those relationships, women have had considerable experience in trying to help others achieve this level of psychological health. While often living within the context of subordination themselves, women of all colors and classes have demonstrated remarkable resourcefulness in combining love and power. A mother with an eighth-grade education somehow manages to raise six children alone on welfare in a housing project riddled by crime and drugs. A single mother on a waitress's salary with little support from anyone else is able to provide medical care for her child who was brain-damaged at birth. A lesbian in a relationship with an alcoholic partner finds the resources to effectively challenge her lover's denial and help her start on the road to recovery. A university administrator puts her own career at risk in bringing charges against a tenured professor for racial and sexist slurs in the classroom. A new mother and successful corporate vice president negotiates for part-time work in order to spend more time with her child. The battered wife of a high-powered executive refrains from using physical punishment when disciplining her children.

These women have greater and lesser degrees of power within our society and within their relationships, but all are trying in their own way to use what power they do have to care for others—even if they themselves are inadequately cared for. Not all women do this, nor is any woman able to do it all the time. Nevertheless, most women—both at home and at work—prefer to use their power in ways that encourage the development of everyone involved.

Unfortunately, women's preferences and expertise are largely ignored or devalued. As they gain access to positions of greater power, women are expected to sacrifice their interest in caring for others and to adopt the behavior of men. Some women comply—willingly or unwillingly—but others manage to resist. While these pioneers could use their authority to dominate others, often they choose to support and guard their values and interests as women.

Women's efforts and expertise in trying to create loving, caring relationships—no matter the circumstances—are valuable assets. Until women are able to use their training and talents without being placed in a subordinate position for doing so, they will continue to experience a disproportionately high rate of psychological distress in comparison to men. Women's distress is a signal that equality has not yet been achieved and that women's values have not yet been fully integrated into the home or the workplace. As women continue to strive for greater social, political, and economic power, they have the opportunity to transform that power into something that really serves human development rather than interferes with it. They will then be able to insist that these values be respected and fully integrated into relationships and institutions.

Trusting ourselves means believing in our own perceptions, our own experience, and our own values as women—even if others see it differently.

Index